Recent Studies in Early Christianity

A Collection of Scholarly Essays

Series Editor

Everett Ferguson

A GARLAND SERIES

Series Contents

Doctrinal Diversity
Varieties of Early Christianity

Edited with an introduction by
Everett Ferguson

GARLAND PUBLISHING, INC.
A MEMBER OF THE TAYLOR & FRANCIS GROUP
New York & London
1999

Library of Congress Cataloging-in-Publication Data

Doctrinal diversity : varieties of early Christianity / edited, with
   introductions by Everett Ferguson.
          p.   cm. — (Recent studies in early Christianity ; 4)
       Includes bibliographical references.
       ISBN 0-8153-3071-5 (alk. paper)
          1. Theology, Doctrinal—History—Early church, ca. 30–600.
   I. Ferguson, Everett, 1933–   . II. Series.
   BT25.D625 1999
   270.1—dc21   99-26311
                                                          CIP

Printed on acid-free, 250-year-life paper
Manufactured in the United States of America

Contents

Series Introduction

Garland published in 1993 *Studies in Early Christianity: A Collection of Scholarly Essays,* an eighteen-volume set of classic articles on the early history of Christianity. The present set of six volumes, *Recent Studies in Early Christianity,* continues that first series by selecting articles written during the last decade. The chronological scope is the same, the first six centuries of the common era. The arrangement once more is topical but with a conflation and realignment of topics to fit the smaller number of volumes. The present series of essays will serve as an important supplement for those who possess the first series. For those without the first series, it will introduce key areas of research and debate on the early history of Christianity.

The growing academic interest in Christianity during its early centuries, as noted in the series introduction to *Studies in Early Christianity,* has greatly accelerated. There has been a proliferation of studies during the last decade on the subject of Christianity in late antiquity. The very popularity of the designation "late antiquity" says something about the current intellectual climate in which these studies arise: a shift from a primary emphasis on Christianity itself to the larger cultural setting of which it was a part, a shift from doctrinal studies to the church as a social institution, and a shift from concern for orthodoxy to the popular religious attitudes and expressions.

The increased study of this period finds expression in more doctoral students, record membership in professional organizations, like the North American Patristics Society and the Association internationale d'études patristiques, and large attendance at the International Conferences on Patristic Studies in Oxford (August 16-21, 1999, marks the thirteenth of these meetings that occur every four years), in addition to participation in specialized conferences on Origen, Gregory of Nyssa, Augustine, and others. Expanded literary productivity is evidenced by new journals (*The Journal of Early Christian Studies,* edited by Elizabeth Clark and Everett Ferguson, a continuation of *The Second Century; Zeitschrift für Antikes Christentum/Journal of Ancient Christianity,* edited by H.C. Brennecke and C. Markschies), new reference works (*The Encyclopedia of Early Christianity* [New York: Garland], edited by Everett Ferguson, first edition in 1990, second and greatly expanded edition in 1997, paperback edition 1998; *The Encyclopedia of the Early Church* [New York: Oxford University Press, 1992], English translation of *Dizionario Patristico e di Antichità Cristiane,* edited by Angelo Di Berardino), and substantial scholarly monographs in the field.

In some ways the selection of articles for six volumes on a decade of scholarship is more difficult than eighteen volumes on a century: We do not have the perspective of time to judge what is of enduring worth. Although some of these pieces will no doubt become classics, the guiding principle in selection has been to point to areas that are drawing the greatest attention. Some subjects have become virtually independent subdisciplines in the study of religion in late antiquity. This is notably true of Gnosticism, although the very term is under attack as a proper category.

The six volumes of this collection of scholarly essays take up the following broad topics: (1) the social setting of the early church, with attention to such matters as women, family, friendship, funerary practices, education, and slavery; (2) the political, cultural, and religious setting of early Christianity in relation to Romans, Greeks, and Jews; (3) the internal development of the church as it recognized its canon of scriptures, interpreted those scriptures, defined its confession of faith, and articulated standards of conduct; (4) the diversity — geographical, doctrinal, disciplinary — that counterbalanced the efforts to achieve a unified orthodoxy; (5) the many expressions of devotion and spirituality that both nourished and manifested faith; and (6) the varied ways in which early Christians wrestled with the limitations of historical existence and human language yet voiced their hopes for another and better world.

These topics represent the emphases in the modern study of early Christianity: social history and the application of the social sciences to the understanding of the historical texts, women's concerns and gender issues, Christians' relations with their Jewish and pagan neighbors, variety in early Christianity (especially fueled by the Nag Hammadi texts but not exclusively so), types of asceticism, literary forms and criticism, and Christianity's relationship to late antiquity and the transition to the medieval world. Some themes long present in the study of early Christianity continue to gain attention: the creedal definition of the faith, the causes and effects of persecution, different approaches to the interpretation of the Bible, forms of worship and spirituality, Christian morality, and the Christian hope.

One person's judgment and one small set of essays cannot do full justice to the rich flowering of studies in the field of early Christianity. We can only point to the areas of emphasis and call attention to some significant studies. These studies will lead teachers and students into the larger field and, we hope, spark their interest in pursuing some of these questions and related matters more extensively, thereby enlarging the number of researchers in a field not only intellectually challenging but also spiritually significant.

Volume Introduction

A principal theme characterizing recent study of early Christianity is the diversity in the Christian movement, present from its beginning and continuing even after orthodoxy was firmly institutionalized. Even among those who established their claim to represent orthodoxy there were differences in the theological interpretation of key doctrines. One study included in this collection (Louth) addresses the general theme of unity and diversity, and of orthodoxy and heresy, in the fourth century.[1]

Then follows a collection of important studies of major doctrines — God, creation, Christ, atonement. For the doctrine of God there is chosen an article on a major Christian thinker, Augustine, by someone acknowledged as a major contemporary Augustine scholar, J.J. O'Donnell. Basic to the Christian world view is the doctrine of creation, and once more Augustine is the object of study (by R. Williams).[2] The bridge between the transcendent God and human beings is supplied in Christian thought by the doctrine of the incarnation of the Word of God.[3] Christ brought reconcilliation between God and humanity by his death on a cross. Eugene TeSelle, himself an important interpreter of Augustine but here dealing primarily with thinkers other than Augustine, looks at the ancient imagery of ransom, now out of favor with most theologians, as a valid contemporary way of describing the effects of the atonement.

On the possibility of divine suffering the Hebrew biblical view of God clashed with the usual philosophical understanding of deity as impassible. This subject has come to prominence once again in modern theology, and this perspective has risen to the surface in the study of the early fathers, especially advocated by Joseph Hallman. In the article chosen to be included here, Hallman finds the logical rigor of the theologians of the Antioch school in refusing to consider the possibility of divine suffering and the guarded openness of the theologians of Alexandria to consider the "paradox of impassible suffering" to be significant for their contrasting approaches to the relation of the divine and human in Christ; Hallman suggests that both viewpoints have something to contribute to the church today.

Other doctrinal topics of recurring interest could not be included in this volume, but some studies may be noted: How the doctrine of original sin emerged,[4] and sin and freedom of the will as related to spirituality.[5] Eschatological topics are treated in Volume VI.

As examples of the varieties in early Christianity, studies are presented on topics of perennial interest — Arianism, Donatism, and the Augustinian-Pelagian conflict — and a newcomer of the last fifty years, Gnosticism. Diversity was already evident in the early history of the church in the differences between Jewish and Gentile believers. The diverse phenomena brought together under the umbrella of "Jewish Christianity" continue to provoke consideration.[6] At one time Gnosticism (the very label for which has become problematic[7]) was considered by most to be the opposite of Jewish Christianity, since it brought heretical teachings into Christianity from the pagan world. Now the Jewish element in Gnosticism is given major consideration. This volume includes survey articles on one of the last half-century's major concerns, Gnosticism, by two of the subject's major students, R. McL. Wilson (a history of research)[8] and Bentley Layton (an introduction to the phenomenon itself).

Arius has been the subject of many studies. These are surveyed by Christopher Stead, who has himself contributed in a major way to a clarification of the issues in the Trinitarian discussions related to Arius and his associates. The reign of Constantine was the setting for a major theological discussion in the East — Arianism — and a major ecclesiological conflict in the West (North Africa) — Donatism. One of the many studies Maureen Tilley has devoted to Donatism in North Africa[9] is included here.

North Africa, too, was the flash point for the outbreak of the Pelagian controversy, which came to embroil much of the western church and to touch on significant questions of human nature and salvation. The two printed lectures of Gerald Bonner are an excellent introduction to the issues involved in the conflict. Patout Burns explains how Augustinianism could rapidly become the majority view when it represented such a reversal of so much earlier Christian thought. Carol Scheppard studies the key issue between Augustine and Julian of Eclanum, who became the literary standard bearer of Pelagius's viewpoint — original sin and its transmission from Adam to all humanity. The Pelagian controversy also raised discussion of the practice of infant baptism and the reasons for it.[10]

Not represented in this volume is the study of schismatic movements. Among these is Novatianism.[11] Especially prominent in recent study is the significant attention given to the Montanist movement, which was forced into schism from the great church. Major publications include collections of source material in English,[12] monographs,[13] and shorter papers on particular topics — challenging the characterization of Montanism as millenarian,[14] arguing that women and not Montanus were its real founders,[15] and attributing to it the occasion for persecution under Septimius Severus.[16] The prominence of women in the Montanist movement, not limited to its beginning, relates to the concerns in Volume I.

Another schismatic movement that was charged with heresy and had some points of kinship with Montanism was Priscillianism. Since the major study over two decades ago by Henry Chadwick,[17] other books have explored other ramifications of Priscillian's movement.[18] This volume includes a study by Ferreiro of the attack on the person of Priscillian made by Jerome, who was notorious for fierce personal attacks on persons with whom he disagreed.

Syriac-speaking Christianity is drawing increasing attention, as a number of western scholars have gained competence in reading Syriac texts, many of which remain unedited. The third annual Syriac Symposium meets June 17–20, 1999, at Notre Dame.

Syriac Christianity is chosen for special treatment because of this burgeoning attention, so that it serves well as an example of the regional and linguistic variety in early Christianity. Moreover, Syriac-speaking Christianity has importance on the world stage as the source of the considerable eastern expansion of Christianity (reaching to China and India) and as the first branch of Christianity to come to grips with Islam, leading to the phenomenon of an Arabic-speaking Christianity.[19]

Christianity made its apearance in Syria early, and Syriac texts preserve important source material, but one must be cautious about the use of this material. David Bundy has employed his amazing linguistic competence to open up many of the eastern manifestations of Christianity. In this collection he looks at the Syriac *Life of Abercius*, finding its setting in fourth-century Phrygia and so not a primary source for early Syriac Christianity. Sebastian Brock is at the forefront of making Syriac texts accessible to western scholars and indeed to members of Syriac-speaking religious communities.[20] His two contributions to this volume provide good introductions to the history and theology of Syriac Christianity. Aphrahat was the first major Christian writer in Syriac whose works survive, and his Christology has great interest as a Semitic counterpart to the developing Christology of the Greek-speaking church.[21] Ephraim, however, was Syriac's most prolific and influential author; Sidney Griffith offers a magisterial introduction to him. The abundant exegetical work that survives in Syriac supplements the western exegesis that is studied in Volume III.[22] Syriac Christianity had its own distinctive ascetic tradition, and notice of this topic here complements attention given to asceticism in Volume V.

NOTES

[1] Alongside this may be placed a similar study for the first three centuries — A.M. Ritter, "'Orthodoxy,' 'Heresy,' and the Unity of the Church in Pre-Constantinian Times," *Studia Patristica* 24 (1993):316–30.

[2] Cf. also, N. Joseph Torchia, "The Implications of the Doctrine of *Creatio ex Nihilo* in Augustine's Theology," *Studia Patristica* 33 (1997):266–73.

[3] Brian E. Daley, "Divine Transcendence and Human Transformation: Gregory of Nyssa's Anti-Apollinarian Christology," *Studia Patristica* 32 (1997):87–95; for Augustine on this subject, idem, "A Humble Mediator: Distinctive Elements of Augustine's Christology," *Word and Spirit* 9 (1987):100–17. Daley has also made important contributions to the understanding of the Christology of Leontius of Byzantium — "'A Rich Union': Leontius of Byzantium and the Relation of Human and Divine in Christ," *Studia Patristica* 24 (1993):239–65.

[4] Jean LaPorte, "From Impure Blood to Original Sin," *Studia Patristica* 31 (1979):438–44.

[5] John J. O'Keefe, "Sin, *Apatheia*, and Freedom of the Will in Gregory of Nyssa," *Studia Patristica* 22 (1989):52–59.

[6] Joan E. Taylor, "The Phenomenon of Early Jewish-Christianity: Reality or Scholarly Invention?," *Vigiliae Christianae* 44 (1990):313–34.

[7] Michael A. Williams, *Rethinking "Gnosticism": An Argument for Dismantling a Dubious Category* (Princeton: Princeton University Press, 1996). For bibliography on "Gnosticism" see the annual updates by David M. Scholer in *Novum Testamentum*.

[8] For another survey, James M. Robinson, "Nag Hammadi: The First Fifty Years," in J.D. Turner and A. McGuire, *The Nag Hammadi Library after Fifty Years: Proceedings of the 1995 Society of Biblical Literature Commemoration* (Leiden: E. J. Brill, 1997), pp. 3–33.

[9] Among these, Maureen Tilley, "From Separatist Sect to Majority Church: The Ecclesiologies of Parmenian and Tyconius," *Studia Patristica* 33 (1997):260–65; see introduction to Vol. II, n. 12.

[10] William Harmless, "Christ the Pediatrician: Infant Baptism and Christological Imagery in the Pelagian Controversy," *Augustinian Studies* 28 (1997):7–34.

[11] Martin Wallraff, "Socrates Scholasticus on the History of Novatianism," *Studia Patristica* 29 (1997):170–77.

[12] Ronald E. Heine, *The Montanist Oracles and Testimonia*, Patristic Monograph Series 14 (Macon: Mercer University Press, 1989) and William Tabbernee, *Montanist Inscriptions and Testimonia: Epigraphic Sources Illustrating the History of Montanism*, Patristic Monograph Series 16 (Macon: Mercer University Press, 1996). Tabbernee uses the inscriptions as the basis for his study of "Montanist Regional Bishops: New Evidence from Ancient Inscriptions," *Journal of Early Christian Studies* 1 (1993):249–80.

[13] Christine Trevett, *Montanism: Gender, Authority, and the New Prophecy* (Cambridge: Cambridge University Press, 1996).

[14] Charles E. Hill, "The Marriage of Montanism and Millennialism," *Studia Paristica* 26 (1993):140–46.

[15] Anne Jensen, "Prisca — Maximilla — Montanus: Who Was the Real Founder of 'Montanism'?" *Studia Patristica* 26 (1993):147–50.

[16] Andrzej Wypustek, "Magic, Montanism, Perpetua, and the Severan Persecution," *Vigiliae Christianae* 51 (1997):276–97.

[17] *Priscillian of Avila* (Oxford: Clarendon Press, 1976).

[18] R. Van Dam, *Leadership and Community in Later Antique Gaul* (Berkeley: University of California Press, 1985); Virginia Burrus, *The Making of a Heretic: Gender, Authority, and the Priscillianist Controversy* (Berkeley: University of California Press, 1995).

[19] Sidney H. Griffith, "Muslims and Church Councils: the Apology of Theodore Abū Qurrah," *Studia Patristica* 25 (1993):270–99; idem, *Theodore Abū Qurrah: A Treatise on the Veneration of the Holy Icons* (Leuven: Peeters, 1997).

[20] Among his many publications note "Syriac Studies in the Last Three Decades: Some Reflections," in *VI Symposium Syriacum (1992)*, ed. René Lavenant, Orientalia Christiana Analecta 247 (Rome, 1994), pp. 13–29, and "Fire from Heaven: From Abel's Sacrifice to the Eucharist. A Theme in Syriac Christianity," *Studia Patristica* 25 (1993):229–43.

[21] William L. Petersen, "The Christology of Aphrahat, the Persian Sage: An Excursus on the 17th *Demonstration*," *Vigiliae Christianae* 46 (1992):241–56.

[22] As a sample, J. Frishman, "Type and Reality in the Exegetical Homilies of Narsai," *Studia Patristica* 20 (1989):169–79.

UNITY AND DIVERSITY IN THE CHURCH OF THE FOURTH CENTURY

by ANDREW LOUTH

To look back to the early Church as a theologian and historian, and ask questions about her unity, is to enter on a long tradition, which goes back at least to the Reformation, if not to the Great Schism of 1054 itself. Once the Church had split, the various separated Christians looked back to justify their position in that tragedy. They scoured the early sources for evidence for and against episcopacy, papacy, authority confided to tradition or to Scripture alone: they questioned the form in which these early sources have come down to us – the sixteenth century saw reserves of scholarly genius poured into the problem, for instance, of the genuineness of the Ignatian correspondence, and what fired all that, apart from scholarly curiosity, was the burning question of the authenticity of episcopal authority on which Ignatius speaks so decisively. Out of that the critical discipline of patristics emerged. It was, in fact, rather later that the fourth century became the focus of the debate about the unity, authority, and identity of the Church – Newman obviously springs to mind and his *Arians of the Fourth Century* (London, 1833) and his *Essay on the Development of Doctrine* (London, 1845). Later on, the fourth century attracted the attention of scholars such as Professor H. M. Gwatkin and his *Studies in Arianism* (Cambridge, 1882), and Professor S. L. Greenslade and his *Schism in the Early Church* (London, 1953), and in quite modern times Arianism, in particular, has remained a mirror in which scholars have seen reflected the problems of the modern Church (a good example is the third part of Rowan Williams's *Arius: Heresy and Tradition* [London, 1987], though there are plenty of others). Continental scholars such as Adolf von Harnack also studied the past, informed by theological perspectives derived from the present; in a different and striking way Erik Peterson turned to the fourth century to find the roots of an ideology of unity that was fuelling the murderous policies of Nazism.[1] In all these cases the

---

[1] Erik Peterson, *Der Monotheismus als politisches Problem*, reprinted in *Theologische Traktate* (Munich, 1951), pp. 45–147. See also A. Schindler, ed., *Monotheismus als Politisches Problem? Erik Peterson und die Kritik der politischen Theologie* (Gütersloh, 1978).

fourth century seemed to be a test case – for questions of *modern* ecclesiology: Rome defended by development in the case of Newman, the justification for the ecumenical movement in the case of Greenslade. As scholars looked back they had various ideas as to how the unity of the Church could be expressed, in what it consisted – Newman was concerned to argue that without the living authority of the papacy none of these add up to very much, Greenslade on the contrary pointed to the very varied ways in which the Church has articulated a sense of its unity and identity and wanted to insist that nothing is a *sine qua non*. There are of course dangers in looking back over the centuries, and I do not wish to suggest that scholars in the past were not aware of them. The main danger is, it seems to me, that things that are obvious to us may never have occurred to those who lived in the past, and contrariwise what seemed pressing to them may be ignored by us because it is not crucial for us. But, conscious, I hope, of the warning of one of my Cambridge professors that one cannot jump out of one's epistemological skin, what I want to do in this paper is to try and recapture something of what unity and diversity in the Church meant to Christians in the fourth century.

But let us begin in the present century. In a survey carried out in Moscow and Pskov in 1992, people were asked where they got their religious and philosophical ideas from. Overall the most influential source of such ideas was newspapers and TV (thirty-nine per cent); even among believers this was still an important source (twenty-seven per cent), running close to relatives and friends (twenty-nine per cent), and the Gospels or other religious literature (thirty-three per cent). The Church, sermons, conversations with clergy were pretty low down the scale (nine per cent overall, only nineteen per cent among believers).[2] What is interesting about these statistics is that they demonstrate the existence of what we could call 'organs of ecumenicity' that the early Church would not even have dreamt of. The 'media' make possible a common pool of ideas, and also a common sense of belonging, that was not there in the fourth century. Many people, even believers, derive their notion of what Christianity is about from the media, and even derive something of their sense

---

[2] Lyudmila Vorontsova and Sergei Filatov, 'The changing pattern of religious belief: *perestroika* and beyond', *Religion, State and Society*, 22.1 (1994), pp. 89–96, table on p. 92.

of identity as religious believers from the same source. And this is clearly something new. It is, of course, the printing press that forms the crucial turning-point in making available ideas in a way that transcends the physical reach of the human communities which originated or fostered them. What that made available was new 'organs of ecumenicity' – a common Bible, printed catechisms, a uniform liturgy – all of these used by religious communities in Western Europe from the early modern period onwards as ways of expressing and nurturing their unity and identity. And none of this was available in that way to the Church of the fourth century: 'would that we were so lucky' must be the view of many in the modern Russian Orthodox Church! It is here that I would locate one of the greatest differences between ourselves and people of the fourth century, differences that have caused our 'world' to shrink, so that our immediate consciousness has expanded to embrace virtually the whole of the globe, and is no longer restricted to the local communities to which we belong.

At this point I think wewneed to remind ourselves just how diverse and disparate the communities of the fourth century – and not just the Christian communities – were. The basic unit was the city – πόλις, *civitas* – with its surrounding countryside. Except in the case of a few great cities, especially Rome and Constantinople, the city and its surroundings were a self-contained economic unit. They were also self-governing, governed by local notables. Their loyalties were primarily local, which found expression in the local religious cults that Christians were to call 'pagan'. The Roman Empire made no attempt to erase this prevailing sense of locality. A variety of languages were spoken but we have little idea about them except when they attained literary expression – something that had already happened to Latin and Greek, and was to happen in the fourth century, largely under Christian auspices, in the cases of Syriac, Coptic, and Gothic. This sense of locality was reinforced by distance, and slowness and difficulty in travelling: we hear of quite a bit of travelling, but it was the preserve of a tiny class. We know, and Peter Brown has recently given eloquent expression to,[3] the problems caused to those who were responsible for governing

---

[3] See P. Brown, *Power and Persuasion in Late Antiquity. Towards a Christian Empire* (Wisconsin, 1992), pp. 3–34.

the empire by poor communications and powerful local interests: a governor could be months away from any confirmation
from the Imperial court, and in many cases it would be safer to
collude with the power of local notables than to risk confrontation in such a vacuum of clear imperial support. There was, of
course, a unified system of public office imposed from above, of
which the governors were the lowest rank. Cities were grouped
into provinces, each subject to a governor appointed for about
two years, provinces into dioceses under *vicarii*, dioceses into
prefectures governed by praetorian prefects, themselves subject
to the emperor (or Imperial college). Emperors often spoke in
their edicts of the empire as a single whole and issued decrees in
respect of it, but recent studies of the fourth century have
emphasized the distance we must recognize between the rhetoric
of imperial decree and political reality: the language may be that
of a 'command economy', but there was not the administrative
machinery for that to be an attainable reality.[4]

It was such a world that the fourth-century Church inhabited,
and whatever unity it experienced had to be something achiev-
able within such a world. The Church's own rhetoric of unity
was considerable. The New Testament fuelled such language and
made it inevitable: the great high-priestly prayer placed on the lips
of Jesus in John 17, the frequent exhortations to unity found in
Saint Paul's epistles, ,together with the powerful imagery he uses
to express it, especially that of the Church as the body of Christ –
all this makes unity an inexorable part of Christian self-conscious-
ness. There were other pressures behind such rhetoric of unity.
Philosophical thinking – both profound, as with Plotinus, and
popular, say in the Hermetic literature – laid great store by unity.
Everything came from unity and was destined for unity. Division
was seen as fragmentation, multiplicity as attenuation.

> The One remains, the many change and pass;
> Heaven's light forever shines, Earth's shadows fly;
> Life, like a dome of many-coloured glass,
> Stains the white radiance of Eternity . . .[5]

---

[4] See, for instance, summarizing much modern research, Averil Cameron, *The Later Roman Empire*
(London, 1993), pp. 113ff., and on Diocletian's 'Price Edict' (301), p. 38.
[5] P. B. Shelley, 'Adonais', stanza 52 (ed. T. Hutchinson, 1904; 1952 edition, Oxford, p. 443).

Morality was defined in terms of unity; singleness – i.e., celibacy – became an ideal that reached beyond the confusing multiplicity of the present. All that only made the Christian rhetoric of the unity of the Church even more compelling. To what, in the real world of the fourth-century Roman Empire, did that rhetoric of unity correspond?

The first thing to be mentioned is, I think, obvious: it is that in the course of the fourth century what was meant by the unity of the Church changed, or rather that the ways in which the Church could express its unity changed – it became 'ecumenical' in the sense that it became an important part of the *oikoumene*, the inhabited world over which the emperor ruled as God's representative. But what did the Church bring into the fourth century? What organs of unity did it already possess, before it had thrust upon it, or found itself thrust into, the imperial structures of unity?

Long before the beginning of the fourth century, the primary, empirical expression of the unity of the Church had emerged. The Christian Church had spread throughout the Roman Empire as an urban phenomenon: it was in the city that the Church flourished. By the end of the second century, at the latest, the unity of the Church in each place had found expression in the fact that each local community, each 'church' in one of the senses of the word *ecclesia*, was led by a bishop, an *episcopus*. It is still not clear what the *essential* role of the bishop was: it is confused by the fact that from the fourth century onwards the bishop became the obvious spokesman for and representative of the local church for almost all purposes in the new 'ecumenical' Church. Dom Gregory Dix has argued,[6] convincingly I think, that the primary and essential role of the bishop in the Christian community was liturgical: he presided over the celebration of the Christian liturgy, nothing took place without his authority, though certainly in larger cities much must have been delegated.

---

[6] In his *Jurisdiction in the Early Church* (London, 1975). For a full, but concise, account of the role of the Christian bishop in late antiquity (mainly, of course, from the fourth century onwards), see H. Chadwick, 'The role of the Christian bishop in ancient society', in *Center for Hermeneutical Studies, Protocol of the 35th Colloquy* (February 1979), 35 (Berkeley, Cal., 1979), pp. 1–14 (reprinted in idem, *Heresy and Orthodoxy in the Early Church* [London, 1991], no. 3).

This principle of 'one city, one bishop' seems to have been adhered to quite strictly: even a huge city like Rome had only one bishop – we know from Eusebius that already by the middle of the third century the single bishop (Cornelius) presided over an establishment of forty-six presbyters, seven deacons, seven sub-deacons, forty-two acolytes, fifty-two exorcists, readers, and doorkeepers, and more than fifteen hundred widows and distressed persons.[7] More than one bishop meant schism, a divided Church (or rather division from the Church): an uncompromising assertion of precisely that by Pope Cornelius is the point of the letter just quoted from Eusebius.

In what other ways was the unity of the Church expressed? The next point that needs to be stressed is something that flows from the liturgical function of the bishop. The celebration of the eucharist itself is an expression of unity – such an idea goes right back to Paul (see I Cor. 10.16–17). But the unity of what – the universal Church, or the local community gathered together with its bishop? One of the earliest eucharistic prayers makes it clear that more is meant than the unity of the local community: 'Be mindful of your Church, O Lord; deliver it from all evil, perfect it in your love, sanctify it, and gather it from the four winds into the kingdom that you have prepared for it.'[8] But as the eucharistic prayers become more expansive, it becomes clear that more is meant than the unity of all Christians who are alive. The Liturgy of St Basil, immediately after the invocation of the Holy Spirit over the worshippers and the holy gifts, prays:

> and unite us all one with another who partake of the one bread and the cup in the communion of the One Holy Spirit . . . that we may find mercy and grace with all the saints who have been pleasing to you from eternity, forefathers, fathers, patriarchs, prophets, apostles, preachers, evangelists, martyrs, confessors, teachers, and every just spirit, all made perfect in faith, and especially our most holy,

---

[7] Cited in Eusebius, *Ecclesiastical History*, VI, xliii, 11 (ed. E. Schwartz, *Die Griechischen Christlichen Schriftsteller der ersten drei Jahrhunderte*, Eusebius Werke, 2 [3 parts, Berlin, 1903–9], p. 618).

[8] *Didache* 10 (F. X. Funk and K. Bihlmeyer, eds, *Die Apostolischen Väter*, 3rd edn [Tübingen, 1970], p. 6).

most pure and ever-blessed Lady, Mother of God and ever-Virgin, Mary . . ."[9]

The one Church into the unity of which we are gathered in the eucharist is primarily the communion of those 'made perfect in faith', secondly it is those gathered together at any particular celebration of the eucharist within that deeper unity, and thirdly (or perhaps: second equal) it is everyone everywhere embraced by that deeper unity. I emphasize this, because the impression is often given that *ecclesia* means either the universal Church (in the sense of geographically universal) or the local Christian community or both: it does indeed mean both, but because first of all it has the meaning just suggested, of unity with the Church already gathered together before the heavenly throne. One might perhaps object that this sense of the Church as embracing those 'beyond the veil' is hardly a sense in which the rhetoric of unity is cashed in terms of the *real* world of the Roman Empire. But I do not think it would have seemed so to Christians of this period. That other world was very real: the Christian cult of saints did not expand into a vacuum, it expanded into another world of whose contours Christians were much more confident than either their modern brothers and sisters in the faith or their pagan contemporaries. And, I might add, they often give the impression that they were more confident of the contours of the realm beyond, inhabited by the saints and patriarchs, and opened up by Christ's resurrection, than of many parts of the Mediterranean world beyond their own immediate locality. The local church, with its growing number of local saints, came to do at least as good a job of defining and expressing local loyalties and local identity as the local pagan cults had done, while at the same time expressing a sense of belonging that transcended the merely local.

In what other ways did the rhetoric of unity find expression? As well as giving expression to a sense of unity with the heavenly courts in the way I have just sketched, the liturgy has historically been used as a way of imposing uniformity and therefore a sense of common unity: one thinks of the place of the Tridentine mass

---

[9] F. E. Brightman, *Liturgies Eastern and Western* (Oxford, 1896), pp. 330f. [my translation].

between Trent and Vatican II,[10] or of the place of the Book of Common Prayer within Anglicanism. In both cases it is widely felt that unity has been made less tangible with the loss of uniformity of liturgical rite. The Church as it embarked on the fourth century had nothing approaching liturgical uniformity: the liturgical variety that becomes manifest with the evidence in the fourth and fifth centuries clearly has deep roots. And yet – sometime towards the end of the second century a Christian bishop, Abercius, whose see was probably Hieropolis in Phrygia (often confused with Hierapolis in the valley of the Maeander), had an inscription set up in which he spoke of his travels to Rome in the West and as far as Nisibis in the East, in which he says,

> He [the pure Shepherd whose disciple Abercius is] also sent me to royal Rome to behold it and to see the golden-robed, golden-slippered Queen. And there I saw a people bearing the splendid seal. And I saw the plain of Syria and all the cities, even Nisibis, crossing over the Euphrates. And everywhere I had associates. In company with Paul I followed, while everywhere faith led the way, and set before me for food the fish from the fountain, mighty and stainless (whom a pure virgin grasped), and gave this to friends to eat always, having good wine and giving the mixed cup with bread.[11]

This text, resplendent with symbolism – the 'splendid seal' is clearly the baptismal seal, the fish a eucharistic reference to Christ (perhaps the earliest) – bears witness to the fact that wherever he was Abercius felt himself at one with other Christians in the celebration of the eucharist. Reading this inscription one might wonder what linguistic diversity Abercius had to cope with in his travels. Greek was clearly the language of his own Church, though it was not the original language of the region.

---

[10] It was pointed out to me that my rhetoric has led me into exaggeration: in many parts of Europe, even by the nineteenth century, the Tridentine mass had only made slow progress in becoming accepted.

[11] Translation taken from J. Lightfoot, *The Apostolic Fathers*, Part II, 1 (London, 1885), p. 480. For his discussion of Abercius, whom he identifies with Eusebius' Avircius Marcellus (see Eusebius, *Ecclesiastical History*, V, xvi; ed. Schwartz, pp. 458–68), see pp. 476–85. A substantial fragment of the inscription survives and was discovered by W. M. Ramsay in 1883.

In the West he travelled as far as Rome, where his Greek would have stood him in good stead: some evidence suggests that Christianity in Rome was Greek-speaking until the beginning of the third century, though other evidence seems to point to Latin Christianity (Hermas refers to a kind of Roman fast as *statio*, a Latin word,[12] and the discovery of the ROTAS-SATOR square at Pompeii is evidence for Latin-speaking Christianity on the Italian mainland by the middle of the first century.)[13] In the East he reached Nisibis, recently (under Verus in the 160s) restored to the Roman Empire: it was presumably Hellenistic, it did not become a centre for Christian Syriac culture until the fourth century.

But the point of this digression is that another way of articulating unity – that of linguistic culture – does not seem to have had any great importance for the early Church. All the original documents of Christianity – the apostolic letters, the Gospels – are, of course, in Greek and the Church was greatly assisted by the widespread use of Greek throughout the Roman Empire. But in the early centuries, where Latin was the local language, Christianity clothed itself in Latin dress. Later on, Christianity adopted the linguistic dress of Syriac, CoCtic, and Gothic: in each case a literature was created, for Christianity was a literary religion, needing at least some of the Scriptures to be available in any language it adopted. Later still, in the ninth century, an alphabet and the basic linguistic structures were created for Slavonic, enabling it to become yet another Christian language. These points seem to me to be worth recalling, since later on various forms of Christianity did identify themselves very closely with a literary culture: Byzantine Christianity for a century or so before the conversion of the Slavs, and Roman Christianity for more than a millenium (though even as late as the ninth century neither Pope Nicholas I nor his successor Pope Hadrian II identified Roman Christianity exclusively with Latin, as their attitude to the Moravian mission of St Cyril and St Methodius makes clear). But there seems to have been no attempt to use

---

[12] Hermas, *Pastor, Simil.*, 5.1.1 and 2 (ed. M. Whittaker, *Die Griechischen Christlichen Schriftsteller der ersten Jahrhunderte*, Die Apostolischen Väter, I. Der Hirt des Hermas [Berlin, 1967], p. 52).

[13] On the Rotas-Sator square, see H. Last, 'The Rotas-Sator Square: present position and future prospects', *JThS*, ns 3 (1952), pp. 92–7.

linguistic culture to express the universality of Christianity in the early centuries, and especially not in the fourth century, when on the contrary the Church seems to have presided over linguistic diversification.

There are also two perhaps more prosaic ways of trying to express the unity of the Church that had been developed before the fourth century. The first is the council or synod (synod is the Christian name, as Ammianus Marcellinus tells us).[14] On several occasions in Eusebius' *Church History* we read of synods of bishops gathered together to deal with some problem. For instance in the 260s several synods seem to have met in Antioch to deal with the problem of Paul of Samosata, who had succeeded Demetrian as Bishop of Antioch. Eusebius' account is confused, and scholarly discussion has probably compounded the confusion. Eusebius at any rate regarded Paul as a heretic whose Christology was inadequate. A synod was required to deal with the problem, since Paul was himself a bishop. We also hear of synods in connection with the problems raised by the Decian persecution and the mass apostasy it occasioned. The synods in Carthage we know from the surviving correspondence of Cyprian, Bishop of Carthage: they met under the chairmanship of Cyprian and reached binding decisions as to how to meet the various problems raised. The Decian persecution also provoked the Novatianist schism in Rome, dealt with by Pope Cornelius by means of a synod with representatives from Italy, Africa and elsewhere. Eusebius tells us of synods from the second century, dealing with issues such as the date of Easter, and the heresy of Montanism. The issues raised vary: sometimes they concern matters of practice – moral or liturgical, sometimes matters of faith. They are concerned with defining the limits of belonging: the sanction is exclusion from communion. Communion is a pre-eminently episcopal matter: it is the bishop who celebrates (or presides over) the eucharist, it is he who baptizes and catechizes (something that remains an episcopal duty until at least the fifth century), and so ultimately decides who shall be admitted to catechesis and baptism. It is not surprising, then, that these

[14] See Ammianus Marcellinus, *Res gestae*, XV, xvii, 7 (ed. J. C. Rolfe, Loeb Classical Library, 3 vols, 1964 edn, 1, p. 162) [*synodus ut appellant*]; cf. XXI, xvi, 18 (Loeb Classical Library, 2, p. 184).

10

synods appear, from the evidence Eusebius gives us, as predominantly episcopal: they are exercises in what is nowadays known as episcopal 'collegiality'. Cyprian, in his *De ecclesiae catholicae unitate*, provides the germ of a theological justification of such episcopal collegiality. Episcopacy is a unity, each bishop holds his part in its totality ('episcopatus unus est cuius a singulis in solidum pars tenetur'). 'So the Church forms a unity, however far she spreads . . . just as the sun's rays are many, yet the light is one.'[15] Synods are a formal expression of such collegiality: Eusebius' *Church History* also reveals informal expressions of such collegiality, exercised through letters, for instance through the letters written by Cornelius of Rome and Dionysius of Alexandria to Fabius of Antioch, who was inclined to take Novatian's part over apostasy.[16] With the synods at Carthage, we have already seen them being used to generate what was to be called canon law, laws concerned with the life of the Church: by the beginning of the fourth century that process had moved a step further, as the canons of the Council of Elvira indicate.[17]

The papacy was another expression of the unity of the church. Because it was later to develop such clearly defined features there has been a tendency to read them back into the earliest period, and a corresponding tendency to refuse to do anything of the sort. But it is difficult not to see Rome already exercising a ministry of unity in the letter Clement wrote, on behalf of the Roman Church, to the Christians of Corinth at the end of the first century, nor to see Rome being conceded some kind of special role when Ignatius addresses the Roman Church as the one who 'presides in love' – προκαθημένη τῆς ἀγάπης.[18] What this amounted to, what it could amount to, is much less clear. One thing, though, I think is certain: Rome neither made nor was conceded any such kind of claim on the grounds that it was the capital of the Roman Empire. There is no evidence either way, but it seems to me unlikely that persecuted Christians

---

[15] Cyprian, *De unitate*, 5 (Cyprian, *De lapsis* and *De ecclesiae catholicae unitate*, ed. and trans. M. Bevenot, SJ, Oxford Early Christian Texts [Oxford, 1971], p. 64).

[16] *Ecclesiastical History*, VI, xlii–xliii (ed. Schwartz, pp. 610–24).

[17] For the canons of Elvira, see M. J. Routh, *Reliquiae Sacrae*, 2nd edn (Oxford, 1846), 4, pp. 255–74.

[18] Ignatius, *Ad Rom.*, prologue (Funk and Bihlmeyer, eds, p. 97).

would have regarded the seat of the persecuting power (which they called 'Babylon') with any religious reverence for that reason – the Church there might have been venerated because of the multitude of Christians who had suffered there, but that is something different. And on the question of Rome's claims, it is striking that Rome always makes a claim on the basis of something that makes some kind of Christian sense – the pope as successor of Peter (already by Pope Stephen's time), as the guardian of the relics of the Roman martyrs, especially Peter and Paul (Pope Damasus' best claim to fame). All I want to claim is that by the beginning of the fourth century the church of Rome, and even the bishop of Rome, have already seen that church, or that office, as exercising a peculiar ministry of unity for the Church as a whole.

So far I have explored – or sketched – various ways in which the unity of the Church was articulated or expressed by the beginning of the fourth century. The points I have made do not constitute any kind of exclusive list: a case can be made (though it is speculative) that until the fourth century various forms of Christian identity existed side-by-side, and in particular that alongside the model of episcopally-defined communion, there existed the model of membership of a doctrinally-defined school. But if that is so then the history of the fourth century is the history of the victory (or final victory) of the bishops.

The fourth century, as everyone knows (though students are constantly tempted to foreshorten the process), saw a dramatic transition in the fortunes of the Church. As the century began, the Church was on the brink of the so-called 'Great Persecution'. That ended with the conversion of Constantine and the beginning of imperial favour for the Christian Church. By the end of the century and the reign of Theodosius, who died in 395, it can be said that the Christian Church had become the official religion of the Roman Empire. The status as object of imperial favour – and even more its final status as official leligion – gave the question of Christian unity a new dimension. If there was schism, if there were rival claimants to an episcopal see, for instance in Carthage, as there were, who was going to receive the imperial bounty? It is not surprising, from what we have seen already, that this question rises in a local context. The attempts to deal with this problem, the problem of Donatism, are a curious mixture of imperial measures – the bishop of Rome appointed as head of an imperial commission – and the traditional methods of the Christian Church – Pope Miltiades inviting other bishops to join him and thus turning the commission into a synod. Although Constantine was able to reach an unambiguous conclusion as to which claimant in Carthage was the real one, the Donatists did not vanish by imperial decree, could not be compelled by anything less than unacceptable force to give up their churches, nor prevented from seizing churches repaired by imperial funds. The schism, as we know, dragged on and on. More serious was the Arian controversy, which reached the attention of the emperor just after he had attained sole control of the Empire with the defeat of Licinius in 324. This, as everyone knows, was dealt with by the calling of the first 'ecumenical' council at Nicaea in 325. Although it w s not called 'ecumenical' for another dozen years (or if it was, that most likely has something to do with the Church's plea for exemption from tax, as Professor Henry Chadwick has suggested),[19] it is not wrong in retrospect to see it as 'ecumenical' and as marking a turning-point. This is not primarily because of its decision about Arianism, though that came to have almost paradigmatic significance too, but because of what was decided in the canons it passed, especially canon 6.[20] 'Let the ancient customs continue' begins the canon, and then goes on to spell them out: the authority customarily exercised by the bishop of Alexandria over Egypt, Libya, and Pentapolis, the 'similar' authority exercised by the bishop of Rome, and finally, 'similarly in Antioch and the other provinces the prerogatives of the metropolises over the churches are to be preserved'.[21] This confirms what has already been affirmed in canon 4 that the right of confirming episcopal appointments lies with the metropolitan bishop. This is seen as the continuation of 'the ancient customs – τὰ ἀρχαῖα ἔθη – but it also conforms the organization of the Church to the existing (and changing) norms of the administration of the Empire: the metropolitans correspond to the governors of the provinces, and

---

[19] See H. Chadwick, 'The origin of the title "Oecumenical Council" ', *JThS*, ns, 23 (1972), pp. 132–5, esp. p. 135 and note.

[20] On canon 6 see H. Chadwick, 'Faith and order at the Council of Nicaea: a note on the background of the sixth canon', *HThR* 53 (1960), pp. 171–95.

[21] Following the text defended by Chadwick, 'Faith and order', pp. 180–1.

their see is the seat of the governor. It seems that something like this had already emerged by the beginning of the fourth century, but this formalized it, and it meant that as the division of the provinces changed, so did the area subject to a metropolitan – as was to happen in Cappadocia in 371/2 to the distress of St Basil of Caesarea.[22] The power of the metropolitan bishop was magnified – bishops become more and more his suffragans – as also emerges from St Basil's reaction to the events of the 370s. In the cases of Alexandria, Rome and Antioch, their jurisdiction extended beyond that of the civil province (though this is stated very unclearly in the case of Antioch, which is perhaps why the original text is no longer preserved in the Greek MSS), corresponding in some way to that of the *vicarii* or even the praetorian prefects. The structure of the Church mirrors that of the Empire, and vice versa: there is more than a suggestion that they are interdependent. What then of the unity of the Church: does it simply reflect the unity of the Empire? There is a good deal of evidence to support such an idea: Christianity, both in the West and the East, identifies itself with the Empire, and has little interest in extending beyond the (old) boundaries (St Patrick, who preached Christianity in Ireland beyond the traditional frontier, seems to have regarded the terms *Romanus* and *Christianus* as synonymous).[23] The idea that the Church reflects the Empire seems to be the reasoning behind canon 3 of the Council of Constantinople (381) – 'because it is new Rome, the bishop of Constantinople is to enjoy privileges of honour after the bishop of Rome' – reaffirmed in canon 28 of the Council of Chalcedon (451), where the parallelism between Church and Empire is expressed in greater detail.[24] This symbiosis between Church and Empire was further deepened by other developments in the fourth century, especially the way in which Constantine's concession to Christian consciences in allowing bishops to function as magistrates[25] had the long-term effect of

---

[22] See B. Gaïn, *L'Église de Cappadoce au iv⁰ siècle d'après la correspondance de Basile de Césarée (330–379)*, Orientalia Christiana Analecta, 225 (Rome, 1985), pp. 306–9, with literature cited there.

[23] See St Patrick, *Ep. 2*, and L. Bieler's note in *The Works of St Patrick*, Ancient Christian Writers, 17 (London, 1953), pp. 90f.

[24] For the texts of the canons, see *DEC*, 1, pp. 32, 99–100.

[25] See A. H. M. Jones, *The Later Roman Empire, 284–602*, 3 vols (Oxford, 1964), 1, p. 480 and n.21 [3, p. 134].

making the bishop an important local figure, exercising imperial authority, at least in his legal capacity, in the city – something that had a profound effect on the daily life of St Augustine, for instance. The Church's own perceptions of unity were being drawn into, perhaps even swallowed up by, the needs of the Christian *oikoumene*.

That is, however, only part of the story of the fourth century. Many Christians were clearly seduced by the tangible import-ance they acquired from these changes. One recalls Ammianus' acid words on the benefits of the papal throne: 'once they have reached it they are assured of rich gifts from ladies of quality; they can ride in carriages, dress splendidly, and outdo kings in the lavishness of their table'.[26] But it was, perhaps curiously, from the bishop of Rome that there emerged resistance to the grow-ing symbiosis of Church and Empire (of course, individual bishops protested and proclaimed the independence of what were to be called priesthood and empire when the imperial embrace sought to constrain them to adopt policies they rejected – one thinks of Athanasius and Ambrose – but that is something different). Rome – whether bishop or church – had never accepted that its authority reflected the authority of the capital, and the canons of Constantinople and Chalcedon, mentioned above, that implied such an argument was never accepted by the pope. Increasingly, from the fourth century onwards, Rome developed a sense of its own authority. The shambles of conciliar ecumenicity in the reign of Constantius, especially – bishops travelling from synod to synod, 'hamstringing the post service', as Ammianus puts it,[27] to devise under imperial pressure one unacceptable doctrinal compromise after another – must have done wonders for Rome's claim to be arbiter of orthodoxy.

But resistance to the growing symbiosis of Church and Empire came from another direction, too. I stressed earlier how import-ant was the sense of unity with the Church 'beyond the veil', and illustrated it from a liturgical text which very likely belongs to the fourth century. The 'local' members of the heavenly court had been the martyrs, and bishops had been able to moderate

---

[26] Ammianus Marcellinus, *Res gestae*, XXVII, iii, 14 (ed. Rolfe, 3, p. 20). Trans. W. Hamilton in Ammianus Marcellinus, *The Later Roman Empire*, Penguin Classics (Harmondsworth, 1986), p. 336.
[27] Ammianus Marcellinus, *Res gestae*, XXI, xvi, 18 (ed. Rolfe, 2, p. 184).

their acknowledged authority by their control of liturgical celebration, though, especially in the heat of persecution, the tensions between bishop and martyr could come into the open, as we know from the case of Cyprian. But normally martyrs were dead, and bishops could c ntrol their cult and their influence. In the fourth century, however, as we know, the mantle of the martyr passed to the ascetic: these men and women stood on the frontier between this world and the next and exercised powers of intercession and healing that were widely acknowledged. They secured their place on the frontier by their rejection of this world, and when they recognized the importance of the Christian emperor, as from the time of St Antony onwards they often did, it was as a servant of the true God to whose court they, the ascetics, had privileged access: think for instance of St Daniel the Stylite's visit to Constantinople, concluding with the emperor, the faithless Basiliscus, and the patriarch prostrate on the ground at the feet of the holy man.[28]

What I have suggested is that in the course of the fourth century there was an attempt to develop an 'ecumenical' understanding of the unity of the Church by assimilating it to the imperial institutions. This was a considerable success: such a church is recognizable in the Church of the Byzantine Empire, and even in the West the Church played a part in the preservation of many of the elements of public order that the successor barbarian states owed to the Roman Empire. But it is only part of the story: the powerful rhetoric of unity had meant something tangible in the pre-Nicene Church, something articulated through the bishop and the liturgy. It is also the case that the attempt to enlist the pope as an imperial servant met with only limited success, though it would be a long time before the papacy was able to offer a ministry of unity in anything other than a piecemeal way – suitable 'organs of ecumenicity' needed to be developed and were only adequately provided by the growth of the new monastic orders of the tenth and eleventh centuries. But what had been most tangible about the unity of the Church – a felt communion through the Eucharist with the

---

[28] *Life of St Daniel the Stylite*, LXXXIII, trans. Ed. Dawes and N. H. Baynes, *Three Byzantine Saints* (London and Oxford, 1948), pp. 57–8.

heavenly court – was something that imperial ecumenicity could not provide, and I have suggested that the ascetics could and did. So, too, could the growing cult of the saints and their relics. The centuries that follow the fourth century see a complex power struggle taking place for the heart of the *Una sancta*. The challenge to a fundamentally secular understanding of unity came from both the pope's growing sense of his Petrine ministry of unity, which resisted assimilation of ecclesiastical authority to state authority, and from the ascetics. One can discern, as one often thinks one can at the end of Late Antiquity, different tracks leading out of Late Antiquity – to Western and Eastern Christendom respectively. If the ascetic challenge differs from the papal challenge in that it preserves the tangible sense of a unity that embraces the heavenly court, whereas the papal challenge simply offers a different understanding of the same kind of coercive authority, that may also suggest something about the differences that emerge as Late Antiquity gives way to the Middle Ages.

Goldsmiths' College, University of London

Augustinian Studies 25 (1994) 25-36

Augustine's Idea of God

James J. O'Donnell
University of Pennsylvania

Best to begin by *hearing* Augustine call on his God.

> quid es ergo, deus meus?

> summe, optime,
> potentissime, omnipotentissime,
> misericordissime et iustissime,
> secretissime et praesentissime,
> pulcherrime et fortissime,
> stabilis et incomprehensibilis,
> immutabilis mutans omnia,
> numquam novus numquam vetus,

> semper agens semper quietus,
> conligens et non egens,
> portans et implens et protegens,
> creans et nutriens et perficiens,
> quaerens cum nihil desit tibi.

> et quid diximus, deus meus, vita mea, dulcedo mea sancta,
> aut quid dicit aliquis cum de te dicit?
> et vae tacentibus de te, quoniam loquaces muti sunt.[1]

The wordplay, the assonance, the alliteration, all disappear in translation.

> What art Thou then, my God?

> Most highest, most good,
> most potent, most omnipotent;
> most merciful and most just;
> most hidden and most present;

most beautiful and most strong,
standing firm and elusive,
unchangeable and all-changing;
never new, never old;

ever working, ever at rest;
gathering in and [yet] lacking nothing;
supporting, filling, and sheltering;
creating, nourishing, and maturing;
seeking and [yet] having all things.

And what have I now said, my God, my life, my holy joy?
or what says any man when he speaks of Thee?
And woe to him who keeps silent about *you*,
since many babble on and say nothing.[2]

The limitations of human language are displayed by the paradoxes in which the divine nature compels Augustine to speak.[3] Not yet for Augustine the mannered style of an Eriugena, for whom God is good, but God is also not good (not good in the human way, at any rate), and God is finally "super-good" (i.e., good in a way that lies beyond the human category of goodness), but some of the same impulse is there. Human words used by humans fail in the presence of the divine, and whatever can be said is only approximation, and most human discourse fails to say anything of God at all, despite endless loquacious efforts.

For a rhetorician as polished as Augustine to admit failure in a matter of rhetoric is a striking thing (more than a rhetorical device here), and not without significance, as most experienced readers of Augustine will always have felt. For all the clarity and definition that Augustine can give to his writing elsewhere, it cannot be without significance that at the center of his concerns lies this finally unsayable Other, who eludes all his attempts to define and delimit. My theme in this essay is that Augustine's elusive God needs to be taken seriously, for all his elusiveness, in order to do justice to the things that Augustine says about *other* things, particularly those things that seem, to us moderns, in one way or another, perplexing or rebarbative. I am fond of saying that whenever Augustine is saying something that moderns find troubling, the best first resort for an interpreter is to look closely to see what text of scripture — not infrequently of Paul — is on the table before him and virtually forcing him — by Augustine's lights — to say what he says. That technique is often powerfully effective and needs to be employed with circumspection when looking at Augustine's views on grace and free will, for example, or on sexuality.[4]

But I find it equally important, time after time in reading Augustine, to remind myself that nothing Augustine writes is intelligible apart from his own experience of God, not only in the pages of scripture, but also in his own life. If we take the trouble to think our way into Augustine's most fundamental religious awe, we will often see a consistency and a clarity in his thought that would otherwise elude us. What I propose to outline here is not systematic. A whole book could and should be written on this theme. These remarks are rather heuristic and occasional, the fruit of spending my adult life reading and rereading Augustine, trying to do justice to him. Isidore of Seville said that the man who claims to have read all of Augustine is a liar and now, having indeed turned over all those pages and passed my eyes over all those words, I know and feel the truth of that more than ever.

It is useful to begin by looking at the narrative Augustine gives in the *Confessions* of his discovery of his God.[5] The sequence emerges if we look carefully at the way he reports the attraction the Manichees had for him and the way he resisted it. The questions the Manichees pressed hardest and with best effect on the adolescent Augustine were these:[6] where does evil come from (in other words, is God good)? does God have a body? how do we understand the seeming inconsistency between Old and New Testament versions of divine justice (in other words, is God just at all)? The short answers to these questions were simple: God is good, God is spirit, God is just.

But to find those answers took Augustine a decade's weary searching that only bore fruit after he came to Milan. Ambrose's sermons, with their emphasis on the Pauline distinction of letter and spirit as a means of interpreting the chasm between the Old and New Testament,[7] rescued God's justice. The first encounter with the books of the Platonists,[8] revealed to him a God who was not like the all-penetrating sea soaking into the sponge of material creation, but who was instead a spirit. The final stage in that revelation came on second look at the Platonists, when the doctrine of evil as a privation of good made itself understood to him, and he could see that all that was created was good, and thus that the creator himself was good.[9]

The justice of God thus revealed was for Augustine an adequate answer to the Jews; the spiritual nature of God, a refutation for the "pagans"; and the goodness of God and God's creation the decisive argument against the Manichees. I think we need to do Augustine the favor of allowing that the questions that long plagued him did indeed speak to the heart of his religious experience of the divine, and that, when he had removed those obstacles and in removing them, found a way to a God who was not a *phantasma* but a real and true God.[10] It was this discovery of the divine nature that made both possible and necessary the further struggle for encounter with the incarnate Word of God that comes to a completion in the famous garden scene in the eighth book of the *Confessions*.[11]

The qualities that persist in Augustine's God, the ones that recur page after page in his work, are reflections of those categories of goodness, justice, and spirituality that enticed him away from the Manichees. I mind particularly that the spiritual nature of God is associated for Augustine with divine immutability. I do not see that we have an adequate study of that theme in Augustine, though many writers have commented on its centrality to his thought.[12] The creative power of God is the correlate of the goodness of God, and God as creator is another role pervasive in Augustine's writing. Similarly, the divine justice leads to an easy acceptance of what is scarcely an exclusively Christian principle, that God cares for and guides the affairs of the created, material world.[13]

One last aspect of Augustine's God seems to me to require highlighting here, and it is a paradoxical one: God's silence. Though God is everywhere, though God watches over and cares for humankind, though God hears human prayers, the response is to every mortal ear silence. For a God whose mediator to humankind is the incarnate Word, this is remarkable, until we realize that for Augustine the continuing incarnation of the Word is twofold: in one place, that Word is encountered in the eucharistic liturgy about which Augustine is (for his time, characteristically) reticent, and in the other, that Word is everywhere in the pages of scripture. A modern must make a special effort that a late antique Christian would not have had to make to realize that the pages of scripture were for Augustine the source of the living, *spoken* Word of God, mediated into sound by the voice of the bishop, or the deacon, or by whatever reader of the scriptural text, a text rarely encountered in silence.[14] Once we bear that in mind, Augustine's God is anything but silent, and it is we who must make an effort to see just how eloquent and omnipresently eloquent Augustine's God can be.

At this point I mean to give only the broadest outline of the implications that I think the study of Augustine's idea of God can hold for Augustinian studies. Each of the few paragraphs that follow could easily be a monograph in itself. My aim in bringing them together and in keeping the scope so limited is precisely to emphasize the connections. Augustine against the pagans, the Donatists, the Manichees, the Pelagians — Augustine the endlessly polemical — is a figure we find sometimes unsympathetic, precisely for what seems so negative about his engagements with his fellow Christians. And if we insist on breaking him up into the subject of disparate scholarly monographs according to his polemical targets, that partial and limited view of him will I think always make him seem less than he was. My sense, after long frequentation of his works, is that we miss something valuable when we do that, and that if we can, here at least briefly, bring together the various sides of Augustine in view of the points I have already made, we can get an idea of a way forward, a way to restore to Augustine a unity of purpose and a dignity of intention that he seems sometimes to have lost in recent generations.

Imagine yourself a fourth-century "pagan",[15] imprudently cast in Augustine's way some afternoon, and challenging him to defend his novel religious ideas.[16] You will suggest to him, as Symmachus had proclaimed in his speech on the altar of Victory in 384, "uno itinere non potest perveniri ad tam grande secretum."[17] Augustine himself might have been open to such argument in his youth, and said something similar himself that he later regretted.[18] As a "pagan", you think yourself a tolerant man, broad-minded in your acceptance of many cults, though in practice you are probably quite snobbish about preferring your own, and curiously disdainful about the excesses of others — perhaps even downright hostile to some. Augustine speaks against you of the unity and spirituality of his God, his ubiquity, and his timelessness — and *thus* of a God who is not the exclusive property of anyone, who forms no closed community, no sect, no cult, but who is in fact accessible to one and all. That is what Augustine was trying to say when young and using language similar to Symmachus', but Augustine's monotheism was far more downright and pastorally practical. "Pagan" monotheism always had something abstract about it: it was a notion about religion, but not a part of the religious experience itself.[19] Augustine's Christianity took philosophical monotheism one step further in the enactment of Christian community.

But Christian community often fractured itself in various ways. The Manichees had their own doctrines, the Donatists their own sense of their special purity and separateness, the Pelagians their own sense of their moral superiority. If "paganism" has few completely wholehearted supporters among Augustine's modern readers, the Christian communities against which he railed, and sometimes did more than rail, have often found and still find sympathetic supporters in modern times. The Donatists, particularly, appeal to a political engagement, the Pelagians to a moral one.[20] If there are two things moderns are slow to forgive Augustine for, it is his use of political power to coerce the Donatists,[21] on the one hand, and his exposition of his views of human sexuality in his combat with the Pelagians and in particular with Julian of Eclanum. Both issues have been heavily ventilated in the last thirty years, though both seem to me susceptible of further investigation. Here I will suggest one theme.

The Donatists made no show of toleration or inclusiveness. They were the party of the saved in Africa, and if the rest of the world was largely unsaved, that was no business of theirs. And they were not without their own coercion. Relatively few individuals, certainly far fewer individuals than in any modern western society, were fully free in their choice of communities. The Donatists were an army of the saved, and an army that had swollen its ranks largely by a kind of benign conscription. If you lived in a Donatist town, or if you were a client of a Donatist patron on the land, you had little choice. Augustine's years-long attempts to negotiate cheerfully with the Donatists sought to loosen that grip, but to little avail. When he finally came to invoke imperial authority, with all the reservations and hesitations that marked that process, and with all the punctilio that marked relations down to the conference of 411, he did so in the name of a style of Christianity that was far more inclusive, whose God was just but not arbitrary, whose God was good, and whose God lay beyond the capacity of a single community to capture him for themselves.

So similarly, the Pelagians used moral superiority, the icy self-control of the ancient aristocrat, as a defining mechanism to separate themselves from their fellow Christians of lesser virtue. Augustine on the other hand, found his God everywhere. More important, he knew the difference between God and man: the qualities he imputed to God were so lofty, so far removed from human capacity, that it was foolish to claim that any human community possessed them fully. If there is a lingering "pagan" stripe to the Donatism and Pelagianism Augustine attacked, it comes from their ability to believe that sufficient excellence, adequate resemblance to the divine, was within human reach. Not so for Augustine, whose God is *so* lofty, so good, so utterly unlike ordinary mortals, that it is only by dint of great generosity that — for all human excellences — it is even possible to talk of salvation. Accordingly, the gap between the most virtuous and the least virtuous member of the community was first of all easily bridged,[22] in both directions, for good and for ill. For him the qualities he venerated were clearly those of his God, not of ordinary people. Religion made a marvelous difference — though, to be sure, Augustine is not quite the patron of the cult of the saints that those who came after him in the west would be — but that difference had its limits. Reformation according to the image and likeness of God never bridged the chasm,[23] and never gave any group of human beings "bragging rights" over against any other. Even those who stood outside the sacramental community of the church merited respect as prospective members or as recipients of yet-hidden grace of God.

It is ironic and appropriate that the image of the Manichees, who drove Augustine to reflect on his ideas of God and seek out the Christian orthodoxy that finally separated him from them decisively, never quite left Augustine alone. The very last words Augustine ever wrote in his *opus imperfectum contra Iulianum* attack not Pelagianism but Manicheism — arguing that it is Julian, not Augustine, who shows signs of the gnostic taint. We are inclined to take this either too seriously (as a sign of a bad conscience) or not seriously enough. My own view is that Augustine fully shook off his Manicheism in every matter of doctrine, but never shook off the questions they had asked. The God he clung to so insistently was precisely the God who would ward off the Manichean God, and so in that way there are dim shadows of Manichee doctrine lying across Augustine's words down through his whole career. In discovering against the Manichees the absolute overweening goodness of God and the contingent, reflected goodness of created things, Augustine succeeded in distancing himself from them, and in embracing all creation. But the chasm between God and creation that the Manichees had exploited remains in that structure of thought: and if there is for many readers a lingering sense that Augustine has somehow or other not gotten it quite right about creation, not *fully* valued the things of this world as they ought to be valued,[24] then here finally we can perhaps see that his *idea* of God needs in the end still to be distinguished from his experience of God. What he thought and said approximated his experience, to be sure, but its imperfection ought, with due charity, to be treated as we consider the tiny deliberate imperfections that Navajo sand-painters included in their designs — as reminders of the fallibility and imperfection of human affairs.

25

For it often seems that Augustine has brought down on himself a surprising reproach — that of being imperfect. For a man who freely confessed from the bishop's residence that he knew not to which temptations he would next submit[25] could scarcely deny the imperfection of his teaching or his life. But his role in the thought of later centuries and the affection (relatively uncharacteristic of Augustine as we have seen) for the cult of the saints grew so strong that he was unable to resist a kind of idealization in the minds of those who came after that first seemed to work to his advantage, but later, as the need for idealization ran afoul of a more mature sense of the risks implicit in such a strategy, rebounded to his seeming discredit.[26]

Perhaps one way past the competing images of Augustine that we receive is precisely to be found in confronting him as he approaches *his* God, however much that God resembles or disresembles one we recognize ourselves. If we make that effort of the imagination, we can leave him in two characteristic poses: of silent listening to the Word in scripture, and in active, vocal response to that Word in the liturgical prayer of the church. Those two Augustines, it seems to me, can and should take precedence over all the other Augustines we know. If we can make that reformation in our sense of who he was and how he lived, then we do a better job of reading what he wrote and of going away form that to write our own lives in or out of his tradition.

For to evoke Augustine in a celebration of a century and a half of Augustinian-led education on a verdant hilltop not far from Philadelphia is to remember that the academic approach to Augustine and his texts has its limits. To know that approach in its excellences *and* to know its limits are both parts of the wisdom that Villanova University exists to foster. The excesses of the academic ideologies of our time are not, happily, failures of enthusiasm but errors of proportion, of not knowing where the academic inquiry becomes part of the life of a larger community. Augustine stood for, and Villanova stands for, as do at least in theory all our institutions of higher learning, a better sense of balance. To study Augustine is to use the disciplines of philology and history to uncover pieces of a long-past life, and in so doing to make possible a better life here and now.

Notes

1. *Conf.* 1.4.4; on this text, and on others from the *Confessions* cited below, I have much more to say in my edition of and commentary on that text (Oxford 1992). If the notes that follow refer to my own writings more abundantly that might be seemly, it is because the opportunity to deliver this lecture just after publication of a work of many years' preparation encouraged me to think back over the *peregrinatio animae* through many encounters with Augustine, from the paperback translation of the *Confessions* that I purchased in high school expecting I know not what lurid revelations through now twenty-five years of assiduous reading, and to attempt to uncover in that experience themes that had been implicit in my reading but hidden to my conscious thought. This paper is one essay in that vein, and meant both to address the concerns of the warmly receptive audience that formed part of Villanova University's sesquicentennial celebrations and to suggest ways for others and above all for myself to go *on* thinking about Augustine in the years to come. I am happy to express my thanks to Fr. John Rotelle, OSA, for the generosity of his invitation, and for many other kindnesses over the years, and similarly to my other friends and colleagues at Villanova, whose support and encouragement has been so valuable.

2. These last words have been particularly controversial, and it would not be fair to fail to mention the alternative interpretation to which they are subjected, as in Pusey's translation: "Yet woe to him that speaketh not, since mute are even the most eloquent." See my commentary for defense of the interpretation I prefer.

3. On paradox as a deliberate rhetorical choice designed to approximate the ineffability of God in Augustine, see my *Augustine* (Boston 1985), pp. 22-24.

4. We may well have other reasons for quarreling with the ideas Augustine expresses, and his reading of scripture, especially of Paul, is not always one that we would give ourselves, but if we make the effort to see scripture through Augustine's eyes, his readings are rarely unintelligible, and making the effort often makes it easier to see what Augustine is really saying. For example, when Augustine, in his *Quaestions on the Heptateuch* 6.10, allows as to how there can be such a thing as a "just war", it is useful to notice that he speaks in the context of Joshua's battle at Jericho. Augustine there is not making some abstract argument, but rather coping with the undeniable fact that in this particular case, God clearly approved war by one people against another; and read in that way, his interpretation is limiting rather than authorizing, concessive rather than encouraging.

5. O. du Roy, *L'intelligence de la foi en la trinité selon saint Augustin: genèse de sa théologie trinitaire jusqu'en 391* (Paris, 1966), pp. 96-106, has argued that Augustine's narrative in the *Confessions* does an injustice to his own theology, in that it assumes that "God" (the trinity) can be known before the Incarnation. I have discussed this in my commentary, vol. 2, pp. 415-16, and still incline to think Augustine can be defended on this point, but for purposes of this paper I will leave the issue to one side and will concede that the relative places of "God" and "Christ"

in Augustine's writings are not always clear and stable with respect to each other, and there is something faintly subordinationist about Augustine's *practice*, though his doctrine is fully orthodox. Bear in mind, for example, that Augustine's church in Africa insisted that prayer at the altar always be directed to the Father, and that it is only centuries later that prayers directed to Christ become commonplace (see T. Klauser, *A Short History of the Western Liturgy* (2nd ed., Oxford, 1979), 30-32).

6. *Conf.* 3.7.12.

7. *Conf.* 6.4.6.

8. I think here of the stage depicted at *Conf.* 7.9.13-15.

9. *Conf.* 7.12.18ff. I thus distinguish between two "tentatives d'extase" in Book 7, separated by this second stage of Platonic analysis; see my commentary *ad loc.*

10. Already at *Conf.* 1.1.1 he adumbrates this theme by showing his caution that ignorant invocation of the divine can get a "wrong number", so to speak, thinking to invoke God but calling in fact on another: he is surely thinking of the errors of his Manichee days here.

11. See my commentary on *Conf.* 8.12.30 for the argument that it is the garden scene in which the incarnate Christ is decisively introduced into Augustine's life.

12. See my commentary on *Conf.* 7.1.1.

13. "Augustine the Epicurean" is an article that can't be written, but there are times when it almost seems it could be. The forms of argument of the Epicureans were, by his own admission, appealing at one stage (see *Conf.* 6.16.26), and the form of Augustine's critique of classical paganism in *City of God* often resembles the Lucretian attack centuries earlier (I have argued, in "Augustine's Classical Readings," *Recherches Augustiniennes* 15(1980) 144-175, that there is more Lucretius in Augustine's memory than had previously been credited).

14. And when encountered in silence, as by Ambrose at *Conf.* 6.3.3 (see again my commentary) or by Augustine in the garden scene at *Conf.* 8.12.30, so encountered precisely so that the one who reads the word can attend to it with a metaphorical kind of hearing more directly than would be possible if he were to read it aloud — the one who *reads* a text in the ancient world is at a disadvantage against the one who listens to it being read.

15. See my "The Demise of Paganism", *Traditio* 35(1979) 45-88; and *"Paganus,"* *Classical Folia* 31(1977) 163-169, for the ways in which "pagan" is a word of limited usefulness to the scholar today, precisely because it embodied a specifically Christian view of late antique society and in its polemical overtones made itself a word that few non-Christians would tolerate being applied to themselves.

16. One of the best examples of such a dialogue of the deaf is the exchange of letters with Maximus of Madauros preserved in Augustine's correspondence, *epp.* 16-17.

17. Symm. *relatio* 3.10.

18. See *sol.* 1.13.23, "sed non ad eam [sapientiam] una via pervenitur", regretted at *retr.* 1.4.3, though *vera rel.* 28.51 echoes the same phrase of Symmachus. Of course both passages were written before Augustine's accession to the Christian clergy.

19. A salutary and sympathetic guide to the lines of non-Christian thought that converge here is J.P. Kenney, *Mystical Monotheism: A Study in Ancient Platonic Theology* (Hanover and London, 1991).

20. W.H.C. Frend has been the most articulate and impassioned partisan of the Donatists in our time, from his *The Donastist Church* (Oxford 1951) onwards, for all that he is a marvelously original and judicious scholar the while, and on the other hand Elaine Pagels, in *Adam, Eve, and the Serpent* (New York, 1988), has emerged as a spokesman for the Pelagian party much less impeded by learning or discretion.

21. Even his most sympathetic interpreter on this point, Robert Markus in *Saeculum* (Cambridge 1969), cannot win him a complete acquittal.

22. Think of the old man Augustine knew, long years in the faith and then suddenly taking up with a young woman not his wife (*c. Iul.* 3.11.22): it is in such pastoral experience that Augustine found his skepticism when faced with the confident virtue of a Julian of Eclanum.

23. Gerhard Ladner, *The Idea of Reform* (Cambridge MA 1959), is the classic study, to be supplemented by R.A. Markus, "'Imago' and 'Similitudo' in Augustine," *Revue des Études augustiniennes* 10(1964) 125-143.

24. I think this is a common modern reading of his work, and precisely because it is common it deserves respect — it may not be an accurate statement of his express doctrine, but it could scarcely manifest itself were there not traits in Augustine's writings that gave occasion for it.

25. *Conf.* 10.4.7.

26. I have approached these issues in my 1991 Augustine Lecture at Villanova, published as "The Authority of Augustine", *Augustinian Studies* 22(1991) 7-35, and also in the commentary in a video presentation of Augustine's life and thought produced in 1992 by Della Robbia Productions of Santa Fe New Mexico, "Augustine: Late Have I Loved Thee."

Augustinian Studies 25 (1994) 9-24

'Good For Nothing'?

Augustine On Creation

Rowan D. Williams
Bishop of Monmouth

'The received view [of the doctrine of creation] consisted of a nest of shared beliefs, but the two most important for our concern are that God created *ex nihilo*, from "nothing", and that God created hierarchically, with the physical subordinated to the spiritual. . . . [T]he imaginative picture it paints is of a God fashioning the world, either intellectually by word (a creation of the mind) or aesthetically by craft (a creation of the hands), but in either case out of what is totally different from God, and in a manner that places humanity above nature, spirit above body'.[1]

'A particular reading of this foundational text [Gen. 1-3] has given Western culture the fundamental idea that the universe is a hierarchy: a system of order imposed by spiritual power from above. . . . There is the idea that the physical world is an artifact, made or constructed by God out of inert matter. . . . Whenever we affirm belief in God as "Maker of the Universe" we are referring to this image, and reinforcing the claim to have and to exercise "spiritual power" over matter'.[2]

Two quotations from fairly recent critiques of certain aspects of traditional theology, both, as it happens, from women theologians with a strong ecological concern. They represent something of a new 'received' view, impatient with what is understood to be involved in the classical doctrine of creation out of nothing; and both — in common, again, with a good many theologians of very diverse complexion — want to remove from our discourse about creation any element of *dualism*, any radical and unbridgeable gap between God and the world. It is just such a gap, we're told, that sanctions or grounds all sorts of other dualisms — not only spirit and body, but man and woman, and humanity and nature;[3] if we *start* with a basic disjunction between an active and a passive partner, and allot a massive metaphysical privilege to the former, we end up associating technocratic humanity, masculinity, and distancing or dominating rationality with God. The result is the mess in which this planet now lives, as well as a model of God that signally fails to offer anyone good news (least of all those historically at the receiving end of manipulative dominance). Our crisis demands new models: both the writers I've quoted argue passionately for giving privilege now to the imagery of a God 'embodied' in the creation or a God who 'gives birth' to creation as something bound in with God's own being.

Augustine's is not a name of good omen in these theological circles.[4] He is regularly held responsible for making canonical all these assumptions about hierarchical dualism, as well as for bequeathing us the doctrine of original sin (or rather original *guilt*) in its most indigestible form, and for involving us in centuries-long muddles about sexuality. If we take, more or less at random, two quotations from his best-known and most accessible discussion of creation (in the last three books of the *Confessions*), we seem to have clear evidence for the prosecution. Here he is, talking about creation and formless matter:

> 'In those days the whole world was little more than nothing, because it was still entirely formless. Yet by now it was something to which form could be added.

> 'For you, O Lord, made the world from formless matter, which you created out of nothing. This matter was itself almost nothing, but from it you made all the mighty things which are so wonderful to us' (XII.8).

And on the radical distance and difference between God and creation:

> 'You had no need of me, nor am I a creature good in such a way as to be helpful to you.

> '. . . [F]or you do not withhold existence from good which neither benefits you nor is of your own substance and therefore equal to you, but exists simply because it can derive its being from you' (XIII.1,2).

Surely these passages bear out the picture given by our contemporary writers? Augustine's creator is wholly alien from what is created, and, when creation is begun, it must be a story of the imposition of spiritual shape or meaning upon a recalcitrant and intrinsically worthless material life. In what follows, I shall argue that this is a complete misreading of Augustine's scheme; whether or not he is right about the relation of God to the world, he cannot simply be charged with inventing or reinforcing a simple matter-spirit dualism. And I want to suggest also that there are dimensions in *any* intelligible Christian theology of creation that oblige us to reckon with some of Augustine's characteristic insights, and so to tread cautiously in exploring some proposed modern correctives, such as those I cited at the beginning of this paper.

To understand what Augustine is saying about creation, we must grasp the way in which he sees both the continuity and the discontinuity between God and the universe. That created things are 'in' God he does not for a moment dispute; indeed (as Books VII and X of the *Confessions* make clear), coming to a Christian mind on the subject of creation involves recognizing that all things are 'in your truth' (VII. 15), in contrast to the Manichaean doctrine that matter is essentially something impenetrable to the divine, though containing 'granules' of divine life, undigested and unintegrated — and also in contrast to the transitional view described in *Confessions* VII. 1 and 5, where the universal presence of God is thought of as a sort of universal permeation of the world by a very refined material stuff.[5] Existing 'in God's truth' is, in the *Confessions*, primarily to do with existing in reality rather than fantasy, and (consequently) existing in coherence: that is to say, the transparency of the world to the prior reality of God lies in the perception of things *actively* existing and maintaining a pattern of interaction that we can follow or chart in certain ways, a pattern of interaction that leaves no room for a final self-fragmentation, a chaos of arbitrary events. This orderliness is the essence of what we call beauty; and our ability to make judgments about beauty, our instinctive appeal to a standard of ideal harmony, is one of Augustine's most familiar grounds for asserting an innate God-directedness in the mind (*Confessions* VII. 17; c.f. for example, *de vera rel.* 21, 56, 67, etc.).

We can say, then, that creation shares or participates in God *by being a coherent system*. It can't participate in any other way, in Augustine's scheme of things: it can't be a literal 'bit' of God, since God is not a material substance, and it can't be an overflow of the divine essence, since Augustine is quite clear that being God is being outside the realm of change and interaction (we shall look at this again later). How this participation is structured Augustine discusses in a number of places by referring to a text from Wisdom (11.21), where we read that God has ordered all things *in mensura, et numero, et pondere.*[6] In perhaps his earliest use of this text, Augustine quotes it as he considers the question of why there are unattractive or repellent animals in the world, and (as in *Confessions* VII. 16) he concludes that their unattractiveness and even their hostility to human beings has to do with our sin and spiritual blindness: 'I can't think of any animal's body or members where I don't find the measure and proportion and order that goes towards harmonious unity. And where all this comes from I can't understand unless it is from the supreme measure, proportion and order that exist in the changeless and everlasting sublimity of God' (*de Gen. c. Man.* 16.26). By the time Augustine came to write Book IV of *de Gen. ad litt.*, fifteen or more years later, the 'measure, proportion and order' of the earlier text have turned into the more familiar alternative of 'measure, proportion and *weight*' — which allows him to make some powerful connections with his use of the metaphor of weight in the *Confessions*, where it may well owe something, directly or indirectly, to Plotinus.[7]

I want now to look at what he has to say in *de Gen.ad litt.* IV.3.7ff. about this text from Wisdom. Obviously, to say that God 'follows' measure, proportion and weight in creating cannot mean that God's creative work is dependent on anything other than God; what God 'follows' is the divine life itself. But this in turn cannot mean that God is identical with measure, proportion and weight as elements in created reality. Rather, God is what fixes a *modus* for everything, a specific way of being; what gives a thing *species*, a formal structure that appeals to both aesthetic and intellectual judgment; and what draws a thing towards a state of equilibrium. God is *qui terminat omnia et format omnia et ordinat omnia* (IV.3.7) — the one who limits all things, gives intelligible shape to all things and directs all things to a goal. We can see that these principles do not apply only to material quantities, but to the active mental subject: the moral or spiritual agent acts (ideally) by measure (action limits itself, it is not a stream of undifferentiated energy), by proportion (wisdom involves an appropriate exercise of feelings and virtues, or, as we might put it, a fitting response to circumstances), and by weight (in choosing or rejecting courses of action according to whether they fit the goals of our love). And here we see more clearly how *our* reality is shaped by a formative agency beyond our minds. For Augustine, to be a thinking being is always to be *responding* to something prior to us, and the ordered shape of mental life (which, remember, includes *emotional* life in this context; Augustine never denies that emotion belongs to the mind), the

34

purposive character of action and our attempts to make sense or balance of our experienced history, shows that the principles of *mensura, numerus* and *pondus* are active in our regard; and since they cannot act on God (nothing acts *on* God), they must be the act *of* God (*ib*.4.8). They represent the direct impact of God on the world, not a sort of afterthought: as a matter of fact, everything in the world has colour, but this is not a sign that colour is a divine activity; the intelligible structure of things does not depend on colour, and so we say that God has organized things in such a way that they are coloured, but not that God made them 'in' or 'according to' a principle of coloration (*ib*.5.11). So the conclusion is that the beauty and intelligibility of the world communicate to us the truth that God's action is the kind of action that produces harmonious effects, and therefore tells us, obliquely but unmistakable, that God's nature is to be, not one harmonious or lovely thing above others, but the cause of all harmony and loveliness.

This is a version of familiar Platonic themes, and picks up the commonplace[8] that when God is called good it is because God is the *source* of good, not one among a class of good things (just as, in Aristotle's famous discussion,[9] you can call food 'healthy' when it is the sort of thing that *produces* health). It is the cornerstone of all classical theories of analogy in speaking of God. So if we say, as we must, that the measure and proportion that govern all things belong in God's life, it is because they represent the way God acts, not the 'rules' dictating how God must act. The natural shape of divine action is what produces beauty; no cause controls this action except the being of God as such. Thus, if the world is orderly and purposive, we can conclude that the activity that moulds it makes for order; and this is brought home to us most vividly in thinking about our own mental life, in recognizing that it is shaped by response to unchanging standards. And if we understand that divine activity is not controlled by anything but God, we shall see that God's *nature* is such as to produce beauty; it is in this way that the world's beauty tells us something of what it is to be God — not because God stands at the summit of an ascending scale of beautiful things, but because we grasp that, whatever God's life is (and we can never catch it in a concept), it is what makes for harmony.[10]

This helps us to negotiate what may seem a difficult corner in the argument. Augustine is not claiming that the world is, crudely, 'like' God, reasonable and harmonious in all ways: of course it isn't. It is a place of risk, frustration and terror from where we stand,[11] as he was to insist with increasing stridency in his later years: a place which is not amenable to our understanding or control, and in which the frustration of purpose by contingent happenings leads to what we call evil.[12] How does this sit with the vision of a world pointing to God by its orderliness? The answer is that, for Augustine, all good except God's is the product of a process; hence the importance of *pondus* as well as *mensura* and *numerus* in his thought. Measure and proportion govern the reality of things that are made to change, and 'weight' is what pulls them to their proper place. Some of this interest in process is of course carried by Augustine's well-known doctrine, Stoic in origin, of *rationes seminales*, the inbuilt principles that regulate the development of organisms according to predictable patterns (acorns grow into oaks, not daffodils or cows). But, more generally (and it is a theme that plays an important part in the discussion of peace and order in *de civ.* XIX), the world is so ordered that at any point in time the balance of things or agencies is being adjusted towards equilibrium: as individual things develop and their relation to other things consequently alters, *pondus* continually guarantees an overall balance, so that there is not, in the natural order, a chaos of conflictual agencies. Energy is conserved, as we might say in the twentieth century. Things are made to change and grow, to realise their optimal form over time; but this change is woven into a universal mobile pattern, consistently reclaiming its stability. In rational beings, as Augustine famously says, *pondus* is *amor* (*Confessions* XII.9.10): it is love that draws us back to our proper place, that pulls us back to stability and harmony. And we know ourselves most fully and truthfully, as he so often says, when we know both that we are desiring beings and that our desire is ultimately and freely itself when it consciously becomes longing for God.

Two points here, then. First, Augustine's is a universe in motion: he takes up a philosophical cliché about regular principles of development, and links it with a more comprehensive picture. Everything 'seeks' its own level or its own place; but that place is a place within a network of sensitive interaction, and to grasp the ordered and purposive beauty of the world is to see this ordered mobility and interdependence as a whole,[13] to see — we could say — what a *world* is, a coherent system. We do not have to be able to chart each process in it to understand that it operates as a whole. Augustine is expressing in a very different idiom the often misunderstood conclusions of the *Tractatus:*[14] 'it is not the *way* the world is, but *that* it is that is mystical. The vision of the world *sub specie aeterni* is a vision of it as a (limited) whole. The sense of the world as a limited whole is what is mystical.' Wittgenstein's analysis of logic requires us to recognise that to talk coherently is to deny that there is such a thing as *pure* contingency, anything that could not in principle be described in some sort of intelligible way: it is not that any given system of description (such as scientific 'laws') delivers a final or exhaustive account, but that we have an irreducible insight or intuition, based in the logical form of our discourse, that coherent description is possible.[15] So what is significant is that we intuit a whole, and that we recognise that we cannot *think* of a particular in isolation (Hegel as well as Wittgenstein is on the horizon here). Augustine's vision has all sorts of points of contact with what has gone before in the Platonic tradition, and his originality cannot be overstated. But the use of *pondus* as a central metaphor, with its connotations of 'finding a level', *seeking* something in shifting circumstances, certainly brings into sharp focus the idea of a purposive totality, rather than just an ensemble of specific orderly processes.

Second, this universal motion of seeking or (analogically) 'desiring' equilibrium is part of the way in which creation manifests God, part of the world's 'continuity' with the life of God. As we have seen, God cannot fall under the same rules as the world; God could not (logically) be simultaneously the cause of a whole interlocking system *and* a member of it, and so we can never talk of features in common between God and the world. If we use the language of continuity, it is as we trace the character of creative action in its manifest effects, in the fact that we can make sense of the flux of things around us. Once again, it is a Platonic commonplace that time is 'the moving image of eternity': Augustine gives a little more edge and definition to this in the idea that God is imaged or reflected in the 'desire' of things for the divine stability.[16] Turn to the *de trin.*, and you will see how this perspective introduces something quite fresh into theological discussion of the image of God in the human subject, which is no longer to be identified with a single feature or cluster of features, but with the orientation of the subject to God, with the radically *unfinished* character of thinking and wanting.[17] Creation, in other words, tells us most about God when it is most clearly *different* from what we conceive to be the divine nature; it speaks of God by being temporal and changeable, a process of endless adjustment that still remains capable of being thought and talked about coherently.

Continuity and discontinuity between God and creation are thus very hard to pull apart in Augustine's thought. The continuities, the ways in which creation shares in the sort of life that is God's, steer us inexorably back to the fundamental difference. But what this secures is a model of creation that should never, in fact, produce the ideas attacked by the writers I quoted at the beginning of this paper. For there to be a world, a limited whole, there must be coherence, a convergence on stability, though it is a stability that continues to alter and reinvent itself at every moment, as time advances: there is no question of 'imposing' anything from 'outside' or 'above', since there is no above or outside the universe in the sense of a rival system acting causally on it from a competing position in logical space. There *is* simply the system, and without intelligibility it cannot be spoken of at all: order is not an extra. But what then does Augustine's language about 'form' and 'matter' mean? This has to be answered by a longer look at the quite complicated arguments of *Confessions* XII, especially 6-13. Having established earlier that creation is not a point at which God changes (since time can only be correlated with the changes of our world, and, once again, God does not share an environment with us and so does not change in response to an environment as we do),[18] Augustine and his readers can only conclude that creation is caused by God's will alone; and what that will establishes as the logical precondition of everything else is that the world will be capable of change (XII.6). We can understand nothing about the world without granting that this is primary. For the world *not* to be God, to be itself as a limited whole, it must be a complex of processes. What does change entail? A *medium* of change or a vehicle of change; or, to put it another way, an interaction between stability and variety. If change were total, global transformation, we couldn't talk about it at all, since there would be no conceptual structures to hold together a before and after. So Augustine proceeds to interpret Genesis 1.1, 'God created the heavens and the earth', in the light of these requirements. We are told that the earth was originally 'without form'; 'heaven', presumably, is at the opposite end of the spectrum from 'earth'. Thus Augustine postulates two extreme cases of created reality — a level at which formal stability is at its highest because the creature is directly open to God, and a level at which there is minimal form, virtually indeterminate reality. The former (the 'heaven of heavens') must be the condition of intelligent agents wholly devoted to the love of God, so that, while still changeable in principle, they are *in fact* unchanging — angels and redeemed souls in the state to which we can now only aspire: they don't need to get better and, if their love is truly purified, they can't get worse; and so they experience a kind of pure duration, beyond 'history' (XII.11). At the other end is matter without form, or rather with hardly any form, minimal stability (we could not give content to the idea of an actually existing state of *total* formlessness, as this would be nothing but potential: what could that mean?): all we can say of it is that it is capable of being further formed (XII.8). The creation we know exists between these two poles, with form constantly and steadily moulding matter into a coherent world. And time, as we experience it, belongs in this in-between. Without form there is no change (XII.11), since there could be no measurement of difference: matter alone could have no history. And a state in which form had attained stability would have no history either, since it would no longer be in search of its optimal condition. In between, form and matter are in ceaseless interrelation: we could, indeed, say that the creation we concretely know *is* the process of form acting on matter, the story of increasingly sophisticated organization and interdependence in the universe.

At this point, we had better pause to clarify what 'form' and 'matter' really mean. The post-seventeenth century mind tends to draw a neat distinction between solid things and ideas, with the result that Augustine's statements about form and matter are read in the way our opening quotations seem to assume — some 'spiritual' force struggling with the world of concrete stuff. But this is a travesty. For Augustine,[19] as for Plotinus,[20] 'matter' is pure potentiality. If we say that matter is not of itself good, or even (as Plotinus very nearly says) that it is the source of evil, we are not saying that there is something wicked about flesh, trees, stones, or even amino acids. This would be nonsense — the kind of nonsense Augustine spent a lot of time exploding in his writings against the Manichees: only minds can be wicked, because moral evaluation is only relevant to beings who have desires and make decisions. The point is that we cannot make any evaluation at all of pure, empty possibility: we can comment on potential only as potential *for* something or other. And once we start talking about potential for something or other, something with recognisable features and structure, we have started talking about *form*. Potential that isn't realised or that is frustrated is, in this perspective, at best a deficit, an incompleteness, and at worst something that erodes the proper purposive action of a thing. The action of form on matter is not the imposition of one thing on another, let alone one system on another: it is simply the process of actualisation itself, the process by which organization appears. In reading these pages of Augustine, we must lay aside the imagery of a primitive stuff shaped into alien structures by God through an act of triumphant power. The point could be better put by saying that God wills that there be reality quite other than God, and that this entails the positing of a reality that can change: if so, it entails also the dialectic of the possible and the actual, it entails a world of purposive fluidity, things becoming themselves, organising themselves more successfully or economically over time. Possibilities are continually being realised, but realised in orderly and intelligible fashion: changes in form mean measurable changes, the only sort of change we can talk about (which is why, incidentally, Aquinas could say[21] that the act of creation was not itself a change or a process).

Creation, then, is the realm in which good or beauty or stability, the condition in which everything is most freely and harmoniously itself in balance with everything else, is *being* sought and *being* formed. This is, of course, why there can be no short route to heaven: we must *grow* into new life, as the *Confessions* constantly reminds us.[22] And we must learn to start where we are, as moving, material beings: God's definitive clue to the divine life, and to how we may open ourselves to it, is the event in which the everlasting Word and Wisdom shapes and speaks in and acts out a human and material history, telling us that there is no way to God but through time. To know God, we must follow the course of the incarnate Word,[23] not look for a timeless penetration of God's mind. Two of Augustine's most important themes converge here: the universal implicit recognition of order in the story of things, and the impossibility of fully living in that order without humility, the recognition that we encounter God truly *only* when we accept our mortal fragility for what it is, do not seek to escape it, but put our trust in a God who speaks and relates to us through flesh. A full exposition of Augustine on creation would have to go hand in hand with an exposition of the role of the incarnate Word; understanding Augustine, especially the Augustine of 395 onwards, has often suffered from a failure to keep these themes in view together. And it is essential, in reading Augustine, to recognise that he becomes more and more preoccupied with growth rather than accomplished vision, so that, at any given moment, we are faced with our inability to master the whole process of things: "As for me, though, I am broken apart in time, whose shape and meaning I do not know; and my thoughts, the most intimate organs of my soul, are split up by time's stormy changes, until, purified and melted by the fire of your love, all of me will flow together into you' (*Confessions* XI.29). Just before this passage, he has been discussing the experience of singing a well-known psalm: bit by bit, expectation shrinks and memory expands. So it is, he says, with the whole of my life and the whole of our common history (XI.28); but in such a perspective, no individual knows the song to its end.

Creation is the constant process of realising potential goods; and that is why the difference between God and creation cannot be elided. There is nothing that is *potentially* good for God. If there were, God's self-realisation would be imperfect; and since the processes of self-realisation are bound up with interaction, an agent bringing some other (passive) entity to its fuller life by supplying what it lacks in itself, this would entail treating God as part of a system, in which independent factors could provide for God what the divine being required and did not possess. This is what Augustine is battling against in *Confessions* XIII. 1-4 in particular, and it remains a fundamental objection to any theory that regards creation as augmenting God's life or consciousness or whatever.[24] Either God has the resource within the divine life for fullness of bliss, in which case no divine act changes or enlarges this in its essence; or God does not have such resource, and this divine lack can only be supplied by another agent — and to postulate such another agent would be to abandon any commitment to the notion of a coherent universe. Hence Augustine's insistence in XIII.1 and 2 on the notion that Creation does not 'benefit' God. This has become a profoundly unpopular doctrine in some circles of late, on the grounds that it builds into the relation between God and world a wholly non-negotiable asymmetry, absolute dependence opposed to absolute self-sufficiency: the problems of dualism and hierarchy or patriarchy are seen as focused here. But what needs to be said is that dualism and hierarchy become problematic as relations *within* a system that ought to be unified and interdependent.[25] Enough should have been said by now to make it clear that God, in Augustine's terms, is in no sense within the same frame of reference. God's action cannot *compete* with created agency, God does not have to overcome a rival presence, the creative power of God is not power exercised unilaterally over some other force, but is itself the ground of all power and all agency within creation. God does not (*pace* McFague, Primavesi and others) make the world by imposing the divine will on some recalcitrant stuff, and no serious theologian has claimed this. Rather, God causes an entire process in which intelligible structure comes to view. In response to the act of God, created life shapes itself as a balanced whole, seeking all the time what the physicists call dynamic equilibrium; but all this, and the possibilities thus realised, is simply the result of the divine freedom.

Thus creation really is 'good for nothing': its *point* is not to serve a divine need. Our difficulty with the idea is (depressingly) the difficulty of imagining a need-free love, and it is a difficulty felt as much by ancients as by moderns. The early Christian claim that God creates out of nothing presupposed the possibility and reality of a love *not* based on kinship or similarity, since it presupposed a God willing to make real something wholly other than the divine life and to endow it with beauty, rationality and liberty. As Clement of Alexandria put it,[26] this is a love that goes beyond the natural claims of *koinonia*. Now *koinonia*, community of kind — perhaps 'solidarity', if you want a fashionable word — is, in the Christian vocabulary, not the ground but the effect of love, of a free reaching-out to what is and remains ineradicably strange and other. So St. Paul implies; so Augustine too implies in his lengthy discussions of love and communion in the anti-Donatist literature.[27] There is a thread of connection between a repudiation of tribal or sectarian accounts of love and what has to be said about the gratuity of creation. It is a point that receives a subtle, almost ironic, twist in the *de doctrina chr.* (I.31-2). If all loving is to be divided into instrumental and contemplative, using and enjoying, loving something for the sake of or in relation to something else and loving something for its own sake, what can be said of God's love for us? If God 'enjoys' us, contemplates us as we do God, that would suggest that God requires us so as to be happy, and so that we augment or enrich the divine life; and this will not do, because light is not kindled by the objects it illuminates. So God's love for us is 'instrumental'? Yes, but God does not 'use' us for the sake of something more ultimate, since God *is* the ultimate good, for whose sake all things in the world are to be loved, and so has no ultimate goal but the self-contemplation of the divine life, which, once again, needs nothing else to complete it. So we must say that God 'uses' us for the sake of our greatest good, which is, of course, loving God: God loves us so that we may come to *our* highest good, not so that *God's* good may be served. Our good is God, and, consequently, the love of one another for and in God. God's love is instrumental for our good, and so is wholly selfless, since my enjoyment of God is the greatest possible bliss for me, but adds nothing to the endless bliss of God.

The pure desire for the joy of another: that is what the Augustinian doctrine of creation presupposes, and that is where it challenges our supposed improvements on his synthesis. There are all sorts of proper objections to a theology that drives a wedge between God and what God makes — and, as we have seen, Augustine would understand and share them. But what is problematic is when these objections lead us towards a theology in which God and creation have virtually indistinguishable interests, and where God's love for creation becomes a function of God's love for God, understood as a furthering of those 'interests'. Ultimately this impoverishes our spiritual and moral imagination in intimating that there is no love beyond kinship and shared interest. I suspect that the difficulty has something to do — in the widest sense — with politics. In the Western world, we have rightly become suspicious of certain models of love that take for granted an unexamined system of power relations — love as the benevolence of the one who possesses towards the one who is dispossessed, a love that does nothing to transform the structures of possession and dispossession. For all kinds of groups, love has been rediscovered in the experience of solidarity, the mutual nurture of those who share the same pain or privation. Such nurture is the source of strength, a beginning of empowerment, and so of transformation. This has been the experience underlying so much of liberation theology, whether in the Third World or among women and black people and others in the global north, and it plays a central role too in various kinds of peace movement. But — as Ellen Charry points out in a powerful and controversial recent essay[28] — there is a risk that different victim groups or marginal groups remain locked in their specific frames of reference, lacking a way of realising a substantive unity with each other, or of imagining a situation beyond the mutual empowerment of those sharing privation. The underlying question of how we love the radical stranger (let alone the oppressor, in some new and rectified order) is evaded if love's paradigms are rooted solely in common experience and common need.

This is not to brush aside — God forbid — the moral weight of solidarity, and the immense force of the discovery of power in powerlessness that emerges from a politics of solidarity. Nor should it lead us to gloss over the fact that Augustine undoubtedly *does* endorse a hierarchical and patriarchal picture of the universe. But his fundamental structures for thinking about creation place firmly on the agenda a set of issues we cannot safely ignore. The desire for the good or the joy of another who *remains* other, perhaps disturbingly, certainly uncontrollably, other, should remind us that solidarity doesn't say everything; and the more that has to be said has a great deal to do with how we understand the love of God in creation and redemption.[29] Without a belief in a love without self-directed interest, we may find that the gospel of a human community beyond faction and rivalry is harder to preach than we might have imagined. Augustine's theology of creation treats the world eminently seriously as the self-communication of God; but, like all God's 'rhetoric', the world does not simply offer a bland reproduction of recognisable and timeless truths.[30] To be serious about creation's meaning and value is to weigh properly its integrity as a moving and changing image, as a limited and fluid whole that is not God, yet is saturated with God. Above all, Augustine invites us to bring our thinking about love under the judgment of a causeless act of origination, whose purpose is nothing but the joy of the other; for him, we can say of creation itself what the poet said of redemption — that it is

Love to the loveless shown,
That they might lovely be.

Notes

1. Sallie McFague, *Models of God. Theology for an Ecological Nuclear Age*, Philadelphia and London 1987, p. 109.

2. Anne Primavesi, *From Apocalypse to Genesis. Ecology, Feminism and Christianity*, London 1991, p. 203.

3. In addition to the works already cited, we might look at Elaine Pagels, *Adam, Eve and the Serpent*, London 1988, for a view of Augustine that tends in this direction; also Rosemary Radford Ruether, *Gaia and God. An Ecofeminist Theology of Earth Healing,* San Francisco and London 1992/3. A more serious engagement with what is believed to be Augustine's legacy for ethics and metaphysics can be traced in the work of Colin Gunton, most recently in "Augustine, the Trinity and the Theological Crisis of the West" *SJTh* 43 (1992) 33-58, and *The One, the Three and the Many. God, Creation and the Culture of Modernity*, Cambridge 1993.

4. It is difficult to construct any profile of what unites the anti-Augustinians of contemporary theology, but it is probably true that they hold in common a radically anti-Cartesian perspective. Perhaps partly because of Descartes' own use of Augustine, Augustine is often read through spectacles strongly tinted by the way in which Descartes set up the problematic of knowledge and certainty. I have attempted to redress the balance a little in 'The Paradoxes of Self-Knowledge in De Trinitate X', *Collectanea Augustiniana* 1993, pp. 121-134.

5. This is, in effect, a Stoic view, though not identified here as such; see, for example, *Stoicorum Veterum Fragmenta*, ed. J. von Arnim, II. 774.

6. *De Gen. c. Man.* I.16.26 and 21.32; for a seminal study of these terms, see W. Roche, 'Measure, Number and Weight in St. Augustine', *New Scholasticism* 15 (1941) 350-376. See also *de nat. boni* for *forma* as a variant of *numerus.*

7. *Enneads* 2.1.3.

8. Articulated, for example, by Albinus, *epitomē* X.5; on the whole question, see R. Williams, *Arius. Heresy and Tradition*, London 1987, III. B and C.

9. *Cat.* I. 1a; for an important expansion and refinement of the point, see Porphyry's commentary on the Categories, esp. 66. 15-21.

10. This is to recognize the (often ignored or minimized) apophatic element in Augustine; see the classic discussion by Vladimir Lossky, 'Les éléments de "théologie negative" dans la pensée de saint Augustin', *Augustinus Magister*, Paris 1954, pp. 575-581.

11. See, for example, *op. imp.con.Jul.* VI, for some of Augustine's most eloquent evocations of the world's miseries.

12. In the sense that we identify as 'evil' the ways in which our wills become incapable of effecting their own good intentions because of the history of fallenness we inherit. Not all sin, Augustine insists, is naked rebellion against God; it may be the simple fact of defeat by reason of intolerable circumstances, by ignorance or by plain weakness; see, e.g., *de nat. et gratia* xxix.33 and Peter Brown's admirable summary in *Augustine of Hippo*, London 1967, p. 350.

13. See Book xix. 12-14 in particular.

14. *de Gen.con.Man.* I.xxii.33.

15. 6.44ff.

16. *Ib*.6.32ff., 6,36ff., 6.362, 6.372.

17. Again, this can be compared with Plotinus' suggestion that the One is somehow mirrored in the *erōs* of intellect toward it; see, e.g. *Enneads* VI.7 and 8.

18. See the article referred to in n. 4 above for a fuller discussion.

19. *Conf.* xi, passim.

20. See, e.g., *Enneads* II. 4 and I.8; J.M.Rist's article, 'Plotinus on Matter and Evil', *Phronesis* VI.2 (1961), pp. 154-166, may be recommended as a thoroughly reliable guide to some of the complexities here.

21. *Summa Theologiae* I.xlv.2 ad 2.

22. E.g. VII.10,20, X, passim; cf. en.in.Ps 37.

23. For the image of the believer running after the incarnate Christ, see *Conf.* IV.12 and *de doct. christ.* I.xxxiv.

24. I should say, in passing, that, while this sets Augustine firmly against all varieties of process theology and any other scheme that proposes to reduce the radical (non-competitive) difference between God and the world, Augustine's relation to Hegel represents a far more complex question, worthy of longer discussion. I do not myself believe that a doctrine of creation faithful to what Augustine and the great majority of traditional theologians take for granted is necessarily hostile to the Hegelian account overall, since this could be read as another way of dealing with what I have called non-competitive difference, in a drastically different idiom. The one thing Hegel does not teach, despite the assumptions of some, is that there is an augmentation of Spirit through the processes of creation, or that God is in any sense a subject of history. But this takes us further afield than is convenient for present purposes. I hope to develop the point more fully in an essay on Hegel's religion for a planned volume on philosophers and faith to be edited by Phillip Blond.

25. For some shrewd observations on this, see M.J. Scanlon, 'The Augustinian Tradition. A Retrieval', *Augustinian Studies* 20 (1989) 61-92, esp. pp. 80-84.

26. *Stromateis* II.xvi (GCS edition, p. 151.27-152-26).

27. See esp. Book III of the *de bapt.*

28. 'Literature as Scripture: Privileged Reading in Current Religious Reflection', *Soundings* lxxiv (1991), pp. 65-99.

29. On the significance of such 'otherness' as fundamental for ethics, see Edith Wyschogrod, *Saints and Postmodernism. Revisioning Moral Philosophy*, Chicago 1990 (allowing for the reservations expressed in my review of this work, *Modern Theology* 8 (1992) 305-307).

30. On God's 'rhetoric', see particularly the 1992 Oxford D. Phil. thesis of Robert Dodaro, OSA, *Language and Justice: Political Anthropology in Augustine's De Civitate Dei.*

The Cross as Ransom

EUGENE TESELLE

It is widely known that the early church interpreted the cross as an event in which human kind was ransomed from captivity to the devil. It is almost as widely assumed that this line of interpretation was logically absurd, morally repugnant, and psychologically childish. This paper attempts to rehabilitate the ransom motif, tracing three variant expressions in patristic literature, then probing the meanings which this "mythic" pattern might suggest to our own age.

When patristic writers treat the cross as a ransoming of sinful humanity from captivity to Satan, it suggests that the chief problem concerning sin is not the wrath of God but bondage to evil. The two problems are not totally isolated—it is separation from God, after all, that leads to bondage to evil. But the ransom model assumes that the latter has a power of its own even when the former is being overcome.

Modern commentators have sensed that this "mythic" pattern probes the depths of evil and suggests how it might be resisted or overcome; but they have not completely articulated it. I shall argue that the patristic discussion brought out the distinctive "logic" of the myth, seeing it as a transaction among several distinct factors, in the course of which a moral victory is achieved and made lasting by bringing evil to limit itself. This logic is not limited to the one case of the cross (we shall explore a number of parallels), but it seems to be expressed with special clarity in this particular doctrinal image.

VARIANT 1: THE METAPHOR OF RANSOM

The fundamental image is, indeed, that of a ransom paid to one who holds a slave or a captive as the precondition for being freed.[1] The owner or

---

1. For discussions of the theme, see Adolf von Harnack, *Lehrbuch der Dogmengeschichte*, 4. Aufl. (Tübingen: J. C. B. Mohr, 1909), I: 683 n. 3; II: 176; Jean Rivière, *Le Dogme de la rédemption. Essai d'étude historique* (Paris: Librairie Victor-

Journal of Early Christian Studies 4:2, 147–170 © 1996 The Johns Hopkins University Press.

captor in this case is the devil, or collectively the demons or the "powers" (especially as referred to in Col 2.13–15 or I Cor 2.8). Origen states the logic of the situation in a way that came to be regarded as authoritative:

> If therefore we were "bought with a price," as Paul agrees [I Cor 6.20, 7.23], then without a doubt we were bought from someone whose slaves we were, and who demanded whatever price he wished in order to release from his power those whom he held. Now it was the devil, to whom we had been sold by our sins, who held us. He demanded therefore as our price the blood of Christic.[2]

The idea of ransom suggests, then, that the problem in salvation, or the obstacle to salvation, is not the wrath of God but the claim of the devil: the human race, by yielding to the devil's tempting, has "justly" fallen under the power or claim of the devil, for although the devil acted "unjustly" in rebelling against God and tempting Adam and Eve, once they have consented to sin they are linked to him as the one to whom they have "sold themselves."[3] Furthermore, the notion of ransom suggests that God ef-

---

Lecouffre, 1905); idem, "Rédemption," DTC 13.2 (1937): 1911–2004; Robert S. Franks, A History of the Doctrine of the Work of Christ, in Its Ecclesiastical Development (London: Hodder & Stoughton, 1918), reprinted under the title The Work of Christ: A Historical Study of Christian Doctrine (London: Thomas Nelson and Sons, 1962); Hastings Rashdall, The Idea of Atonement in Christian Theology, Bampton Lectures 1915 (London: Macmillan, 1920); Gustaf Aulén, Christus Victor: An Historical Study of the Three Main Types of the Idea of the Atonement, trans. A. G. Hebert (London: SPCK, 1931); Martin Werner, Die Entstehung des christlichen Dogmas problemgeschichtlich dargestellt (Bern and Leipzig: Paul Haupt, 1941), 238–71, abridged in The Formation of Christian Dogma: An Historical Study of Its Problems, trans. S. G. F. Brandon (London: Adam & Charles Black, 1957), 95–106); H. E. W. Turner, The Patristic Doctrine of Redemption: A Study of the Development of Doctrine during the First Five Centuries (London: A. R. Mowbray, 1952), chapter 3; Werner Elert, "Redemptio ab hostibus," TLZ 72 (1947): 266–270; J. N. D. Kelly, Early Christian Doctrines, 5th ed. (New York: Harper & Row, 1976), 382–94; Hans Kessler, Die theologische Bedeutung des Todes Jesu. Eine traditionsgeschichtliche Untersuchung (Düsseldorf: Patmos-Verlag, 1970); idem, Erlösung als Befreiung (Düsseldorf: Patmos-Verlag, 1972); Linwood Urban, A Short History of Christian Thought (New York: Oxford University Press, 1986), 109–116; Neil Forsyth, The Old Enemy: Satan and the Combat Myth (Princeton: Princeton University Press, 1987). The social customs involved in the ransom of slaves and captives, and the use of ransom as a religious metaphor, are surveyed in Gerhard Barth, Der Tod Jesu Christi im Verständnis des Neuen Testaments (Neukirchen-Vluyn: Keukirchener, 1992), 71–75.

2. Comm. in Rom. 2.13 (PG 14.911). The other classic passage in Origen is comm. in Mt. 13.8–9 (PG 13.1111–19), where all the major biblical texts are brought together.

3. Gregory of Nyssa, or. catech. 22 (PG 45.60); Augustine, psal. 125.2 (CCSL 40.1846; Trin. 4.13.17 [CCSL 50.182–84]).

fects the liberation of human kind not by violence, not by powe
a manner that expresses goodness, justice, and wisdom.[4]

VARIANT 2: ABUSE OF POWER

The image of ransom, when it is taken literally, suggests too mu
equality between God and the devil, or too amicable a relationsl
the general patristic view involves a more complex scenario, or
Rivière differentiated by calling it not "ransom" but "abuse of
or Kelly characterized as not a "satisfaction of the Devil's s
rights" but "his proper punishment for going beyond them."[6] It
knowledged that the devil has a claim over sinful humanity. But
il has no rights over Christ, the Second Adam, who was conceiv
Holy Spirit, was not overcome by sin, and never yielded to t
temptations.[7] In the case of Christ, therefore, the devil overste
prerogatives and misused his power in condemning and executi
one who was sinless. On the widespread assumption that death
penalty or natural consequence of sin, the accusation and exe
Christ is not only inappropriate but unjust, an "abuse of powe
result the devil forfeits his rights, not only over Christ (over who
er had "rights," although he did have the power to tempt and e
cuse and torment and kill), but over all those who attach ther
Christ and adhere to the one in whose case the devil became guil
accusation.[9] This scenario is at least part of the background

4. Gregory of Nyssa, *or. catech.* 22 (PG 45.60–61); Dionysius Areopagi
5. Adamantius, *dial.* I.27 (PG 11.1756–57), criticizes the notion of :
though it were between two friends, or as though the devil were somehov
Human beings are the ones who have "sold themselves" through sin, "alien
selves" from God. The devil does not sell them in any sense. Furthermo
"gave" his blood as a ransom, then he would have "received it back" in l
tion; one cannot suppose the devil giving back his ransom so easily, and
Christ had "power to put his life aside and take it back" (Jn 10.18), thus
own power alone.
6. Kelly, *Doctrines,* 387.
7. Hilary, *psal.* 68.8 (PL 9.475); Ambrosiaster, *ad Col.* 2.13
81/3.184–87); Augustine, *Lib.* 3.10.31 (CSEL 74.116–17; *Trin.* 13.1
(CCSL 50A.402–8); *Eu. Io.* tr. 95.4 (CCSL 36.567).
8. Rivière suggests ("Rédemption," 1939–40) that this theory, while
in the East, is more characteristically Latin (see passages cited there).
9. This can happen because the believer is "Christo indutum" (Aug
13.16.21 [CCSL 50A.410]) or is linked to Christ "uinculo fidei" (*conf.* 9.
27.153]).

, but in

renunciation of the devil and his "works" or
y) at baptism,[10] the exorcism of demons in
e use of the sign of the cross in an apotropa-
t bay.[12]

ild blunder into a situation filled with disas-
eral explanations. The best known is that of
according to which the incarnation is a mys-
powers.[13] In its classic statement during the
of Christ functions as a kind of bait hidden

:h of an
ip,[5] and
e which
power,"
ipposed
s still ac-
the dev-
d by the
e devil's
pped his
ig some-
s the just
ution of
:."[8] As a
n he nev-
en to ac-
iselves to
y of false
for early

ica, e. h. 3.
"sale," as
converted.
iting them-
e, if Christ
is resurrec-
in any case
rises by his

15 (CSEL
2.16–15.19

·ell attested

istine, Trin.
2.36 [CCSL

il at Baptism: Ritual, Theology, and Drama (Ithaca:
f., notes that the renunciation of Satan was the one
ismal rituals. Possible Jewish backgrounds are ex-
)unce Satan, His Pomps and His Works," in Bap-
posium, trans. David Askew (Baltimore: Helicon,

is is found already in the gospel tradition; in the
i gloats about the power of Jesus' name over the
; (2 apol. 6) and Jews (dial. 85).
F. J. Dölger entitled "Beiträge zur Geschichte des
imes of the JAC. In the fourth of these, 4 (1961):
sign of the cross is first attested in the Gnostic
it was widely used for apotropaic purposes. See

Werner, Entstehung, 243 (ET, 97); Turner, chap-
s: Die Anschauung von Christus als Bote und En-
hen Literatur des christlichen Altertums, Theo-
1), 297–310; and Georg Kretschmar, Studien zur
!1 (Tübingen: J. C. B. Mohr, 1956), 49–53. Paul
sdom of God, concealed in the Christ who is cru-
first puts on and then puts off the Adamic body
ee Ernst Käsemann, Leib und Leib Christi. Eine
lichkeit (Tübingen: J. C. B. Mohr, 1933), 140–46,
l Liturgy," Essays on New Testament Themes,
on: SCM Press, 1966), 162–63. Ignatius (Eph
if a cry" which were "hidden from the ruler of
ig birth, and the death of the Lord. The disguise
s, moves from hinting at a mysterious "beyond"
the tradition that Christ descends through the
ugh them, "putting on" and then "putting off,"
; principalities and powers. This is found in Si-
iC 264.316–18]), Basilides (haer. 1.24.6 [SC
–14 (Hennecke-Schneemelcher I.256–57), and
uses this tradition to interpret Col 2.15. Dis-
demons about Christ's true identity continues
iture and art. See Ruth Mellinkoff, The Devil
lief in Grünewald's Altarpiece (Berkeley: Uni-
l.

in a trap (this is the usual Western imagery) or covering the fishhook of the divine nature (Gregory of Nyssa's notorious comparison).[14] Another favorite explanation is that there was a tragic overstepping or *hamartia* on the part of the devil. On this view the devil was not deceived by God but erred because of jealousy or ambition.[15]

Sharing some features of both of these, but distinct from them, is the suggestion of Gregory of Nyssa that the master of a slave can be given whatever ransom he may "accept," knowingly or unknowingly. God in justice offered a repayment "adequate to the debt," and in this sense one can even speak of the devil's accepting an exchange in which he believes he will receive something more valuable than what he already has. It is still a "deception of the deceiver," and the devil is misled by his own pride and desire for power; but the stress is upon the justice and goodness of the transaction, since it is to the benefit not only of those who are enslaved but even, Gregory thinks, of the enslaver, the devil himself, when life is introduced into the realm of corruption and righteousness purges out the accretions of sin.[16]

VARIANT 3: OVERCOMING DEATH

The notion of ransom to the devil, even in this more sophisticated "abuse of power" form, was occasionally criticized in antiquity (the patristic writers were not as naive as critics sometimes imply). Gregory Nazianzen objects to the idea of *payment* and asks *to whom* it would be made. He rejects payment either to the Evil One or to the Father. And yet he goes on to speak of Christ's "overcoming the tyrant." His own resolution is that *death* is overthrown by the cross, killed by the giver of life.[17] John of Damascus likewise objects to the language of ransom, yet he still speaks of the deception of the devil and acknowledges that there is a ransom that frees from condemnation. It is not that Christ's blood was offered to the

---

14. *or. catech.* 24 (PG 45.65).

15. Augustine, *serm.* 134.4 (PL 38.744): "Erras, deceptor, non fallitur Redemptor: erras. Vides in Domino carnem mortalem, non est caro peccati: similitudo est carnis peccati." The devil's envy had already been suggested as the reason for the sin and death of Adam and Eve (Sap 2.23–24), the sin of Cain (Theophilus of Antioch, *Autol.* 2.29), and a whole series of sins in subsequent human history (*I Clem* 4). See Willem Cornelis van Unnik, "Der Neid in der Paradiesgeschichte nach einigen gnostischen Texten," in *Essays on the Nag Hammadi Texts in Honour of Alexander Böhlig*, Nag Hammadi Studies III (Leiden: E. J. Brill, 1972), 120–32. Its extension to the crucifixion, therefore, is not surprising.

16. *or. catech.* 26 (PG 45.69).

17. *or.* 45.22 (PG 36.653).

tyrant, but that *death* seized the bait of his flesh and could not contain divinity. Thus corruption was overcome by life, as darkness is by light.[18] These writers appear to view the ransom or abuse of power imagery as an excessively dramatic expression of a conviction which they also share, but which they think can be stated more soberly: that death and corruption are conquered by the incarnate Word, and that Christian experience includes a sense of being freed from death, which is, of course, the consequence of sin and guilt.[19] While Christ's victory over death is usually attributed to the power and righteousness of the divine Word, Origen took note of the statement (Mt 20:28) that the Son of Man came "to give his *soul* as a ransom for many," and applied to Christ passages like "free among the dead" (Ps 88|87|.5 LXX) and "You did not leave my soul in Hades" (Ps 16|15|.10 LXX). He insisted, then, that neither the Word nor the body is the ransom. At the same time he refused to "divide Jesus from Christ" and affirmed that Christ is "one whole."[20]

Athanasius offers the most impressive of the "demythologized" accounts of redemption, in the sense that the devil is not explicitly involved in either the captivity or the ransoming. Using a different kind of language, drawn from Paul, Athanasius speaks of the curse of the Law. God willed that the human race live in communion with God; but when they "devised and imagined" that which had no being,[21] God allowed them to lapse into their natural condition of corruption and mortality, thus enforcing the earlier threat that death would be the consequence of disobedience.[22] But now God faces a dilemma: death has gained a "legal hold,"

---

18. *f. o.* 3.27 (PG 94.1096–97).

19. Perhaps the earliest Christian expression of this theme is Paul's conviction that Christ dies to sin and the "body of sin," so that death "no longer rules" (Rom 6.5–11; cf. I Cor 15.45–50, II Cor 5.14–15). The power of life over death is elaborated by taking over the pre-Christian theme of a "descent into Hades," literature on which is surveyed by Gerhard Barth, *Tod Jesu Christi*, 85–97. This was developed in highly mythic form in the narrative of the "harrowing of Hell" in the apocryphal *Acts of Pilate*, which probably comes from the second half of the second century. Here Satan, who has both tempted Adam and inspired the crucifixion of Christ, is differentiated from Hades, who senses the power of one who could raise Lazarus with only a word and warns Satan against bringing Christ into the realm of death. Christ, "the king of glory," breaks the gates of Hades (cf. Ps. 24[23].7–10), seizes "the chief ruler Satan" and confines him to Hades until his second coming, takes Adam by the hand and leads out all those who have been held in the underworld. The passage is translated in *New Testament Apocrypha*, rev. ed., ed. Wilhelm Schneemelcher, English trans. ed. R. McL. Wilson (Philadelphia: Westminster/John Knox Press, 1991), I:524–25.

20. *comm. in Mt.* 16.8 (PG 13.1397–1400).

21. *gent.* 7 (PG 25.16) and the entire section, 3–7 (PG 25.8–16).

22. *inc.* 4–5 (PG XXV.104–5).

since God had declared what would happen in the event of transgression and cannot be false to God's own word; yet it is inappropriate that a creature made for communion with God remain under the power of death, and it seems unworthy of God's goodness to neglect the misery of the human condition.[23] God must be true to the law already laid down, and to accept mere repentance would neither uphold the "reasonable expectation concerning God"[24] nor reverse the natural power of corruption. Since human nature cannot renew itself, divine power is needed to create it afresh. But this cannot occur until death and corruption—which are not merely natural or factual, but the just consequence of transgression—are abolished.[25]

Therefore the Word assumed a body which could die, and "offered it to death";[26] in this way the *prohibition* against transgression is maintained and even fulfilled,[27] but the *punishment*, the "law involving the ruin of human beings,"[28] the law "which was against us,"[29] is ended. Indeed, Christ suffered death "on behalf of all" so that the "debt" might be paid;[30] all were freed from the curse in that they died "in him";[31] he received not his own death but the death of others,[32] inflicted by others in their hostile counsel, and even received it as a curse.[33] How does this happen? Athanasius uses the metaphor that the power of death was "spent" or "used up" in the death of Christ,[34] but this seems to mean more prosaically that Christ "offered an equivalent" and thereby "satisfied the debt by his death"[35] or repaid the debt "owed by all."[36] Death itself can no longer be the same, for it ceases to be condemnation under the Law; now it is not corruption but only dissolution, not a perishing but a sowing.[37]

---

23. *inc.* 6 (PG 25.105–8).
24. "*To eulogon to pros ton theon,*" three times in *inc.* 7 (PG 25.108–9).
25. *inc.* 13 and 44 (PG 25.120 and 173–76).
26. *inc.* 8, 9, 16, 20, 25, 31 (PG 25.109, 112, 124, 132, 140, 149).
27. *inc.* 8 (PG 25.109).
28. *inc.* 8 (PG 25.109).
29. *inc.* 10 (PG 25.113).
30. *inc.* 20 (PG 25.132).
31. *inc.* 8 (PG 25.109).
32. *inc.* 22 (PG 25.136).
33. *inc.* 24–25 (PG 25.137–40).
34. *inc.* 8 (PG 25.109).
35. *inc.* 9 (PG 25.112).
36. *inc.* 20 (PG 25.129). George Dion Dragas, "St Athanasius on Christ's Sacrifice," in *Sacrifice and Redemption: Durham Essays in Theology,* ed. S. W. Sykes (Cambridge: Cambridge University Press, 1991), 94–95, emphasizes that the role of death, and certainly of the devil, is derived from the law of God, which gives death its power and is used by the devil to keep humanity under his control.
37. *inc.* 21 (PG 25.132).

We find, then, three variants of the ransom motif: "ransom" described in such fashion that the captor agrees to accept the payment that is offered; the more complex sequence involving an "abuse of power" through which the devil forfeits his just claim; and a somewhat more demythologized version which emphasizes an exchange of death for life or a shattering of death by life. The first, we might say, is an overly literal elaboration of the metaphor of ransom; the second offers a more carefully reasoned scenario; the third focuses upon the human predicament and its resolution in Christ's death and resurrection. But their "family resemblance" is clear.

RELATION TO SACRIFICE

It must be acknowledged that the ransom motif does not stand alone. The early church had to deal with the sacrificial language in both the Jewish and the Christian Bible. The two motifs met in the Exodus Passover narrative, where the positive goal is to worship God in the wilderness (Ex 3.7–12, 5.3, 9.1), but Pharaoh keeps them captive until he is "compelled by a mighty hand" (Ex 3.19). Because Pharaoh has refused to release Israel, God's "firstborn," God will slay Pharaoh's firstborn (Ex 4.22–23). So God "ransoms" or "redeems" Israel from its captivity (Ex 6.6; cf. Dt 15.15, 24.18) through a complex process: the "Destroyer" kills all the firstborn, but "passes over" those households where the blood of the sacrificed lamb has been placed on the doorposts (Ex 12.23).[38] Hippolytus

---

38. Jon D. Levenson, *The Death and Resurrection of the Beloved Son: The Transformation of Child Sacrifice in Judaism and Christianity* (New Haven and London: Yale University Press, 1993), notes several distinct strands in ancient Israel: (1) unequivocal evidence of child sacrifice in Ex 22.29b, Jer 19.5–6, Ezek 20.26, and Mic 6.7; (2) the possibility of offering an animal substitute, as evidenced in Ex 13.13 and 34.19–20 as well as the *aqedah* (Gen 22.1–19); (3) prophetic criticism of child sacrifice, leading Jeremiah and Ezekiel, Deuteronomy and the Holiness Code, to omit all mention of either a divine claim upon firstborn human males or their redemption by offering an animal substitute; and (4) the failure of such attempts to *eradicate* the motif and its lasting *transformation* into the sacrifice of an animal substitute, as evidenced by the late Priestly document to which Ex 12–13 belongs (43–52). Levinson thinks in sacrificial terms, overlooking the possible "ransom" overtones in this troubling tradition. As a consequence he must identify YHWH with El, who in Canaanite myth sacrifices his son or a younger deity to slavery or death (32–35), or with the "Destroyer" (45–46), when it would be possible to see a tension between two aspects of deity—or of the human situation. He moves in the latter direction only toward the end, where he focuses attention on the Joseph story with its emphasis on sibling rivalry and its consequences (226–32). Levenson's book is discussed from several Christian and Jewish perspectives in the Winter 1994 issue of *Dialog*, 52–66.

linked this apotropaic practice with the sign of the cross,[39] and Origen identified the Destroyer, like other threatening figures in the biblical narratives, with Satan.[40] Augustine pointed out that Christians, from the catechumenate on, bear the sign of the cross on their foreheads, like the blood on the doorposts; but this sign drives away the Destroyer only because Christ dwells in their hearts.[41]

The passage about the scapegoat—actually two goats (Lev 16.7–10), one "for the Lord," sacrificed as a sin offering, and one kept alive "for taking away sin" (thus called the *chimaros apopompaios, caprus emissarius*), which is driven into the wilderness carrying the people's sins— was understood during the first two centuries as a discrediting of persecutors. The Epistle of Barnabas (7.9) says that the accursed goat is later crowned, and those who have abused it (or him, since it is a foreshadowing of the cross) say, "Is not this the one whom we crucified and rejected and pierced and spat upon?"[42] Justin interprets the two goats as the two advents of Christ, one on the cross and the other as judge.[43] Origen seems at first glance to abandon these earlier suggestions of a complex interrelationship between the two goats, and instead follow the path of diremption, viewing the two goats as symbols of the radically different "lots"

39. *trad. ap.* 42 (SC 11bis.134–36).

40. *princ.* 3.2.1 (GCS 5.244–45); *Cels.* 6.43 (GCS 2.113–14). It is to be noted, however, that in these passages the Destroyer is mentioned only in order to reinforce the contrast between God and the "opposing powers," and there is no reversal of the kind typical of ransom. Origen also speaks of a "double crucifixion," visibly of Christ, invisibly of the devil (*hom. 8 in Jos.* 3 (SC 71.222–24). But he goes on to moralize it, in a way typical of his homilies: the Christian is "crucified to the world" when the prince of the world finds nothing in us; the world, like the devil, is "crucified to us" when we do not respond to sinful desires. In his allegorical interpretation Origen spiritualizes even more: Christ's sacrifice is really for those who have an attitudinal change, when faith destroys the power of the Destroyer and they can pass over into the presence of God (*Peri Pascha: Christianisme Antique* 2:15–16,25,46–47; ACW 54.36,41,54).

41. *eu. Io. tr.* 50.2 (CCSL 36.433–34).

42. See especially *Épître de Barnabé*, Introduction, traduction et notes par Pierre Prigent, texte grec établi et présenté par Robert A. Kraft, SC 172 (Paris: Éditions du Cerf, 1971), 132–35, and James Carleton Paget, *The Epistle of Barnabas: Outlook and Background* (Tübingen: J. C. B. Mohr, 1994), 136–40. John Dominic Crossan, *Who Killed Jesus: Exposing the Roots of Anti-Semitism in the Gospel Story of the Death of Jesus* (San Francisco: HarperSanFrancisco, 1995), 122–25, suggests that this passage in Barnabas reflects Jewish and early Christian midrash on the scapegoat passage, and that this midrashic tradition actually *shaped* the passion narrative as we find it in the gospels.

43. Justin, *dial.* 40.4; 111.1 (Goodspeed 137, 227); Tertullian, *Marc.* 3.7.7 (CSEL 47.387–88).

and destinies of the good and the evil.[44] But then he goes on to speak of Christ's descent into the underworld as a sharing of the destiny of the scapegoat, after which he goes into the heavenly sanctuary to make a propitiatory offering for those who choose to come back from the desert and stand before the altar.[45]

Augustine, who began with an emphasis upon ransom,[46] wrestled with its connection with sacrifice, which he understood as reconciliation and reunion with God.[47] Particularly problematical to him was Paul's statement that God "made him who knew no sin to be sin for us" (II Cor 5.20–21). While this could suggest ransom from the devil, Augustine felt compelled to read it as a reference to the sin offering (Lev 4.29), called *hattath* in Hebrew and duly translated *hamartia* in the Septuagint and *peccatum* in the Old Latin.[48] But in these very same discussions we see that the ransom motif remains important.[49] His concern, briefly, is to find a place for sacrifice (which is offered to God in behalf of sinful humanity) without losing the role of ransom (by which bondage to sin, guilt, or the devil is cancelled). Rivière argued[50] that sacrifice came to have priority, and he cited a passage in which Augustine seems to set them in a causal sequence: "The blood of the Redeemer is poured out, and the bill of debt is cancelled."[51] His point is that sin as separation from God must be abolished before its penalty of bondage to sin and the devil can be relaxed. Be that as it may, the obverse also needs to be said. Even when God is ready to take a sinful humanity back into fellowship, the devil has "just claims" which can be cancelled only through a transaction like that sketched in

44. *hom. 9 in Lev.* 3–4 (SC 287.80–86). In *hom. 10 in Lev.* 2 (SC 287.136) he even compares Barabbas to the goat which is kept alive but goes into the wilderness, and Christ to the goat which is sacrificed as a propitiation.

45. *hom. 9 in Lev.* 5 (SC 287.90–96).

46. Especially *arb.* 3.10.31 (CCSL 29.293–94).

47. The principal passages in Augustine concerning sacrifice are *conf.* 10.43.69 (CCSL 27.278–79), *Trin.* 4.14.19 (CCSL 50.186–87), *civ.* 10.5–6 (CCSL 47.276–79), *eu. Io. tr.* 41.5 (CCSL 36.360–61), *enchir.* 13.41 (CSEL 46.73). A classic discussion is Joseph Lécuyer, "Le sacrifice selon saint Augustin," *AM* II:905–914. See also P. Eijkenboom, "Christus Redemptor in the Sermons of St. Augustine," in *Mélanges offerts à Mademoiselle Christine Mohrmann* (Utrecht-Anvers: Spectrum, 1963), 233–39, and most recently Gerald Bonner, "The Doctrine of Sacrifice: Augustine and the Latin Patristic Tradition," in *Sacrifice and Redemption: Durham Essays in Theology*, ed. S. W. Sykes (Cambridge: Cambridge University Press, 1991), 101–17.

48. *serm.* 134.5 (PL 38.745); *serm.* 152.9–11 (PL 38.823–25); *serm.* 155.8–11 (PL 38.845–47); *c. du. ep. Pelag.* 3.6.16 (CSEL 60.504–5).

49. The two themes of ransom and sacrifice are intertwined in *Trin.* 4.12.15–14.19, written about 406, and *Trin.* 13.10.13–20.26, written about 417–18.

50. Rivière, *Dogme* 181–85.

51. *Serm.* 134.5 (PL 38.745).

the ransom narrative.[52] Augustine seems to assume, furthermore, that reconciliation is not actualized until it takes place in each individual, in the new community of the church.[53] And even then it is necessary to rely upon the ransom achieved in the cross, as Augustine says in a very "Lutheran" passage referring to his mother:

> Let no one tear her away from your protection; let not him who is at once lion and serpent [Ps 91(90).13] bar the way, either by force or by guile, for she will answer, not that she has no debt to pay, lest she be convicted and taken into custody by the cunning accuser, but that her debts are cancelled by Christ, who cannot be repaid the price which he paid for us when the debt was not his to pay.[54]

ORIGINS OF THE MOTIF

In the ransom motif we have an interesting case in the development of doctrine, one in which, as Rashdall puts it in his unfriendly way, "there was gradually evolved a scheme in which all the vague, confused, more or less metaphorical expressions of earlier writers are taken in grim earnest, and hardened into a definite and very astonishing theory."[55]

The motif probably developed among groups that came to be considered heterodox. Among the Gnostics—and among Catholic writers, too—there are suggestions that Christ disguised himself and overcame the powers. Disguise can be linked, in fact, with every feature of the life of Christ: the incarnation (an infiltration through the cordon of besieging powers), the temptations, his silence at his trial, the descent into Hades,[56] and finally the ascension (the obverse of his entry into the world).

It has long been recognized that the motif came to full expression among the Marcionites.[57] According to their theology the Demiurge, the

---

52. I have argued this at greater length in *Augustine the Theologian* (New York: Herder and Herder, 1970), 172–75.

53. In *conf.* 5.9.16 Augustine, speaking of his own past, says that *at that time* God had not yet forgiven, "in Christ," any of his sins and had not yet dissolved, "in his cross," the enmity which he had caused through his sins. The allusion is to Eph 2.16, which speaks of God reconciling Jews and Gentiles through the cross and "killing the enmity" through Christ. Apparently reconciliation is *not* fulfilled until it happens in the lives of individual persons within the Catholic Church, which alone has "the unity of the Spirit in the bond of peace" (Eph 4.3).

54. *conf.* 9.13.36 (CCSL 27.153–54).

55. Rashdall, *Idea of Atonement*, 243.

56. For the development of this motif see Forsyth, *The Old Enemy*, 231, n. 37, and the texts cited in note 19 above.

57. Harnack, *Dogmengeschichte*, I: 683, n. 3; Franks, *History*, 14–15; Rashdall, *Idea of Atonement*, 245.

Just Creator, violated his own law of justice in causing Christ's death; in compensation he had to free all those who believe in Christ. Thus Jesus is the ransom which redeems believers from the Just Creator and frees them for the Good God.[58]

But we have also begun to see that the Marcionites, like the Gnostics, salvaged some features of the New Testament (specifically Paul and the Fourth Gospel) which were not being taken seriously by other segments of the Christian movement.[59] Anti-heretical writers like Justin, Theophilus, Irenaeus, and Hippolytus assimilated Gnostic and Marcionite themes in the process of refuting them. And of course these groups continued to be a vivid presence to Catholic writers. During the third century Manichaeism absorbed the Marcionite movement and posed its own challenge to orthodoxy up to the time of Augustine and his Pelagian opponents. At the very least it must be said that Gnosticism, Marcionism, and Manichaeism emphasized certain features of redemption that might not otherwise be taken into account.[60]

Irenaeus is the first of the Catholic writers to anticipate the ransom theme. He speaks of the Word's "giving himself as ransom for those who had been led into captivity,"[61] places responsibility for sin more upon the devil than upon the childlike Adam and Eve,[62] and suggests, "Justly he who led humankind captive is again brought into captivity, and humankind, which was led captive, is freed from the chains of condemnation."[63] And yet, neither in these passages nor elsewhere does he state the complete "ransom" scenario. His strongest statement of the "logic of re-

58. See especially Esnik, quoted by Franks, *History*, 14. Patristic testimonies include Origen, *hom. 6 in Ex.* 9 (PG 12.338), and Adamantius, *dial.* 1.27 (PG 11.1756–57). See Adolf von Harnack, *Marcion: Das Evangelium vom fremden Gott. Eine Monographie zur Geschichte der Grundlegung der katholischen Kirche*, TU 45 (Leipzig: J. C. Hinrichs, 1921), 111–12 and 171–72, for the various testimonies that Christ "buys" the redeemed through the cross. This implies, according to the Marcionites, both that they belong to another (since one does not buy what is one's own) and that Christ does not have anything to do with this Creator but comes from elsewhere.

59. Luise Schottroff, *Der Glaubende und die feindliche Welt. Beobachtungen zum gnostischen Dualismus und seiner Bedeutung für Paulus und das Johannesevangelium*, Wissenschaftliche Monographien zum Alten und Neuen Testament 37 (Neukirchen: Neukirchener Verlag, 1970); Elaine Pagels, *The Gnostic Paul: Gnostic Exegesis of the Pauline Letters* (Philadelphia: Fortress Press, 1975).

60. Carl Andresen, "Erlösung," *RAC* 6: 130.

61. *haer.* 5.1.1 (SC 153.18).

62. Irenaeus, like the apologists before him, takes great interest in the demons and places the responsibility for sin upon them, not upon any corruption of human nature. Human beings are assumed to be free to respond to good and evil powers; but their freedom, which is both finite and fallible, is unequal to the task.

63. *haer.* 3.23.1 (SC 211.446).

demption"—that the devil is refuted and exposed to ridicule, being bound
with the same chains of transgression and apostasy with which he bound
human beings—applies to the temptations in the wilderness, not to the
cross.[64] Irenaeus' emphasis is upon the "recapitulation" effected in the
Second Adam, the transformation brought about through the incarnation, life, death, and resurrection of the Word. The disobedience at the
one tree is reversed through obedience at another tree,[65] and it becomes
effective for others through "persuasion"[66] or "experience";[67] indeed,
God permitted sin for the education of the human race through "experience," first of evil, then of good.[68] Irenaeus' chief contribution was to re-
state the ransom theme, no longer in terms of the cosmic *dualism* of the
Gnostics and Marcionites, but in the language of *apostasy* from the one
Creator, and God's corresponding action against "the apostasy" which
tyrannized over the human race.[69] He seems, furthermore, to be the in-
ventor of the dictum that what the devil did "unjustly" is overcome "justly"
by Christ.

It was Origen who, as Harnack says, "fixed and transmitted through
his disciples" the theme of a ransom from the devil;[70] Harnack adds that
this is an example of Origen's "conservatism," his unwillingness to abandon something which was part of the tradition.[71] We could add to this his
comprehensiveness, which impelled him to consider many different traditions of interpretation.[72] His "fixing" of the ransom motif must be set
alongside his use of other traditions which go well beyond it, if they do
not conflict with it, such as his use of the Gnostic interpretation of Colos-
sians 2.15[73] and his belief in the gradual conversion of the powers.

UNDERSTANDING THE RANSOM IMAGE

The ransom metaphor, as we have seen, was expressed in three basic variants in patristic writings: (1) a literal use of the notion of ransom or sale

64. *haer.* 5.21.3 (SC 153.274–78).
65. *haer.* 5.16.3 (SC 153.218).
66. *haer.* 5.1.1 (SC 153.20).
67. *haer.* 5.21.3 (SC 153.278).
68. *haer.* 3.20.2 (SC 211.388), 4.39.1 (SC 100.962).
69. Forsyth, *The Old Enemy*, 334–42, citing *haer.* 5.1.1 (5.21.3 could also be
added).
70. Harnack, *Dogmengeschichte*, II: 176.
71. *Dogmengeschichte*, I: 683, n. 3.
72. Wesley Carr, *Angels and Principalities: The Background, Meaning and Development of the Pauline Phrase hai archai kai hai exousiai* (Cambridge: Cambridge University Press, 1981), 168–71, 174–76.
73. *Cels.* 2.64 (GCS 2.186). See note 13 above.

or exchange; (2) the more complex scenario of an "abuse of power" through the failure of the powers to recognize the true character of the situation; and (3) a "demythologized" version making the transaction a victory of good over evil, life over death. The first is excessively literal and seems rarely to have been taken seriously even in the early centuries. The third has the advantage of probing the meaning of the mythos for the believer; it is the approach taken by most modern writers who have been appreciative of the ransom theme.[74] Its ontological claims (such as the power of life over death or the capacity of good to absorb evil) are rhetorically impressive. But they are scarcely self-evident.

This third way of speaking may be convincing, then, only because it is a rationalization of the metaphor on which it depends—or, to go back to its apparent source, only because Paul focused attention upon the cross as the point of transition from the old age to the new. Athanasius still follows the logic of an exchange, under which the penalties of the law are both satisfied and ended.[75] Gregory of Nyssa insists that the infinite power of good is manifested only after evil does its worst and finds its "limit."[76] Luther rediscovered the ransom motif in his struggle over the works of the Law and justification by faith.[77] Calvin, whose "penal substitution" understanding of the cross has more similarities to the ransom tradition than to the Anselmian, thinks of Christ as bearing the full force of the

74. Aulén, *Christus Victor*, 75–76, 123–124, 128–131, 162–172; Paul Tillich, *Systematic Theology* II (Chicago: University of Chicago Press, 1957), 171–72, 173–76.

75. Athanasius' achievement is all the more impressive because he thought of Christ as the divine Word in human flesh; it was the Word, not a human mind or soul, which descended into Hades to free the spirits there. See Aloys Grillmeier, *Christ in Christian Tradition. Volume I, From the Apostolic Age to Chalcedon (451)*, 2nd rev. ed., trans. John Bowden (London: A.R. Mowbray, 1975), 315–17. Athanasius could have made much of the divine power of the Word in overcoming death and Hell, as Aulén later does. Instead he operated on the principle that, since corruption and death had become endemic to the human situation, life must encounter and overcome death in the same realm (*inc.* 44 PG 25.140–41). Note also the passage, cited n. 20 above, in which Origen emphasizes that the ransom is paid by the *soul* of Jesus.

76. For this image in Gregory see especially Jean Daniélou, "Comble du mal et eschatologie chez Grégoire de Nysse," in *Festgabe Joseph Lortz*, ed. Erwin Iserloh and Peter Manns (Baden-Baden: Bruno Grimm, 1958), II: 27–45.

77. In the 1535 Commentary on Galatians, writing on Gal 3.13 and 4.4–5 (WA 40/1.437–450, 560–71 [American Edition 26.280–89, 367–74]), he sets up a contest between the "curse" and the "blessing." Christ associates himself with those who are under the curse by assuming their flesh and blood, or assuming their "person"; in assuming and bearing the sins of the whole world in this way, he lets the Law gain a certain "right" over him. He did not become a new teacher of the Law; rather he subjected himself to it, became its disciple or even its slave, performed it and bore its consequences (567–69 [372–73]). The curse of the Law must even complete its work

curse upon sinful humanity, experiencing it to the full, and thereby break-ing it.[78] In other words, even this "demythologized" variant must be un-derstood, not as a general metaphysical truth, but as the conceptualiza-tion of a concrete interaction among several distinct factors or "agents."

Therefore I propose to explore primarily the second variant, the "abuse of power" scenario, because of its evident importance in most of the pa-tristic statements about redemption, its explication of the "logic" of ran-som, and its intractably narrative form. Precisely because it is the *lectio difficilior* it demands consideration, on the suspicion that it expresses some pattern of meaning which could not be easily stated in any other way.

Let us seek comparisons or analogues in more general types of experi-ence (political, social, psychological), not as though the religious symbols are reducible in their meaning to general processes which can be more ac-curately named in other ways, but just the reverse: basic issues can be at stake in a range of familiar experiences.[79]

The most evident parallel is in the sphere of social relationships and in-teractions. Abuse of power—overstepping one's authority and conse-quently being discredited—is common in human interactions. In the fo-rum of public opinion, all that one needs to do is mention a past event which is morally debatable ("The Holocaust"; "Hiroshima"; "Vietnam"; "Watergate"; "Chappaquiddick") to compromise a claim to legitimate authority. After Three Mile Island and Chernobyl the political rhetoric of nuclear power can never be the same. People prefer to link themselves with those whom they call, rather vaguely, the martyrs—a Dietrich Bon-hoeffer, a Martin Luther King, Jr., the Kennedy brothers, an Oscar Romero, the six Jesuits in San Salvador—rather than their opponents, even when the perpetrators cannot be identified precisely. The name of

---

by accusing Christ of blasphemy and sedition and all other sins (448 [288], 565 [370]). But the Law is able to find nothing in him; it has no basis on which to defend itself, and consequently it loses its jurisdiction over Christ—who was subject to it only be-cause of his voluntary subjection, not because of what he was—and over all who be-lieve in him (564–65 [369–70]). Then the Law, which had been able to accuse and ter-rify the conscience, loses its power and is displaced by faith as the only instrument of justification.

78. Calvin, *Inst. Chr. Rel.* 2.14.3–12.

79. If we need New Testament warrant for considering other kinds of undeserved suffering, we find it, for example, in the narrative of the "slaughter of the innocents" (Mt 2.16–18), which makes the point that their mother Rachel "refused to be con-soled" (in other words, did not allow it to be explained or justified in providential terms), and the magi are said to return to their homeland "by another way" (Mt 2.12), not cooperating with the political system of the tyrant.

John Birch gained currency as the first U.S. citizen to be a victim of the People's Republic of China; it was used, like the sign of the cross, to ward off any claims of legitimacy which that government might attempt to wield. The pink triangle has been adopted by gay men and lesbians to associate themselves with one set of victims of the Nazi regime—and their opponents with Adolf Hitler.

As we consider the various examples, it is clear that sometimes there is a *total and permanent* discrediting of a person, regime, or cause, but more often it is only a *partial and temporary* loss from which public figures have a way of recovering. The parallels with the patristic ransom theme are most striking when we find ourselves dealing with "systems of domination," which may be political or ideological or psychological in character. But those highly dramatic parallels should not distract us from other possibilities: value judgments about priorities or the direction of one's own life; considerations about what constitutes "death" and "life"; fears of "returning to bondage" if one follows a particular orientation; even the possibility of "conversion" on the part of the powers that rule life, for the ransom model does not require us to "demonize" even the most powerful and intractable systems. What is central to the ransom model, in other words, is not *irreversible condemnation* but *unavoidable moral confrontation*, and the outcomes can vary.

Perhaps the most dramatic form of moral confrontation in our day— and a clear parallel to the "abuse of power" scenario—is non-violent resistance.[80] Here a claim of higher validation is made to bring an end to a legalized pattern of oppression. Very often the judicial process itself has been manipulated for political ends, with ample opportunity for abuse of power by both the prosecutor and the judge.[81] Non-violent direct action takes control of the situation away from the ruling powers, poses a dilemma to them, puts them in a double bind: they must either consent to an act of

80. The parallel is drawn, with quotations from Martin Luther King, Jr., in Urban, *A Short History of Christian Thought*, 115–16.
81. The justice meted out by colonizers and by conquerors would supply many examples. For instances in the legal history of Europe and the U.S., see Otto Kirscheimer, *Political Justice: The Use of Legal Procedure for Political Ends* (Princeton: Princeton University Press, 1961). The political calculations that led to the Nuremberg trials, and the legal complications created when the victors prosecute the defeated enemy, are explored in Bradley F. Smith, *The Road to Nuremberg* (New York: Basic Books, 1981). Celebrated (and controversial) examples in the U.S. include the trials of the "Boston Five," traced in Jessica Mitford, *The Trial of Dr. Spock, the Rev. William Sloane Coffin, Jr., Michael Ferber, Mitchell Goodman, and Marcus Raskin* (New York: Knopf, 1969), and the "Chicago Seven," traced in Jason Epstein, *The Great Conspiracy Trial: An Essay on Law, Liberty, and the Constitution* (New York: Random House, 1970).

disobedience (and thus appear weak, or give legitimacy to the dissenters) or exert their authority against it (and thus seem bullying and be morally discredited). It is a kind of moral "ju-jitsu" that uses an opponent's strength to defeat him.[82]

It is often pointed out, however, that Gandhi's nonviolence movement was aided by the British sense of fair play and the publicity that his actions received in the press, just as the civil rights movement owed much of its success to the fact that it was the first long-term "media event" covered by the television networks. In other words, a wider forum of public opinion is crucial if the process of discrediting is to occur. Usually it does not happen within the closed setting of a legislature or the councils of government. Considerations like these warn us, then, that the "abuse of power" transaction, while it can occur, is not inevitably successful. What is it that makes the difference?

THE FREEING EVENT

The experiences which we have been examining all have to do with a shift of legitimation. When the change is a morally convincing one, there has been a complex "transaction" which we are trying to map.[83] In all such experiences we are not dealing with a mere physics of power relationships. The maintenance of one order, the rise of another, and the transition from the one to the other are all valuational in character. There is, furthermore, a forum of public opinion within which events are judged; it is given voice by the astonished crowd, the chorus of Greek tragedy. What is of special interest is that, from time to time, some event makes the public aware of criteria which may have been only implicit before hand and enables that public to change its loyalties.

What is it that changes the situation? The ransom scenario highlights three factors, all of which, I think, must be present for it to be coherent and to be effective, morally, socially, and psychologically.

1. *Knowledge, exposure, demystification* are often assumed to be enough to alter the balance of forces. René Girard has developed a wide-

82. Saul Alinsky, introduction to *Reveille for Radicals* (New York: Vintage Books, 1969), x.

83. The term "transaction" has perhaps overly rich connotations. Its Latin root was *transigo*, to "carry through" a controversy and bring it to a resolution. It has to do, then, with conflict and negotiation and an eventual resolution, which need not be the preferred outcome, of course, for every party. "Transaction" as I use the term refers both to the *social interactions* that are symbolized in the ransom scenario and to the *moral and psychological process* in which bondage is overcome by discovering its limits and moving on to a new stage of inner courage and reintegration.

ranging theory—one that has many resonances with the ransom scenario—that "sacred violence" is the basis of most societies. As he explains it, community, a sharing of the same tangible reality or professed ideal, inevitably gives rise to rivalry and competition over the shared object. The contradiction between communion and rivalry is resolved by transferring all the guilt for the rivalry to the scapegoat.[84] Girard seems to assume, however, that it is enough for this situation to be "exposed," "unmasked," brought to consciousness—something that first occurred, he says, in the biblical narratives, especially that of the cross. He does not give much attention, in other words, to the process of change, either in the event which accomplishes the unmasking or in the subjective conversion of the person.

Similarly Paul Ricoeur, in dealing with the "myth of punishment," calls it a "logic" and suggests that it can be vanquished only with a new logic, a logic not of equivalence but of superabundance, the reversal of values suggested frequently by Paul ("the gift is not like the transgression," "how much the more," "but now").[85] To take such statements by themselves would be merely to dissolve the old logic and arrive at a new stage of insight.

But there is ample evidence that awareness of the existing situation is not enough to break its power, even over those who have explicit "knowledge." It seems more convincing when the old law is led to *condemn itself*, the old logic to *refute itself*; this is a large element in the "abuse of power" version of the ransom theme. Yet even self-condemnation or self-refutation may not seem "logically compelling" to all who are involved. The ruling powers may be quite credible in their own applications, and even reversals, of the moral criteria. More than exposure or plausible logic is needed.

2. How does it happen that a transformation is brought about in the spectators, the beholders, the "public"—those who, while not at the center of the drama, become convinced that a powerful authority has been discredited and shift their loyalties to the victim of an abuse of power? It seems to be the result of a *public presence* which challenges the prevail-

---

84. René Girard, *Violence and the Sacred*, trans. Patrick Gregory (Baltimore: Johns Hopkins University Press, 1977). See also *Things Hidden Since the Foundation of the World*, trans. Stephen Bann and Michael Metteer (Stanford: Stanford University Press, 1987) and *The Scapegoat*, trans. Yvonne Freccero (Baltimore: Johns Hopkins University Press, 1986).

85. Paul Ricoeur, "Interpretation of the Myth of Punishment," in *The Conflict of Interpretations: Essays in Hermeneutics*, ed. Don Ihde (Evanston: Northwestern University Press, 1974), 368–75.

ing system of values. The "public presence" of which we are thinking is not simply a matter of outward confrontation and inward courage, both of which can waver or be misused; it also involves a *symbolic presence*— in this case, of the cross, preached and visually represented. Even the cross, as we know very well, can be misused.[86] But it also has the potentiality to bypass conventional interpretations, tapping deeper emotions and realigning the tensions that pervade the human situation.

Even to speak can be a "political" act, at once challenging, offending, and—if successful—transforming. Judith Lewis Herman, who played a major role in bringing incest to public attention,[87] reminds us of three relatively recent challenges to the conspiracy of silence about trauma: the first when psychiatrists sought to understand hysteria in the late nineteenth century, the second when Vietnam veterans struggled for recognition of post-traumatic stress disorder, the third when sexual and domestic violence was forced upon the attention of the public.[88] As these and other examples demonstrate, it cannot be taken for granted that the truth will be told, or, when told, will be believed. The situation is even worse than this. To continue with a contemporary example, battered women are *not* entirely captive or silent; they often stand up to their abusers and leave the situation. But this, counselors say, is when they are followed, "stalked," hunted down, and attacked with an even more explicit and public violence. And battering men, they add, are rarely held accountable by friends and family, law officers or judges.

Facts like these reinforce the importance not only of "speaking," of giving public testimony, but of having a "support system" that can deal with psychological obstacles and offer, in the most contemporary case, legal protection, housing, and economic assistance. Discrediting and a change in loyalties, in other words, are not enough. When we think of the early church, or of more recent examples of nonviolent social change associated with Gandhi, or with Martin Luther King, Jr., or with several anti-war movements, the existence of an alternative community is crucial not only

86. The ironies become overwhelming in the Crusades (which were not limited to the Holy Land, of course, but were also waged in Spain and in the Baltic lands); or when conquerors planted the cross as a sign and justification of their possession of the New World; or when Jews, accused of "deicide," were put under pressure to convert, as in medieval Germany, and the offer of the crucifix could only be responded to by spitting on it, inviting martyrdom as the only remaining way to "sanctify the Holy Name." See Jacob Katz, *Exclusiveness and Tolerance: Jewish-Gentile Relations in Medieval and Modern Times* (Oxford: Oxford University Press, 1961), 82–92.

87. Judith Lewis Herman, with Lisa Hirschman, *Father-Daughter Incest* (Cambridge: Harvard University Press, 1981).

88. *Trauma and Recovery*, 9.

for its testimony—which helps to ensure that there will in fact be a public forum in which issues of comparative justice can be raised—but for the example and support it offers to its own adherents. It is not inappropriate, then, when J.B. Metz speaks of the "subversive memory" of Christ's death and resurrection,[89] or Sharon Welch suggests the broader notion of "communities of resistance and solidarity,"[90] for this was one of the accomplishments, sociologically and culturally, of the early church.

3. A moral or psychological *change of posture* is also involved, and it does not take place until it becomes unavoidable. How does it occur? Some contemporary psychological theories are actually based upon a consideration of Paul or Irenaeus and attempt to explore the psychodynamics of the changes which they expressed in religious terms.

Psychologists usually link the imagery of bondage to the devil with the legalistic posture, sometimes in the active mode, sometimes in the passive. David Bakan has developed a theory of the devil as a personification of the self's attempts at mastery and self-justification, which are projected, "cast out" of the self when these attempts at mastery fail.[91] What is needed, he says, is a "surrender of the ego," a recognition that regions which have been denied by the ego must be brought back into awareness. Greater openness and receptivity, reunion with what has been separated through projection, is achieved with the aid of a "healer" like Jesus, who can "untie sin from suffering"—who shows that one can face what is repugnant in oneself because it is no longer linked with suffering, or rather because suffering and death are no longer understood simply as punishment for sin.[92] Don Browning offers a contrasting but complementary perspective, looking to the supra-individual powers which impose demands ("conditions of worth" in his parlance) upon the self, both binding and thwarting its deeper tendencies toward self-actualization.[93] Browning also speaks of the healer, who in this case mediates God's "unconditional empathic acceptance" of the sinner and of the most hostile human feelings.

89. Johannes Baptist Metz, *Faith in History and Society: Toward a Practical Fundamental Theology* (New York: Seabury Press, 1980), 66–67, 100–118.

90. Sharon D. Welch, *Communities of Resistance and Solidarity: A Feminist Theology of Liberation* (Maryknoll: Orbis Books, 1985).

91. David Bakan, "The Projection of Agency on the Figure of Satan," in *The Duality of Human Existence: An Essay on Psychology and Religion* (Chicago: Rand McNally and Company, 1966), 50. See also Henry A. Murray, "The Personality and Career of Satan," *Journal of Social Issues* 18 (1962): 41.

92. Bakan, "Projection of Agency," 97; cf. also his *Disease, Pain, and Sacrifice: Toward a Psychology of Suffering* (Chicago: University of Chicago Press, 1968), 126–27.

93. Don S. Browning, *Atonement and Psychotherapy* (Philadelphia: Westminster Press, 1966), 183–87, and also 104–7.

He senses the drama of the ransom motif, which he rehabilitates as the expression of the abreaction in which bondage to the conditions of worth is broken:

> The cross of Jesus Christ stands for a massive attempt on the part of these supra-individual conditions of worth to "fend off" God's incarnate uncondi-tioned empathic acceptance.[94]

When it is learned that God can accept all feelings and yet remain loving, it becomes possible to repudiate the conditions of worth; they are "de-feated and rendered impotent."[95]

Erik Erikson, in his discussion of Luther's overcoming of the accusing conscience, formulates a psychological version of *simul iustus et pecca-tor*:

> A predominant state of mind in which the ego keeps the superego in victori-ous check can reconcile certain opposites which the negative conscience rig-idly keeps separate; ego dominance tends to be holistic, to blend opposites without blunting them. . . . Our ego is most powerful when it is not burdened with an excessive denial of our drives, but lets us enjoy what we can, refute what we must, and sublimate according to our creativity—always making due allowance for the absolutism of our conscience, which can never be ap-peased by small sacrifices and atonements, but must always remain part of the whole performance. . . . [T]he ego gains strength *in practice* and *in affectu* to the degree to which it can accept at the same time the total power of the drives and the total power of conscience. . . .[96]

Or is it even more complex, a strengthening, not of the ego (which main-tains the autonomous role of negotiator) but, as the later Erikson will say, of the "self," deeper than the ego?[97] "Self psychology" speaks of differ-ent, even conflicting, "selves," different unifications of one's energies and one's values. Under the pressure of changed external circumstances, what had been "peripheral" may become the "nuclear" self without becoming the sole and all-encompassing self.[98] This way of putting it may be closer

---

94. Browning, *Atonement and Psychotherapy*, 245.
95. Browning, *Atonement and Psychotherapy*, 246.
96. Erikson, *Young Man Luther: A Study in Psychoanalysis and History*, 216–217.
97. Erik Erikson, *Identity, Youth, and Crisis* (New York: W.W. Norton, 1968), chap-ter 5. Even in the earlier passage in *Young Man Luther* (212–14), Erikson highlights the internalization of, even identification with, cultural and social tensions which are ordinarily ignored or suppressed.
98. See Heinz Kohut, *Self Psychology and the Humanities: Reflections on a New Psychoanalytic Approach*, ed. Charles B. Strozier (New York: W. W. Norton & Com-pany, 1985), specifically the chapter on courage, heroism, martyrdom, and tragedy, which are analyzed in terms of "the continuation of the two great narcissistic config-

to the abiding tenuousness of human life and the dramatic interactions among one's own psychic functions and the external forces to which they are linked.

Ricoeur recognizes that the logic of punishment survives at the heart of the new logic, as something which must be remembered even in the proclamation of that which has superseded it, something which is needed in order to understand the new: "If the wrath of God had no more meaning for me," he suggests, "I would no longer understand the import of pardon and grace."[99] One remains, so to speak, at the point of transition between bondage and freedom, old and new, the community of evil and the community of good. To this extent, at least, one must always operate in terms of the Pauline and Lutheran distinction between Law and Gospel, which are not susceptible of being resolved into a higher unity, or, even if they can be resolved in insight or concept, remains bifurcated in our existence.[100] It is not enough to speak only of self-integration, or moving to a "higher stage," whether it is understood psychoanalytically or existentially or conceptually, for there continue to be relationships to symbolic events, some signifying release, others signifying the imposition of bondage or a return to bondage.

One of the emphases of "self psychology" is its recognition of the role of the "self-object," the ideal self which gives coherence to one's life and does so all the better if it is sufficiently broad and complex to include life's crises within its scope. While the ideal self may be one's own creation (and this is the achievement conventionally attributed to "heroes" and "geniuses"), ordinary mortals depend first upon the idealized parent, then upon culture heroes and religious figures. Heinz Kohut discusses the tragic hero whose central self is realized in death, often because of a "code-

---

urations of early life: the grandiose self and the idealized parent imago" (35). On this theory the archaic function of the "self-object," which gives coherence and meaning during the early years, is transformed and becomes much more complex as a unifying set of values and ideals to which one's life can be devoted—and for the sake of which one can give up other rewards or even sacrifice one's life.

99. "Interpreting the Myth of Punishment," 376.

100. Compare the analogous comment by John Hick, *Evil and the God of Love* (New York: Harper & Row, 1966), 395, on the difference of vantage point in viewing evil which gives rise, respectively, to dualistic and processive conceptions of it: "Experienced from within the stresses of human existence, evil *is* a sheerly malevolent reality, hostile alike to God and His creation. It is a threat to be feared, a temptation to be resisted, a foe to be fought. . . . Seen, on the other hand, in the perspective of a living faith in the reality of the great, ongoing, divine purpose which enfolds all time and all history, evil has no status in virtue of which it might threaten even God Himself. It has an interim and impermanent character which deprives it of the finality that would otherwise constitute so much of its terror."

transgressing deed," and whose death both confirms that sense of self and gives permanence to the achievement.[101] He comments that Jesus in Gethsemane, at the trial, and on the cross has functioned, psychologically speaking, as a "self-object" giving meaning and coherence in the most difficult situations of life and death.

To explore the social and cultural and psychological dynamics of a religious symbol, as I have been doing in this last section, is not to be "reductive." It is, rather, to trace, more accurately and more fully, how the cross has often enabled people to face the conflicts and contradictions of their situation, redescribe them, and deal with them in a new and different way.

APPRAISAL

Let us summarize the difficulties many have had with the ransom motif—which also highlight its advantages—under five headings:

1. Its mythic character. All versions of the ransom theme utilize mythic narratives, seemingly in an irreducible way; this is true even of the more "demythologized" or "ontologized" versions of Athanasius and others. This fact suggests, on the other hand, that the ransom theme taps depths of imagery which cannot be reduced to concepts because they reflect fundamental features of the human situation. It is susceptible of conceptual thematization, however, along lines which may help to clarify certain aspects of the human situation.

2. Its view of evil. The ransom motif seems, in an almost Manichaean fashion, to ascribe too much power, or too many "rights," to evil. But in fact most explications of the ransom motif derived the "power" or "rights" of evil from God or from the Law, misused through apostasy. Within that framework they felt compelled to acknowledge the power of evil and to recognize, in a fashion close to the tragic view of life, that evil does have consequences, which cannot be either ignored or easily overcome. It denies the adequacy of notions that the good can simply drive out the bad; it recognizes instead that evil has irreversible consequences and that it must be brought to defeat itself.

3. Its approach to salvation. The ransom motif regards a transaction with evil as central to the work of Christ; it presupposes that the problem of a broken relationship with God has already been dealt with. In its defense it can be argued that evil is *the* problem in thinking about salvation, and (by contrast with "satisfaction" theories) that God is *not* the chief problem.

101. Kohut, *Self Psychology*, 37–39.

4. Its conceptual thematization. The ransom motif, especially in its "abuse of power" formulation, adopts a juristic/forensic framework, with all the difficulties of "legalism" and the additional absurdities of a mythic narrative. In its defense, however, two things must be said: first, the forum of judgment, by the logic of the argument, is one shared among God, the powers of evil, and the human self; second, even in utilizing a juristic/forensic framework ("law," "guilt," "punishment") that framework is broken. Whereas the Anselmian theory posits three alternatives—obedience, punishment, or satisfaction—all of which are applications of the same legal framework, the ransom scenario suggests that "death is overcome by death," that is, the curse or sentence or punishment which had hung over sin loses its claim precisely through being executed, finding its limit, refuting its applicability to all cases, creating an exception which breaks its hold.

5. Its meaning for human life. The ransom theme plays out many of the moral tensions that are experienced both in social and political life and in the internal dynamics of the psyche. It is not dependent upon revelation and faith to set the context; it addresses a ubiquitous human issue and attempts to make it more explicit. These tensions are realigned (it would be too much to say that they are overcome) through a drama enacted in the forum of public judgment which not only offers a new kind of personal orientation but ensures that certain dimensions of human experience will not be met with total silence in the public realm.

Eugene TeSelle is Professor of Church History and Theology in the Divinity School, Vanderbilt University

The Seed of Fire: Divine Suffering in the Christology of Cyril of Alexandria and Nestorius of Constantinople

JOSEPH M. HALLMAN

For as if one took a spark and buried it amid much stubble, in order that the seed of fire preserved might lay hold on it, so in us too our Lord Jesus Christ hides life through his own flesh, and inserts it as a seed of immortality, abolishing the whole corruption that is in us.
Cyril of Alexandria, *Commentary on John* 6.54

Beginning with the Apologists of the second century Christian thinkers have continually defended the immutability and impassibility of God. The tradition has absorbed a philosophical understanding of the divine which is difficult to square with some elements of the scriptural portrait. There God has a steadfast love for his people, but is taken by surprise by human evil. God swears new covenants, becomes angry at human disobedience, is sorrowful, feels grief, forgives.

Divine immutability also seems to contradict the Christian confession of faith dogmatized in the fourth and fifth centuries which states that God has become flesh in Jesus of Nazareth. All four gospel authors show that Jesus had emotions, changed his mind and experienced weaknesses, even ignorance and fear. Nevertheless, the majority of writers argue, God does not change. Yet in spite of the dominant philosophical understanding, there is a faint dissonant chorus in the Christian tradition made up of minor voices. For them the God of Jewish and Christian faith is a fellow-sufferer.[1]

---

1. This is the main thesis of my book, *The Descent of God: Divine Suffering in History and Theology* (Minneapolis: Augsburg/Fortress Press, 1991). Theological

Journal of Early Christian Studies 5:3, 369–391 © 1997 The Johns Hopkins University Press

Celsus, the middle Platonic critic to whom Origen responded called attention to immutability when he objected to Christian belief in a divine descent.

> God is good and beautiful and happy, and exists in the most beautiful state. If then He comes down to men, He must undergo change, a change from good to bad, from beautiful to shameful, from happiness to misfortune, and from what is best to what is most wicked. Who would undergo a change like this? It is the nature only of a mortal being to undergo change and remoulding, whereas it is the nature of an immortal being to remain the same without alteration. Accordingly, God could not be capable of undergoing this change.[2]

Origen replies to Celsus that although Celsus' statement is true in general, the case of Christian faith is different. Celsus does not grasp "how because of his great love to man, God made one special descent in order to convert those whom the divine scriptures mystically calls 'the lost sheep of the house of Israel.'"[3]

Arians again raised the issue by arguing that if the Logos *became* flesh or suffered, the Logos could not be divine. Hence the question of divine immutability became an important theme in the disputes of the fourth and fifth centuries. Underlying the Arian contention was a long and honorable philosophical tradition beginning with Plato which insisted that rational descriptions of the absolute must include immutability and impassibility. Change, emotion, and suffering belonged only to limited temporal beings.[4]

Arius like Celsus, believed that whatever suffers, changes, or feels emotions cannot be divine. Since the Arians taught the suffering of the Logos, this could be the main reason they concluded that the Logos could not be divine in the strict sense.[5] It is because of soteriology that

---

literature devoted to the subject of God's suffering is currently voluminous so I will not attempt to cite it. For a recent bibliography, see the published thesis of Marcel Sarot, *God, Passibility, and Corporeality* (The Netherlands: Kok Pharos Publishing House, 1992). Various writers appeal to scripture, religious intuition, spirituality, theodicy, philosophy, and liberation theology to defend divine passibility, but seldom to the history of Christian doctrine.

2. Origen, *Cels.* 4.14 (GCS 1:284). Translation from Henry Chadwick, *Origen: Contra Celsum* (Cambridge: University Press, 1955), 192–93.

3. Origen, *Cels.* 4.17, (GCS 1.286); Chadwick, 195.

4. See *Descent of God*, chapter 1.

5. See, for example, Homily 2, 22, and 25 of Asterius the Sophist in Marcel Richard, *Asterii Sophistae commentariorum in Psalmos quae supersunt accedunt aliquot homiliae anonymae* (Oslo: A. W. Brogger, 1956). Also the two Arian homilies

the divinity of the Incarnate Logos became dogmatized in the orthodox Alexandrian response to Arianism through the Council of Nicea. Unless the Logos is divine, Athanasius argues against them, we are not saved. There is no salvation without Incarnation. In spite of the contradiction that the descent of an impassible and immutable God seems to imply, the Logos is divine.

The Christological question in the strict sense arose when early thinkers from Antioch beginning with Eustathius (bishop of Antioch from 324–330), examined the Arian position: the human soul of Jesus was missing.[6] And this seemed to be the case among the orthodox as well! Assuming that the Logos is immutable and impassible, the change, emotion, and suffering of Jesus described in the gospels must belong to something else in Jesus besides the divine Logos. All agreed that the body of Jesus suffered. But Antiochene theologians argued that the Alexandrians, whether they adhered to Nicea or not, neglected explicit recognition of a finite spiritual principle to which Jesus' mental and psychological feelings and ultimately his experience of physical sufferings could be attributed. If Jesus had no human soul or personality, his sufferings became the sufferings of God.

Cyril of Alexandria and Nestorius occupied the center of this controversy in the fifth century. I believe that we will better understand their fundamental disagreement if we place the issues of divine immutability and impassibility in the forefront of discussion.

CYRIL OF ALEXANDRIA

There is good evidence that the early Cyril regularly attributed emotion to the one God when he interpreted the Old Testament. This is surprising given his Alexandrian background, but probably springs from a general lack of interest in the questions of Greek philosophy. Cyril simply takes the many texts ascribing emotion to the deity at face value. The *De adoratione in spiritu et veritate* (written between 412 and 429) often

---

in J. Liébaert (ed.), *Deux homelies anomeenes pour l'Octave de Pâques* (SC 146). Finally, see the Arian *Opus imperfectum in Matthaeum* (PG 56:612f.). I am following the thesis of the late R. P. C. Hanson, *The Search for the Christian Doctrine of God: The Arian Controversy 318–381* (Edinburgh: T & T Clark, 1988); *Descent of God*, 79–82; also Rowan Williams' criticism of Hanson's thesis as too simplistic in "R. P. C. Hanson's Search for the Christian Doctrine of God," *SJT* 45 (1992): 101–11.

6. See Aloys Grillmeier, *Christ in the Christian Tradition*, Second Edition, vol. 1 (Atlanta: John Knox Press, 1975), 296–301.

mentions the divine anger to which scripture testifies.[7] Statements indicating that the God of Scripture has emotions also occur in two early texts which deal with the Abraham and Isaac story.[8]

It is clear that Cyril defends the absolute immutability and impassibility of the Logos from his early anti-Arian writings through his later works. There is no doubt that for him, the Word had to be immutable and impassible in order to be divine. In the famous *Epistola dogmatica* approved unanimously at the first meeting of the council of Ephesus, then by Pope Leo in 451 and at Chalcedon and Constantinople, for example, Cyril denies the mutability and passibility of the Word in no uncertain terms. He writes:

> For we do not say that the nature of the Word was changed
> (*metapoietheisa*) and made flesh, nor yet that it was changed (*meteblethe*)
> into whole man, of soul and body . . . the Word did not suffer in the divine
> nature because it was impassible and non-physical.[9]

Cyril is completely consistent in holding that the act of generation does not result in divine mutability because divine mutability is self-contradictory. Hence generation must be without change of the divine nature. Essentially Cyril is only repeating the position of Athanasius and of Nicene orthodoxy.

Various important gospel texts, however, attribute emotion and psychological suffering to Jesus. Cyril confronts these passages for the first time in the *Thesaurus* (written no later than 425), then in his early *Commentary on John* (before 429). He discusses them several times later in the three texts entitled *De recte fide* (c. 430) and in the *Scholia de incarnatione Unigeniti* (sometime after 431). Yet these texts offer solutions which differ considerably from each other. In one of his last works, *Quod unus sit Christus*, Cyril has still not resolved the problem. This lack of resolution on Cyril's part provides a key element in understanding both Nestorianism and the rise of Monophysitism.

7. 153D–155A (PG 68); 169D in reference to the sins of the Sodomites; 364C which discusses Jos 7.1b: "the anger of the Lord burned against the Israelites"; 378C-D; 381D; 389C. I have avoided discussion of the dating of Cyril's works by following the general consensus among scholars and by giving the earliest and latest possible years of authorship within that consensus. See J. Quasten, *Patrology*, vol. 3 (Westminster, Md., 1983), 116–42.

8. From the same period as *De adoratione*, see *Glaphyra in Genesim* 140B-C (PG 69); 145D; 148A; *Festal Letter* 5.6, in Pierre Evieux et al. (eds.), *Cyrille D'Alexandrie: Lettres festales*, 30–32 (SC 372).

9. Also in this letter God is completely *atreptos* and *analloiotos*. P. E. Pusey (ed.), *The Three Epistles of S. Cyril* (Oxford and London: James Parker and Co., 1872), 6–8. See also G. M. de Durand (ed.), *Deux dialogues christologiques* 683E (SC 97).

THE EARLY CYRIL

Because scripture ascribes both human and divine things to Jesus, Cyril says in the *Thesaurus* that we should not be confused by passages describing the agony in the garden and Jesus' fear of death. Examples of acting in a divine manner include the raising of Lazarus from the dead and changing water into wine; it is the human which agonizes and fears death.[10] We cannot ascribe suffering and death to the Word.[11] We should not be bothered by scriptural shifts of voice between the speech of the Son as Word and as human however. Statements such as "let this cup pass from me" during the agony in the garden (Mt 26.39) are proper to the flesh, not to the Logos.[12] This does not necessarily mean that Cyril in his early writing denies that Jesus has a human soul. He uses *sarx* in a sense that includes the soul, and says so explicitly in his early *Commentary on John* when he interprets John 1.14.[13]

After arguing against the Arians that the Logos is divine, and therefore cannot grow, Cyril asserts that the human nature is perfected by the divine Word. Hence growth in wisdom and grace (Lk 2.52) is not the result of moral development in the give-and-take world of human experience, but the gradual elevation of the humanity of Jesus by the Logos. This becomes Cyril's constant theme when discussing the issue of Jesus' emotions, such as fear of death, sadness, and being troubled.[14] The

10. *Thesaurus de Sancta et Consubstantiali Trinitate* 393A (PG 75). For a discussion of this section of the *Thesaurus* and Athanasian parallels, see Jacques Liébaert, *La doctrine christologique de Saint Cyrille D'Alexandrie avant la querelle Nestorienne* (Lille: Facultes Catholiques, 1951), 114–25.

11. 396A-D (PG 75).

12. 397A (PG 75).

13. P. E. Pusey, *Cyrilli Archiepiscopi Alexandrini in D. Joannis Evangelium* (Bruxelles: Culture et Civilisation, 1965), vol. 1, 140. The English translation is by the same author, *Commentary on the Gospel according to St. John*, 2 vols. (Oxford: James Parker & Co., 1879). I will provide the volume and page numbers for Pusey's Greek text first, then for the translation in parentheses. Contrary to Liébaert, I do not believe that *sarx* and *soma* are equivalent terms for Cyril. Liébaert thinks that Cyril used *sarx* in *Thesaurus* 24 (from which the *Thesaurus* passages above are taken) only once in the general sense of human nature. I cannot see how one can make that determination. It is interesting to note how seldom Cyril uses *soma* (twice) in comparison to *sarx* (27 times!) in that text in comparison to Athanasius (see 124 of Liébaert). Could this be a subtle but purposeful shift on Cyril's part to a use of *sarx* which included the soul? For a recent discussion of Jesus' soul in Cyril's early Christology, see Lawrence J. Welch, "Logos-Sarx? Sarx and the Soul of Christ in the Early Thought of Cyril of Alexandria," *St. Vladimir's Theological Quarterly* 38 (1994): 271–92.

14. See 444A; Liébaert, *Doctrine christologique*, 118–19.

Logos perfects the humanity of Jesus, and as a result raises up the entire human race. There are some good examples in the *Commentary on John*.

DIVINIZATION IN THE COMMENTARY ON JOHN

Cyril's view of salvation grounds his early understanding of the Incarnation and his resistance to the Christology of Nestorius. Like Augustine, he believed that all of human nature was affected by the sin of Adam as well as by the enfleshment of the Logos. The Logos could not be intimately united to *all* of human nature unless it united with the human nature of Jesus. Although Cyril uses a wide range of soteriological imagery in the *Commentary on John*, the perfection of humanity is one of his favorites.[15]

"The Word became flesh" means that the Logos assumed a soul as well as a body. Importantly, John writes that the Word "became" flesh, not that it "came into" flesh. Otherwise you might suppose that

> he came to it as in the case of the prophets or other of the saints by participation. . . . Wherefore he is also God by nature in flesh and with flesh, having it as his own, and conceived of as being other than it.[16]

Cyril also adds, however, that God did not leave the divinity to be changed into flesh and to suffer. This is impossible, "for Godhead is far removed from all variableness (*alloioseos*) and change (*metaboles*)." Cyril's analysis of the "dwelt among us" in John 1.14 brings out his soteriological concern most clearly.

> For we were all in Christ, and the community of human nature rises up to his person; since therefore he was named *the last Adam* giving richly to the common nature all things that belong to joy and glory, even as the first Adam [gave] what pertained to corruption and dejection. *The Word* then *dwelt* in all through one so that the one being *declared the Son of God with power according to the Spirit of holiness*, the dignity might come to all human nature. . . . Therefore in Christ the bond is truly made free, mounting up into mystic union with him who had *the form of* the *servant*.[17]

---

15. See Joseph L. McInerney, "Soteriological Commonplaces in Cyril of Alexandria's *Commentary on John*," in *Disciplina Nostra*, ed. Donald F. Winslow (Philadelphia: Patristic Foundation, 1979), 179–85.

16. Pusey 1:140 (1:109).

17. Pusey, 1:141 (1:110). For the Adam-Christ typology of Cyril, see especially Robert L. Wilken, *Judaism and the Early Christian Mind: A Study of Cyril of Alexandria's Exegesis and Theology* (New Haven: Yale University Press, 1971), 93–142.

For Cyril human beings by nature are rising up through our likeness to Christ. Much later in the *Commentary* when he interprets John 10.28, he writes that "because he has become man, he brought all men into friendly relationship by being of the same race, so that we are all united to Christ in a mystical relationship."[18] According to Cyril, all of us, both good and evil persons, will rise from the dead as a result. Physical immortality is now assured for all because of the Incarnation. In a statement made in connection with the lifegiving qualities of the Eucharist he develops a striking analogy. The saving power of Jesus is hidden like a spark in the stubble of human nature. It is a seed of fire. He writes:

> For as if one took a spark and buried it amid much stubble, in order that the seed of fire preserved might lay hold on it, so in us too our Lord Jesus Christ hides life through his own flesh, and inserts it as a seed of immortality, abolishing the whole corruption that is in us.[19]

An important soteriological text occurs in Cyril's spiritual interpretation of the miracle of Cana. The deeper meaning of the change from water into wine relates to the Incarnation in which God "rendered all our nature whole, raising it from the dead in Himself."[20] Further on when he interprets the passage on Nicodemus he writes that

> we become partakers of the divine nature, as enjoying Him who proceeds from it essentially, and through him and in him re-formed (*anamorphoumenoi*) to the Archetype-Beauty, and thus re-born (*anatiktomenoi*) unto newness of life, and re-molded (*anaplatomenoi*) to the divine sonship.[21]

DISPUTED FRAGMENTS IN BOOK EIGHT

There are several texts which discuss the soul of Jesus in book eight of Pusey's edition of the *Commentary on John* which Liébaert thinks are problematic because they come from *catenae*.[22] The early Cyril has

18. Pusey 2:252 (2:100). See also the references in H. Chadwick, "Eucharist and Christology in the Nestorian Controversy," *JTS*, n.s. 2 (1951): 154, note 1.

19. Pusey 1:533 (1:421). For Eucharist in Cyril, see Chadwick, "Eucharist," 145–64.

20. Pusey 1:204 (1:157).

21. Pusey 1:219 (1:168). In his recent book on Cyril's Christology John A. McGuckin emphasizes its soteriological importance (*St. Cyril of Alexandria: The Christological Controversy, Its History, Theology, and Texts* [New York/Cologne: E. J. Brill/Leiden, 1994], 173–226).

22. Liébaert, *Doctrine christologique*, 129–37.

nothing to say about the soul of Christ in the *Thesaurus* or in *De Trinitate* (written shortly after *Thesaurus*). But he does mention the soul at least twice in his pre-Ephesus period.[23] And we have seen that *sarx* includes the soul in Cyril's interpretation of John 1.14. Is it possible that because of some texts in John's gospel, Cyril developed his thoughts on the soul of Christ even further before the confrontation with Nestorius? Or are the texts discussing the soul of Christ in the *Commentary* inauthentic?

The text which raises the question about the soul of Christ in book eight is John 12.27: "Now my soul is troubled. And what should I say— 'Father, save me from this hour'? No, it is for this reason that I have come to this hour." Cyril" can see from the first part of the statement that the human nature of Jesus was affected by trouble and fear. Because these are human emotions, they are controlled by the Logos, "cut short" (*diakoptetai*) as he puts it, "by the power of the Word."[24] The trouble and fear are overcome. Hence the second part of the statement: "It is for this reason that I have come to this hour." Nevertheless, "Cyril" writes:

> He feels as a human characteristic the mental trouble that is caused by suffering. Yet he is not agitated like we are, but only just so far as to have undergone the sensation of the experience; then again immediately he returns to the courage befitting to himself.[25]

The text continues: "From these things it is evident that he indeed had a rational soul." Being troubled by thinking of terrible things, such as his coming death, "must be the suffering of the rational soul, by which alone in truth a thought can enter into us through the processes of the mind."[26]

> For the suffering of dread is a feeling that we cannot ascribe to the impassible Godhead, nor yet to the flesh; for it is an affection of the cogitations of the soul, and not of the flesh.[27]

This dread is a human psychological emotion precisely because it involves "anticipation of coming suffering" which animals cannot have. Besides this, the text does not say "my flesh is troubled" but "my soul."[28] If we do not attribute suffering to the soul of Jesus, we fall into the docetism of Manes; we must hold that the entire human nature has been

23. In the Easter Festal letter of 420 (PG 77:573B); *Glaphyra in Genesim* 6 (PG 69:297C). See Grillmeier, vol. 1, 415, note 4.
24. Pusey 2:316 (2:150).
25. Pusey 2:317 (2:151).
26. Ibid. This certainly does not sound like the early Cyril.
27. Ibid.
28. Ibid.

made one with God, "for that which has not been taken into his nature, has not been saved."[29] This discussion ends with a strong statement about the necessity for the Logos to be united to a human soul, and the saving result of this union. These do not seem to be the thoughts and words of the Cyril of this period as Liébaert convincingly argues. Yet the argument is soteriological and in this respect does sound like Cyril.

> For unless he had felt dread, human nature could not have become free from dread; unless he had experienced grief, there could never have been any deliverance from grief; unless he had been troubled and alarmed, no escape from these feelings could have been found. . . . The affections of his flesh were aroused, not that they might have the upper hand as they do indeed in us, but in order that when aroused they might be thoroughly subdued by the power of the Word dwelling in the flesh, the nature of man thus undergoing a change for the better.[30]

FRAGMENTS FROM BOOK SEVEN

It is interesting to contrast how Cyril deals with the human knowledge and emotions of Jesus in John's account of the raising of Lazarus from the dead in fragments from book seven of the *Commentary*. According to this text, Jesus asks "where have you laid him ?" (11.34). Cyril claims that Jesus must have feigned ignorance and finds a parallel in God's question to Adam—"Adam, where are you?"[31] He also has a problem with Jesus being troubled by Lazarus' death, since God cannot feel grief. "Surely it is an infirmity of human nature to be overcome by grief abjectly, but this as well as the rest is brought into subjection, in Christ first, that it may be also in us."[32]

Jesus weeps for Lazarus, but only a little, Cyril says, "lest he might seem to be cruel and inhuman." He did this to instruct us not to weep too much over the dead. "For it is one thing to be influenced by sympathy, and another to be effeminate and unmanly." Hence Jesus permitted his *sarx* to weep a little even though it was "in its nature tearless and incapable of any grief, so far as regards its own nature."[33]

---

29. Pusey 2:318 (2:151). For a French translation and a detailed analysis of the relevant texts of book eight, see Liébaert, *Doctrine christologique*, 131f.

30. Pusey 2:320 (2:154). See the important parallel in *Thesaurus* 14 (PG 75:397C). Liébaert thinks that this is the same text but that it has been misplaced in the *Commentary*. Whatever the truth of the matter, it is authentically Cyril's because of this parallel.

31. Pusey 2:281 (2:123). Liébaert takes this fragment to be authentic.

32. Pusey 2:280 (2:122).

33. Pusey 2:282 (2:123).

Perhaps the fragments from both books seven and eight are all from Cyril, perhaps not. When emotions are attributed to the human soul of Christ in the fragments from book eight, they are "cut short" and held under control by the impassible Logos. If the Logos merely permits the flesh to weep a little as in book seven, grief is also held in check. Aside from the uncharacteristic emphasis on the soul in the fragments from book eight, conceptually the two passages are in agreement. If *sarx* includes the rational soul for Cyril in book seven, and there is good evidence in the *Commentary* that it does, the two texts say the same thing in different words. It is also important to note the emphasis on soteriology: Christ must feel emotions in order that emotions be brought into subjection, and their subjection is the way that they are divinized by the Logos both in Christ and in us.

THE LOGOS FEELS EMOTION

Book nine contains one of the most surprising passages in the entire *Commentary*. In discussing John 13.21 (parallel 12.27) which states that "Jesus was troubled in spirit," Cyril strongly insists that divine attributes are not like ours. *But they do include some kind of emotion (kinesis)*! "The divine nature is exceedingly terrible in uttering reproofs, and is stirred to violent emotion (*kinoumenon*) by unmingled hatred of evil."[34] Scripture expresses God's anger and wrath (*orgen kai thumon*) in human language even though the divine essence is not subject to these feelings "in any way that bears comparison with our feelings, but is moved to indignation (*kinoumenes*) the extent of which is known only to itself and is natural to itself alone."

> And it certainly seems as though the emotion (*kinesin*) of the Godhead, intolerant of the restraint of the flesh, did really bring about a slight shuddering and an apparent condition of disturbance, exhibiting the outward signs of anger (*orges*); doubtless similar to what is recorded also at the raising of Lazarus where we read that Jesus went to the tomb "groaning in himself."[35]

34. Pusey 2:363 (2:193). Pusey's translation may render *kinesis* too strongly. Nevertheless even at its weakest the term suggests divine emotion, hence change.

35. The emphasis is mine, citing Pusey 2:363 (2:194). Liébaert's translation (p. 128) is slightly, but insignificantly different. He concentrates solely on the issue of the human soul of Christ, hence does not see the importance of this unique text for Cyril's view of impassibility.

In the last reference Cyril returns to the Lazarus event with an even stronger sense that it is necessary to attribute some type of mutability, not just to the human soul of Jesus but to the divine Logos itself! Interestingly, in the only other text from the non-catena section of the *Commentary* which discusses the emotions of Christ, Cyril states that "God the Word, immortal and incorruptible, and life itself by nature could not shudder at death," and assigns the shuddering only to the flesh.[36] We have come upon exactly the dilemma which the early Cyril had to face. Either he attributes emotion and mutability to the Logos and risks condemnation for Arianism, or he assigns them to the human soul. At this point Cyril cannot decide how to resolve this dilemma. I do not believe that he ever did.

THE EPHESUS PERIOD

In the *De recte fide* addressed to the Emperor and written around the year 430 Cyril mentions the soul of Christ in passing in several places.[37] Here he gives it theological significance by attributing anxiety, fear, sadness, and the agony of Jesus to it.[38] In a letter to the emperor's wife, he writes:

> It is therefore evident that the only begotten Son has become man in taking on a body, not without a soul or mind, but on the contrary, a body animated by a rational soul and having the perfection of what comes to it by nature. And just as he has made his own all bodily properties, just so he made his own all those of the soul . . . thus just as according to the economy he granted to his body to suffer on occasion what comes to it, just so he granted to his soul to suffer what is proper to it.[39]

Here we see a full awareness on Cyril's part of the importance of the soul of Christ. Yet a short time later in the *Scholia on the Incarnation* he can reverse his position and argue that the soul of Jesus does not suffer in its own nature![40] In the *Scholia*, Cyril writes:

36. A comment on John 6.38–39. Pusey 1:487 (1:384). See Liébaert, *Doctrine christologique*, 127–28.
37. 45.19 (ACO 1.1.1); 52.12; 53.21. Also *Oratio ad Pulcherium et Eudociam augustus de fide* 26–61 (ACO 1.1.5).
38. 55 (ACO 1.1.1).
39. 58–59 (ACO 1.1.5).
40. Chadwick, "Eucharist," 158–62. See G. Joussard, "'Impassibilité' du Logos et 'impassibilité' de l'âme humaine chez saint Cyrille d'Alexandrie," *RSR* 45 (1957): 209–44. Mainly from the *Scholia* 8 (ACO 1.5.220) Joussard argues that for Cyril, the soul does not suffer. It is by nature impassible.

> Even though the body is weighed down or tortured and the soul indeed feels pain because its own body suffers, still it will itself not allow any torment into its own nature.[41]

In spite of not suffering any torment, however, the soul does have a certain sympathy (*synalgein*) for the sufferings of the flesh, i.e., a certain consciousness of what is happening to the body.[42]

> For the body is moved to physical desires; and the soul follows but not as a participant because it is outside of these desires.[43]

The question regarding the suffering of the soul is intrinsically related to the question about whether and how the Logos suffers the sufferings of the body.

> But it is out of place to say that God the Word feels the sufferings; the Godhead is impassible and is not of us. But having a rational soul united with the body, he himself impassibly knew things happening within the body while it suffered, and he was doing away with the weaknesses of the flesh as God, but making them his own because they came from his own body. Thus also he is said to have hungered, been tired, and suffered for us.[44]

Here as elsewhere Cyril vigorously denies that the Logos suffered. Unlike the soul, the divinity does not perceive the body's pain. The divinity is not of us (*kath hemas*), but is united with the body which possesses the rational soul. Yet while the body suffered, the Logos knew impassibly what was happening within it. The Word cannot be ignorant of the sufferings of the flesh, so it knows of them impassibly.[45]

Cyril gives several analogies for the effect that the divine has on the human. One comes from the hot coal which touched Isaiah's lips (Is 6.6–7) to purify him before he began his preaching. Other analogies include that of fire touching wood, the odor of a lily (here the fragrance is

---

41. "Et si forte a suo corpore deprimatur aut torqueatur, condolet quidem, quod suum corpus patiatur, ipsa vero in suam naturam nullum patitur omnino tormentum" (189.1–3 [ACO 1.5]). See the stronger version in F. C. Conybeare, *The Armenian Version of Revelation and Cyril of Alexandria's Scholia on Incarnation and Epistle on Easter* (London: Text and Translation Society, 1907), 176.

42. 220.34 (ACO 1.5).

43. 188.33 (ACO 1.5). The soul is "nulla quidem modo participans" in the sufferings of the body; see also Conybeare, *Armenian Version*, 176.

44. 221.3–5 (ACO 1.5); R. Hespel, *Le florilège cyrillien*, in *Bibliothèque du Muséon* (Louvain: Publications Universitaire, 1955), 154, line 3–6; Conybeare, *Armenian Version*, 176.

45. 221 (ACO 1.5); Hespel, 154, line 3–6.

incorporeal, hence like the divine) and the divine presence in the ark of the covenant.[46] Although the sufferings of the body do not affect the Logos because it is by nature impassible, the Logos does affect the body. This explains the miracles that Jesus worked through his body. The body belongs to the Word

> not in the same way as laughing is proper to a man or neighing to a horse, but because it was made His by true union, to possess and accomplish its uses as an instrument for whatever was its nature to do. . . ."[47]

Near the end of the *Scholia* Cyril asks how we can attribute suffering to Christ and still consider him impassible as God.[48] God remains impassible insofar as his nature is concerned, for God is impassible.[49] The soul does not suffer in its own nature, but it is not outside of passion insofar as it belongs to a body which suffers. Cyril reaches for more analogies, such as the water from the Nile which turns into blood in Ex 4.9 and the two birds which are part of the ritual for the cleansing of leprosy in Leviticus 14.4–7. Both of these seem to limp badly! Again he insists that the sufferings of the Logos are truly his, but that he does not suffer in the divine nature.[50] Succinctly he writes:

> he suffers and does not suffer in one way and another: he suffers humanly in the flesh as man; he remains impassible in a divine way as God.[51]

46. 189–90 (*ACO* 1.5); 221–22; Conybeare, *Armenian Version*, 178. The Latin and Armenian versions give even more examples. For a discussion of the analogies for the Incarnation in Cyril, see John A. McGuckin, *Christological Controversy*, 196–212.

47. Conybeare, *Armenian Version*, 197; 203.28–30 (*ACO* 1.5). The most recent and definitive work on Cyril's understanding of the unity of person in Jesus comes from the following authors: R. A. Norris, "Toward a Contemporary Interpretation of the Chalcedonian *Definition*," in *Lux in lumine: Essays to Honor W. Norman Pittenger*, ed. R. A. Norris (New York: Seabury, 1966), 62–79; idem, "Christological Models in Cyril of Alexandria," *Studia Patristica* 13/2, ed. E. A. Livingstone (Berlin: Akademie-Verlag, 1975), 255–68; Ruth M. Siddals, "Oneness and Difference in the Christology of Cyril of Alexandria," *Studia Patristica* 18/1, ed. E. A. Livingstone (Kalamazoo, Mich.: Cistercian Publications, 1985), 207–11; eadem, "Logic and Christology in Cyril of Alexandria," *JTS*, n.s. 38 (1987): 341–67. See also G. Joussard, "Une intuition fondamentale de saint Cyrille d'Alexandrie en christologie dans les premières années de son épiscopat," *Revue des Études Byzantines* 11 (1953): 175–86, esp. 179 and 183.

48. "Quonam modo et passionem ipsi deputemus et inpassibilem servemus ut deum?" (209 [*ACO* 1.5]; Conybeare, *Armenian Version*, 205).

49. "Inpassibilis enim deus est" (209.14–15 [*ACO* 1.5]).

50. 210 (*ACO* 1.5); Conybeare, *Armenian Version*, 207–08; 210–11.

51. "Patitur et non patitur secundum aliud et aliud: patitur quidem humane caro, eo quod homo sit; inpassibilis autem divine manet ut deus" (211.9–10 [*ACO* 1.5]).

The *Scholia* seems to end on a note of desperation when Cyril insists over and over again that his position does not force him to hold that God suffers. He probably has his Antiochene opponents in mind who say the exact opposite about his Christology, thereby accusing him of heresy.

THE LATE CYRIL

In a treatise written late in his career, the *Quod unus sit Christus*, Cyril mentions the soul of Christ several times, but makes almost no explicit appeal to it to solve his exegetical problems with texts ascribing sorrow or fear to Jesus.[52] Jesus' cry of dereliction from the cross does not express Jesus' own feeling of despair but was spoken as an example for us. "It was meant so that we should learn something from it."[53] Rather than a doubt arising in the human soul of Jesus, the statement "My God, why have you abandoned me?" is the question asked by a human race mired in the sin of Adam.[54] After wrestling with the issue of divine suffering repeatedly throughout this treatise, Cyril seems to end on a note of desperation similar to that expressed at the end of the *Scholia*. The flesh suffers, he says, the deity does not. But there are no examples one can use to express this. Cyril now thinks only one of his examples from the *Scholia* is appropriate: it is as if iron is heated by a flame. The flame, which represents the Logos, does not become less hot when heating the iron. Only the iron, the humanity of Jesus, changes.[55]

Hence throughout his career Cyril gives a variety of interpretations, some of which suggest that the Logos suffers, at least by implication, and others which assert that mental and psychological sufferings should be attributed to the human soul of Jesus. Commonly, whether Cyril mentions the soul of Jesus or not, the Logos is divinizing Jesus' humanity as well as ours, always acting for a salvific purpose by elevating what it touches. It is the spark in the stubble, the seed of fire.

For Cyril the theology of Antioch ignored the self-abasement which the incarnation implies, a self-abasement necessary for salvation.

---

52. G. M. de Durand (ed.), *Deux Dialogues Christologiques* 728D, 238; 736C-E, 348 (SC 97).

53. Durand 755D, 438–756D, 442. Quoted from the translation of J. A. McGuckin, *St. Cyril of Alexandria on the Unity of Christ* (Crestwood, N.Y.: St. Vladimir's Seminary Press), 103.

54. McGuckin, *On the Unity*, 105–06.

55. Durand, 776A, 504, and following. McGuckin, *On the Unity*, 130–31.

The death of a man, however righteous, cannot have any redemptive value. So Cyril's problem is to find a form of words which preserves the impassibility of the Logos while at the same time affirming that in some sense the Logos suffered. If he did not suffer, we are not saved.[56]

Chadwick holds that Cyril reached a "not very illuminating conclusion: the Logos suffered impassibly," *epathen apathos*.[57] Aside from the irresolution evident in Cyril's texts, I believe the *epathen apathos* is quite illuminating in the context of the hidden insight of divine suffering found in Alexandria beginning especially with Athanasius. Because of this insight a logical problem arises which Cyril recognizes only dimly. His statement is "not very illuminating" because it does not satisfactorily explain how the Logos is impassible and simultaneously able to suffer. Although the paradox of Cyril expresses the theological distinctiveness of the Christian view of God compared to those of Plato and Aristotle, philosophical conceptuality to express this incarnational understanding was unavailable.

For McGuckin the statement *apathos epathen* although paradoxical is not a "meaningless conundrum."[58] "God suffered impassibly" is only apparently contradictory "because the word 'God' is being used in a different way to normal."[59] In this statement Cyril is referring to God-in-the-flesh, not God-in-himself.

McGuckin is correct, but does not go far enough. Unless one shows definitively that they are using one of the two terms, either *epathen* or *apathos* in a sense different from the other, there *is* a contradiction. Hence what must be found is a way of understanding suffering which is appropriate to the divine, one which does not limit God, or take away divine attributes. In other words, the statement must mean that God

---

56. Chadwick, "Eucharist," 158. One of the phrases in the dogmatic epistle is particularly interesting in this regard. "He was the one, incapable of suffering, in the body which suffered." Pusey, *Three Epistles*, 8. Also "in the crucified body he was impassibly making his own the sufferings of his own flesh." See also Pusey, *Three Epistles*, 24. These statements indicate that for Cyril, the sufferings of Jesus had to belong to the Logos in some way, even though he was impassible. The salvation offered by Christianity depended upon this.

57. Chadwick, "Eucharist," 159. So far as I can ascertain, the phrase is not found in Cyril's Greek. Chadwick cites R. V. Sellers, *Two Ancient Christologies* (London: SPCK, 1940), 88; to Sellers' references Chadwick adds *Scholia* 37 (ACO 213.7) which has "patiebatur autem inpassibiliter."

58. McGuckin, *Christological Controversy*, 185.

59. McGuckin, *Christological Controversy*, 191. Nestorius argued that impassible suffering was a logical absurdity. See the fragment in Friedrich Loofs, *Nestoriana: Die Framente des Nestorius* (Halle: Niemeyer, 1905), 333, 21ff.

suffers in one sense, and in another sense does not. Later in the book McGuckin writes:

> Cyril says he suffers impassibly. That does not mean it is a play act; it means he does suffer, but does so *qua* man, not *qua* God, but neither, because of the intimate union, does he suffer in a discontinuous (or unengaged) way, rather in a direct fashion in so far as he has made the body his very own and because of it now exists in two conditions. . . . Cyril understands the suffering as a mode of God's very impassibility . . . the passivity is an expression of the perfect power of the Godhead whereby it appropriates to itself the fragile and powerless flesh.[60]

Cyril's thoughts on divine suffering and the human soul of Jesus developed over time as I have shown and it is necessary to appreciate the inner dynamic of his continuing search for a rational solution as well as his ultimate failure. In a footnote to the text quoted above McGuckin comes close to proposing a rational way to overcome this apparent contradiction. The incarnation

> is a real but not an absolute limitation on the Godhead because the Godhead chooses to adopt the limitations that apply to humanity as an exercise of its omnipotent freedom.[61]

McGuckin does not pursue this thought any further. The author of an ancient work attributed to Gregory the Wonderworker entitled *Ad Theopompum* argued that God's suffering was appropriate because, unlike ours, it was useful, salvific, and freely chosen. Yet this does not distinguish sufficiently between divine suffering and the suffering of holy people. Perhaps there is a more appropriate way to think of the divine as a fellow-suffer by developing these ideas further and with more logical rigor than the *Ad Theopompum* or Cyril used.

Because Cyril never resolves the question of the suffering of the Logos or of the human soul of Jesus, his Christology opens the door both to the critique of Antioch with its emphasis on the suffering of the human soul of Jesus on the one hand, and to the suffering of the divine Logos in Monophysitism on the other. It is not enough to say *apathos epathen*. Because Cyril simultaneously affirms and denies divine suffering, his logic fails. Nestorius upholds the *apathos* of the Logos denying the *epathen*, the Monophysites uphold *epathen*, denying *apathos*.

---

60. McGuckin, *Christological Controversy*, 202–03.
61. McGuckin, *Christological Controversy*, 201, note 47.

NESTORIUS

The usual approach to the differing Christologies of Cyril and Nestorius is to try to determine where orthodoxy lies. Even today there is a tendency to take sides. The recent translator of Cyril's letters in the *Fathers of the Church* series states about one of Nestorius' responses to Cyril that "Nestorius replied arrogantly . . . and in his answer favored blasphemies similar to the earlier ones."[62] In an appendix to the English translation of the Book or the *Bazaar of Hericleides*, one of the editors proposes a choice between "Cyril's inconsistency" and "the barren coherence of Nestorius."[63] Bebis has a negative evaluation of Nestorius as a theologian and of his orthodoxy as well. He writes: "A pupil of Theodore of Mopsuestia, he had not the power and the intuition to see the value of the Apophatic Theology of the Fathers."[64] Bebis describes Nestorius' soteriology as "weak, deficient, and one-sided" because it does not measure up to the divinization theology of Athanasius and Cyril.[65] Nestorius is the prime example of "complete failure to see that behind the Christological controversy of his times the whole theology of the Church on the redemption of mankind could stand or fall."[66]

To ask how Nestorius deals with the issue of divine suffering may provide a less polemical and more fruitful understanding of the difference between him and Cyril than these contemporary writers offer. How does Nestorius attempt to reconcile the demands of ancient philosophy that God can neither change nor suffer in any way with the Athanasian intuition dogmatized by Nicea that Christian faith is incarnational, that the God of Christianity has drawn near in the human person of Jesus? We should presume that neither Nestorius nor Cyril "favored blasphemies" and that Nestorius certainly did not intend a so-called "barren coherence," nor was he at all unaware of the importance of soteriology. In fact, his entire project can be seen as an attempt to construct a soteriology which preserved human freedom of will and resisted the notion of divine absorption which he thought Cyril taught.[67] And if Cyril

62. John I. McEnerney (trans.), *St. Cyril of Alexandria: Letters* (Washington, D.C.: CUA Press, 1987), vol. 1, 50, note 7.
63. G. R. Driver and Leonard Hodgson (eds.), *The Bazaar of Heracleides* (Oxford: Clarendon Press, 1925), 420.
64. G. S. Bebis, "The Apology of Nestorius: A New Evaluation," *Studia Patristica* 11/2, ed. F. Cross (Berlin: Akademie Verlag, 1972), 107–12.
65. Bebis, "Apology," 110.
66. Bebis, "Apology," 111.
67. See R. A. Norris. Jr., "The Problem of Human Identity in Patristic Christological Speculation," *Studia Patristica* 17/1, ed. E. A. Livingstone (Oxford: Pergamon Press, 1982), 155.

is inconsistent on the question of divine suffering and change, it should be no surprise. He merely reflects the continuing inconsistency of the entire tradition as it first repeated, then came partially to react against, the twin philosophical axioms of divine immutability and impassibility in the light of the Incarnation.

A. Grillmeier reviewed the literature about Nestorius written from the seventeenth century until the 1970s in an appendix to the second edition of his *Christ in Christian Tradition*.[68] A sampling of this literature shows that the scholarly community has continued interest in the historical question of the justice of Nestorius' condemnation. Some wonder whether Nestorius is more theologically in line with tradition than previously thought. This question is especially important because of the recent discovery of a Syriac text, originally in Greek from Nestorius' own hand, entitled in its English translation, *The Bazaar of Heracleides*, dated 451. We now have some direct access to the later thought of Nestorius.[69] Before this there were mainly the fragments collected by Friedrich Loofs and others.[70]

In several of these fragments Nestorius' insistence on divine immutability and impassibility in the Incarnation is quite clear. We shall see that this is also the case in the *Bazaar*. Like many writers before him, Nestorius often cites Malachi 3.6 and Ps 101.28 as evidence that the divine excludes change and suffering.[71] Neither John 1.14 nor Phil 2.5–7 can be interpreted to mean that the Logos changes or suffers as a result of the incarnation.[72]

The ideas of the *Bazaar* are especially relevant if as Scipione argues the first part was actually written by Nestorius. Scipione argued against the thesis of L. Abramowski who held that the first 125 pages came from the monastery of the *Akoimetai* between 523 and 533. If Scipioni is correct that we are hearing from Nestorius in part one, the *Bazaar* explains why

68. A. Grillmeier, *Christ*, vol. 1, 559–68.

69. G. R. Driver and Leonard Hodgson, *Nestorius: The Bazaar of Heracleides* (Oxford: Clarendon Press, 1925). Hereafter I will refer to this work as DH. There is a French translation by F. Nau, *Le Livre d'Heraclide de Damas* (Paris: Letouzey et Ane, 1910).

70. Most importantly Loofs, *Nestoriana*. Also see the others as noted in Quasten vol. 3, 515–16. Whether interpolated or not, the *Bazaar* allows us access to sustained arguments by Nestorius. See McGuckin, *Christological Controversy*, 126–30, for a recent discussion of the sources for Nestorius.

71. Loofs, *Nestoriana*, 193.5–6; 267.5; 320.28–321.1.

72. Loofs, *Nestoriana*, 176.6–19; 306–07; 254.4, 13, 16. This last fragment is taken from the first homily against the *Theotokos*.

Nestorius found the Christology of Cyril so objectionable and how he himself attempted to deal with the issue of divine suffering in the Incarnation.[73] Since the second part of the treatise discusses immutability more than twenty times, however, whether Nestorius wrote part one or not has little effect on my contention that immutability was his major concern.

THE BOOK OF HERACLEIDES

The first part of the book is written as a dialogue with a certain Sophronius, Nestorius' opponent. It contains an important discussion which is reminiscent of a work mentioned above, the *Ad Theopompum* ascribed, probably erroneously, to Gregory the Wonderworker, a pupil of Origen.[74] For Sophronius a single argument provides for the possibility of the Incarnation: God can do whatever God wills.

> It pertains to the omnipotent and infinite nature to be able to do everything . . . all other things are limited while it is not limited by anything, and it, as God, can do what cannot be done by anyone else.[75]

Everything God wishes to do, God does. Hence God can become flesh.[76] Nestorius replies that although God can do whatever God wants to do, God cannot become flesh. If God became flesh, God would be limited. Flesh cannot do everything "in that it is flesh and not God. For it pertains to God to be able to effect everything, and not to the flesh; for it cannot do everything it wishes."[77]

To this Sophronius replies that God is only able to will to become what he is not, not what he is. God became flesh but the divine nature did not change. God must have become flesh in some other way. Nestorius thinks that this implies two essences in the Incarnation, one which God

---

73. Luise Abramowski, *Untersuchungen zu dem Liber Heraclidis des Nestorius* (CSCO 242, Subsidia 22), questioned the authorship of the first part. I. Scipioni, *Nestorio e il concilio di Efeso: Storia dogma critica* (Milan: Vita e pensiero, 1974), defended it as authentic. He argues that these pages were Nestorius' own reworking of another work of his with the title *Theopaschites*. The Syriac translator refers to this work in his preface. For a complete discussion, see Grillmeier, *Christ*, vol. 1, 501–19; also Roberta C. Chesnut, "The Two Prosopa in Nesorius' *Bazaar of Heracleides*," *JTS*, n.s. 29 (1978): 392–98.

74. See my book *Descent of God*, 46–49.

75. DH 10. I have altered this quotation slightly and will continue to do so to avoid archaic turns of phrase.

76. DH 13.

77. DH 14.

was by nature, one which God became, which was of flesh. Sophronius denies this implication, and offers the analogy of water, which can be frozen or running. Water has one essence, but two forms. Nestorius suggests that this view is docetist. Sophronius replies that Nestorius prefers logic over faith, and repeats his contention that because God can do anything, God can become flesh. He gives three more examples: God could raise up children of Abraham from stones; turn a human body into a pillar of salt; create a man from dust.

In these examples, Nestorius says, the former essence is lost and replaced by another. Sophronius appeals to Moses' staff which became a serpent, then a staff again, and to the Nile which turned to blood, then returned to water. Nestorius maintains that in these examples as well, there is a change of essence.[78] He thinks that the two essences in the Incarnation cannot be combined without loss of the singularity of each essence, and must be united in some other way. It is here that the importance of divine immutability appears. Nestorius wonders how anyone could think that the Creator changed the divine being into a created nature.

> For in that God is Creator, God is unchangeable, and works by an unchangeable nature. . . . In effect either God is what God is by nature, eternally God, and did not become another nature while remaining in the essence of God; or, not having the nature of God, was made and is not the Creator, which is absurd and impossible.[79]

The logic of Nestorius is apparently unshakable, because it reduces Sophronius to an hour of silence![80] Nestorius argues that those who propose a combined nature after a hypostatic union are teaching divine passibility.[81] His own theory of union is difficult to understand, but rests on a theory of a combination of two *prosopa* in the incarnation rather than two *ousia*.[82]

---

78. DH 15–17.

79. DH 27. I altered this and the following passages from the *Bazaar* to make them gender-neutral and to avoid archaic language.

80. DH 28.

81. DH. 35–41.

82. Rowan A. Greer, "The Image of God and the Prosopic Union in Nestorius' *Bazaar of Heracleides*," in *Lux in lumine: Essays for W. N. Pittenger*, ed. R. A. Norris (New York: Seabury, 1966), 46–61; H. E. W. Turner, "Nestorius Reconsidered," *Studia Patristica* 13 (1971): 306–21; Roberta C. Chesnut, "The Two Prosopa," 392–409; J. A. McGuckin, "The Christology of Nestorius of Constantinople," *Patristic and Byzantine Review* 7 (1988): 93–129.

In the second part of part one of the *Bazaar* Nestorius lists the human experiences of Jesus that his opponents assign to God:

> the human fear and the betrayal, the interrogation, the answer, the smiting upon the cheeks, the sentence of the cross, the way of the cross, the setting of the cross upon his shoulder, the bearing of his cross, the removal (of it) from him that it might be set on another, the crown of thorns, the robes of purple, the raising up on the cross, the crucifixion, the fixing of the nails, the gall which was offered unto him, the other distresses, the surrender of his spirit to the Father, the bowing down of his head, the descent of his body from the cross, the embalming, his burial, the resurrection on the third day, his appearance in his body, his speaking and his teaching. . . .[83]

According to Nestorius they have "God suffering the sufferings of the body . . . thirsting, hungering, in poverty, in anxiety, meditating, praying . . . the properties of God the Word they ignore and make them human."[84] It is an "aweful and dreadful thing" to tell others that the Son "has been changed from impassible to passible and from immortal to mortal and from unchangeable to changeable." Nestorius dramatizes what he considers the glaring contradiction: his opponent holds that the divine can neither suffer nor change, but the hypostatic union means that the sufferings and changes described by the gospels must have happened to the eternal Logos. "They make use indeed of the name of orthodox, but in fact they are Arians."[85]

Nestorius is able to argue effectively against Cyril's favorite analogy for the unity of Christ, that of the soul and the body. If the union is natural like that of the soul and body, when the body suffers, the Logos suffers just like the soul.[86]

> As the soul naturally gives perception to the body, so by means of this perception it experiences the sufferings of the body, so that the perception of the sufferings of the body is given by the soul and to the soul; for it is passible.[87]

83. DH 92.
84. DH. 93.
85. DH 94. See also 178 and 181.
86. DH 162.
87. DH 172; McGuckin (*Christological Controversy*, 198–201) does a fine job expressing the importance for Cyril of the soul/body analogy for the union of the divine and human in the Incarnation. Yet he does not mention the problem which it presents, a problem which Nestorius saw clearly: if the union is reciprocal, when one suffers or changes, so does the other. But as we saw above, Cyril does not think of the union as completely reciprocal in either case.

The union of Logos and the human is not hypostatic for Nestorius, but voluntary "as consisting in a property of the will and not of the nature."[88] As we saw above in the *Scholia*, Cyril argues that the soul does not suffer in the same manner as the body, thereby attempting to avoid Nestorius' conclusion regarding natural union.

For Nestorius, orthodoxy demands that one holds to the impassibility of the Logos in the Incarnation. The Logos "by nature is impassible and unchangeable and invariable, does not even suffer in any manner in the human nature, since it is not his to suffer in his nature."[89] Cyril has "made even God the Word passible."[90] The orthodox are those who consider the Word "unchangeable and invariable," not those who attribute "birth and growth and upbringing and gradual advance in stature and in wisdom and in grace and the commandments and their observance and their fulfillment and the suffering and the cross and the death and the resurrection" to it.[91] In a comment near the end of the book, Nestorius captures the dilemma of Cyril who implies that God changes, while "ten thousand times you say that he is unchangeable!"[92]

Scholars usually study Nestorius' *Bazaar* to analyze his version of the unity of person in the Incarnation, but do not pay sufficient attention to the underlying issue of divine immutability and impassibility. This focus is understandable if the question is one of Chalcedonian orthodoxy. Yet if one simply reads this book as it now stands, divine impassibility is clearly the single most important issue in it, discussed repeatedly throughout the treatise. Depending upon how one numbers the passages, Nestorius discusses impassibility in part two alone, for example, more than twenty times![93]

CONCLUSION

McGuckin makes an important point concerning the historical importance of Cyril's Christology.

> It is highly doubtful whether a prophetic or charismatically based
> Christology, such as that favoured by several of the Antiochenes . . . would

---

88. DH 179.
89. DH 212.
90. DH 173. Although this passage does not name Cyril, it clearly refers to him as "this man" and as "one who lied concerning the fathers." See also 174 and 177.
91. DH 212; also 219.
92. DH 250.
93. Pages I have not yet cited: DH 226, 230, 232, 237, 240, 243, 244, 247, 258.

ever have survived its reinterpretation by Islam. This is another way of saying that it was Cyril's vision and concept of the divine Lord that authentically articulated the faith of the entire eastern church, and gave voice to the warmth of his people's religious commitment to a God who had so willingly, and personally, committed himself to the vagaries of their life.[94]

Belief in the descent of God in Jesus of Nazareth expresses the essence of Christian faith and needs to be preserved to adhere to the fullness of that faith. Working out the theological question of divine passibility is intimately related to the intelligible defense of the Christian confession. This confession may appropriately begin with a paradox of impassible suffering, but must ultimately make use of rational systematic categories and distinctions to express it. Otherwise belief in a divine descent can be dismissed by intelligent and thoughtful people as contradictory. And this is the importance of the critique of Nestorius who in the spirit of rational theology, demanded consistency.

A contemporary systematic soteriology and Christology in the spirit of Alexandria but with the critique of Nestorius is an appealing project, something which is far removed from the recent work on Jesus in the Jesus Seminar. Surprisingly, the stubble of post-modern post-twentieth-century life might contain a divine incarnate spark which lies buried in it, and given the widespread spiritual malaise evident in Western civilization, Cyril's divine "seed of fire preserved" could "lay hold" on this stubble once again. This stubble will never flame up, however, without the cool breeze of logical rigor.

Joseph M. Hallman is Professor of Theology at the University of St. Thomas.

94. *Christological Controversy*, 223–24.

R. McL. Wilson

Half a Century of Gnosisforschung – in Retrospect

At the Stockholm Colloquium on Gnosticism in 1973, Hans Jonas was invited to be Honorary President of the Colloquium and to deliver the closing address. It was suggested that he might provide »in short, some fragments of your autobiography as a scholar« – hence the title of his address: A Retrospective View.[1]

At one point Jonas recalls his efforts to establish some contact with British scholars in the field of Gnosticism, after his departure from Germany in the thirties, and in particular the response he received in a letter from F. C. Burkitt, which »opened my eyes for the first time to how nationally determined the different views of one and the same subject were at that time«.[2] The letter, he says, was to the effect: »I have read your manuscript with interest, but I must tell you frankly that with this kind of view of the matter, which is completely in the German vein, you cannot hope to cut any ice here.« Jonas adds that he could even remember the sentence, »Of what audience are you thinking? Who should read that here?«

It is evident that Jonas felt Burkitt's response to be something of a rebuff, but it is open to question whether Burkitt intended it in that way, and not rather as a friendly word of advice and warning. Just a few years before, Burkitt had published his own *Church and Gnosis*, in which he urged that the best way in which to approach the second century systems was to regard them as Christian systems: Valentinus and others were Christians who sought »to set forth the living essence of their Religion in a form uncontaminated by the Jewish envelope in which they had received it, and expressed in terms more suited (as they might say) to the cosmogony and philosophy of their enlightened age«.[3] Burkitt's arguments for the essential Christianity of Valentinus were still accepted as convincing by C. H. Dodd

---

1   *Proceedings of the International Colloquium on Gnosticism*, Stockholm, August 20-25, 1973 (Stockholm: Kungl. Vitterhets Historie och Antikvitets Akademien 1977) 1-15. The »half a century« in the title of the present paper relates to the fact that the writer took his first tentative steps into this field in 1942.

2   *Proceedings...*, 9. The subsequent account of a meeting with Evelyn Underhill is a further illustration of »cultural difference«: there is a time and a place for everything, and afternoon tea was not the time or place for an extended discussion of Gnosticism, particularly with non-specialists present! To English eyes that was an opportunity for Jonas to »break the ice« and make himself known; once introduced, he could have sought opportunity for extended discussion at some later date.

3   *Church and Gnosis* (Cambridge 1932) 27 f. – J. F. Bethune-Baker however (*Introduction to the Early History of Christian Doctrine*, London 1903, [7]1942, 76) speaks of the Gnostics as »starting from Oriental principles« .

some twenty years later,[4] but it is rather his view of the priority of the philosophical over the mythological Gnosticism with which Jonas takes issue. In *Gnosis und spätantiker Geist*, he quotes from Burkitt a passage referring to the gnostic representations as »explanations of the particular mystery presented by Christianity«, and adds the comment »An dieser These hält B. in striktem Gegensatz zur neueren deutschen Forschung fest«.[5] The quotation from Burkitt continues: »Only a philosophy can explain a mystery: a mythology may embody a philosophy, but does not in itself explain it. For this reason I regard the more or less philosophical Gnosticism – i. e. Valentinus – as original and the mythological Gnosticism as on the whole derivative and degenerate.« The first volume of Jonas' book, of course, bears the sub-title »Die mythologische Gnosis«; the first part of the second, published in 1954, is headed »Von der Mythologie zur mystischen Philosophie«.

Jonas' remark about the »nationally determined« views of the subject is certainly correct, and is confirmed by A. D. Nock's review in *Gnomon*,[6] of which Jonas observed: »the one extensive review in Germany of ›Gnosis und spätantiker Geist‹ was in the English language and by a British scholar living in America«.[7] In this review Nock wrote that Jonas' real interest »lies in an attempt to make a synthesis. He does this with concepts of Spengler and Heidegger. Frankly, I cannot understand what he does in this direction. He is a metaphysician trying to shake off the yoke of history and to lead us to a higher level of comprehension; I am left in a terminological fog, and I know that I am not alone in this situation«.[8] In a review of the second edition, R. M. Grant similarly wrote that the attempt to explain Gnosticism in terms of existentialism was not likely to be illuminating for many readers – including the reviewer.[9] After three introductory paragraphs, Nock abandons detailed criticism and strikes out on his own. Finally he writes »A phenomenon such as Gnosis can be studied in a vertical section or in a horizontal section. The work of Dr Jonas should be of value to those who are looking at Gnosis in the second way and wish to follow a topic through the different related movements. But they should not regard it as in any sense superseding Harnack, de Faye or Burkitt.«[10] This, it should be remembered, relates to a book »das wohl«, as Professor Rudolph puts it, »zu den bekanntesten Gnosisbüchern überhaupt zählt«. »Man kann ohne Übertreibung sagen, daß durch Jonas eine neue, die vierte Stufe in der neuen Gnosisforschung eingeleitet wurde, da er das Wesen der Gnosis und ihrer Aussagen in einer Analyse zu bestimmen suchte, die zwar vom Existentialismus getragen war, mit der er aber erstmalig eine Zusammenschau des bis dahin Unter-

---

4 C. H. Dodd, *The Interpretation of the Fourth Gospel,* Cambridge 1953, 100, note 4. Cf. also G. Lüdemann, *ZNW* 70, 1979, 86-114.

5 H. Jonas, *Gnosis und spätantiker Geist,* Göttingen ²1954, 256, note 1.

6 A. D. Nock, *Gnomon* 12, 1936, 605-612; reprinted in *Essays on Religion and the Ancient World,* ed. Z. Stewart, Oxford 1972, 444-451. German translation in K. Rudolph (ed.), *Gnosis und Gnostizismus,* (WdF cclxii, Darmstadt 1975), 374-386 (the reference there to volume 3 is incorrect).

7 *Proceedings...,* 10.

8 Nock, *Essays...,* 444.

9 R. M. Granz, *JTS NS* 7, 1956, 308-313 (see pp. 310, 313).

10 Nock, *Essays...,* 451.

suchten bot und damit der Forschung ein Mittel in die Hand gab, sich über die Eigenart des Gegenstandes klar zu machen.«[11]

British scholars at that time were still working with the view which in R. P. Casey's words[12] prevailed »from Irenaeus to Harnack«: Gnosticism was »an attempt to inject into Christianity more Greek thought than it was able to assimilate; hence (Harnack's) description of Gnosticism as *die akute Hellenisierung des Christentums*«.[13] The ideas of the *religionsgeschichtliche Schule*, headed by Reitzenstein and Bousset, were viewed with considerable reserve. »Paul might testify that to the Greeks his gospel was mere ›foolishness‹, but Reitzenstein and others knew better. It was not merely a matter of Paul's having borrowed odd words from the mysteries: his mysticism, his doctrine of baptism as a dying and rising with Christ, his sacramental conception of the Eucharist, his worship of Jesus as ›Lord‹ – all sprang from the same source, the Greek mysteries. They did not stop to consider that their knowledge of these mysteries was really very scanty, that all this amazing transmogrification of the gospel must have taken place within twenty years, that, if Paul derived his message from his environment, he did what no other missionary has ever done – borrowed his gospel from the people among whom he worked.«[14] Reitzenstein in particular was often the target for criticism: »In matters of chronology he was singularly cavalier and raised the subjective criticism of documents to a high imaginative art.«[15] Moreover, Gnosticism was for many British scholars no more than a minor deviation in the course of Church history, easily described as the result of a fusion of Christianity and Greek philosophy – which allowed the historian to proceed immediately to more important matters such as the Arian controversy. Many would have echoed the words of Charles Bigg, considering it merely bizarre and grotesque: »The ordinary Christian controversialist felt that he had nothing to do but set out at unsparing length their tedious pedigrees, in the well-grounded confidence that no one would care to peruse them a second time« – but they did not always pay heed to the context, with its perceptive

---

11 K. Rudolph, *Die Gnosis*, Leipzig 1977; Göttingen [3]1990, 38 (English Translation Edinburgh 1983, 33).

12 R. P Casey, *JTS* 36, 1935, 45-60 (see pp. 55 f.); German translation in Rudolph (ed.), *Gnosis und Gnostizismus...*, 352-373 (see p. 367). Casey writes (p. 60; German version p. 373): »It should be recognized that ›Gnosticism‹ is a modern, not an ancient category, that its use has frequently obscured more than it has illuminated the picture of early Christianity, but that behind it lies a definite historical reality: a group of theologians and sects characterized (a) by their obligations to Christianity, (b) by the autonomous quality of their systems which made them rivals of orthodox Christianity rather than modifiers of it in points of detail, and (c) by a demand for theological novelty which their frequent appeals to a remote antiquity have obscured but not concealed.«

13 R. P. Casey, in: *The Background of the New Testament and its Eschatology* (FS Dodd), ed. W. D. Davies and D. Daube, Cambridge 1954, 52.

14 A. M. Hunter, *Interpreting the New Testament 1900-1950*, London 1951, 70. Hunter mentions H. A. A. Kennedy (*St. Paul and the Mystery Religions*, 1913) and Schweitzer (*Paul and His Interpreters*, 1912) as subjecting the theory to »very damaging criticism«. On the whole question of Christianity and the Mystery Religions, see now A. J. M. Wedderburn, *Baptism and Resurrection*, Tübingen 1987.

15 Casey, in: *The Background...*, 53.

observation »It was an attempt, a serious attempt, to fathom the dread mystery of sorrow and pain, to answer that spectral doubt, which is mostly crushed down by force – Can the world as we know it have been made by God?«[16]

With the benefit of hindsight, it can now be seen that the difference is largely one of approach and presuppositions. British scholars were working largely in terms of *Kirchengeschichte*, treating Gnosticism as simply an episode in Church history, whereas the *religionsgeschichtliche Schule* and their successors were trying to set the New Testament and early Christianity in its proper context in the life of the wider world of the first century.[17] Nock, as already noted, wrote perceptively of a vertical and a horizontal section. British scholars were interested largely in the »vertical«, the historical development from the New Testament through inter-action with Greek philosophy to the Nicene and Chalcedonian creeds; Jonas' concern was with the delimiting and understanding of »the gnostic phenomenon«.[18] For him it was important to cast as wide a net as possible, drawing in the relevant material from diverse sources to illuminate obscurities. From this point of view chronology and historical filiation are not of immediate importance, but for a complete picture both the horizontal and the vertical aspects require to be taken into account.

In the thirties, Bultmann was recognised by British scholars as one of the leading figures in the New Testament field, but still with certain reservations. His use of Form Criticism appeared to be unduly radical, as did his proposals for »demythologizing« the New Testament, and not everyone could share his enthusiasm for the existentialist approach, or accept his view of the »gnostic Redeemer« myth.

---

16 Ch. Bigg, *The Christian Platonists of Alexandria*, Oxford 1886, 28. Cf. G. A. G. Strousma, *Another Seed*, Leiden 1984, 17: »At the root of the Gnostic rejection of the material world and its creator lies an obsessive preoccupation with the problem of evil.« Bethune-Baker (note 3) quotes »one of the soundest and soberest of modern scholars« as saying »The time is gone by when the Gnostic theories could be regarded as the mere ravings of religious lunatics. The problems which taxed the powers of a Basilides and a Valentinus were felt to be amongst the most profound and difficult which can occupy the human mind [...] It is only by the study of Gnostic aberrations that the true import of the teaching of catholic Christianity [...] can be fully appreciated.«

17 Professor Rudolph has recently applied this distinction not only to terms like Gnosis but also to »Christian« (in: *Apocryphon Severini* [FS Giversen], Aarhus 1993, 192-213): »Einerseits ist sie [die Gnosis, R. McL. W.] ... aus deutlich vorchristlichen Quellen gespeist, andererseits hat sie eine offensichtlich ›christliche‹ Geschichte, weshalb sowohl literarisch als auch inhaltlich von »christlicher Gnosis« gesprochen wird« (195). »Das Problem stellt sich nun nicht nur, wie bisher meist immer wieder diskutiert, ob Gnosis vor-. neben- oder nachchristlich einzustufen ist, sondern was eigentlich im ersten und zweiten Jahrhundert (n. Chr.!) als ›christlich‹ zu verstehen ist, sofern man sich nicht auf die kirchen- geschichtlichen und theologischen Urteile, die von ›Rechtgläubigkeit‹ und ›Häresie‹ bestimmt sind, stützen will.« The historian of religion employs ›christlich‹ for both ›Grosskirche‹ and ›Sekte‹ without importing the distinction of apostolic ›orthodoxy‹ and non-apostolic ›heresy‹ into the early history of Christianity (195). In the eyes of their contemporaries, »alle, für die irgendwie Jesus Christus eine Bedeutung hat, gelten als ›Christen‹, zum Ärger natürlich der Apologeten und Häresiologen« – cf. Celsus and Porphyry (196).

18 Cf. his Messina paper, »Delimitation of the gnostic phenomenon – typological and historical«, in: U. Bianchi (ed.) *Le Origini dello Gnosticismo*, Leiden 1967, 90-104. German translation in Rudolph (ed.), *Gnosis und Gnostizismus...*, 626-645.

Another point of criticism was his use of Mandean material,[19] and Jonas too made extensive use of Mandean documents. Burkitt in 1928 pointed out that Mandean texts showed evidence of knowledge of the Peshitta,[20] and Lietzmann in 1930 demonstrated the influence of Syriac liturgy.[21] Taken together, these seemed to indicate that Mandean sources were too late to be given any consideration. It was only in 1965 that Professor Rudolph, in his *Theogonie, Kosmogonie und Anthropogonie in den mandäischen Schriften,*[22] demonstrated the possibility of identifying stages of development in the Mandean literature – which opens up again the whole question of Mandean origins: we now know that there was development and modification at later stages, and that at an earlier point there was influence from Syrian Christian sources, but of what kind were the ideas of the group before these modifications took place? That is a question we cannot answer, but the possibility remains that Mandean literature correctly preserves a tradition of an origin further to the west some centuries before the earliest recorded mention; elements in that literature may thus conceivably go back to a very early date. In any case, Mandean sources may legitimately be used as comparative material;[23] what we may not do is to assume that similarity implies relationship, and that if the relationship involves dependence then the dependence is wholly on the Christian side. That was the fundamental error which British scholars saw in the work of the *religionsgeschichtliche Schule.*[24] As Earle Ellis wrote many years ago, »Because of its emphasis on placing Scripture in its historical environment modern biblical scholarship has often tended to convert parallels into influences and influences into sources«.[25] Parallels may be entirely coincidental, and something more than mere parallelism is required before we can speak of influence; to claim one text as the source of another, one movement as the forerunner of another, is to go further still.

A further point relates to the terminology employed: British scholars tended to use the term »Gnosticism«, with reference particularly to the developed Gnosticism of the second century systems. From this point of view, naturally, there could be no talk of »gnostic« influence upon the New Testament. German scholars on the other hand preferred to speak of »Die Gnosis«, and in general to use it in a rather wider sense, to cover the whole gnostic phenomenon. There were however differences of opinion as to what was covered by the term – in 1956 H. J. Schoeps wrote »Die meisten Autoren operieren nämlich mit so ungeklärten Begriffen, daß die Polemiken, die sie führen, zu Scheingefechten werden, da jeder unter Gnosis offenbar

---

19 Cf. Dodd, *The Interpretation...,* 115-130, esp. his conclusion p. 130.
20 F. C. Burkitt, *JTS* 29, 1928, 228.
21 Lietzmann, *SB Berlin,* 1930, 596.
22 Göttingen 1965.
23 Cf. Dodd, *The Interpretation...,* 130, who speaks of Mandean literature as »a valuable addition« to the literature of Gnosticism, yet for his purposes of limited value, because of the late date to which most of it must be attributed.
24 Cf. C. Colpe, *Die religionsgeschichtliche Schule. Darstellung und Kritik ihres Bildes vom gnostischen Erlösermythus,* Göttingen 1961.
25 E. Ellis, *Paul's Use of the Old Testament,* Edinburgh 1957, 82.

etwas anderes versteht.«[26] A particular source of confusion was the use of the term »Gnosticism« to render »die Gnosis« when a German book was translated into English: in some cases the choice was accurate enough, when the German author was dealing with the second-century systems, but when he was employing »die Gnosis« in a wider sense the result could be disastrous. A case in point is Bultmann's *Primitive Christianity in its Contemporary Setting*,[27] which contains a chapter headed »Gnosticism«. This was a natural enough rendering at the time, but the German title of the chapter is »Die Gnosis«, and this makes a subtle but significant difference. To say the least, an earlier section makes curious reading: it mentions in succession the mysteries, Gnosticism, »finally« the Christian gospel, and closes with a quotation from Christian Gnosticism. Bultmann could not have been attacked as he was by some scholars had they realised that at some points he was speaking not specifically of the second-century Gnosticism but of Gnosis in the wider sense.

At the Messina Colloquium in 1967 an attempt was made to clarify the situation, by defining »Gnosticism« as referring to the second-century systems and identifying »gnosis« as »knowledge reserved for an elite«, with the further qualification that not every gnosis was a »gnostic« gnosis, but only such as met certain criteria.[28] For elements of a »gnostic« type, which had long been recognised to exist in the first century, even by those who held to a narrower definition of Gnosticism and regarded it as a Christian heresy, the terms »pre-gnostic« and »proto-gnostic« were suggested. This definition was immediately rejected by Professor Rudolph,[29] on the ground that it involved an *Auseinanderreißung* of things that belonged together, and in fact it has never become established. As it happens, French-speaking scholars like Lucien Cerfaux and Jean Daniélou had long used both terms, »la gnose« in a wider sense corresponding to the German use of »Die Gnosis«, and »le gnosticisme« in a narrower sense corresponding to the British use, and such a distinction still seems to meet requirements. In a paper delivered in 1964, Jonas wrote »A Gnosticism without a fallen god, without benighted creator and sinister creation, without alien soul, cosmic captivity and acosmic salvation, without the self-redeeming of the Deity – in short: a Gnosis without divine tragedy will not meet specifications«.[30] This provides a few criteria for making just such a distinction

---

26 H. J. Schoeps, *Urgemeinde, Judenchristentum, Gnosis*, Tübingen 1956, 30. The list presented for »Gnosis« by H. M. Schenke (*Kairos* 7, 1965, 114-123, reprinted in Rudolph (ed.), *Gnosis und Gnostizismus...*, 585-600; reference to p. 588) corresponds to the »Gnosticism« of the narrower definition, with the addition of some Hermetica.

27 English Translation London 1956; the chapter on »Gnosticism« is on pages 162-171, and quotes Mandean and Hermetic as well as gnostic texts; the passage referred to below is at pages 154-155.

28 See the documento finale in Bianchi (ed.), *Le Origini...*, xx ff. (English version xxvi-xxix; German xxix-xxxii); for the qualification of gnosis see paragraph B II.

29 K. Rudolph, *ThR* 36, 1971, 18-19, in the context of an extended review of the Messina volume; cf. also Rudolph, *Die Gnosis...*, 64.

30 H. Jonas, in: J. P. Hyatt (ed.), *The Bible in Modern Scholarship*, Nashville 1965, 293; this was directed originally against Scholem's treatment of Hekhaloth mysticism as a »Gnosis«,

between a wider and vaguer Gnosis and the specific and developed Gnosticism of the second-century systems – but, it is important to note, without tearing them apart; there is something new, but there is also a certain continuity. Professor Rudolph comes close to this position when he writes that by Gnosis and Gnosticism he understands the same thing: »erstere als Selbstbezeichnung einer spätantiken Erlösungs-religion, letzterer als neuere Bildung davon.«[31] This at least allows for the possibility of some difference between them. Unfortunately this distinction has been confused in certain quarters with the Messina definition, although in fact it is a distinction specifically rejected by Ugo Bianchi in his introduction to the Messina volume.[32]

By way of contrast to the general British approach, it may be noted that the Scottish theologian Hugh Ross Mackintosh wrote, in *The Person of Jesus Christ*: »More and more it is being felt that Gnosticism – an atmosphere rather than a system – is more easily comprehensible in the light of the general history of religion than as a form of Christianity. Looming on the horizon by the year 60, it became really dangerous in the first half of the second century, striving as it did to capture the Gospel for the philosophy of the age. The Church was to be turned into a mystery society or a speculative school.«[33] The reference to »an atmosphere rather than a system« immediately reminds one of the title of Jonas' *Gnosis und spätantiker Geist*; but Mackintosh was an exception, and clearly shows some sympathy with the *religionsgeschichtlich* approach. In 1964 Nock wrote »I should say that in general apart from the Christian movement there was a Gnostic way of thinking, but no Gnostic system of thought with its ›place in the sun'; a mythopoeic faculty, but no specific Gnostic myth«;[34] that reference to »a Gnostic way of thinking« appears to make some concession to the German point of view, but at an earlier point Nock observed that the relation of some of the new texts to the New Testament »seems to me to vindicate completely the traditional view of Gnosticism as a Christian heresy with roots in speculative thought«.[35] At that stage however he could refer to only a few of the Nag Hammadi documents. What is important here is the increasing recognition, even among those who adhered to the traditional definition, that even in the first century there was already a good deal of thought which shows affinities with the later Gnosticism. An atmosphere, an attitude, a way of thinking, trends and tendencies in the direction of the later Gnosticism – all recognise that there is something suggestive of Gnosticism in the narrower sense, yet not enough to permit any claim that a full-scale developed Gnosticism is already present. The problem of definition is quite simply to find some way of cov-

---

and more generally against claims for a Jewish origin of Gnosticism, but would seem to have relevance in a wider context.

31 Rudolph, *Die Gnosis...*, 64.

32 Bianchi (ed.), *Le Origini...*, 3 f.

33 H. R. Mackintosh, *The Person of Jesus Christ*, Edinburgh 1912, reprint 1937, 134; cf. Bethune-Baker, *Introduction...*

34 Dodd, *Essays...*, 958.

35 Ib. 956. German translation in Rudolph (ed.), *Gnosis und Gnostizismus...*, 554-584 (see pp. 582, 580).

ering such elements without incurring the danger of reading first-century documents with second-century spectacles. It is difficult, if not impossible, to give
firmer shape and contours to the first-century Gnosis without introducing elements
from the second century. The terminology may already be present, but does it already have the gnostic connotation which it has in the context of the second-century systems? It is often said that the ingredients of the later Gnosticism are already present; but the ingredients are not yet the finished dish: they require to be
combined in the proper proportions, and the mixture cooked.

The major change in *Gnosisforschung* since the thirties is the result of the publication of new material. First there was the Berlin Codex 8502, known as far back as
1896, when Carl Schmidt identified one of the texts it contains, the Apocryphon
Johannis, as Irenaeus' source for a part of the *Adversus haereses*.[36] With the discovery of three further copies in the Nag Hammadi library, and further investigation, it is now clear that this document should not be directly identified as
Irenaeus' source, but as Sagnard shows it certainly presents the same system.[37]
More to the point, it is now generally regarded as prior to Valentinus, a system
taken over, developed and elaborated in the Valentinian system – which entails a
departure from Burkitt's view of the priority of the philosophical over the mythological. Secondly, there was the eventual publication of the Nag Hammadi library
itself, ably deployed by Professor Rudolph in his magisterial volume *Gnosis*.[38]
This discovery made available over forty original gnostic texts, most of them previously unknown. Prior to 1955, our resources for the study of Gnosticism consisted of the refutations of the Church Fathers, which were inevitably suspect as
the propaganda of the opposition, written to denounce and destroy a hated heresy,
and by men who were not always entirely scrupulous in their choice of weapons.
The only original gnostic material was contained in the Bruce and Askew codices,
documents in Coptic from a period when Gnosticism had long run to seed.[39] Now
we have four copies in all of the Apocryphon Johannis, in two different recensions,
which opens up the possibility of detailed comparison to determine the course and
nature of its development; duplicate copies, more or less fragmentary, of other
documents; also texts like the Letter of Eugnostus and the Sophia Jesu Christi,
which are so closely parallel that they must be related – in this case the general
consensus regards the Sophia as developed out of Eugnostus; and various other
documents, some of which are clearly gnostic whereas others have been recognised
as more or less »orthodox« in character. In view of the emphasis sometimes placed
on the contribution of Greek philosophy, and particularly Platonism, to the development of Gnosticism, it may be worthy of note that one is a rather poor translation of part of Plato's Republic.

---

36   *Philotesia, Paul Kleinert ... dargebracht*, Berlin 1907, 315 ff.
37   Sagnard, *La gnose valentinienne et le témoignage de saint Irénée*, Paris 1947, 439 ff. pre-
     sents a summary of the two texts in parallel columns.
38   For bibliography see D. M. Scholer, *Nag Hammadi Bibliography 1948-1969*, Leiden 1971,
     with the annual supplements in Novum Testamentum. The list now extends to 7628 entries.
39   Cf. W. C. Till in *La Parola del Passato*, 1949, 230 ff.

On the whole it may be said that where parallel passages make comparison possible the Nag Hammadi texts tend to confirm the accuracy of the quotations in the earlier Fathers (Epiphanius remains a more doubtful witness). In some cases indeed it is a patristic quotation that provides the clue to the understanding of an obscure Coptic text. On the other hand it is no longer possible to work simply with the patristic classification: the texts do not fit neatly into the system, for sometimes elements ascribed by patristic authors to one gnostic school are found in texts which appear to belong predominantly to another.[40] A more positive aspect is that the new documents have led to some revisions in our conception of the nature of Gnosticism: where once it appeared to be largely a counsel of despair, some passages proclaim Gnosis rather as a religion of hope. »The gospel of truth is joy for those who have received from the Father of truth the grace of knowing him« (NHC I 16.31-33). There are texts which speak of gnosis in terms of deliverance, of liberation, of waking out of sleep and the terrors of a nightmare into a new life of light and joy and gladness: »He who shall receive that light will not be seen, nor can he be detained. And none shall be able to molest such a one, whether he (still) dwells in the world or departs from the world. He has already received the truth in the images. The world has become the aeon; for the aeon has become a Pleroma for him. And as such it is visible to him alone, not hidden in the darkness and the night, but hidden in a perfect day and a holy light.«[41]

Another area in which the Nag Hammadi library has made reconsideration necessary is that of gnostic ethics. Formerly it was common enough for scholars to note the curious phenomenon that asceticism and lubricity could both spring from the self-same root, the gnostic disparagement of this world, the body, and all that belongs to them. On the one hand the inference was that the gnostic should have nothing to do with the things of this world, which pointed to asceticism; on the other the conclusion that nothing of this world was of any relevance to salvation, and the gnostic was therefore free to please himself – if he did not, as in some views, have a positive duty to disobey the commands of the Demiurge. In the light of the Nag Hammadi texts it appears that the evidence leans rather toward asceticism.[42] Similarly, it was often affirmed that the gnostics claimed to be »saved by nature«, because of their consubstantiality with the world of Light, and that conduct was therefore irrelevant. Now, as Professor Rudolph has demonstrated, it is clear from the new texts »daß die ›Pneuma-Natur‹ des Gnostikers einerseits durchaus auch als Gnade Gottes verstanden werden kann, andererseits das Heil nicht automatisch sicher ist, sondern von einem entsprechenden Lebenswandel begleitet sein muß [...] Die Gnosis ist keine ›substanzhafte Heilstheologie‹, wie sie die Häre-

---

40 Cf. F. Wisse, »The Nag Hammadi Library and the Heresiologists«, in: *Vig. Chr.* 25, 1971, 205-23.

41 *Gospel of Philip* 86.7-18 (Translation after H. M. Schenke, from *NT Apocrypha* i, ed. W. Schneemelcher [English Translation Cambridge 1991] 206).

42 Cf. F. Wisse, »Die Sextus-Sprüche und das Problem der gnostischen Ethik«, in: Böhlig; Wisse, *Zum Hellenismus in den Schriften von Nag Hammadi* (Göttinger Orientforschungen VI. Reihe, Bd. 2), Wiesbaden 1975, 70; also Wilson, »Ethics and the Gnostics«, in: *Studien zum Text und zur Ethik des Neuen Testaments* (FS Greeven, BZNW 47), Berlin 1986 440-449.

siologen karikieren [...] Natürlich bleibt es dabei, daß das ›Pneumatische‹ nicht zugrunde gehen kann und sein Eingang ins Pleroma vorbestimmt ist, aber das Warum und Wie ist vom rechten Verhalten des Trägers nicht unabhängig.«[43]

One thing the new documents have not done is to resolve the long-debated question of the origins of Gnosticism, but in the nature of the case that is only to be expected: in their present form the Nag Hammadi texts are fairly late Coptic versions, in manuscripts from the early fourth century. On the other hand these documents go back to Greek originals, probably of the second century, and in some cases it has been claimed that they may even go back to the first; but such claims are generally treated with reserve. We still in any case have no gnostic documents which in their present form can be dated earlier than the New Testament. For the same reason we are no nearer to settlement of the vexed question of a pre-Christian Gnosticism: what is clear is that there was no developed system that we can identify, although even the most doughty supporters of the traditional view admit that there was a good deal of »gnosticising« thought in the New Testament period.[44] What we do have is evidence to suggest a substantial Jewish contribution to the development of Gnosticism, although the significance of that contribution has been the subject of debate: was it mediated through Christianity, or is the very origin of Gnosticism to be sought in Judaism?[45] What is not in doubt is the presence of Jewish elements in the gnostic texts and systems, but these Jewish elements have frequently been subjected to a substantial re-interpretation.[46] The new documents have also provided examples of gnostic exegesis and use of Scripture, and the fact that in some cases we have duplicate or parallel versions makes it possible to investigate the development of some gnostic texts from earlier to more developed forms.

From some points of view it might appear that the new discoveries, and the researches of half a century, have not after all made a great deal of difference, but that would be a superficial judgment. Much has been done, and in particular there

---

43 *Die Gnosis* (note 11) 134 f.

44 For detailed discussion see E. M. Yamauchi, *Pre-Christian Gnosticism. A Survey of the Proposed Evidences*, Grand Rapids ²1983. Simone Pétrement also (*Le Dieu séparé*, Paris 1984) consistently maintains the view that Gnosticism is post-Christian and sees it as originating within Christianity itself.

45 M. Friedländer long ago argued for a Jewish origin, but without great success. The new material has prompted reconsideration of his views. See »Friedländer Revisited: Alexandrian Judaism and Gnostic Origins« in: B. A. Pearson, *Gnosticism, Judaism and Egyptian Christianity*, Minneapolis 1990, 10-28. Several other articles in this volume are relevant to the discussion. Cf. also K. W. Tröger, »Gnosis und Judentum« in: *Altes Testament, Frühjudentum, Gnosis*, Berlin 1980, 155-168, and other articles in that volume. Both Jonas in: Hyatt, *The Bible...*, and W. C. van Unnik (*Vig. Chr.* 15, 1961, 65-82, reprinted in Rudolph [ed.], *Gnosis und Gnostizismus...*, 476-494) expressed reservations.

46 See A. Böhlig, »Der jüdische und judenchristliche Hintergrund in gnostischen Texten von Nag Hammadi«, in: Bianchi (ed.), *Le Origini...*, 109-140 (reprinted as two chapters in Böhlig, *Mysterion und Weisheit*, Leiden 1968, 80-111); he concludes »Es ist ganz eindeutig festzustellen, dass die Gnosis mit der Umwertung der religiösen Traditionen aus Judentum und Judenchristentum zwar Vorstellungen übernommen, aber aus ihnen Neues geschaffen hat.«

is no longer quite the same gulf between scholars from different countries and different backgrounds. There are of course still differences of nuance, shades of opinion, but there is also a large measure of agreement. The last word has not yet been written, but there is now a greater consensus of opinion among scholars in many respects.

Prolegomena to the Study
of Ancient Gnosticism

Bentley Layton

INVESTIGATIVE PROCEDURE

1. The aim of these prolegomena is to propose a means of identifying the data that can be used to write a history of the Gnostics, and thus to define the term Gnosticism (§23). The subject of Gnosticism will be treated here as part of the social history of ancient Mediterranean antiquity, because the data make it clear that the word "Gnostic" primarily denoted a member of a distinct social group or professional school of thought (§9), not a kind of doctrine. It was people who were called Gnostics. The artifacts of these people, especially their literary and intellectual artifacts, can be called Gnostic only in a secondary way, by reference to the name of the ancient group whose members produced them. The grounds for such a conclusion are presented below.

2. Any account of the Gnostics can only be tentative. As will be seen below, the data regarding the ancient Gnostics are sparse and survive out of context; are unrepresentative and come from tendentious sources; or else are pseudepigraphic mythography and completely disguise their real author, audience, and place, date, and reason of composition. No historical interpre-

Earlier versions of this text were read as public lectures at the École biblique et archéologique française de Jérusalem, the Israel Academy of Sciences and Humanities (in honor of Gershom Scholem), the Annual Meeting of the Society of Biblical Literature, the University of Illinois classics department (in honor of Miroslav Marcovich), the University of Pennsylvania, the Oriental Club of New Haven, and the graduate philosophy faculty of the New School for Social Research (in honor of Hans Jonas). I am grateful to various colleagues for critical discussion of the paper, and most recently to Zlatko Pleše, Thomas Jenkins, and Stephen Emmel for comments on the final draft.

tation of inadequate data is likely to produce clear and certain results, even if the best procedure of investigation is followed. Yet this accident of the data does not diminish the historical importance of the subject, nor lessen the urgency with which the results are needed for historical understanding.

3. The word "Gnosticism" is a modern word, created by the Cambridge Platonist Henry More in the seventeenth century through application of a productive modern desinence -*ism* to the scholarly loanword *Gnostick* (which itself had been taken directly from ancient Greek texts); see Appendix below. There is no equivalent of the word "Gnosticism" in ancient Greek, Latin, or Coptic. The history of the word "Gnosticism" from the seventeenth century to 1995 is fundamentally irrelevant to the historical study of antiquity (though it might be an appropriate topic in modern intellectual history).

4. However, the word *gnōstikos* (γνωστικός) occurs in Classical and Postclassical Greek (from there, borrowed into Latin), and so this is the term, as describing members of an ancient group called the Gnostics (see §9), that historians will have to interpret before they can draw any inductive conclusion about a characteristic category or ism of the ancient Gnostics, the ancient Gnostic ism, or Gnosticism (§23).

5. The historical investigator of a social group will pay considerable attention to how its members characteristically constituted, constructed, defined, and designated themselves as a specific group. If they had a distinctive proper name (*nomen proprium*, personal name) for themselves, obviously this is the appropriate label for the modern historian to use when referring to them. Furthermore, the modern historian must avoid using that word in any other sense, because ambivalent usage would introduce disorderliness into the historical discourse.

6. In general, proper names and epithets of ancient groups vary among themselves linguistically in formation, syntax, translatability, jargon character, range of reference, and so on. Some have one set of characteristics, while others have another. For example, some proper names of social groups are translatable—that is, allow a possible translation into another language as a common-noun substantive (e.g., οἱ Μεθοδικοί, a first-century medical *hairesis* [αἵρεσις]; cf. μέθοδος, μεθοδ-ικός, "systematic"), while others are not (e.g., οἱ Πλατωνικοί denoting adherents of the school of Plato); some epithets were relatively distinctive group jargon ("the seed of Seth"), while others were less distinctive ("the saved"); and so on. Bearing in mind the existence of a scale of naming words that ranges in gradation from extreme properness to extreme commonness with many points along the

way, the historical analyst should look carefully for the privileged, most distinctive (most "proper") name by which the members of any distinct group designated themselves as a group.

7. The common-noun meaning of any translatable proper name of a social group requires special consideration: (a) whether the common noun already existed before the word's appearance as a proper name; and, if so, the meaning, usage, and connotation of the common noun at the very moment it was adopted as the proper name of a group, that is, the intention of the leader who coined the proper-name usage; (b) whether the common-noun meaning was, or continued to be, vivid to members of the group beyond the moment of its coinage or the moment of their adhesion or rather, faded from consciousness; that is, whether the common-noun meaning tells us anything about typical attitudes or practices of group members. As will be seen below, two more issues arise in the study of "Gnostic" as a proper name in antiquity: (c) possible restoration of the vividness of the common-noun meaning by hostile opponents for the purpose of vilification; (d) possible adoption of the name (including but not necessarily limited to ad hoc borrowing), with possible restoration of the vividness of the common-noun meaning, by a person who did not count as a member of the group. Various ancient social group names presumably differed from one another as to these four points.

Illustration of the four points: (a) The adoption of the common-noun substantive γνωστικός as a proper name is discussed below, §§9–10. (b) Do members of the modern Christian Protestant denomination named Methodists think or talk about themselves as being methodical and do they act methodically? (c) Irenaeus mockingly suggests that the Gnostics do not really supply *gnōsis* when he speaks of "that which is falsely called gnosis" in the full title of his work *Adversus Haereses*. (d) Clement of Alexandria's description of "the *gnōstikos*" (typically in the singular) is of a spiritual type, not a member of a haeresis (see §12).

8. The original meaning of Greek *gnōstikos* was a common-noun meaning. Its history began in the fourth century B.C.E., not as a word of everyday speech but rather as a technical term that belonged to philosophy, as philosophical diction, the language of intellectuals. This flavor clung to the word throughout its entire ancient history. The word made its first appearance in a dialogue of Plato (the *Statesman*) and was invented by him through the process of combining the very productive adjectival desinence *-(t)ikos* (-[τ]ικος) with the stem *gnō-* (γνω-) plus (*-s-* [-σ-]), which is found in γνῶναι ("know"), γιγνώσκειν ("know"), γνῶσις ("knowledge"), and so on (*gnōstikos* would have been perceived as deriving from the stem *gnō-* [γνω-] and not from any specific word.) Plato invented several hundred new Greek terms with the ending *-ic* (in Greek *-*[τ]ικος), and in this case, as often, he

explained what the new word was supposed to mean. The literary context is a dialogue about the qualities of an ideal ruler. First, the discussants distinguish two possible kinds of science (ἐπιστήμη): one kind is termed *praktikos*, "practical" (πρακτική scil. ἐπιστήμη), for example, the skill of a carpenter. For the opposite kind of science, Plato invents the new word *gnōstikos* (γνωστική scil. ἐπιστήμη). This made-up word, he explains, describes the pure sciences such as mathematics, which merely lead to knowledge, not to practical activity, τὸ δὲ γνῶναι παρέσχοντο μόνον, "they merely furnish the act of knowing" (*Statesman* 258e), παρεχόμενός γέ που γνῶσιν ἀλλ᾽ οὐ χειρουργίαν, "providing knowledge, not manual skill" (259e). Since the science that characterizes a ruler has to do with the "intelligence and strength of his soul," it is more akin to the *gnōstikos* type of science than to the *praktikos*: it supplies knowledge instead of showing how to practice a craft; it is more like mathematics than like carpentry. The science of an ideal ruler must be γνωστική; it must supply the ruler with knowledge. This passage from the *Statesman* with its explicit definition of *gnōstikos* sets the usage of the word for the next five centuries. Like many of the new words formed with *-(t)ikos*, *gnōstikos* was never very widely used and never entered ordinary Greek; it remained the more or less exclusive property of Plato's subsequent admirers, such as Aristotle, Philo Judaeus, Plutarch, Albinus, Iamblichus, and Ioannes Philoponus. Most important of all, in its normative philosophical usage *gnōstikos* was never applied to the human person as a whole, but only to mental endeavors, faculties, or components of personality.

The productive adjectival desinence *-(t)ikos* (-[τ]ικος) basically conveys no more than "(somehow) related to . . ." (rather like the Greek genitive) and is thus ambiguous. Its ambiguity made it widely useful for the creation of new technical vocabulary in Greek; according to Adolf Ammann's count, from the classical period down to the end of late classical antiquity about five thousand new technical terms with the desinence *-(t)ikos* were coined. Because of this inherent ambiguity, when Plato coins a new word in *-(t)ikos* he usually stops to explain exactly what he wants it to mean: word and technical definition are created at the same moment. Such is the case with *gnōstikos*: both the new technical word and its technical definition (τὸ γνῶναι παρεχόμενος, "furnishing the act of knowing," "knowledge-supplying") are launched in the same passage of text. For the rest of its rarefied lexical history, the word was only used as a Platonist technical term. Its adoption in Platonizing (§29) Christian circles as a proper name belongs precisely to this philosophical history.

9. The application of *gnōstikos* to persons as social entities was therefore a significant deviation from established usage of this technical term. The personal application of *gnōstikos* first occurs in the second century C.E., in reference to Christians whom Irenaeus, bishop of Lyons, attacks (180 C.E.) in his work *Adversus Haereses* (he may be using a now lost composition by Justin Martyr, written about 150 C.E., that had been directed against various

schools of thought or *haireseis* [αἱρέσεις]). These persons are collectively called by the plural of *gnōstikos* (οἱ Γνωστικοί scil. ἄνθρωποι, *Adv. Haer.* 1.29.1; etc.) and are said to constitute "the so-called 'Knowledge-Supplying' school of thought" (ἡ λεγομένη Γνωστικὴ αἵρεσις, *Adv. Haer.* 1.11.1). A century later a pagan Neoplatonist observer, Porphyry, also speaks of Gnōstikoi as members of a *hairesis* (αἱρετικοί, *Vita Plotini* 16). In one passage Irenaeus (1.25.6) refers explicitly to those who "call themselves" Gnōstikoi; a contemporaneous non-Christian Middle Platonist Celsus also knows of people "who profess to be" Gnōstikoi (apud Origen, *Contra Celsum* 5.61). About the same time Clement of Alexandria speaks of the leader (προϊστά-μενος) of a certain *hairesis* who "calls himself" a Gnōstikos (*Strom.* 2.117.5); elsewhere, of followers of Prodicus who "call themselves" Gnōstikoi. Passages such as these indicate that Gnōstikos was a self-designating proper name referring to a haeresis. This is the only proper-name usage of the word *gnōstikos* in classical or late classical antiquity, and we may conclude that it was the Gnostics' own professional school name for themselves, rather than a descriptive epithet formulated by their enemies. This conclusion is suggested not only by outright statements of the kind cited above. It is suggested also by the history, meaning, and connotations of the common-noun usage of *gnōstikos* at the time that the proper name was coined, since the quality expressed by the common noun *gnōstikos* was clearly a desirable one: Plato had first illustrated its meaning with the example of an ideal ruler, and subsequent users of the common noun never strayed too far from Plato's passage. Thus, in the second century C.E. the effect of its neologistic application to persons must have been admirative, not pejorative, and so it was presumably a self-applauding designation. Applied to persons, "Gnostic" meant "belonging to the 'Knowledge-Supplying' school of thought," the Γνωστικὴ αἵρεσις.

10. The specific reason why the creator of this *hairesis* chose the name Gnōstikē ("Knowledge-Supplying") is not clear. Actually, the claim to possess and teach *gnōsis* ("knowledge") was certainly common enough in Christian (and Hellenistic Jewish) circles, including nonphilosophical ones, as was the insistence that one's religious opponents did not have it. Thus any implied claim to supply or to have *gnōsis* ("knowledge") was not at all a distinctive claim. The only innovative element in the proper name Gnōstikoi was a matter of word usage: its application for the first time in the history of the word to a school of thought, and (by extension) to members of that school. This application to persons as social entities was a neologism; it must have sounded strange and thus (because of the word's philosophical connotations) very much like professional jargon. The professional or technical sound of the term was also conveyed by the desinence *-(t)ikos* (§8, end). These factors made Gnōstikē eminently suitable as a distinctive pro-

fessional self-designation, despite the absolute banality of the idea of supplying or having *gnōsis* ("knowledge").

11. The only people called by the *proper name* "Gnostics" in late antiquity are members of this *hairesis*. Provisionally, all these references will be considered to attest in some sense to a single Gnostic *hairesis* developing over time in many places and also using or getting additional names.

Critical evaluation of the *Adversus Haereses* literature is made difficult by the polemical strategy of Irenaeus (following Justin Martyr or Hegesippus?), which strings together and homogenizes a largely fictitious *successio haereticorum* from the first-century mythical figure of Simon Magus down to the second generation of Valentinians, sometimes under the extended rubric of Gnōstikoi. But references by Irenaeus and Celsus (both using Justin Martyr's lost *Syntagma?*) to a contemporaneous group that *called themselves* "the Gnostic *hairesis*" or "Gnostics" can be taken as the starting point for social historical investigation.

12. Clement of Alexandria's description (ca. 200 C.E.) of an ideal type called "the *gnōstikos*" (usually in the singular, sometimes qualified as ἡμῖν ὁ γνωστικός, "our [kind of] gnostic") does not refer to membership in a social group and is not a proper name (see §7[d]); Clement does not, for example, call his own contemporary church hoi Gnōstikoi. His use of "gnostic" is comparable to general descriptions of the behavior of *ho sophos* (ὁ σοφός), the ideal "wise person," in Stoic ethical writings.

In Clement's works, five categories will clearly account for most uses of γνωστικ-, of which the first three express Clement's own neologistic meaning. Much of his largest work, the *Stromateis*, is devoted to explaining this neologism. (a) Substantive ὁ γνωστικός in Clement's special sense; defined as ὁ τῆς παντοδαπῆς σοφίας ἔμπειρος οὗτος κυρίως ἂν εἴη γνωστικός (*Strom.* 1.58.2); opposed to ὁ ἄπειρος καὶ ἀμαθής (*Strom.* 5.57.1–2). He once contrasts οἱ γνωστικοί (Christians who might conform to his ideal type) with αἱ αἱρέσεις (*Strom.* 7.94.3). More than 150 instances, mostly singular. (b) Modifying adjective, γνωστικός -ή -όν, with reference to (a). Modifies a wide variety of substantives. More than fifty instances. (c) Adverb γνωστικῶς, with reference to (a). About two dozen instances. (d) Neuter substantive τὸ γνωστικόν, opposed to τὸ ποιητικόν, somewhat like Plato's usage (§8) (*Strom.* 6.91.2). (e) Substantive Γνωστικός -οί. Members of a school that calls itself the Gnōstikoi (*Strom.* 2.117.5; 3.30.2; 4.114.2; 4.116.1; 7.41.3; cf. *Paedagogus* 1.52.2). Among these are the followers of Prodicus οἱ ἀπὸ Προδίκου (*Strom.* 3.30.1).

In Greek literature down to the seventh century, there seems to be no other record of *gnōstikos* applied to specific people. Two apparent exceptions to this statement turn out to be irrelevant or nonexistent upon closer inspection. First, in the manuscripts of Diogenes Laertius, *Vitae Philosophorum* 1.114 (second century C.E.), Epimenides the Presocratic shaman and seer is called γνωστικώτατον. However, editors following J. J. Reiske (*apud* H. Diels, *Hermes* 24 [1889] 307), have been unanimous in emending the transmitted text to ‹προ›γνωστικώτατον. This conjecture is supported by the fact that in Roman Greek literature at least two other figures of remote antiquity, namely, Anaxagoras and Democritus, are called προγνωστικός.

The second passage is in the Greek Alexander Romance, which comes down to us in several distinct ancient recensions, whose interrelationships have been investigated by textual scholars. Recension γ, book III (ed. F. Parthe, p. 452,20) contains an episode in which Bucephalus avenges Alexander's death in the manner of "those people who are λογικώτατοι and γνωστικώτατοι." Whatever the correct text of this passage may be, recension γ has been shown by its modern editors to be an expansion of the somewhat earlier recension ε (ed. J. Trumpf, p. 177,6), which has this same passage verbatim but without the phrase containing γνωστικώτατοι. Since the author of recension γ has been dated to the seventh century C.E. (because of details that are mentioned in describing a chariot race), the phrase containing the word γνωστικώτατοι must be regarded as a seventh-century Byzantine revision. In any case the word as used in recension γ designates an ideal type and not a social group. A third passage has been adduced by Morton Smith, from Ps.-Ecphantus, ed. H. Delatte, but in fact this passage does not contain the word in question, nor does Delatte defend it as a conjecture (*pace* Smith).

13. Where does the social historian find data describing the Gnostics (see §4)? The most certain place to start is the ancient references that mention them explicitly by their own professional name (§9), *hoi Gnōstikoi*. These can be called the *direct testimonia*. Despite the tendentious sources in which they are preserved, the direct testimonia are the fundamental and most certain core of information about the Gnostics, but they are very meager and give an extremely inadequate (and partly contradictory) historical picture. It is therefore desirable to use a compensatory procedure of investigation that will increase the amount of available data that can be associated with the social group called Gnostics and so thicken the ultimate description of the Gnostics (even at the cost of introducing greater uncertainty into the results).

14. All the direct testimonia occur in works by the enemies of the Gnostics, especially Irenaeus, Celsus, Clement of Alexandria, Hippolytus, Plotinus, Porphyry, and Epiphanius, and they report, in a very reduced and ironic way: doctrines (mostly isolated) of the Gnostics, liturgical and sexual practices of the Gnostics, and cosmological myth read by the Gnostics. Of these three, the reports of Gnostic cosmological myth have the greatest chance of being distinctive, because myth is an orderly system with characters, plot, an elaborated structure, a functional narrative dynamics, and a philosophical point of view; because reports of a cosmological myth are, at least in the second century, liable to be based on written works of a philosophical character; and because a myth of origins often functions as part of the apparatus of group maintenance, in a way that abstract philosophical doctrines do not—whereas isolated doctrines are hard to interpret without their full context, and stories about sexual customs and liturgical practices are not likely to be based on very accurate or firsthand information. A priori, then, the summarized reports about Gnostic myth have a special likelihood of being

a touchstone by which other, undenominated textual material can be recognized as being Gnostic and thus added to the Gnostic data base.

15. Also present in the direct testimonia are some lists of titles of Gnostic literary works (§18), and also lists of other names by which the Gnostics were called (either by themselves or by their enemies).

16. The compensatory procedure consists of five steps, in which various textual features are assumed to be a distinctive sign that a work emanates from, or that a testimonium refers to, the Gnostic *hairesis* even though the proper name "Gnostic" does not appear. Using these features, the entire body of surviving ancient Christian literature is surveyed, and those items which show a distinctive feature are added to the corpus of Gnostic data. The uncertainty of this procedure relates to the difficulty of proving that the indicative textual features are *distinctive* indicators of Gnostic authorship.

The procedure is like the method of field archaeologists, who use purely formal archaeological means when they establish which artifacts belong to one and the same stratigraphic level, and only afterwards interpret and describe the culture that these artifacts represent. In the present case the aim is to establish, by formal philological means, which data can be linked with the direct testimonia explicitly naming the Gnostics, and only after these have all been collected, to draw conclusions about the Gnostic *hairesis*.

17. *Step 1.* The first step is collection and critical use of the direct testimonia, to which reference has already been made (§§13–15). These convey five kinds of information: doctrines; liturgical and sexual practices; a summary of Gnostic philosophical myth; lists of some Gnostic books by title; and other names by which the Gnostics also were known.

18. *Step 2.* Here two comparisons are made. First, summaries of Gnostic myth that were registered in step 1 are compared to all the vast corpus of surviving Christian literature (including the manuscript hoard from the Nag Hammadi region), to see if any correspondences can be found, and one such correspondence is easily identified. In his direct testimonium about the Gnostic *hairesis*, Irenaeus (*Adv. Haer.* 1.29) summarizes part of a work (unnamed) which, he says, belongs to the Gnostics; comparison shows that the unabridged version of this work survives elsewhere in no fewer than four manuscript witnesses: in the manuscripts it is entitled *Secret Book According to John*, and it contains an elaborate philosophical creation myth. Irenaeus notes (1.30–31) that several versions of Gnostic myth were circulating about 180 C.E.

Second, the direct testimonia refer to several Gnostic works by title only. A number of these occur in a testimonium by Porphyry in his life of the

Neoplatonist philosopher Plotinus. The circumstances that he describes are those of Plotinus's seminar in Rome, between 262 and 270: "In [Plotinus's] time there were among the Christians many others, members of a school of thought (αἱρετικοί), who were followers of Adelphius and Aquilinus and had started out from classical philosophy. They possessed many works by Alexander of Libya, Philocomus, Demostratus, and Lydus; and they brought out revelations of Zoroaster, of Zostrianus, of Nicotheus, of the Foreigner, of Messus, and of other such figures. They deceived many people, and themselves as well, in supposing that Plato had not drawn near to the depth of intelligible essence" (*Vita Plotini* 16). Three of the works whose titles are mentioned in this testimonium are preserved or excerpted in the Nag Hammadi hoard. They are the *Oracles of Truth of Zostrianos; The Foreigner;* and the *Book of Zoroaster.* Formally this identification is made only by title; however, the contents of all three have significant points of contact with the *Secret Book According to John,* tending to confirm their identification as Gnostic. Thus, in step 2, four surviving Gnostic works have been added to the meager direct testimonia: *The Secret Book According to John, Zostrianos, The Foreigner,* and the *Book of Zoroaster* (the latter known only in excerpted form).

19. *Step 3.* In step 3, attention shifts to the content of these four Gnostic works, and here a common, distinctive system of mythographic features is registered. Hans-Martin Schenke was the first to describe this distinct common system (which he variously called the Sethian Gnostic system or the Gnostic Sethian system). It expresses with more or less variation a distinct type of cosmography and philosophical creation myth, and it has its own general structure, imagery, and cast of characters. It can be considered Gnostic because of Irenaeus's statement that a myth which he summarizes, from the *Secret Book According to John,* belongs to the Gnostics (§18). The distinctive Gnostic mythographic system is now compared with all works of ancient Christian literature in search of correspondences of content, especially similarities of mythical structure (for the reasons stated in §14). This comparison yields an expanded corpus of works; the exact membership of this corpus is to some degree debatable, but the type of myth that it displays seems to stand distinct within ancient Christian literature. Provisionally, ten additional works are added to the corpus in this step: nine are known from the Nag Hammadi hoard and a tenth can be recognized in an Oxford manuscript, and they can be properly described as literary artifacts of the Gnostics. Adding these ten works to the four registered in step 2 of the procedure, a corpus of some fourteen works of Gnostic scripture is accumulated. The method elaborated by Schenke needs further evaluation and refinement, and at present its results (including the exact composition of the corpus) are merely provisional.

Provisionally the fourteen works are the following: *The Secret Book According to John (Apocryphon of John), The Book of Zoroaster* (excerpted in the longer version of the *Secret Book According to John*), *The Revelation of Adam* (*Apocalypse of Adam*), *The Reality of the Rulers* (*Hypostasis of the Archons*), *First Thought in Three Forms* (*Trimorphic Protennoia*), *Thunder: Perfect Mind* (*Thunder, Perfect Intellect*), *The Egyptian Gospel* (*Gospel of the Egyptians*), *Zostrianus*, *The Foreigner* (*Allogenes*), *The Three Tablets of Seth* (*Three Steles of Seth*), *Marsanes*, *Melchizedek*, *The Thought of Norea*, and the untitled text in the Bruce Codex.

The structure of the Gnostic type of myth also has striking parallels in Valentinian mythography, just as Irenaeus (*Adv. Haer.* 1.11.1) states that the Valentinian *hairesis* derived historically from the Gnostic *hairesis*. But many aspects of Valentinian mythography are also significantly different from Schenke's Gnostic type of myth, so that Valentinus and his followers can best be kept apart as a distinct mutation, or reformed offshoot, of the original Gnostics.

20. *Step 4.* Now this enlarged corpus of fourteen works is compared with all ancient testimonia or summaries of esoteric Christian mythmakers, no matter what sectarian name they bear in the sources. This time the goal is to look for two things: first, distinctive parallels to the Gnostic type of myth and cosmography; second, any references to the titles of the corpus of fourteen surviving Gnostic works that were not already registered in step 1. At this point, several more testimonia are added, including Irenaeus's summary of Satorninus of Antioch, Epiphanius's so-called Sethians, his Archontics, and the group called Audians by Theodore bar Konai. These can be called the *oblique testimonia*, since they are not transmitted under the name of the Gnostics, but nevertheless seem to refer to the Gnostics under other names.

21. *Step 5.* In the last step of the procedure, the "other names" registered in step 4 (§20) are assembled with the "other names" registered in step 1 (§17), and compared with all surviving information about early Christian sects called by these names, in order to collect additional testimonia, even if this information does not agree with the distinctive Gnostic type of myth, as represented in steps 3 and 4. The inclusion of information under names other than Gnōstikoi may mean that the result of the survey is a species containing several varieties. It may, of course, also mean that the survey contains some irrelevant data.

22. In the center of the Gnostic corpus is the *Secret Book According to John*, which Irenaeus's summary explicitly assigns to the Gnostics. Around the periphery are works, titles, testimonia, and names whose pertinence will remain a matter of greater uncertainty. Each step of the procedure leads to more comprehensiveness and less certainty.

23. If the proposed procedure is correct, then *only data identified by these five steps should be assumed to describe the Gnostics.* "Gnosticism" thus means an *inductive category based on these data alone* (cf. §§3–4). (Other data, and induc-

tive categories based on different data bases, would have to be called by some other name.)

24. The question is sometimes raised of why the self-designation "Gnostic" does not occur in the corpus of Gnostic writings (as opposed to the testimonia). The answer lies in the fact that the name Gnostic was the name par excellence of the members of the *hairesis*, their most proper name (§6). As such, its function was not to convey information about what they were like, but rather to express their distinctiveness as a group; not to say what they were, but who they were. The claim to supply (or have) *gnōsis* was absolutely banal, but the use of Gnōstikos *as a proper name* was distinctive (§10, end). Now, the works in the Gnostic mythographic corpus are pseudepigraphic and mythic in literary character, disguising their real author, audience, and place, date, and reason of composition. They do not speak of second- and third-century school controversies (as do the testimonia of Irenaeus, Porphyry, or Epiphanius), but rather of primordial, eschatological, and metaphysical events and relationships. In such compositions, there is no context in which a second-century school name such as Gnōstikos might naturally occur. Thus, the absence of the proper name "Gnōstikos" in the mythographic corpus is not a significant absence.

In Gnostic mythography the enlightened religious person *as a type* is described by other terms, which occur there as epithets (i.e., as "less proper" nouns than the term Gnostic, §6): "the offspring of Seth," "the immoveable race," etc.

On the basis of the Gnostic mythographic corpus, it is therefore impossible to comment on whether or not the common-noun meaning of Gnōstikos was vivid to members of the Gnostic *hairesis* (cf. §7[b]). Within some non-Gnostic circles, the polemics of Irenaeus and the other heresiologists (§7[c]), as well as Clement of Alexandria's ad hoc adoption of the term *gnōstikos* for his ideal spiritual type (§7[d]), must have heightened awareness that a claim to bestow knowledge (*gnōsis*) could be implied in the common-noun meaning of the name. Yet this says nothing about the Gnostics' own conscious evaluation of their name.

SOCIAL HISTORY

25. Because of its pseudepigraphic character (§24), the Gnostics' mythographic corpus cannot provide data for a social history of the Gnostics, that is, a thick description of the *hairesis* over time. The historian has to depend entirely on the meager direct (§13) and oblique (§20) testimonia, supplemented by any information known about the textual transmission of the mythographic corpus (region and language of transmission, scribal names, etc.). The testimonia include a great deal of information about Gnostics said to be known (at least by hostile observers) under other names. To some degree these names appear to be pejorative labels used by the enemies of the Gnostics (e.g., Borborites, "filthies"); others may be self-appellations

used by offshoots or subgroups within the Gnostic movement; still others may be the names of groups mistakenly included within the survey. In sum, the term "Gnostic" may turn out to name a species containing several varieties. Ancient names for the Gnostics may have included Archontics, Barbelites, Borborians, Borborites, Coddians, Levites, Naasenes, Ophians, Ophites, Phibionites, Satornilians, Secundians, Sethians, Socratites, Stratiotics, and Zacchaei (Valentinians are purposely omitted from this list, cf. §19, end). At least some of these names, especially Borborites, were polemical tags devised by enemies of the Gnostics.

26. A social history of the Gnostics has not yet been written. Provisionally, the information of the testimonia may be summarized as follows. This summary is not such a history, but it may serve to demonstrate the kind of data that are collected by application of the procedure. Three points should be noted. First, this data base is only provisional, subject to possible refinement and reapplication of the procedure that is described above. Second, the rich data on the Valentinian *hairesis*, which developed out of the Gnostics ca. 150 C.E., are not included here (testimonia on the later history of the Valentinians have been collected by Koschorke). Third, Gnostics under all their "other names" known from the direct and oblique testimonia (§25) are simply called "Gnostic" in the following summary. This simplification probably conceals important distinctions felt and observed at some level by the ancient persons themselves.

(a) The Pre-Constantinian Period, before 325 C.E.

Before 325, Gnostics are noted in Antioch, Alexandria (?), Rome, and probably Coptic-speaking Egypt. The first to be mentioned are Satorninus (Satornilus) of Antioch (sometime before 155), and the Gnostics who influenced Valentinus, either in Alexandria or Rome. The Valentinian reformation of the Gnostic *hairesis* occurs about 150, in Rome. The ascetic ethics of Gnostic piety is noticed by Irenaeus: vegetarianism, celibacy, and (presumably) sexual continence: "[Satorninus] says that marriage and the engendering of offspring are from Satan. And most of his followers abstain from (the flesh of) living things" (*Adv. Haer.* 1.24.2). The mythography, Christology, and soteriology of Gnostics (including the so-called "Satornilians") are attacked in a flood of anti-sectarian publications. The translation of Gnostic literature from Greek into the Egyptian language, Coptic, almost certainly occurs before Constantine's final victory.

(b) The Post-Constantinian Period, after 325 C.E.

The post-Constantinian evidence portrays a situation that has changed. Now Gnostics are noted not only in the Greek-speaking East but also in

Aramaic and Armenian linguistic areas. They are an element *lodged within* non-Gnostic Christianity, both parochial and monastic. As such, they suffer more and more violent forms of ecclesiastical persecution, which is now backed up by the power of imperial Christian Orthodoxy and the Zoroastrian court of Persia. Gnostics are noted in Egypt (335 C.E.), Palestine (350), Arabia (among the Ebionites, 340), various parts of Syria (later fourth century to 578), Cilicia (340), Galatia (350), Constantinople (422), Lesser or Byzantine Armenia (350), Osrhoëne (370 to 436), and Greater or Persian Armenia (360 to 578). In Egypt, Epiphanius finds them "hidden within the church." Peter the Archontic Gnostic is an ordained priest in the Orthodox church, and later he lives undetected as an ascetic in Judean desert monasticism. Fourth-century Gnostics use the canonical Old and New Testaments allegorically to justify or disguise their views. Theodore of Mopsuestia (400 C.E.) considers them difficult to distinguish from non-Gnostics; while Nestorius (422) is said to have found Gnostics freely attending Orthodox services in Constantinople and even to have detected crypto-Gnostics among the clergy of that city. The ascetic or monastic associations of Gnostics, already noted in the case of second-century "Satornilian" Gnostics, are attested from Epiphanius's sojourn in Egypt about 335 down to the flight of Persian Gnostic monks into Syria, about 570. The later phase of the ascetic Audian movement uses the Gnostic *Secret Book According to John* and *The Foreigner*, and teaches a creation myth based on these. Attacks on Gnostic myth and scripture continue strong in the antisectarian literature. A public debate is reported between a Gnostic and a non-Gnostic opponent in Cilicia, about 340. In fourth- to sixth-century Orthodox sources, innuendo is added to substance, and the Gnostics are mainly called Borborites or Borborians, from Greek *borboros*, "filth," "muck"—clearly a satire on the name of Barbēlō or Barbērō, the primary hypostatic aeon in Gnostic myth (the term also evokes *barbaros*, "barbarian"). Together with this innuendo goes a slanderous tradition alleging the existence of sexually promiscuous worship services, which has its origins in the pre-Constantinian period. However, the tenor of such stories is at odds with the asceticism of Gnostic piety and with the participation of Gnostics in Orthodox Christian worship. The only detailed report of Gnostic sexual rituals is given by Epiphanius; its veracity is indeed a matter of dispute. And, of course, sexual innuendo about Christian worship services of all denominations is centuries older than Epiphanius.

With the gradual establishment of an imperial Christian Orthodoxy the established religious party could more and more effectively take legal measures against the Gnostics. Gnostics are "detected" within Orthodox parishes and monasteries and are excommunicated, starting about 335 C.E.; a priest is defrocked as being a Gnostic in 340; scripture manuscripts are now in danger of destruction, as the burial of the Nag Hammadi hoard may suggest; Gnostics are forbidden by imperial law to build churches or conduct services; their baptism is nullified (Syria, late fifth century); and their legal testimony is declared universally invalid. The most violent persecutions occur in Byzantine Armenia, where with imperial backing Bishop Mesrop imprisons, tortures, physically mutilates, and exiles Gnostics (about 400). In Osrhoëne, about the same time, Bishop Rabbula also exiles them, while in northwestern Sassanid Persia at royal instigation they are persecuted and forced to flee abroad (565–578).

Thus, the activity of the Gnostics, in parts of the Roman, Byzantine, and Persian empires, is attested from the early second to the late sixth centuries C.E. Although their mythography is best known from apocrypha transmitted in the Coptic language (among those discovered near Nag Hammadi), the original language of the *hairesis* was clearly Greek, and its scope, international.

27. Accidentally, only a few Gnostic teachers are known by name: Saturninus of Antioch (before 155 C.E.); Adelphius, Alexander of Libya, Aquilinus, Demostratus, Lydus, Philocomus (all before 251); Eutactus of Satala, Peter the Archontic (both about 350); and possibly one Gnostic scribe, an Egyptian named Concessus Eugnostus (the copyist of Codex III from the Nag Hammadi hoard).

28. All ancient opponents of the Gnostics in both these periods, whether Christian or pagan, treat them as a species of Christian—a *hairesis* (αἵρεσις), "sect," "school of thought." However, the exact social relationship of Gnostics to non-Gnostic Christians is unclear. The surviving Gnostic mythography—all of which predates Constantine's victory—shows certain features that look in some sense to be exclusionary: a complex and distinctive myth of origins; a strong expression of group identity; a special jargon or in-group language; and talk about a Gnostic initiatory sacrament of baptism. Pre-Constantinian testimonia do not necessarily tell us whether the Gnostics had separate parishes, or, rather, like the Valentinians of that period, tried to exist undetected as a component of mixed congregations. Certainly the post-Constantinian sources depict them as an unwanted element within the established Orthodox church at large, though fourth-century Gnostic missionary efforts are also recorded. Thus, although the Gnostics may conveniently be called a "*hairesis*," no precise sociological limitation of that term is immediately obvious from the testimonia. Designations and self-designations of medical and philosophical schools would provide very pertinent comparative data for the further study of this question.

INTELLECTUAL HISTORY

29. An intellectual history approach to Gnosticism would have as its main data the evidence of the Gnostics' mythography rather than the testi-

monia, because the mythic data provide extensive firsthand, completely narrated structures, as opposed to very brief, secondhand, tendentious testimonia recorded without context (§14). The Gnostics' mythography consists of multiple versions of a cosmogonic myth of origins, which is reminiscent of Plato's *Timaeus*. Therefore this approach would situate the various versions of the myth within the history of Hellenistic and late antique Greek philosophy, including its orientalizing representatives such as Philo Judaeus, Plutarch, and Numenius. The most obvious comparanda are the interpretations and retellings of the *Timaeus* in the period from Xenocrates to Plotinus. The obviously Platonist context of the Gnostics' mythography on the plane of intellectual history, goes hand in hand with the Platonist context of the common noun *gnōstikos* and the proper name "Gnostic" (§§8–9) on the plane of lexicography. This helps us to understand, at least in terms of school politics, how the Platonic technical term *gnōstikos* might have seemed appropriate as a distinctive proper name when it was coined— strange as it may have sounded—by the founder of the Gnostic school of thought.

A substantial supplement, if used thoughtfully and critically, to the Gnostics' own mythography would be the works of Plotinus (especially *Enneads* 3.8; 5.8; 5.5; and 2.9 [nos. 30–33 in chronological order]) that were written in response to Gnostic myth. The detailed assimilation of this Plotinian evidence has hardly yet begun.

Furthermore, because all ancient observers, whether Christian or pagan, treat the Gnostics as a Christian *hairesis* (§28), the intellectual history approach would also situate the Gnostics' mythography within the development of Christian doctrines, Christian interpretations of the Bible (especially Genesis), and, more generally, the Christian uses of myth. On the functions of myth in ancient Christianity, see recently Wayne A. Meeks, *Inventing Christian Morality*, passim.

APPENDIX: HENRY MORE'S COINAGE
OF THE WORD "GNOSTICISM" (§3)

Henry More (1614–1687), the author of *An Exposition of the Seven Epistles* (1669), stood in a learned tradition that exegeted the New Testament book of Revelation, especially the seven letters to the churches of Asia (Rev 2:1–3:22), partly by reference to Epiphanius's lurid description of the Nicolaitans and Gnōstikoi, two groups that Epiphanius (*Panarion* 25–26) had equated. Among More's sources was Henry Hammond (1605–1660) (*A Paraphrase and Annotation upon All the Books of the New Testament* [2nd ed. 1659]), whose work shows acquaintance with ancient Christian heresiological literature and takes a broad view of "Gnosticks" as a generic name for "all the Heresies then abroad" in ancient Christianity, emphasizing the moral depravity of the "Gnostick-heresie" (p. 878). More, writing English Protestant polemic, interprets the seven letters allegorically as signifying seven periods of church history. In interpreting the church at Thyatira (Rev 2:18–29) he coins the term "Gnosticism" with roughly the same generic meaning as Hammond's "Gnostick-heresie":

> This Woman of Thyatira [Rev 2:20], (whether the wife of the Bishop of Thyatira, or some other Person of quality, for Interpreters of the letter vary in that) according to the Literal sense, is described from her acts, as onely guilty of pretending her self to be a Prophetesse, and that thereby she seduced the servants of Christ to commit fornication and to eat things sacrificed to Idols, which is a chief point of that which was called Gnosticisme. (*Exposition*, 99)

He repeats the new ism word (with a slightly different spelling) in a polemical tract against Roman Catholicism entitled *Antidote Against Idolatry*, which is printed with the *Exposition* as an appendix (unpaginated):

> [fo. O1 verso] 8. The truth is, most men are loath to be μάντεις κακῶν, to be messengers of [fo. O2 recto] ill news to the greatest, that is to say, to the corruptest, part of Christendome; but rather affect the glory and security of being accounted so humane, of so sweet and ingratiating a temper, as that they can surmize well of all mens Religions; and so think to conciliate to themselves the fame of either civil and good Natures, or of highly-raised and released Wits, (though it be indeed but a spice of the old abhorred Gnosticism,) that can comply with any Religion, and make a fair tolerable sense of all. 9. But these are such high strains of pretense to Wit or Knowledge and Gentility as I must confess I could never yet arrive to, nor I hope ever shall: though I am not in the mean time so stupid in my way, as to think I can write thus freely without offence. And yet on the contrary, I can deem my self no more uncivil then [*sic*] I do him that wrings his friend by the nose to fetch him out of a Swound. 10. I am not insensible how harsh this charge of Idolatry against the Church of Rome will sound in some ears, especially it being seconded with that other [fo. O2 verso] of Murther, and that the most cruel and barbarous imaginable, and finally so severely rewarded with an impossibility of Salvation to any now, so long as they continue in Communion with that Church.

On More's life and works, see *Encyclopedia Brittanica*, 11th ed. (1911), s.n.

ANNOTATED BIBLIOGRAPHY

Ammann, Adolf. -ΙΚΟΣ *bei Platon: Ableitung und Bedeutung mit Materialsammlung*. Freiburg: Paulusdruckerei, 1953. Reliable account of derivation and meaning of Greek adjectives in -(t)ikos.

Chantraine, Pierre. *La formation des noms en grec ancien*. Société de linguistique de Paris, Collection linguistique 38. Paris: Honoré Champion, 1933. Pp. 384–96 ("Dérivés thématiques en -κος"). Best history of Greek adjectives in -(t)ikos.

———. *Etudes sur le vocabulaire grec*. Paris: Klincksieck, 1956. Pp. 97–171 ("Le suffixe grec -ικος").

Gero, Stephen. "With Walter Bauer on the Tigris: Encratite Orthodoxy and Libertine Heresy in Syro-Mesopotamian Christianity." In *Gnosticism and Early Christianity*, edited by Charles Hedrick and Robert Hodgson, 287–307. Peabody, Mass.: Hendrickson, 1986. Oblique testimonia concerning "Borborite" Gnostics; many of the data summarized above in §26 were collected by Gero.

Koschorke, Klaus. "Patristische Materialien zur Spätgeschichte der valentinianischen Gnosis." In *Gnosis and Gnosticism: Papers Read at the Eighth International Conference on Patristic Studies (Oxford, September 3rd–8th, 1979)*, edited by Martin Krause, 120–39. Nag Hammadi Studies 17. Leiden: Brill, 1981.

Layton, Bentley. *The Gnostic Scriptures: A New Translation with Annotations and Introductions*. Garden City, N.Y.: Doubleday, 1987. Part I "Classic Gnostic Scripture" (pp. 3–214). Annotated translations of some, but not all, of the Gnostic mythographic works; and some, but not all, of the direct and oblique testimonia to the Gnostics.

Meeks, Wayne A. *The Origins of Christian Morality: The First Two Centuries*. New Haven: Yale University Press, 1993. Ancient Christian uses of myth.

More, Henry. *An Exposition of The Seven Epistles To The Seven Churches; Together with A Brief Discourse of Idolatry; with Application to the Church of Rome*. London: James Flesher, 1669. Copy in the McAlpin Collection of Union Theological Seminary, New York, New York. First appearance of the term "Gnosticism."

Schenke, Hans-Martin. "Das sethianische System nach Nag-Hammadi-Handschriften." In *Studia Coptica*, edited by Peter Nagel, 165–73. Berliner byzantinistische Arbeiten 45. Berlin: Akademie-Verlag, 1974. Pioneering attempt to describe a set of distinctive features defining a corpus of Gnostic mythography, which Schenke calls "the Sethian system"; cf. step 3 of the procedure described above.

———. "The Phenomenon and Significance of Gnostic Sethianism." In *The Rediscovery of Gnosticism: Proceedings of the International Conference on Gnosticism at Yale, New Haven, Connecticut, March 28–31, 1978*, edited by Bentley Layton, Vol. 2, *Sethian Gnosticism*, 588–616 (and discussion, pp. 634–40, 683–85). Studies in the History of Religions 41, vol. 2. Leiden: Brill, 1981. Further elaboration of his "Das sethianische System."

Smith, Morton. "The History of the Term Gnostikos." In *The Rediscovery of Gnosticism: Proceedings of the International Conference on Gnosticism at Yale, New Haven, Connecticut, March 28–31, 1978*, edited by Bentley Layton, Vol. 2, *Sethian Gnosticism*, 796–807. Studies in the History of Religions 41, vol. 2. Leiden: Brill, 1981. Fundamental history of the common noun *gnōstikos*.

Von Staden, Heinrich. "Hairesis and Heresy: The Case of the *haireseis iatrikai*." In *Jewish and Christian Self-Definition*, edited by Ben F. Meyer and E. P. Sanders, Vol. 3, *Self-Definition in the Greco-Roman World*, 76–100. Philadelphia: Fortress, 1982. Extremely pertinent information on various uses of the term *hairesis* in medical school polemics.

ARIUS IN MODERN RESEARCH

THERE is no need to argue the crucial importance of the Arian controversy in the early development of Christian doctrine, and much new light has been thrown on its history in recent years. Yet the motives and intentions of Arius himself are still disputed. I have taken the opportunity to reconsider them in a fairly non-technical style, reproducing a lecture generously commissioned by the University of Mainz. I shall consider three subjects: our evidence for Arius' doctrine; the main intention of his theology; and his relation to earlier thinkers. I will make some introductory remarks on each of these points.

1. Arius' writings have not survived *in extenso*. Our knowledge of his thought depends on three sources.

(*a*) We have letters written by Arius, which differ notably in their occasion and their emphasis. The earliest, Optiz *Urkunde* 1, is a short note written to an influential friend, in which Arius complains that he has been unjustly treated by his bishop, Alexander, and sets out some points of disagreement. The next, *Urkunde* 6, is a respectful approach to Alexander in which Arius explains his theology in more accommodating terms, apparently in the hope of securing toleration. The third, *Urkunde* 30, is a short credal statement addressed to the Emperor Constantine, which avoids all controversial points. The first two letters were written *c.*320 A.D., the third, I believe, *c.*333;[1] it resulted, of course, in the Emperor's withdrawing the condemnation imposed on Arius by the Council of Nicaea. A few phrases from a fourth letter are quoted by Constantine; see Opitz *Urkunde* 34.

(*b*) We have some remains of the *Thalia*, a composition in verse in which Arius presents his theology in forcible terms. The first seven lines are quoted by Athanasius in his 'First Oration against the Arians', published perhaps *c.*340 A.D., some twenty years after the poem was written. Twenty years later again Athanasius quoted some forty-two lines in his work *De Synodis*, along with other Arian documents. This, I believe, is valuable evidence.

(*c*) There is a great mass of material in the form of reports and criticisms of Arius' doctrine by Alexander and especially by Athanasius. It includes two letters written in the name of Alexander and numerous summaries by Athanasius, all phrased in roughly similar terms. The most influential of these has been the report, based on the *Thalia*, which Athanasius presents in his

---

[1] See Annik Martin, *RHE* 34.2 (1989), 319 n. 2, against Opitz (327).

© Oxford University Press 1994

[Journal of Theological Studies, NS, Vol. 45, Pt. 1, April 1994]

'First Oration', chapters 5 and 6. Not all of this report is reliable. It includes quotations, or alleged quotations, from the writings of Arius and of his colleague Asterius. But these are interspersed with hostile comments, and we also hear of remarks thrown off in conversation by unnamed Arian partisans. Scholars in the past have been far too ready to treat all this evidence as equally valid. In particular, they have preferred the indirect evidence of Athanasius to probable quotations from Arius, who is a heretic.

2. Arius' chief theological interest, it has long been supposed, was to uphold the unique dignity of God the Father, especially in comparison with the divine Logos. Alexandrian theology at this time was pluralist; it insisted that the Second and Third Persons of the Trinity were real and substantial beings, and not mere energies or functions of the Father. Alexander followed Origen in holding that the Logos was eternally generated from the Father; he differed from Origen in ascribing to him equal dignity and power. Arius rejected both these doctrines. To make the Logos coeternal and equally divine, he thought, was to preach two Gods; the Logos must be seen as junior, as radically inferior and subordinate to the Father. This view is strongly expressed in Arius' first letter and in the *Thalia* fragments.

Nevertheless Arius expresses this doctrine within certain limitations. He describes the Logos, in Isaiah's words, as 'a mighty God'. Although junior to the Father, and created by him, the Logos was called into being before all creation and executed the Father's creative work. So much is repeatedly disclosed by Athanasius.

But Arius appears to have been inconsistent. He emphasized the lesser dignity of the Logos by pointing to human limitations which he underwent as incarnate in Jesus: suffering, uncertainty, the need for decision, and the like.[2] It might seem that a Logos who was, next to the Father, the supreme architect of the universe should *eo ipso* be wise and powerful and proof against human weakness. Nevertheless Arius, or some of his followers, described the Logos as, in important respects, subject to our infirmities; the opposing party seized on these admissions, and complained that he considered the Logos a mere man, no more than a man.

It was this side of Arius' doctrine that was taken up by two American scholars, Robert Gregg and Dennis Groh.[3] In their view the main concern of Arius was not to subordinate the Logos to the Father, but to offer a distinctive approach to salvation. The

---

[2] R. Lorenz, 'Die Christusseele im arianischen Streit', *ZKG* (1983), 1–51; 36 n. 198 citing Urk. 30.2; 34.14, 32; also much indirect evidence.

[3] R. Gregg and D. Groh, *Early Arianism, a View of Salvation* (London, 1981).

Arian Logos, they think, is conceived as a morally perfect man, subject to our human limitations, and showing us by his example how those limitations can be overcome. This view has met with some criticism; but it has been given a cautious welcome by Dr Rudolf Lorenz. He has expressed it in the pregnant phrase 'Arius ist Isochrist'.[4] He does not mean, of course, that Arius was the equal of Christ; nor indeed that he claimed to be so. He means that, in Arius' view, men are capable of attaining equality with Christ; and this entails, conversely, that Arius assigns no greater dignity to Christ than a perfect man could attain.

3.   Lorenz agrees with Gregg and Groh that Arius' main interest lies in Christology; and he seems to accept their view that Arius' Christology is an adoptionist one, '*adoptianistisch*'.[5] These points are associated with a distinctive view of Arius' antecedents. Lorenz holds that Arius' doctrine of the Logos is influenced by Origen's teaching on the soul of Christ, rather than by Origen's Logos doctrine itself. Furthermore, he believes that Arius stands in a line of tradition which derives from Paul of Samosata.[6] Both these suppositions lend support to the view that Arius teaches an adoptionist Christology.

I have described these points very briefly, as I mean to return to them later. For the moment I will say that the suggestion about the soul of the Logos is most interesting and suggestive; but it involves complications which Dr Lorenz may perhaps have overlooked. But to present Paul of Samosata as a forerunner of Arius is an idea which, I must confess, I believe to be totally misconceived.

I now return to my first topic, our evidence for Arius' theology. Scholars in the past have relied on the testimony of Athanasius and Alexander, and Lorenz followed them in his fascinating book *Arius Judaizans?* written in 1979. He exhibited this testimony in a system of eight headings, which has been widely adopted. Since that time he has done me the honour of giving careful attention to an essay of mine in which I put forward a very different view.[7] In fact I have entered this discussion with three principal contributions.[8] My essay of 1976, 'Rhetorical Method in Athanasius', attempted to show that Athanasius was not objectively reporting facts for the benefit of future historians; he was engaged in a bitter

---

[4] 'Christusseele' 3, cf. 41 n. 250.
[5] Ibid. 3, cf. 40 f., 48.
[6] R. Lorenz, *Arius Judaizans?* (Göttingen 1979) 128, cf. 'Christusseele' 48.
[7] See n. 2.
[8] *Vig. Christ.* 30 (1976), 121–37; *JTS*, NS, 29 (1978), 20–52; ibid. 39 (1988), 76–91.

controversy, and was not above using the polemical devices allowed by the conventions of his time. If misrepresentation served his turn, he would misrepresent. A second essay of 1978, on the *Thalia*, claimed that our best information on that work is the extracts preserved in Athanasius *de Synodis* 15, to which I will return. Most recently, in 1988, I argued that one of the letters attributed to Bishop Alexander, beginning ʿΕνὸς σώματος, is in fact the work of Athanasius. This also affects Lorenz's argument, since he could claim that on some points the testimony of Athanasius is confirmed by that of Alexander. But their agreement is much reduced if we admit that only the longer letter, ʿΗ φίλαρχος, was actually composed by Alexander. Lorenz cites it much less, and its agreement with Athanasius is indeed much less close. The linguistic arguments for my view, I still think, are irrefutable; if some scholars have been sceptical, it is mainly because my view conflicts with a common view of Athanasius' activity, namely that he wrote nothing until after he became bishop in 328; whereas I present him as writing an important dogmatic letter at the age of little more than twenty; in Charles Kannengiesser's words, I make him a sort of theological Mozart!

Accordingly, next to the letters of Arius himself, our most reliable source is the *Thalia* fragments of *de Synodis* 15. We have some forty-two lines written in rather crude verse. I was wrong in trying to identify their metre as anapaestic; since then Professor M. L. West has described it as Sotadean, which agrees with Athanasius' remarks in the 'First Oration' and elsewhere.[9] But a metrical structure, whatever it be, suggests that Arius' text has been preserved without substantial change. I myself see these lines as a sequence of disconnected fragments; Athanasius has in fact selected those lines which give an opening to criticism, so that almost all of them correspond to objections which he has developed elsewhere. It is most unlikely that Arius could have written a theological poem in which every line was offensive to orthodox sentiment; but if there were inoffensive lines, it would suit Athanasius' purpose to omit them. What then was the extent of the original poem? We have no means of knowing. If pressed for an answer, I would consider it unlikely that it was less than 100 lines or more than 500; but I must emphasize that this is mere conjecture.

The doctrinal importance of this finding is that the *Thalia* fragments provide a check on Athanasius' testimony, particularly in the 'First Oration', chapters 5 and 6, which has long been taken

[9] *JTS* 32 (1982), 98–106.

to be the best source. At one point it is completely confirmed: Arius does indeed, in his own words, proclaim the inferiority of the Logos and his substantial unlikeness to the Father in just the way that Athanasius condemns; though no doubt he also praised the Father in lines which we have lost.[10] At another point Athanasius is clearly at fault; Arius describes the many ἐπίνοιαι of the Son in terms which resemble Origen's; the ἐπίνοιαι are functional titles of dignity. But Athanasius treats these ἐπίνοιαι as mere fictions or pretences, an interpretation of the word which is possible in itself but entirely unjustified in this context. It is a disconcerting thought that Athanasius insists on an interpretation which will later be found in Eunomius, whereas Arius agrees with St Basil. In general, one might summarize the position by saying that Athanasius has slightly, but persistently, exaggerated the extent of Arius' unorthodoxy. No apology can turn Arius into a Christian Father. But he is nothing like the villain that tradition has made of him; and at certain points, where he made unwise pronouncements, he was later willing to retract them.

But can my reading of the *Thalia* be confirmed on critical grounds? I am not aware that there was widespread dissent from my 1978 paper. Nevertheless there are two scholars at least who hold strongly dissenting views, which I will attempt to discuss.

First, my greatly respected friend Charles Kannengiesser maintains the traditional view that our prime source for Arius' teaching is the 'First Oration', chapters 5 and 6; but he has proposed an entirely novel explanation of the *de Synodis* material.[11] He sees it as an artistic composition displaying a unified structure, which I myself cannot detect. It seems to me to contain a number of fresh starts and unexplained transitions, as was observed long ago by Bardy,[12] and as I have already agreed.[13] As to its content, Kannengiesser thinks that it is a reformulation of the original *Thalia*, made shortly before Athanasius wrote the *de Synodis*, by a writer who was moving towards a neo-Arian position. This view, I believe, is wholly disproved by metrical considerations. The original *Thalia* was composed in verse, as Athanasius reports. But the version of it presented in his 'First Oration' is almost entirely unmetrical. It must therefore have diverged to some extent from

---

[10] Cf. Urk. 6.2; Alexander, Urk. 14.46.

[11] C. Kannengiesser, *Holy Scripture and Hellenistic Hermeneutics* (Berkeley California, 1982), 14–20; R. C. Gregg (ed.) 'Arianism' *PMS* 11 (1983), 59–78; E. Lucchesi and H. D. Saffrey (eds.) *Memorial A. J. Festugière* (Genève, 1984), 143–51.

[12] *Lucien*, 255–7.

[13] *JTS* 38 (1987), 199–201.

the original text. Yet we are told that a later writer both reformul-
ated Arius' verses with a new theology in mind and reintroduced
the original metre. Whether he based his work on the original text
or on Athanasius' paraphrase, such a procedure defies belief.

Kannengiesser's account might perhaps be thought more
acceptable if taken in conjunction with the analysis of the 'First
Oration' itself proposed in his *Athanase, Évêque et Écrivain*, which
suggests that chapters 1–10 are a later addition, composed perhaps
in the 350s (op. cit. p. 402). This would make them roughly
contemporaneous with the major works in which Athanasius cites
a number of documents *verbatim*. And the solitary appearance of
ὁμοούσιος at i.9 could be simply explained on the hypothesis of
a later date. But, as I have argued when reviewing the book in
this journal (36.1 (1985), 226 f.), the subtraction of chapters 1–10
(with 30–34 and parts of Book ii) does not leave a convincing
remainder.

Kannengiesser argues for his redating of chapters 1–10 on the
ground that their content is not discussed in the later chapters,
which are mainly concerned with Asterius. But this fact, I think,
can be simply explained without resorting to theories of dislo-
cation. If the 'First Oration' appeared, as we agree, during
Athanasius' Second Exile, it would be natural for him to begin
writing with the Alexandrian situation in mind and make Arius
his principal target. But before long he was at Rome in the company of Marcellus, who had provoked a furore by his attack on
Asterius; in fact this work, and the replies by Eusebius of Caesarea,
were a major cause of strained relations between Rome and the
East. Asterius' theology therefore must have been actively debated
at Rome, as well as Marcellus' attack, and Athanasius' shift of
objectives is thereby explained.

Secondly, Dr Rudolf Lorenz has done me the honour of subjecting my 1978 paper to very careful discussion; he treats it,
indeed, with respect, besides offering valuable corrections. Yet for
all its acuity and learning, his paper shows signs of piecemeal
composition. He begins by stating his view of Arius, using the
traditional material and the well-known eight headings. He then
deals very fully with my critical work, and accepts some of my
arguments; but this does not lead him to reconsider the rather
conservative account of Arianism that he has previously given.
His conclusion is presented in notably moderate terms:
'Athanasius' reports contain important information, which should
not be disregarded. Arianism is not an invention of orthodox
polemics; and Arius is not to be bracketed with Eusebius of
Caesarea.' But this sentence leaves important truths unsaid.

Athanasius' information is of course important and would be indispensable if we had no better sources by which to correct it. But at certain points, I have argued, we have better sources, which enable us to detect the element of misrepresentation that runs through so much orthodox polemics, and so come closer to the real Arius. Dr Lorenz's impressive construction is not fully reliable because it uses material for which, unfortunately, such correctives are lacking. I agree, of course, that Arius made provocative claims which Eusebius avoided; but neither of them was wholly consistent or wholly intractable. The comparison is introduced, presumably, because Lorenz thinks I have been too kind to Arius. But he surely will not claim that I have been careless in scrutinizing the evidence?

This account must suffice; it cannot be stretched to include a detailed discussion of texts. We turn, then, to the remaining topics, the intentions of Arius and his antecedents.

Here Dr Lorenz makes the following four points.

1. Arius derives his view of the Logos from Origen's teaching on the *soul* of the Logos, rather than the Logos himself.
2. In Origen, this soul gains divine status by adoption.
3. Arius in the *Thalia* declares that the Son was adopted.
4. This is confirmed by Alexander's report (Urk. 14.35 f.) which links Arius with Paul of Samosata.

It may be convenient to begin with a remark on the term 'adoptionism', since Lorenz has attributed this view to the Arians. English scholars spell the word with a second 'o', 'adoptionism', so that it has no apparent connection with the heretical Adoptiani like Elipandus. In practice it suggests that someone attains a status which is not his by nature through his own moral effort and achievement. It seems that the German term *Adoptianismus* gives much the same impression. But a higher status need not be gained by adoption; some men became Roman emperors simply by seizing power on the strength of their military prestige. Conversely, if adoption takes place, it need not be a response to recognized merit. Normally, of course, it will take place on the double ground of merit in the past and promise for the future. But adoption where there is no promise is possible; one might in sheer pity adopt a hopelessly difficult child. Adoption on performance only is also unlikely; yet a king might adopt an honoured counsellor, say, on his deathbed, so as to cheer his last hours with the thought that his children would enjoy royal honours. The normal situation is adoption *ex praevisis meritis*, rather as Samuel judged that David would make a good king.

But if the essential point is that someone attains divinity by his own effort, we need a better term; in English we might perhaps speak of 'promotionism', in German perhaps of *Verbesserungstheologie*; this would correspond with Athanasius' accusations that Arius conceived Christ's goodness in terms of προκοπή and βελτίωσις. I think there must be some truth underlying these charges; but we cannot be sure, since at this point there is no first-hand evidence to provide a check on the opponents' reports. What can be said with some assurance is that it is most unlikely that Arius thought of salvation exclusively in exemplarist terms. Almost all Christian thinkers employ a variety of concepts and symbols to interpret the mystery of our salvation.[14] An Arius who relied on one alone is hardly a credible figure.

Let us turn, then, to the suggestion that Arius' view of the Logos derives from Origen's treatment of the soul of Christ. Lorenz provides a very careful and well-documented study, which cannot be fully considered in this paper; but I will summarize it as follows.

1. For Origen, this soul, like other souls, is a created being; though its creation must be seen as a timeless condition.
2. Like other souls, it has free will, and can act either for the better or the worse.
3. But the soul of Jesus consistently adheres to the Logos in love, and so becomes totally fused with him in one spirit.
4. This soul therefore receives all the honorific titles that originally belonged to the Logos.
5. The Logos assumed this soul in order to become incarnate. But the Logos remains distinct, and is unaffected by the human emotions that attach to his soul.
6. This soul's persistence in well-doing is held out to mankind as an example for us to follow.

Dr Lorenz then argues, in a much briefer paragraph, that Arius' teaching reproduces the pattern just set out.

I find this argument impressive and largely convincing. Nevertheless there are some reservations that need to be made.

1. Origen's account is not as consistent as Lorenz makes out. In some contexts he emphasizes the total fusion of the soul of Christ with the Logos; they become 'one spirit', they need not be separately named, and so on. Elsewhere, he draws clear distinctions: the soul is an instrument of the Logos; the soul is passible,

---

[14] In some unpublished notes I have summarized Athanasius' salvation doctrine under some twenty headings. Exemplarist teaching is widespread. For Origen, see *Princ.* iv.4.4, p. 354–26. For Athanasius, *EF* 2.5, 10.7, *Ep. Marc.* 13 (of Christ's earthly life); also c. Ar. iii.20 (ὑπογραμμός from 1 Pet. 2: 21) of Christ's unity with the Father.

the Logos impassible.[15] Moreover, Origen is unclear as to the moment at which their union takes place. In the *de Principiis* ii.6.3, in Rufinus' translation, it takes place *principaliter*; Lorenz paraphrases it 'von Anfang der Schöpfung an hängt sie unzertrennlich dem Sohn Gottes an', etc.[16] But in c. Cels ii.9 it is united 'after the Incarnation'. How then was it before? Was it not yet in being, or not yet obedient?

There is a complication here. Origen holds that our actions are free, but yet are fully foreseen by God. I do not myself think this conjunction is possible; but for the moment let us accept it. It does not then follow that a good action eternally foreseen by God ensures unchanging goodness. It might be negated by another action which God equally foresees. But *undeviating* goodness foreseen by God is quite another matter. There is no uncertainty here which needs to be dispelled. It may be that Athanasius has missed this point. He argues, absurdly I think, that on the Arian view the Saviour did not become Logos until he had performed the good works which secured his divinity.[17] This is like saying that David did not become king until he had succeeded in ruling wisely, as Samuel foretold.

2. Some of Origen's assumptions are clearly not shared by Arius, a fact which counts against Lorenz's emphasis on his dependence. Arius clearly did believe in God's total foreknowledge; this plays an important part in his conception of the Son's moral condition, as free in principle but undeviating in fact. He clearly did not believe in the eternity of God's creative action, and of the creatures themselves. Time is part of the order of creation, and outside the temporal order such words as 'before' and 'after' become obscure and uncertain in their application. Nevertheless Arius insists on asserting the priority of God over his creatures, including even his Son, who is prior to all time, yet ἀχρόνως γεννηθεὶς ὑπὸ τοῦ πατρὸς ... οὐκ ἦν πρὸ τοῦ

---

[15] Origen seems to hold both (i) that the soul of Christ is by nature like other souls, and so permanently distinct from the Logos, and (ii) that its moral union is unshakeable, so that it is permanently united. For (i): it is created by the Logos, *Princ.* i.7.1, Lorenz n. 208. By nature intermediate: flesh/spirit, *Co. Rom.* 1.7.45; flesh/deity, ibid. i.7.55, *Princ.* ii.6.3. So can do good or evil, *Princ.* ii.6.5, Lorenz n. 226, 235. Not by nature God, *Cels.* ii.9 init, cf. *Princ.* ii.6.5. Doesn't change its (created?) essence *Cels.* iv.18. For (ii): It is united to God by its free choice, *Princ.* ii.6, iv.4.4 (354.13), *Cels.* v.39; but its obedience has become second nature, *Princ.* ii.6.5; it is so fused that it need not be distinguished or separately named, *Cels.* vi.47, *Princ.* iv.4.4 and fr. 37; it is in substance divine, *Princ.* ii.6.6. For the notion of acquired substance or 'second nature' see my *Divine Substance* p. 148 n. 18.
[16] 'Christusseele' 38.
[17] C. Ar. i.38.

γεννηθῆναι.[18] Here Lorenz very perceptively points out observations by Origen which do not square with his general picture, but are not unlike Arius' opinions.[19]

3. There is one obvious objection to Lorenz's view. Arius plainly believed in the pre-existence of the Logos, though not in his eternity; this is shown by his literal acceptance of Prov. 8: 22. But he cannot have believed in the pre-existence of souls. For Peter of Alexandria is known to have attacked Origen's doctrine at this point, and Athanasius repeats his condemnation.[20] If Arius had accepted that doctrine, it is surely inconceivable that Athanasius should have missed the opportunity to condemn him.

If is of course a common opinion that Arius did not acknowledge *any* soul in Jesus. But I do not rely on this opinion. Our only firm evidence for it is a statement by Eustathius of Antioch.[21] But Arius must have found some means of interpreting the New Testament passages which refer to Christ's soul. He could well have accepted Origen's dictum: 'When Scripture wishes to indicate any suffering or trouble that affected him, it uses the word "soul", as when it says "Now is my soul troubled"', and so on. Origen thus dissociates the Logos from suffering. Athanasius carries this process further, and assigns the Lord's sufferings to his 'flesh'. He could thus complain that the Arian exegesis of such texts associates the Logos too closely with suffering; he does not, and presumably could not, complain that the Arians fail to grant the Logos a soul.

To summarize: Arius' doctrine of the Logos was indeed influenced by Origen's views on the soul of Christ. But one must not suppose what a careless reading of Lorenz might easily suggest, that he simply adapted Origen's teaching. He plainly diverges at a crucial point, over the pre-existence of souls in general; and he has no concern to insulate the Logos from suffering. The truth is rather that Origen expressed a number of sharply divergent views; Arius adapted some and rejected others to form his own synthesis.[22]

I shall deal rather briefly with Lorenz's third point. He detects an act of adoption in the well-known couplet from Arius's *Thalia*:
ἀρχὴν τὸν υἱὸν ἔθηκε τῶν γεννητῶν ὁ ἄναρχος
καὶ ἤνεγκεν εἰς υἱὸν ἑαυτῷ τόνδε τεκνοποιήσας.

[18] *Urkunde* 6.4.
[19] 'Christusseele' 38 n. 223. On time see R. Williams *Arius* p. 122 nn. 55, 56; also 'Christusseele' 38 n. 218 ref. *Princ.* ii.9.1 p. 164.1, ἐπινοουμένη ἀρχή.
[20] Peter: Leontius of Byzantium *c. Monoph.*, Fr. in Routh *Rel. Sacr.* iv.50. Athanasius *ad Epict.* 8, *Vit. Ant.* 74.
[21] Fr. 15, de Riedmatten p. 100. It was of course upheld by some later Arians.
[22] So Lorenz, 'Christusseele' 38 n. 223.

Argument naturally arises on two points: does τεκνοποιεῖν mean 'to beget' or 'to adopt'? And does the couplet refer to two separate divine acts, or to a single act with a double description? Lorenz thinks that the first line denotes the begetting of the Son, and the second refers to a subsequent act of adoption.[23] But this interpretation is directly contradicted by a phrase in Arius' letter to Alexander, *Urkunde* 6.3: the Son received from the Father his life and being and his dignities, which the Father brought into being simultaneously with him, τὰς δόξας συνυποστήσαντος αὐτῷ τοῦ πατρός. Of course theologians can be inconsistent, as I have shown; but I doubt if Arius would have contradicted himself at this vital point in a carefully phrased dogmatic letter.

There remains the question of Paul of Samosata. We may start from some acknowledged facts. Lucian was highly regarded by Arius and his sympathizers. Lucian is described as a successor of Paul by Alexander of Alexandria; though this report lacks confirmation. Arius is portrayed by Athanasius as sharing the errors of Paul, but we have no surviving statement by Arius in his favour.

My difficulty in following Dr Lorenz is that at a crucial point Arius seems to have agreed with Paul's accusers, rather than with Paul himself. Certainly we must not make the mistake of thinking that, whatever his accusers believed, Paul always took the opposite view. There are, in fact, several points of agreement. Paul's accusers apparently held a pluralistic theology resembling that of Dionysius of Alexandria. Paul agreed with them to the extent of making the Logos a distinct personal being, identifiable with the divine Wisdom, and substantially distinct from the Father. The main point of difference was that the accusers held that the divine Wisdom was substantially present in the man Jesus, or essentially united with him. Paul complained that this was equivalent to making the two identical, so that the human sufferings of Jesus impinge directly on the divine Wisdom. He himself drew a sharp distinction between the divine Logos and the man born of Mary; yet he protested that he had an adequate concept of their union, which avoided the error of making them identical. The man Jesus was not pre-existent; on the other hand his coming was foreseen and appointed by the Father.

But this sharp distinction between the Logos and the man is wholly foreign to Arius' thought. If we think that he used the human sufferings of Christ to prove the inferiority of the Logos, this argues something like a substantial union between them; we

---

[23] Better in R. Williams *Arius* p. 102, n. 40.

have shown that he did not use the soul, or the flesh, of Christ as an effective barrier between them; this is the truth underlying Eustathius' complaint. But the lack of an adequate distinction also explains the fact that it was possible to misrepresent Arius as a follower of Paul. One of them appeared to believe in a man guided merely by external inspiration; the other in a passible Logos too much entangled in human limitations. Both then were accused, though on totally different grounds, of making Christ a mere man.

I have had to present Paul's opinions briefly and dogmatically, in a form appropriate to a lecture. I have consulted the texts as presented by de Riedmatten, which I believe to be authentic, though no doubt selective.[24] And I have tried to avoid some common misconceptions. I remember my pupils at Oxford asking me whether I thought Paul an adoptionist or a Sabellian. The answer I should have given is that these are not true alternatives; but both are polemical statements which are extremely remote from the facts. Paul no doubt attached importance to the human acts of Jesus, instead of making him a mere mouthpiece of the divine Wisdom. But he did not make him simply an inspired man. Paul's Wisdom figure is a substantial being, she has a dignity which must be upheld, she dwells in the man Jesus as in a temple. Once these facts are admitted, the charge of Sabellianism also collapses.

Where then does Lucian fit into the picture? Here I am less certain; but I will make a suggestion. I start from the following facts. Arius regarded Lucian as a respected teacher. Next, the views of the Lucianist party show some resemblance to those of Paul's accusers. But the contemporary bishops of Antioch, Philogonius and Eustathius, are opposed to the Lucianists, though they are not, of course, prepared to defend the memory of Paul. At some time, then, there must have been a reversal of theological tradition at Antioch. But we do not hear of any break in the episcopal succession. It may be, therefore, that Bishop Domnus, who succeeded Paul, was not an outright opponent, but an uncontroversial figure calculated to appeal to moderate men on both sides. This would explain why the ambitious and influential Paul left behind him no strong body of sympathizers, but only a quite insignificant group of Paulianists.

[24] For a telling defence see M. Simonetti 'Per la Rivalutazione di alcuni Testimonianze su Paolo di Samosata', *RSLR* 24 (1988), 177–210. He criticizes M. Richard's attack on the reliability of the fragments, in 'Malchion et Paul de Samosate, Le témoinage d' Eusèbe de Cesarée', *Eph. Theol. Lov.* 35 (1959), 325 ff. I hope to reinforce this criticism; see H. C. Brennecke *et al.* (edd.), *Logos, Festschrift für Luise Abramowski*, Göttingen 1993, 140–50.

As for Lucian, if he really was excommunicate for the duration of three episcopates, his fall must have taken place very soon after Paul's expulsion. We may see him, then, as an uncompromising pluralist, strongly *opposed* to Paul, who was condemned because he refused to accept the policy of peace and accommodation. By representing him as a successor to Paul, Bishop Alexander means no more than that he was the next prominent troublemaker.[25] Alexander needed to gain the support of Eustathius and his allies, who would not altogether approve of his pluralistic Trinity, with its barely-concealed doctrine of three hypostases; so he takes the opportunity to dissociate himself from two teachers whom Eustathius is sure to dislike. But we need not accept his insinuation that the two agreed with each other.

In arguing this case, I have diverged a little from my principal theme. My purpose has been to argue that the traditional estimate of Arius is the right one. His main concern was to uphold the unique dignity of God the Father in the face of attempts to glorify the Logos, as he thought, unduly. This interest is abundantly attested in his surviving fragments. It is allowable, if rather strained, to say that his main interest was Christology. But the idea that he was mainly concerned to propound an exemplarist theory of salvation finds little or no support in his surviving fragments. I venture to think that we have seen the end of a most interesting episode in the history of Arian scholarship; and that after Dr Lorenz no scholar of equal distinction will come forward to support this theory.

CHRISTOPHER STEAD

[25] I agree with Bardy (*Lucien* 48) in seeing Lucian as an opponent of Paul, and in not pressing the sense of Alexander's διαδεξάμενος (*Urkunde* 14.36) to indicate a formal succession (*Lucien* p. 51 n. 66); but I see no need to imagine two Lucians, which would rob Alexander's remark of its point in seeking to discredit a teacher revered by his Arian opponents.

Revue des Études Augustiniennes, 39 (1993), 309-332

Jerome's polemic against Priscillian in his *Letter* to Ctesiphon (133, 4)*

In the fourth-century Priscillianism was the major heretical group in the Iberian Peninsula widely accused of embodying the teachings of the Gnostics and Manichaeans[1]. Priscillian's asceticism and oratory skills won him many admirers and numerous opponents. The Priscillianist controversy ended tragically with his execution at the hands of the Emperor in 385/86[2].

Priscillian's opponents consistently charged him of both moral and doctrinal lapses. One of his critics was none other than Jerome who joined the concerted effort to extirpate the Priscillianists. The principal focus of this article is a letter

---

* I wish to thank Professors Jeffrey B. Russell, Glenn Olsen, and the editors at the Institut d'Études Augustiniennes for their useful and constructive critique of earlier versions of this paper.

1. A few examples are : AUGUSTINE, *De haeresibus* 70, *CCSL* 46. *Aurelii Augustini Opera*, Pars XIII, 2. p. 333. PROSPER OF AQUITAINE, *Chronicum integrum pars secunda*, *MGH AA* IX, pp. 460 and 462 ; SULPICIUS SEVERUS, *Chron.* II, 46, *CSEL* 1. pp. 99-100 ; Finally, ISIDORE OF SEVILLE, *Etymologiarum* VIII, *De haeresibus Christianorum*, 8, 5. 54 in *San Isidoro de Sevilla. Etimologías.* vol. 1 (Libros 1-X), edición bilingüe, (ed. J. OROZ RETA, et al), *Biblioteca de Autores Cristianos*, 433. Madrid, 1982, pp. 698-701. ¡Hereafter *San Isidoro de Sevilla*]. Noteworthy is Filastrius of Brescia, who alluded to the Priscillianists without referring to them specifically by name : *Diversarum hereseon liber*, 84, *CCSL* 9, pp. 253-254.

2. On the execution, W.H.C. FREND observed, «for the first time, a Christian had been condemned to death on what appeared to be a religious issue», in *The Rise of Christianity*, Philadelphia, Fortress, 1984. p. 713 ; For Priscillian in general consult the groundbreaking study by H. CHADWICK, *Priscillian of Avila. The Occult and the charismatic in the early church*, Oxford, 1976 ; An enlightening recent study is by R. VAN DAM, «The heresy of Priscillian», chapter 5 in his book *Leadership and Community in Late Antique Gaul*, «The Transformation of the Classical Heritage, 8», Berkeley, University of California Press, 1985, pp. 88-114. For the most complete bibliography on Priscillian up to 1984 see A. FERREIRO, *The Visigoths in Gaul and Spain A.D. 418-711: A Bibliography*, Leiden, E.J. Brill, 1988. pp. 197-203, and J.E. LOPEZ PEREIRA, «Prisciliano de Avila y el Priscilianismo desde el siglo IV a nuestros días : Rutas bibliográficas», *Cuadernos Abulenses* 3 (1985), pp. 13-77.

that Jerome wrote to Ctesiphon, approximately in 415, or about three decades after Priscillian's execution. The letter in general has received limited commentary from modern researchers who oftentimes repeat in uncritical fashion what Jerome says about the moral and doctrinal errors of Priscillian[3]. Given Jerome's polemical style and tempestuous attitude are we wise to dismiss any possibility of exaggeration on his part ? The letter, as a polemical document, indulges in a typological attack of Priscillianism, and as such raises questions about how accurately he portrays the sect. As David S. Wiesen reminds us about Jerome's literary style, «St. Jerome was uniquely suited by his learning as well as by his temperament to combine the inherited body of pagan satire with a new and vigorous Christian satiric spirit into a literary attack on the vices of society and of personal enemies[4]».

Jerome's attitude towards Priscillianists shifted from an ambiguous stance in his *De viris inlustribus* which goes up to the year 393, to one of definite rejection in his *Letter* to Ctesiphon, written around 415. In the former work Jerome refused to outright condemn Priscillian nor even to link him to Gnosticism[5]. In the letter to Ctesiphon, as this study will confirm, Jerome linked Priscillianists not only to Gnosticism, but much more besides. I am not convinced that Jerome's change of mind was based on a better understanding of Priscillianism. It seems more plausible that Jerome joined at that latter date an already pervasive condemnation of Priscillian by the Church at large.

---

3. For critical discussions of the letter see M. J. RONDEAU, «D'une édition des "Lettres" de Saint Jérôme», *Revue des Études Latines* 42 (1964), pp. 166-184, especially pp. 180-181. P. DEVOS, «La date du voyage d'Égérie», *Analecta Bollandiana* 85 (1967), pp. 165-184, especially pp. 180-182 ; H. CHADWICK, *Priscillian of Avila*, pp. 37-38 ; V. BURRUS, *The making of a heresy. Authority, gender and the Priscillianist controversy.* Unpublished doctoral dissertation, Graduate Theological Union, Berkeley, July-1991, II-262 p., especially pp. 207-211. The author's treatment of the letter is couched within the broader goal of expounding the feminist issues surrounding the controversy with Priscillian. Also the preliminary foundation article by A. FERREIRO, «Sexual Depravity, Doctrinal Error, and Character Assassination in the Fourth Century: Jerome against the Priscillianists», *Studia Patristica* (in the press). Due to constraints imposed by the publisher I only focused upon the figures of Simon Magus and Nicolas of Antioch, which are undoubtedly to be viewed as foundational for the remainder of Jerome's exegesis in section four of the *Letter* to Ctesiphon. For the Latin edition consult *Epistula* 133. 4, *CSEL* 56, pp. 247-248. In regard to Ctesiphon, J.N.D. Kelly observed: «We have no certain clue to Ctesiphon's identity, but Jerome's jibes at his 'religious illustrious house' where the 'heretic' holds forth, and at people who supply him with money, suggest that he was one of Pelagius's wealthy lay supporters (*Jerome: His life, writings and controversies*, New York: Harper and Row, 1975, p. 314). The author does not address Jerome's commentary on Priscillian at all in this work.

4. *St. Jerome as a Satirist: a study of Christian thought and letters*, Cornell University Press, 1964. pp. 6-7.

5. *De viris inlustribus*, 121, in *Hieronym: De viris inlustribus* (ed. W. HERDING) *Bibliotheca Scriptorum Graecorum et Romanorum Teuberiana* Leipzig, 1879, p. 162 = *PL* 23, c. 750. See D.G. HUNTER, «Resistance to the Virginal Ideal in Late Fourth-Century Rome : The Case of Jovinian», *Theological Studies* 48 (1987), pp. 56-60, especially at 57.

Jerome primarily discussed Pelagianism, not Priscillian, in the letter to Ctesiphon, and his remarks need to be considered within that broader dialogue. While Jerome refuted Pelagianism he directed Ctesiphon's attention to Priscillianism as an example of a sect that has likewise lapsed morally and doctrinally. Presumably whatever Jerome attributed to the Priscillianists he impugned upon the Pelagians as well[6]. Jerome's attack upon the moral/doctrinal errors of Priscillian revolved heavily on the 'types' of men and women that not only characterize the sect but all heretics in general. The typological heretical men and women Jerome associated with Priscillian represent the many 'faces' of heresy that Ctesiphon is warned to avoid.

Jerome focused his attack on Priscillianist women by interweaving key passages from Scripture. What emerges from his biblical exegesis is a devastating typological attack upon women. He singled out women led astray by Priscillian, and by all previous male heresiarchs. The first of the scriptural references is a combination of *Ephesians* 4: 14 and *2 Timothy* 3: 6-7 wherein emerges the image of weak women led astray by false male teachers. David Wiesen, however, reminds us that Jerome did not have only one view of women, anymore than he did of men[7]. Jerome's combined passages read : «silly women burdened with sins, carried about with every wind of doctrine, ever learning and never able to come to the knowledge of the truth[8]». The women that Jerome paraded in the letter embody all of the characteristics and behavior unacceptable to the orthodox. They are arrogant and presumptuous women illegitimately seeking to abrogate the power of the Holy Spirit.

Jerome continued with a paraphrase of *2 Timothy* 4: 3, which he rephrased now to shift the focus upon 'vulnerable men' deceived by heretical women primarily because they are «men with itching ears who know neither how to hear nor how to speak[9]». As in the case of women Jerome only singled out men lured into spiritual deception. The male heretics represent individuals whose

---

6. V. BURRUS, *Making of a heresy*, pp. 185-253.

7. *Ephesians* 4: 14 refers to "men" in non-gender specific fashion. Women are not singled-out as the main perpetrators of false doctrine. *2 Timothy* 3. 6-7 focuses upon "weakwilled" women, yet these passages are within a broader context. The verses preceding and following address males and females engaged in spiritual and carnal depravity. The section begins with the all inclusive "people", but it is men who violate, control, sway, and lead women astray. Once again, D. S. WIESEN notes that Jerome's most loyal supporters were women (*Jerome as a Satirist*, p. 164).

8. «Quid uolunt miserae mulierculae oneratae peccatis, quae circumferuntur omni uento doctrinae, semper discentes et nunquam ad scientiam ueritatis peruenientes», *Ep*. 133. 4, *CSEL* 56, p. 247.

9. «Et ceteri muliercularum socii, prurientes auribus et ignorantes quid audiant, quid loquantur, qui uetustissimum caenum, quasi nouam suscipiunt temperaturam», *Ep*. 133. 4, *CSEL* 56, p. 247. Scripture refers to men in gender free fashion, and Jerome departs from this sense to chastise specifically males. The 'hearing' and 'speaking' Jerome mentions was intended to convey the inability of heretics to hear the voice of Christ (See the *Gospel of John* 10. 4-5). Heretics do not hear the voice of Christ, neither do they speak his truth.

pride leads them to abuse the Word of God and lure spiritually weak people. All of them are tools of the Evil One intent on destroying the flock of God.

Jerome's biblical exegesis includes a reference from the Old Testament prophet *Ezekiel* 13: 10-16. 17. False prophets consciously mix old mire with a new form of [weak] cement to foster and whitewash falsehood. The passages in Ezekiel speak prophetically of a cleansing that God will send in the form of 'overflowing showers' ; one that will tear down the edifice of falsehood. Jerome perceives his role, so it seems, as the prophet of God's cleansing power to bring down all of the errors brought together by Priscillian[10].

Jerome closed the section on Priscillian with two scriptural references from the New and the Old Testaments, respectively. He quotes *2 Thessalonians* 2: 7 focusing on the warning 'Now also the mystery of iniquiry is working'[11] alerting his readers that Satan and heretical teachers were alive and well in his own day as they had been in apostolic times. Here Jerome layed the culpability for spiritual error evenly at both men and women. Jerome, with prophetic condemnation, concluded with an admonition and quote from Jeremiah 17: 11. In his own words :

> «Men and women in turn "lay snares for each other till we cannot but recall the prophet's words the partridge has cried aloud, she has gathered her young which she had not brought forth, she unrightfully gets riches ; in the midst of her days she shall forsake them, and in the end she shall be a fool[12]"»

Succinctly heretics are spiritually barren, abandoned, and in the end fools. The reference to Jeremiah served well his purpose to establish the deviancy of Priscillian and his followers, whom he charged of :

(a) Spiritual kidnapping - 'quae non peperit'

(b) Illegitimate riches - 'faciens divitias suas, non cum judicio'

(c) Not true devotion - 'In dimidio dierum derelinquet eas'

[Unlike Christ who promised never to abandon his sheep, John 10: 11-15].

(d) Their fate is foolishness - 'et novissimum ejus erit insipiens'

The scriptural references cited by Jerome set the tone for the remainder of the letter. The cardinal focus of Jerome's polemic against Priscillianism is the material couched between these scriptural references. Let us now turn our attention to the heart of Jerome's arguments, which he expounded in the form of a heresiarchical list.

---

10. *Ep.* 133. 4, *CSEL* 56, p. 247.

11. «Nunc quoque mysterium iniquitatis operatur», *Ep.* 133. 4, *CSEL* 56, p. 248.

12. «Duplex sexus utrumque supplantat, ut illud propheticum cogamur adsumere : clamauit perdix, congregauit quae non peperit, faciens diuitias suas non cum iudicio. in dimidio dierum derelinqunt eum, et nouissimum eius erit insipiens», *Ep.* 133. 4, *CSEL* 56, p. 248.

It is well known that some Church Fathers compiled lists of heretics intended for circulation in the Church[13]. I intend to investigate : Why Jerome singled out only a 'select few' of the heretics for his own list ? Of the heretics Jerome includes what deeper spiritual meaning do they signify, if at all, other than face value identification by the reader ? Lastly, how does each sect correspond to the actual charges against Priscillian as found in the major sources other than Jerome ? From Jerome's letter the following list of heretical men and women with accompanying accusations emerges:

Male	Female	Accusation
Simon Magus	Helena	A sect
Nicolas of Antioch	Bands of Women	uncleanness
Marcion	a woman (unidentified)	mindsnares
Apelles	Philumena	false doctrine
Montanus	Prisca / Maximilla	pervert churches
Arius	Constantia	lead world astray
Donatus	Lucilla	polluting baptism

Agape/Elpidius form the only exception where Jerome altered the gender of the list.

Agape	[Elpidius]	Spiritual blindness
Priscillian	Galla and her sister	Zoroaster/magic

The deeper meaning of each heretic, including their corresponding error, lies in the patristic sources from which Jerome carefully selected so as to develop a critique directed at both the Pelagian and Priscillianist sects[14].

---

13. These are the major heresiarchical lists that I will make reference to in this study, along with a variety of other relevant sources : IRENAEUS OF LYON, *Contre les hérésies*, Livre 1. 2 (ed. A ROUSSEAU), *Sources Chrétiennes* (= *SC*), 264, Paris, 1979 ; CLEMENT OF ALEXANDRIA, *Stromata* III, Cap. IV, *Die griechischen Christlichen Schriftsteller* (= *GCS*) 2 band (ed. O. STÄHLIN), Leipzig, 1906, 1, pp. 207-208. HIPPOLYTUS, *Refutatio omnium haeresium, GCS* 3 band (ed. P. WENDLAND), Leipzig, 1916. *Les Constitutions Apostoliques,* Tome II, Livres III-VI. (ed. M. METZGER), *SC* 329, Paris, 1986. FILASTRIUS OF BRESCIA, *Diversarum hereseon liber, CCSL* 9, pp. 227-ff. ; EPIPHANIUS OF SALAMIS, *Panarion haer.* (1-64), *GCS,* 2 band (ed. K. HOLLAND and J. DUMMER), Leipzig, 1915 and 1980. AUGUSTINE, *De haeresibus, CCSL* 46, pp. 283-358 ; VINCENT OF LÉRINS, *Commonitorium Excerpta, CCSL* 64, pp. 127-195. ISIDORE OF SEVILLE, *Etymologiarum* VIII, *De haeresibus Christianorum*, in *San Isidoro de Sevilla*, pp. 692-702.

14. Jerome more than any other contemporary writer of Priscillian went beyond the Manichaean-Gnostic association, although not everyone after him followed closely the arguments he brings forth in the letter. For example, AUGUSTINE, *De haeresibus*, 70, *CCSL* 46, p. 333. The *Constitutions of the Holy Apostles* identified a succession of all heretics from Simon Magus, 6. 8. 1, *SC* 329, pp. 314-317. Vincent of Lérins well after Jerome mentioned

Jerome began his list with a reference to Simon Magus, and for good reason. In all of the heretical lists Simon Magus consistently tops the list of Christian heresies and Irenaeus is the earliest source for this tradition[15]. The Church Fathers unanimously taught that Simon Magus is the 'spiritual father' of all heresy. Some sources such as Hippolytus's *Refutation of all Heresies*, *Constitutions of the Holy Apostles*, and the *Commonitorium* of Vincent of Lérins explicitly teach that all subsequent heretics either spiritually derive indirectly from Simon or are his direct 'successors'[16]. All of the heretics Jerome identified are understood to be pseudo-"spiritual successors" of Simon, and they all are spiritually embodied in Priscillian[17]. The position of both Simon and Priscillian at opposite ends of the list is not incidental. Simon and Priscillian appear as the Alpha and Omega of heresy, for all heresies ultimately are traceable to Simon. Jerome was quite conscious of the fact that in the New Testament it was the Apostle Peter that confronted, rebuked, and silenced Simon Magus[18]. Thus, Simon the "rock" crushed by his apostolic authority the other Simon, the 'magician', the anti-apostle who established a parallel pseudo-apostolic succession[19]. Again, the sources are clear on this encounter between Peter and

---

the succession, but Jerome provided in the letter the 'specific heretical links', between Simon and Priscillian, *Commonitorium*, *CCSL* 64, pp. 148-149, pp. 181 and 182.

15. IRENAEUS, *Contra haereses*, 1. 23. 1, *SC* 264, pp. 312-313. See A. LE BOULLUEC, *La notion d'hérésie dans la littérature grecque IIe-IIIe siècles*, vol. 1 : *De Justin à Irénée*, Paris, 1985, pp. 481-483 and 558, for further discussion on the concept of heretical succession.

16. Hippolytus voiced a similar opinion : *Refutatio omnium haeresium* 6. 7, *GCS* 3, pp. 134-135. *Constitutions of the Holy Apostles*, 6. 8. 1, *SC* 329, pp. 314-317, Eusebius of Caesarea had the same views : *HE*, 2. 13 (ed. G. BARDY), *SC* 31, pp. 66-68. [This edition reproduces the *GCS* text]. Pseudo-Tertullian called Simon Magus the "first" of all heretics : *Adversu.s omnes haereses. Tertulliani Opera,* pars II *opera Monastica, CCSL* 2. 2. p. 1401. VINCENT OF LÉRINS, *Commonitorium, CCLS* 64. p. 181.

17. The absence of specific language pointing to "succession" or "successors" of Simon Magus is readily evident in many early works on heresy, notably those by : IRENAEUS, *Contra haereses*, 1. 23. 2, *SC* 264, pp. 314-315, comes very close by saying that all heresies are "derived" from Simon Magus ; FILASTRIUS OF BRESCIA, *Diversarum hereseon liber*, 29, *CCSL* 9, p. 228. AUGUSTINE, *De haeresibus*, 1, *CCLS* 46, p. 290 ; They all gave Simon heretical primacy by positioning him first on their list of Christian heresies. Epiphanius of Salamis in the *Panarion* offers a more extensive dialogue on Simon and he used explicit language, but one that is still shy of the language that we find in the *Constitutions* or in Vincent of Lérins. Epiphanius said of Simon, «Simon Magus's makes the first sect to begin in the time since Christ», *Panarion haer.* 21, 1. 1, *GCS* 1, p. 238. The only 'succession' in Epiphanius is in regard to the Gnostics.

18. *Acts of the Apostles* 8. 9-25. The Simon Magus tradition in the *Apocryphal New Testament* has its own separate development which does not contribute directly to the pseudo-apostolic succession that we are pursuing in this portion of the article. I am, however, currently working on a booklength monograph on the figure of Simon Magus from the Early Church to the Reformation.

19. The idea of pseudo-apostolic succession is implicit in the heretical lists, particularly the early ones. The *Constitutions of the Holy Apostles*, voiced the precise language that

Simon, notably Eusebius of Caesarea ; and in Priscillian we find, spiritually speaking, an enemy of the apostles - and no less than the Apostle Peter - the one chosen by Christ to build his Church. Jerome in one stroke condemned Priscillian and advanced Petrine supremacy[20]. That Priscillian was considered by some to be the conglomeration of all previous heresies, thrown together, so to speak, is attested in a letter that Pope Leo I wrote against the Priscillianists[21]. In the preface to his lengthy critique of Priscillianism, the pope expressed his anguish over a heresy which combined the error of all previous heretical teaching. He warned : «Indeed, if all the heresies which have arisen before the time of Priscillian were to be considered diligently, hardly any error will be found by which this impiety has not been infected[22]».

Simon Magus is also accused of being intimate with a woman named Helena, who was his co-partner in propagating perverse doctrines[23]. Priscillian was likewise accused first of leading women astray into doctrinal error, and second of cavorting with these women in orgiastic fashion[24]. The patristic reference to

---

Jerome infused into his own list, see 6. 9. 6, *SC* 329, pp. 320-321. Consult A. LE BOULLUEC, *La notion d'hérésie* cited above in note 15.

20. Most of the sources remain true to the account in the *Acts of the Apostles*, but Eusebius used expressions like no other to describe the confrontation between Simon Peter and Simon Magus, for example, where he speaks of Simon and his followers negatively : *HE*, 2. 1. 10-12, *SC* 31, p. 51. Eusebius devoted chapter 13 to the origins of Simon, then, in chapter 14 he turned to Peter's ministry at Rome. Simon is considered the most formidable enemy of the Apostles : *HE*, 2. 13. 1 and 2. 14. 1, *SC* 31, p. 66-67 and 68, respectively. Finally Eusebius depicted Peter as the greatest of all Apostles who vanquished Simon Magus ; see *HE*, 2. 14, *SC* 31, pp. 68-70. For a partial discussion of Simon Magus and Eusebius, see B. PEARSON, «Eusebius and Gnosticism», in *Eusebius, Christianity and Judaism* (H.W. ATTRIDGE and G. HATA, eds.), *Studia Post Biblica*, 42, E.J. Brill, 1992, pp. 291-310.

21. In the letter Pope Leo I did not spare colorful graphic language to expose the depravity of the Priscillianists, *Ep.* 15, *praef, PL* 54, c. 678-679.

22. «Denique si universae haereses quae ante Priscilliani tempus exortae sunt diligentius retractentur, nullus pene invenietur error de quo non traxerit impietas ista contagium : quae non contenta eorum recipere falsitates qui ab Evangelio sub Christi nomine deviarunt, tenebris se etiam paganitatis immersit, ut per magicarum artium profana secreta et mathematicorum vana mendacia, religionis fidem morumque rationem in potestate daemonum, et in effectu siderum collocarent». (*Ep.* 15, *praef., PL* 54, c. 679).

23. JUSTIN MARTYR, *Apologia* 1. 26. *Florilegium Patristicum* (ed. G. RAUSCHEN), Bonnae 1904, pp. 39-42. IRENAEUS, *Contra haereses*, 1. 23. 2-4, *SC* 264, pp. 314-321. TERTULLIAN, *De anima*, 34, *CSEL* 20, pp. 358-360 ; HIPPOLYTUS, *Refutatio omnium haeresium*, 6. 19-20, *GCS* 3, pp. 145-148. EUSEBIUS OF CAESARIA, *HE*, 2. 13, *SC* 31, pp. 66-68. FILASTRIUS OF BRESCIA, *Diversarum hereseon liber*, 29, *CCSL* 9, p. 229 ; EPIPHANIUS, *Panarion haer.* 21, 2. 2-3. 6, *GCS* 1, pp. 239-242.

24. Sulpicius Severus reported the sexual deviancy of Priscillian : «Inde iter coeptum ingressi, turpi sane pudibundoque comitatu, cun uxoribus atque alienis etiam feminis, in quis erat Euchrotia ac filia eius Procula de qua fuit in sermone hominum Priscilliani stupro grauidam partum sibi graminibus abegisse», *Chron.* II, 48, *CSEL* 1, p. 101, and in 50, p. 103 ; Jerome elsewhere echoed this behavior : «soli cum solis clauduntur mulierculis et illud eis inter coitum amplexusque», *Ep.* 133. 3, *CSEL* 56, p. 245 ; Pope Leo I chastised the

---

Helena brought a deeper moral dimension to Jerome's commentary on Simon Magus. Jerome refered to Helena as a 'harlot', an insulting remark that invoked the sexual improprieties that accompany such an accusation. Irenaeus portrayed Helena as a woman created by the mind of Simon, and he seemed to have meant this quite literally. He also states that both were worshipped by their followers as Jupiter and Minerva, respectively[25]. Additionally, those who followed them built statues in their honor, and they made liberal use of love potions on each other, presumably to engage in illicit sexual activities[26]. Patristic writers were able to embody in Helena the sex, magic, and idolatry repeatedly associated later with the Priscillianists. Jerome never entertained the possibility that Helena, who accompanied Simon Magus, was initiating or participating in a "female succession" of heretics. The doctrine of apostolic succession, even in its pseudo-heretical form, is definitely confined to males. Helen although a culprit along with Simon Magus is perceived as dependent on him.

Jerome remained faithful to the patristic tradition in regard to Nicolas's strict succession from Simon Magus, but he shifted to the moral realm rather than doctrinal error only. Jerome did not ignore the moral dimension in Simon but his attention there was more on Simon as originator of doctrinal error. With

---

immorality of the Priscillianists, too : «Videbant enim omnem curam honestatis auferri, omnem conjugiorum copulam solvi, simulque divinum jus humanumque subverti», *PL* 54, c. 679-680. Also his remarks in 54, c. 683-684, 689 and 691. Finally, the Council of Braga (561) made the same accusations in canons 11 and 15, in *Concilios Visigóticos e Hispano-Romanos*, José VIVES (ed. et al), Barcelona-Madrid, 1963. pp. 68-69 [Hereafter *Concilios Visigóticos*].

25. *Contra haereses*, 1. 23. 4, *SC* 264, pp. 318-319. The most significant research on Simon Magus and Helena is : H. WAITZ, «Simon Magus in der altchristlichen Literatur», *Zeitschrift für die neutestamentliche Wissenschaft und die Kunde des Urchristentums* 5 (1904), pp. 138-140 ; L. H. VINCENT, «Le culte d'Hélène à Samarie», *Revue Biblique* 45 (1936), pp. 221-232, with plates of statuary ; G. QUISPEL, «Simon en Helena», *Nederlands Theologisch Tijdschritt* 5 (1951), pp. 339-345 ; L. CERFAUX, «Simon le Magicien à Samarie», *Recherches de Science Religieuse* 27 (1937), pp. 615-617 = reprinted in *Recueil L. Cerfaux*, Ed. J. DUCULOT & GEMBLOUX, 1954, pp. 259-262 ; G. ORY, «Le mythe Samaritain d'Hélène», *Cahiers du Cercle Ernest Renan* 3, 12 (1956), pp. 1-32 ; There are scattered references to Helena in J.M.A. SALLES-DABADIE, *Recherches sur Simon le Mage. 1, L'Apophasis megalè*, Cahiers de la Revue Biblique, 10, Paris, 1969 ; One of the most thorough treatments is by K. BEYSCHLAG, *Simon Magus und die Christliche Gnosis*, Wissenschaftliche Untersuchungen zum Neuen Testament, 16, Tübingen, 1974 ; G. LÜDEMANN, *Untersuchungen zur simonianischen Gnosis*, Göttingen, 1974, pp. 55-65. K. RUDOLPH, «Simon Magus oder Gnosticus ?», *Theologische Rundschau* 42 (1977), pp. 328-351 ; R. BERGMEIER, «Die Gestalt des Simon Magus in Act 8 und in der simonianischen Gnosis-Aporien einer Gesamtdeutung», *Zeitschrift für die Neutestamentliche Wissenschaft und die Kunde des Älteren Kirche*, 77 (1986), pp. 273-275 ; J. FOSSUM, «The Simonian Sophia Myth», *Studi e Materiali di Storia delle religioni , L'Aquila* 11 (1987), pp. 185-197. All of these studies provide extensive references to the sources and pertinent secondary literature.

26. *Contra haereses*, 1. 23.4, *SC*, 264, pp. 318-319. See also HIPPOLYTUS, *Refutatio omnium haeresium*, 6. 19-20, *GCS* 3, pp. 145-148, and for a summary of Simon's doctrines, p. 143.

Nicolas, Jerome did not bypass the doctrinal concerns altogether, yet it is abundantly clear that Nicolas embodies a "type" of all future moral heretics and that is why he called Nicolas the "deviser of all uncleanness[27]". As Simon is the font of doctrinal error, Nicolas is the wellspring of immorality. Jerome associated immoral behavior amongst the heretics every bit as much as doctrinal error.

The patristic commentary on Nicolas brings to the surface what Jerome wished to convey to Ctesiphon. Irenaeus established the tradition that Nicolas was one of seven deacons appointed by the apostles at Jerusalem[28]. In his *Against Heresies* he accused Nicolas and his followers of leading lives, "of unrestrained indulgence", which also included idolatry[29]. According to Irenaeus, the *Apocalypse* of John singled out Nicolas and the Nicolaitans for their immorality. Clement of Alexandria is less sure whether Nicolas actually founded the sect of the Nicolaitans[30]. Clement reports an incident, which he doubts to be true, and it is apparently the source of all of the negative rumors about Nicolas[31]. Nicolas allegedly brought his wife to the apostles, to whom he offered her up in marriage and encouraged her to "abuse the flesh", which Clement understood to mean Nicolas's renunciation of his own passions. Clement continued by pointing out that Nicolas never married again, his daughters remained virgins, and that even his son remained chaste[32]. In the latter tradition, Isidore of Seville in the *Etymologies* opted for the morally lapsed view

---

27. «Nicolaus Antiochenus, omnium inmunditiarum repertor, choros duxit femineos», *Ep.* 133. 4, *CSEL* 56, p. 248.

28. IRENAEUS, *Contra haereses*, 1. 26. 3, *SC* 264, pp. 348-349. PSEUDO-TERTULLIAN, *Adversus omnes haereses*, *CCSL* 2. 2, pp. 1402-1403.

29. *Contra haereses*, 1. 26. 3, *SC* 264, pp. 348-349.

30. CLEMENT OF ALEXANDRIA, *Strom.*, 3, 4, *GCS* 1, pp. 207-208. *The Constitutions of the Holy Apostles*, likewise cast doubt over the connection between Nicolas and the Nicolaitans, 6. 8. 2, *SC* 329, pp. 316-317. Epiphanius did not question this tradition, *Panarion haer.* 25, *GCS*, 1, pp. 267-274. In the latter tradition Nicolas is credited with the foundation of the sect, for example, Filastrius of Brescia seems to have adopted a neutral position - whether by intent is difficult to ascertain -, since he focused only on the 'person' rather than the 'sect'. *Diversarum hereseon liber*, 33, *CCSL* 9, p. 231. AUGUSTINE, *De haeresibus*, 5, *CCSL* 46, p. 291. ISIDORE OF SEVILLE followed the Augustinian tradition faithfully in Spain : *Etymologiarum* VIII, *De haeresibus Christianorum*, 8. 5. 5, in *San Isidoro de Sevilla*, pp. 693-695. On the Nicolaitans see P. PRIGENT, «L'hérésie asiate et l'église confessante de l'Apocalypse à Ignace», *Vigiliae Christianae* 31 (1977), pp. 1-22, especially pp. 10-22. Also his more comprehensive *L'Apocalypse de Jean. Commentaire du Nouveau Testament*, sér. II, 14, Genève, Labor et Fides, 1988.

31. *Strom.*, 3, 4, *GCS* 1, pp. 207-208.

32. *Strom.*, 3, 4, *GCS* 1, pp. 207-208. See also EUSEBIUS OF CAESAREA, *HE*, 3. 29. 1-4, *SC* 31, pp. 139-140. EPIPHANIUS OF SALAMIS, *Panarion haer.* 25, *GCS* 1, pp. 267-274. Some convey only that Nicolas had been a deacon, chosen by the Apostles, and who subsequently fell into doctrinal error. For example, see HIPPOLYTUS, *Refutatio omnium haeresium*, 7. 36, *GCS* 3, pp. 222-223. *Constitutions of the Holy Apostles*, 6. 8. 2, *SC*, 329, pp. 316-317. FILASTRIUS OF BRESCIA, *Diversarum hereseon liber*, *CCSL* 9, pp. 231-232. AUGUSTINE, *De haeresibus*, 5, *CCSL* 46, p. 291-292.

of Nicolas. Isidore repeated his appointment by Peter as deacon in Jerusalem, and he uncritically cited the doubtful story that Nicolas gave up his wife to be seduced by the apostles[33].

Jerome chose to ignore Clement and embrace the Irenaean tradition in which Nicolas was reprimanded for perverted sexual behavior. Priscillian was, then, the spiritual descendent of Simon in doctrinal error and of Nicolas in immorality. If one accepts Irenaeus's account, as with Simon, Nicolas was confronted, repudiated, and cast out by one of the most prominent apostles, John the beloved of Christ. With this line of reasoning the Priscillianists, as all heretics, are opposed to apostolic teaching and morality.

Jerome associated Nicolas with the companionship of "bands of women", a view that ignored a good portion of patristic writers, notably Clement but again borrowing heavily from Irenaeus[34]. This view of Nicolas cavorting with numerous women is consistent with the alleged behavior associated with Priscillian, especially in Sulpicius Severus and Pope Leo I[35]. Sulpicius singled out specific women supposedly sexually involved with Priscillian, such as Procula, who allegedly became pregnant and had an abortion[36]. In other places, Priscillian is depicted participating in sexual orgies and nude liturgical services. These allegations are echoes of the somewhat obscure Adamite sect frequently mentioned in some heretical lists[37]. Such rumors seems to have been behind the conciliar prohibition at the Council of Zaragoza (380) that women should stay away from other men [Priscillianists][38]. At the outset Jerome established the two

---

33. *Etymologiarum* VIII, *De haeresibus Christianorum* 8. 5. 5, in *San Isidoro de Sevilla*, p. 694. The bishop of Seville closed his observations with the Apostle John's condemnation of Nicolas, a clear scriptural reference to the Nicolaitans in the Apocalyse. *Ibid*, «Quos Iohannes in *Apocalypsi* inprobat dicent (2. 6) : 'Sed hoc habes quod odisti facta Nicolaitarum'».

34. *Ep*. 133. 4, *CSEL* 56, p. 248.

35. See note 27 above.

36. «Cum uxoribus atque alienis etiam feminis, in quis erat Euchrotia ac filia eius Procula, de qua fuit in sermone hominum Priscilliani stupro grauidam partum sibi graminibus abegisse», SULPICIUS SEVERUS, *Chron*. II, 48, *CSEL* 1, p. 101. See note 24 above.

37. Sulpicius referred to nude prayer services, *Chron*. II, 50, *CSEL* 1. p. 103. Jerome specifically mentioned this practice. *Ep*. 133. 3, *CSEL* 56, p. 245. What is readily evident from this study is the fact that most heretical sects were accused of nudity, sexual liberties, and other related practices. Augustine included the Adamites in his list, *De haeresibus*, 31, *CCSL* 46, pp. 304-305.

38. «Ut mulieres omnes ecclesiae catholicae et fideles a vivorum alienorum lectione et coetibus separentur, vel ad ipsas legentes aliae studio vel docendi vel discendi conveniant, quoniam hoc Apostolus iubet. Ab universis episcopis dictum est : Anathema futuros qui hanc concilii sententiam non observaverint», canon 1, *Concilios Visigóticos*, p. 16. The most thorough treatment of the Council of Zaragoza is the collection of essays in *I Concilio Caesaraugustano. MDC Aniversario*, Zaragoza, 25-27 de septiembre de 1980, Zaragoza, 1980. In the same volume, see specifically the essay by J.M. BLÁZQUEZ, «Prisciliano, introductor del ascetismo en Hispania. Las fuentes. Estudio de la investigación moderna», pp. 65-121. See also F. BOLGIANI, «La polemica di Clemente Alessandrino contra gli gnostici

major foundations upon which the remaining heresiarchical structure rests, and he found his pillars in the men Simon/Nicolas, and the women Helena/Bands of Women.

Jerome accused Marcion and an unidentified woman of collaborating together to deceive men, particularly at Rome[39]. Marcion certainly represents more than a male who cavorted with questionable women, for he was better known for his role in the debates over the Canon of the New Testament, and its relationship with the Old Testament.

Irenaeus mentioned Marcion, within the context of other heretics, whom he also accused of being disciples and successors of Simon Magus. Concerning any immoral behavior with women, or of employing female emissaries, he is completely silent[40]. The Pseudo-Tertullian reported that Marcion was "excommunicated because of a rape committed on a certain virgin[41]". Jerome's belief that Marcion sent a woman to Rome to deceive men is equally isolated and is not corroborated by any previous or contemporary writers. In this manner Jerome was able to maintain both the male heretical successions and the parallel list of female "followers". The male line with Marcion is based firmly on a well established growing tradition ; whereas the female line is more the imagination of Jerome, and one that certainly modified the story of the virgin related by Pseudo-Tertullian. I believe that Jerome's reference to Rome is an allusion to St. Peter, symbolically pitting Marcion against the "Chief of the Apostles[42]".

There is more, typologically speaking, to consider about Marcion and for what he was best known, the debate over the Canon of Scripture. According to the tradition, Marcion had rejected the Old Testament as inconsistent with the spirit and message of the New Testament ; furthermore his selection of the latter testament was to be found within an even narrower corpus of gospels and epistles. As far as Jerome was concerned the question of the Canon was a closed topic settled by the Church in earlier times. The case of Priscillian is an example

---

libertini nel III libro degli Stromati», in *Studi in onore di A. Pincherle. Studi e Materiali di storia delle religiosi*, 38, 2 vols., Roma, 1967, pp. 86-136.

39. «Marcion Romam praemisit mulierem, quae deceptarum sibi animos praepararet», *Ep*. 133. 4, *CSEL* 56, p. 248. See also A. SALLES, «Simon le Magicien ou Marcion ?», *Vigiliae Christianae* 12, 4 (1958), pp. 197-224.

40. IRENAEUS, *Contra haereses*, 1. 27. 1-4, *SC* 264, pp. 348-355. The same is true of the testimony found in Hippolytus and Eusebius who did not intimate that Marcion had misbehaved with any women. HIPPOLYTUS, *Refutatio omnium haeresium*, 10. 19, *GCS* 3, pp. 279-280. EUSEBIUS OF CAESAREA, *HE*, 4. 11. 8-10, *SC* 31, pp. 175-176. Filastrius of Brescia, Augustine, and Isidore of Seville likewise did not connect Marcion with any female followers. FILASTRIUS OF BRESCIA, *Diversarum hereseon liber*, 44, *CCSL* 9, p. 236. AUGUSTINE, *De haeresibus*, 22, *CCSL* 46, pp. 299-300. *Etymologiarum* VIII, *De haeresibus Christianorum*, 8. 5. 21, in *San Isidoro de Sevilla*, p. 695.

41. PSEUDO-TERTULLIAN, *Adversus omnes haereses*, *CCSL* 2. 2, p. 1408.

42. *Ep*. 133. 4, *CSEL* 56, p. 248. A tantalizing element in Irenaeus and Eusebius is the specific inclusion of Rome and the papacy in their entries on Marcion. In Irenaeus, Cerdo and Marcion are treated together : *Contra haereses* 1. 27. 1-4, *SC*, 264, pp. 348-355. Eusebius quoted Irenaeus on these matters as his chief source : *HE*, 4. 11, *SC* 31, pp. 173-176.

that for some the Canon was still a matter of discussion, and a dialogue filled with controversy. Jerome spoke for what was rapidly emerging as the consensus Catholic view of the Canon, whereas Priscillian - as Jerome saw him - was the symbolic Marcionite vestige who would violate the Scripture as found in both testaments. There is a consistent litany of charges levelled against Priscillian for his use of apocryphal or non-canonical books[43]. The reference to apocryphal works seems to point to Priscillian's own writings and Gnostic gospels and epistles. The First Council of Braga (561) whose primary agenda was to deal with an apparently strong persistent Priscillianism in Galicia, referred to these books :

«It is not proper to recite in church psalms composed by laymen nor to read books that are outside the canonical books of the New and Old Testament[44]».

The subject of the Canon was continued with vigor by Jerome in the section on Apelles and the prophetess Philumena, about whom he says, "Apelles possessed in Philumena a companion in his doctrines[45]". The parallel with Jerome's earlier comments about Simon and Helena is striking.

---

43. Irenaeus singled out this issue, too, *Contra haereses*, 1. 27. 2, *SC* 264, pp. 350-351. Filastrius of Brescia also commented on Marcion's canonical preferences : *Diversarum hereseon liber*, 44, *CCSL* 9, p. 236. Also relevant is his entry, 88, pp. 255-256. Some of the testimony includes Pope Leo I, in an indirect reference to tampering with the holy books, «per ipsos doctrinae Priscillianae Evangelium subditur Christi, ut ad profanos sensus pietate sanctorum voluminum depravat, sub nominibus prophetarum et apostolorum non hoc praedicetur quod Spiritus sanctus docuit, sed quod diaboli minister inseruit», *Ep.* 15, *praef.*, *PL* 54, c. 680, see also c. 687-688. Augustine devoted an entire letter to this topic : *Ep.* 237, *CSEL* 57, pp. 526-532 ; and *De haeresibus*, 70, *CCSL* 46, pp. 333-334. There are other references in VINCENT OF LÉRINS, *Commonitorium, CCSL* 64, p. 182. More explicitly at the First Council of Toledo (400) : «Et cum accepisset chartulam, de scripto recitavit: Omnes libros haereticos, et maxime Priscilliani doctrinam, iuxa quod hodie lectum est», and in the same council, «nullis libris apocryphis aut novis scientiis, quas Priscillianus composuerat involutum... quaecumque contra fidem catholicam Priscillianus scripserat cum ipso auctore damnasse», *Concilios Visigóticos*, pp. 29, 30-31 and 33, also the First Council of Braga (561), *Concilios Visigóticos*, pp. 69, 73. Jerome addressed the use of extra-biblical sources and the writing of books by the Priscillianists in several works, and in some cases indirectly, such as, his *Commentariorum in Esaiam. Libri XII-XVIII, CCSL* 73A. S. *Hieronymi Presbyteri Opera*, Pars 1, 2 A, p. 735. Another indirect citation is in *Praefatio S. Hieronymi in Pentateuchum*, *PL* 28, c. 180-181. Also, but more directly, in *De viris inlustribus*, 121, 122, 123, (ed. W. HERDING), pp. 62-63, = *PL* 23, c. 750-751. See the edition by R. BRAUN, *Contre Marcion*, 2 t., *SC* 365, 368, Paris, 1990, 1991.

44. Canon 12, p. 73, note in the same council, canon 17 which was directed at Priscillian : «Si quis scribturas, quas Priscillianus secundum suum depravarit errorem vel tractatos Dictinii quos ipse Dictinius antequam converteretur...», *Concilios Visigóticos*, p. 69.

45. «Apelles Philumenem suarum comitem habuit doctrinarum» : *Ep.* 133. 4, *CSEL* 56, p. 248. A rather startling gap in the testimony on this sect is the absence of Philumena, for example : FILASTRIUS OF BRESCIA, *Diversarum hereseon liber*, 47, *CCSL* 9, p. 237 ; EPIPHANIUS, *Panarion haer.* 44, *GCS* 2, pp. 189-199 ; AUGUSTINE, *De haeresibus*, 23, *CCSL* 46, p. 300 and ISIDORE OF SEVILLE, *Etymologiarum* VIII ; *De haeresibus Christianorum*, 8. 5. 12, in *San Isidoro de Sevilla*, p. 695.

Tertullian in several works directed his attention to Apelles and Philumena. Firstly, he established the heretical lineage, that Jerome found useful in his polemic. Tertullian in his *On Prescription Against Heretics* taught that Apelles had been a disciple of Marcion, but that Apelles forsook continence ; thus precipitating a schism between them, a story he repeated in the *On the Flesh of Christ*[46]. In the former work Tertullian identified the woman as being from Alexandria, and in both works he says that Apelles forsook her in order to take up an affair with Philumena, whom he colorfully calls "an enormous prostitute", and in either case both were illicit unions[47]. It is rather surprising in view of what the Pseudo-Tertullian *Against All Heresies* said about Marcion earlier that he appears as more sexually continent than Apelles. The Pseudo-Tertullian was not consistent here, although most of the remaining sources do repeat the continence of Marcion[48]. It is also here that we are introduced to the spiritual dimension of this heresy. Pseudo-Tertullian, after alerting the readers to the carnality of these heretics, continued to call Philumena a prophetess that apparently seduced Apelles[49]. Jerome who was well acquainted with this commentary helped Ctesiphon make the spiritual associations between them and the Priscillianists.

Hippolytus elaborated the spiritual dimension of Apelles and Philumena in his work *Refutation of all Heresies*. Apelles «devotes himself to the discourses of a certain Philumena as to the revelations of a prophetess, and to a book which he calls *Revelations*[50]». The reference to a prophetess and a book called *Revelations* is clearly an issue directly related to the question of Canon. Again, as far as Jerome was concerned there were no other books outside of the Vulgate Canon that could be legitimately called upon as authoritative, much less apostolic. Add to all of these concerns the woman, Philumena. the "enomorous prostitute" (as Tertullian called her), the mediatrix of these prophecies. Jerome had about as tight a case against this heresy as any orthodox zealot could ever wish for, and the connections he made with Priscillian require little imagination on our part.

The moral impropriety of Apelles and Philumena, along with the prominent role of the latter, are similar to practices associated with Priscillian. The question of the Canon in relation to Philumena's book of *Revelations* is

---

46. *De praescriptione haereticorum*, 30, *CSEL* 70, p. 37 in the same work, 33, pp. 41-42 ; also his, *De carne Christi* 6, *CSEL* 70, p. 203 in the same work chapter 8, pp. 212-214. See also, J.P. MAHÉ, *La chair du Christ*, 2 t., SC 216, 217, Paris, 1975. Tertullian referred to Apelles and Philumena in *Adversus Marcionem*, *Tertulliani Opera*, *pars* 1, 3, 11. and 4, 17, *CCSL* 1, pp. 521-523 and 585-588. And, *De anima*, 23 and 26, *CSEL* 20, pp. 335-336 ; 362-363.

47. «Postea vero immane prostibulum et ipsam» : *De praescriptione haereticorum*, 30, *CSEL* 70, p. 37. Eusebius adds little to the previous commentary in general, but he too did not spare negative language concerning Philumena : *HE*, 5. 13. 2, *SC* 41, pp. 42-43.

48. See note 40 above.

49. PSEUDO-TERTULLIAN, *Adversus omnes haereses*, *CCSL* 2. 2, p. 1409.

50. HIPPOLYTUS, *Refutatio omnium haeresium*, 7. 38, *GCS* 3, p. 224 and 10. 20, *GCS* 3, pp. 280-281.

certainly reflected in the apocryphal books associated with Priscillian. Jerome also maintained the succession of heretics since it was widely believed that Apelles had been a disciple of Marcion. Jerome did depart from the patristic commentary in how he depicted the relationship between Apelles and Philumena. Jerome spoke of Philumena as an "associate" of Apelles, whereas, in Hippolytus, Apelles is virtually led and spellbound by Philumena[51]. The relationship Jerome espoused was especially consistent with the Priscillian tradition regarding the woman Agape as we shall see below. Priscillian is spoken of as both leading astray or being swayed by women, but he is most frequently portrayed as the "man" in charge[52]. Jerome obviously desired to maintain at this juncture a line of male heretics assisted by women who propagate the message of their male teachers.

In Montanus Jerome arrived at the end of what he called "ancient history", and in numerous ways he continued to challenge the question of extra-biblical revelation as before with Marcion and Apelles. Jerome singled out both spiritual and moral lapses, calling Montanus "that mouthpiece of an unclean spirit", who was also guilty of leading astray "two wealthy and high born ladies, Prisca and Maximilla[53]". Montanus allegedly used the two women to bribe and sexually pervert many churches[54]. In summary, Jerome alerted his readers that the Montanists gave women a prominent role, claimed to have additional messages from God, and much more besides.

As with Apelles and Philumena, the primary practice of the Montanists that Jerome focused upon was their self-proclaimed belief that God spoke to them directly as he had done with the apostles. Tertullian in *A Treatise on the Soul* reported that a Montanist woman claimed to receive visions, to talk to angels - even Jesus himself - and to be able to discern people's hearts[55]. Hippolytus taught that Montanists preached a message which they believed superceded that given by Christ[56]. Apollonius in *Concerning Montanism* accused Montanist women of leaving their husbands, taking gifts and money, lending on interest ;

---

51. Jerome used "comitem habuit" to describe their relationship, such an association is certainly not reflected in most of the sources, *Ep.* 133. 4, *CSEL* 56, p. 248.

52. Especially in the *Chronicon* of Sulpicius Severus : «Is ubi doctrinam exitiabilem aggressus est, multos nobilium pluresque populares auctoritate persuadendi et arte blandiendi allicuit in societatem. ad hoc mulieres nouarum rerum cupidae, fluxa fide et ad omnia curioso ingenio, cateruatim ad eum confluebant» (*Chron.* II, 46, *CSEL* 1, pp. 99-100).

53. «Montanus, inmundi spiritus praedicator, multas ecclesias per Priscam et Maximillam, nobiles et opulentas feminas, primum auro corrupit ; dein heresi polluit. dimittam uetera, ad uiciniora transcendam», *Ep.* 133. 4, *CSEL* 56, p. 248. AUGUSTINE, *De haeresibus* 26 and 27, *CCSL* 46, pp. 302-303.

54. In Sulpicius the charge of bribery is singled out as yet another of the moral lapses of the Priscillianists. Some examples in the *Chronicon* are 48 and 49, *CSEL* 1, pp. 101-103.

55. *De anima*, 9, *CSEL* 20, p. 310.

56. HIPPOLYTUS, *Refutatio omnium haeresium*, 8. 19, *GCS* 3, p. 238. Also, EPIPHANIUS, *Panarion haer.* 4. 8, *GCS* 2, p. 219-241.

and if that were not enough, a weakness for expensive clothes, jewelry, including an appetite for gambling[57].

Jerome revealed some of his views on the Montanists in *Letter* 41, wherein he targeted the prophetic-revelation message of this sect. He commenced with a reference to the "Day of Pentecost" as a unique event that in itself was a fulfilled final event[58]. Apparently, if we are to believe Jerome, the Montanists claimed a somewhat similar outpouring of the Spirit, which *de facto* made their message equal to the apostles, if not superior[59]. The True Church, continued Jerome, was inaugurated at Pentecost, and it is from those apostles *only* that legitimate successors proceed. Jerome qualified his previous statements, where he affirmed that he did not oppose prophecy, only that type which claimed to supercede the revelation of Scripture[60]. He fully agreed with previous commentators who attacked the Montanist claim of an exclusive fullness of apostolic knowledge not possessed or received by anyone else.

The parallels that Jerome desired to make between the Montanists and Priscillianists seemed to be the following. Earlier in section three of *Letter* 133 Jerome said Priscillianists «are rash enough to claim for themselves the twofold credit of perfection and wisdom[61]». When Priscillian was blamed for leading women astray, these were usually socially high born and wealthy, like Prisca and Maximilla. Sulpicius Severus similarly attributed to the Priscillianists bribery and other forms of irresponsible uses of money to buy influence and power[62]. The 'unclean spirit' that spoke through Montanus was Jerome's way of establishing the satanic origins of both Montanists and Priscillianists.

The prominent role of women in both sects is all too obvious. Equally significant was the widely held tradition that Montanus and Maximilla committed suicide and died a tragic death, as all heretics, figuratively speaking, ultimately do. In both incidents the heretics met death and Jerome's statement that Priscillian was «condemned by the whole world and put to death by the

---

57. EUSEBIUS, *HE*, 5. 18. 3-4, *SC* 41, p. 56. Consult, Asterius Urbanus in EUSEBIUS, *HE*, 5. 16-17, *SC* 41, pp. 46-54.

58. *Ep.* 41, 1, *CSEL* 54, pp. 311-312.

59. Hippolytus shared this opinion, *Refutatio omnium haeresium* 8. 19, *GCS* 3, pp. 238. FILASTRIUS OF BRESCIA, *Diversarum hereseon liber*. 49, *CCSL* 9. p. 238. There is a rich tradition on the biblical exegesis of 'Babel and Pentecost' see my «Linguarum diversitate : 'Babel and Pentecost' in Leander's homily at the Third Council of Toledo», *Actas del XIV Centenario del Concilio III de Toledo 589-1989*, Toledo 10-14, May, 1989. Toledo 1991 pp. 237-248. JEROME, *Ep*. 41, 1, *CSEL* 54, pp. 311-312.

60. JEROME, *Ep*. 41, 1, *CSEL* 54, p. 312. Augustine repeated with no innovation the corpus of earlier writers, *De haeresibus*, 26 and 27, *CCSL* 46. pp. 302-303. Isidore of Seville referred to the alleged Montanist belief that they possessed a superior revelation, *Etymologiarum* VIII, *De haeresibus Christianorum* 8. 5. 27, in *San Isidoro de Sevilla*, p. 696.

61. «uerbum perfectionis, et scientiae sibi temere uindicantes», *Ep.* 133. 3, *CSEL* 56, p. 245.

62. See note 54 above.

secular sword» should be interpreted within this framework[63]. And from this point onward Jerome turned his attention to heretical groups that flourished in his own words, "to times nearer to our own", and so he set his sights upon Arius[64].

Arianism in Jerome's day was a heresy that still raged in the East and one contemporaneous with Priscillianism. Jerome blamed Arius for leading the world astray, and also for "beguiling the Emperor's sister[65]". This sister was Constantia, who exemplified yet another "high born woman", led astray by a heretic. Briefly told, Constantia was deceived by a presbyter in the royal palace, who was, in a sense, a "closet" Arian, one who believed that Arius had been misrepresented and unjustly condemned at Nicaea. It seems the presbyter persuaded Constantia of Arius' innocence, then she in turn made efforts to convince her brother, the Emperor, to reconsider Arius' condemnation[66].

Jerome was intent on associating Priscillian with the Arian heresy especially its Trinitarian theology. It was exceedingly desirable, if not crucial, for Jerome to establish a "heretical" link between Priscillian and Arianism, the most explosive theological heresy of the fourth century[67]. Jerome's direct association of Arius with Priscillian is unique since the major contemporary sources, notably Sulpicius Severus and the Council of Zaragoza (380), do not specifically call Priscillian an Arian.

Such Arian associations were creatively made in the latter sources, such as, the First Council of Braga (561) and the letter of Pope Leo I[68]. At the First Council of Braga Arius is not specifically mentioned by name in relation to Priscillian, but such an omission is not insurmountable. The initial four canons that condemn Priscillian address his Trinitarian doctrine, and if what they relate is accurate, they are without question Arian views[69]. I have noted elsewhere that Arianism, which had been pervasive in Galicia prior to the council, is not mentioned specifically in the least. The bishops, as I have argued, believed that Arianism was dead, at least officially, since the Suevic monarchy no longer

---

63. See EUSEBIUS OF CAESARIA, *HE* 5.16. 13, *SC* 41, p. 50.

64. *Dimittam uetera, ad uiciniora transcendam, Ep.* 133. 4, *CSEL* 56, p. 248.

65. *Arius, ut orbem caperet, sororem principis ante decepit, Ep.* 133. 4, *CSEL* 56, p. 248.

66. See, SOZOMEN, *HE*, 2. 27, *SC* 306 (trans. André-Jean FESTUGIÈRE) Paris, 1983. pp. 348-355. The editor notes that Sozomen is following both Rufinus (*HE* 1 (x), 12) and Socrates Scholasticus (*HE* 1, 25), p. 349. Constantia is not mentioned in FILASTRIUS OF BRESCIA *Diversarum hereseon liber* 66, *CCSL* 9, p. 244. AUGUSTINE, *De haeresibus*, 49, *CCSL* 46, pp. 320-321. ISIDORE OF SEVILLE, *Etymologiarum* VIII, *De haeresibus Christianorum* 8. 5. 43, in *San Isidoro de Sevilla*, p. 698.

67. The literature on Arianism is extensive. For an introduction in a broader context and with detailed current bibliography see, W.H.C. FREND, *The Rise of Christianity*, Philadelphia, Fortress Press, 1984. Consult R.P.C. HANSON, *The Search for the Christian Doctrine of God. The Arian Controversy 318-381*, Edinburgh, T&T Clark, 1988, pp. 516-530.

68. Pope Leo I, *Ep.* 15, *PL* 54, c. 678-695. First Council of Braga (561), *Concilios Visigóticos*, pp. 65-77.

69. First Council of Braga (561), *Concilios Visigóticos*, pp. 67-68.

claimed to be followers of Arianism[70]. In Galicia bolder claims for the eradication of heresy, both Arian and Priscillianist, were announced at the Second Council of Braga of 572. In the opening speech it was declared «through the help of Christ's grace there is no doubt about the unity and orthodoxy of the faith in this province[71]». It was alarming enough to admit to the possibility of one heresy in that province [Priscillianism], it was quite another matter to affirm Arianism, particularly in view of its most recent official extirpation. In the four canons of the First Council of Braga Priscillian was associated with numerous heretics, they are all 'safely' in the distant past, however[72].

A letter of Pope Leo I was read by the bishops at the First Council of Braga (561), and it appears to have been the singular major document used against the Priscillianists[73]. The pope mentioned these heretics by name in regard to the Trinity : Sabellius, Paul of Samosata, and Photinus, all later identified at the Council. He pressed further on the Trinity to refute Priscillian when he said : "In this they also pursue the Arian's mistake". We are to understand "also" as a reference to an earlier section in the letter where Pope Leo I had already dealt point by point with Priscillianist Trinitarianism[74]. The bishops gathered at Braga chose not to mention Arianism specifically as found in Leo's letter.

Constantia does not occupy a central role in Arianism, but for Jerome's purposes she became an important feminine connection with the preceding male heretics and their female companions. She is also exemplary of a heretical woman easily swayed into heresy and scheming behind the scenes.

Jerome moves on to address the Donatists. Donatus and Lucilia are blamed for «defiling with his polluting baptism many unhappy people in Africa», and what that baptism entailed theologically is what Jerome wanted to bring to the surface[75]. The Donatist debate centered upon the legitimacy of bishops, who had lapsed during persecution and then after the persecution lifted asked to be reinstated. The Donatists argued against the *traditores* [bishops] who cooperated with the Imperial authorities in handing over religious books. The Donatist church emphatically required re-baptism as a necessary prerequisite to mend the treasonous past of the *traditores* ; the Catholics argued otherwise on all of these

---

70. «The Missionary Labors of St. Martin of Braga in 6th Century Galicia», *Studia Monastica* 23, 1 (1981), pp. 19-20.

71. *«Et quia opitulante Christi gratia de unitate et rectitudine fidei in hac provincia nicil [sic] es dubium»*, *Concilios Visigóticos*, p. 79.

72. For example «sicut Sabellius et Priscillianus dixerunt», canons 1, 2, 3, and 4, *Concilios Visigóticos*, pp. 67-68.

73. First Council of Braga (561), *Concilios Visigóticos*, p. 66.

74. «Quod blasphemiae genus de Sabellii opinione sumpserunt» (15, 3) ; «Quod utique non auderent dicere, nisi Pauli Samosateni et Photini» (15, 2), And more directly on the Arian affiliation : «In quo Arianorum quoque suffragantur errori» (*Ep.* 15, 1, *PL* 54, c. 681).

75. «Donatus, per Africam ut infelices quosque fetentibus pollueret aquis, Lucillae opibus adiutus est», *Ep.* 133. 4, *CSEL* 56, p. 248. Consult also, AUGUSTINE, *Contra Litteras Petiliani Libri Tres* 1, *CSEL* 52, pp. 3-23. *S. Optati Milevitani Libri VII* 1, 16-20, *CSEL* 26, pp. 18-22.

points[76]. I have reduced the complexities of Donatism to single out those areas that Jerome could have associated with Priscillian. Four areas that serve Jerome's intent were : the concept of *traditores* ; the illegitimacy of bishops ; the sectarian nature of Donatism ; and the role of Lucilla.

The denunciation of *traditores* leveled by the Donatists was a charge readily reversed by the Catholics and applied to all heretics. In the spiritual sense heretics have betrayed the sacred message that had been given to the Church, and they have 'chosen' not to maintain the whole counsel of God. The Donatists were rebuked for calling themselves the 'True Church' and excluding all others who were not of their [true] fold. Donatism was meant by Jerome to force this message : the Priscillianists are traitors of the faith who have falsely passed themselves off as the 'true heirs' of apostolic teaching.

The second issue in Donatism focused upon the legitimacy of bishops. The posture of the Donatists rejected *in toto* the ecclesiastical structure of the Catholics, for that matter of any other 'church' as well. A major episode in Priscillian's career was his consecration as bishop of Avila[77]. Priscillian was consecrated by bishops who had abandoned Catholic orthodoxy to pursue him as their leader. The emergence of a parallel Church, accompanied with its own episcopacy, was a major concern of Sulpicius Severus[78]. Priscillian could not claim any apostolic legitimacy as a bishop, nor could those who were consecrated by him, nor any self-styled successors after his death. Jerome would have Ctesiphon recall that the only succession these bishops belonged to was the pseudo-apostolic one inaugurated by Simon Magus. Jerome apparently really believed, in the spiritual sense, that there existed an antiapostolic succession parallel to that of the Apostles. In both successions it is the Holy Spirit and the spirit of the Evil One that propagate them, respectively. Like the Donatists, the Priscillianists do not have a theological apostolic foundation to legitimize the existence or propagation of their church. Priscillian seemed to have required re-baptism, as the Donatists had done, but the canons of the First Council of Toledo (400) do not specify what distinguished the rite of baptism of the Priscillianists and Catholics[79].

An important corollary issue invoked in such debates between Catholics and heretics, before and after this era, has to do with the sectarian nature of heretics. Jerome deliberately mentioned Africa not just for geographical accuracy ; rather, to draw attention to the parochial nature of this sect, which unlike the Catholics had a more limited following. In the final analysis, not a single heresy

---

76. See the seminal study by W.H.C. FREND, *The Donatist Church*, 2nd ed. Oxford, 1971.

77. SULPICIUS SEVERUS, *Chron.* II, 47, *CSEL* 1, pp. 100-101.

78. Sulpicius described graphically the deep division Priscillianism caused, even well after the execution : «At inter nostros perpetuum discordiarum bellum exarserat, quod iam per quindecim annos foedis dissensionibus agitatum nullo modo sopiri poterat», *Chron.* II, 51, *CSEL* 1, p. 105.

79. The reference to baptism is in canon 18 : «Si quis in his erroribus Priscilliani secta sequitur vel profitetur, ut aliud in salutare baptismi contra sedem sancti Petri faciat, anathema sit», *Concilios Visigóticos*, p. 28.

could claim universal acceptance, an argument frequently voiced by the Catholics. Jerome applied such a judgment to this local sect in Spain. Although Priscillian did claim a following in Gaul, the Priscillianists could never in good faith claim universal acceptance. The frequent allusions to St. Peter via Simon Magus, the reference to Rome, and the sectarianism of this sect that are couched in Jerome's letter were intended to pit Priscillian in opposition to the universal church, a position pressed increasingly by the bishops of Rome[80]. Finally, as with Arius and Constantia, Lucilla did not occupy a very significant place in the Donatist debate. We do know that she was a noble woman from Carthage and a strong supporter of the Donatists against the Catholics[81]. Jerome did not fail to make the typological connection between Lucilla and the women who followed Priscillian.

Jerome finally focused upon the Iberian Peninsula, where «in Spain the blind woman Agape led the blind man Elpidius into the ditch[82]». There is a remarkable resemblance in this relationship with that of Apelles and Philumena. In this section, however, Jerome introduced some very interesting twists to the relationship between Agape and Priscillian. Agape, the woman, is the primary culprit who leads Elpidius astray into spiritual blindness, but there is more. Jerome also adds in what is a remarkable departure from his list of previous heretics *successoremque sui Priscillianum habuit*. If *habuit* has Agape as the subject then this makes Priscillian her successor, and this is the most likely reading according to Virginia Burrus[83]. Agape is culpable of deceiving both Elpidius and Priscillian. Agape's alleged engendering of a successor in Priscillian provides the 'type' of a woman pretending to be a teacher of men and propagating spiritual offspring. At this point in the letter Jerome has reached the apogee of his narrative and Agape's activity is the most damning evidence of heretical behavior, an indictment against Pelagian and Priscillianist women. Jerome gave Agape the principal credit for being a teacher of Priscillian as an example of the grossest violation of apostolic succession. Agape is also Jerome's 'spiritual link' to connect Priscillian with Marcus of Memphis. We also do not need to hold Jerome here to fostering an *immediate* succession from

---

80. In the First Council of Braga (561), the bishops gathered specifically pointed out that Pope Leo I was [about or approximately -Latin *-Fere*] the fortieth successor of St. Peter *beatissimus papa urbis Romae Leo, qui quadragesimus fere extitit apostoli Petri successor*, *Concilios Visigóticos*, p. 66. Also in canon 18 of the First Council of Toledo (400) it is expressed specifically that Priscillian is in direct opposition to St. Peter, *Concilios Visigóticos*, p.28.

81. Lucilla is not reported at all by Filastrius of Brescia, Augustine, nor by Isidore of Seville. Filastrius devotes little space to the Donatists : *Diversarum hereseon liber* 83, *CCSL* 9, p. 253. Augustine's entry on the Donatists is one of his lengthiest : *De haeresibus*, 69, *CCSL* 46, pp. 331-333. Isidore is very brief : *Etymologiarum* VIII, *De haeresibus Christianorum* 8. 5. 51, in *San Isidoro de Sevilla*, p. 698.

82. *In Hispania Agape Elpidium, mulier uirum, caecum caeca duxit in foueam*, *Ep*. 133. 4, *CSEL* 56, p. 248.

83. *Ep*. 133. 4, *CSEL* 56, p. 248. See V. BURRUS, *Making of a heresy*, pp. 210-211, note 90.

Agape ; rather it seems to be a 'typological' succession, just as Priscillian is a successor of all of the heretics in the list. Jerome brings this novel "succession" to an abrupt halt in his ensuing statement where he says that Priscillian engendered the woman 'Galla' and in this fashion reestablishes the masculine succession. Jerome may have borrowed his information from Sulpicius Severus and the latter created a nexus between the Gnostics and Priscillian, a link that by his own admission was "not at all easy to explain[84]". According to Sulpicius, a Gnostic Marcus of Memphis was the first to introduce Gnosticism into the Iberian Peninsula, and Agape and Elpidius were his first pupils. They, in turn, were the teachers of Priscillian. Another unique aspect about them is that neither are found in any other heretical lists.

Of Agape and Elpidius we know nothing else, but of Marcus there is plenty in the patristic sources, and Jerome had already identified Marcus in his *Commentaries on Isaiah* (17. 64. 4-5) as the Gnostic heretic 'behind' Agape. In a letter to Theodora, Jerome commented more about Marcus, citing Irenaeus as his major source. He erroneously called Marcus a disciple of Basilides. In the remainder of his exposition Jerome was consistent with the previous commentaries on Marcus. Jerome accused Marcus of misleading unlearned men and high-born women, and of engaging in unlawful intercourse[85]. The *Constitutions of the Holy Apostles* called Marcus a spiritual successor of Simon Magus and Hippolytus reports that Marcus even allowed women to offer up the Eucharist[86]. For Jerome's purpose Marcus confirms the illicit sexual behavior of heretics, the sexually loose women heretics tend to attract, the seduction of weak-minded uneducated men, and lastly but no less important, the unbroken succession with Simon Magus.

The reference to Marcus is not without its problems as Virginia Burrus alerts us. Jerome links Priscillian with the Marcus identified by Irenaeus in several places. Sulpicius made a similar connection identifying Marcus as the originator

---

84. «Qui quidem et partem habent Gnosticae haereseos de Basilidis inpietate uenientem», *Ep.* 133. 3, *CSEL* 56, p. 245. Here Jerome seems to be drawing directly from Sulpicius Severus who attributed the arrival of Gnosticism not to Marcus of Memphis but to Priscillian's teachers Agape, and Elpidius. See *Chron.* II, 46, *CSEL.* 1, pp. 99-100.

85. «Quod Marcus quidam de Basilidis Gnostici stirpe descendens primum ad Gallias uenerit...maximeque nobiles feminas quaedam in occulto mysteria repromittens hoc errore seduxerit magicis artibus et secreta corporum uoluptate amorem sui concilians», *Ep.* 75, 3, *CSEL* 55, p. 72. Again, the primary source for the entire tradition was Irenaeus, *Contra haereses*, 1. 13-15, *SC* 264, pp. 188-253. See also EPIPHANIUS, *Panarion haer.* 34, *GCS* 2, pp. 5-39.

86. 6. 8. 1, *SC* 328, pp. 316-317. HIPPOLYTUS, *Refutatio omnium haeresium*, 6. 40, *GCS* 3, pp. 171-172. Eusebius added to all of these deviant practices the charge that Marcus was remarkably skilled in magic arts, *HE*, 4. 11. 4, *SC* 31, p. 174. Isidore of Seville in *De viris illustribus* mentioned Marcus specifically in his entry on Priscillian, whereas Filastrius of Brescia, Augustine, and Pseudo-Tertullian did not contribute any novelties on Marcus : *De viris illustribus*, C. CODOÑER MERINO (ed.) p. 135. FILASTRIUS OF BRESCIA, *Diversarum hereseon liber*, 42, *CCSL* 9, p. 235. AUGUSTINE, *De haeresibus* 14, *CCSL* 46, p. 296. The PSEUDO-TERTULLIAN, *Adversus omnes haereses*, focused only on doctrinal error : *CCSL* 2. 2 pp. 1407-1408.

of Gnosticism in the Iberian Peninsula, yet he does not say that Marcus taught Priscillian directly[87]. Recall that Agape and Elpidius were taught by Marcus according to Sulpicius. Some scholars have argued back and forth on the question whether there are indeed two traditions of Marcus ; the one of Irenaeus, and the one described by Jerome and Sulpicius[88]. The problem seems to be exarcebated, I believe, by an insistence on a strict literal reading of the chronology in these passages. Jerome is creating in the letter and elsewhere typological spiritual links with previous heretics and this is especially true in the case of Marcus of Memphis, as Virginia Burrus notes, Jerome was intent on creating a "gnosticized portrait of Priscillian[89]". This liberty is evident in his *Commentaries on Isaiah* where he quotes Irenaeus regarding Marcus's activity in Gaul, but Jerome extends it into Iberia as well[90]. The use of typological rhetoric and arguments allows for such flexibility and is not necessarily to be dismissed as only willful distortion, although it was not beneath Jerome to exaggerate or invent details. Sulpicius offers a working chronology and links which Jerome greatly exploits in the letter.

Since Jerome had already acknowledged the connection between Marcus and Agape he did not need to repeat it in rote fashion in the letter because he had a different agenda here. Jerome wanted a female Gnostic culprit identified with Priscillian in the list and Agape was that person. Jerome was not thinking in absolute chronological fashion ; he was thinking of spiritual typological connections.

In the concluding entry Jerome reported that Priscillian, was a zealous devotee of a magician of Zoroaster and became a bishop through him[91]. The censure of Zoroastrianism associated Priscillian directly with the magical arts. Jerome's fixation on Priscillian's fascination with magic and magicians is well-founded, or at least consistent with other testimony, whereas no other writer attaches explicitly Zoroastrianism to Priscillian. The brief reference to Zoroaster is another example of the literary freedom Jerome indulged in to attack the Priscillianists. As I have stated before, a literalistic pursuit of the minute facts, strict chronology, and exact descriptions of practices matter little in this style of polemic. Jerome wants to associate Priscillian with magic : Why not with one of the most notorious magicians, Zoroaster ? Noteworthy in the entry is Jerome's condemnation of Priscillian's ordination as a bishop which he says was the work of a Zoroastrian bishop.

The accusation of the magical occultic background of Priscillian was one of several essential offenses that permitted the Emperor Maximus to arrest, try, and execute Priscillian at Trier in 385. Jerome, therefore, boasted with self-righteous indignation that the "whole world" justly punished Priscillian by death with the

---

87. *Ep.* 133. 4, *CSEL* 56, p. 248. V. BURRUS, *Making of a heresy*, pp. 200-201, note 52.

88. V. BURRUS, *Making of a heresy*, pp. 189-191, note 13.

89. *Ibid.,* p. 194.

90. *Commentariorum in Esaiam, CCSL* 73A, Pars 1, 2A, p. 735. See note 86 above. V. BURRUS, *Making of a heresy*, p. 191, note 12.

91. *Ep.* 133. 4, *CSEL*, 56, p. 248 ; V. BURRUS, *Making of a heresy*, p. 209.

secular sword. That Priscillian was rejected by all of the major ecclesiastics of his day and that he was put to death is absolutely true, but Jerome deliberately chose not to mention their unanimous opposition to the execution[92].

Of 'Galla' and the 'sister' we know absolutely nothing else. What Jerome mentions here is all that we possess, for they are absent in the entire corpus of sources. As with Marcus the exact meaning of the phrase, *Galla non gente sed nomine germanam huc illucque currentem alterius et vicinae haereseos reliquit haeredem* has been the source of much discussion. The word seems to refer to a 'Gallic woman' that formed part of the band of women that followed Priscillian in Gaul. In either case, whether the citation refers to a specific woman Galla or a generic group from Gaul, Jerome is still able to accomplish his overall purposes[93]. The Gallic woman and the 'sister' that perpetuate heresy have all of the heretical characteristics of Agape and is once again a visible manifestation of Priscillian's spiritual fruit. He was not only taught and deceived by Agape, Priscillian now deceives a 'woman' or 'women', and they in turn take the initiative to propagate heresy. Just what the second heresy of kindred form was is also unknown, for Jerome does not explicitly expound, presumably we can infer a version of the teachings of Priscillianism. I maintain that one of Jerome's messages here is to affirm the continued proliferation of heretical teachings, for he closed the letter with *2 Thessalonians* 2: 7: «Now also the mystery of iniquity is working», a forceful affirmation that the spirit of Simon Magus was alive and in Priscillian. It was Vincent of Lérins who expressed this thought so well : *a*

---

92. *Chron.* II, 48, *CSEL* 1, p. 101. Martin of Tours, Pope Damasus, and Ambrose of Milan condemned the audacious behavior of the Emperor. Martin of Tours even implored the Emperor not to shed blood. According to Sulpicius, the Emperor delayed the trial until the aging Martin of Tours had passed away. «Namque tum Martinus apud Treueros constitutus non desinebat increpare Ithacium, ut ab accusatione desisteret, Maximum orare, ut sanguine infelicium abstineret, satis superque sufficere, ut episcopali sententia haeretici iudicati ecclesiis pellerentur : saeuum esse et inauditum nefas, ut causam ecclesiae iudex saeculi iudicaret. denique quoad usque Martinus Treueris fuit, dilata cognitio est : et mox discessurus egreria auctoritate a Maximo elicuit sponsionem, nihil cruentum in reos constituendum», *Chron.* II, 50, *CSEL* 1, p. 103. Pope Leo I, in like manner as Jerome, spoke uncritically of Priscillian's execution, nor did he even hint about the uproar against these unfortunate events by the leading members of the Church in that era, *Ep.* 15, *praef.*, *PL* 54, c. 679. Sulpicius expresses his disgust of Hidacius and Ithacius, Priscillian's main accusers, *Chron.* II, 50, *CSEL* 1, p. 103. Ambrose voiced similar outrage, *Ep.* 30 (Maur. 24) 12, in *Sancti Ambrosii Opera, pars decima. Epistulae et Acta*, Tom. I. *Epistularum Libri I-VI*, *CSEL* 82, 1, pp. 214-215 and also in *Ep.* 68 (Maur 26), *CSEL* 82, 2, pp. 169-178.

93. «Et uicinae hereseos reliquit heredem», *Ep.* 133. 4, *CSEL* 56, p. 248. Sulpicius Severus identified two women named Euchrotia and her daughter Procula, but not one by the name Galla. V. BURRUS, *Making of a heresy*, p. 211, notes 91 and 92. See also pp. 211-212 where the author argues that the reference to Galla is to a proper name following Ferdinand CAVALLERA, «Galla non gente sed nomine», *BLE* 38 (1937), pp. 186-190. For relevant bibliography on Galla see, M.-J. RONDEAU, «D'une édition», pp. 180-181 and Paul DEVOS, «Date du voyage d'Égérie», pp. 180-181. Also H. CHADWICK, *Priscillian of Avila*, pp. 37-38. The concensus seems to be that Galla is a proper name. I concur on the grounds that it is consistent with Jerome's identification of specific proper names in his list, with one exception, the anonymous woman he associated with Marcion.

quo vetus ille turpitudinum gurges usque in novissimum Priscillianum continua et occulta successione manavit. (From whom the old stream of disgrace [heresy] flows and persists in uninterrupted and secret succession in the most recent [heretic], Priscillian[94].)

Conclusion

The letter to Ctesiphon as a source of Priscillianism has numerous limitations. Jerome's principal agenda is to launch an attack on Pelagians and not the Priscillianist sect directly. On account of its polemical intent the letter is filled with typological language that does not necessarily contain an accurate portrayal of the Priscillianists. Jerome's selective use of patristic sources, his limited first-hand acquaintance with the sect, and not the lease his inflammatory rhetoric casts serious doubts on the veracity of the moral and doctrinal lapses he attributes to the Priscillianists.

The letter also sheds light on Jerome's attitude towards women. The heretical women represent 'typologically' behavior unbecoming of orthodox women. Each of them embody various aspects of a negative feminine tradition ; for example : Helena and the Bands of Women are the originating types of doctrinal/sexual depravity. Marcion's unidentified woman is guilty of 'seducing' others at Rome, while Constantia and Lucilla engage in similar sinister activities behind the scenes. Philumena and Prisca/Maximilla are excellent examples of demonically seduced women who believe God is speaking through them in prophetic fashion. They also falsely imitate the apostolic duties of legitimate bishops. Agape seems to personify the most damnable example of a woman 'out of place' as she audaciously teaches Priscillian and pretends to perpetuate a legitimate succession of apostolic truth. Jerome, in a sense, left the best for last in Agape, a Gnostic woman as the quintessential exemplar of the female heretic. 'Galla' and the 'sister', encouraged by Priscillian, are presented by Jerome of perpetuating heresy freely without any seeming reliance [submission] on male authority. Jerome presented to Ctesiphon a 'hall of fame' of women clearly out of place in the Church, and his warning is that Pelagius and his female followers, like the Priscillianists, have overstepped the acceptable boundaries of orthodox definitions of the role of women.

The men paraded by Jerome from Simon Magus down to Elpidius, all represent typologically moral and doctrinal behavior associated with the Priscillianists. Simon and Nicolas are responsible for giving 'birth', so to speak, to the doctrinal and moral errors of all heretics. Marcion reminds the reader of Priscillian's appetite for non-canonical books. With Apelles and Montanus Jerome continued the theme of extra-biblical revelation which he wants to associate with all heretics, especially Pelagius and Priscillian. Arius the most well known heretic in Jerome's day is creatively associated with Priscillian in so far as Trinitarian errors are concerned. Donatus is a fine example Jerome employs to bring to the surface the parochial nature of *all* heretics who cannot

---

94. *Commonitorium, CCSL* 64. p. 181.

claim the universal proliferation of the Catholics, and Priscillian similarly is guilty of perpetuating doctrines in a 'corner' of the world. Elpidius exemplifies a weak male seduced by a Gnostic woman who in his blindness, along with Agape, deceives Priscillian, a clear expression of the 'blind leading the blind'.

The letter to Ctesiphon is useful as an example of the polemical style of Jerome. It also reveals his mastery and selective use of patristic sources. As a Priscillianist document Jerome's treatment is rather unique in that he established extensive 'typological' heretical links between Priscillian and previous heresies. What Jerome does not confirm is the moral and doctrinal error of Priscillian, rather in rote fashion he repeats the ubiquitous negative rumors about the sect.

Alberto FERREIRO
Seattle Pacific University
Department of History
Seattle, WA 98119 U. S. A.

ABSTRACT : The fourth-century Priscillianist controversy in the Iberian Peninsula and Gaul drew much attention from admirers and opponents. One formidable voice opposed to Priscillian was Jerome. In his *133 Letter* written to Ctesiphon, approximately in 415, Jerome launched an attack against Priscillianists in section four of that letter. Jerome utilized mainly typology to associate Priscillian with the previous major heresies going ultimately back to the 'Father' of Christian heresy, Simon Magus. This study proposes for the first time an in-depth exploration of Jerome's polemic to discredit the Priscillianists.

Dilatory Donatists or Procrastinating Catholics: The Trial at the Conference of Carthage

MAUREEN A. TILLEY

In the year 411 the bishops of Christian North Africa, Augustine among them, assembled in Carthage to debate whether Catholics or Donatists should be recognized as the true Christian church in North Africa. Although most biographies of Augustine and histories of Christianity in North Africa mention this conference, they spend little time on the substance of the discussion which took place between the two parties. Accusations by fourth-century Catholics, especially Augustine, and remarks by modern commentators often charge the Donatists with delaying the debate on the real issues of the Conference by interventions and procedural motions which served no useful purpose. Even W. H. C. Frend in *The Donatist Church*, and Peter Brown in his biography of Augustine take Catholic propaganda on this issue at face value.[1]

But there is more to the historical record than the Catholic accusations. Rarely do scholars make use of extant documentary evidence, specifically the proceedings of the Conference itself. The *Gesta*, a transcription of the steno-graphic record of the debates, or at least most of them, does exist.[2] It offers one key source for material on the Donatists which has not been filtered through the biases of their victorious Augustinian opponents.[3] Using the

1. W. H. C. Frend, *The Donatist Church: A Movement of Protest in Roman North Africa* (Oxford, 1952), p. 279; Peter Brown, *Augustine of Hippo: A Biography* (Berkeley, 1969), p. 334. See also Remi Créspin, *Ministère et sainteté: Pastorale du clergé et solution de la crise donatiste dans la view et la doctrine de Saint Augustine* (Paris, 1965), p. 91; and Paul Monceaux, *Histoire littéraire de l'Afrique chrétienne depuis les origines jusqu'a l'invasion arabe,* 7 vols., (Paris, 1901–1922; reprint Brussels, 1963), 6:71.
2. The *Gesta* are printed in Serge Lancel, *Actes de la Conférence de Carthage en 411*, 3 vols. (Sources chrétiennes 194, 195, and 224) (Paris, 1972 and 1975), in *Gesta Conlationis Carthaginensis Anno 411*, volume 149A of *Corpus Christianorum Series Latina*, also edited by Lancel (Turnhout, Belgium, 1974); J.-P. Migne, *Patrologia, Series Latina* 11.1257–1418 (Paris, 1844–) (hereafter cited as PL); and in J. D. Mansi, *Sacrorum conciliorum nova et amplissima collectio* 4.19–246 (Florence, 1739–1798; reprint and continuation: Paris, 1901–1927). This paper uses Lancel's *Sources chrétiennes* edition of the Latin and the author's own English translation.
3. Emin Tengström, *Die Protokollierung der Collatio Carthaginensis: Beitrage zur Kenntnis der römischen Kurzschrift nebst einem Exkurs über das Wirt sceda (schedula)* (Studia Graeca et Latina Gothoburgensia) (Göteburg, 1962), pp. 20–34, raises the possibility of the

Ms. Tilley is assistant professor of religion in the Florida State University, Tallahassee, Florida.

Gesta, this essay highlights the substantive issues as they are found in the debates. It also challenges the usual interpretation of the Conference, that the Donatists avoided the issues at stake. The first section of this article reviews the background of the Conference; the second advances some important judicial considerations and applies them to the theological questions of the Conference; the third focuses on the question of *persona*, the issue at the heart of the Conference. Together they demonstrate how, contrary to received historical wisdom, the Donatists did try to discuss the issues for which the Conference was called, but the differing agenda of both parties prevented not only a resolution of the issues but even a recognition that the parties were addressing the same question.

1.

In 311 a Carthaginian named Caecilian was ordained bishop by, among others, Felix of Abthungi, a man charged with handing over the scriptures to the civil authority during the persecution under Diocletian. As a *traditor*, Felix would be excluded from the episcopate and anyone he ordained would not be considered a true bishop by orthodox Christians.

However, there was some debate about whether Felix really had handed over the scriptures. Consequently, the validity of Caecilian's ordination was in question. Since the local church could not settle the question to the satisfaction of all involved, both sides appealed to the emperor Constantine to adjudicate the issue. The recognition of Caecilian or his recently ordained rival, Majorinus, would dictate who could claim the properties and privileges of the church of Carthage and who would receive imperial largesse as a support for a state-recognized cult. This was a major civil suit with religious implications.

Despite Felix's vindication by an imperial commission, his opponents, the supporters of Majorinus, refused to accept the validity of Caecilian's ordination and to hold communion with him or anyone who associated with him. His ordination was not the only issue. His enemies censured him for the lack of respect shown imprisoned confessors by the hierarchy of Carthage.[4] Advocates of Majorinus and supporters of Caecilian kept ordaining their own

---

emendation of the *Gesta* of the Conference in the process of stenographic transcription citing specific allowances for such in Hermogenianus *Digest* 42.1.46 and *Codex Theodosianus* I 1.6.1 (hereafter cited as *Cod. Theod.*). Such suspicions might cast some doubt on the accuracy of the record as it currently exists. Yet in the *Gesta* themselves there are indications of the correction of the record by the speakers themselves (such as in I 55). One should also note that each party at the conference was allowed to have representatives to check the record. In addition, since not all the bishops could read shorthand, or read at all (*Gesta* I 133, II 43), there was a delay between the second and third sessions for the production of a regular record which could be checked by conference participants (*Gesta* II 43–48). All of these militate against suspicions such as Tengström's.

4. See the *Passio ss. Dativi, Saturnini Presb. et aliorum*, Migne, PL 8.689–703.

lines of rival bishops. The schism continued with more or less hostility for a century until the latter party petitioned the emperors Honorius and Theodosius to settle the issue once and for all.

The emperors responded, issuing their rescript on 14 October 410. They appointed Count Flavius Marcellinus judge and commanded the Catholic and Donatist bishops to assemble in Carthage to determine the cause of the schism and to establish orthodoxy by a discussion between the two parties. Refusal to attend would be considered contumacy.[5] Marcellinus issued his own edict, setting the precise date for the Conference, 3 June 411. At that meeting reason, he said, would vanquish heresy.

In the past, each side had advocated such a conference when the timing was favorable to their position. Now the successors of Caecilian's supporters, the self-styled "Catholic" party, could approach such a conference in confidence. Episcopal commissions at Rome in 313 and at Arles in 314 had vindicated Caecilian, and recently the emperors had imposed and reimposed sanctions against their opponents, led by Bishop Donatus, depriving them of their churches and levying fines on their partisans.[6] So the Catholics were not so much looking for justice anew as the full enforcement of earlier decisions in their favor.[7] The Donatists, as they were called by their opponents, were in a more precarious position. Although the laws against them were held in abeyance for the duration of the Conference, the appointment of Marcellinus as judge did not bode well for their side.[8] They could not be sanguine about their prospects when the judge's rhetoric was so prejudicial to their cause.[9]

Nonetheless, they acknowledged the imperial instruction and came to Carthage expecting a church council. However, while they were on their way to Carthage, Marcellinus issued a new instruction.[10] In it he laid out the methods of operation at the Conference. He called for the delegation of authority on each side to seven bishops, seven counsellors, and four observers for the stenographic team. The Donatists arrived in Carthage to find circumstances far different from what they expected. They objected to this novel procedure, for they found themselves not equal partners with the

5. *Gesta* I 4.
6. Optatus, *S. Optati Milevitani Libri VII*, edited by Carolus Ziwsa, volume 26 of *Corpus Scriptorum Ecclesiasticorum Latinorum* (Prague, 1893), pp. 204–206 and 208–210; *Cod. Theod.* 16.5.37–39 and 16.6.3–5, all from the year 405; 16.5.401 (407); *Constitutiones Sirmondianae* (hereafter cited as CS) 12 (407); *Cod. Theod.* 16.5.44–45 (408); CS 14 (409); *Cod. Theod.* 16.5.51 (410).
7. Brown, p. 331, quoting Augustine, *Ep.* 88.5 and 10; and Créspin, p.78.
8. *Gesta* I 4; See Créspin, p. 75.
9. *Gesta* I 4, where the following are used against the Donatists: *errore suo, scaeva donatistarum,* and *superstitionibus.* See especially *Gesta* II 15–30 for the prejudicial assessment of the Donatist bishops.
10. See *Gesta* I 10 and 14. On the timing of Marcellinus's edict and the arrival of the Donatists in Carthage, see Lancel I:38, 338.

Catholics in a church council but participants in a formal court case.[11] They had come for a conference of bishops, a *collatio* or comparison of positions. When they settled down in Carthage they realized that they were involved not in an ecclesiastical meeting but in an imperial administrative process.

On the first day of the Conference, 3 June, the Donatist bishops contemplated a formal complaint against the change in ground rules. However, when the Catholics arrived with their delegates chosen and an elegant *mandatum* prepared, and a Donatist protest against the format of the Conference was to no avail, the Donatists entered into the legal case as best they could.[12]

2.

It may seem strange to discuss legal issues in the midst of a theological debate. It may seem ridiculous to do so in the context of a church which produced the question "*Quid Hierusalem Athenis?*" Yet one should notice two things about the link between North African Christianity and Roman culture. First, denigration of that link in third- and fourth-century writings is always expressed in eminently classical terms and prose. Second, as Peter Brown has persuasively shown, the acceptance of Christianity by non-Romans often meant the concomitant adoption of the Latin language and all of its cultural baggage.[13] No matter how western Christians tried to disown Roman culture, it was theirs. Thus one should not find it incongruous that in the gathering of North African bishops in 411 Roman judicial rhetoric and procedure played a theological role.

The society of Roman North Africa was a traditional one in which dress, conduct and, above all, legal customs were dictated by the *mos maiorum*.[14] The Conference of Carthage was not exempt from traditional emphases. Even the posture of the participants at the Conference of Carthage was dictated by custom.[15] So also did legal custom provide for the conduct of the Conference.

---

11. *Cum hoc nec mos publicus habeat nec iudicium consuetudo* (*Gesta* I 14).
12. *Gesta* I 16.
13. "Christianity and Local Culture in Late Roman North Africa" in *Religion and Society in the Age of Augustine* (London, 1972) which is equivalent to the *Journal of Roman Studies* 58 (1968): 85–95.
14. Créspin, pp. 116–120, citing the illiteracy of one bishop (see n. 3 of this paper) thinks most of the bishops were not especially learned and that their flocks were unappreciative of the finer points of rhetoric. Yet, the illiteracy of the population of the Roman Empire, including North Africa, is still a matter of great debate. In addition, in a society which is primarily oral, there is little material on which to base a direct correlation between literacy and the appreciation of either the greater or smaller points of oral communication. See also Monceaux, 6:4, for an assessment of the education of Primianus, the Carthaginian primate.
15. See *Gesta* II 3–5 wherein Marcellinus, the presiding officer respectfully refuses to sit in the presence of standing bishops. The Donatist bishops had refused to take their seats

Yet the Conference was not conducted under the centuries-old formulary process. That method had been officially abolished by Constantius II in 342.[16] Instead it was conducted as a *cognitio extraordinaria*. This procedure differed from the ancient process in several ways that are germane to this case. First, the judge was no longer an intermediary between the plaintiff and the defendant; he was an imperial administrative officer and could rule on procedural matters. Second, if the person who initiated the complaint did not appear on time, the case could be decided for the other party.[17] Third, unlike the older formulary procedure, the roles of plaintiff and defendant were not clearly defined. It was not necessarily the person who brought the case to the attention of the magistrate who automatically became the plaintiff; either the accuser or the accused could become the defendant. The judge was generally free to determine the issue.[18] Fourth, the execution of the sentence of the court was no longer a private or even civic affair, but the business of the imperial government.[19]

In this case the Conference was called by an imperial edict. Many of its procedures were established by the mandate given by the Augusti, the Emperors Honorius and Theodosius, to its judge Marcellinus. It was he who determined the date for the various sessions, called together the affected parties, summoned any necessary witnesses, and decided procedural rules. While all of these legal issues were important at this Conference, three issues, the identity of the defendant and plaintiff, the matter of the rules of procedure, and the issue of *persona* are of prime importance.

First, there is the question of plaintiff and defendant. Under the old formulary procedure the plaintiff would simply be the person wronged, the person who brought the charges to the attention of the court. On this issue the old formulary tradition, despite its legal abolition, influenced the progress of the Conference. Hence, there was wrangling over who had called for the intervention of civil authority on earlier occasions and who would make the first accusation on the floor of the Conference. These were of paramount importance in showing who was the defendant and who the plaintiff.[20]

As Marcellius claimed that his mandate to conduct the Conference con-

---

in the presence of the Catholics on the ground that they could not sit with the wicked (Psalm 1:1). See p. 12 of this article.
16. *Codex Iustinianus* 2.57.1.
17. *Cod. Theod.* 2.6.1.
18. J. A. C. Thomas, *Textbook of Roman Law* (Amsterdam, 1976), pp. 71–72.
19. For a history of the *cognitio extraordinaria* and its relationship with the formulary system, see H. F. Jolowicz, *Historical Introduction to the Study of Roman Law* (Cambridge, 1932), especially p. 405; Thomas, pp. 120–122 and A. Guarino *Storia del Dritto Romano*, 4th edition (Naples, 1969), pp. 592–594.
20. *Gesta* I 5; III 41, 46, 49, 74, 106, 119–124, 141, 200–202, and 215–220. The dispute appears to extend back as far as the year 313. See Créspin, pp. 78–89, and Monceaux, 6:164–165, for an analysis of the documentary history leading up to the Conference.

tained no specific authority for him to decide the plaintiff and defendant, he declared that it would be the duty of the participants themselves to decide the matter.[21] Naturally each side was hesitant to claim the role of accuser. The party of Caecilian balked at claiming the status of plaintiff. It would have to prove itself the true Church in order to claim it constituted the injured party under civil law.[22] The party of Majorinus also hesitated. For these people being the true Church meant being the persecuted church.[23] Therefore it would be unthinkable for them to make the first accusation.

This reluctance to claim the legal status of plaintiff illuminates incidents occurring during the first two sessions of the Conference. During the first session bishops in the party of Majorinus and Donatus refused to be seated. This gesture was a physical manifestation of an argument *a majore ad minorem*: as the persecuted Christ stood before Pilate, so they would not sit in the presence of their persecutors.[24] During the second session, they used verses of psalms to make the same point. They, the innocent, would not sit in the company of evil doers.[25] Even when the members of both parties were identifying themselves to authenticate the signature on their mandates, Donatists used the process to assert their status as true Church. Often when a Caecilianist rival identified himself as the bishop of a certain town, the Donatist bishop would acknowledge his identity as resident of the city and "my persecutor."[26]

Given their conduct in these legal circumstances, it is easy to see why the two parties were so careful about how they signed the records of the minutes of the Conference. Petilian, one of the Donatists' most able debaters, quickly switched from his simple *"Recognaui* (I certify)" to *"Petilianus, episcopus recognaui."*[27] Moreover, he found that his opponents had been designated in the *Gesta "N., episcopus ecclesiae catholicae,"* and that members of his party had been identified merely as *"episcopus"* or as a member of the Donatist party. He pinpointed this as a prejudicial action on the part of the Conference secretaries and insisted, to little avail, that if members of his party were called Donatists after their previous leader, his opponents should be called Mensurists or Caecilianists after the leaders of their party.[28] The Donatists properly insisted that the right to use the appellation "Catholic" was a central issue of the Conference.[29] So it seems that rather than being delaying tactics, as

21. *Gesta* III 126; see III 51. Marcellinus could have decided the question, called a *iudicium duplex*, by lot as Ulpian, *Disputationes* II recommended. See *Digest* 5.1.14.
22. *Gesta* III 200; *Cod. Theod.* 11.39 and following.
23. *Gesta* III 22, 25–27, 30; compare with III 258.
24. *Gesta* I 145.
25. *Gesta* II 3–5 (Psalms 1:1 and 25:4–5).
26. For instance, *Gesta* I 188–189, 191–192.
27. *Gesta* I 7 and 9.
28. *Gesta* III 22, 30–35 and 91–95.
29. *Gesta* III 91–97 and 258.

historians who depend on Augustine have said, motions on the identification
of the participants as defendant and plaintiff were germane to the very issue
for which the Conference was called. Each side was simply doing its best to
cast the other as plaintiff.

After the question of the identity of the participants, the second issue was
that of the ground rules for procedure. While Marcellinus's edict characterized the *Collatio* as a civil procedure and not a church council, the participants
themselves debated how the Conference should be run. Raising this point
was not a temporizing tactic of the Donatists. It was an attempt to discuss an
issue inextricably intertwined with that of the identity of the Church and with
the previous question of identity. The crux of the procedural issues revolved
around the question of person or persona. In a legal and religious sense,
persona was a specification of identity. It indicated the character of the
person under consideration. In a legal context the examination of the
persona would judge the fitness of the person to execute a contract or to
appear in court in whatever capacity. In a religious sense, person indicated
the moral character of an individual. Petilian exposed the double nature of
the concept and its implications in an unequivocal manner. Bishops might
gather to discuss a theological issue, but Christians, he said, do not go to civil
court with one another. He demanded a resolution of the problem. The very
option of resorting to civil law, especially on a religious matter, by any
so-called Christian participant appeared in Petilian's eyes as an abdication of
the claim to be a Christian: "Using a mandate in these procedures is not
taking up the issue according to ecclesiastical usage but wasting time in legal
contests . . . If [my opponent] separates himself from the Law [of God], he
shows he is not a bishop; if he truly adheres to the Law, then I ought to
respond to him since he desires to be a Christian".[30] "Now, yes again, I am
demanding that they set forth which they choose, whether they are going to
deal with me in a legal case or whether they will make their argument
according to divine law."[31]

The outcome of the discussion on the manner of pleading, one of the most
basic of ground rules, would go a long way toward settling the question of
what evidence would be admissable, and therefore, what charges each side
would be willing to make. So Petilian observed: "Therefore, noble sir [Marcel-
linus], if the course of this case has been consistent from the beginning, either

---

30. *Nam uti mandato, his formulis praesumere non est ecclesiasticae consuetudinis sed forensis ludi
    atque certamine . . . si a lege discesserit, episcopum se non demonstret; si uero legem tenuerit, tunc
    et ut illi qui christianus esse desiderat debeam respondere* (Gesta I 53). Compare with *Gesta* I
    44–46.
31. *Et nunc etiam atque etiam flagito ut promant quid eligant, utrum forensi actione mecum agant, an
    legla [diuino] concertatione disceptent* (Gesta III 149). Note here and in the selections which
    follow that Donatist speakers consistently use "law" for scripture. For them civil law is
    law only in a derivative sense.

they [his 'Catholic' opponents] should throw out these scraps of paper [the *mandatum*] and proceed with the debate according to [divine law], or if they want to use them, they should throw out divine law."[32]

Augustine articulated the response of the Catholic side. He had a firm grasp on what the choice between civil and divine law meant. As representative of the Catholic bishops, he was ready to agree with the Donatists to use scriptural evidence (in an ecclesiastical process) if the Donatists on their part would promise not to bring up the question of specific persons, that is, evidence about Caecilian and the *traditores*, evidence which the Catholics considered part of a civil suit settled in 314.[33]

Marcellinus brought the issue into even clearer focus: if the parties opted for a civil case, the issue could be argued on questions of person with evidence from archival sources; if they chose the rules of an ecclesiastical assembly, the question would be that of the nature of the Church and it would be argued with evidence from the Bible.[34]

The Donatists were on the horns of a dilemma. On the one hand, if they opted for the method of argumentation they preferred, Scripture, they would lose some of their best evidence, the very basis of the schism as far as they were concerned, namely, the Caecilianist controversy. On the other hand, if they introduced material from their Caecilianist dossier, they would find themselves engaged in a civil suit and unable to use Scripture as the basis for their case. Neither alternative was satisfying because their ecclesiology was both scriptural and exceptionally personal. It was scriptural because Donatists believed that every text of the Bible could speak to them of the nature of the Church.[35] It was personal because they saw the Church not so much as a hypostatized institution, as Augustine did, but as the people who professed Christianity.

3.

All the legal motions thus far presented can be seen and have been seen by earlier scholars as delaying tactics. But given that the rules of the *cognitio extraordinaria* were more fluid than the old formulary process, it is better to interpret them as Donatist attempts to force the Conference to discuss as procedural issues exactly what they considered the real issue. It was the very issue for which the Conference had been called, the issue the Catholics would most have liked to omit from the agenda, the question of person.

---

32. *Igitur, uir nobilis [Marcellinus], si tenor se ita habet causae sicut ab initio uidetur esse formatus, aut iacturam cartulatarum istarum publicarum faciant et ad legalem disceptationem ueniant, aut, si his rebus ut desiderant faciant legis diuinae iacturam (Gesta III 153).*
33. *Gesta* III 187 and 201. See p. 10 of this article.
34. *Gesta* III 156.
35. See the Donatist exegete Tyconius, *Liber Regularum*, passim.

The question of person was both a legal and a theological one. From a judicial viewpoint, the question of person could be raised in two ways. It could be raised as a preliminary item at the beginning of the trial or it could be brought to the attention of the judge during the body of the trial as a piece of evidence. In either case, the question of person played a major role in the strategy of the Donatists.

If the question of person were raised at the beginning of the trial, it acted as a consideration of either the identity of participants or their fitness to take part in the trial. This was the issue the Donatists raised in their identification of each and every individual in the Catholic party who signed the *mandatum*. This was one of the reasons why they opposed the use of representatives instead of the whole body of bishops during the first session. Secondly, the Catholic *mandatum* in which they delegated their authority to representatives could be a proper legal document only if it represented real people, so each bishop who signed the Catholic mandate was called upon to identify himself.[36] This is also why there were challenges to signatures of the illiterate and the dead or of bishops who had no congregations.[37]

Alternatively, the question of person could be introduced as part of the evidence within the trial itself and it is here that the theological aspects of persona are most important. While information on the character and past acts of the defendant or plaintiff is of limited acceptability as evidence in modern American jurisprudence, it was a keystone for any Roman trial.[38]

The Donatists had asked for the personal identification of all those who had signed the mandate to see who constituted the Catholic party and to recognize its members individually as the descendants of *traditores*. This personalist line of reasoning even led to Petilian's acerbic challenge to Augustine: "What are you? Are you a son of Caecilian or not?" For one of Augustine's consecrators had been ordained by a *traditor*, and the Donatists contended that his evil was contagious.[39] This *ad hominem* argument about who ordained Augustine reveals the centrality of the personal for Donatists. Motions which began as attempts to identify participants and to decide whether they were accuser or accused, *legal* procedures, were at heart

---

36. *Gesta* I 65, 114, 116, 126, 176, 181, 184–185. To avert problems for the Catholic party, Marcellinus worked out a compromise whereby the total number of signatures accepted would be based on the total number of Catholic bishops present even though some of the signatures represented persons who were absent or deceased and some of the Catholic bishops who were present had not signed the mandate.
37. *Gesta* I 133, 181–182, 208. Quintillian, *Institutio Oratoria* V.5.2, on impugning the evidentiary quality of documents by alleging that the signatories had been absent or dead.
38. For the theory see [Cicero], *Ad C. Herrenium* II.6.9 and III.6.10 and Quintillian, *Institutio Oratoria* V.7.3, 26–30 and 34; for the practice, the orations of Cicero.
39. *Gesta* III 221–247. Petilian to Augustine: "*Tu quid es? Filius es Caeciliani, an non? Tenet te crimen Caeciliani an non.*"

questions of substance, the deepest questions the Conference was called to decide: who and what was the Church; in what did the holiness of the Church consist? The Donatists saw the holiness of the Church and its members as inextricably linked. Hence, it mattered terribly to the Donatists what Augustine's ecclesiastical lineage was. Once the personae of the Catholic bishops were recognized, the Donatists could proceed to use the identification of the *traditores* and their sons to lay the groundwork for a discussion of the nature of holiness in the Church.[40]

On the other hand, the Catholics took every opportunity they could to assert that the holiness of the members of the Church had little to do with the holiness of the institution.[41] For example, in their letter to Marcellinus, also part of the *Gesta*, they defended their claim by appealing not to the holiness of the members of their church but to the universality of its communion. The Catholic party argued against what they perceived as the Donatist conception of the Church, that of a small African community allied with a few churches abroad.[42] The warrant for the Catholic view of the Church as universal was Scripture itself: "and to preach in his name repentance and the remission of sins *to all nations* beginning *from Jerusalem.*"[43] That universality impelled a recognition of communities with a far greater spread than that of the Donatists and their allies. It meant the recognition of communities with individual members who had been identified clearly as sinners.

The Catholic acceptance of communities with sinful members permitted their controversial exegesis of the parable about the threshing floor: for the Catholics, that floor on which both chaff and wheat lay was the Church. The wheat and the chaff represented saints and sinners within the Church.[44] The Donatists, with their emphasis on the holiness of the Church, were able to interpret the same parable (and similar ones) as referring not to the Church but to the world at large.[45]

The usual analysis of the debate at the Conference of Carthage characterizes the Church according to the Donatists as one in which no one was sinful, and the Church of the Catholics as one spread throughout the world, one in which saints and sinners are thoroughly integrated. However, both the longer speeches and the short interventions of the Donatists offer a more nuanced view.

40. *Gesta* III 258.
41. See Créspin, pp. 86–90.
42. *Gesta* I 18.
43. *Et praedicari in nomine eius paentientiam et remissionem peccatorum per omnes gentes incipientibus ab Hierusalem* (Luke 24:27 in *Gesta* I 18). See also *Gesta* I 48, III 7 and 228.
44. Matthew 3:12 and Luke 3:17; *Gesta* III 261.
45. *Gesta* III 258. James S. Alexander, "A Note on the Interpretation of the Parable of the Threshing Floor at the Conference of Carthage of A.D. 411," *Journal of Theological Studies* n.s. 24 (1973): 512–519, 513, n. 1, reviews the debates between the two parties and the North African precedents for the Catholic position.

The Donatists did not claim that there were no orthodox churches outside North Africa and the orbit of the Donatist allies. They may even have agreed with the quotation used by the Catholics on recognizing the true Church by its universality. They merely stated that it was their opinion that those in communion with the Catholics of North Africa were in communion with the wrong party.[46] It was the very question of which North African community represented the true Church which they insisted was the question to be resolved by the Conference.[47]

The idea that the Donatists represented their church as perfectly pure is an overstatement of what was actually presented at the Conference. In their debate with the Catholics Donatists emphasized an issue which was not germane in Catholic eyes: the ability of the Church to deal with individual sinners in her midst. Here one encounters the crucial juncture of the Latin legal concept of person and the Donatists' scriptural and personal ecclesiology. Since the life and character of a person may be counted as evidence in support of a person's legal claims, the Donatists might have argued from the conduct and character of their opponents to the status of their claim to be the true Church in North Africa. And these heirs of Roman culture did just that. They corrected the Catholic interpretation of the parable of the dragnet wherein bad or useless fish are not identified but remain together with the good ones until the boat reaches land. The Catholics highlighted the timing of the separation of the fishes, the end of the voyage, which they interpreted as the end of the world. This interpretation justified the existence of many sinners in the Church.

The Donatists countered the interpretation and conclusions with an emphasis on the timing of act of separation: as soon as the fish are raised above the waterline and the boat reaches land. By emphasizing timing, they capitalized on the very words of the gospel: "The Evangelist labels 'hidden' those you called 'mixed.' " For the Donatists, only when the character of the fish or the sinner became *known* was that identity crucial.[48] The Catholics, in Donatist eyes, were unable to deal with evil even when it had been identified. On these grounds the Donatists could claim to be the true Church even if their congregations contained sinners, for they dealt with them as soon as they were identified. On the same grounds, the Catholic claim to be the true Church was vitiated. The Catholic claim that the Church could and did contain malefactors without prejudice to its holiness indicated a fatal laxity in Donatist eyes. The persona of the Catholics revealed their lack of fitness to make accusations at the trial of Donatists.

---

46. See the argument advanced by Robert B. Eno for "Some Nuances in the Ecclesiology of the Donatists," *Revue des études augustinennes* 18 (1972): 46–50.
47. *Gesta* III 99.
48. *De occultis reis dixit Euangelista, non de euidentibus quos tu [Augustine] uis tecum esse permixtos* (*Gesta* III 263). See Eno, pp. 49–50.

In reply, the Catholics pointed to Jesus' toleration of Judas. "The Lord Jesus Christ himself, a singular example of patience, not only knew that this most evil traitor was in the midst of his disciples, but already fully aware of this, he admitted him to the number of his disciples."[49]

In response, the Donatists were happy to associate their opponents with that infamous *traditor*: "Then let them go with Judas their patron, these enemies of the truth of the Lord."[50] To add to this "guilt by association," the Donatists charged the Catholics with accepting the baptism of groups with whom they did not hold communion. If the Catholics in reply could point out that even the demons confessed Christ, the Donatists were ready to acknowledge the Catholic willingness to be associated with demons.[51] The Donatists' most damning evidence regarding the Catholic church was its inability deal effectively with evil persons within its ranks, and its association with Judas and the demons. All these, in Donatist eyes, convicted it of being anything but the true Church. This was the very same point the Donatists repeatedly tried to raise through procedural motions.

4.

It has often been asserted that the Donatists avoided the issue of Caecilian because his vindication by imperial authority marked the beginning of their persecution.[52] Yet it is the Donatists who repeatedly brought up the issue associated with Caecilian, that of person, the very issue the Catholics despite their earlier legal victory hesitated to raise.[53] When he could no longer escape the discussion, Augustine declared that even if Caecilian had been guilty, his guilt was not germane to the agenda of the Conference. He maintained this in the face of a concerted Donatist effort to focus on that very question as the major substantive issue of the Conference. Catholic refusal to admit the question of person, which was the origin of the schism, is key to an accurate interpretation of the rhetoric of the Conference. Whether holiness was an attribute of the Church as an institution or as a group of individuals was the issue which broke apart the North African church. Procedural motions made by the Donatists at the Conference have been characterized as dilatory, but this is not the case. Rather they were, in the main, attempts to raise this issue of personal holiness in the only way it could be raised, procedurally. Rather than labelling the Donatists obstructionists for constantly bringing the ques-

---

49. *Ipse dominus Iesu Christus, exemplum singulare patientiae, traditorem suum utique pessimum, non solum cognitum in discipulorum numero pertulit, uerum etiam praecognitum in discipulorum numerum adsumpsit (Gesta* I 55).
50. *"Vadant ergo cum suo Iudo patrono inimici dominicae ueritatis" (Gesta* III 258).
51. *Gesta* III 258.
52. For instance in Brown, p. 332.
53. *Gesta* III 201, 214, and especially 222.

tion to the floor, historians would do just as much justice in applying the label to the Catholics for refusing to discuss it either procedurally or substantially.

In any event, Donatist legal maneuvers at the Conference of Carthage in 411 in no way merit the description "dilatory." On the contrary, they repeatedly attempted to discuss the central problem for which the Conference was called. Any equitable evaluation of the Conference must recognize that Catholic failure to perceive the issue allowed them to procrastinate their way to victory.

The Atmosphere of Election: Augustinianism as Common Sense *

J. PATOUT BURNS

Augustine's teaching on gratuitous divine election, with its supporting doctrine of inherited guilt and necessary grace, challenged the established interpretation of Paul's teaching in the Western Church. These innovations quickly achieved widespread acceptance in Africa but were questioned or rejected in Italy and Gaul. The difference in response can be correlated with contrasting social settings of the churches. The continuing conflict between the Donatists and Catholics in the towns of Roman Africa over the efficacy of baptism and the necessity of belonging to the proper eucharistic communion created uncertainty about the functioning of the Christian economy of salvation. As a result, behavior was disconnected from salvific effects and God's governance appeared arbitrary. Under these conditions, a doctrine of election without regard to merit could take root and flourish.

When Prosper wrote to Augustine in 429 to report on the opposition to his theory of predestination then solidifying in Provence, one charge detailed was that Augustine was reading the letter to the Romans in a way that no Christian had ever read it before, including its author and original addressees.[1] Vincent of Lerins' principled denunciation would certainly have applied: this doctrine had not been taught always, everywhere, and by everyone.[2] In a fifth-century perspective, Augustinianism was innovation or, more likely, aberration.

Aberration, of course, occurs regularly, and some of it is recurrent. Innovation, however, takes hold; it addresses a new situation effectively

*1993 NAPS Presidential Address
1. Augustine's *Ep.* 225.3 (CSEL 57.457–459).
2. *Commonitorium* 1.2 (PL 50.637–38).

Journal of Early Christian Studies 2:3, 325–339 © 1994 The Johns Hopkins University Press.

and designs the future. Paul's teaching on the Mosaic Law and the gospel of Christ provides an instance of innovation. The complex of ideas which comprise Augustine's theory of election—the inheritance of Adam's guilt, the impotence of fallen and even created nature, the necessity and gratuity of divine grace, divine control of human decisions—constitutes what can also be recognized as a genuine innovation. When Augustine was reborn in Christ, this was not Christian doctrine; by the time he died in Christ, most of it was generally accepted, at least in Africa.[3] A hundred years later, it had begun to pass from doctrine to dogma, at least in the Western Church.[4]

Augustine's intellectual biography has been carefully researched. The genesis of his new reading of Romans and its elaboration into a coherent doctrine of divine operation have been chronicled. The inner workings of his intellectual development have been traced and the way one idea led to another and the whole was constructed has been mapped.[5] Yet the very success of this intellectual history raises a different sort of question which cannot be answered by these techniques—why a radically new idea or worldview takes root and flourishes, while another remains tucked away in a treatise, waiting to be ferreted out centuries later and displayed as a curiosity. Augustine's theory of predestination was nearly such. He reached a new understanding of Romans in his response to Simplician's questions, finished about 396.[6] He then used that reading to shape the narrative of conversion in the Confessions[7] but otherwise said almost nothing about it for the next twenty years.[8] Then during the last decade and a half of his life, he not only promoted but insisted on this radically different understanding of the relations between divine governance and human freedom. A whole segment of the Christian world, moreover, agreed with him. Augustine's own sudden shift might be explained in terms of some new intellectual development, such as the abandoning of the notion that the soul entered the earthly body by sinning, or the demands of

---

3. See, for example, the decisions of the African regional councils of 416 which are reported in Augustine's *Epp.* 175–176 (CSEL 44.652–668) and the decrees of the Council of Carthage of 418 (CCSL 149.67–77).

4. In the declarations of the Council of Orange (CCSL 148A:55–76).

5. On which see Patout Burns, *The Development of Augustine's Doctrine of Operative Grace* (Paris: Etudes Augustiniennes, 1980).

6. *Simpl.* 1.2 (CCSL 44.24–56).

7. Burns, *Development*, 47.

8. Even in the initial stages of the Pelagian controversy, in *Spir. et litt.* 34.60 (CSEL 60.226), *Perf.* 19.40–42 (CSEL 42.42–45) and *Gest. Pelag.* 16.39–17.41 (CSEL 42.94–97), Augustine passed by opportunities to explain the way in which God effectively calls the chosen.

the controversy with the Donatists and Pelagians.[9] But these hypotheses do not account for the idea taking hold in the North African church and spreading north across the Mediterranean.

So the question of the social context of the doctrine of divine election forces itself forward: in what type of world would Augustinianism be plausible and become the common sense? The following analysis is totally dependent upon the theory of social organization proposed by the British cultural anthropologist, Mary Douglas.[10] The reader will, however, be spared a full elaboration of this system. Its relevant elements will be explained in their applications.

Before moving to the social setting of the doctrine of election, however, the patterns of thought which it disrupted should be reviewed. First, the way of reading Paul's reflections on Israel and the nations in Romans which was standard in the West at the end of the fourth century must be detailed. Next, attention will be directed to Augustine's initial acceptance of this tradition and then his radical rejection of it. The reactions to Augustine's theory of predestination, in Africa and in Gaul, will be noted. Only then will the social context of the two different responses to Augustinianism, in Europe and in Africa, be examined.

1. READING PAUL IN THE WESTERN CHURCH

In dealing with the election of the nations and rejection of Israel in Romans, Paul was attempting to make sense of the destinies of peoples, not of individuals. In the fourth and fifth centuries, however, the focus was no longer on nations but on individuals. The Christian church was a voluntary society to which individuals committed themselves, often in stages which culminated in baptism as they approached death and judgment. Faith in Christ, observance of the natural moral law, and reception of baptism were generally recognized as necessary conditions for attaining salvation. These assumptions guided the interpretation of Paul's writings which were being produced at that time. In general, these commentaries reflect a confidence in the intelligibility of the divine governance and the justice of the economy of salvation. Behavioral expectations were clear and their fulfillment was expected to gain a person access to eternal life.

Origen's commentary on Romans was still available in the Greek origi-

9. See Robert J. O'Connell, S.J., *The Origin of the Soul in St. Augustine's Later Works* (New York: Fordham University Press, 1987) and Burns, *Development*.

10. The more recent and more elaborate exposition is in "Cultural Bias," reprinted in Mary Douglas, *In the Active Voice* (London, Boston and Henley: Routledge & Kegan Paul, 1982), 183–254.

nal and was translated into Latin by Rufinus at the end of the fourth century. Since Rufinus' translations are often adaptations, his text provides some evidence of Origen's third-century eastern views but a clear indication of what Rufinus judged acceptable to a Roman audience. Rufinus' Origen acknowledged that faith in Christ, which can come only through the preaching of the church, was necessary for salvation.[11] Thus, he asserted, no individual may be denied the opportunity to hear, to believe, and to call upon the name of the Lord. In the time before Christ, all the nations except Israel followed their governing angels into the practice of idolatry and thus forfeited the salvation offered to Israel through practice of the law and trust in the prophecies.[12] Since the coming of Christ, God has sent preachers to everyone, thereby either responding to a good purpose of worshiping the true God or removing any excuse from a hardened heart. Thus he concluded that nations and individuals are responsible for their failure to attain salvation.[13]

The theory of preexistence which Origen used to explain differences in people's situations and opportunities in Rufinus' translation of *On First Principles* is not put forward in the translation of the *Commentary on Romans*.[14] Both works, however, uphold the principle that God elects only on the basis of decisions which are actually made by individuals.[15] Even the election of Israel from among the nations was justified by its singular refusal of idolatry—a thesis which must have required no small adjustment of the thesis of the Deuteronomic history.[16]

The first complete commentary on Paul was produced by the writer now known as Ambrosiaster. He provided multiple versions of that commentary but no variation in his explanation of human access to salvation. He carefully explains why faith, and not simply the observance of the natural law, is required for salvation.[17] Baptism provides forgiveness of past sins and a call to live according to Christ's teaching.[18] Ambrosiaster accepted

---

11. *Orig. Rom.* 1.9–10, 2.7, 4.5 (PG 14.855B–D, 887C–888C, 976D–977A).

12. *Orig. Rom.* 8.9 (PG 14.1186B–C).

13. *Orig. Rom.* 8.5–6 (PG 14.1167–1168A, 1171C–1175A).

14. As a result, the exposition of the distinction between Esau and Jacob is abbreviated and assigned to foreknowledge, *Orig. Rom.* 7.15 (PG 14.1142A–1143B), see the parallel in *Orig. Princ.* 2.9.5–7 (SC 252.360–371).

15. *Orig. Rom.* 1.3, 7.7–8, 8.11 (PG 14.842A–847B, 1121B–1127C, 1191A–1195A).

16. *Orig. Rom.* 8.9 (PG 14.1186B–C).

17. The fulfillment of the law can be required as a debt of nature itself but faith goes beyond the natural operation of the intellect, by affirming what is not evidently true, and thereby earns a reward. *Comm. Rom.* 4.4 (CSEL 81.128–131).

18. *Comm. Rom.* 6.1–8, (CSEL 81.1.188–197), *Comm. Gal.* 3.27 (CSEL 81.3.42),

Paul's assertion in Romans 10[19] that the gospel of Jesus had been spread all over the world either through the missions of his disciples or by accounts and rumors of their preaching and miracles.[20] Salvation was made available to those who had already died through the descent of Christ into their place of confinement before his resurrection.[21] Thus he was able to interpret divine election as foreknowledge of the decisions which persons would make when the opportunity was provided to them.[22] Finally, the privileged status of Israel was presented as the reward for its acceptance of the Mosaic Law, which had been rejected by each of the other nations.[23] Like Rufinus, Ambrosiaster believed that the economy of salvation operates by discernible rules of impartial justice.

In his gloss on the letters of Paul, Pelagius insisted that God wills the salvation of every person and never does anything which would hinder it.[24] Pelagius acknowledged what Augustine would make a significant problem: that the gospel has not been preached to every individual, even since the coming of Christ. Even so, he explained, God knows those from whom the message would elicit a salvific response and calls foreknown believers from among the nations.[25] Thus he implied that God knows and judges others on the basis of decisions and actions which they never actually have the opportunity to make or perform.[26] The complexity introduced by this theory would play a role in the subsequent debate over election.

The Christian society which was served by these three commentators on Paul must have assumed that God gives every human being the appropriate opportunity to attain salvation. God's demands were clearly articulated in the moral law and the ritual practices of the church. Even the forgiveness of sins and the granting of divine mercy could be shown to be just.[27] Although Douglas' theory does not permit an inference from views of the cosmos to the structures of a particular society, it may be presumed

---

Comm. Col. 2.11–12 (CSEL 81.3.183–184). He also referred to it as a putting on Christ, the promise of resurrection and liberation from idolatry. The question of its necessity for salvation was not addressed.

19. Rom. 10:18–20.
20. Comm. Rom. 10.18 (CSEL 81.1.354–357).
21. Comm. Rom. 5.15, 10.7, 14.9 (CSEL 81.1.180–181, 344–347, 438–439).
22. Comm. Rom. 8.28–30, 9.11–17 (CSEL 81.1.288–293, 312–325).
23. Comm. Rom. 2.12, 3.9 (CSEL 81.1.72, 104–105).
24. Exp. 1 Tim. 2.4 (PLS 1.1348).
25. Exp. Rom. 8.29–30, 9.10 (PLS 1.1149–1150, 1153).
26. Comm. Rom. 9.15, 11.2, 11.33 (PLS 1.1153, 1159, 1163).
27. See, for example, Ambrosiaster's redemption theory in Comm. Rom. 3.4–5, 24, 5.9–10, 7.4 (CSEL 81.1.96–103, 118–121, 160–161, 214–217).

that the Christians for whom these texts were written experienced the church as a well ordered and predictable organization.[28]

2. AUGUSTINE'S READING OF PAUL

Augustine's early attempts to deal with the text of Paul generally follow the pattern which has been found in his European contemporaries. Though Augustine placed more stress on the gratuity of the call to faith, he insisted that God does indeed call every individual and that the individual's response determines reward or punishment. Like Pelagius, Augustine was aware of the geographic and temporal limits of the gospel preaching but he claimed that God's call was universal, though it was mysterious and was sometimes given even before birth.[29] In *On Various Questions to Simplician*, he reversed course partially and asserted divine control over the decision to accept the call to faith. Still, he continued to claim that God does in fact invite the nonelect and that they refuse because their dispositions are contrary to God's offer.[30]

Through the writing of the *Confessions*, Augustine continued to assume that God calls everyone and that responsibility for failure remains with the individual. He appealed to a divine knowledge of how a person might respond only to account for the efficacy of preaching, not as a basis for God's giving or withholding the call itself.[31] At this point, he may have had a secret solution to the questions posed to the divine justice by the limited availability of the necessary means of attaining Christian salvation during earthly life. Robert O'Connell has argued that until about 418, when the Pelagian controversy was already well underway, Augustine held or at least considered plausible the Origenist theory that souls descend into

---

28. Some societies profess an egalitarian principle but undermine its effect by permitting competition which inevitably produces and sustains inequality. Other societies use equality of rights to restrain autonomy and domination. Further analysis of these commentaries, particularly that of Pelagius, would probably reveal the individualistic and competitive worldview which characterized the Empire itself.

29. *Quest.* 68.6 (CCSL 44A.182–183).

30. God cannot be charged with responsibility for anyone's failure to attain salvation. Still, Augustine noted that God could find a way to move even the non-elect to salvation. *Simpl.* 1.2.13–15 (CCSL 44.38–39).

31. *Conf.* 8.2.4, 8.6.15, 8.12.29–30, 9.8.18, 6.7.11 (CCSL 27.115–116, 122–123, 131–132, 144–145, 80–81). In fact, when considering infants who die before having made any decisions, he admitted that he could not understand how they would be judged by God. He did not suggest that God would know and judge the life they might have led had they survived. *Lib.* 3.23.66–69 (CCSL 29.314–316).

various earthly situations as a consequence of sin in a prior existence.[32] Thus he might have believed that God had acted on every soul before its coming into the body and thus had already provided each individual an opportunity for a salvific response.[33]

During the first decade of the fifth century, the controversy with the Donatists moved baptism into greater prominence in Augustine's thinking. He asserted that good works could not save without baptism;[34] nor could even faith, as long as the sacraments were available.[35] He also decided that dying infants could be saved through baptism, though he did not yet pronounce on the fate of infants who die unbaptized.[36]

In response to a Porphyrian objection to the plausibility of the Christian claim to provide exclusive access to salvation, Augustine began to shift his position on the universality of the call to faith. He maintained that the prophetic promise or the apostolic report of Christ's saving work was available in every age, from the creation to the judgment. Even before the coming of Christ, the prophecies had actually been heard in some nations beyond Israel. Yet he recognized the validity of the objection: the gospel had not been and still was not being preached throughout the world. In this apologetic context, he could not appeal to a call given in mysterious ways or before birth, so he used a solution based on the divine knowledge of human response, which had been employed earlier.[37] God knows what acceptance the gospel would meet in every situation and thereby ensures that it is preached wherever it would have a salvific effect. For purposes of

32. O'Connell places the definite rejection in 417 or 418, at the latest, using *Serm.* 165.6 (PL 38.905–906) and *Pecc. or.* 31.36 (CSEL 42.195), in summer 418, after having argued that the "earlier" rejections in *Peccat. merit.* were actually subsequent emendations of that text. See *Origin,* 183–187 and 114–115.

33. The Origenist position itself was still viable, as Elizabeth Clark demonstrates in *The Origenist Controversy: The Cultural Construction of an Early Christian Debate* (Princeton: Princeton University Press, 1992).

34. *Petil.* 3.56.68 (CSEL 52.222), *Cresc.* 2.13.16 (CSEL 52.375).

35. *Cons.* 4.6.7 (CSEL 43.400–403), the case being Christian catechumens who lose the reward of assisting missionaries if they die without actually receiving baptism and joining the community. *Bapt.* 4.24.31 (CSEL 51.259–260) speaks of the thief who died with Jesus, in faith but without the opportunity for baptism. Augustine later revised this judgment, claiming uncertainty that the thief was in fact unbaptized, *Retract.* 2.18 (CCSL 57.104).

36. *Bapt.* 4.24.31 (CSEL 51.259–260), *Ep.* 98 (CSEL 34.520–533).

37. Augustine had used divine foreknowledge of a person's response to the call as the basis for election in *Quaest.* 68.3 (CCSL 44A.177–179) and *Rom.* 47.4, 52.11, 53.6 (CSEL 84.30, 35, 36). Subsequently, in *Simpl.* the same kind of knowledge was used to make a call effective by adapting it to the elect's dispositions, *Simpl.* 1.2.13 (CCSL 44.37–38).

argument, he suggested, the objector should assume that everyone would have rejected the gospel in those locales where it was unknown, as most do wherever it is actually preached.[38]

On the eve of the Pelagian controversy, therefore, Augustine seems to have been operating on the common assumption of Western Christians that faith in Christ and baptism were necessary for entrance into the Kingdom of God. Further, he asserted that an opportunity for attaining this faith was either provided to everyone or that those to whom it was not given were known by God to be unwilling to receive it. Unlike his fellow Christians, a careful reading of the text of Paul had led Augustine to realize that divine election was not simply foreknowledge of human decisions. As yet, however, he avoided an open advocacy of the doctrine of gratuitous predestination.[39]

3. EQUAL OPPORTUNITY DENIED

In his initial attacks on the Pelagians, Augustine insisted on the necessity of receiving both baptism and the eucharist for salvation. Considering the case of infants, he rejected any alternative between the baptized being admitted to the Kingdom of Christ and the unbaptized being condemned to eternal punishment.[40]

In an abrupt about-face, however, he categorically denied that God judges impartially and provides an opportunity for salvation to every individual. In certain regions of the world, he observed, the gospel of Christ has never been preached and even now the sacraments are not celebrated. Thus he concluded: because the gospel and the sacraments are not offered to them, no one living in those places—adult, youth or infant—can be saved.[41] His earlier apologetic appeal to God's knowledge of possible responses was brushed aside: was it truly plausible that no one in all those lands and ages was as deserving of God's mercy as some of his own fellow Christians? The claim that God chooses to make salvation

38. *Ep.* 102.8–15 (CSEL 34.551–558). For Augustine's later revision of his interpretation of this passage, see *Praed.* 9.17–18 (PL 44.973A–974C) and *Perseu.* 9.23 (PL 45.1005C–1006D).

39. He let a number of occasions pass without even mentioning it: *Spir. et litt.* 34.60 (CSEL 60.220–221), *Perf.* 19.40–42 (CSEL 42.42–45) and *Gest. Pelag.* 16.39–17.41 (CSEL 42.94–97).

40. The position was taken firmly in *Peccat. merit.* 1.12.15, 3.4.7 (CSEL 60.15–16, 133–134).

41. *Nat. et grat.* 2.2, 4.4, 8.9, 9.10 (CSEL 60.234–236, 238–239). This may indeed be the first treatise against the Pelagians to be completed. The same position is taken in *Peccat. merit.* 1.21.29–1.22.32 (CSEL 60.27–32) but O'Connell argues that this section was part of a subsequent revision of the text, *Origin*, 114–15, 198–200.

available because of its foreknown acceptance or rejection was plainly preposterous.[42]

Turning from faraway lands to the realm of immediate and undeniable Christian experience, Augustine pointed to the fate of infants. Some are baptized, die immediately and attain salvation; others die as they are being brought to baptism and must be condemned; still others receive baptism in illness but survive only to fail in faith and die in sin, losing the salvation they might have gained by dying as children. Yet every Christian must acknowledge that the timing of these deaths and the consequent difference in destinies lie within God's providential control. They cannot be correlated with the merits or efforts of the infants, their parents or the clergy.[43]

By such experiential appeals, and a mass of scriptural citations, Augustine drove home his theses: God does not give every individual the opportunity to attain salvation; God chooses those to whom salvation is to be offered; God bestows salvation on at least some without any decision or merit on their own part. Those whom God has not chosen die and are condemned for the guilt inherited from Adam and the sins they have added as occasion provided.[44] On this experiential foundation, he then erected the doctrinal structure of gratuitous divine election: inherited guilt, natural impotence, the necessity and gratuity of grace, the divine operation of human willing.

4. REACTION TO AUGUSTINE'S INNOVATION

The African church was convinced that God rather than humans—infants or adults—controls individual destinies. If Augustine's sermons provide an indication of the mind-set of his audiences, the faithful found the teaching acceptable, once it was repeated a few times.[45] Their bishops, meeting by provinces in 416 and in plenary session in 418, backed Augustine's teaching and insisted on the condemnation of the traditional position represented by Pelagius.[46] Fortunately the report of one monastic reaction

---

42. *Peccat. merit.* 1.22.31 (CSEL 60.29–31).

43. *Peccat. merit.* 1.21.29–30 (CSEL 60.27–29), *Ep.* 194.7.31 (CSEL 57.200–201), *Grat.* 22.44–23.45 (PL 44.909–911). See also *Corrept.* 7.11–13 (PL 44.923–924), where the argument was extended to those who are not chosen for salvation.

44. At just this point, according to O'Connell's thesis, Augustine rejected the Origenist theory of a sinful descent of the soul into the body; see *Origin*, 179–200.

45. See, for example, *Serm.* 294 (PL 38.1335–1348) on the baptism of infants and original sin, where Augustine used extensive repetition.

46. The decisions of the African regional councils of 416 are reported in Augustine's *Epp.* 175–176 (CSEL 44.652–668) and the decrees of the Council of Carthage of 418 (CCSL 149.67–77).

also survived. At Hadrumetum the brethren were so completely convinced that they refused to be corrected by their abbot and suggested that he pray for them instead, since only God could improve and save them.[47]

Outside Africa, however, Augustine's theories were greeted with amazement and disbelief, even by many of his admirers. The Roman bishop agreed to condemn Pelagius but let the theory of inherited guilt pass without comment.[48] Prosper's and Hilary's letters report that the monastic and episcopal establishment of Provence both agreed that God does require Christian faith and baptism for salvation and conceded that, in fact, the gospel is not preached everywhere and the sacraments are not universally celebrated. Yet these traditionalists refused to recognize that God does not give each individual the opportunity to be saved.[49]

In an attempt to return Augustine to his senses, the learned Christians of Provence reminded him of his own earlier reflections on these questions. They recalled that in responding to Porphyry, he had asserted that the gospel is preached wherever God knows it will meet with some acceptance and not preached where God knows it will be rejected by everyone. On the fate of infants, they suggested that Augustine admit the ignorance he had professed thirty years earlier in *On Free Choice*. If he insisted on pursuing the question, however, they proposed an extension of his answer to Porphyry: God gives and denies baptism to dying infants depending on how they would have acted had they been allowed to live longer. In brief, they were uncomfortable arguing about marginal cases and more secure in the traditional teaching which covered the broad range of Christian practice quite well. They recommended that Augustine conform to the established Christian principles of individual responsibility and divine impartiality.[50]

In responding, Augustine called attention to the inconsistency which was introduced by these attempts to establish impartiality. God, he retorted, has stated that each person will be judged on the basis of what had actually been done during earthly life; no one would be required to answer for what he or she might have done by living longer.[51] Without these limits on responsibility, no Christian could die securely in faith and love since

47. Augustine then had to show the relevance of human ministry to the divine operation in *Grat.* and *Corrept.* The whole incident was chronicled in *Epp.* 214–216 (CSEL 57.380–402), and in the additional material provided in the Bibliothèque augustiniennes edition (BA 24.46–73, 228–245).

48. Among Augustine's letters, *Ep.* 181 (CSEL 44.701–714).

49. Among Augustine's letters, *Epp.* 225, 226 (CSEL 57.454–481). See also Cassian's *Coll.* 13 (CSEL 13.361–396).

50. Similar arguments were presented by Vitalis, a layman writing from Carthage. Augustine responded in *Ep.* 217 (CSEL 57.403–425).

51. He cited 2 Cor. 5:10; *Praed.* 12.24–13.25 (PL 44.977–979).

they might be condemned for sins they had not actually committed but would have committed during later—possible but not actual—years of life.[52] These learned Christians must acknowledge that, like himself, they really did not understand the way God selects individuals to become Christian. Furthermore, he argued, they must recognize that by the same mysterious justice, God preserves some Christians to salvation while allowing their fellow communicants to sin and die. Once human instability and divine control over the time and circumstances of death were granted, the doctrine of election followed inexorably.[53] In the insistence of that response one hears not only the retort of a seasoned controversialist but the deeply held hope of a father whose only son had died as an awe-inspiring youth shortly after his baptism.

In contrast to what had been a consensus among Western Christians, an irreducibly different mind-set had developed in Africa. Augustine insisted and his fellow Christians agreed that God controls the destinies of individual human beings and operates by a justice which not only surpasses but contradicts their own understanding. The Africans knew by experience that God's ways were mysterious and believed that they were just. The Europeans, in contrast, insisted that God rewards and punishes according to rules which are both clearly announced and reasonably intelligible.

5. SOCIAL ORGANIZATION AS A MATRIX OF INTERPRETATION

Augustine used arguments from both authority and experience to develop and defend his innovative reading of the Pauline corpus. The scriptures and, to a lesser extent, their received interpreters were cited extensively. More important, from the current perspective, was the attention he focused on the practice of baptism in which Christians crossed the boundary which separated the Catholic communion from the demonic realm. He then argued that God determines salvation by control over who enters and remains in the communion of the church, demonstrating that the tradi-

52. *Praed.* 14.26 (PL 44.979–980); the same argument is used in *Ep.* 217.5.16, 6.22 (CSEL 57.414–416, 418–419). This reflected one of his major problems with the Origenist theory, that salvation was not secure. Indeed, by controlling the time of death God protects from temptation, forestalls an impending sin, and thereby grants salvation to the chosen. The coup de grace was given by appealing to Christ's statement that the miracles performed in Galilee would have provoked conversion in Tyre and Sidon, where they were never performed, *Perseu.* 9.22–10.24, 14.35 (PL 45.1005–1007, 1014).

53. This argument was developed in *Corrept.* 8.18–19 (PL 44.926–927) and *Ep.* 217.6.19–21 (CSEL 57.417–418).

tional teaching did not fit African experience. The conflict over the doctrine of predestination, therefore, might be correlated with different experiences in the crossing of the boundary which defined the Christian churches and regulated their interaction with both the Empire and competing religious groups.

In Africa, Gaul and Italy, the Catholic community had lost that sharp sense of social boundary which had characterized Christianity before the Constantinian and Theodosian establishment, that separateness to which the Donatists in Africa still clung. The church no longer considered itself an island of religious and moral purity in a sea of idolatry and corruption. Its rituals, baptism and eucharist, no longer established and delimited a social body, protecting and preserving the whole community from the pollution of the Roman world. Instead, the rituals were provided for individual use in gaining access to the truly blessed realm, the Kingdom of Heaven. In this, the European and African communities were alike but one was secure in this experience and the other not.[54]

The review of contemporary Pauline commentaries and of objections to Augustinian innovations clearly indicates that European Christians had a firm grasp on the rules by which God expected them to act and the consequent rewards or punishments God would visit upon them. Above all, they perceived the rules as equitable; everyone had a fair chance and was to make the most of it. Their lives were complex, however, because their responsibilities to the church and to the Empire regularly conflicted. Few could combine exemplary Christian virtue with outstanding achievement in the Empire. Some accepted baptism early in life and strove to secure their salvation by a full-time Christian commitment, as ascetics or clergy. Many more lived as catechumens and turned to baptism at the appropriate moment to gain forgiveness for their sins and the right to enter heaven upon death. None doubted either the necessity or the efficacy of baptism. The consequences of bad timing could be terrible: for the humblest monk or the most exalted emperor.[55] Success or failure, however, was a matter of individual decision and responsibility, not the outcome of some cosmic plot.

As they looked outside the community, among their fellow citizens Eu-

---

54. To use Douglas' terms, the cosmic justification for church practices was holding firm in Europe but had failed in Africa.

55. Consider the case of the catechumen revived by Martin of Tours and the emperor Valentinian II. Martin's extraordinary power was demonstrated by his winning an exception to this rule; Sulpicius Severus, *Mart.* 7 (CSEL 1.117–118). Ambrose struggled to console the sister of Valentinian, who had died before baptism, *Valent.* 51–54 (CSEL 73.354–356).

ropean Christians saw only individuals who had rejected Christianity, even in the face of legal disabilities, to follow the cult of the demons. Such experience as they had of people living outside the Roman order was apparently adequate to convince them that none would embrace salvation. In short, these Christians experienced the church as a well-ordered economy, perhaps even more reasonable than the Empire from which it was not completely segregated. Living in such a society, they could hardly entertain the uncertainty and even irrationality of the Augustinian worldview.[56]

The African experience of the church and the economy of salvation, in contrast, was marked by incoherence and insecurity. Consider first the African Catholic's sense of identity. The most significant difference between European and African Catholic experience in the fourth and fifth centuries was the success of the Donatist church. Augustine's finely crafted responses to the Donatist challenges to the holiness of the Catholic church and the efficacy of its rituals certainly impressed the later ages which adopted his sacramental teaching. His elegant solutions, however, could not be translated into patterns of social experience and organization by his contemporaries. The true church, the society of saints, was not an identifiable group but an invisible communion of all who shared the interior disposition of charity. The unvarying effect of baptism was a spiritual tattoo on the soul rather than admission to membership in a social organization. Charitable intention, which only God could verify, rather than proper performance made the observance of the moral law truly good and its absence vitiated all the moral actions of schismatic Christians.[57] None of these notions corresponded to formal criteria which could be verified in behavior, certainly not by the general run of African Catholics.

The strength of the Donatist church, which seems to have been a solid social institution, created a great deal of confusion and uncertainty for African Catholics. By baptism the Donatists claimed to make a convert part of a pure community, which enforced the standards of fidelity to Christ. Its clergy professed freedom from entanglement in the idolatry and persecution of the Roman Empire. Its communion symbolized the Kingdom of Heaven, whose entranceway it claimed to be. Membership in that church meant friendship with the martyrs and fidelity to Christ: it counted for something as the Christian approached the judgment seat.

56. Thus in Douglas' categories, the European Church was lower on the group scale than its African counterparts and individuals could negotiate their salvation according to established rules. By using the status of catechumen, and to a lesser extent that of ascetic, persons could belong to the church without submitting to its disciplinary standards and the pressures which the bishops could bring to bear on the baptized.

57. For a review of these issues, see Burns, *Development*, 59–71.

African Catholics, in contrast, were required to recognize Donatist baptism, though the Donatists denied the validity of their own. They seem to have received the sacrament earlier than their European counterparts,[58] but they could place much less trust in the efficacy of the ritual.[59] For Catholics, therefore, group membership was functionally determined not by baptism but by the eucharistic communion.[60] Yet they knew that unlike the Donatists, their church did not maintain the standards of Christ by excluding the unworthy from communion, or even from among the clergy. Only Christ, they were reminded, was competent to sort out the wheat from the weeds, as he would surely do in the judgment. As a result, the Catholic communion did not symbolize the Kingdom of God on earth, with the saints in the center and the sinners excluded or in penance on the fringe. Could these Catholics approach the judgment with the presumption that their good standing within the church entitled them to line up on the right side?[61]

When African Catholics looked out from their church's communion, how did the world appear? That God would condemn the self-satisfied Roman traditionalists, the terrifying barbarians to the south, and the Arian Vandals moving eastward across Africa made perfect sense, since they were aggressively opposed to the true faith. As disciples of Cyprian, the patron saint of all African Christians, these Catholics were also expected to believe that their God-fearing, Christ-worshiping, martyr-loving Donatist neighbors would also be sent to hell for the sin of schism. Yet those Donatists shared the same creed, the same sacraments, and the same moral observance. One or the other, but not both, would be saved because the true church could be found in only one of the competing communions. Did the identity of the true church, as the Donatist claimed, really rest on whether Caecilian, the bishop of Carthage a century earlier, had been tainted by sacrilege? Or was that question really irrelevant and foolish, as the Catholic bishops claimed after laboring to prove Caecilian innocent? In the absence of regular, reassuring experience, even in the face of its

58. Augustine's arguments for the timing of death deal with the baptism of infants but with the postbaptismal sin or repentance of adults rather than their baptism.

59. Some Catholics had themselves and their children baptized in the Donatist church, trying to make sure.

60. Augustine even argued that sharing in that communion could replace a missing or invalid baptism, *Bapt.* 5.2.2 (CSEL 51.263–264).

61. Augustine's instructions for teaching the doctrine of election to the community are, in this regard, instructive: the people are to be exhorted to thank God for the gifts received and ask for those still needed. He was attempting to provide an experience, fallible though it might be, of God's intention to save each of the believers. *Perseu.* 22.57–62 (PL 45.1028–1032).

opposite, African Catholics had to believe with full heart that somehow they, and not their Donatist rivals, had been guided by God into the proper church. Could the Catholics be sure that their Donatist neighbors would be condemned and they saved?

That Augustine would argue from extreme cases, such as unbaptized infants, unevangelized pagans and Christians dying after a sudden fall into sin, would not have surprised his African audience at all. Those hearers could not hope to find clarity and certitude in their ordinary experience of the economy of salvation. Augustine asked the African Catholics to believe that God had somehow chosen them to belong to the right church and had let the rest of Adam's children go wandering off to perdition. That did not startle or surprise them at all; on reflection, they realized that they had already believed it. The only alternative was to believe the reverse, and immediately join either the Donatists or the pagans. Once the impartiality of divine justice was undermined, moreover, the entire Augustinian system became obvious: inherited guilt, necessary and gratuitous grace, divine operation of both the faith and the perseverance of the elect.

When the Vandals turned their world upside down, our African Catholics may have been prepared for the ensuing chaos. They could continue to trust that the grace which had brought them so far would surely see them home. A century later, the dying of the Roman order in Europe might have moved their Gallic confreres to join in on a chorus of that old Augustinian hymn, "O altitudo divitiarum sapientiae et scientiae Dei! How inscrutable are his judgments, how unsearchable his ways!"[62]

J. Patout Burns is Thomas and Alberta White Professor of Christian Thought, Washington University, St. Louis

62. Rom. 11:33.

Augustinian Studies 23 (1992) 33–51
Gerald Bonner

Pelagianism and Augustine*

Among the many achievements of twentieth-century ecclesiastico-histori-
cal research has been the advance made in Pelagian studies. By this I do not
mean simply, or even primarily, the identification and publication of Pelagian
writings, fundamental as such researches are, but even more the attempt to
understand the phenomenon of Pelagianism as the Pelagians understood it, to
see them as they saw themselves. In company with other theological schools,
like Arianism and Nestorianism, condemned in their own age as heresies and
for centuries treated as such by scholars, we now seek to see Pelagianism as a
religious tendency existing in its own right and not as mere opposition to
prevailing doctrine; believing itself to be orthodox and not setting out
deliberately to pervert Christian truth — it has, after all, been fairly remarked
that the one sin to which one cannot logically admit is that of being, as opposed
to having been, a heretic, because this would imply that one is deliberately
believing doctrines which one recognizes to be false. This does not mean, of
course, that it is now impossible for a scholar to hold that the ancient heresies
were erroneous; but it does require that they must be allowed a fair hearing on
their own terms, and not on what their opponents regarded as their own terms.
I think that B. R. Rees, in the title of his book, *Pelagius: A Reluctant Heretic*,
has very fairly caught the spirit of the contemporary approach to Pelagianism
by scholars who would still wish to regard themselves as orthodox Christian
believers.

It is for this reason that in these two lectures I want to begin from a
consideration of Pelagianism as a movement in itself and not to see it, as it has

so often in the past been seen, as a kind of appendage to the career of Augustine. This does not mean that Augustine now becomes irrelevant to the history of Pelagianism. On the contrary, as I hope to suggest later on, it was he, more than any other individual, who ensured that it was to have a permanent place as an event in ecclesiastical history; but it does mean that, in considering the Pelagian movement, we should avoid the temptation of seeing it negatively, as being aimed primarily at Augustine, and try to understand it in positive terms, as seeking to build, rather than to destroy. It may, of course, be our final conclusion that Pelagianism was, in essence, a negative influence, that its assumptions, carried to their logical conclusion, would have turned the Catholic Church into a tiny assembly of saints rather than a large school for sinners; but it would be unfair to the Pelagians to suppose that their goal was anything other than the advancement of Christian truth and morals, as they understood them. A generation ago the Swedish scholar, Torgny Bohlin, drew attention to the fact that Pelagius, in his Pauline commentaries, had two theological opponents principally in mind: Arianism and Manichaeism. In choosing these two, Pelagius displayed a concern for Christian doctrine as well as for Christian morals. The Arians denied the full divinity of the Word and so assailed the foundation of Christian faith. The Manichees, as dualists, denied the goodness of matter and therefore, since they saw man as a compound of matter and spirit, it logically followed that he must inevitably sin because of the material element in his nature. It was this assumption of the inevitability of sin because human beings have material bodies that Pelagius and his supporters attacked. Against Manichaean determinism they asserted the freedom of the human will, and it was because of their determination to assert the freedom of the human will that they denied the doctrine of Original Sin, which they saw as impugning the goodness of God as creator and as implying a Manichaean view of the human body as being something evil. Unless we keep this double concern in Pelagian theology in mind: to maintain right doctrine and to encourage men and women to live the Christian life in accordance with what they believed to be the teaching of the Gospel, we shall fail to understand the movement. In their appeal to Pope Zosimus in 418 both Pelagius and Caelestius submitted professions of faith in which, said Augustine, Pelagius held forth upon many matters which were irrelevant to the dispute.[1] We may reasonably hold that they did not seem so to Pelagius, who sought to vindicate himself in respect of both faith and works, in the belief that the one depends upon the other.

It was this emphasis upon man's essential goodness which, being God's creation, cannot be destroyed by sin, and upon the freedom of the human will, given by God and equally invulnerable, that constituted the foundation of Pelagian ethics, and explains why Pelagius, even before controversy began, reacted so violently to Augustine's prayer in the *Confessions*: "Give what Thou dost command and command what thou wilt."[2] It was not, I suggest, simply that it seemed to give excuse to the slothful and hypocritical; rather, that it struck at the whole basis of moral theology as Pelagius understood it. The Pelagians were not innocently unaware of human weakness.[3] They knew that, in practice, even good Christians sinned and needed to do penance; but they were utterly opposed to making human weakness the measure of human achievement: the only acceptable goal was perfection and, as the Pelagian author whom I call the Sicilian Anonymous says, in his treatise *On the Possibility of Not Sinning*,[4] if someone is told that he is capable of avoiding sin, he will be encouraged to make every effort to avoid it, with the result that, even if he does sin, his sins will be less frequent and less serious.[5] The traducian theory of the physical transmission of Adam's primal sin seemed to the Pelagians a recipe for disaster. If you start off persuaded that you are going to fail, then fail you undoubtedly will.

It is the denial of any doctrine of Original Sin which constituted the one essential article of belief for any would-be Pelagian. Once there is agreement on that point there is a reasonable margin for different tendencies and emphases. In general Pelagianism seems to have commended a strong asceticism, though Pelagius himself took care to defend the lawfulness of marriage, even though, like other, more orthodox theologians, he preferred virginity and chaste widowhood.[6] Again, although their denial of Original Sin removed the urgent necessity for infant baptism felt by Augustine, the Pelagians were quite prepared to accept the practice as part of the custom of the Catholic Church. They certainly did not regard their own foundation doctrine of the denial of Original Sin as a ground for separation from the Great Church. At his trial at Carthage in 411 Caelestius, perhaps the ablest Pelagian leader, charged with holding that the sin of Adam injured only himself and not the human race, was content to argue that doctrine concerning the transmission of sin as a matter of opinion, not of heresy. "I have always said that infants need baptism and ought to be baptized. What more does he want from me?" he demanded.[7]

The Pelagians, then were a body within the Church, holding opinions which they sought to commend to their fellow-Christians though without any desire to depart from Catholic unity. One might, in modern terminology, call them a pressure-group. But how strong was this pressure group? It is here that we encounter a question which is rarely discussed, presumably because of the sparsity of evidence, but which is of great importance in evaluating the movement. Augustine apparently considered that Pelagians were very numerous in Africa,[8] a view which was shared by the bishops of Proconsular Africa in their letter to Pope Innocent of 416.[9] If this was indeed the case, it is surprising that we hear so little of them during the Controversy, especially after the condemnation of Caelestius in 411 and Pelagius and Caelestius together in 417. Perhaps the African bishops panicked and saw Pelagians where they were not. There was a group at Rome sympathetic to Pelagius, as Aurelius of Carthage, Augustine, and their fellow-signatories recognized in their letter to Pope Innocent in 416[10] (though Innocent expressed ignorance of any Pelagian presence in the city),[11] and this group was sufficiently numerous to engage in open violence with its opponents in 418,[12] thus finally persuading the imperial government to intervene;[13] but rioting was as popular an activity in the Roman world as it would be in Boston, Massachusetts, and London, England, in the eighteenth century, and it may well be that many of those who indulged in violence were as much motivated by the excitement of the proceedings as by sympathy with Pelagian theology. The same may apply to the motives of those who assaulted Jerome's monastery at Bethlehem in 416. Jerome made enemies, and not a few persons might have been happy to join in an attack on him without being much concerned about his theology. Accordingly, we do not need to regard Jerusalem as a Pelagian stronghold. The writings of the Sicilian Anonymous and the statement of Augustine's correspondent, Hilary, that certain Syracusan Christians hold that a rich man could not enter the Kingdom of God unless he abandoned his wealth[14] — one of the Sicilian Anonymous's doctrines[15] — point to the existence of a Pelagian party in Sicily but give no indication of its strength. Again, there was a Pelagian group in the East, at Constantinople, which suffered from the attentions of the Patriarch Atticus,[16] but once more we have no information about its numerical strength.

It might be argued that the considerable quantity of Pelagian writing which has survived points to the existence of a reasonably large body of sympathizers, but this hardly amounts to proof. In the first place, the mass of Pelagian literature, though considerable, is not overwhelming. Some of it can be confidently assigned to individual authors, much remains of doubtful authorship, but the total number of Pelagian writers is not likely to have been large.

Furthermore, the fact that certain writings have been preserved tells us nothing about the readership which they enjoyed in their own day, and since a number of them are letters, their survival may well have been fortuitous. In short, there is nothing in the evidence available to us to suggest that Pelagianism was ever a mass movement like Donatism, or later movements like Nestorianism or Monophysitism. What really alarmed the African bishops, who were its earliest and most indefatigable opponents, was its theology, which went directly counter to their own. African concern, it may reasonably be suggested, arose from the conviction of their own rightness with regard to the doctrine of Original Sin, and a refusal to allow that there could ever be any compromise on this matter. Scholars today are wisely cautious about seeing heresies and schisms in the early Church as expressions of latent nationalism; but whatever the explanation, the ability of the African Catholic episcopate to stand together to defend what it believed to be the doctrine of the universal Church is both obvious and impressive.

Thus the struggle between the Pelagians and their opponents was essentially a literary — one might almost say, a pamphlet — war, were it not for the enormous size of the writings of the later contributors, notably Julian of Eclanum and Augustine, and it may be that the quantity of our source-material has helped to create the impression, at least in Western Christendom, that the Pelagian Controversy had an epic quality, comparable with the earlier struggle against Arianism. This seems to me to be untrue; and I would further utter a warning against any assumption, from the quantity of our documentation, that we can now reconstruct the people and the events of the Controversy with considerable exactitude. Such a supposition is too optimistic; and it remains true that the principal actors in the Controversy, on the Pelagian side, remain shadowy figures. Let us look at one or two, starting with Rufinus of Syria, the man who, according to Marius Mercator, first sowed the seeds of Pelagianism at Rome by corrupting Pelagius and using him as the agent for spreading heretical views which he was too astute to proclaim openly. Is he to be identified with the "Rufinus, a priest of the province of Palestine" who is alleged to be the author of the *Liber de Fide* by a colophon in St. Petersburg MS. Q.v.1.6, which is the sole existing witness to this anti-traducian work? And is he further to be identified with the priest Rufinus sent by Jerome from Bethlehem to Milan in 399, to give assistance at the trial of a certain Claudius, who was arraigned on a capital charge? I think that he may be; but there is a very large element of conjecture in this identification.[17] Again, let us consider

Pelagius. Apart from his Pauline commentaries, which are now generally accepted as genuine, and fragments quoted by Augustine, a question-mark hangs over the very large corpus of writings which have been attributed to him since the pioneering work of George de Plinval in the 1940s. Most people today seem to accept the arguments of Robert F. Evans, which identify a limited number of works as being by Pelagius himself - a list accepted by B. R. Rees in his recent volume of translations of Pelagian writings; but a recent, and very learned, work by three Italian scholars[18] expresses reservations about whether the *Letter to Celantia*, preserved among the works of Jerome but certainly not by him,[19] can safely be assigned to Pelagius. Again there is the treatise *On the hardening of Pharoah's heart*, discovered by Germain Morin and eventually published by Georges de Plinval, which some have wished to see as an answer to Augustine's two books *To Simplicianus on various questions* (396)[20] and which may be − but there is no proof. In short, much of the writing which has, from time to time, been ascribed to Pelagius is dubious; and the man himself, apart from a few moments of self-revelation, as in his vehement rejection of Augustine's petition: "Give what Thou commandest and command what Thou wilt" or his defiant question at the Synod of Jerusalem: "What is Augustine to me?",[21] displays few positive qualities and was certainly not the leader of the Pelagians once the battle began. His disciple, Caelestius, is a more impressive personality, the most effective man of action which the movement produced, but we have far too little material from his pen to evaluate him adequately. The writer whom John Morris called the Sicilian Briton, and I the Sicilian Anonymous, and B. R. Rees the Pelagian Anonymous, is a powerful writer with well-defined and remarkably radical views, which bring out the strongly ascetic tendency in Pelagianism; but we do not know who he was, and the writings which are attributed to him are attributed on stylistic and theological grounds, and if he played any active part in the controversy once it had broken out, we know nothing of it. Julian of Eclanum, is of course, familiar to us thanks to his own ready pen and the fact that Augustine preserved large portions of his writings in the *Opus Imperfectum*; but he only emerged as the active part of the Controversy drew to a close, and so only played a limited - but important - part in its events, as opposed to being a very sharp thorn in Augustine's flesh for the last decade of the saint's life.

With these reservations − and they are very considerable reservations − about our sources, which are usually established for us by others and which we are then all too often inclined to accept and to use without question, let us try to consider the thought-world and career of Pelagianism. I have already suggested that there is no reason to think that it was a mass movement. I have also maintained that it had no characteristic theology, other than a denial of any transmission of Original Sin, so that individual Pelagian writers show individual emphases in their thought. I would be inclined to regard Pelagius as being the theoretician of the movement, in that he, more than anyone else, tried to provide a general theological basis for its practical program. Julian of Eclanum is another theoretician, perhaps the ablest brain that Pelagianism produced; but he is more limited in scope than Pelagius, a polemicist rather than a constructive theologian.[22] Rufinus the Syrian, though he may be the inspirer of the movement, is a one-treatise man, who is at least as much concerned with denouncing Origen as with denying the transmission of Original Sin. The Sicilian Anonymous is the revivalist author of Pelagianism, enthusiastically denouncing riches and commending virginity. In his uncompromising asceticism he goes further than Pelagius, but his attitude reflects a very real tendency in Pelagianism: a rejection of any compromise in Christian living. The Pelagians were not monks; but their program, if it had been carried through uncompromisingly, would have turned the entire Christian Church into a monastery.

Let us now attempt to plot the outline of the history of Pelagianism. As a movement, it enjoyed a very short existence, between 408, when Pelagius first comes on to the stage, and 431, when it was condemned, in the person of Caelestius, by the Council of Ephesus, though its ghost was to haunt theologians for centuries. As regards its place of origin, there seems no reason to dispute the view that it arose in Rome and in aristocratic circles, largely female, to which Pelagius seems to have been a sort of lay spiritual director. Pelagius' own relationships suggest this interpretation, from his lost letter of 406 to Paulinus of Nola,[23] and his famous letter of 413 to Demetrias, the daughter of Anicia Faltonia Proba,[24] to his appeal, after his condemnation in 418, to Albina, Pinianus and Melania the younger.[25] Like his enemy Jerome before him, Pelagius had a liking for devout women of high rank, and they, equally, seem to have responded. At the same time, it would be unwise to overestimate the prestige enjoyed by Pelagius in Rome, outside the aristocratic circles which patronized him. In 416 Pope Innocent I expressed ignorance as to whether or not there were any Pelagians in the city,[26] though in 418-9 Augustine was to write at length to the presbyter Sixtus (a future pope), who was suspected of being too much inclined to Pelagian theology.[27] It may be that the great emigration of Roman aristocrats from 408 onwards, in the face of the threat to Rome of Alaric the Goth, effectively dissolved the Pelagian presence there.

Paradoxically, however, it was precisely this emigration which brought Pelagianism to the notice of the African bishops and so brought about the Pelagian Controversy. Indeed, but for Alaric Pelagianism, as we have come to understand it, might never have existed. As late as 412, when he embarked on the composition of the third book of *De Peccatorum Meritis et Remissione*, Augustine knew Pelagius only by repute, as a holy man of no small spiritual advancement, whose commentaries on the Pauline Epistles he had only recently read. Without laboring this piece of information, it at least implies that Pelagius' writings had not, at this time, achieved any particular fame outside his own circle except, perhaps, with the jealous Jerome, who may have had personal reasons for disliking Pelagius and his theology. Furthermore, it was not Pelagius who had provoked the attack on Pelagian doctrine in North Africa but his disciple Caelestius, who had been accused of teaching heresy by the Milanese deacon Paulinus, generally identified with the biographer of Saint Ambrose. I have long thought it probable that Caelestius' attitude to paedobaptism would have attracted attention in Africa, where the theology of baptism had played so important a part in the dispute with Donatism.[28] Caelestius, at his trial at Carthage, argued that the reason for infant baptism (a practice of which he approved) was not a matter of dogma, but admitted of a number of differing theological explanations. It was here, however, that he came up against African dogma, looking back to the teaching of Saint Cyprian, and was condemned. Significantly his personal opinion, so unacceptable to the Africans, proved to be no bar to his subsequent ordination at Ephesus.

The condemnation of Caelestius at Carthage apparently left the African bishops in a permanent state of concern about any denial of their theological expertise in general and of traducian doctrine in particular. However, they did not immediately launch an offensive against Pelagian teaching. Even Augustine, later to be the implacable opponent of anything Pelagian, contented himself with answering Pelagian doctrines brought to his attention, like that reported to him from Sicily by Hilary[29] and Pelagius' treatise *De Natura*, sent by Timasius and James.[30] With Pelagius himself he remained on civil terms, as is shown by his Letter 146 (413). But perhaps the best evidence of Augustine's desire to avoid an open breach with Pelagian theologians in revealed by his famous treatise, *On the grace of the New Testament* (Letter

140), written probably in the early months of 412, in response to an enquiry from a certain Honoratus regarding the meaning of five passages of Scripture. In his reply, Augustine added a sixth question of his own: *What is the grace of the New Testament?*, asked with Pelagianism in mind. In his work Augustine makes no reference to Pelagian denial of Original Sin or the need for infant baptism; rather, he is concerned with what he saw as the implications of Pelagian doctrine: a false self-sufficiency, resulting in a lack of humility. At its deepest level, Augustine's concern was with the sin of pride, which he believed, rightly or wrongly, to be the consequence of the train of reasoning initiated by Pelagius.

It was not, then, in Africa that a direct assault was first launched upon Pelagius himself, but in Palestine, for it was here that Jerome pursued a campaign which may have been of long standing, if we are to accept the suggestion that the unnamed monk who criticized the extreme views of Jerome's denunciation of Jovinian may have been Pelagius. Whether this is the case of not, there is substance in Robert F. Evans's suggestion that Jerome's *Dialogue against the Pelagians*, which we know from Orosius to have been in process of composition in July 415,[31] was inspired by Pelagius who had revived charges of Origenism, and undue disparagement of marriage.[32] It was, indeed, Jerome, rather than Augustine, who was the first opponent of Pelagius, albeit without naming him, and an explanation is clear: in Jerusalem Pelagius was an all-too-close neighbor of Jerome at Bethlehem and was supported by sympathetic elements of the Roman aristocracy, who like him, had preferred the safety of the East to the perils of life at Rome, threatened by the Goths. Augustine, in Africa, still at this time preoccupied by the attempt to bring the Donatists into unity and with the composition of the *De Civitate Dei*, to say nothing of smaller writings, like that against the Origenists and Priscillianists composed for Orosius, had far less motive than Jerome to embark upon a campaign against Pelagius, a man with a reputation for piety, as Augustine himself recognized, and who enjoyed the friendship of many of Augustine's friends. Perhaps by 415 Augustine's views were changing. In the letter to his friend Evodius, written at the end of 415, he referred to having recently written a large book "against the heresy of Pelagius,"[33] that is, the *De Natura et Gratia*. Nevertheless, in that work he was careful to attribute the erroneous opinions of Pelagius (whom he does not name) to a "burning zeal" (*zelo ardentissimo*) against the excuses of those who try to extenuate their sins by attributing them to the weakness of human nature and not to their own will.[34] Similarly, in the

De Perfectione Iustitiae Hominis, written at approximately the same time as the *De Natura et Gratia* and aimed at certain propositions attributed to Caelestius, Augustine was careful to say, with regard to the view that even before the coming of Christ there had been men free from actual, as opposed to Original, sin, that he dared not reprehend this view, although he was not able to defend it.[35] Among the charges leveled against Caelestius at his trial at Carthage in 411 was the allegation that even before the coming of Christ there had been sinless men — wholly sinless, that is to say, given Caelestius' denial of Original Sin. Augustine would not accept such a denial; but if the notion of sinlessness implied not giving consent to the lusts which Original Sin necessarily engendered, he was prepared to tolerate this view, even though he could not personally accept it. This particular doctrine was to be denounced by the pan-African Council of Carthage of May 1, 418, canons 6 and 7. In 415 Augustine was prepared to tolerate it as an opinion, while rejecting it personally.

Let us, at this point, consider the position of the Pelagian party — and the word party must, in this context be used with care, because it implies a degree of organized relationship which, so far as we can tell, was wholly lacking in the associates of Pelagius at this time — in the summer of 415, the point at which the campaign against Pelagian theology is set in motion by the behavior of Paul Orosius. Caelestius, condemned by a Carthaginian synod, has contrived to get himself ordained at Ephesus. Pelagius is at Jerusalem, in the congenial company of other Roman refugees and on good terms with the bishop, John, whose high opinion of him may not be wholly uninfluenced by the fact that he, too, has suffered from the attacks of Jerome during the Origenistic Controversy at the end of the fourth century. Furthermore, Jerome himself seems to have seen his own debate with Pelagius as being in part an extension of the earlier controversy; hence his interpretation of Pelagius' doctrine of *impecantia* (the view that a man is able to live without sin if he chooses) as being equivalent to the Stoic philosophical ideal of *apatheia* — freedom from passion.[36] Again, Jerome fastened on the deficiency of the Pelagian conception of grace, declaring that for Pelagius it was no more than free will and God's law.[37] Interestingly, however, although a believer in the guilt of Adam inherited by humanity, he made no reference to the issue of infant baptism until Orosius brought it to his notice, when he arrived in Bethlehem in the spring or early summer of 415, equipped with copies of Augustine's anti-Pelagian writing to that date, including the letter to Hilary

(Letter 157). Jerome had been first in the field in opposing Pelagius; but his activity had been essentially local, and he had not covered the whole range of Pelagian interest.

Such was the situation in the ecclesiastical world in the middle of 415. There was disagreement; there was suspicion; but there was no reason to expect the sequence of violent events which marked the three following years.

The initiator of the period of violence which was to come was Paul Orosius. He belongs to that category of individuals — John Wilkes Booth is another — whose influence on the course of history is out of all proportion to the time which they occupy the stage. To say that no one could have caused more trouble than Orosius in the Pelagian affair would be rash, give the talent of human beings to cause trouble. Let it suffice that his contribution was outstanding and may have been decisive. "Talented, opinionated, narrowly orthodox, impetuous"[38] — to these qualities ascribed to him by J. N. D. Kelly we may add another, which was to prove decisive: utter lack of tact. Orosius came to Bethlehem, according to his own account, to see Jerome. He was also the bearer of two long letters from Augustine, and had perhaps been asked to warn Jerome about the pernicious views of Rufinus the Syrian, the alleged inspirer of Pelagius and perhaps a monk from Jerome's monastery.[39] But Avitus of Braga, Orosius' fellow-countryman, says that Orosius was sent to Palestine by the African bishops, which may imply that he was deputed to make common cause with Jerome against the doctrines which had been condemned in Caelestius.[40] At all events, Orosius arrived in Bethlehem full of anti-Pelagian zeal. Invited to a diocesan synod at Jerusalem on July 30, 415 he behaved with astonishing arrogance, taking the line that the decisions of the synod of Carthage of 411 and the teaching of Jerome and Augustine were not open to discussion, but merely required endorsement by the Palestinian synod. His impertinence to Bishop John was amazing, reaching its high point in his celebrated retort to John, when the latter declared: "It is I who am the Augustine here," "If you are Augustine, follow his opinion!"[41] It was no wonder that Pelagius enjoyed the sympathy of the synod and that Orosius was only able to avert his acquittal by proposing that the matter, as a Latin affair, had best be referred to Innocent of Rome for his judgment. It was, however, the sequel to the Jerusalem synod which was decisive. When Orosius came to Jerusalem for the Feast of the Dedication of the Church of the Holy Sepulchre on September 12, he was publicly denounced by Bishop John as one who held that an individual could not avoid sin even with God's help. Nothing could have been further from Augustine's thought than such a doctrine of total corruption, but the fact that such a charge could be made at all was horrifying. The *débâcle* at Jerusalem in the summer of 415 was consummated by the fiasco at Diospolis in December, when Pelagius was exonerated from all the charges brought against him. The fact that he achieved his acquittal only by disowning Caelestius and by being economical with the truth regarding his own writings was not known to the African bishops in general and to Augustine in particular until some time afterwards. If Caelestius were now to make an appeal to Rome and if the Carthaginian decision of 411 were to be set aside, African theological rectitude would receive a disastrous blow and the Catholic faith — at least in the eyes of the Africans — would be imperiled.

So the African bishops arose, terrible as an army with banners, to crush one lay-theologian of the second rank and a maverick Roman aristocrat who, since his condemnation in 411, had been living an apparently blameless life at Ephesus, not giving offence to anybody. In their letter to Pope Innocent the bishops of Proconsular Africa declared that Pelagian error had many defenders, widely dispersed,[42] although they provided no evidence to support this assertion; while their colleagues from Numidia stated that, although Pelagius in Jerusalem was said to have deceived some hearers, the opposition to his views was far stronger.[43] Aurelius of Carthage, joined by Augustine, Alypius, Evodius and Possidius — all personal friends of the bishop of Hippo — declared that they had heard that Pelagius had some supporters in Rome[44] but went on to speak of many others who ensnared and made captive weak souls.[45] This letter, clearly influenced if not drafted by Augustine, provides in succinct form the doctrine which Pelagius and Caelestius are said to be attacking and is an excellent statement of Augustinian theology. What the Africans desired, however — no doubt sincerely — was that it should be forced on the Pelagians as the only acceptable form of orthodox doctrine.

What would have happened if Innocent had declined to fall in with these African proposals we cannot tell, though it is a reasonable guess that their rejection would have provoked a crisis far greater than than occasioned by the dispute between Saint Cyprian and Pope Stephen in the third century. The inflexible determination of the Africans was shown after Innocent's death when his successor, Zosimus, attempted to reopen the question, only to be met by a flat refusal. *Causa finita est* — "the matter is settled" — was their argument, and they did not hesitate to obtain the support of the secular arm for their contentions and, in the hour of victory, to issue a series of canons expressing African doctrine in its most extreme terms.[46] It would be going too far to regard the Pelagian affair as a case of deliberate empire-building on the part of the Africans; but their intolerance of any opinion other than their own and the ruthlessness of their methods cannot be denied.

It is curious that it is only after the condemnation of Pelagius and Caelestius in 418 that we begin to find evidence of some real support for their theology. This was provided by eighteen Italian bishops, of whom Julian of Eclanum is the leading spirit and the one antagonist who seems to have really shaken and irritated Augustine. The reason for this, apart from Augustine's understandable resentment that he, the great theological expert of the West, should be_contradicted and insulted by a much younger man (and Julian's polemical style was undoubtedly offensive), lay in the fact that Julian was a really able controversialist, who chose the ground for debate very skillfully, by representing Augustine's understanding of sexual concupiscence as Manichaean, and thereby changing Pelagian tactics from a defensive to an offensive stance. Augustine and the Africans had called the Pelagians *inimici gratiae* — "enemies of grace"[47] – a charge which had a good deal of plausibility; it was very difficult to find confession of grace in Pelagian writing in any form other than grace of creation, illumination, and remission of sins in baptism, since their denial of any transmission of Original Sin postulated a self-sufficiency in man's created nature. Pelagius and Caelestius had behaved in a passive fashion in the face of such charges, defending themselves but not denouncing their accusers. Julian went on the offensive, attacking Augustine's preoccupation with sexual concupiscence as the medium by which Original Sin was transmitted as being a species of Manichaean dualism, which regarded the flesh as inherently evil. Julian was able to point to the fact that Augustine was a former Manichee and suggest that he had never ceased to be one at heart — the Ethiopian cannot change his skin or the leopard his spots.[48] If for Augustine the Pelagians were *inimici gratiae*, for Julian and his supporters Augustine and his party were *illi Manichaei, quibus modo non communicamus* — "Manichees with whom we do not now communicate."[49] It was unfair, of course. Augustine had waged an implacable war with the Manichees from 388 onwards; but Julian did not intend to be fair. He wanted to win, and his tactics were very effective. In 415 John of Jerusalem had accused Orosius of holding that man could not be free from sin even with God's help.[50] Julian, whether consciously or unconsciously, had developed the accusation in the most damaging way, by associating Augustine's theology with the heresy which, more perhaps than any other, horrified the Fathers of the Church. It may well be that Augustine's virtual obsession with Julian sprang from embarrassment at the charges which Julian leveled. His Manichaean past was still haunting him, however strongly he anathematized it.

Unfortunately for Julian, impressive as his tactics were, they came too late. If he could only have intervened earlier, before the condemnation of Pelagianism, he might have affected the course of debate, but once Pelagianism had been proscribed by pope and emperor alike and the resources of the state directed to its suppression, no argument or eloquence on his part could avail to turn the clock back. It is significant that his writings survive in large measure only because Augustine adopted the technique, which he had previously employed when answering Faustus the Manichee, of reproducing long passages from Julian before giving his own reply. Augustine apart, we have effectively no knowledge of how influential Julian's writings were in his own lifetime. Undoubtedly they were read in some circles, but how large were these circles? There was certainly a Pelagian circle at Constantinople, which included the Pelagian bishop Florus, who found a copy of Mani's *Letter to Menoch* there and dispatched it to Julian, thereby providing him with what he regarded as decisive evidence that Manichaeism and Traducianism taught the same doctrine.[51] This group was persecuted and expelled by the Patriarch Atticus,[52] perhaps as a sequel to the Emperor Honorius' edict of June 9, 419, which threatened penal sanctions against Pelagians and instructed Bishop Aurelius of Carthage to make this decision generally known.[53] However, the most remarkable feature of the sequel to the condemnation of Pelagius and Caelestius and their supporters in 418 is a negative one: the absence of any strong reaction from the movement at large. It was not the Pelagians but the Massilians, the so-called Semi-Pelagians of Southern Gaul, who had no sympathy with Pelagius but who were horrified by the implications of Augustine's predestinarian theology, which seemed to take away all freedom from the individual, who constituted the most formidable opposition to the triumph of Augustinian deterministic theology.

Unlike Pelagius and Caelestius, John Cassian and his supporters were too famous, and too much respected, to be suppressed by strong-arm measures. Prosper of Aquitaine, Augustine's admirer, might see their teaching as no more than the remains of Pelagian depravity (*reliquiae Pelagianae pravitatis*),[54] but this was far from being a universal opinion. Thus Vincent, a Semi-Pelagian monk of the famous island monastery of Lérins, while dismissing both

Pelagius and Caelestius as introducers of impious novelty in his *Commonitorium*[55] and adding an even briefer reference to Julian of Eclanum,[56] nevertheless, significantly, omits the name of Augustine from a catalogue of defenders of Christian orthodoxy which includes names like Athanasius, Gregory of Nazianzus, Basil of Caesarea, Gregory of Nyssa, Cyprian of Carthage, an Ambrose of Milan, and in a short, but vicious paragraph, expresses a condemnation of a predestinarian heresy which looks uncommonly like the teaching of Augustine as seen by a Semi-Pelagian.[57]

Augustine's literary duel with Julian of Eclanum has provided material for theological discussion over the centuries; but there is no proof that it had more than a parochial interest during the last decade of his life. This, indeed, is the problem. After 418 effective opposition to predestinarian theology came from the Semi-Pelagians. Julian is the only impressive campaigner on the Pelagian side and Julian, interestingly, reflects the oriental, Greek outlook, which emphasized free-will and recoiled with horror from the rigor of Augustine's extreme predestinarian teaching. Cyril of Alexandria, a correspondent of Augustine, who forwarded to him a copy of the minutes of the Synod of Diospolis,[58] was later to use Pelagianism as a charge with which to smear Nestorius: Pelagianism (called by Cyril Caelestianism) and Nestorianism are one and the same, in that both ascribe man's salvation to his own action, since for Nestorius Christ is not the Son of God born of Mary but a man who was by his own choice united to the eternal Son of God[59] (hence Bishop Gore's famous *mot* that "the Nestorian Christ is the fitting savior of the Pelagian man").[60] The third Ecumenical Council of Ephesus of 431 included anathemas of Caelestius, now regarded as the leader of the Pelagian party, in its first and fourth canons, but these were probably intended more as a gesture to the West than as an expression of Cyril's opinions. As Lionel Wickham has put it: "If Nestorius was, in some sense as a pupil of Theodore [of Mopsuestia], anti-Augustinian, Cyril was certainly not an Augustinian".[61] and this judgment would seem to apply to the Eastern Orthodox Church to this day. Augustine is not much of a hero there.

But what of Pelagianism in the West? So far as I can see from the evidence, it was represented only by a small group of theological writers and a handful of their supporters. It was never a mass-movement. (I ignore the suggestion initiated by J. N. L. Myres, supported by John Morris and approved by Peter Salway in *The Oxford History of England* vol. I (1981), that Pelagianism was a movement against political corruption which exercised a powerful influence in Britain after the Roman withdrawal from the island, because I simply cannot believe it.) The Africans over-reacted against the movement after the failure of the prosecutions of Pelagius in Palestine in 415 because they saw their own theology in danger. In consequence they ascribed to Pelagius and Caelestius and their supporters an importance that they never in fact possessed, and this belief was sustained for centuries by the influence of Augustine's writings. Augustine, certainly, came to see Pelagianism as a deadly menace – "the proudest heresy of all" – and his criticism of its theology, whether we accept it or not, has played a decisive rôle in religious thought in Western Christendom. Peter Brown has said that "Pelagianism as we know it, that consistent body of ideas of momentous consequence, had come into existence; but in the mind of Augustine, not of Pelagius [in the winter of 411-412]."[62] I think that this date is too early, and would consider that Augustine's formal systematization of Pelagianism came to birth later, in the period 416-417, with Paul Orosius as midwife; but I accept Brown's view that historians and theologians have too long tended to form their image of Pelagianism by looking through Augustinian spectacles.

Notes

* The first of the two Otts Lectures for 1992, delivered at Davidson College, North Caroline, on March 25, 1992. The second lecture will be published in the next issue of *Augustinian Studies*.

1. *De Gratia Christi et de Peccato Originali* 1, 32,35; *CSEL* 42, 152.

2. *Confessionum libri XIII* 10, 29, 40; *CCSL* 27, 176; *De dono perseuerantiae* 20, 53; *PL* 45, 1026.

3. Nevertheless, both their denial of any transmission of Original Sin and their indignation at the excuses of sinners inevitably made them rigorist in their approach, with little inclination to accept the necessity of those 'daily light and trivial sins' from which, according to Augustine, life here on earth is never exempt (*Enchiridion ad Laurentium* 19, 71; *CCSL* 46, 88.

4. *De possibilitate non peccandi* 3, 2; *PLS* 1, 1460. Translated by B. R. Rees, *The Letters of Pelagius and his Followers* (Woodbridge: The Boydell Press 1991).

5. One may here note some psychological understanding on the part of the Pelagians, at least in the case of the Sicilian Anonymous.

6. Pelagius, *Epistula ad Celantiam* 28: "apostolicae doctrinae regula nec cum Ioviniano aequat continentiae opera nuptiarum nec cum Manicheo coniugia condemnat." *Inter* Jerome, *Epistula* 148; *CSEL* 56, 352.

7. *De Gratia Christi* 2, 3, 3; *CSEL* 42, 169.

8. *De Gestis Pelagii* 35, 62; *CSEL* 42, 116.

9. *Inter Aug.*, *Epistula* 175, 4: "impietas, quae iam multos assertores habet per diuersa dispersos;" cf. 6: ". . . multi, qui eorum perhibentur esse uel fuisse discipuli, haec mala, quibus fundamenta Christianae fidei conantur euertere, quacumque possunt, adfirmare non cessant." *CSEL* 44, 658, 661-662.

10. Augustine, *Epistula* 177, 2; *CSEL* 44, 670.

11. *Inter Aug.*, *Epistula* 183, 2; *CSEL* 44, 725-6.

12. Marius Mercator, *Chronicon*, s.a. 418. *MGH. Chronica Minora*, ed. T. Mommsen (Berlin 1892) i. p. 468.

13. See Honorius, *Rescript* of April 30, 418. *PL* 45, 126-7; 48, 39-86.

14. Augustine, *Epistula* 156; *CSEL* 44, 448.

15. *De Diuitiis* 18, 1-11; *PLS* 1, 1407-11; Tr. Rees, *The Letters of Pelagius* 200-05.

16. Celestine, *Epistula* 13, 1. 8; *PL* 50, 469B; 481B. See Gerald Bonner, "Some remarks on Letters 4* and 6*" in *Les lettres de Saint Augustin découvertes par Johannes Divjak: Communications présentées au Colloque des 20 et 21 sept. 1982* (Paris: Etudes Augustiniennes 1983), 161-2.

17. I made this suggestion in my Augustine Lecture, *Saint Augustine and Modern Research on Pelagianism* (Villanova: Villanova University Press 1972), 26-7. It remains no more than an hypothesis.

18. Rees, *op. cit.* (note 4 above). Writing in Washington, D.C., unable to remember the names of the scholars, and with my copy of their book in England, I shall have to give the reference with the text of the second lecture.

19. I accept the arguments of Robert. F. Evans, *Four Letters of Pelagius* (New York: The Seabury Press 1968).

20. See G. Martinetto, "Les premières reaction de Pelage", *Revue des Etudes Augustiniennes* (1971) 83-117. His attribution is accepted by Juan B. Valero, *Las bases antropologicas de Pelagio en su tratado de las Espositiones* (Madrid: Universidad Pontificia Comillas de Madrid 1980).

21. *De dono perseuerantiae* 20, 53; *PL* 45, 1026; Orosius, *Apologeticus Liber* 3; *CSEL* 5, 607.

22. This is not to deny Julian's originality as a polemicist. See Elizabeth A. Clark, "Vitiated seeds and holy vessels: Augustine's Manichaean past" in *Ascetic Piety and Women's Faith. Essays on Late Ancient Christianity* (Studies in Women and Religion v. 20 -- Lewiston, NY: The Edward Mellen Press 1986) 291-349.

23. See Augustine, *De Gratia Christi* 1, 35, 38; *CSEL* 42, 154.

24. *PL* 30, 15-45; 33, 1099-1120. Tr. by Rees, *op. cit.*, 35-70.

25. Augustine, *De Gratia Christi* 1, 1, 1; *CSEL* 42, 125.

26. Inter Aug., *Epistula* 183, 2; *CSEL* 44, 726.

27. Augustine, *Epistula* 194; *CSEL* 57, 176-214.

28. See Bonner, *op. cit.* (note 17 above) p. 36.

29. Inter Aug., *Epistula* 156; *CSEL* 44, 448-9; Augustine, *Epistula* 157; *CSEL* 44, 449-88.

30. *De natura et gratia* 1, 1; *CSEL* 60, 233.

31. Orosius, *Apologeticus Liber* 4, 6: ". . . et in libro, quem nunc scribit . . ." *CSEL* 5, 608.

32. Robert F. Evans, *Pelagius. Inquires and Reappraisals* (New York: The Seabury Press 1968) 6-25.

33. *Epistula* 169, 4, 13: "scripsi etiam grandem quendam librum aduersus Pelagii haeresim cogentibus nonnullis fratribus" *CSEL* 44, 621.

34. *De natura et gratia* 1, 1; *CSEL* 60, 233.

35. *De perfectione iustitiae hominis* 21, 44; *CSEL* 42, 48.

36. See Evans, *op. cit* (note 32 above) pp. 21-4.

37. Jerome, *Epistula* 133, 1-3; *CSEL* 56, 241-7; *Dialogus aduersus Pelagianos* 1, 1-5; *PL* 23, 495A-501B. See J. N. D. Kelly, *Jerome* (London: Duckworth 1975) 319.

38. Kelly, *op. cit.*, p. 317.

39. See J. A. Davids, *De Orosio et sancto Augustino Priscillianistarum et Origenistarum aduersariis: commentatio historica et philologica* (The Hague 1930) 23.

40. Avitus, *Epistula ad Palchonium*, *PL* 41, 805-06. See Davids, *op. cit.*, pp. 23-4.

41. Orosius, *Apologeticus Liber* 4; *CSEL* 5, 608.

42. See above, note 9.

43. Inter Aug., *Epistula* 176, 4; *CSEL* 44, 667.

44. Inter Aug., *Epistula* 177, 2; *CSEL* 44, 670.

45. *Ibid.*, 3; *CSEL* 44, 671.

46. See F. Floeri, "Le Pape Zosime et la doctrine augustienne du péché originel" in *Augustinus Magister* (Paris: Etudes Augustiniennes 1954), ii. pp. 755-61; G. Bonner, "Les origines africaines de la doctrine augustinienne sur la chute et le péché originel", *Augustinus* (1967) 102-03; Pier Franco Beatrice, *Tradux Peccati. Alle fonti della dottrina agostiniana del peccato originale* (Milan: Università Cattolica del Sacro Cuore 1978) 288-95; J. Patout Burns, "Augustine's role in the imperial action against Pelagius", *The Journal of Theological Studies*, NS 30 (1979) 67-83.

47. Augustine, *Epistula* 176, 2; *CSEL* 44, 664; *Contra duas epistulas Pelagianorum* 1, 1, 2; *CSEL* 60, 424.

48. *Opus imperfectum contra Iulianum* 4, 42; *PL* 45, 1361.

49. *Contra duas epistulas Pelagianorum* 1, 2, 4; *CSEL* 60, 425.

50. Orosius, *Apologeticus Liber* 7, 1-3; *CSEL* 5, 611.

51. *Opus imperfectum contra Iulianum* 3, 166. 187; *CSEL* 85, 469. 485-8.

52. Celestine, *Epistula* 13, 1. 8; *PL* 50, 469B. 481AB.

53. *Inter Aug.*, *Epistula* 201, 1-2; *CSEL* 57, 296-9.

54. Prosper, *Epistula ad Augustinum* 7; *PL* 51, 72C.

55. Vincent, *Commonitorium* 24, 8-9; *CCSL* 64, 181.

56. *Ibid.*, 28, 15; *CCSL* 64, 188-9.

57. *Ibid.*, 26, 8-9; *CCSL* 64, 185. On Gallic Opposition to Augustinian predestinarian theology, see the papers by Ralph W. Mathisen. "For Specialists only; The Reception of Augustine and His Teachings in Fifth-Century Gaul" in *Presbyter Factus Sum*, edd. by Joseph T. Lienhard, Earl C. Muller and Roland J. Teske (*Collectanea Augustiniana*, edd. by Joseph C. Schnaubelt and Frederick van Fleteren, vol. II) Villanova, PA: 1992), 29-41 and Thomas A Smith, "Augustine in Two Gallic Controversies: Use or Abuse", *op. cit.*, pp. 43-55. Also Robert Markus, "The Legacy of Pelagius" in *The making of orthodoxy: Essays in honour of Henry Chadwick*, ed. by Rowan Williams (Cambridge University Press 1989), 214-34.

58. Augustine, *Epistula* 4*, 2; *CSEL* 88, 26-7. BA 46B, 108-10.

59. Photius, *Bibliotheca* 54; *PG* 103, 93C-97A. See Lionel Wickham, "Pelagianism in the East" in *The making of orthodoxy*, 204-05.

60. Charles Gore, "Our Lord's Human example", Church Quarterly Review 16 (1883) 98.

61. Wickham, *art. cit.* (note 59 above), p. 211.

62. P. Brown, *Augustine of Hippo: A Biography* (London: Faber 1967) 345.

Augustinian Studies 24 (1993) 27-47

Augustine and Pelagianism*

Gerald Bonner
The Catholic University of America

In my previous lecture I offered you an interpretation of Pelagianism which regarded it as a literary movement, which has achieved a rather unhappy immortality by coming into conflict with the African bishops, who saw their dogma of Original Sin called into question by the conciliar decisions in Palestine in 415, which declared Pelagius to be orthodox. Alarmed by these developments, the Africans ruthlessly exerted all their considerable influence to crush Pelagius and his disciple, Caelestius, procuring their excommunication by Pope Innocent and refusing to consent to any reopening of the case by Innocent's successor, Zosimus. In this they succeeded so well that in the aftermath of the condemnations of 418 the real opposition came, not from the handful of Pelagian supporters and their indefatigable literary spokesman, Julian of Eclanum, but from the so-called Semi-Pelagian theologians of Southern Gaul, who were alarmed by the implications of Augustine's predestinarian theology, and who were too distinguished a group to be repressed by the methods which had been applied to the Pelagians. As a result of the influence exercised by Augustine's writings over Latin Christianity in the following centuries, a kind of heroic picture of the Pelagian Controversy was constructed, which seemed to be confirmed by the condemnation of Caelestius and his supporters at the Third Ecumenical Council of Ephesus in 431, though there is no particular reason to suppose that Cyril of Alexandria was much concerned with Pelagianism, except as another indictment to urge against Nestorius. In short, I sought to argue that the importance of Pelagianism as a movement, as opposed to its undoubted importance as a theological tendency, has been exaggerated by Church historians, both old and new, who have taken their estimate of it from the extreme opinions of Augustine and his African colleagues.

A criticism that could be levelled against my view, even by those who would be willing to give it a generally favorable reception, is that it underestimates the active — as opposed to the literary — role of Augustine in the Controversy and over-emphasizes the contribution of the African episcopate. I recognize the force of this argument, since nobody can ignore the part played by Augustine in pressing the campaign against Pelagius from the year 416 onwards. I think that he had good reason for his zeal, since the acquittal of Pelagius at Diospolis in 415 seemed to call into question, not only Augustine's personal theology but also his conviction, which had played so large a part in his arguments with the Donatists, that there was one Catholic faith, maintained from East to West by the undivided Church of Christ, and it was essential for him to have that conviction reaffirmed by the Roman see, the senior see of Christendom. Nevertheless, I remain persuaded that Augustine's African colleagues were not mere followers of their brilliant spokesman, but people with minds of their own and firmly-held beliefs about the rightness of African doctrine. The history of African Christianity, from the days of Cyprian to its fall to the Arab invaders in the seventh century, reveals a Church determined to maintain its own convictions against pope and emperor alike, not by disowning these authorities, but by insisting that they should recognize the correctness of African understanding of the faith. It has been suggested that the medieval Papacy only became possible because the African Church, the one Western local Church which had the prestige and the self-confidence to oppose Roman pretensions, had been destroyed by the Arabs. This has long seemed to me to be a very plausible hypothesis.

Nevertheless, even if one does not accept the view that Augustine was, from the first, the prime mover of the campaign against Pelagius, there can be no question of his importance in it, and this raises the question: What precisely was the effect upon him of the challenge of Pelagianism? One answer to this question was given by Martin Luther who, in his forthright way, suggested that the Pelagians "made a man of Augustine" who, but for them, would have been "a very dry and thin teacher."[1] Considering that the *Confessions* were written before Pelagius appeared on the scene of Augustine's life, and that the *De Trinitate* and the *De Civitate Dei*, although composed during the Controversy, were certainly not inspired by it, one can only say that Luther's opinion was a very personal one, reflecting the interests and preoccupations of the speaker. However, like many other sweeping generalizations, Luther's is not without an element of truth. The Pelagian Controversy had its effect upon Augustine, producing in him a theological hardening, pleasing to some in his own time and in later centuries, repulsive to others; and the hardening was of a different order from that produced by other controversies. It is an unhappy fact that Augustine, although never descending to the sort of controversial vituperation which disfigures the works of certain other patristic writers when disputing with theological opponents, tended as time wore on to become increasingly bitter. Thus, at the beginning of his anti-Donatist campaign, in the *Psalmus abecedarius*, composed in 394, he was to lament the alleged cruelties perpetrated upon the Donatists in 347, in the so-called Macarian persecution.[2] In his last anti-Donatist work, the *Contra Gaudentium* of 419-20, he had come to approve imperial coercion to bring the separatists back into the Catholic fold and could tell Gaudentius, the Donatist bishop of Thamugadi, who had threatened to burn himself and his congregation in his church, rather than give up that church to the Catholics, that it was better for a few abandoned people to perish, than for a multitude of souls, whose way to salvation they impeded, to burn with them in hell for ever.[3] But Augustine's hardening in the Pelagian Controversy went deeper. He became progressively more and more persuaded that the sovereignty of God had to be maintained against all human notions of love and justice. Julian of Eclanum observed that Augustine worshipped a God who was a *nascentium persecutor* — a tormentor of neonates.[4] Such an accusation cannot fairly be levelled against Augustine himself — the fate of unbaptized infants was a source of anguish for him; but he accepted the doctrine and expressed it in terrible language. Let me cite one example, taken from a letter of 418.

> God by His creation, has willed so many souls to be born who, He foreknew, would have no part in His grace, so that they might, by an incomparable multitude, outnumber those whom He has deigned to predestinate as children of promise in the glory of His kingdom, in order that it might be shown, by the very multitude of the reprobate, that the number of those who are most justly damned, whatever it may be, is of no concern with the righteous God; and that those who are redeemed from condemnation should thereby also understand that only damnation, which they see bestowed upon so large a part of humanity, was due to the whole lump, not only to those who, by the choice of an evil will have added many sins to the Original Sin, but also to so many little children who, being bound only by the chain of Original Sin, are snatched from this [mortal] light without the grace of the Mediator. Indeed, this whole lump would receive its debt of just damnation unless *the potter*, who is not only just but also merciful, should make some *vessels to honor*, according to grace (Rom. 9:21) and not according to what was due, while

> He relieves some little children, to whom no merits can be ascribed, and anticipates some adults, so that they may have some merits.[5]

This uncompromising declaration on Augustine's part shows that nine years of anti-Pelagian polemic had, indeed, in Luther's words, "made a man of him." During the next, and final, decade of his life, Augustine was to display an ever-increasing rigor, which justified John Calvin's claim: "If I wanted to weave a whole volume from Augustine, I could readily show my readers that I need no other language than his. But I do not want to burden them with wordiness."[6] If Calvin's assertion seems exaggerated, consider this passage from the *De Praedestinatione Sanctorum*, composed in 429, the year before Augustine's death.

> Let us therefore understand the calling by which the elect are made. They are not chosen because they have believed, but in order that they may believe. . . . And so they were chosen before the foundation of the world, by that predestination by which God fulfilled what He had preordained. *For those whom he had predestined, he also called*, by that calling according to His plan, and not therefore any others, but *those whom he called, he justified* (Rom. 8:30). Nor did He call any others but those whom he had predestined, called and justified, those also he glorified, by that end which has no end. God therefore chose the faithful; but in order that they might be faithful, not because they were already faithful.[7]

This passage well exemplifies the hardening in Augustine's pronouncements in the years following the condemnation of Pelagius and Caelestius. Many readers will find it distasteful, if not horrifying. Thus John Burnaby, one of the great exegetes of Augustine's theology of love, was moved to observe that "nearly all that Augustine wrote after his seventieth year [i.e. 423-424] is the work of a man whose energy has burnt itself out, whose love has grown cold," though he qualified this allegation by the admission that "not even in the *De Correptione et Gratia* [written in 426] is the Augustine of the *Confessions* altogether unrecognizable."[8] This is true; but it is true in a particular way, which Burnaby did not dwell upon. The fact is that the doctrines which Augustine maintained against the Pelagians, with all their implications, had been formulated long before Pelagianism came to Augustine's notice. Controversy constrained him to draw out the implications and to affirm them with a steadily increasing dogmatism, which admitted of no other understanding than his, a dogmatism which alarmed the Semi-Pelagian theologians of Marseilles, because it seemed to take from the individual any element of free choice and to leave him a puppet in the hands of his Creator, and their view is surely correct. Augustine never forgot the words of Romans 9:20-21: *Shall what is made say to the potter, Why hast*

*thou made me thus? Does not the potter have power out of the same clay
to make one vessel to honor and another for ignoble use?* It is a feature
of Augustine's theological development that he came increasingly to em-
phasise the absolute power of God. It is true that he always insisted that
this absolute power was not, as it might appear, exercised in an arbitrary
and tyrannical way, and that at the Last Day the justice of God will be
revealed, by which one soul is taken and another left; but in the meantime: *Does not the potter have power out of the same clay to make one
vessel to honor and another for ignoble use?*

Let us endeavor to follow the development of Augustine's thought as
it is revealed in the Pelagian Controversy.

It may reasonably be said that the foundation of Augustine's anti-
Pelagian polemic is his belief in the need for baptism for all ages as a
remedy for the guilt inherited from Adam, *in whom all sinned.*
Augustine's first anti-Pelagian treatise, the *De Peccatorum Meritis et
Remissione*, significantly, has for a subtitle: *De Baptismo Parvulorum.*
The issue with Pelagian theology was one of principle, not practice.
Caelestius, the man who initiated the debate in Africa, and Julian of
Eclanum at later date, accepted the desirability of infant baptism, but
denied that this had any particular theological implications. Augustine,
and the other African bishops, insisted that it did. They could point to
Letter 64 of their hero, St Cyprian, conveying the decision of an African
council of sixty-six bishops, which probably met in the spring of 252.

> No one is denied access to baptism and grace. How much less reason is
> there then for denying it to an infant who, being newly born, can have
> committed no sins! The only thing that he has done is that, being born
> after the flesh as a descendant of Adam, he has contracted from that first
> birth the ancient contagion of death. And he is admitted to receive remis-
> sion of his sins all the more readily in that what are being remitted to him
> are not his own sins but another's.[9]

Such was the doctrine of the African Church with which Augustine
would have been familiar from the time of his return to Africa in 388. He
may have learned it earlier, from the instruction of Ambrose, at Milan.
(It is significant that the first attack on Caelestius in Africa for denying
the need for infant baptism for the remission of sins came from the Milanese deacon, Paulinus.) In Augustine's case, however, the notion of an
inherited sin is tied to another, and more terrible, theological conception:
the idea of the *massa*, the lump of sin, to which all human beings adhere,
because of their seminal participation in the Fall, and from which only a
very small minority is liberated. The notion of the *massa* is not
Augustine's invention. He inherited it, possibly from the unidentified

theologian traditionally known as Ambrosiaster whom he calls Hilary; but for Augustine the notion had a more sinister connotation than it had for his predecessor, and this has caused some scholars — probably wrongly — to see in it a reflection of the *bôlos*, the lump of sinful, dark matter, from which, in the Manichaean theology, the imprisoned light-particles could not be set free, but were lost for ever.[10]

The doctrine of the *massa* first appears in Augustine's writings in Question 68 of the *De Diversis Quaestionibus LXXXIII*, published by him in 395/6, and must therefore have been formulated at some time before that date, probably when Augustine was presbyter of Hippo. To quote Question 68:

> For *just as we have borne the image of the earthly man* (I Cor. 15:49) let us now bear *the image of the heavenly man* (ibid.), *putting off the old man and putting on the new* (cf. Col. 3:9-10), so that no one may say to us, as to a vessel of clay, *Shall what is made say to its maker, Why hast thou made me thus?* (Rom.9:20) And in order that it may be made clear that these words are not said to a sanctified spirit but to fleshly clay, see what follows: *Does not the potter have power out of the same clay to make one vessel for honor and another of ignoble use?* (Rom.9:21) Therefore from the time that our nature sinned in paradise, we are formed by the same divine providence, not according to heaven, but according to earth, that is, not according to spirit, but according to the flesh by mortal generation, and we are now made from the same lump of slime, which is the lump of sin. Since therefore we lost our merit by sinning, and lacking God's mercy nothing is owed to sinners but eternal damnation, what does a man from this mass do, when he answers God back and says: *Why hast thou made me thus?*[11]

At about the time when Augustine was preparing *De Diversis Quaestionibus LXXXIII* for publication, or perhaps a little earlier — we cannot be more precise than this — he was completing the second and third books of his treatise *On Free Choice*, begun at Rome in 388. Of this work, Augustine specifically declares in the *Retractations* that it was directed against the Manichees, to discuss the question: *quid sit malum?* — what is evil? Augustine's concern was with the primal sin of Adam. If evil is not something positive, as the Manichees taught, but a non-entity, a negation, how did it come about that Adam, who was created by a good God, ever fell into sin? Augustine begins his enquiry from the orthodox Christian principle that God cannot be the source of evil: "We believe that everything that exists is created by the one God, and yet that God is not the cause of sin. The difficulty is: if sins go back to souls created by one God, and souls go back to God, how can we avoid tracing sins back to God?"[12] Augustine's answer is that sin arises from a movement in the soul which he calls *libido*, an evil form of *cupiditas* (desire).[13] *Libido* is, indeed, a blameworthy form of *cupiditas*.[14] In view of the importance which the word *libido* will subsequently have on Augustine's later works, whether as *libido dominandi*, the lust for rule which is so forcefully denounced in *The City of God*, or as *libido carnalis*, sexual lust, which is to figure so prominently in his later anti-Pelagian writings, it should be made clear that, in the *De Libero Arbitrio*, the word is not to be identified directly either with disordered sexuality (which did not exist before the Fall) or with lust for power and domination (which equally did not then exist). Essentially, *libido* is a desire for lower good things, good in themselves, but not supremely good, in preference to the Supreme Good, which is God (a theme which will become familiar in Augustine's later writings). In the *De Libero Arbitrio*, however, Augustine is not concerned with the consequences of Adam's sin, but with its cause. As he says in Book III: "It is more important to enquire in what state the first man was created than how his descendants have been propagated,"[15] and his opinion is, that Adam was created neither wise (*sapiens*) — for if he had been, he would not have fallen into sin — nor foolish (*stultus*) — for if he had been, God his creator would have been the cause of sin and not himself. Instead, Adam was created in a midway condition (*media adfectio*),[16] which could neither be called wisdom nor folly — the will is a certain midway good (*medium quoddam bonum*).[17] Free choice in Adam, Augustine was later to declare in the *De Spiritu et Littera*, was a *media vis*, a neutral power capable of being turned towards God for good or away from Him and so to sin.[18] Augustine never resolved the fundamental question of why this power, which was bestowed upon Adam by a good and loving Creator, should have led to sin rather than to obedience nor, in the *De Libero Arbitrio*, did he greatly care to do so.

> What need, then, is there to seek the origin of the motion, by which the will turns from the Unchangeable to a changeable good? We admit that it is a movement of the soul, that it is voluntary, and therefore culpable. All useful learning in this matter has its object and its value in teaching us to condemn this movement and to restrain it, and to turn our wills from falling into temporal pleasures to the enjoyment of the Eternal Good.[19]

The *De Libero Arbitrio* was destined to play an important role in the development of Augustine's view of Pelagianism, because a passage from it was quoted, together with those of other Christian authors, by

Pelagius in his work *De Natura*, in support of his own view that sin could be avoided, if an individual chose.

> Whatever is the cause of the will, if it cannot be avoided, there is no sin in yielding to it. If it can be resisted, then there must be no yielding and there will then be no sin. Or perhaps it may trick the unwary? Then care must be taken not to be tricked. Or is the trickery such that it cannot possibly be guarded against? In that case there is no sin, for who sins in committing what he cannot guard against? But since sin is committed, it therefore can be avoided.[20]

This quotation may well have been decisive in determining Augustine's later attitude to Pelagius; its citation seemed to imply that his own earlier theology had, in effect, been Pelagian. In fact, throughout the treatise *De Libero Arbitrio*, Augustine was discussing Adam's nature before the Fall and not as it exists today, in a vitiated state, among his descendants. Augustine had made this abundantly clear, in passages which he subsequently quoted in the *De Natura et Gratia*, written in 415 in reply to Pelagius' *De Natura*.

> There are two punishments for every sinful soul: ignorance and difficulty. Because of ignorance, error puts us to shame; because of difficulty, anguish afflicts us. But it is not the nature of man, as he was created, but rather the pain of man under condemnation to approve the false for the true, and not to be able to refrain from lustful action on account of the insistence and torturing anguish of the flesh.[21]

And again:

> Properly, we speak of nature in one way when referring to that nature in which man was first made guiltless as the first of his race, and in another way when we speak of that nature in which we are now born, condemned by the sentence passed upon Adam, ignorant and enslaved in the flesh, in the manner of which the Apostle says: We were by nature children of wrath, even as the rest (Eph.2:3).[22]

Given such specific declarations in the *De Libero Arbitrio*, it is difficult not to feel that Pelagius was either disingenuous, or at least grossly careless, in choosing quotations from Augustine to support his own position which Augustine did not hold. It is true that we have only Augustine's reference as evidence; but since Augustine's treatise was addressed to Timasius and James, the two former disciples of Pelagius who had brought the *De Natura* to Augustine's attention and asked for his comments, there seems every reason to assume the fundamental reliability of his evidence. The fact that Pelagius had cited the *De Libero Arbitrio* in support of his arguments would particularly concern Augustine, because he obviously thought well of the work. He had recommended its reading to Secundinus the Manichee in 405/6;[23] had defended its content in a letter addressed to Count Marcellinus in 412;[24] and had referred to its wide circulation in a letter to Jerome in 415.[25] In a letter to Paulinus of Nola, written in the middle of 417, he declared that it was Pelagius' *De Natura* which first opened his eyes to the dangers of Pelagian doctrine, which threatened to destroy any belief in the grace of God bestowed upon humanity through the one Mediator, Jesus Christ.[26] It is, of course, true that Pelagius, since he denied any transmission of Original Sin from Adam to his descendants, might have replied that what Augustine said about Adam's nature would be equally applicable to human nature today; but for Augustine such misrepresentation of his doctrine was more than misunderstanding: it was a perversion of his teaching which appeared to ascribe to him a theology which he held to be wholly wrong.

At the same time, it would be a mistake to suppose that the emphasis of the *De Libero Arbitrio*, completed at some time between 391 and 393, was exactly the same as that of Augustine's later anti-Pelagian writings. Because Augustine was dealing with the initial cause of sin in Adam, and not with its subsequent manifestations in the human race, and because when he wrote it there was no opposition of a Pelagian character to his assumptions, he did not, when he composed it, feel the same necessity to emphasis the need for grace as he did later.[27] But there was another consideration: in the period 391-395 Augustine's view on the overriding power of grace had still not fully developed. Evidence of this is to be found in his *Expositio in Epistulam ad Romanos*, composed in 394/5, in which he speaks of the *massa luti* — "the lump of slime" — from which the potter makes one vessel to honor and another to dishonor[28] and quotes Romans 9:20-21: *O man, who art thou, that repliest unto God?* But he also asserts the power of free choice, by which a person may believe and receive grace,[29] and speaks in a Semi-Pelagian fashion of grace being given as a reward for the faith which God foresees that an individual will have[30] — language which he was later to explain in the *Retractations:* "I had not yet sought diligently enough or discerned up to this time what is the nature of 'the election of grace,' concerning which the same Apostle says: *There is a remnant left selected out of grace* (Rom.11:5). This certainly is not grace if any merits precede it."[31] Augustine's thought in 395 is, indeed, very like the theology of the Semi-Pelagians of Marseilles, which he opposed some thirty years later.

A year after writing the *Expositio in Epistulam ad Romanos,* Augustine's attitude changed, with portentous consequences. Having been asked by his old pastor Simplicianus, the presbyter of Milan who succeeded St. Ambrose as bishop in 397, to explain certain passages of Scripture, Augustine suddenly came to comprehend, with an absolute clarity, what he believed to be the full significance of I Corinthians 4:7: *For who singles thee out? Or what hast thou that thou didst not receive? And if thou hast received it, why dost thou boast, as if it were not a gift?*[32] As an intellectual conversion, this illumination while writing to Simplicianus in 396 falls only a little short of that experience at Milan ten years before, for by it Augustine came to perceive that the elect are not chosen because they believe, but in order that they may believe. Put in another way, a conviction of God's absolute power took possession of Augustine's mind, and what he was to write subsequently in the later stages of the Pelagian Controversy represented a restatement, with increased emphasis and harshness, of the conclusions to which he had come in 396.

Augustine himself certainly did not underestimate the significance of his conversion, which marked for him the triumph of divine grace over human free choice, and acceptance of the absolute power of God over His creation, including human beings. At the end of his life, in the *De Dono Perseverantiae*, he cited the *Ad Simplicianum*, followed by the *Confessions*, as works which had opposed Pelagianism long before Pelagius had written.[33] One can see the *Confessions*, indeed, as the exemplification in Augustine's own career, up to his baptism, of the message of the illumination of 396. *What hast thou, that thou didst not receive? And if thou hast received it, why dost thou boast, as if it were not a gift?* "Give what thou dost command, and command what thou wilt." Is not this famous prayer effectively a practical application of the text of I Corinthians 4:7?[34]

I have, in my previous lecture,[35] spoken of the restraint exercised by Augustine in his early dealings with the Pelagians in the period 411-415: he sees them as brethren to be persuaded, rather then as heretics to be suppressed, even though their convictions went clean against his own. I have long been persuaded that the change in his attitude from fraternal remonstrance to implacable hostility, made clear when, after the condemnation of Pelagius, Albinia, Pinianus and Melania attempted to approach him on Pelagius' behalf,[36] was not simply due to the fact that he had lost trust in Pelagius' honesty. Behind this obvious reaction we may, I suggest, see evidence of deep-seated alarm. The events of the year 415, notably the apparent endorsement of Pelagius' theology by the two Palestinian synods, seemed to call into question Augustine's assumption of the universality of Christian doctrine, including the African understanding of the doctrine of Original Sin. Although this initial impression was erroneous, as Augustine subsequently discovered by reading the minutes of the Synod of Diospolis, the fear persisted, and could be exorcised only by the formal confirmation of African — that is, Augustinian — theology by the Apostolic See. Hence the pressure on Pope Innocent in 416 and the unyielding opposition to Pope Zosimus, when he sought to reopen the case in 417. Furthermore, Augustine could not afford, for his own peace of mind, to tolerate any differences of opinion on the two great issues which were to preoccupy the last years of his life: the divine decree of predestination; and the problem of the transmission of Original Sin.

With regard to predestination, I have already quoted the terrifying letter of 418, in which Augustine declared that "by the very multitude of the reprobate" it is shown that "the number of those who are most justly damned, whatever it may be, is of no concern with the righteous God."[37] I have also quoted the assertion made at the end of his life in 429, in the *De Praedestinatione Sanctorum*, in which he declares that the elect "are not chosen because they have believed, but are chosen in order that they may believe."[38] One has only to compare these pronouncements with the language of his *Expositio in Epistulam ad Romanos* of 395 to see the change which has come over his thinking. Thus, in the Expositio, Augustine can quote Romans 9:20: *O man, who art thou who replies unto God?*[39] and speak of the *massa luti,* to which all pertain who are not brought to spiritual things;[40] but he can also say:

> For it is ours to believe and to will, but God's to give to those who believe and will the power of doing good through the Holy Spirit, through whom charity is poured into our hearts (Rom.5:5)[41]

and again:

> We cannot will if we are not called, and when, after the call, we have willed, our will and our course do not suffice, if God does not give strength to the runners and lead whither He calls. It is clear, therefore, that it is not *of him who wills or of him who runs but of God showing mercy* (Rom.9:16) that we do mercy[42]

both of which passages he sought to explain in the *Retractations,*[43] since he felt that each left a loophole for human initiative, however small. The conversion experience of 396 swept away all such scruples. We have freedom only because God gives us freedom, and we are saved, only because God wills us to be saved. The elect are not chosen because they have believed, but in order that they may believe.

221

It was this apparent denial of any possibility of human initiative in the response to the call of God which produced the reaction which is commonly, but misleadingly, called Semi-Pelagianism, and which may more accurately be described as a reassertion and defense of the same principles which Augustine had himself affirmed in his *Expositio in Epistulam ad Romanos* in 395.

> Man has it in his power by free choice to believe the Liberator and to receive grace, that with Him who now bestows it setting him free and aiding him, he need not sin, and thus he may cease to be under the Law, but rather with the Law or in the Law fulfil the Law by the love of God, which he could not do by the fear of God.[44]

This view had vanished, for Augustine, with the illumination of 396. Certain individuals, both in Africa and in Gaul, found his later theology, as expressed in the treatises *De Correptione et Gratia* and *De Dono Perseverantiae*, intolerable: it removed all freedom from man, so that he could not even respond to the Gospel, unless God gave him the power to do so, a power that was not simply free choice, but a specific and deliberate act of grace accorded to only the elect, who had been chosen by God without any regard to foreseen merit. The essence of the dispute between Augustine and the Semi-Pelagians turns on the beginning of faith (*initium fidei*). For the mature Augustine, this is solely the action of God. For the Semi-Pelagians, such an understanding was both too limited and too limiting. John Cassian of Marseilles, the most distinguished name among them, maintained that although God works in all men, it sometimes happens that the beginning of good works comes from individuals, as a result of the natural good which God has implanted in them in their creation — examples would be Zacchaeus the publican; the Penitent Thief; Abraham; and Cornelius, the centurion — while in other cases God's grace anticipates the human will — examples here would be Paul; Matthew; Peter; Andrew; and the rest of the Apostles.[45] Accordingly, divine grace is dispensed to humanity in various ways and according to the capacity of the individual.

The difference between the views of the Semi-Pelagians and Augustine might be explained as being due to their different pastoral experience: Cassian and the Messalians looked to the Egyptian Desert, where the monk waited upon God and needed to be reassured that, if God found even a tiny spark of faith, He would blow it into a flame, and the individual must therefore not lose heart if his prayers appeared to go unanswered; while Augustine, laboring in a parish with its usual quota of Laodicean souls, did not so easily assume that everyone of his flock was striving to make progress in the Christian life; but this explanation is too easy, and ignores the significance of the conversion of 396: *What hast thou, that thou didst not receive? And if thou hast received it, why dost thou boast, as if it were not a gift?* and the brutal words of the letter of 418: "The number of those who are most justly damned, whatever it may be, is of no concern with the righteous God."[46] Augustine believed that, since the Incarnation, with the particular and peculiar exception of the martyrs, there was no admission to the Kingdom of Heaven except by the reception of the sacrament of baptism, which Christ Himself had instituted. He was well aware that, in his day, the great majority of human beings went out of the world without receiving the sacrament. Accordingly, they were damned; though infants who had committed no personal sins would be afflicted with only the mildest penalties.[47] Augustine was, nevertheless, persuaded that there is no injustice in God.

> Likewise, as the Apostle says: *Not of him who wills nor of him who runs, but of showing mercy* (Rom.9:16). He also comes to the aid of some infants, although they do not even will or run, when He wishes to aid them, whom He chose in Christ before the foundation of the world. To these He gives grace graciously, that is, with no preceding merits on their part, either of faith or of good works. But He did not come to the assistance of those adults whom He did not will to aid, even when He foresaw that they would have believed His miracles, if they had been worked among them. In his foreknowledge He judged otherwise about them, secretly indeed, but justly, for there is no injustice in God for *inscrutable are his judgements and his ways* past finding out (Rom.11:33) and *all the ways of the Lord are mercy and truth* (Ps.24 [25]:10).[48]

Between such a view and that of the Semi-Pelagians there was no reconciliation. Augustine had no doubt about the harshness of his doctrine and recommended that it should be proclaimed discreetly;[49] but he never questioned its rightness — hence his attempts to explain away the words of I Timothy 2:4: *God willeth all men to be saved and to come to the knowledge of the truth* by declaring that "all" in this context means "many" or "all who are saved"[50] or "all, because no one is saved except those whom God wills to be saved." One may well believe that Augustine's sudden understanding of the significance of I Corinthians 4:7 when writing to Simplicianus had made him impervious to any argument pointing in another direction.

> And so let truth be expressed, especially when some disputed question demands it, and let those who are able, accept it, lest perhaps while it is passed over in silence because of those who cannot accept it, those who *can* accept truth as the means of avoiding falsehood will not only be defrauded of truth but will even be engulfed by falsity.[51]

Augustine had been accused by the Semi-Pelagians of teaching new and unsound doctrine[52] — a charge which he naturally denied. He recognized the pastoral difficulties raised by his theology — hence his suggestion that predestination should be preached discreetly, to avoid unsettling tender minds;[53] but his conviction of the truth of his position was absolute. It may be that his final position was an overreaction to Pelagian theology, as the Semi-Pelagians claimed; but it was nonetheless a logical development of the conclusions to which he had come more than thirty years before.

There is another example of the development of Augustine's opinions through controversy with Pelagianism: his emphasis upon sexual concupiscence in the transmission of Original Sin. This is a vast topic, has been much discussed in the past, and will probably continue to be much discussed, given the popularity of the study of sexuality and psychology in contemporary society, and it has implications for Augustine's social and moral teaching, with which I am not now concerned. We will here confine our discussion to the topic of sexual concupiscence in the debate with the Pelagians.

Let me begin by reminding you that Augustine has two words to describe sexual desire as experienced in our fallen world: *libido* and *concupiscentia*. Neither of them is limited to sexual desire, and *libido* in particular plays a major role in *The City of God* as *libido dominandi*, the lust for rule. There is a linguistic difference between them, in that *libido* is a classical word, while concupiscentia derives from the ecclesiastical vocabulary of the Latin Church.[54] We have seen that, in the *De Libero Arbitrio, libido* is the desire for a lower good thing, which drew Adam from his obedience to the command of God and so brought about the Fall.[55] In that context, *libido* is not sexual desire, but rather a self-assertive impulse on the part of the human soul — it is, indeed, a manifestation of *superbia,* pride, the head and fount of all sin and, by the just judgement of God, the pride which brought Adam to sin and fall becomes the punishment of the fallen human condition: the sexual instinct, which should have been the servant of the will, becomes a rebel against that will. The famous sixteenth chapter of Book XIV of *The City of God,* with its denunciation of orgasm because it overpowers the control of the mind, excellently expresses Augustine's mature view of human sexuality.

It is not, however, so much Augustine's view of the character of fallen sexual activity which is important here, but its corollary: Augustine's belief that the guilt inherited from Adam, "in whom we all were when we were all that one man,"[56] is passed to his descendants in the (for him) necessarily sinful concupiscence which accompanies the act of procreation. It was this view of concupiscence, which had been present in Augustine's outlook from the beginning of the Pelagian Controversy, which found expression and publicity in the two books, *On Marriage and Concupiscence,* addressed to Count Valerian in 418/9 and 419/20 respectively. These attracted the attention of the Pelagians, and especially of Julian of Eclanum, and provided an issue over which Augustine and Julian were to wrangle at tedious length during the last ten years of Augustine's life.

Julian of Eclanum is not a man to be easily evaluated. As a personality he is not endearing — an aristocrat, he adopted the superior tone of a cultured patrician talking down to a country parson. Estimates of his theological ability vary (for myself, I dislike him, but consider him to have an able intellect). He certainly had powers of initiative and leadership; considerable learning; and the ability, as a controversialist, to see the weak point in the adversary's argument and so to fight his battles on ground of his own choosing and on issues where his opponent was most vulnerable. These were, in Augustine's case, the doctrine of Original Sin and its consequences, which seemed to make God unjust[57] — by what equity can an infant be damned, who has committed no sin other than that of having been born? — and the origin of evil — if God is seen as the author of evil He is, by Julian's reckoning, no different from the Prince of Darkness, the Evil Principle of the Manichees. In short, the Augustinian view seemed to Julian to turn Manichaean Dualism into a Monotheism with a self-contradictory God who is both good and evil.[58] Traducianism — the transmission of Original Sin by physical generation — is simply a new form of Manichaeism, the Manichaeism which Augustine had allegedly renounced, after having professed it for a decade in his youth.[59]

Augustine provided Julian with an opening in 418/9 by writing the first book of the *De Nuptiis et Concupiscentia* in which, in his own words, he "defended the good of marriage to prevent the belief that marriage is vitiated by the concupiscence of the flesh" and showed that "conjugal chastity makes good use of the evil of lust (*malo libidinis*) for the procreation of children."[60] In this work, Augustine did not affirm anything more than he had previously said about the element of concupiscence in Christian marriage; but he said it here specifically, in a treatise addressed to Valerian, the Count of Africa, a high official who was strongly anti-Pelagian. Julian saw his opportunity. He identified Augustine's teaching with that of Mani — an excellent controversial tactic, but one which ensured that there could be no question of any reconciliation between the two controversialists. Once again Augustine's orthodoxy, which meant so much to him, was impugned, and in a manner which, so far as he was concerned, utterly misrepresented his way of thinking.

It is possible, even easy, when reading Julian's criticisms of Augustine, to see him as a reasonable man who tried to bring an element of common sense into the Pelagian debate, as when, for example, he countered Augustine's argument that the general human desire for privacy when engaging in sexual intercourse is proof of a sense of shame induced by concupiscence, by observing that, equally, we do not care to relieve ourselves in public — an example of modesty which has nothing to do with concupiscence.[61] It would, however, be unwise to suppose from this that Julian's outlook was "modern" in a way that Augustine's was not. Julian was a man of his time, influenced alike by Stoic and Aristotelian philosophical principles and by the Christianity of the day. His thought was based on certain fairly simple assumptions: that God cannot be unjust or the author of evil; that while man possesses a material body, in common with the animals, he is distinguished from them by the God-given faculty of reason, whereby he can recognize moral principles; and that the mature human being is endowed with the power of free choice, a quality which cannot be nullified or weakened by any previous action. As a Pelagian Julian naturally rejected any suggestion that Adam's primal sin passed to his descendants, and he goes to considerable trouble to argue that the word "all" (*omnes*) in Romans 5:18 is to be understood in the sense of "many" — if, he says, we speak of a solitary schoolmaster in a certain city and say that he teaches all the inhabitants, we mean by that all who study, and not all who live there.[62] Again, he explains (correctly) the phrase of Romans 5:12: *in quo omnes peccaverunt*, which Augustine misunderstood, as meaning "in that all sinned" — that is, by imitation — and not "in whom all sinned" — that is, in Adam — as Augustine wished to understand it.[63] Given such views, it naturally followed for Julian that infants did not, and could not, share in Adam's sin; and since they were unable to exercise a free choice of the will, they clearly were unable to sin, since Julian, in defining sin, borrowed Augustine's own definition in his anti-Manichaean treatise *On the Two Souls*, composed in 392: "Sin is the will to admit or to maintain what justice forbids and from which one is free to abstain."[64] But Julian went further. He pointed out that the Apostle had said that the free grace of Christ had abounded for many more that the sin of Adam had been able to destroy (Rom. 5:15).[65] Accordingly, he altogether rejected Augustine's view of the damnation of the greater part of the human race.

226

One might say, allowing for the distortion imposed by any literary quotation, however apposite, that Julian's attitude is

God's in His heaven, all's right with the world,

in contrast to Augustine's:

And yet we trust that somehow good will be the final end of ill.

Augustine's reaction to Julian's assaults was defensive, but completely confident. He had absolute assurance of his own understanding of Scripture as a justification of his own opinions (a confidence which, it may be observed, he shared with Julian) and saw himself supported by a host of famous Christian theologians: Irenaeus of Lyons; Cyprian of Carthage; Reticius of Autun; Olympius of Spain; Hilary of Poitiers; Ambrose of Milan; Gregory of Nazianzus; Innocent of Rome; John Chrysostom; Basil of Caesaria; and (of course) Jerome.[66] Particularly he appealed to Ambrose of Milan, "whom I reverence as a father, for in Christ Jesus he begot me through the Gospel, and from this servant of Christ I received the laver of regeneration,"[67] as a guarantor of his orthodoxy and right belief; but even without this formidable cloud of witnesses (not all of whom, incidentally, were as favorable to his opinions as he believed), it is all but impossible to believe that Augustine would have been swayed by Julian's arguments. Between him and Julian a great and unbridgeable gulf had been fixed.

If one considers Augustine's role in the Pelagian Controversy, it is difficult not to be impressed by his overwhelming energy. Between 411 and his death in 430, treatises flowed, at his dictation, from the pens of his amanuenses, even when, at the end of his life, he was fighting a war on two fronts maintaining, against the Semi-Pelagians, the absolute decree of God over human initiative, and defending, against Julian, his own understanding of the transmission of Adam's sin and denying that there could be any injustice in the apparently undeserved fate of unbaptized infants. Nevertheless, in all this productivity, Augustine was essentially re-stating the arguments which he had employed at the very beginning of the controversy in the *De Peccatorum Meritis et Remissione;* and these arguments in turn derived from the theological conclusions which he had reached in 396 when answering the questions of Simplicianus. But these conclusions would appear from Augustine's subsequent explanations to have been not so much the result of a course of reasoning and argument as of a sudden illumination, which may have resembled the illumination which came to him at Milan about the nature of evil, as a result of the ascents of the mind brought about by reading the Neoplatonists. We do not have sufficient evidence available to test this hypothesis, but it is to be observed that in the *De Praedestinatione Sanctorum,* composed in 429, at the end of his life, Augustine states that God revealed the truth to him when writing to Simplicianus. It may be that Augustine's unyielding obduracy in the last decades of his life is to be explained by an interior conviction, brought about by a conversion experience, against which no counter-argument, however distinguished its source, could hope to prevail.

Notes

* The second Otts Lecture, delivered at Davidson College, North Carolina, on March 26, 1992. The first Lecture was printed in *Augustinian Studies* 23 (1992), 33-51. Please note that the reference that was not included in the first lecture (p. 38 note 18) is *La coppia nei Padri.* Introduzione, traduzione e note di Giulia Sfameni Gasparro, Caesare Magazzù, Concetta Aloe Spada. Milan: Edizione Paoline 1991, pp. 135-6, 364-66. In my lecture, referring to this work from memory, I suggested that they called into question the Pelagian authorship of the *Letter to Celantia.* This was incorrect. What they said was that most scholars would attribute the letter to Pelagius, but this hypothesis could be overturned by later investigations. It might be well to quote them: "Nonostante che — é bene sottolinearlo — le consonanze tematiche o stilistiche lascino sempre un margine di ipoteticità che altre fortunate scoperte potreberro fugare completamente, si può ritenere tuttavia con buona dose di verosimiglianza che la *Lettera a Celanzia* appartengna a Pelagio" (pp. 365-6).

1. Luther, *Tischreden (D. Martin Luthers Werke,* Weimer 1883), IV, 56: "Augustinus nihil acriter de fide scribit, nisi cum contra Pelagianos scribit: *sie haben* Augustinum *auffgeweckt und zum manne gemacht;"* V, 414-5: "Augustinus, *wenn er die Pelagianer nit het wider sich gehabt, so wers ein ser aridus und tenuis doctor worden."*

2. Psalmus abecedarius, lines 157-8: "Nolite nobis iam, fratres, tempus Macarii imputare/ Si crudeles erant illi, et nobis displicent valde." *CSEL* 51, 9.

3. *Contra Gaudentium* 1,22,25. *CSEL* 53,224.

4. *Opus imperfectum contra Iulianum* 1,48: IUL. (4). *CSEL* 85,38.

5. Augustine, *Epistula* 190,3,12. *CSEL* 57,146-7.

6. *Institutio Christianae Religionis,* edd. P. Barth & W. Wiesel, *Iohannis Calvini Opera Selecta*3 (Munich 1931), 389. Translated by Ford W. Battles, *Calvin: Institutes of the Christian Religion* (The Library of Christian Classics Vol. XXI) (Philadelphia: The Westminster Press 1961), 942.

7. *De Praedestinatione Sanctorum* 17,34 PL 44,985; 986 (My translation).

8. Burnaby, *Amor Dei. A study in the religion of Saint Augustine* (London 1936), 231.

9. Cyprian, *Epistula* 64,5.2. *CSEL* 2,720-21. Translated by G.W. Clarke, *The Letters of St Cyprian of Carthage*. Vol. III (Ancient Christian Writers Vol. 46) (New York/Mahwah, N.J. 1986), 112.

10. The originator of this suggestion seems to have been Ernesto Buonaiuti, *La genesi della dottrina agostinian intorno al peccato originale* (Rome 1916), repeated in the "The genesis of St. Augustine's idea of Original Sin," *Harvard Theological Review* 10 (1917), 159-75. Augustine cites Ambrosiaster under the name of Hilary in *Contra duas epistulas Pelagianorum* 4,4,7 (*CSEL* 60,528), composed in 420/421, but seems to have known him earlier; see N. Cipriani, "Un' altra traccia dell' Ambrosiaster in Agostino (*De pecc.mer.remiss.* 2,36,58-59)", *Augustinus* 24 (1984), 515-25. Augustine could have derived his doctrine of the *massa damnata* and its implications from Ambrosiaster; but it could equally well have been inspired by African tradition and St Ambrose, and the Ambrosian influence would seem more likely, given Augustine's personal contact with, and deep veneration for, the great Bishop of Milan. See P.F. Beatrice, *Tradux Peccati, Alle fonti della dottrina agostiniana del peccato originale* (Milan 1978), 159 ff. On the *bôlos*, see Buonaiuti, "Manichaeism and Augustine's idea of *massa damnationis*," *Harvard Theological Review* 20 (1927), 117-27.

11. *De diversis Quaestionibus LXXXIII*, q.68,2,3. CCSL 44A, 176-7 (My translation).

12 *De Libero Arbitrio* 1,2,4. CCSL 29,213. Translated by Mark Pontifex, *St. Augustine. The Problem of Free Choice* (Ancient Christian Writers Vol. 22) (Westminster, MA./London 1955), 38.

13. *Ibid.* 1,4,9. CCSL 29,215.

14. See the note by Pontifex, *op. cit.* note 12, pp.239-40.

15. *De Libero Arbitrio* 3,24,71. CCSL 29,317. Pontifex, p.212.

16. *Ibid.*, Pontifex, pp.212-3.

17. *Ibid.*, 2,19,53. CCSL 29,272. Pontifex, p.134.

18. *De Spiritu et Littera* 33,58. CSEL 60,216.

19. *De Libero Arbitrio* 3 1,2. CCSL 29,276. Translation by John H.S. Burleigh, *Augustine: Earlier Writings* (The Library of Christian Classics Vol.VI) Philadelphia: The Westminster Press 1953), 171.

20. *Ibid.*, 3,18,50. CCSL 29,304. Quoted by Pelagius in *De Natura*. See *De Natura et Gratia* 67,80. CSEL 60,293. Cf. *Retractationes* I,9 [8]. CCSL 57,25-6 (My translation).

21. *Ibid.*, 3,18,50. CCSL 29,306; *De Natura et Gratia* 67,81. CSEL 60,296 (My translation).

22. *Ibid.*, 3,19,54. CCSL 29,307; *De Natura et Gratia* 67,81. CSEL 60,296 (My translation).

23. *Contra Secundinum* 11. CSEL 25 (2),923.

24. Augustine, *Epistula* 143,5. CSEL 44,255.

25. Augustine, *Epistula* 166,3,7. *CSEL* 44,555-6.

26. Augustine, *Epistula* 186,1,1. *CSEL* 57,45-6. Cf. *Retractationes* II, 42 [68]. *CCSL* 57, 124.

27. Cf. *Retractationes* I,9 [8], 4: " . . . quamvis et in his libris, qui non contra illos [sc. Pelagianos] omnino, quippe illi nondum erant, sed contra Manichaeos conscripti sunt de libero arbitrio, non omnimodo de ista dei gratia reticuimus, quam nefanda impietate conantur auferre." *CCSL* 57,26.

28. *Expositio in Epistulam ad Romanos* 54 (62),18-19. *CSEL* 84,38-9.

29. *Ibid.*, 37 (44),3. *CSEL* 84,19.

30. *Ibid.*, 54 (62),9. *CSEL* 84,37.

31. *Retractationes* I,23 [22],2. *CCSL* 57,68-9.

32. *Ibid.*, 2,1 [27]. *CCSL* 57,89-90.

33. *De Dono Perseverantiae* 20,52-53; 21,55. *PL* 45,1026; 1027.

34. *De diversis Quaestionibus ad Simplicianum* 1,2,9. *CCSL* 44,34; *Confessionum Libri XIII*, 10,29,40. *CCSL* 27,176; cf. *De Spiritu et Littera* 13,22. *CSEL* 60,175-6.

35. See *Augustinian Studies* 23 (1992), 40-42.

36. *De Gratia Christi et de Peccato Originali* 1,35,38-37,41. *CSEL* 42,154-6.

37. See p. 29 above and note 5.

38. See pp. 30 above and note 7.

39. *Expositio in Epistula ad Romanos* 54 (62),18. *CSEL* 84,38.

40. *Ibid.*, 19. *CSEL* 84,39.

41. *Ibid.*, 53 (61),7. *CSEL* 84,36 (My translation).

42. *Ibid.*, 54 (62),3. *CSEL* 84,36 (My translation).

43. *Retractationes* 1,23 [22],3. *CCSL* 57,69-70

44. *Expositio in Epistula ad Romanos* 37 (44),3. *CSEL* 84,19 (My translation).

45. Cassian, *Collationes* 13,11; 14 and 15. *CSEL* 13,375-8; 384-90.

46. Augustine, *Epistula* 190,3,12. *CSEL* 57,146-7.

47. Augustine, *Epistula* 184A,1,2. *CSEL* 44,732-3; *Enchiridion* 23,93. *CCSL* 46,99.

48. *De Dono Perseuerantiae* 11,25. *PL* 45,1007 (My translation).

49. *Ibid.*, 22,58-62. *PL* 45,1029-31.

50. *Contra Iulianum* 4,8,44. *PL* 44,760; *Enchiridion* 27,103. *CCSL* 46,104-06; *De Correptione et Gratia* 15,47. *PL* 44,945.

51. *De Dono Perseuerantiae* 16,40. *PL* 45,1017 (My translation).

52. *Inter Augustini Epistulae* 225,2; 226,2. *CSEL* 57,455-6; 469-70.

53. See quotation from *De Dono Perseuerantiae* 16, 40 (note 51 above).

54. See G. Bonner, *"Libido* and *concupiscentia* in St. Augustine, *"Studia Patristica VI,* ed. F.L. Cross (Texte und Untersuchungen zur altchristlichen Literatur Bd 81) (Berlin: Akademie Verlag 1962), 303-14; *Saint Augustine of Hippo. Life and Controversies*[2] (Norwich 1986), 398-401.

55. See pp. 33 above.

56. *De Civitate Dei* 13,14. *CCSL* 48,395-6.

57. *Opus imperfectum* 1,67 (5): "Non potest autem deus nisi iustus et pius esse, quod est deus meus Iesus Christus." *CSEL* 85,68.

58. *Ibid.*, 3,172-177. *CSEL* 85,473-8.

59. *Ibid.*, 6,18. *PL* 45,1535-6. For a discussion of the debate between Julian and Augustine, see Elizabeth A. Clark, "Vitiated seeds and holy vessels: Augustine's Manichean past" in *Ascetic piety and woman's faith. Essays on late ancient Christianity* (Studies in Women and Religion Vol.20), Lewiston: New York 1986, 291-349.

60. *Retractationes* 2,53 [79]. *CCSL* 57.131.

61. *Opus imperfectum* 4,37. *PL* 45,1356-7.

62. *Ibid.*, 2,135;144. *CSEL* 85,174.

63. *Ibid.*, 2,174. *CSEL* 85,174.

64. *De Duabus Animabus* 15. *CSEL* 25 (1),70; *Opus imperfectum* 1,44. *CSEL* 85,31.

65. *Opus imperfectum* 2,85; 96-98. *CSEL* 85,222-3; 228-30.

66. *Contra Iulianum* 2,10,33; 37; 3,17,32;. *PL* 44,697; 709; 719.

67. *Ibid.*, 1,3,10. *PL* 44,645.

The Transmission of Sin in the Seed:
A Debate between Augustine of Hippo
and Julian of Eclanum

Carol Scheppard

University of Pennsylvania

The debate between Augustine of Hippo and Julian of Eclanum spanned ten years, dominating the final phase of Augustine's conflict with the Pelagians, and consuming the later years of his life. Much of recent scholarship concerning this debate has been influenced by the work of Peter Brown, who portrays the conflict as a battle between a seasoned campaigner, Augustine, and an opportunistic young upstart, Julian. While derogatory comments made by both Augustine and Julian certainly have encouraged this form of interpretation, the emphasis upon it has tended to privilege the personalities involved over the concerns they expressed. It is necessary, therefore, to set aside temporarily the obsession with egos, and focus on the issues which the men themselves debated at length.

The heart of Augustine's conflict with Julian was rooted in his disagreement with Pelagius over the origins of sin, the power of the human will and the effects of baptism. Among the many consequences of this disagreement was Augustine's insistence that sin is transferred in the human seed. Julian protested vehemently, raising many difficult questions for Augustine and ultimately accusing him of retaining the Manichean beliefs of his early life. While later Catholic theology supported Augustine and condemned Julian, the conflict itself has never been completely laid to rest. Thus, the specific points raised in the debate warrant our careful attention. Once we have so studied the particulars of the debate and their implications, we stand better able to reassess the forces which fueled the intensity of the dialogue. For what was at stake for both men was not only personal satisfaction or the establishment and maintenance of orthodoxy, but also the model by which each man constructed his ideal notion of the nature of the Christian Church.

The Transmission Of Sin In The Seed

The debate between Julian and Augustine is directly related to the conflict between Augustine and Pelagius over the origins of sin, the power of human will and the effects of baptism. Pelagius maintained that humanity does not sin through an inheritance from Adam, but rather merely through imitation of his behavior. Thus, humanity *is* capable of not sinning. As a result, for Pelagius, baptism constituted the central event of the Christian life because it marked the end of life absorbed in imitation of Adam and the beginning of life entirely dedicated to the imitation of Christ. Baptism carries with it the potential for a radical change to a sinless life. Augustine is adamantly opposed to this position. He insists that through Adam humanity has fallen victim to lust and no longer exercises control over the will. All children born are thus born through concupiscence and are therefore born in sin. As a result, for Augustine, baptism constitutes merely the first step on a long road to perfection. It is in the context of this confrontation that the debate between Augustine and Julian ensues.

The debate between Augustine and Julian spread over ten years, from 419 to 430 CE, comprising the final chapter of Augustine's long standing battle with the Pelagians. Unfortunately, Julian's two main works against Augustine, "To Turbantius" (419 CE) and "To Forus" have been lost. What we know of these letters comes in the form of extracts from Augustine's two major works against Julian, *Contra Julianum* and *Opus Imperfectum Contra Julianum*. The argument presented here is a reconstruction of Augustine and Julians' debate over the transmission of sin in the seed drawn extensively from these latter two documents. [1]

---

1. The line of reasoning which I follow here is influenced by an essay by Elizabeth Clark entitled "Vitiated Seeds and Holy Vessels: Augustine's Manichean Past," in *Ascetic Piety and Women's Faith: Essays on Ancient Christianity*, pp 291-325, Lewiston: Edwin Mellen Press, 1986.

Julian, given his Pelagian notion of baptism as complete cleansing, opens the discussion on the transmission of sin in the seed by asking Augustine why, according to Augustine, baptized people have sinful children. Is not the whole person cleansed in baptism? Augustine responds that only the carnal nature is transferrable. Spiritual rebirth is only possible through grace. He offers the example of the olive tree. No matter how much olive trees are cultivated, they produce only wild olive trees.[2] What is underscored here is that, for Augustine, purity is only accessible through divine grace. No righteous human behavior can ever undo the loss of the control of the will and the stain of concupiscence incurred by Adam at the Fall.

Julian finds this unacceptable, for he insists that concupiscence is not a sin. It existed as one of the original senses before the Fall of Adam. Using the Aristotelian model as support, he claims that the "genus" of concupiscence is its vital fire, its "species" is the genital motion, its mode is the conjugal work, and its excess is intemperate fornication.[3] Thus, only in excess is concupiscence problematic. Augustine is not swayed by this line of reasoning, and asserts again the post-Fall introduction of concupiscence. He claims that the seed was created by God without lust, but through the Fall it came to be soiled by the Devil. It is only by God's grace that God continues to be active at all in the lives of those born of the soiled seed.[4]

Julian is not satisfied and continues arguing along Aristotelian lines. He points out Aristotle's teaching that the "accidents" inhere to their subject. If this is true, then sin can not be transferred from parents to children — the sin would inhere to the parents. Even more, when dealing with baptized parents, no sin can be passed on to their children because there is no sin to be passed on. One can not mix the will and the creation

---

2. Augustine, *De nuptiis et concupiscentia*, CSEL vol 42, pp 211-319, Book 1. Abbreviations: *Corpus Christianorum*, Series Latina (CCL); *Corpus Scriptorum Ecclesiasticorum Latinorum (CSEL); Patrologia Latina (PL)*.

3. Augustine, *Contra Julianum*, PL 44: 641-880, 4:65, 3:26.

4. Augustine, *Contra Julianum*, 4:12, 3:51.

of seeds.[5] There are two very important things to note here. First of all, it is quite clear that Julian has not been convinced by Augustine's olive tree explanation of baptism, and continues to press his initial point that baptized parents can not bear sinful children. Secondly, Julian's comment on mixing the will and the creation of seeds is a reference to Pelagius' teaching that it is not in the nature of the body to have "sin mixed in." As Julian sees it, Augustine's claim that children inherit sin from their parents is dangerously close to the Manichean claim that one inherits sin in the sinful body.

Augustine responds to Julian by citing both Aristotle and Paul. Following Aristotelian teachings, Augustine explains that the accidents do inhere to their subject, but that sin is transferred by "affectation" and "contagion." He states further that sin is indeed mixed in with the seed, because without it children would not be born dead as Paul claims in 2 Corinthians 5:14 when he says, "quoniam si unus pro omnibus mortuus est, ergo omnes mortui sunt/since one died on behalf of all, therefore all died."[6]

Instead of arguing with the biblical references, Julian continues with the Aristotelian discussion and shifts the focus a bit from sinful humanity to the sinless Jesus. Pushing the notion of affection and contagion, he asks Augustine to explain how Jesus could have been born of Mary, a human, and not acquire sin by affection or contagion. Augustine explains that Jesus received the pure seed of the Holy Spirit, not the soiled seed of Joseph. Thus, Jesus was not conceived in concupiscence.[7]

Here Julian feels he has something on Augustine. Since, as Julian is confident he has already shown using Aristotelian logic, concupiscence in an original sense, then Jesus had to have concupiscence or he would not be fully human. If Augustine is indeed claiming Jesus to be anything other than fully human, then Augustine is an Apollinarian! Augustine, of

---

5. Augustine, *Contra Julianum*, 16:15 & 18, 5:51.

6. Augustine, *Contra Julianum*, 6:24.

7. Augustine, *Contra Julianum*, 5:52, 54, 55.

course, is quick to counter. He insists that Jesus was human in the same way that Adam was before the Fall. Jesus had senses but he did not have concupiscence for he was born of no *conmixtio* of the flesh. He always had control of his will and was never plagued by lust. Jesus could have procreated but he chose not to.[8]

Julian, now turning to the Bible himself, addresses another issue raised by Augustine's sinful seed. He quotes from Romans 5:12, ". . . just as sin came into the world through one man, and death came through sin, and so death spread to all because all have sinned." Julian focuses on the first phrase, "just as sin came into the world through one man," and claims that this obviously can not refer to sin entering the world through generation as that requires two people involved in a sexual act. Thus, this has to prove the Pelagian teaching that sin comes into the world through humanity's *imitation* of one man, Adam.[9]

Augustine responds claiming that when Paul says "through one man" he means the *"semen generationis/*the seed of procreation"[10] Augustine here is assuming a current medical position on conception. According to Aristotle, the womb merely receives the semen; the woman has no part in generation. He describes how the semen acts as an artist on the woman's blood. The blood provides the matter and the semen the active principle. Augustine describes this as children being "poured off" (*transfussus/ transfuduntur*) from the man to the woman.[11] Augustine thus goes on to claim that the beginning of conception is *"a viro seminante/*by male insemination"*,*[12] that women conceive and bear children but they do not generate them,[13] that women receive the sinful seed from men,[14] and that Jesus was not created *"ex semine/*from the seed" so he

---

8. Augustine, *Opus imperfectum contra Julianum*, CSEL vol 85, PL 45: 1049-1608, 4:48, 122.

9. Augustine, *Opus imperfectum contra Julianum*, 2:56.

10. Augustine, *Opus imperfectum contra Julianum*, 2:56.

11. Augustine, *Opus imperfectum contra Julianum*, 2:178.

12. Augustine, *Opus imperfectum contra Julianum*, 2:83.

13. Augustine, *Opus imperfectum contra Julianum*, 3:85.

is "liber a nexu seminatricis concupiscentiae/ free from the connection of concupiscence of the seminator."[15]

Elizabeth Clark observes that at this point Augustine seems close to one of two conclusions: either the transmission of sin is solely a male responsibility (Jesus was born without sin because Joseph was not involved), or there is something not quite fully human about Mary (Jesus was born without sin because his mother carried no sin),[16] Augustine seems comfortable with the idea that Adam carries the sinful seed and that it is men, therefore, who transfer sin to their offspring, but he does not absolve women of sin entirely. In fact, he points out that Eve carries a heavy responsibility for the Fall, and thus constitutes a particularly bad of example for how to behave.[17]

The issue of the sinfulness of Mary is a tricky one. Augustine comments, *"Non transcribimus diabolo Mariam conditione nascendi; sed ideo, quia ipsa conditio solvitur gratia renuscendi/*we do not convey Mary to the Devil by the condition of her birth, because that condition was loosed by the grace of regeneration."[18] There seems in Augustine's mind to be something special about Mary. In *Nature and Grace* 36.42, he comments,

> We except the holy Virgin Mary, concerning whom I wish to raise no question when it touches the subject of sin, out of honor for the Lord. From Him we know what abundance of grace for overcoming sin in every particular was conferred upon her who had the merit to conceive and bear Him who undoubtedly had not sin.[19]

---

14. Augustine, *Opus imperfectum contra Julianum*, 2:179.

15. Augustine, *Opus imperfectum contra Julianum*, 4:104.

16. E. Clark, "Vitiated Seeds and Holy Vessels..." pp 312-313.

17. Augustine, *Opus imperfectum contra Julianum*, 2:56.

18. Augustine, *Opus imperfectum contra Julianum* 4:122.

19. J. O'Donnell, *Augustine*, Boston: Twayne Publishers, 1985, p 135.

Augustine does not claim Mary to be immaculate, but he certainly puts her in a class by herself.

While these issues are interesting and warrant some careful pondering, they remain somewhat minor ones for Augustine and Julian. The charge underlying Julian's line of attack consistently has been that Augustine has never really given up his Manichean beliefs, and that his teachings on the origin and transference of sin are essential Manichean. Julian points particularly to the Manichean belief in the degenerative nature of the world, and in their identification of concupiscence as the origin of sin.[20] The Manicheans claimed that evil had entered the world through a primordial conflict between the forces of Light and Darkness, and that human bodies were a product of that evil. Pelagius had been particularly upset with the Manichean belief that "it was the nature of the body to have sin mixed in."[21] Pelagius emphatically countered that "the flesh itself is not hostile to God, as the Manicheans say, but the carnal mind is."[22] What is important to note here is that, given the central concerns both Pelagius and Julian had with Manichean beliefs, it is quite understandable that Julian would take issue with Augustine's position. Julian believes that concupiscence is natural and an original bodily sense created in humans by God before sin entered the world, and that sin is not inherited, but rather a willful choice of the carnal mind. It is logical, therefore, that he would view Augustine, who claims this original bodily sense is the mark and carrier of sin, as someone who holds the Manichean view that the body is sinful and has "sin mixed in."

For his part, Augustine, who equates concupiscence with the transference of sin, sees it as an unnatural drive which entered the world after the Fall, bringing sin and suffering into God's perfect world. Anyone who would view this sinful force as present before the Fall must view Paradise as full of sin and suffering. Thus Augustine reaches the logical

---

20. Augustine, *Opus imperfectum contra Julianum*, 3:187.

21. Pelagius, *Expositiones xiii epistularum Pauli: Romanos*, ed. A Souter, Expositions, vol ii, Cambridge, 1926, Theodore De Bruyn (trans), Oxford: Clarendon Press, 1993, 6:16.

22. Pelagius, *Expositiones...*, 8:7.

conclusion that Julian holds the Manichean view that the world was a sin filled place long before Adam's arrival. In addition, the Pelagian teaching that the body does not sin, but the carnal mind does, constitutes a reverse form of Manichean body-mind dualism. Augustine found Manichean body-mind dualism particularly offensive because he believed that they used it as an excuse to increase perversity. Given Augustine's central tenet that concupiscence is the mark of the loss of control of the will, and given his major concerns with the Manichean viewpoint, it is not at all surprising that that he should find Julian's position problematic and somewhat Manichean.

Thus, from the beginning, the debate between Augustine and Julian had no chance of resolution. It was a debate between individuals whose foundational tenets could not be reconciled, and so it dragged on for years. The question which then arises is why? Why put so much energy into perpetuating an irreconcilable conflict? Why not simply agree to disagree? Obviously, the stakes are extremely high. While there were certainly personal issues between them, both Augustine's and Julian's positions carried with them powerful socio-political implications.

Issues At Stake For Augustine And Julian

The views Augustine and Julian held concerning the relationship between sex, the individual and society have interesting implications when one begins to examine their models for what the Church should be. These conflicting models are readily evident in Augustine's earlier debates with Pelagius. Augustine raged at what he deemed to be Pelagius' over-estimation of the power of the will and lack of reliance on God's grace. Pelagius, for his part, was very angry at the way that Augustine's *Confessions* seemed to popularize the growing trend in Roman society toward a half-hearted form of piety. Pelagius called on individuals to insist on a new set of values in a world which he saw as weighed down by convention. As he saw it, new Christians, becoming Christian largely through marriage, remained Roman citizens at heart who simply began using new names for the same old behaviors.

Pelagius responded to this by claiming that Christians need to do more than say they believe, they need to live out their belief. No double standard was to be allowed — every Christian must be a monk. Pelagius

240

put heavy emphasis upon the responsibility of the individual. Humans have no excuse for sinning.[23] Thus, for Pelagius the emphasis fell much more heavily on righteousness than on grace.

As Peter Brown has explained, the implication here is that Pelagianism does not constitute an open model for what the Church should be. Instead, it presents an elitist model made up of those special individuals who are able to lead nearly sinless lives.[24]

Seen in this light, one begins to understand Augustine's intolerance for the Pelagian position. For him it was the Donatist battle all over again. By denying both that humans are born unable not to sin and that they are thus completely reliant on the grace of God for salvation, the Pelagians were creating divisions within the church body and were endangering Christian unity in Christ. For Augustine, in-born concupiscence was the great leveler. Not one person is able to stand righteous before the community and before God, and thus all are united in their contrition and need for God's grace. Christianity is not an elitist movement, but rather a majority religion made up entirely of convalescents. While Augustine was very harsh in demanding baptism for all those outside the church, he showed great moral tolerance for those within the church.[25] Baptism was essential for it necessitated a change of attitude and a turning to God. Still, salvation was for those who God had chosen, not for those who by their own choosing set themselves apart. For Augustine, the emphasis fell much more heavily on grace than on righteousness.

Conclusion

Thus, we see how Augustine and Julian's debate over the transmission of sin in the seed involved not only issues of personal satisfaction and the establishment and maintenance of orthodoxy, but also the model

23. P. Brown, *Augustine of Hippo: A Biography*, Berkeley: University of California Press, 1967, pp 343-349.

24. P. Brown, "Pelagius and His Supporters: Aims and Environment," *Journal of Theological Studies*, 1968, n.s. 19: 93-114, pp 98-99.

25. Brown, "Pelagius and His Supporters..." pp 111-112.

by which each man constructed his ideal notion of the nature of the Christian church. The debate itself proved to be irreconcilable. Julian believed that concupiscence was an original sense created by God as natural in humans before the Fall. Augustine insisted that concupiscence entered the world as a result of Adam's disobedience and forever after acted as the carrier of sin from generation to generation. From these starting places, neither man could help but reach the conclusion that the other was a Manichee and a heretic. Still, they battled on for years because giving up meant giving up on their central visions for the Christian community. Augustine believed that the sin transferred in the seed through the concupiscence involved in conception created a mass humanity united in its utter reliance on God's saving grace. As he aged Augustine became increasingly wedded to this belief, for the world he lived in made him increasingly doubtful about the power of the human will to overcome evil. Julian, on the other hand, believed that the human will was indeed powerful enough to overcome evil, but that those who were committed to a life of purity had to separate themselves from others and build each other up in the ascetic practices which could lead to perfection. For Julian, ceding to Augustine meant giving up his vision of the church as the lauded spriitual elite living a life of radical renunciation and separation.

The *Life of Abercius*: Its Significance for Early Syriac Christianity

DAVID BUNDY

Historians concerned with the history of early Christianity in northern Mesopotamia are confronted with two problematic and inter-related sources, the Abercius inscription and the *Life of Abercius*. The Abercius inscription is a burial inscription, fragments of which were discovered in Phrygia Salutaris by William Ramsay in 1883.[1] It must be dated before 215 C.E. when the peripatetic affluent Christian's grave epigram was plagiarized by a certain Alexander, son of Antonius, whose longer name destroyed the meter of the earlier text but preserved eight lines of the original.[2] It becomes significant for early Syriac Christianity because of the mention of Nisibis as the easternmost limit of Abercius' travels to visit Christian communities. As such, it is the earliest reference to Christians residing in Nisibis. The Christians mentioned by Abercius antedate by at least a century the earliest details provided by Ephrem the Syrian in his reminiscences of the exploits of the bishops of Nisibis.[3]

This inscription was also known because of its inclusion in the *Life of*

DAVID BUNDY is Research Librarian, Asbury Theological Seminary, Wilmore, KY 40390.

[1]William M. Ramsay, "Cities and Bishoprics of Phrygia," *Journal of Hellenic Studies* 4 (1883): 424–427; A. Abel, "Étude sur l'inscription d'Abercius," *Byzantion* 3(1926): 324–325.

[2]A. Abel, "Étude," pp. 321–323; H. Leclercq, "Abercius," *DACL* 1(1907), cols. 68–69; William M. Ramsay, "Trois villes phrygiennes," *Bulletin de correspondance Hellénique* 6(1882): 518–520, no. 6. Cf. also the analysis of P. Batiffol and G. Bareille, "Abercius (inscription d')," *DThC* (1909) 1.57–66, and K. P. Kirsch, "1. Abercius," *DGHE* (1912) 1.104–106.

[3]*Des Heiligen Ephraem des Syrers Carmina Nisibena*, hrsg. Edmund Beck, I (CSCO 218–219, Syr. 92-92; Louvain: Secr. du CorpusSCO, 1961), hymns nos. xiii–xvi. Ephrem mentions three bishops, all of whom would have held the position at Nisibis during Ephrem's lifetime (circa 306–373 C.E.). It is impossible to know the identity of the mysterious Palut who was considered by Ephrem's religious rivals to have been influential in early Syriac Christianity.

Abercius, a text which has long been part of the Christian literary tradition. This work, which bears all the structural components of fourth to sixth-century hagiography, recounts Abercius' struggle against heretics in Asia Minor, his voyages to Rome and, eventually, to Nisibis. On the way, he engages in a dialogue with a Marcionite and recites passages from the work of Bardaisan, the late second and early third-century Edessan theologian. He eventually meets Bardaisan himself before finally returning to Hieropolis in Phrygia Salutaris, where he composed his epitaph.

The inscription and *Life* were not used by Labourt and Burkitt in their histories of early Syriac Christianity.[4] Both Bauer and Turner ignored the documents in their efforts to interpret early Syriac Christianity in the larger context of Christian origins.[5] Specialists in Syriac literature have tended to cite the text but with a high degree of tentativeness, probably because the inscription so radically predates any confirmatory evidence for Christianity in Nisibis and because hagiographical texts are historiographically problematic. Ortiz de Urbina cited the inscription as evidence for Christianity in Edessa,[6] and his conclusion was cited approvingly by Kristen.[7] Vööbus, Segal, Murray, and Fiey cite the inscription and the mention of Nisibis, but without commenting on the historiographical issues raised by the text.[8] None of these writers attempted to deal with the *Life of Abercius.*

---

[4]J. Labourt, *Le christianisme dans l'empire perse sous la dynastie sassanide (224–632)* (Bibliothèque de l'enseignement de l'histoire ecclésiastique; Paris: Victor Lecoffre, 1904); F. C. Burkitt, *Early Eastern Christianity. St. Margaret's Lectures 1904 on the Syriac Speaking Church* (London: John Murray, 1904). Many authors have posited the origins of Christianity in Northern Mesopotamia as a development of Judaism in the region, thus, G. Quispel, "The Discussion of Judaic Christianity," *Vigiliae Christianae* 22(1968): 81–93, and L. W. Barnard, "The Origins and Emergence of the Church in Edessa During the First Two Centuries, A.D.," *Vigiliae Christianae* 22(1968): 161–175, along with most scholars of the period.

[5]Walter Bauer, *Orthodoxy and Heresy in Earliest Christianity* (The New Testament Library; London: SCM, 1972); H. E. W. Turner, *The Pattern of Christian Truth: A Study in the Relations Between Orthodoxy and Heresy in the Early Church* (London: Mowbray, 1954). This neglect is interesting considering that contemporary analyses of the Abercius material could have been mustered to support both positions.

[6]Ignatius Ortiz de Urbina, "Le origini del cristianesimo in Edessa," *Gregorianum* 15(1934): 82–91.

[7]E. Kristen, "Edessa," *RAC* (1959) 4. 569.

[8]A. Vööbus, *History of the School of Nisibis* (CSCO 266, Subsidia 26; Louvain: Secr. du CorpusSCO, 1965) does not refer to Abercius, but he does mention (without commentary) the text in his *Celibacy, A Requirement for Admission to Baptism in the Early Syrian Church* (PETSE, 1; Stockholm: n.p., 1951); J. B. Segal, *Edessa, "The Blessed City"* (Oxford: Clarendon, 1970) 69; Robert Murray, *Symbols of Church and Kingdom, A*

Drijvers took a different approach. In his study of Bardaisan, he argued that the *Life* contained accurate information about Bardaisan and his meeting with Abercius and concluded that "there would seem to be no reason to doubt the historicity of this passage. . . ,"[9] He cited the text in articles on Edessa and on orthodoxy and heresy in early Syriac Christianity,[10] and returned to it again in his magisterial address to the Ninth International Conference on Patristic Studies held at Oxford in 1983. This was published as an article, "East of Antioch, Forces and Structures in the Development of Early Syriac Theology."[11] In this essay, Drijvers used the *Life* as: (1) indicative of the persistence of Marcionite beliefs in Syria about C.E. 200; (2) suggestive of inter-Christian relations of the same period; and (3) evidence for the bilingual skills of both Abercius and Bardaisan. Drijvers concludes, "Aberkios like Bardaisan surely knew Syriac, otherwise his action against the Marcionites in the East Syrian and Northern Mesopotamian area would have been ineffective."[12] The recounting of the travels and experiences of Abercius in the east is accepted as an accurate account of historical events.

The task of this essay is to examine the viable uses of the *Life of Abercius* as a source for Christianity in Asia Minor and northern Mesopotamia. The method is to analyze briefly the texts under consideration, indicate how these have been interpreted by historians, and examine the texts in their contexts, before suggesting an alternative interpretation of the significance of this data in the study of early Syriac Christianity.

Study in Early Syriac Tradition (Cambridge: University Press, 1975) 6; J. M. Fiey, "Les marcionites dans les textes historiques de l'église perse," *Le Muséon* 83(1970): 183; *idem, Nisibe, metropole syriaque orientale et ses suffragants des origines à nos jours* (CSCO 388, Subsidia 54; Louvain: Secr. du Corpus SCO, 1977) 19–21. Margherita Guarducci, "L'iscrizione de Abercio e Roma," *Ancient Society* 2(1971): 174–203, sees the line on Rome as a poetic rendering of a period conceit, but significant for understanding how the Roman church was viewed in the second century. In *Epigrafi sacre pagane e cristiane* (*Epigrafia greca* 4; Rome: Istituto Poligrafico dello Stato, 1978) 377–386, Guarducci draws attention to the credal elements of the inscription.

[9]H. J. W. Drijvers, *Bardaisan of Edessa* (Studia Semitica Nederlandica, 6; Assen: Van Gorcum, 1967) 170–171.

[10]H. J. W. Drijvers, "Edessa und das judische Christentum," *Vigiliae Christianae* 24(1970): 21, repr. H. J. W. Drijvers, *East of Antioch* (Collected Studies Series, 198; London: Variorum Reprints, 1984), art. II; *idem,* "Rechtglaubigkeit und Ketzerei in ältesten syrischen Christentum," *Symposium Syriacum 1972* (OCA 197; Roma: Pont. Inst. Ori. Stud., 1974) 299, repr. Drijvers, *East of Antioch,* art. no. III.

[11]H. J. W. Drijvers, "East of Antioch: Forces and Structures in the Development of Early Syriac Theology," *East of Antioch* (Collected Studies Series, 198; London: Variorum Reprints, 1984) 1–27.

[12]Ibid., pp. 5–6.

I

THE ABERCIUS INSCRIPTION

The Text

The inscription has been the subject of extensive study.[13] This translation is based on the text as reconstructed by Abel on the basis of the research of Leclercq and Nissen:[14]

> Citizen of a distinguished city, I have made this while living in order to have one day[15] a place for my body. My name is Abercius;[16] the disciple of a chaste pastor who pastures his flock of sheep on the mountains and in the plains, who has great eyes seeing everything from above; it is he who taught me the true letters; he who sent me to Rome to contemplate the king and to see a queen with golden clothing and shoes of gold. I saw there also a people who wear a shining seal. And, I saw the plain of Syria and all the villages, Nisibis across the Euphrates. Everywhere I found people with whom to speak. Paul, I had (with, upon). . . .[17] The faith preceded me everywhere and served me as nourishment a fish from the spring, very large, pure, which the chaste virgin received. And she provided it continuously as food to friends; having a precious diluted wine which she provided with the bread. I, Abercius, dictated these things to be written, I being actually seventy-two years of age, that the one who understands this might think to pray for Abercius. However let no one place another in my tomb, and if he does, he will pay two thousand pieces of gold to the treasury of the Romans, and to my beloved hometown Hieropolis, one thousand pieces of gold.

Interpretation of the Text

The text, reconstructed from the inscription of Alexander son of Antonius, two fragments of the inscription of Abercius itself, and the texts

---

[13]A. Abel, "Étude," pp. 221–411, provides a thorough and detailed *status quaestionis* as well as an analysis of the textual and historical issues. The extensive bibliography, 406–411, is helpful but fraught with bibliographical errors. For more recent bibliography, see Wolfgang Wischmeyer, "Der Aberkiosinschrift als Grabepigramm," *Jahrbuch für Antike und Christentum* 23(1980): 22–47.

[14]Abel, "Étude," pp. 323–324; Leclercq, "Abercius," cols. 69–74; Theodor Nissen, *S. Abercii Vita* (Bibliotheca auctorum graecorum et romanorum Teubneriana; Leipzig, Berlin: G. B. Teubner, 1912) 53–54. On the Armenian text of the inscription as attested by the Armenian version of the *Life of Abercius* (see below note 27) from *B. N. Arm.* 46 fol. 100v, see F. C. Conybeare, "Harnack on the Inscription of Abercius," *Classical Review* 9(1896): 295–297. See *Bibliotheca Hagiographica Orientalis* (Subsidia Hagiographica, 10; Bruxelles: Soc. des Bollandistes, 1910) 2–3.

[15]William M. Ramsay, *The Cities and Bishoprics of Phrygia* Vol. I, Part II: *West and West-Central Phrygia* (Oxford: Clarendon, 1897) 710–711, suggests the text read φανερῶς, thus, "in order to have a visible place for my body."

[16]With regard to the ethnic background of the name, Abercius, see the summary of the discussion by Wischmeyer, "Aberkiosinschrift," pp. 26–27.

[17]The missing word after the mention of Paul's name may well indicate that the inscription was understood as a comment on, and therefore fell victim to, the Marcionite or Montanist controversies.

of the inscription recorded in the various recensions of the *Life of Abercius*, is quite reliable. The interpretation of the inscription and the identification of Abercius' religious community have remained unresolved issues, especially if they are investigated independently of the context provided by the *Life of Abercius*.

The inscription has been interpreted both as pagan and as a marginally Christian syncretistic text which uses language and images borrowed from the Sibylline traditions and other cultic (mystery) traditions of Asia Minor.[18] It has also been understood as an "orthodox" treatise which uses available terms in Christian contexts.[19] The latter interpretation drew support from the identification of Abercius with Avircius Marcellus, a late second–century Phrygian recipient of a treatise against Montanism mentioned by Eusebius (*H.E.* V.16).[20] However, there is nothing in the inscription which demonstrates the conformity of Abercius to later canons of orthodoxy. The available evidence indicates that the province of Phrygia experienced considerable religious activity during the second and early third centuries, much of it non-conformist. *If* we can exclude the possibility of Abercius having been a Montanist on the basis of the dedication of the anti-Montanist treatise recorded by Eusebius, we cannot exclude the possibility that he was a Marcionite. The reference to Paul is perhaps an allusion to the Marcionite or Montanist controversies, although it is too laconic to suggest a perspective on the discussions. Abercius may well have been an adherent of any Christian group. Very probably, Abercius' Christianity was as eclectic as the language and symbolism of his burial epitaph. Such was certainly the case in other areas where Christian communities were found "East (and north) of Antioch." For example, at Edessa, during the late second and early third century, Bardaisan borrowed the language and science of the Hellenistic synthesis in northern Mesopotamia, as did his contemporary Julius Africanus.[21] Ephrem inveighed against the eclecticism of his Christian community at Nisibis as late as 358–359 C.E. in the *Mēmrē on Nicomedia*.[22]

---

[18]See the excellent survey of Abel, "Étude," pp. 382–389.

[19]This identification, apparently first suggested by William M. Ramsay, "Tale of Saint Abercius," *Journal of Hellenic Studies* 3(1882): 350, became an accepted scholarly conclusion. More recently this has been challenged, with justice, by Wischmeyer, "Aberkiosinschrift," p. 27.

[20]Wischmeyer, *Aberkiosinschrift*, pp. 22–47; Abel, *Étude*, 389–395.

[21]Drijvers, *Bardaisan, passim*. D. Bundy, "Criteria for being *in communione* in the Early Syriac Church," *Augustianum* 25(1985): 600–602.

[22]*Ephrem de Nisibe, Mēmrē sur Nicomédie*, ed. Charles Renoux (Patrologia Orientalis, 37, 2–3; Turnhout: Brepols, 1975), *passim;* D. Bundy, "Christianity and Paganism in

The inscription alone provides no data about the Christians in Nisibis before 216 C.E. It does suggest that no simple theory describing the ideological affiliations, social status, ethnic identity, and organizational structures of the Nisibean Christian community will be adequate.

II
THE LIFE OF ABERCIUS

The Narrative

The *Life of Abercius* contains the text of the inscription and purports to be a narrative of the life of this same Abercius. As the story goes,[23] during the reign of Marcus Aurelius and Lucius Verus, an edict was promulgated which required sacrifice to idols. Abercius, bishop of Hieropolis, became angry at the crowds submitting to the requirement. Taking matters into his own hands as directed in a dream, he destroyed the statues of the false gods during the night. Confronted by the temple staffs, he cursed them and rejected the advice of friends to flee before they could retaliate. Instead he went to the city square to preach. The crowds planned to lynch him, despite pleas for calm by the city's leaders. At the height of the crisis, three demon-possessed persons walked by and Abercius healed them with a prayer. The crowd became subdued, listened to his exposition of the faith, and Abercius was able to baptize five hundred persons.

His fame grew to the extent that crowds came from Phrygia Magna and Lydia to hear him preach. One day, as they listened, Phrygella, mother of a certain Euxeinianos, a person of high social standing, came requesting healing of her blindness. She was healed and confessed the true Christian faith. Three other blind women came for healing and, with their sight, received visions of Christ as an older man, as an adult, and as a youth.

When Euxeinianos heard of his mother being healed, he came to talk with Abercius. The dialogue (§§ 31–38) focused on several issues: (1) the attributes of God which appear contradictory, (2) the necessity of evil,

---

Northern Mesopotamia during the Fourth Century," Paper presented to the Twelfth Annual Byzantine Studies Conference, Bryn Mawr, PA, Oct. 10–12, 1986.

[23]This summary is based on the edition of *Paris Gr. 1540* by Nissen, *S. Abercii Vita*, pp. 1–55. On the versions and editions, see Francois Halkin, ed., *Bibliotheca Hagiographica Graeca*, 3rd ed. (Subsidia Hagiographica, 8a; Bruxelles: Soc. des Bollandistes, 1957) I. 1–2; idem, *Auctarium Bibliothecae Hagiographicae Graecae* (Subsidia Hagiographica 47; Bruxelles: Soc. des Bollandistes, 1969) 13; idem, *Novum Auctarium Bibliothecae Hagiographicae Graecae* (Subsidia Hagiographica 65; Bruxelles: Soc. des Bollandistes, 1984) 11.

(3) Christian ethical responsibility, (4) the role of the will in the process of salvation, and, (5) the freedom of the will.

Later, while traveling on a healing mission, Abercius became aware that the area needed a public bath. He uttered a prayer and hot water erupted from where he had knelt. After this feat a demon endeavored to tempt the saint but was sent fleeing to Rome, daring the saint to follow. In Rome the demon entered Lucille, daughter of Marcus Aurelius, and announced that it could only be cast out by Abercius. A letter from Marcus Aurelius to Euxeinianos (quoted, §§ 47–48) brought Abercius to Rome, dispensing miracles as he traveled. The demon was cast out and ordered to return to Hieropolis carrying on its back a large stone altar to be erected in the village. As payment for exorcism rendered, Abercius asked that a bath be built at the site of his hot spring and that the poor receive an annual distribution of wheat.

Led by a dream, Abercius left Rome for Syria, passing through Antioch, Apamea, and Edessa to Nisibis (§ 69). Everywhere he sought to resolve the disputes within the Christian communities and fought against the Marcionites. After leaving Nisibis to return west, he met a delegation led by "Bardaisan who was distinguished from all others by his descent and wealth" (§ 70). Bardaisan offered Abercius a gift of money, and when the saint politely refused the sum, gave instead the title ἰσαπόστολος because of his efforts on behalf of his co-religionists.

Abercius then returned to his flock where he wrote a volume on the obligations of the clergy, caused another spring to flow, wrote his epitaph (§ 77), and died in the faith.

The Life of Abercius: Its Text and Historical Situation

The text is preserved, most completely, in *Paris Gr. 1540*. It is supported by a Russian version which Nissen collated against *Paris Gr. 1540*.[24] It is also attested by two abbreviated versions, the one found in *Coislinianus 110*, the other in *Hierosolymitanus Sabaeus 27* and *Mosquenses 397*.[25] Another Greek witness is the tenth-century revision by Simeon Metaphrastes, who deleted a portion of the dialogue between Abercius and Euxeinianos.[26] Surius made a Latin translation of this revision.[27] As

[24]See the discussion of the importance of the Russian version by Nissen, *S. Abercii Vita*, xix–xxi, and the text, retroverted to Greek, collated pp. 1–55.

[25]Abel, "Étude," pp. 328–329; Nissen, *S. Abercii Vita*, pp. 56–86.

[26]Abel, "Étude," p. 326.

[27]Conybeare, "Harnack," p. 296. The Armenian version of the *Life of Abercius* was edited by N. Akinian, "The Life of Aberkios (in Armenian)," *Handes Amsorya* 25(1911): cols. 89–98. Akinian also proffered an analysis of the Armenian version and its significance for the textual tradition in his article, "Studies on the Life of St. Aberkios (in Armenian)," *Handes Amsorya* 27(1913): cols. 325–344, 515–520.

well, an Armenian version is extant which Conybeare suggested to be
translated from a Syriac rendition of the version of Simeon Metaphrastes.[28] No trace has been found, to my knowledge, of the Syriac text.
Orthodox calendars celebrate Saint Abercius on October 22.

Analysis of the sources used by the author has yielded some results,
and the date of composition can be fixed within a relatively narrow margin. It has been demonstrated that the *Life of Abercius* cites, in addition
to the New Testament (Matthew, Mark, Luke, John, Acts, 1 Cor., Eph.),
Bardaisan's *Book of the Laws of the Countries,* and the *Acts of Peter.*[29]
Conybeare pointed out a narrative in the Babylonian Talmud in which a
demon is forced to carry a stone on its back.[30] The topographical allusions
as well as the text of the inscription indicate that the author was thoroughly familiar with the city of Hieropolis in Phrygia Minor.[31] The data
about contemporary political and historical events has been examined in
detail.[32] The imperial personages named obviously existed. However, the
activities attributed to them are not always consistent with what can be
ascertained from more reliable records. There are numerous anachronisms
in the narrative. The political demarcations described in the text provide
a *terminus a quo* of C.E. 297 for the composition of the text. The apparant
reference to Julian's stopping of the grain subsidies would support a date
after 363.[33] The designations "Phrygia Minor," if not glosses, could suggest a *terminus ad quem* of C.E. 385.[34] With regard to Abercius himself,
the *Life* adds little substantive data to what is found in the inscription.
We are informed that Abercius was a bishop active in the conversion of
the region from paganism, a philosopher (!), theologian, and author. The
story of his excursions are summarized in the inscription. The data about
his ecclesiastical status and literary prowess reflect, however, concerns
of the fourth century rather than the second.

Interpretations of the Life of Abercius

Scholars have interpreted this text in various ways. Duchesne, who
proffered the first serious examination of the text, indicated numerous

[28]Nissen, *S. Abercii Vita,* 87–123.

[29]Theodor Nissen, "Die Petrusakten und ein bardesanitischer Dialog in der Aberkiosvita," *ZNTW* 9(1908): 190–203, 315–328; idem, *S. Abercii Vita,* pp. 1–55, notes.

[30]F. C. Conybeare, "Talmudic Elements in the 'Acts of Abercius'," *The Academy* (1896):
468–470. Brian McNeil, "Avercius and the Song of Songs," *Vigiliae Christianae* 31(1977):
23–34, explores vocabulary shared with other texts from the early Christian period.

[31]Ramsay, *Cities and Bishoprics of Phrygia,* Vol. I, Part II, pp. 711–715.

[32]Abel, *Étude,* pp. 396–404.

[33]Ramsay, "Tale," pp. 339–341.

[34]Abel, "Étude," p. 399. Cf. L. Duchesne. "Saint Abercius, Évêque d'Hiérapolis en
Phrygie," *Revue des questions historiques* 34(1883): 16–21.

historiographical errors in the text and attributed the present form of the *Life* to the sixth century. He frequently refers to the *Life* as a legend but, impressed by the inclusion of the inscription, did not deny the partial historicity of the *Life*.[35] Ramsay, discoverer of the fragments of the inscription, suggested that, "in the *Acta* the historical Avircius Marcellus is transformed into the legendary St. Abercius," although the text may contain local traditions.[36] Nissen identified the borrowings from Bardaisan and the *Acts of Peter* but made no judgments of the text's historical value.[37] Leclercq argued that the "historical value of the text has been rehabilitated, at least for one of its parts, so that one cannot treat it with the disdain it appeared until recently to deserve."[38] After the publication of the masterful edition of the three Greek recensions of the *Life* by Nissen in 1912,[39] the text attracted little attention by historians. A. Abel provided evaluation of the texts: "through his inscription and the details of his life confirmed in it, we have access to the most ancient symbolism and Christian activity in Asia Minor."[40] He was less sanguine about the *Life of Abercius* and argued that it was constructed during the fourth century on the basis of the inscription and local information.[41]

Strathmann and Klauser found the *Life* did not contribute to understanding Abercius and accepted the fourth-century date.[42] Grégoire asserted the historicity of the *Life*, arguing, against Delehaye[43] (whose position he overstates), ". . . (he) is incorrect to consider the *Life of Saint Abercius* as a hagiographical novel with no historical basis and having no source other than the inscription. . . ."[44] Grégoire focuses discussion on the description of the role of Abercius as a colleague of Bardaisan in

[35]Duchesne, "Saint Abercius," pp. 5–33.

[36]Ramsay, *Cities and Bishoprics of Phrygia*, Vol. I, Part II, p. 713.

[37]Nissen, "Die Petrusakten."

[38]Leclercq, Abercius, col. 67.

[39]Nissen, *S. Abercii Vita*.

[40]Abel, "Étude," p. 405.

[41]Ibid., p. 404.

[42]H. Strathmann, Th. Klauser, "Aberkios," *RAC* (1950) 1. col. 12. The same is true of M. V. Brandi, "Abercio," *Bibliotheca Sanctorum* (1961) 1. col. 68–75. W. M. Calder, "Early Christian Epitaphs from Phrygia," *Anatolian Studies* 5(1955): 25 n. 4, describes the *Life of Abercius* as "largely legendary," noting the data borrowed from the inscription. Wischmeyer, "Aberkiosinschrift," 23, describes the *Life* more negatively: ". . . die Aberkioslegende selbst sehr fabulös ist, . . ."

[43]Hippolyte Delehaye, *The Legends of the Saints* (New York: Fordham, 1962) 65: "With the help of various episodes which are mostly reminiscences from other legends, the hagiographer produced a very detailed narrative which was very successful."

[44]H. Grégoire, "Bardesane et S. Abercius," *Byzantion* 25–27(1955): 364.

the battle against the Marcionites, but suggests that the real opponents of Abercius in Hieropolis may have been Montanists. He also argues that the text provides important data for the history of the persecution of Christians in Asia Minor during the second century.[45]

Drijvers, in his effort to identify all early sources relevant to Bardaisan, drew upon the *Life of Abercius*. He arrived at much the same conclusion as Grégoire. He argues that, whereas, (1) the speeches of Euxeinianos repeated in the text demonstrate a literary relationship between the *Book of the Laws of the Countries* and the *Life*, (2) the description of Bardaisan (§ 70) accords with what is known from the Syriac tradition, (3) "the geographical indication of the place of meeting corresponds with Bardaisan's dwelling place," and, (4) the author correctly indicates Bardaisan's and Abercius' common antipathy for the Marcionites; therefore, the historicity of the Bardaisan section of the *Life* is not to be doubted.[46]

However, *contra* Grégoire and Drijvers, it can be argued that the data in the texts to which they appeal in arguing for at least a limited historicity can be found in many texts of the fourth century. Eusebius and Ephrem were aware of the tradition of Bardaisan reflected in the *Life of Abercius*.[47] Bardaisan's anti-Marcionite predilections were reported by Eusebius.[48] His relationship to Edessa and his writings appear to have been widely known during this period. His writings were used by Eusebius and by *De Recta Fide in Deum* attributed to a certain Adamantius.[49] The most that can be affirmed is that the text confirms what was widely known from widely circulated literature. The writer of the *Life of Abercius* was aware of these traditions and incorporated them in the narrative, even as the burial inscription and topographical and geographical data of Hieropolis and its surrounding area were included. To use the *Life* as a mass of historical detail in search of either the historical Abercius or the historical Bardaisan is not productive, although the examination of the level

---

[45]Ibid., pp. 363–368.

[46]Drijvers, *Bardaisan*, pp. 170–171.

[47]Eusebius, *H. E.* IV.30, "Bardaisan . . . wrote dialogue against the followers of Marcion." Ephraem's statements on the person of Bardaisan and his followers have been assembled by Drijvers, *Bardaisan*, pp. 161–165. See also the section in Drijvers, *Bardaisan*, dealing with the later Syriac tradition, pp. 185–199, and Th. Nissen, "Die Petrusakten und ein bardesanitischer Dialog in der Aberkiosvita," *ZNW* 9(1908): 190–203, 315–328.

[48]Eusebius, *H. E.* IV.30.

[49]A. von Harnack, *Marcio, das Evangelium vom fremden Gott. Neue Studien zu Marcion* 2nd ed. (*TU* 45; Leipzig: J. C. Hinrich, 1924) 60*. D. Bundy, "Marcion and the Marcionites in Early Syriac Apologetics," *Le Muséon* 101(1988): 21–32. *De Recta Fide in Deum* attributed to Adamantius needs to be more thoroughly examined.

of the author's historical awareness and accuracy is an important first step toward allowing the *Life* to be used as a historical document.

The Structure of the Life of Aberkios

The *Life* is part of the large corpus of hagiographical texts composed between the fourth and sixth centuries. Their function appears to have been primarily didactic. The genre provided a vehicle for addressing contemporary problems and issues, often in the guise of an archaizing narrative. The literary genre and its function in this period suggest that an examination of the literary structure may provide access to the issues in discussion.

The *Life of Abercius* is composed of five narrative units and a conclusion. Each of the narrative units has an independent coherent narrative line and its own characters. However, each unit deals with an aspect of issues which recur throughout the larger narrative.

(1) Paragraphs 1–19.   Here are recounted the struggle against paganism in the city of Hieropolis in Phrygia Minor and the effort of Abercius to convince the populace that there is but one true God. The three men "with unclean spirits" are healed when they challenge Abercius on the issue of the unity of God and end up confessing the "one true God." The crowd is overwhelmed by this healing, and many forsake paganism and are baptized. This then leads to a healing ministry in the region. The healing appears to have been a healing from the pagan (Marcionite, or perhaps Manichaean) affirmation of the plurality of divinity. The theological observations attributed to Abercius are those of Judaeo-Christian monotheism.

(2) Paragraphs 20–30.   As the peripatetic healer continues his ministry, Phrygella comes before Abercius and requests healing from her blindness. It is not stated that Phrygella holds questionable beliefs, but the text makes clear that an affirmation of faith congruent with that of Abercius is a condition for being healed. She affirms, "I believe on the Lord ($\delta\epsilon\sigma\pi\acute{o}\tau\eta\nu$) Jesus Christ our God," and as she is healed, sees a great light (probably an allusion to Paul's conversion, Acts 9:3–19). The name Phrygella is probably to be understood as signifying Phrygia. After her healing, three blind women come to be healed. The three women in the narrative *may* signify the three Montanist prophetesses of Phrygia. Their vision of Christ in three forms seem to indicate that though Christ may appear differently to different people, it is still the same Christ.

(3) Paragraphs 31–38.   Euxeinianos, son of Phrygella, after hearing of his mother's healing, comes to discuss doctrinal and philosophical issues with Abercius. The text makes clear that the discussion is but another facet of Abercius' healing ministry—a healing from doctrinal error. The perspective articulated by Euxeinianos is distinctly Marcionite. Indeed,

the name of the Marcionite is an allusion to Marcion, who came from Sinope on the Pontus Euxeinos. Euxeinianos is convinced of the correctness of Abercius' understanding. He becomes a vigilant believer and is later described by Marcus Aurelius as a "good man" (§ 47). The suggestion is that a Marcionite believer can accept the "true faith" and become an Abercius-type believer, while retaining his social status.

(4) Paragraphs 39–66. During his multi-faceted ministry of healing in Phrygia, he cast out a demon which went to Rome and infected the daughter of the emperor. Like Paul and Marcion, Abercius is summoned to Rome. The letter (obviously a forgery) from the emperor requesting Abercius' help is sent to Euxeinianos, who impels Abercius to accept. Abercius leaves Trophimus[50] in charge of the parish. The emperor and empress Faustina are not described as heretics, but the empress must indicate that she agrees with Abercius' understanding of the faith in order to expedite the healing. The demon (Marcionism?) is expelled from Rome and must return to Phrygia. Gifts are accepted which benefit Abercius' parish but not him personally.

(5) Paragraphs 67–75. Christ then tells Abercius to go to Syria to aid the believers.[51] He obeys and travels through Syria combatting the "heresy of the Marcionites." This is the first time in the text that the Marcionites are mentioned by name. Common cause is made with Bardaisan against the heretics and disunity in the church. Many are dissuaded (healed) from their heresies. Bardaisan's offer of gold is refused, but the title ἰσαπόστολος is conferred and accepted. The conferring of this title, reserved during this period for Constantine, brings to a climax the theme which has been developed throughout, that of true apostolicity.[52] The confirmation of the title is an anti-Marcionite gesture. Abercius, not Marcion, is like the apostle Paul!

The concluding paragraphs (§§ 76–80) take Abercius back to Hieropolis, where he confirms the faith of his parish before dying a victorious death.

Issues Raised

The *Life of Abercius* thus addresses four primary issues: (1) the revival (or continuation) of paganism in Phrygia; (2) the prevalence of Marcionite

---

[50]Probably an allusion to 2 Tim. 4:20 and Acts 20:4; 21:29.

[51]Probably an allusion to Paul's "Macedonian call," Acts 16:9.

[52]The issue of "apostolicity" was central to the Marcionite controversy. For a presentation of relevant data, see the work of R. Joseph Hoffmann, *Marcion: On the Restitution of Christianity. An Essay on the Development of Radical Paulinist Theology in the Second Century* (AAR Academy Series, 46; Chico: Scholars Press, 1984) 101–153, *et passim.*

ideas and, perhaps, of the Marcionite church; and (3) the question of true apostolicity, that of Paul-Abercius over against Paul-Marcion; (4) the mission of the "true apostle"—to heal people of "blindnesses," "unclean spirits," "demons," and "heresies."

Hieropolis of Phrygia Salutaris is the significant recurring geographical feature of the narrative. The early ministry and miracles are centered there, and even when in Rome, Abercius is thinking of Hieropolis. While in Syria, he remembers his obligations as representative of the community to which he must return before his death.

One unanswered question is the significance of the writer's identification of Bardaisan. Bardaisan is depicted in nearly regal terms, a Christian statesman who is not required to affirm faith before healing can take place. As well, Bardaisan's work provides the response for Abercius against the Marcionites. The approach of the author of the *Life of Abercius* is quite different from that of Adamantius (*De Recta Fide*), who uses passages from Bardaisan's writings and then attacks Bardaisan. Did the community in Phrygia recognize the words as Bardaisan's? Probably the intellectuals of the community would have known the source of the dialogue. It is also significant that the anti-Marcionite *Acts of Paul* are cited. While one might see in this text a Bardaisanite document, it is more probably an indication that the negative evaluation of Bardaisan by Ephrem, Adamantius, and others had not replaced the positive analysis reflected in Eusebius.

III
CONCLUSION

This analysis argues against Drijver's use of the *Life of Abercius* as a source for early Christianity in Syria, although it may be used to demonstrate the influence of Syriac writers and traditions and their appropriation beyond the traditionally assumed linguistic frontiers of Syriac Christianity. The issues in discussion, however, relate to fourth-century Phrygia, not to Syria. This is not to suggest that all the historical details and allusions to local cultural practices are fictitious. The author took considerable care with the narrative and the framework within which it is set. However, the historical data in the *Life* about Syria and Bardaisan are literary devices, as is the narrative about Marcus Aurelius and the imperial family, designed to lend credibility and interest to the story. They conform to and expand upon the Abercius inscription. They must be considered as functions of the text in which they are found.[53] The *Life* sug-

[53]There have been some attempts to rehabilitate hagiographical texts as historical sources,

gests that the ideological identity of the Phrygian church was still in flux during the late fourth century. It is what other data, from writers as different as the Cappadocians and the emperor Julian, would lead us to expect. What is significant is that the Marcionites and Marcionite ideas were still significant forces in Phrygia.

---

and certainly they are crucial to any historical analysis. However, the assumption is often made that accuracy in geographical (and/or historical) detail guarantees the authority of other data in the narrative. Such an assumption skirts the issues raised by the complex genre that is hagiography. For different historiographical approaches to hagiographical texts, see, for example: Stephen Mitchell, "The Life of Saint Theodotus of Ancyra," *Anatolian Studies* 32(1982): 93–113; Frank R. Trombley, "Paganism in the Greek World at the End of Antiquity: The Case of Rural Anatolia and Greece," *Harvard Theological Review* 78(1985): 327–352; and, David Bundy, "The *Acts of Saint Gallicanus:* A Study of the Structural Relations," *Byzantion* 57(1987): 12–31.

Eusebius and Syriac Christianity

SEBASTIAN BROCK

At the outset it is necessary to recall that Eusebius' *Ecclesiastical History* is essentially a history of the Christian church within the bounds of "our οἰκουμένη," i.e., the Roman Empire. Since the Christianized Roman Empire served for Eusebius as an εἰκών of the Kingdom of God, what lay outside the empire was a potential source of detriment and danger, and it is significant that in his only reference to "the land of the Persians" (*HE* 7.31.2) he speaks of it as a place from which "deadly poison" comes (he is referring to the teaching of Mani).

This model set by Eusebius, whereby "Church History" is limited to the history of the church within the Roman Empire, has had an insidious effect on almost all subsequent histories of the early church down to modern times, for these normally leave the reader with the impression that Christianity was essentially a phenomenon restricted to the Graeco-Latin cultural world, once it had broken loose of its Jewish roots.

The all-pervasive influence of Eusebius has meant that the existence of a third cultural tradition, represented by Syriac Christianity, has consistently been neglected or marginalized by church historians, both ancient and modern. Eusebius is indeed aware of the existence of Syriac-speaking Christian communities in the eastern provinces of the Roman Empire, but these, with the one exception discussed below, are of very peripheral interest to him. As for Syriac Christianity beyond the eastern boundaries of the Roman Empire, that is, within the Persian, or Sassanid, Empire (approximately modern Iraq and Iran), he has not a single word to say, even though Christianity was certainly already well established there by his time (however unclear the details may be).

In the following pages our concern will primarily be with Eusebius' sole detailed reference to Syriac Christianity, centered around the alleged correspondence between Abgar Ukkama ("the Black"), king of Edessa (Syriac Urhay, modern Urfa in southeast Turkey), and Jesus. After looking at this and the parallel account in the early fifth-century Syriac work known as the *Teaching of Addai* (*Doctrina Addai*), we shall need to consider briefly the other scanty evidence available for the early history of Syriac Christianity prior to the fourth century; only then will it be possible to assess what, if any, historical value Eusebius' account may have.

Eusebius' narrative concerning King Abgar appears right at the end of Book 1 of his *Ecclesiastical History* (1.13). First of all he gives a general account (1.13.1–5) of how Abgar, having heard of Jesus' healings, sent a letter "asking to find relief from his disease." Jesus sent a letter in reply, promising to send one of his disciples. In due course, after the resurrection the apostle Thomas sends Thaddaeus, one of the seventy, to preach in Edessa. Eusebius then names as his source for all this a Syriac document kept in the archives of Edessa. From this document he then provides a translation of the two letters, from Abgar to Jesus (1.13.6–9), and from Jesus to Abgar (1.13.10). Following these two documents he gives an extended narrative extract from his Syriac source, recounting Thaddaeus' arrival and preaching in Edessa (1.13.11–22). Subsequently, in *HE* 2.1.6–7, Eusebius provides a retrospective summary of his earlier account; since, however, this adds no new material, discussion below will be confined to the longer passage in 1.13.

Eusebius' claim to have used a Syriac document from Edessa can be accepted, though it is improbable that it was kept in the town's archives, and unlikely that he himself made the translation into Greek. This Syriac document from which Eusebius quotes in fact survives, albeit in a later and somewhat expanded form, incorporated into a much longer work known as the *Teaching of Addai* (where Addai is the same person as Eusebius' Thaddaeus). The Syriac *Teaching of Addai* is preserved in a manuscript of about 500 CE, and the work in its present form probably dates from the first decades of the fifth century.[1] The author of the *Teaching of Addai* evidently had access to the Syriac original underlying Eusebius' Greek, for his wording differs in a number of significant details from that of the early Syriac translation of Eusebius' *Ecclesiastical History* (which might otherwise have been supposed to have been the sole source of the relevant sections of the *Teaching of Addai*).[2] Although the initial pages of the *Teaching of Addai*, where the account runs closely in parallel with Eusebius' account, can thus be taken back to some time prior to the publication of Eusebius' *Ecclesiastical History*,[3] the remainder of the *Teaching of Addai* contains materials, some of which can only belong to the late fourth or early fifth century, while others are of indeterminate date.

The extent of the additional material in the *Teaching of Addai* can best be seen from a summary listing of the contents:

(1) Introductory narrative, providing an account of how Abgar came to send a letter to Jesus at the hands of Ananias/Hannan[4] (trans. Phillips, pp. 1–3; trans. Howard, pp. 3–7); although the general tenor of this is implied by Eusebius' opening sections (*HE* 1.13.1–5), many new details have clearly been added.

(2) The text of Abgar's letter (trans. Phillips, p. 4; trans. Howard, pp. 7–8); this is very close to Eusebius, with only minor differences in wording.

(3) The text of Jesus' reply in the form of an oral message, not a written letter (trans. Phillips, pp. 4–5; trans. Howard, p. 9);[5] although in Eusebius this is given as a letter by Jesus himself, the wording of the contents is again very close in the two texts, except that the *Teaching of Addai* adds a blessing at the end for the city of Edessa.

(4) A brief account of how Abgar's messenger, Hannan, painted Jesus' portrait and presented it to Abgar (trans. Phillips, p. 5; trans. Howard, pp. 9–11); this is absent from Eusebius.[6]

(5) The narrative of Addai's arrival and healing of Abgar (trans. Phillips, pp. 5–10; trans. Howard, pp. 11–21); this corresponds very closely with Eusebius' narrative, with only some rather minor differences.

(6) Addai tells the story of how Protonike, wife of Claudius, was converted by Simon Peter and went to Palestine where she discovers the true cross in Jerusalem (trans. Phillips, pp. 10–16; trans. Howard, pp. 21–35); this is not to be found in Eusebius, and is clearly a later insertion, for it presupposes a Christian building on the site of Golgotha.[7]

(7) Abgar arranges for Addai to preach to the whole city; his long sermon is then given (trans. Phillips, pp. 16–30; trans. Howard, pp. 35–63). Since Eusebius' narrative breaks off with the plans for Addai to preach to the whole city, it is likely that his source document also contained Addai's sermon; it is unfortunately not possible to say for certain whether the sermon in the *Teaching of Addai* preserves the original document intact, or whether it has altered and expanded it. If, however, the author of the *Teaching of Addai* continues here to follow the same practice as in the earlier sections, then it would seem likely that he would have kept

to his source fairly closely, though there is the possibility that he may have inserted some new material.

The remainder of the *Teaching of Addai* has nothing corresponding in Eusebius' account, and is likely to be the work of the person who produced the *Teaching* in its present form, probably early in the fifth century.

(8) Narrative concerning conversions of local nobles; Addai's church building and his ordinations; Abgar's correspondence with Narse, "king of the Athoraye (Assyrians)," concerning Addai (trans. Phillips, pp. 30–36; trans. Howard, pp. 63–75);

(9) Abgar's correspondence with Tiberius, urging him to punish the Jews of Jerusalem for crucifying Jesus (trans. Phillips, pp. 36–38; trans. Howard, pp. 75–81);[8]

(10) Addai's illness and arrangements before his death (trans. Phillips, pp. 38–39; trans. Howard, p. 81);

(11) Addai's final address to the nobles of Edessa (trans. Phillips, pp. 39–45; trans. Howard, pp. 83–95);

(12) Addai's death and burial (trans. Phillips, pp. 45–47; trans. Howard, pp. 95–99);

(13) his successor Aggai's ministry and martyrdom (trans. Phillips, pp. 47–50; trans. Howard, pp. 99–105);

(14) the ordination of his successor Palut by Serapion, bishop of Antioch, who in turn had been ordained (literally, "received the hand") by Zephyrinus of Rome, in the line of succession from Simon Peter (trans. Phillips, p. 50; trans. Howard, p. 105;[9]

(15) Lebubna is stated to be author of the account of Addai (trans. Phillips, p. 50; trans. Howard, pp. 105–7).

Thus of these contents of the *Teaching of Addai* only (2), (3) and (5) correspond closely to material in Eusebius, and for these sections the two texts are translated in parallel below.[10] The beginning and end of Eusebius' narrative also presuppose the general background of (1) and the existence of a sermon corresponding to (7) in the *Teaching of Addai*.

(a) *Letter of Abgar to Jesus*[11]

Eusebius, *HE* 1.13.6–9	*Teaching of Addai*
6. Abgar Uchama, the toparch,	Abgar Ukkama
to Jesus the good Saviour	to Jesus the good Doctor
who has appeared in the district	who has appeared in the district
of Jerusalem, greeting!	of Jerusalem, my lord, greeting!
I have heard concerning you	I have heard concerning you

and your cures, how they are accomplished by you without drugs and herbs. For, as the story goes, you make the blind regain their sight, the lame to walk, and you cleanse lepers	and your healing, that you are not healing with drugs and herbs. For by your word you open [the eyes of] the blind, you cause the lame to walk, and you cleanse lepers, and the dumb you cause to hear,

and cast out unclean spirits
and demons, and you cure those
tormented by long disease,
and you raise the dead.
7. And when I heard all these things
concerning you
I decided that it is one of the two,
either that you are God and
came down from heaven
to do these things,
or are a son of God
for doing these things.
8. For this reason I write to
beg you to hasten to me
   and heal the suffering
which I have.
   Moreover I have heard
   that the Jews are murmuring
against you,
	and spirits and demons and the
	tormented by your very word you
	heal;
	even the dead you raise.
	And when I heard the wonderful
	great things which you are doing
	I decided
	either that you are God who
	came down from heaven and have
	done these things,
	or you are the Son of God
	who do all these things.
	For this reason I have written to
	beg you to come to me, as I worship
	you, and heal a certain sickness
	which I have, as I have believed in
	you. Moreover I have heard this
	too, that the Jews are murmuring
	against you
	and are persecuting you
	and even want to crucify you

and wish to illtreat you. 9. Now I have a city, very small and venerable which is enough for both.	and are intent on harming you. Now I hold a city small and beautiful which is enough for both to live there in quiet.

(b) *Jesus' reply to Abgar*[12]

Eusebius, *HE* 1.13.10	*Teaching of Addai*
10. Blessed are you who have believed in me, not having seen me, for it is written concerning me[13] that those who have seen me will not believe in me, and that those who have not seen me will believe and live. Now concerning what you wrote to me to come to you, I must first complete here all for which I was sent, and after thus completing it, to be taken up to him	Blessed are you who, not having seen me, have believed in me, for it is written concerning me that those who see me will not believe in me, and those who do not see me will believe in me. Now concerning what you wrote to me that I should come to you: that concerning which I was sent here is henceforth completed, and I am going to ascend to my

who sent me, and when I have been taken up I will send you one of my disciples to heal your suffering and give life to you and those you.	Father who sent me, and when I have ascended to him I will send you one of my disciples who will heal and restore the sickness you have, and everyone who is with you he with will convert to eternal life. And your town shall be blessed, and an enemy shall not have dominion over it ever again.[14]

(c) *Narrative*

Eusebius, *HE* 1.13.11–22	*Teaching of Addai*

11. Now after Jesus had ascended
Judas, who is also Thomas, sent
to him Thaddaeus as an apostle
being one of the Seventy
    And he came
              and stayed
with Tobias, son of Tobias.
	After Christ had ascended to heaven
	Judas Thomas sent
	to Abgar Addai the apostle
	who was one of the Seventy-Two[15]
	apostles. And when Addai came
	to the town of Edessa, he stayed
	at the house of Tobia, son of Tobia,
	a Jew who was from Palestine.[16]

Now when news of him was heard, it was reported to Abgar	And when news of him was heard in all the town, there entered one of Abgar's nobles and he spoke about Addai—his name was ʿAbdu, son of ʿAbdu, one of Abgar's leading men who sat on bended knee:
that an apostle of Jesus has come here, as he wrote to you.	"Look, a messenger has come and stayed here, the one concerning whom Jesus sent (a message) to you, (saying), 'I am going to send you one of my disciples.'"
12. So Thaddaeus began in the power of God to heal every disease and weakness so that all marvelled. And when Abgar heard the great and wonderful deeds that he doing, and how he was working cures	And when Abgar heard these things and the mighty deeds which Addai was was doing, and the wonderful cures which he was effecting,
he began to suspect that this was he of whom Jesus had written, saying, "When I have been taken up, I will send you one of my disciples who will heal your suffering." 13. So he summoned Tobias with whom Thaddaeus was	he was of the firm opinion that "Truly, this is the man of whom Jesus had sent (a message), 'When I have ascended to heaven, I will send you one of my disciples.'" Now Abgar sent and summoned Tobia

EUSEBIUS AND SYRIAC CHRISTIANITY | 217

staying, and said,
"I hear that a certain man of
power has come, and is staying in
your house. Bring him up to me."

And Tobias came to Thaddaeus and
said to him, "The toparch, Abgar,
summoned me and bade me bring you
to him in order to heal him." And
Thaddaeus said, "I will go up since

I have been miraculously sent to him."
14. So Tobias rose up early the next
day and taking Thaddaeus came to Abgar.
Now as he went up,

while the king's magnates
were standing present, as soon as
he entered a great vision appeared
to Abgar on the face of the apostle
Thaddaeus. And when   Abgar
saw this   he did
reverence to Thaddaeus, and wonder
held all those who were standing by
        for they had not seen
the vision which appeared only to
Abgar. 15. Then he asked Thaddaeus,
"Are you of a truth a disciple
of Jesus,
the son of God who said to me
'I will send you one of my disciples
who will heal you and give you life'?"
And Thaddaeus said, "Since you have
        had great faith in him who
sent me, for this reason I
was sent to you. And again, if
you believe in him, the request of
your heart shall be to you as
you believe."
16. And Abgar said to him, "I have
such belief in him as to have
wished to take   force and
destroy the Jews who crucified him,
had I not been prevented from this

and said to him,
"I hear that a certain man of
power has come and is staying in
your house. Bring him up to me.
Maybe there shall be found for me
some good hope of healing from
him."

And Tobia rose up early the next day
and brought Addai the apostle,
taking him up to Abgar, while Addai
knew that "it is by the power of God
that I have been sent to him."

And when Addai had gone up and
entered
Abgar's presence, with his nobles
standing by him, at his entrance
to him a wonderful vision appeared
to Abgar from the face of
Addai. And the moment Abgar
saw that vision he fell down and did
reverence to Addai, and great wonder
held all those who were standing in
his presence, for they did not see
the vision which had appeared to
Abgar. Then Abgar said to Addai,
"Are you of a truth the disciple
of Jesus that man of valor,
the Son of God, who sent to me
'I will send you one of my disciples
for healing and for life'?"
Addai says to him, "Since you have
from the first had faith in him who
sent me to you, for this reason I
was sent to you. And when again
you believe in him, everything that
you shall believe in shall be to
you."
Abgar says to him, "I have
such belief in him as to have
wished to take me a force and go and
destroy the Jews who crucified him,
but I abstained from doing this

by the Roman Empire."

And Thaddaeus said, "Our Lord
has fulfilled the will of his
Father, and after fulfilling it
                has been
taken up to the Father."

17. Abgar said to him, "I too have
believed in him and in his Father."
And Thaddaeus said, "For this cause
     I lay my hand on
you in his name."

And when he did this
immediately he was healed from
the disease[17] and the suffering which
he had.
18. And Abgar   wondered
that just as he had heard concerning
Jesus
        so he had in fact received
through his disciple Thaddaeus who
cured him without drugs and herbs,

and not only him, but also Abdus
the son of Abdus who had the gout;
     for he too came and fell at
his feet and received his prayer at
his hands, and was healed.

And the same Thaddaeus healed
many others of their fellow citizens,
performing many wonderful deeds
and preaching the word of God.
19. And after this Abgar said,

"O Thaddaeus, it is by the power
of God that you do these
things and we ourselves have
wondered.
But in addition to this, I beg you
narrate to me concerning the coming
of Jesus, how it happened, and
concerning his   power
and by what power he did these

because of the Roman Empire and
the covenant of peace which had
been established by me with our lord
Caesar, Tiberius, like my former
ancestors."
And Addai says to him, "Our Lord
has fulfilled the will of his
Father and having completed the
will of his begetter, has been
raised to his Father, and is seated
with him in the glory in which he
was from eternity."
Abgar says to him, "I too
believe in him and in his Father."
And Addai says to him, "Because you
have thus believed I lay my hand on
you in the name of him in whom
you have believed."
And immediately he laid his hand on
him he was healed from the harm of
the disease   which
he had had for a long while.
And Abgar was amazed and wondered
that just as he had heard concerning
Jesus, that he was performing and
healing, so
                        Addai too
        without drugs of any kind
was healing in the name of Jesus,
                including ᶜAbdu
the son of ᶜAbdu who had the gout
in his feet. And he too proffered
his feet, and he laid his hand on
them and healed him, and he no
longer had the gout.
And also in the whole city

he performed mighty healings,
manifesting wondrous powers in it.
Abgar says to him,
"Now that everyone knows that
                it is by the power
of Jesus Christ that you do these
wonders and we ourselves have
wondered at your works,
        I beg you, therefore,
narrate to us concerning the coming
of Christ, how it happened, and
concerning his glorious power,
and concerning the wonders which

things of which I have heard."

20. And Thaddaeus said, "I will
now be silent,
but since I was sent
to preach the word,

tomorrow summon for me an assembly
all your citizens and I will
preach before them, and sow in them
the word of life,

concerning the coming of Jesus,
how it happened, and concerning his
mission, and for what reason he was
sent by the Father,
and concerning his power and his
    deeds and the
mysteries
which he spoke in the world
and by what power he did these things
and concerning his new
preaching and concerning his lowliness
and humiliation, and how he humbled
himself and put aside and made small[18]
his   divinity,

and was crucified and descended into
Hades,   and rent
the partition which had not been
rent from the beginning of the world,
and raised the dead,
        and he went down alone, but
ascended with a great multitude to his
        Father."
21. So Abgar commanded his citizens to
assemble in the morning to hear the
preaching of Thaddaeus, and after
this he ordered him to be given
gold and silver, but he did not
receive it, saying, "If we have left
our own things, how shall we take
those of others?"

we have heard that he was doing,
which you saw along with the rest
of your companions."
Addai says to him, "Of this I will
not be silent from preaching,
because for this reason I was sent
here to speak and to teach everyone
who is willing to believe like you.
Tomorrow assemble for me all the of
    city
        and I will sow in it
the word of life in the proclamation
which I shall preach before you both
concerning the coming of Christ,
how it happened, and concerning his
glorious power, and concerning his
Sender, why and how he sent him,
and concerning his power and his
wonderful deeds and concerning the
glorious mysteries of his coming
which he spoke in the world

and concerning the exactitude of his
preaching, and he
        made himself small and humbled

his exalted divinity in the body
[var. humanity] which he had
assumed
and was crucified and descended to
the place of the dead, and rent
the partition which had never been
rent,
and revived the dead by his being
killed, and he went down alone, but
ascended with   many to his
glorious Father."

And Abgar ordered him to be given
silver and gold.
    Addai says to him,
"How can we take what is not ours,
for our own things we have left, as
we were commanded by our Lord, to
be without purses and without
wallets; rather, carrying crosses on
our shoulders, we have been
commanded to preach his gospel in

	all creation...."
	[At the opening of the *Teaching of*
22. These things were done in the	*Addai*] In the 343rd year of the
340th year.	kingdom of the Greeks....[19]

What are we to make of this account? While no serious scholar would accept it at face value, there is the possibility that this legend (for such it must be classed) might contain some grains of historical value. On this point scholars generally fall into one of two camps: thus some consider the entire narrative to be a fabrication dating from about 300, while others prefer to see the narrative as reflecting the supposedly historical conversion of King Abgar VIII, "the Great," at the end of the second century, but transposed to Abgar V, "the Black," in order to take back the conversion of the royal house to apostolic times. The first view was propounded by W. Bauer in 1934, while the second was argued by F. C. Burkitt in his influential book *Early Eastern Christianity* (1904); subsequent scholars have generally followed either Bauer or Burkitt in their basic attitude to the account.[20] Here we need only note that Burkitt's interpretation assumes that Abgar VIII (Burkitt referred to him as Abgar IX),[21] who reigned from ca. 177–212, did indeed convert to Christianity—something which is, as we shall see, far from certain.

At this point, before proceeding any further in an attempt to assess the historical value, if any, of the story of Addai's mission in Edessa as recounted in the narrative common to Eusebius and the *Teaching of Addai*, it will be helpful to glance at the other surviving evidence for Syriac Christianity as a whole prior to the fourth century. It will rapidly become clear how very meager this evidence is: only with the *Demonstrations* of Aphrahat (composed in the Sassanid Empire between 337 and 345), the acts of the Christian martyrs under Shapur II (339–379), and the extensive corpus of prose and poetry by Ephrem (active until 363 in Nisibis, and thereafter in Edessa, until his death in 373), does Syriac Christianity at last emerge from obscurity.[22] All the evidence for the period prior to the fourth century is exceedingly limited, and usually of uncertain interpretation.

The main witnesses for this early period, apart from the account of Addai's mission in Eusebius and the *Teaching of Addai*, are the following passages:

(1) The *Chronicle of Edessa*, dating from the mid sixth century, opens with an account of a flood in Edessa in November 201 CE, during the reign of Abgar (VIII).[23] In the course of this narrative, which is certainly derived from the town archives, it is mentioned that the flood waters damaged "the sanctuary [*haykla*] of the church of the Christians." Although it has been suggested[24] that the words are an interpolation, since there is no mention of

a Christian church in a similar account of a flood in the *Chronicle* of Ps.-Dionysius of Telmahre,[25] the passage should be accepted as original since the account in the other chronicle probably refers to another flood (the local river Daisan caused a number of serious floods until it was diverted round the town by Justinian in the mid sixth century).

The only other references to Christianity prior to the fourth century in the *Chronicle of Edessa* are: (a) the expulsion of Marcion "from the catholic church" (without reference to Edessa) in 137/138 CE; and (b) the birth of Bardaisan on 11 July 154.[26] Only with Bishop Qona's "laying the foundations of the church of Edessa" in 312/313 CE do references to the Christian history of Edessa become the norm. The silence concerning Addai and the conversion of Abgar in this important local source is significant.

(2) In the course of his account of the Paschal controversy (ca. 190 CE) Eusebius has a passing reference to the presence, at a meeting in Palestine, of bishops "in Osrhoene and the cities there" (*HE* 5.23.4; the Syriac translation has "of the churches of Mesopotamia and the cities there"). Since, however, the words do not feature in Rufinus' Latin translation (made in 402/403), they could be an early interpolation into the extant Greek text of Eusebius.[27]

(3) The inscription of bishop Abercius of Phrygian Hierapolis (died ca. 200) describes in symbolic language his travels to Rome and to Nisibis, thus providing evidence for the existence of a Christian community in that town at the end of the second century; although it is likely he would have passed through Edessa, no mention is made of it.

(4) The chronographer Julius Africanus, whose *floruit* belongs to the early decades of the third century, has two passages where mention is made of King Abgar (VIII), with whose court he was clearly very familiar:

> (a) In an excerpt on the subject of archery, derived from his *Kestoi*,[28] Julius Africanus mentions Abgar, his son Maᶜnu, and Bardaisan "the Parthian." The passage shows that Bardaisan (whose skill at archery is praised) frequented Abgar's court, and that Julius Africanus was probably tutor to Maᶜnu, and so would have known the royal family well. No mention of Christianity is found in the passage.

> (b) The Byzantine chronographer George Syncellus quotes Julius Africanus as describing Abgar (VIII) as ἱερὸν ἄνδρα, "a holy man."[29] This has often been taken as a reference to Abgar's conversion to Christianity, but this is by no means a necessary inference; indeed ἱερὸν would be a rather surprising term to be used for a prominent convert.

(5) The Syriac *Book of the Laws of the Countries*,[30] composed in the early third century by a pupil of Bardaisan, contains the following passage (§ 45):

> In Syria and in Edessa people used to cut off their privy parts for Tār‘ata [Atargatis]; but when King Abgar believed, he gave orders that anyone who cut off his privy parts should have his hand cut off. And from that day until the present no one cuts off his privy parts in the region of Edessa.

On the surface this looks like a clear reference to Abgar's conversion (it is usually assumed that the Abgar in question is Abgar VIII), but the words "when he believed" are absent from Eusebius' quotation of the passage (*PE* 6.10.44); this means that it is very likely that they represent an interpolation in the Syriac text, made by some copyist familiar with the *Teaching of Addai* (who would have identified the Abgar as Abgar V).

In the next section (46) of the *Book of the Laws of the Countries* there is an important testimony to the extent to which Christianity had spread in the East:

> What should we say about the new family of us Christians, whom Christ established at his coming everywhere and in every region: we are called Christians after the single name of Christ, and we assemble on the same one day of Sunday, and on fixed days we abstain from food. Our brothers in Gallia [Gaul] do not take males as consorts, nor do those in Parthia marry two wives, nor are those in Judaea circumcised, nor do our sisters among the Geli and Cushans sleep with strangers; those in Persia do not marry their daughters, and those in Media do not run away from their dead, or bury people alive, or give them as food for dogs; and those in Edessa do not kill their wives or sisters who commit adultery, but they simply distance themselves from them, handing them over to the judgment of God; nor do those in Hatra stone to death thieves. In every place they happen to be, the local customs do not cause them to depart from the law of their Christ.

(6) Of the local Edessene martyr acts, two are entirely fictional: the *Acts of Sharbel* and the *Acts of Bishop Barsamya*[31] both claim to be contemporary accounts of events under Trajan and in the reign of "Abgar the Seventh," dated to September 104; in fact both texts are clearly from the same circles that produced the *Teaching of Addai* and belong to the early fifth century. Much more impressive for the historian are the *Acts of Shmona and Gurya*, martyred probably in 297, and of the deacon *Habbib*, martyred probably in 309.[32] Although the two *Acts* in their present form present some problems, there is no serious doubt that these martyrdoms took place. It is significant that Ephrem knows of these three (*Carmina*

Nisibena 33:13), but nothing of Sharbel and Barsamya (or, for that matter, of Addai); likewise the calendar of martyrs preserved in a manuscript written in Edessa in November 411 includes only Shmona, Gurya, and Habbib as martyrs of Edessa.[33]

(7) One other source has often played an important part in the discussion of early Syriac Christianity, i.e., the *Chronicle of Arbela*.[34] This work, available only in an early twentieth-century manuscript, purports to relate the history of Christianity in Arbela, capital of Adiabene, up to the mid sixth century; included in this is a (suspiciously) detailed account of the succession of bishops of Adiabene going back to Peqida "upon whom Addai the apostle personally laid hands." Some scholars have given credence to this account (notably P. Kahle in his influential book *The Cairo Geniza*)[35] and have gone on to suppose that Christianity reached Adiabene at an early date, as a result of the conversion of the Jewish ruling family, and that the Edessene Abgar legend really had its origin in Arbela and was only adapted to Edessa at a later date. *The Chronicle of Arbela*, however, which is the main basis for this speculative reconstruction, is a highly problematic text, and even if it turns out to be a medieval compilation rather than a modern forgery (as has been claimed),[36] it is generally agreed now that its account of Christianity in the Parthian period (up to 226) is little more than wishful thinking; even for the account of the local fourth-century martyrs, for whom independent accounts survive, the evidence of the *Chronicle* proves unreliable.

(8) Many other later sources, such as the *Acts of Mari* (a disciple of Addai) and the various later chronicles,[37] offer information on the early spread of Syriac Christianity, but their evidence is either problematic or manifestly an elaboration of the Addai tradition.

Account also needs to be taken of extant early Syriac literature, much of which has been connected with Edessa by modern scholars. It is, however, essential to remember that these connections which have been adduced with Edessa often rest not on any secure evidence, but solely on speculation— speculation, moreover, which has largely been invited by the assumption that the Abgar narrative contains an element of historicity. There is thus a clear danger here of circularity of argument.

The only early texts for which an Edessene origin is assured are: (a) the account of the flood at Edessa in October 201, preserved in the *Chronicle of Edessa*; (b) the scant fragments of Bardaisan's works preserved by later polemicists from Ephrem onwards; and (c) the *Book of the Laws of the Countries*, from the School of Bardaisan. As we have seen, these are in fact the texts which provide the earliest unambiguous evidence for Christianity at Edessa (all belong to the early third century).

Other texts for which an Edessene origin is often posited, but without the support of any real evidence, are: the Peshitta Old Testament, the Diatessaron, the Old Syriac Gospels, the *Odes of Solomon*, the *Gospel of Thomas*, the *Gospel of Philip*, and the *Acts of Thomas*. Each of these may be considered briefly.

The Peshitta Old Testament is of course not a unified work, and the origins of its various constituent parts remain extremely obscure.[38] All that can be said, on our present knowledge, is that an Edessene origin for at least some books is a possibility (but no more).

Although the Syriac Diatessaron was the standard Gospel text in Edessa in the third quarter of the fourth century (assuming that Ephrem's *Commentary on the Diatessaron* dates from his last years in Edessa), there is no evidence that it must also have been composed there.[39] Similarly, the Old Syriac Gospel text, preserved in two famous fifth-century manuscripts (the Curetonianus and Sinaiticus), was quoted occasionally by Ephrem in his *Commentary on the Diatessaron*, but again there is no positive evidence that this translation was made in Edessa: this is certainly a possibility—but nothing more than that.[40]

As far as the *Odes of Solomon* are concerned, everything remains totally uncertain: they are variously dated by scholars, ranging from the late first to the late third century, and it is far from assured that their original language was Syriac (though this is the majority opinion at present).[41] In any case, the suggestion that Ode 6 alludes to the flood at Edessa in 201 is entirely misguided.

The *Gospel of Thomas*, the *Gospel of Philip*, and the *Book of Thomas the Contender*, preserved in Coptic among the texts from Nag Hammadi, all display features which suggest a Syrian origin, or links with Syria. The only specific evidence which might point to Edessa is the use (in the *Gospel of Thomas* and the *Book of Thomas*) of the name "Judas Thomas," for this occurs in the narrative common to Eusebius (*HE* 1.13.11) and the *Teaching of Addai*, and is otherwise only to be found in pre-fourth-century literature in the *Acts of Thomas*. It is very unlikely, however, that this double name was confined just to Edessa.[42]

The *Acts of Thomas*, which are usually dated to the third century, may have been among the "certain texts pertaining to St. Thomas" which the western pilgrim Egeria states that she read at Edessa during her visit there in 384, and already in Ephrem's lifetime Edessa boasted the presence of the apostle's bones, brought there by a merchant from India (*Carmina Nisibena* 42:1–2). But even though the *Acts of Thomas* may have been well known in Edessa in the fourth century, there is no real evidence that they were written there (Edessa certainly does not figure in its contents).

One last piece of evidence requires considering: that of the Syriac language itself. Syriac is nothing other than a literary dialect of Aramaic which possesses its own distinctive script. Early Syriac writers use a variety of terms to refer to the language, but besides the more general terms "Aramaya" (Aramaic) and "Suryaya" (Syriac), a third term stands out, "Urhaya," the dialect of Urhay/Edessa, or "Edessene (Aramaic)." The existence of this term must indicate that Syriac, which came to be adopted as the literary and cultural language of Aramaic-speaking Christians throughout the eastern provinces of the Roman Empire and over the border in the Sassanid Empire, started out as the local Aramaic dialect of Edessa. This consideration might then lead one on to claim that all the early Syriac texts enumerated above can, after all, validly be linked with Edessa. Such an assumption, however, is unwarranted, for we now know from pagan inscriptions of the first, second, and third centuries CE from the Edessa region, and from the Syriac document of sale written in Edessa in 243, that written Syriac underwent some dialectal changes between the epigraphic texts of the first to third centuries (termed "Proto-Syriac") and the standard Syriac common to all the literary texts which have come down to us.[43] In view of this epigraphic evidence it is likely that the few surviving literary texts written before ca. 300 have had their dialect "updated" to conform to the standard literary Syriac of the fourth century onwards; this means that we have no means of saying whether their original dialect was that of the early Edessene inscriptions ("Proto-Syriac"), or not.[44] Conversely, neither can we claim that, because an early text such as the *Acts of Thomas* is in standard, or Edessene Syriac, that it must accordingly have originated from Edessa.

The importance of the specification of standard Syriac as "Edessene" in fact lies elsewhere, for it provides us with clear evidence that, at the time when standard Syriac/Edessene emerged out of Proto-Syriac (perhaps by about 300) and became the literary language of Aramaic-speaking Christianity throughout the Middle East, Edessa must have been the most prominent Christian center in the whole area.

We are now in a position to return to the narrative of Addai's mission common to Eusebius and the *Teaching of Addai*. The silence concerning Addai in all the early sources enumerated above is highly significant; in particular, had the document preserved in Eusebius and the *Teaching of Addai* really been kept in the archives of Edessa, it is inconceivable that use would not have been made of it by the *Chronicle of Edessa*, which definitely did draw on the town's archives. Equally telling is the silence of Ephrem, who spent the last ten years of his life in Edessa.[45] Outside Eusebius, the earliest mention of the legend is in the diary of Egeria (384; she in fact never mentions Addai, only Abgar and his emissary Ananias).

Though attractive at first sight, the attempt by Burkitt and others to rescue an element of historicity in the Addai legend by supposing that it reflected the conversion of Abgar VIII, rather than Abgar V, likewise runs into serious trouble, for the evidence for Abgar VIII's conversion also proves to be extremely flimsy: if we accept, as surely we must, that the words "when he believed" are an interpolation in the *Book of the Laws of the Countries*, then everything hangs on Julius Africanus' ambiguous description of Abgar VIII as "a holy man." Here again silence is significant: if Abgar VIII had really converted, Julius Africanus (who, as we have seen, knew him personally) would certainly have mentioned this dramatic event in his *Chronography* in much clearer terms, and it is idle to suppose that such a mention simply happened not to be preserved among the surviving fragments of this work, for later Syriac chroniclers clearly drew on his work, and if any such passage had ever existed there, they would undoubtedly have taken it over into their own chronicles. Important too in this connection is the negative evidence of the coins of the kings of Edessa, none of which bear any hint of a Christian symbol;[46] similarly none of the funerary mosaics of the Edessene nobility, dating from the late second and the third centuries, offers any indication that Christianity had reached these families yet (one of these mosaics may even include a portrait of Abgar VIII).[47]

In the light of the evidence set out above there seems to be no choice for the historian but to reject Eusebius' account of Thaddaeus' mission to Edessa as a legend without historical basis. We can only speculate on the reasons why it was invented and promoted (with immense success, as it turned out!). One quite likely suggestion is that early Christianity in Edessa covered a wide spectrum of groups, some of whom (such as the followers of Marcion and of Bardaisan) later came to be regarded as heretical; according to this view, members of the group which emerged in the late third and early fourth century as "orthodox" sought to promote their authority by circulating a narrative concerning Addai's mission to Edessa in order to provide themselves, not only with a respectable apostolic origin, but also with a direct link with Jesus himself.[48] Whether or not the promoters of the legend also intended to provide Christian counter-propaganda to early Manichaean missionary work[49] is hard to say: while it is possible that Addai of the legend was created to counterbalance the historical Addai/Adda, one of Mani's chief missionaries, it is also conceivable that Mani, who saw himself as the paraclete promised by Jesus (John 16:7), deliberately gave his own apostle the name of Addai in order to counter the Edessene legendary tradition (to which Mani would then be the earliest witness).

When the Addai legend was taken up and expanded by the author of the *Teaching of Addai*, some slightly different interests can be discerned, two of which deserve mention here. First is the concern to establish a link with the see of Rome, which is achieved by the statement[50] that Addai's second successor, Palut, was consecrated bishop by Serapion of Antioch (190/191–211/212), who was in turn consecrated (a patent anachronism!) by Zephyrinus of Rome (198–217), whose priesthood went back to Simon Peter. Such a concern with the Petrine apostolic succession also finds expression in what must be a nearly contemporary letter by Pope Innocent I (402–417);[51] its occurrence in an eastern writer from the patriarchate of Antioch must point to a date of composition for the *Teaching of Addai* after the reconciliation between Rome and Antioch, which took place during the episcopacy of Alexander of Antioch (acceded about 414).[52] Exactly the same line of succession reappears at the end of the *Acts of Barsamya*.[53]

A second special interest of the *Teaching of Addai* concerns the nobility of Edessa, several of whom are named as being the first converts to respond to Addai's preaching.[54] The appearance of exactly the same names in the legendary *Acts of Sharbel* and of *Barsamya*[55] suggests that all three documents in fact emanate from the same circles. Since several of these names appear on second- and third-century pagan inscriptions from the Edessa region,[56] and are rarely if ever found in Syriac sources of the fifth century and later, it may safely be deduced that the names are genuine names of ancestors of the people who produced the *Teaching of Addai* and the *Acts of Sharbel* and of *Barsamya*; what is not likely to be genuine, however, is their alleged conversion to Christianity. Since the *Acts of Sharbel* and of *Barsamya* both make use of motifs to be found in the *Acts of Shmona and Gurya* and those of *Habbib*, it looks as if the authors of the *Acts of Sharbel* and of *Barsamya* were seeking to promote the view that (a) their pagan ancestors had converted to Christianity at a much earlier date than was in fact the case, and that (b) the upper classes of Edessa had produced a martyr and a confessor long before the (historical) martyrdoms of Shmona, Gurya, and Habbib, who all came from surrounding villages. The first of these aims is clearly shared by the author of the *Teaching of Addai*.

It emerges, then, that the Syriac document used by Eusebius and the expanded form of this document as it appears in the *Teaching of Addai* are both the products of tendentious propaganda. Standing a little over a century apart, their intentions are different, and this means that, when dealing with the *Teaching of Addai*, it is important to keep these two elements apart.

It is of course disappointing to see our single detailed source of information about early Christianity in Edessa relegated to the realm of unhistorical legend, leaving us with only a few scattered hints concerning the early spread of Christianity in the area. We can only speculate about the date when Christianity first reached Edessa: a late first-century date is of course possible, but no satisfactory evidence for this survives;[57] all that can be said with certainty is that by the end of the second century Christianity was well established in Edessa (probably in various forms), and that by the end of the third century it had spread to the surrounding villages. With the fourth century one particular form of Christianity emerges as "orthodox" and from that date on we become much better informed, since later generations were only concerned to transmit literature of this particular provenance.

Notes

[1] Edited, with English translation, by G. Phillips, *The Doctrine of Addai, the Apostle* (London: Trübner, 1876). A new translation, with Phillips' text reproduced, is given by George Howard, *The Teaching of Addai* (SBLTT 16, Early Christian Literature Series 4; Chico: Scholars, 1981). Several excerpts in fifth-century manuscripts survive besides the one complete manuscript in Leningrad; for the latter there is also a photographic edition by E. N. Meščerskaya, *Legenda ob Avgare* (Moscow: Akademiya Nauk SSSR. Institut Vostokovedeniya, 1984) 119–84. Papyrus fragments of what appear to be a Greek version survive, edited by R. Peppermüller, "Griechische Papyrusfragmente der Doctrina Addai," *VC* 25 (1971) 289–301. There is also an expanded Armenian translation. See further H. J. W. Drijvers, "Abgarsage," in W. Schneemelcher, ed., *Neutestamentliche Apokryphen* (5th ed.; Tübingen: Mohr [Siebeck], 1987) 389–96. A new edition of the Syriac text is being prepared by A. Desreumaux. For the date, see n. 52.

[2] This was in fact the opinion of E. Schwartz, "Zu Eusebius Kirchengeschichte: II, Zur Abgarlegende," *ZNW* 4 (1903) 64; for the view expressed here see also H. J. W. Drijvers, "Facts and Problems in Early Syriac-Speaking Christianity," *The Second Century* 2 (1982) 160; reprinted in idem, *East of Antioch: Studies in Early Syriac Christianity* (London: Variorum, 1984). The earliest surviving manuscript of the Syriac translation of the *Ecclesiastical History* dates from 461/462 CE.

[3] This is usually thought to be 311 CE; though T. D. Barnes has argued for an earlier date (late 290s), he thinks the excerpt on Edessa may not have featured in the first edition; see his *Constantine and Eusebius* (Cambridge: Harvard University Press, 1981) 128.

[4] In Eusebius he is described as a ταχυδρόμος, "courier" (likewise Egeria calls him a *cursor*), whereas the *Teaching of Addai* calls him an "archivist" (*tabulara = tabularius*). The source of the difference lies in a confusion between *tabularius* and *tabellarius* (to which ταχυδρόμος corresponds).

[5] It is possible that the *Teaching of Addai* preserves an older stage of the legend on this point; it is certainly surprising to find this in a document which must postdate the visit of Egeria (384), when she was given a copy of both letters. Further evidence that the two letters, and especially the second, were soon transmitted separately is provided by the five inscriptions of the fifth/sixth centuries (Edessa, Ephesus, Philippi, and two from the Pontus region), and by later texts on papyrus. Normally Eusebius' text is followed, but with the protective blessing added at the end (see n. 12). The most detailed study of the development of the literary transmission of the letters remains that by E. von Dobschütz, "Der Briefwechsel zwischen Abgar und Jesus," *ZWT* 43 (1900) 422–86.

[6] Although some have seen this as a deliberate omission by Eusebius (who is known to have held views hostile to the portrayal of Christ), it is more likely that this episode represents a later development. Subsequently the portrait was upgraded to an icon

"not painted by human hand," and eventually into the *mandylion*, transported to Constantinople in 944. This last has recently been identified, on no solid grounds, as the Turin Shroud: for a refutation of this see Averil Cameron, *The Sceptic and the Shroud* (London: King's College Inaugural Lecture, 1980); reprinted in her *Continuity and Change in Sixth-Century Byzantium* (London: Variorum, 1982) chap. 5. The sixth-century developments are illuminatingly discussed by A. N. Palmer, "The Inauguration Anthem of Hagia Sophia in Edessa," *Byzantine and Modern Greek Studies* 12 (1988) 117–67, esp. 119–30. The relevant texts, accompanied by a fundamental study, are given by E. von Dobschütz, *Christusbilder: Untersuchungen zur christlichen Legende* (TU 18, n.F. 3; Leipzig: Hinrichs, 1899).

[7] This story also exists independently in some later Syriac manuscripts; it is an early variant of the legend of the finding of the cross by Queen Helena, a narrative which first emerged at the end of the fourth century and which quickly took on many forms.

[8] This is also found in an early Syriac form of the history of the Dormition of the Virgin Mary (W. Cureton, *Ancient Syriac Documents* [London: Williams & Norgate, 1864; reprinted, Amsterdam: Oriental Press, 1967] 111), and elsewhere.

[9] For interest in the succession, see below. Palut is likely to be a historical person and, to judge by Ephrem's mention of him (*Hymns against Heresies* 22:5–6), he was at one time leader of the group which eventually emerged as the "orthodox" church in Edessa.

[10] The translation by Kirsopp Lake in the LCL has been slightly modified here and there in order to bring out material common with the *Teaching of Addai*.

[11] The following differences are the most notable: Eusebius may have added "toparch" and changed "Doctor" (a common title of Christ in early Syriac literature, e.g., *Act. Thom.* 143, and common in Ephrem) to "Savior" for the benefit of his Greek readers; on the other hand the *Teaching of Addai* adds to the anti-Jewish element.

[12] The most notable differences are at the end, where the *Teaching of Addai* adds the famous blessing. Most of the later Greek texts of the letter, whether literary, or in inscriptions and on papyri, contain the blessing (with various forms of wording). It may be deduced that a blessing had already been added by 384 when Egeria visited Edessa, for she noticed that the form of the letter with which she was already familiar at home (Spain?) was shorter than the text she read at Edessa; see P. Devos, "Égérie à Édesse: S. Thomas l'apôtre, le roi Abgar," AnBoll 85 (1967) 381–400, esp. 397–99. By the mid sixth century the letter had been inscribed on the very walls of Edessa according to Procopius, *History of the Wars* 2.12.26 (this cannot be the surviving inscription from Edessa).

[13] Not biblical; evidently an anti-Jewish development based on John 20:29.

[14] The word "again" may have in mind the events of 259/260 when Edessa was probably briefly in the hands of Shapur I after his capture of the emperor Valerian nearby.

[15] The same variant, 70/72, occurs at Luke 10:1, 17, on which see B. M. Metzger, "Seventy or seventy-two disciples," in his *Historical and Literary Studies, Pagan, Jewish and Christian* (NTTS 8; Leiden: Brill, 1968) 67–76.

[16] It is important to note that this is absent from Eusebius, for several scholars have used it as the basis for their hypothetical reconstruction of the earliest mission from Palestine to Edessa. See the entirely justified criticisms of J. C. L. Gibson, G. Quispel, L. W. Barnard, and others in H. J. W. Drijvers, "Jews and Christians at Edessa," *JJS* 36 (1985) 92.

[17]Never specified in either text; later forms of the legend transfer ʿAbdu's gout to Abgar, or offer other identifications.

[18]This is language characteristic of much early Syriac theology, e.g., *Od. Sol.* 7:3, *Act. Thom.* 80, and often in Ephrem.

[19]The Seleucid era dates here represent 29 (probably) and 32 CE as the date of the Passion; several different dates for the Passion were current (a more commonly found one was 31).

[20]Walter Bauer, *Rechtgläubigkeit und Ketzerei im ältesten Christentum* (BHT 10; Tübingen: Mohr, 1934; 2d ed. 1963); ET: R. A. Kraft and G. Krodel, eds., *Orthodoxy and Heresy in Earliest Christianity* (Philadelphia: Fortress, 1971; London: SCM, 1972) chap. 1 (quoted below from the English edition). F. C. Burkitt, *Early Eastern Christianity* (London: John Murray, 1904) chap. 1. Notable followers of Bauer's basic position are H. Koester, "ΓΝΩΜΑΙ ΔΙΑΦΟΡΟΙ," *HTR* 58 (1965) 279–318, and H. J. W. Drijvers (in many studies); British and American scholars tend to follow Burkitt (who took his cue from R. A. Lipsius), notably H. E. W. Turner, *Patterns of Christian Truth* (London: Mowbray, 1954) 39–46, 85–94, and L. W. Barnard, "The Origins and Emergence of the Church in Edessa during the First Two Centuries A.D.," *VC* 22 (1968) 161–75 (both of which are unreliable on many points). Some recent variations of this second approach, none carrying conviction, are J. J. Gunther, "The Meaning and Origin of the Name 'Judas Thomas,'" *Le Muséon* 93 (1980) 113–48; E. Peretto, "Il problema degli inizi del cristianesimo in Siria," *Augustinianum* 19 (1979) 197–214; and J. B. Segal, "When Did Christianity Come to Edessa?" in B. C. Bloomfield, ed., *Middle Eastern Studies and Libraries: A Felicitation Volume for Professor J. D. Pearson* (London: Mansell, 1980) 179–91.

[21]Older writers (and some more recent ones) refer to Abgar the Great as Abgar IX; the revision of Edessene chronology, made possible by the discovery at Dura Europos of a parchment deed of sale written in Edessa in 243 CE (P. Dura 28), shows that he should be called Abgar VIII: see A. R. Bellinger and C. B. Welles, "A Third-Century Contract of Sale from Edessa in Osrhoene," *Yale Classical Studies* 5 (1935) 93–154.

[22]For an excellent orientation see R. Murray, *Symbols of Church and Kingdom: A Study in Early Syriac Tradition* (Cambridge: Cambridge University Press, 1975), and idem, "The Characteristics of the Earliest Syriac Christianity," in N. G. Garsoïan, T. F. Mathews, and R. W. Thomson, eds., *East of Byzantium: Syria and Armenia in the Formative Period* (Washington, DC: Dumbarton Oaks, 1982) 3–16. For Ephrem, S. P. Brock, *The Luminous Eye: The Spiritual World Vision of St. Ephrem* (Rome: Centre for Indian and Inter-Religious Studies, 1985).

[23]There are several editions, the most accessible being that of L. Hallier, *Untersuchungen über die Edessenische Chronik* (TU 9; Leipzig: Hinrichs, 1892). An English translation of the passage will be found in J. B. Segal, *Edessa, "The Blessed City"* (Oxford: Clarendon, 1970) 24–25. For the date of the chronicle (soon after 540), see W. Witakowski, "Chronicles of Edessa," *Orientalia Suecana* 33–35 (1984–1986) 487–98.

[24]By Bauer, *Orthodoxy and Heresy,* 13–14 (but with weak arguments).

[25]Latin translation by J. B. Chabot, *Incerti Auctoris Chronicon Pseudo-Dionysianum Vulgo Dictum* I (CSCO, Scriptores Syri 3.1; Louvain: Durbecq, 1927) 98.

[26]Bardaisan (154–222) is known from many other sources and is the one personality to loom out from the fog of uncertainty surrounding early Syriac Christianity. A cultured Christian belonging to the aristocracy of Edessa, he was evidently a familiar figure at the court of Abgar the Great (see n. 28). Owing to their speculative nature, his

writings (in Syriac) were not transmitted by later generations who regarded his views as heretical; as a result, only hostile accounts of his teaching survive. A good account is given by H. J. W. Drijvers, *Bardaisan of Edessa* (Assen: Van Gorcum, 1966).

[27]Thus Bauer, *Orthodoxy and Heresy*, 9 (probably correctly).

[28]*Kestoi*, fragment I.20, in J.-R. Viellefond, *Les "Cestes" de Julius Africanus* (Firenze: Edizioni Sansoni Antiquariato; Paris: Didier, 1970) 183–85.

[29]Georgius Syncellus, *Ecloga Chronographica* (ed. A. A. Mosshammer; Leipzig: Teubner, 1984) 439 (Dindorf, p. 676). Later writers (such as Epiphanius, *Pan.* 56.1) elaborate on this. In the past some scholars, taking (b) as referring to Abgar's supposed conversion, have gone on to suggest that the document common to Eusebius and the *Teaching of Addai* was known to, or ultimately derived from, Julius Africanus, thus taking it back to the early third century. Such suggestions are willful and irresponsible, and have rightly been abandoned by more recent scholars.

[30]There is a convenient English translation by H. J. W. Drijvers, *The Book of the Laws of Countries* (Assen: Van Gorcum, 1965).

[31]An English translation is given by Cureton, *Ancient Syriac Documents*, 41–72.

[32]English translation in F. C. Burkitt, *Euphemia and the Goth with the Acts of Martyrdom of the Confessors of Edessa* (London: Williams & Norgate, 1913) 90–128.

[33]F. Nau, *Un martyrologie et douze ménologes syriaques* (PO 10/1; Paris: Firmin-Didot, 1912) 7–26 (Habbib, 2 Sept.; Shmona and Gurya, 15 Nov.).

[34]There is a recent photographic edition, with German translation, by P. Kawerau, *Die Chronik von Arbela* (CSCO, Scriptores Syri 199–200; Louvain: Peeters, 1987).

[35]P. Kahle, *The Cairo Geniza* (London: The British Academy, 1947; 2d ed., Oxford: Blackwell, 1959) chap. 3C.

[36]By J.-M. Fiey, "Auteur et date de la Chronique d'Arbèles," *OrSyr* 12 (1967) 265–302. The matter must be considered as still *sub judice*.

[37]A survey of some of the later Syriac texts can be found in F. Haase, *Altchristliche Kirchengeschichte nach orientalischen Quellen* (Leipzig: Harrassowitz, 1925) 70–73. The Addai legend is imaginatively adapted to Armenian interests in Moses Khorenatsi's *The History of the Armenians* 2.26–35 (probably a work of the eighth century): see R. W. Thomson, *Moses Khorenatsʿi: History of the Armenians* (Cambridge: Harvard University Press, 1978) 39–41, 163–77.

[38]See S. P. Brock, "Bibelübersetzungen I.4, Die Übersetzungen ins Syrische," *TRE* 6 (1980) 181–85, and the *Anchor Bible Dictionary*, s.v. "Syriac Versions" (ed. David N. Freedman; Garden City, NY: Doubleday, forthcoming).

[39]It is still disputed whether Tatian wrote his Diatessaron in Greek or in Syriac. If he wrote it in Syriac, then his epithet ὁ ’Ασσύρος, "the Assyrian," is of possible relevance; unfortunately, however, the term is too vague to be of assistance, for it can cover anywhere from western Syria to Adiabene (north Iraq). If, on the other hand, the Syriac is a translation, then the epithet "Assyrian" is of no relevance to the place of origin of the Syriac Diatessaron. On the whole subject see W. L. Petersen, *An Introduction to the Diatessaron* (Supplements to *VC*, forthcoming).

[40]For the Old Syriac, see B. M. Metzger, *The Early Versions of the New Testament* (Oxford: Clarendon, 1977) 36–48.

[41]An invaluable survey of the secondary literature on the *Odes of Solomon* is provided by M. Lattke, *Die Oden Salomos in ihrer Bedeutung für Neues Testament und Gnosis*, Vol. 3: *Forgschungsgeschichtliche Bibliographie 1799–1984 mit kritischen*

Anmerkungen (OBO 25/3. Freiburg: Universitätsverlag; Göttingen: Vandenhoeck & Ruprecht, 1986).

[42]For a balanced discussion see H. J. W. Drijvers, "Edessa und das jüdische Christentum," *VC* 24 (1970) 4–33, esp. 13ff., reprinted in idem, *East of Antioch*, chap. 2.

[43]See H. J. W. Drijvers, *Old-Syriac (Edessean) Inscriptions* (Semitic Studies Series n.s. 3; Leiden: Brill, 1972) xii (with literature).

[44]Although the two Old Syriac Gospel manuscripts contain a number of nonstandard morphological features, the small extent of the epigraphic texts from Edessa, and the almost entire lack of comparative materials, make it impossible to state whether these nonstandard features belong specifically to Edessa. (For another possibility which has been suggested, see n. 57.)

[45]Two texts have sometimes been adduced as witness, but neither is genuinely by Ephrem; these are (a) the *Testament of Ephrem*, of which the most recent edition is that by E. Beck, *Des heiligen Ephraem des Syrers Sermones IV* (CSCO, Scriptores Syri 148–49; Louvain: Secretariat du CSCO, 1973), where lines 233–36 refer to the blessing of the town; and (b) the appendix to the Armenian translation of Ephrem's *Commentary on the Diatessaron*, Latin translation by L. Leloir, *S. Ephrem: Commentaire de l'Evangile concordant, version arménienne* (CSCO, Scriptores Armeni 2; Louvain: Imprimerie Orientaliste, 1954) 248, where the use of the name Thaddaeus and Abgar's title of "toparch" clearly shows that the material derives from Eusebius and has nothing to do with Ephrem's *Commentary*.

[46]The inscriptions and coin legends are collected by Drijvers, *Old-Syriac (Edessean) Inscriptions* (coins, pp. 58–59, with references to the standard works). Segal (*Edessa*, 27–35) gives a good general discussion (and several of the mosaics are illustrated in his plates).

[47]Published by H. J. W. Drijvers, "A Tomb for the Life of a King: A Recently Discovered Edessene Mosaic with a Portrait of King Abgar the Great," *Le Muséon* 95 (1982) 167–89; for some doubts about the identification of the king see J. B. Segal, "A Note on a Mosaic from Edessa," *Syria* 60 (1983) 107–10.

[48]See H. J. W. Drijvers, "Rechtgläubigkeit und Ketzerei im ältesten syrischen Christentum," in *Symposium Syriacum 1971* (Orientalia Christiana Analecta 197; Rome: Pontificium Institutum Orientalium Studiorum, 1974) 291–308, reprinted in his *East of Antioch*, chap. 3; this is basically a modification of Bauer's view.

[49]This is proposed by H. J. W. Drijvers, "Facts and Problems in Early Syriac-Speaking Christianity," 160–66. An excerpt from Mani's letter to the Edessenes is quoted in the Cologne Mani Codex (64:8–65:20): English translation by Ron Cameron and Arthur J. Dewey, *The Cologne Mani Codex "Concerning the Origin of His Body"* (SBLTT 15; Early Christian Literature Series 3; Missoula, MT: Scholars, 1979) 50–53.

[50]Trans. Phillips, p. 50; trans. Howard, p. 105.

[51]PL 20.548 (letter to Alexander of Antioch). For the later concern for apostolicity in the East see F. Dvornik, *The Idea of Apostolicity in Byzantium* (Cambridge: Harvard University Press, 1958) chaps. 2–3, esp. pp. 15, 47.

[52]This is a slightly later date than the one usually given for the *Teaching of Addai* (late fourth century), but agrees with that proposed (on quite different grounds) by T. D. Barnes in a paper given at the Patristic Studies Conference, Oxford 1983.

[53]Trans. Cureton, *Ancient Syriac Documents*, 71. A similar interest in apostolic succession, but taking the Edessene episcopate directly back to Addai (without the

Antioch-Rome connection), is found in the *Teaching of the Apostles*, of which the oldest manuscript is British Library Add. 14644 of the fifth/sixth century which also contains the *Teaching of Addai* and the *Acts of Sharbel*. The *Teaching of the Apostles* is dated to the (mid?) fourth century by W. Witakowski, "The Origin of the 'Teaching of the Apostles,'" in *IV Symposium Syriacum 1984* (Orientalia Christiana Analecta 229; Rome: Pontificium Institutum Studorium Orientalium, 1987) 161–71; he rightly sees some connection with the circles which produced the *Teaching of Addai* (both Addai and Aggai are mentioned), but his dating is perhaps too early.

[54]Trans. Phillips, pp. 17–18, 39; trans. Howard, pp. 35–37, 81.

[55]Trans. Cureton, *Ancient Syriac Documents*, 45, 63. The relationship between the three texts has often been noted. The manuscript tradition suggests that certain other documents may have originated in these circles; see M. van Esbroeck, "Le manuscrit syriaque nouvelle série 4 de Leningrad (Ve siècle)," in *Mélanges Antoine Guillaumont: Contributions à l'étude des christianismes orientales* (Cahiers d'Orientalisme 20; Geneva: Patrick Cramer, 1988) 210–19.

[56]E.g., Bar Kalba: Drijvers, *Old-Syriac (Edessean) Inscriptions*, nos. 6–8; Ḥafsai: Drijvers, no. 6; ʿAbshlama: Drijvers, no. 52; Shmeshgram: Drijvers, no. 28.

[57]Some have claimed that the Old Syriac Gospels contain morphological elements reflecting Palestinian Aramaic, which could point to an early mission from Palestine; thus Matthew Black, *An Aramaic Approach to the Gospels* (3d ed.; Oxford: Clarendon, 1967) 281–86. The interpretation of this evidence is, however, extremely problematic. Much will depend on whether one considers the Judaic features in fourth-century Syriac Christianity to be late arrivals (so Drijvers, "Jews and Christians at Edessa" and elsewhere), or whether one sees these as going back to the very origins of Syriac Christian tradition; some possible examples will be found in S. P. Brock, "Jewish Traditions in Syriac Sources," *JJS* 30 (1979) 212–32, and "The Lost Old Syriac at Luke 1:35 and the Earliest Syriac Terms for the Incarnation," in William L. Petersen, ed., *Gospel Traditions in the Second Century* (Christianity and Judaism in Antiquity Studies 3; Notre Dame, IN: University of Notre Dame Press, 1989) 117–31. There is probably much to be said for Segal's suggestion ("When Did Christianity Come to Edessa?") that there were two major evangelizing movements in Edessa, of different origin and of different date. The details of his reconstruction, however, are open to serious objections.

THE CHRISTOLOGY OF THE CHURCH OF THE EAST IN THE SYNODS OF THE FIFTH TO EARLY SEVENTH CENTURIES: PRELIMINARY CONSIDERATIONS AND MATERIALS

By

Dr Sebastian Brock

Oriental Institute, Oxford

Among Archbishop Methodios' many publications his *The Person of Jesus Christ in the Decisions of the Ecumenical Councils* (1976) provides a valuable collection of the main documents on the Christological controversies of the fifth century, together with information on modern initiatives leading to theological dialogues between the Oriental Orthodox Churches and both the Orthodox and Roman Catholic Churches. Similar theological discussions involving the Church of the East have not so far been held in modern times, and this is of course a Church with a very different tradition of Christology from that of the Oriental Orthodox Churches. The present article, which is offered as a modest tribute to Archbishop Methodios' concern for ecumenical matters, attempts to provide some preliminary considerations and documentation in the hopes that these might prove of use when such discussions with the Church of the East do eventually take place. My concern here is solely with the period that proved formative for the Christological position of the Church of the East, namely, the fifth to the early seventh centuries; and at the outset it should be stressed that my aim is merely to put forward some suggestions for ways towards a constructive understanding of the Christology of the Church of the East, and not to offer any judgement on that position.

The presentation follows the following pattern:

I *Sources*
 (a) Synods
 (b) Individual writers

II *Preliminary considerations*
 (a) Geographical
 (b) Political
 (c) Linguistic
 (d) Variety of positions within the Christological spectrum.

III *Translations of the main Christological statements in the Synodicon of the Church of the East.*

(a) Synod of 410
(b) Synod of 486.
(c) Synod of 544.
(d) Synod of 554.
(e) Synod of 576.
(f) Synod of 585.
(g) Synod of 598.
(h) Synod of 605.
(i) Assembly of bishops in 612.

Sources

(a) *Synods*

Our most important source of knowledge of the official Christology of the Church of the East during the formative period of the fifth to seventh centuries[1]. is provided by a collection of synodical texts usually known as the Synodicon Orientale, following the title employed by its editor, J.B.Chabot[2]; in the course of these are to be found a number of credal statements, and it is these that are translated below in III. The texts published by Chabot in fact constitute just a part of a vast synodical collection (of eighty items) which is transmitted in a number of nineteenth and twentieth-century manuscripts copied from a manuscript of the thirteenth or fourteenth century (Alqosh

---

1. For the background J. Labourt's *Le christianisme dans l'empire perse sous la dynastie sassanide* (Paris 1904) is still fundamental; his work is brought up to date in certain respects by J.M. Fiey, *Jalons pour une histoire de l'église en Iraq*(Corpus Scriptorum Christianorum Orientalium 310, 1970). In English the best works are W.A. Wigram, *An Introduction to the History of the Assyrian Church* (London 1910) and W.G. Young, *Patriarch Shah and Caliph* (Rawalpindi 1974).

2. J.B. Chabot, *Synodicon Orientale* (Paris 1902).

AKSUM–THYATEIRA. *A Festschrift* for Archbishop Methodios of Thyateira and Great Britain.

281

ms 169, perhaps of AD 1298/9); the collection was put together in its present form in the eleventh century.[3] The following synods contain texts of relevance for our present purposes:

(1) *Synod at Seleucia-Ktesiphon held under the Catholicos Isaac in 410.*

It was at this synod, summoned on the initiative of Marutha bishop of Martyropolis, that the Council of Nicaea was officially recognized by the Church of the East. Prefaced to the canons of the synod is a credal profession whose Syriac text comes down in two different recensions, of which the one is transmitted in Syrian Orthodox sources[4], while the other is to be found in the manuscripts of the East Syrian Synodicon; the latter gives the Nicene Creed in its 'pure' form.

There has been a long controversy over the relationship between these two texts, Some have held that the Acts of the Synod of 410 were originally prefaced by *both* creeds, while others have claimed that the West Syrian recension represents a late interpolation (largely on the grounds of the occurrence of phraseology that seemed reminiscent of the *filioque* clause). Very recently, however, A. de Halleux[5] has demonstrated that it must in fact be the West Syrian text, and not the form in the Synodicon Orientale, that is the original; this is shown (a) by the presence of archaic phraseology in the West Syrian recension, and (b) by the appearance in the East Syrian text of certain neologisms which otherwise first occur in texts from c.A.D. 500 onwards.

The West Syrian recension concludes with the statement that "we are in agreement with the faith of the 318 bishops in the city of Nicaea; this is our confession and our faith, which we have received

from our holy fathers". De Halleux very plausibly suggests that this profession of faith made at the Synod of 410 represents an adaptation of a local Persian creed made by the council fathers in the light of the Nicene Symbol.

(2) *Synod at Seleucia-Ktesiphon held under the Catholicos Akakios in 486.*

Although synods had met in 420 and 424 no credal statements were issued. Two further synods were convened in 484 and 485, during the course of a feud between the Catholicos and Barsauma, metropolitan of Nisibis.[6] The Synod of Beth Lapat in 484 evidently included a Christological statement expressed in Antiochene terms, by way of reaction against Zeno's religious policies across the border, in the Roman Empire; the canons of this synod,[7] however, along with those of a further synod in 485, were not preserved, although in all probability the tenor of their theological position is reflected in the important credal statement issued at the synod of Seleucia–Ktesiphon in 486, translated in III(b). The importance of this text lies in the fact that it is the first such statement that we possess from the Church of the East from the period subsequent to the Councils of Ephesus and Chalcedon; its language markedly belongs to the Antiochene tradition of Christology, but it can in no way be described as openly 'Nestorian'.[8] The accompanying anathemas are anti-'Theopaschite' in character.

(3) *The synod held under the Catholicos Aba in 544.*

The learned Catholicos and confessor Aba had travelled widely in the Roman Empire prior to his elevation, and it was while he was in Alexandria that he met Kosmas, author of *Khristianike topographia.* Kosmas clearly held Aba (to whom he refers as Patrikios) in high esteem.[9] It was Aba who brought back to Persia various works by Nestorius and had

3. The contents of this collection are well described by W.Selb, *Orientalisches Kirchenrecht, I. Die Geschichte des Kirchenrechts der Nestorianer* (Österreichische Akademie der Wissenschaften, phil.–hist. Klasse, Sb. I, 1981).

4. In Syrian Orthodox eyes the Church of the East in Persia was orthodox until the end of the fifth century, when it was 'nestorianized' as a result of the nefarious influence of Barsauma, metropolitan of Nisibis. As is pointed out below, the language of the synod of 486 is Theodoran, not Nestorian, but since Theodore was seen by the Syrian Orthodox as implying Nestorius, the epithet 'Nestorian' was misleadingly applied. (This synod was further held in abhorrence by the Syrian Orthodox since it allowed the clergy (including bishops) to marry–a canon which was invoked in recent times by Mar Shem'on XXIII, with tragic results).

5. ¸Le symbole des évêques perses au synode de Séleucie–Ctésiphon (410)', in ed. G. Wiessner, *Erkenntnisse und Meinungen II* (Göttinger Orientforschungen, I. Reihe: Syriaca, Band 17; 1978), pp. 161–90. The west Syrian recension has recently been re-edited by A.Vööbus, 'New sources for the Symbol in early Syriac Christianity', *Vigiliae Christianae* 26 (1972), pp. 291–6; the two oldest manuscripts belong to the eighth century. See also J. Gribomont, 'Le symbole de foi de Séleucie Cté-siphon (410)', *A Tribute to A Vööbus* (ed. R. H. Fissher), (Chicago, 1977), pp. 283–94.

6. For the background see S. Gero, *Barsauma of Nisibis and Persian Christianity in the Fifth Century (Corpus Scriptorum Christanorum Orientalium* 426; 1981).

7. The synod of Gregory I (605) states that at the synod of 484 Barsauma upheld the teaching of Theodore of Mopsuestia against the accusations of 'heretics' (perhaps he had Philoxenus in mind: see his letter to the monks of Beth Gogal, recently published by A. de Halleux in *Le Muséon* 96 (1983), pp. 5–79).

8. As, for example, W. de Vries in *Das Konzil von Chalkedon* (Würzburg 1951), I, p. 683. In this connection it might be noted that W. Macomber's study of this synod's Christological position ('The Christology of the Synod of Seleucia–Ctesiphon AD 486', *Orientalia Christiana Periodica* 24 (1958), pp. 142–54) gives an unnecessarily hostile interpretation of the text; his approach serves as a good modern example of how a theological statement can be understood wherever possible *in malam partem* (Macomber's later writings show more sympathy).

9. Cp. M. Wolska, *La topographie chrétienne de Cosmas Indicopleustes* (Paris 1962), pp. 63–73 etc.

them translated into Syriac (the extant Book of Hera-kleides was translated in 539/40[10]).

The Acts of the Synod of 544 themselves contain no Christological statement, but the Synodicon Orientale preserves a letter on 'orthodoxy of faith' by Aba, addressed to the clergy of Susa. The theological language is surprisingly traditional for the man who brought Nestorius' writings to Persia, and the profession of faith perhaps deliberately avoids any of the contentious technical terms.

(4) Synod held under the Catholicos Joseph in 554.

The profession of faith from this synod (held the year after the Fifth Council) is very close in tenor to the Chalcedonian definition. While the terms 'natures' and 'properties' feature in it, no mention is made either of *qnoma* (i.e. hypostasis) or *prosopon*. Those who speak of 'two Christs' or 'two Sons' are specifically anathematized.

(5) Synod held under the Catholicos Ezekiel in 576.

Although the synod issued no formal profession of faith, the preamble to the canons includes some passages of Christological relevance. Once again the absence of the terms *qnoma* and *prosopon* may be noted; on the other hand, at one point the phraseology „Christ who is in the flesh, *who is known* and confessed *in two natures*, God and Man, *a single Son...*" seems to echo directly the wording of the Chacedonian definition.

(6) Synoder held und the Catholicos Isho'yahb I in 585.

Two professions of faith are preserved, one belonging to the synod itself, the other to be found in an accompanying document which evidently belongs to the occassion of Isho'yahb's diplomatic mission to the emperor Maurice. According to the medieval chronicle known as the Liber Turris Isho'yahb's profession of faith was accepted as orthodox by the patriarchs of Constantinople and Antioch. As will be seen, the language is indeed far more Chalcedonian than Theodoran in spirit.

(7) Synod held under the Catholicos Sabrisho in 598.

Although no formal profession of faith is preserved the preamble contains some relevant passages.

(8) Synod held under the Catholicos Gregory I in 605.

It was at this synod that it was laid down that "each of us should receive and accept all the commentaries and writings of the blessed Theodore the Interpreter". The credal statement, however, is not distinctly Theodoran; it speaks of the "single union of one prosopon"; no mention is made of the term *qnoma*.

(9) Assembly of bishops held during the interregnum in 612

After the death of the Catholicos Gregory I in 608 the Persian Shah Khosroes II refused to let the bishops of the Church of the East to elect a successor, and during the period while the patriarchate remained vacant (till the Shah's death in 628) the affairs of the Church of the East were run by Babai the Great (see II.b.4) and Aba, Archdeacon of Seleucia. In 612, instigated by his influential Christian doctor, Gabriel of Sinjar (who was a Syrian Orthodox), Khosroes ordered that a disputation take place between representatives of the Church of the East and the Syrian Orthodox; from this occasion the Synodicon Orientale preserves a profession of faith presented by the bishops of the Church of the East to the Shah. As might be expected in the context of such a confrontation the position adopted is a hard–line one, expressed in fairly uncompromising Antiochene phraseology.

In the Synodicon Orientale there follows a series of objections against the tenets of the "Severan Theopaschites",[11] as follows:

–against those who confess a single nature and a single *qnoma* in Christ;

–against those who say that God suffered in the flesh and died in the flesh;

–against those who ask whether the holy Virgin gave birth to the God or gave birth to the Man;

–against those who falsely accuse us of confessing a quaternity in God, instead of a Trinity;

–against those who accuse us of (confessing) a duality of Sons".

These in turn are followed by a reply to two questions (clearly posed by their opponents): "Is it the Nestorians or the monks[12] who have turned aside from the foundations of the faith transmitted by the teachers of old", and „Previous to Nestorius, is there anyone who says that Christ is two natures and two *qnome*, or not?" The reply to these questions takes the form of a florilegium, and in the preamble to this there occurs an important passage which shows that the Church of the East understands the term *qnoma* in a Christological context in a markedly

---

10. The English translation by G.R. Driver and L. Hodgson (*The Bazaar of Heraclides*, Oxford 1925) needs to be used with caution: see R.H. Connolly in *Journal of Theological Studies* 27 (1926), pp. 191–200.

11. Chabot *(Synodicon Orientale*, p. 586) already noted that many of the arguments also occur in St. John of Damascus, *Contra Jacobitas*.

12. i.e. the Syrian Orthodox.

different sense from that of *hypostasis* in the Chalcedonian definition.[13]

(b) *Individual writers*

Besides the Synodicon Orientale there also survives
a number of other texts which deal directly or indirectly with Christology; the most important of these,
for the period late fourth to early seventh century,
are:

(1) *Narsai*

Narsai, the famous East Syrian poet, taught at
the 'Persian School' in Edessa until c. 471, when
local hostility from his theological opponents led
him to make a hasty move, across the Roman border,
to Nisibis, where he was welcomed by the metropolitan, Barsauma, and where he eventually became
head of the renowned theological School of Nisibis.
He died at a great age soon after the turn of the sixth
century (the exact date is not known). The following
of his verse homilies, or *memre*, are of particular
relevance:
–Verse homilies on the Nativity, Epiphany, Passion, Resurrection and Ascension, edited with English
translation by F.G. McLeod in *Patrologia Orientalis*
40, fasc. 1 (1979)[14].
–Verse homily on the Three Doctors (Diodore,
Theodore, Nestorius), edited with a French translation by F. Martin in *Journal Asiatique* IX. 14–15
(1899–1900)[15].

(2) *Cyrus of Edessa*

Cyrus, who belongs to the mid sixth century,
wrote six 'Explanations of the Liturgical Feasts'
which have been edited with an English translation
by W. Macomber in the *Corpus Scriptorum Christianorum Orientalium* 355–6 = *Scriptores Syri* 155–6
(1974). Although these are not directly concerned
with Christology, the background which they provide is helpful for gaining an understanding of the
general theological approach of writers in this tradition; a useful outline of this will be found in W. M-
comber's article "The theological synthesis of Cyrus
of Edessa", in *Orientalia Christiana Periodica* 30
(1964), pp. 5–38, 363–84.

(3) *Discussions between Paul, Metropolitan of
Nisibis and the Chalcedonians*

The text of an official theological discussion arran-
ged by Justinian which took place soon after 561
between the Chalcedonians and Paul, the representative of the Church of the East, is preserved in a
Syriac manuscript of Monothelete provenance.[16]
It has been published with a French translation by
A. Guillaumont, "Justinien et l'église de Perse",
in *Dumbarton Oaks Papers* 23/4 (1969/70), pp. 39–66.

(4) *Babai the Great*

Babai (died 628) was a prolific author who exercised a profound influence on the Church of the East,
and his treatise „On the Union" (sc. of the two natures
in Christ) is the one major statement on Christology
that we have from the Church of the East in this period.
This work was edited, with a Latin transation, by A.
Vaschalde in *Corpus Scriptorum Christianorum Orientalium* 79–80 = *Scriptores Syri* 34–5 (1915), together
with a short treatise „Against those who say that,
just as the soul and the body are one *qnoma*, so too
God the Word and the Man are one *qnoma*". A useful,
and sympathetic,[17] English presentation of Babai's
Christology is given by G. Chediath, *The Christology
of Mar Babai the Great* (Kottayam, 1982).
Whereas for most East Syrian writers it is Theodore
of Mopsuestia who is the prime formative influence,
Babai's Christology is clearly also influenced by the
Syriac translation of Nestorius, Book of Herakleides.[18]

(5) *Martyrius/Sahdona* (early seventh century)

Martyrius, the author of a fine work on monastic
spirituality, The Book of Perfection, is to be identified
with the bishop Sahdona ('little martyr'), whose expulsion from the Church of the East for 'heresy'
is related by Thomas of Marga and others.
Martyrius' Christological position is outlined in
chapter 1 of Part II of his Book of Perfection (edited
with French translation by A. de Halleux in *Corpus
Scriptorum Christianorum Orientalium* 214–5 = *Scriptores Syri* 90–91 (1961)). It was his formulation of
a single *qnoma* in Christ (consonant with the wording

13. Translated below, III.i.2.

14. McLeod gives a short introduction; more detailed studies are provided by his dissertation, *The Soteriology of Narsai*
(Pontifical Oriental Institute, Rome 1968) and in that by I.
Ibrahim, *La doctrine christologique de Narsai* (Angelicum, Rome
1974/5).

15. Cp. G. Sfair, 'L'ortodossia di Narsai rilevata dalla sua
omelia sui Dottori greci', *Bessarione* 33 (1917), pp. 313–27; L.
Abramowski, 'Das Konzil von Chalkedon in der Homilie des
Narsai über die drei nestorianischen Lehrer', *Zeitschrift für
Kirchengeschichte* 66 (1954/5), pp. 140–43; K. McVey, ‚The
memra of Narsai on the three Nestorian Doctors as an example
of forensic rhetoric', *Orientalia Christiana Analecta* 221 (1983),
pp. 87–96.

16. For this aspect see my 'A Monothelete florilegium in
Syriac', in *Orientalia Lovaniensia Analecta* (forthcoming).

17. The author is a Syro–Malankara priest (and so belongs
to a Church with an Alexandrian Christological position).

18. For this aspect see L. Scipioni, 'Il Libro di Eraclide di
Nestorio e il Liber de Unione di Babai il Grande', in his *Ricerche
sulla cristologia del 'Libro di Eraclide' di Nestorio* (Fribourg
1956), pp. 110–58. Other important studies of Babai's Christology are by L. Abramowski, 'Die Christologie Babais des Gros-
sen' *Orientalia Christiana Analecta* 197 (1974), pp. 219–45, and
'Babai der Grosse: Christologische Probleme und ihre Lösungen',
Orientalia Christiana Periodica 41 (1975), pp. 290–343; V.
Grumel, 'Un théologien nestorien, Babai le grand', *Echos d'
Orient* 22 (1923), pp. 153–81, 257–80; 23 (1924), pp. 9–33,
162–77, 257–74, 395–99.

of the Chalcedonian definition, but going against the traditional usage of the Church of the East) that led to his condemnation by the authorities of that Church; in all other respects his Christological language remains characteristically Antiochene, as is shown by A. de Halleux in an article, "La christologie de Martyrios/Sahdona dans l'évolution du nestorianisme", in *Orientalia Christiana Periodica* 23 (1957), pp. 5–32.

(6) *Isho'yahb II*

Isho'yahb II was Catholicos from 628–646, years which witnessed the change from Persian to Arab rule. His interesting letter on "How we should confess the single propopon of Christ", addressed to a certain Rabban Abraham, has recently been published, with a French translation and good introduction, by L.R.M. Sako, *Lettre christologique du Patriarche syro-oriental Isho'yahb II de Gdala* (Rome, 1983).[19]

(7) *Miscellaneous Christological texts*

An important collection of East Syrian Christological texts, perhaps put together about the 9th century, includes a number of pieces belonging to the late sixth and the seventh centuries; these have been published with an English translation, by L. Abramowski and A.E. Goodman, *A Nestorian Collection of Christological Texts* (2 vols, Cambridge, 1972)[20].

(8) *Liturgical texts*

Since liturgical texts often contain important doctrinal testimony, these should not be overlooked; in particular attention should be drawn to the prayers introducing the Institution Narratives in the Anaphoras attributed to Theodore and to Nestorius, both translated into Syriac in the sixth century. A recent English translation can be found in K.A. Paul and G. Mooken, *The Liturgy of the Holy Apostles Adai and Mari together with the Liturgies of Mar Theodorus and Mar Nestorius* (Trichur, 1967), pp. 76–7, 94–6.

II

Preliminary Considerations

When studying the Christology of the Church of the East, and especially when comparing it with western positions and developments (whether Greek or Latin), a number of important considerations need to be held in mind.

(a) *Geographical*

Since the Church of the East functioned within the Sasanian Empire, and thus outide the bounds of the Roman Empire, it was not directly involved in any of the general Councils convened by imperial command. The canons and the symbol of the Council of Nicaea are indeed recognized by the Church of the East, but this was only achieved 85 years later, at the Synod of Seleucia–Ktesiphon in 410, thanks to the initiative of Marutha, bishop of Martyropolis. The Council of Ephesus (431) is specifically rejected,[21] but a more ambivalent attitude, *post eventum*, is taken to the Council of Chalcedon; thus Isho'yahb II (628–46) comments:[22]

Although those who gathered at the Synod of Chalcedon were clothed with the intention of restoring the faith, yet they too slid away from the true faith: owing to their feeble phraseology, wrapped in an obscure meaning, they provided a stumbling block to many. Although, in accordance with the opinion of their own minds, they preserved the true faith with the confession of the two natures, yet by their formula of one *qnoma* (hypostasis), it seems, they tempted weak minds. As an outcome of the affair a contradiction occurred, for with the formula 'one *qnoma*' they corrupted the confession of 'two natures', while with the 'two natures', they rebuked and refuted the 'one *qnoma*'. So they found themselves standing at a cross roads, and they wavered[23] and turned aside from the blessed ranks of the orthodox, yet they did not join the assemblies of the heretics; they both pulled down and built up, while lacking a foundation for their feet. On what side we should number them I do not know, for their terminology cannot stand up, as Nature and Scripture testify: for in them many *qnome* can be found in a single ,nature', but that there should be various 'natures' in a single *qnoma* has never been the case and has not been heard of.

Likewise the eighth–century writer Shahdost[24]

---

19. In 630 during the course of an embassy from Persia, Isho–'yahb met the emperor Heraklios at Aleppo; there his profession of faith was accepted by the Greeks and he was invited to celebrate the Liturgy, at which both the emperor and his clergy received communion (the sources are translated in Sako, pp. 42, 46–50, 53–7, 59–60).

20. For some corrections to the translation see the review by T. Jansma in *Journal of Semitic Studies* 20 (1975), pp. 93–109.

21. For a recent statement see Mar Aprem, *The Council of Ephesus of* 431 (Trichur 1978).

22. Ed. Sako, sections 42–49.

23. The French translation (p. 147) misrepresents the sense here.

24. In Abramowski–Goodman. *A Nestorian Collection*, II, p. 20. The 'falsification' of the Chalcedonian definition in the text of the East Syrian Synodicon will evidently be a subsequent development; for this 'revised' text, see A. de Halleux, 'La falsification du symbole de Chalcédoine dans le Synodicon nestorien', *Mélanges offerts à Jean Dauvillier* (Toulouse 1979), pp. 377–84 (the alterations include a change to 'two *qnome*'). Cp. also W. de Vries, 'Die syrisch–nestorianische Haltung zu Chalkedon, in *Das Konzil von Chalkedon*, I, pp. 603–35.

says that "although they (sc. the Catholicos Akakios and the Metropolitan Barsauma of Nisibis) did not accept the Synod of Chalcedon... nevertheless they did not entirely reject it".

Justinian's ecclesiastical policy, culminating in the 'Three Chapters' and the Fifth Council, not surprisingly comes under sharp attack, above all from Babai.

In all this it should always be kept in mind that, from the point of view of the Church of the East, these Councils were far from being truly ecumenical, seeing that they were only of direct concern to those living within the Roman *oikoumene*.

(b) *Political*

It was only after Christianity had been adopted as the official religion in the Roman Empire that persecution of Christians took on serious dimensions in the Sasanian Empire. It was certainly the case that, in the fourth and fifth century, persecution was a likely concomitant of any outbreak of hostilities between the two empires; indeed Persian Christians were sometimes suspected of being secret sympathisers of the enemy.[25] It is, then, possible that *one* of the reasons why the Church of the East chose to adopt a markedly Antiochene position on Christology at the Synod of Seleucia–Ktesiphon in 486 was the conscious desire to disassociate Persian Christianity from the official Christological position in the Roman Empire at the time.

The combination of geographical and political separation of the Church of the East from Christianity in the Roman Empire had a further important consequence from the point of view of Christology: since the Church of the East was not directly involved in the fierce Christological controversies taking place in the Roman Empire from the 430s onwards, its theological language and its understanding of certain technical terms remained comparatively'old fashioned'. Any awareness of developments within the Greek–speaking world would come primarily by way of the Persian School of Edessa (closed in 489) and its successor, the School of Nisibis, and the flavour of this theological language was thus going to be essentially Antiochene, and specifically Theodoran. An Antiochene slant to Christology having been initially accepted, it is not surprising that subsequent influences from across the border should have been from theologians writing in that tradition, one of whom, of course, was Nestorius.

It is a fact that Nestorius was held in high regard by Narsai,[27] and that Nestorius' Book of Herakleides (not translated into Syriac until half a century after the Synod of 486) exerted a strong influence on the Christology of Babai,[28] but at the same time it needs to be remembered that Nestorius never came to hold anything like the position of authority that was accorded to Theodore of Mopsuestia, the 'Exegete' *par excellence*. Accordingly, it is misleading in the extreme to speak (as is often done) of a 'nestorianization' of the Persian Church over the course of the century and a half that followed the synods of the 480s; to do so is to be beguiled by the rhetorical hyperbole of the theological opponents of the Church of the East, who regularly labelled anything to do with Theodore as, by implication, Nestorian.

(c) *Linguistic*

It is well known that one of the complicating factors in the Christological controversies of the fifth and sixth centuries lay in the varying understandings that different parties had of the central technical terms οὐσία, φύσις, ὑπόστασις and πρόσωπον. This situation became all the more complex when the controversy was being conducted in Syriac rather than Greek, for two different reasons: (i) The standard equivalent terms in Syriac had a rather different semantic range from that of their Greek counterparts;[29] thus, for example, the connotations of Syriac *kyana* and *qnoma* are by no means precisely the same as those of φύσις and ὑπόστασις which they regularly represent (see further below); (ii) Over the course of the late fifth to the seventh century Syriac translation technique underwent many refinements, above all in West Syrian circles.[30] Theologians of the Church of the East, however, living outside the Roman Empire, were not always aware of these developments which took place in the eastern provinces of the Roman Empire, and chiefly in Syrian Orthodox circles.

In the Chalcedonian definition the words μία ὑπόστασις proved a stumbling block just as much to the Church of the East as they did to the Syrian Orthodox, for both groups shared the view that φύσις implied ὑπόστασις (and vice versa). Thus, to the Syrian Orthodox, ἐν δύο φύσεσι was the illogical element, since for them μία ὑπόστασις implied their own starting point μία φύσις τοῦ θεοῦ λόγου σεσαρκωμέ-

---

25. Occasionally this was justified, cp my ,Christians in the Sasanian Empire: a case of divided loyalties', *Studies in Church History* 18 (1982), pp. 7–9, reprinted in *Syriac Perspectives on Late Antiquity* (London, 1984), ch. VI.

26. And perhaps earlier, at the Synod of Beth Lapat in 484; this was certainly how later Syriar Orthodox writers explained the matter (e.g. Barhebraeus, *Chron. Eccl.* III, col. 65).

27. His homily on the Three Doctors, however, suggests that he had little or no direct knowledge of Nestorius' works; probably Narsai (and others in the Church of the East) saw him as a martyr for the cause of Antiochene Christology.

28. See note 18.

29. This was an old problem that had already been highlighted by the Greek translators of the Hebrew Bible (e.g. when they rendered Torah by Nomos).

30. Cp. my 'Towards a history of Syriac translation technique', *Orientalia Christiana Analecta* 221 (1983), pp. 1–14.

νη;[31] to the Church of the East, on the other hand, it was the μία ὑπόστασις that was illogical,[32] since their starting point was the two natures, which for them implied two *qnome (qnoma* being the regular translation of ὑπόστασις).

In East Syrian understanting *kyana* ('nature', φύσις) is generic, while *qnoma* is an individual manifestation of a *kyana*;[33] thus the two *kyane* in Christ are often specifically described as being 'the divinity and the humanity', and correspondingly the *qnoma* of the divinity is God the Word, perfect God, and the *qnoma* of the humanity is the Man Jesus, perfect Man; and here it needs emphasizing that 'the Man'[34] is definitely never thought of as having any separate pre-existence, prior to the Union.[35] Furthermore, for all the traditional dislike of theopaschite language in writers of the East Syrian tradition, there is never any doubt that God the Word, in his humanity, suffered and died: there is no question of two subjects, as will be clear from the texts translated below in III.

Underlying the varying opposing formulations are several different understandings of the connotations of the term 'nature': to the Church of the East *kyana* 'nature' is associated much more closely with *ituta* ('essence', οὐσία)[36] than with *prosopon*, while in Syrian Orthodox tradition οὐσία and φύσις are sharply distinguished, and φύσις is associated rather with πρόσωπον.[37] This difference of usage is reflected very clearly in sixth-century translation practice in connection with the term ὁμοούσιος:

(1) East Syrian writers normally preserve the older, fifth-century, usage whereby ὁμοούσιος is translated by *bar kyana*, 'of the same nature' (lit. 'son of nature'), or by *bar ituta*, 'of the same essence' (lit. 'son of essence').

---

31. E.g. Severus, *ad Nephalium* (Corpus Scriptorum Christianorum Orientalium 119), p. 16: 'It is obvious to all who have just a modicum of training in the teachings of true religion that it is contradictory to speak of two natures with reference to the one Christ, he being one hypostasis; for whenever one speaks of one hypostasis, one must necessarily also speak of one nature'.

32. E.g. Isho'yahb II, quoted above in II.a.

33. Thus we often encounter the phrase 'the two *kyane* and *their qnome*'.

34. In East Syrian terminology 'the Man' means 'an individual human being' (in the abstract), and definitely *not* a specific person: see, for example, Babai, *Liber de Unione* (ed. Vaschalde), p. 160. Thus the phrase 'He put on the Man' in sixth-century East Syrian writers corresponds to 'He put on Adam/our humanity/ (our) body', characteristic of early Syriac authors. Cp also note 60.

35. So Babai repeatedly, e.g. *Liber de Unione* (ed. Vaschalde), pp. 59, 91ff, 100, 111, 116, 244 etc.

36. Thus, from the East Syrian point of view, Cyril's μία φύσις τοῦ θεοῦ λόγου σεσαρκωμένη was barely different from saying μία οὐσία –a formulation that Cyril's expositor par excellence, Severus, of course firmly rejected.

37. Here it should be noted that normally East Syrian writers speak of three *qnome* in the Trinity (rather than three *parsope*).

---

(2) West Syrian writers refine the translation usage and provide the more precise equivalents *shawe b–ituta* or *shawe b-ousia*, 'equal in essence'. Thus, in sixth-century Syrian Orthodox usage *kyana* 'nature' is kept firmly separate from *ituta* 'essence'.

On occasion some awareness is shown of the existence of an understanding of key technical terms that differs from that which the writer himself employs: thus Babai at one point[38] explains why 'the former fathers' used the formula 'one *qnoma* from two natures' (i.e. the Syrian Orthodox position); this he explains, was because they were countering Arius, Eunomius and Apollinarius who denied that Christ was either complete God or complete Man. Babai goes on to say that these fathers sometimes used *qnoma* and *parsopa* interchangeably 'just as happens now, so they say, in Roman territory'; such usage, however, is to be avoided, according to Babai, in order to counter theopaschite teaching.

In the translations in III below I regularly employ the following formal translation equivalents:

itya	(divine) Being
ituta	(divine) essence
kyana	nature
qnoma	(transliterated)
parsopa	person, prosopon.

I have preferred to leave *qnoma* untranslated in order to draw attention to the difference in sense that it has in sixth–century East Syrian texts from ὑπόστασις in contemporary Greek writers (even though it is the standard translation equivalent). It should be noted that modern translators have sometimes rendered *qnoma* in a Christological context as 'person': this is to be deplored, since it can lead to obvious misunderstandings (in none of these East Syrian texts do we ever encounter the 'Nestorian' formula of 'two prosopa')[39]

(d) *Variety of positions within the Christological spectrum*

In seeking to understand the ecclesiological dimensions of the controversies of the fifth and sixth centuries it is essential to avoid the simplistic threefold model of 'Nestorian –Chalcedonian– Monophysite'. Matters are far more complex. For present purposes one might propose the following spectrum,

---

38. Ed. Vaschalde, pp. 305–6.

39. For studies on the East Syrian understanding of the various technical terms reference may be made to Anon., 'On the history of the Syriac terms *ithutha, kyana, parsupa and qnuma*', in J.F. Bethune-Baker, *Nestorius and his Teaching* (Cambridge 1908), pp. 212–32, and W.A. Wigram, *An Introduction to the History of the Assyrian Church* (London 1910), pp. 279–85, besides the monographs on individual writers mentioned in I.b. Cp also J. Pelikan, *The Spirit of Eastern Christendom* (600–1700) (Chicago/London 1974), pp. 39–49.

moving from extreme Antiochene to an extreme Alexandrian Christological position:

(1) True 'Nestorians' (two prosopa).
(2) Strict Dyophysites outside Roman Empire: Church of the East.
(3) Strict Dyophysites within Roman Empire: e.g. Theodoret, Akoimetai, Roman Church.
(4) Silence over Chalcedon: e.g. Henotikon, Dionysios the Areopagite.
(5) Neo-Chalcedonians.
(6) Henophysites:[40] Timothy Ailouros,Philoxenos, Severos.
(7) Eutychians (true Monophysites).

It should of course be kept in mind that even this seven-fold model is an oversimplification in that it glosses over the various shades of opinion within each group: thus, for example, it is clear that within the Church of the East itself there were several stances, with Babai representing the strictest dyophysite position, openly rejecting the Chalcedonian position (and so presumably even those of group 3), while others[41] were evidently very close to the position of those in group 3, within the Chalcedonian camp.

Within this sevenfold model the various positions can be seen as dividing up in different ways, depending on the criterion by which they are being judged; thus, for example:

–acceptance of Chalcedonian definition:	groups 3–5
–Antiochene Christological tradition:	1–3
–Alexandrian Christological tradition:	4–7
–anti–Theopaschite:	1–3
–single subject in Christ:	2–7
–Christ is ὁμοούσιος ἡμῖν as well as ὁμοούσιος τῷ πατρὶ	1–6

Writers belonging to the Neo-Chalcedonian position had already conceded that the Chalcedonian definition was not an exclusive criterion of orthodoxy: ἐκ δύο φύσεων was, in their eyes, also acceptable, provided that ἐν δύο φύσεσι was not itself rejected.[42] This last point was a stumbling block for the Henophysites in the sixth century, and it remains a problem in at least some Oriental Orthodox circles today as well[43] (owing to their rather different understanding of the terminology).

With the Church of the East there is a similar problem of verbally conflicting formulae (two *qnome*

against μία ὑπόστασις). Clearly if progress in dialogue is to be made, several things need to happen:

(1) The clue offered by the Neo-Chalcedonians, that orthodoxy in Christology does not necessarily have to be confined to adherence to the Chalcedonian definition, needs to be followed up and developed.[44] In other words, a criterion of orthodoxy other than that of Chalcedon needs to be applied to the sevenfold model suggested above; as a beginning one might propose the last two of the various criteria mentioned above (a single subject in Christ, and Christ as ὁμοούσιος ἡμῖν as well a ὁμοούσιος τῷ πατρί.

(2) A serious attempt must be made to penetrate behind the wording of the various formulae in order to discover how they were arrived at and (above all) the way in which they were understood by those who put them forward. And here two basic points need to be kept constantly in mind: firstly, that the central technical terms were understood in markedly different ways by the different parties;[45] and secondly, that each position was developed by way of reaction against a particular trend that was (rightly) seen as dangerously heretical: the existence of different bêtes noires led to the emergence of different emphases. With the benefit of hindsight we are able to see that, at the roots of the tragedy of these fifth and sixth-century schisms, lay the failure on all sides to make the necessary effort of imagination: each party saw its opponent's position only in the light of its own understanding of the technical terminology and only in the light of its own fears and preoccupations. A clear example of such misunderstanding is provided by the two sides of the so-called Theopaschite controversy.

(3) The concentration of attention on a restricted area of Christological terminology needs to be avoided. Thus, in the case of the Church of the East, it would be unfair to find fault with its favoured imagery of 'the temple' or 'the clothing', taken in isolation; it so happened that, for various reasons, this imagery (which had perfectly respectable Biblical origins) came to be dropped in the sixth century by virtually everyone living within the Roman Empire, and was thus preserved and developed only by the Church of the East, beyond the borders. Furthermore we should remember, not only that this imagery is archaic, but also that its advocates themselves insist that no one image should be taken in isolation: each image needs to be used in conjunction with a variety of others as well, seeing that no single image can provide an adequate analogy to the nature of the union of the two natures in Christ.[46]

---

40. It is very important to avoid the term ,Monophysites' for this group.

41. These will have included Henana and Martyrius.

42. This was also Justinian's position at the conversations with the Syrian Orthodox in 532: see the text translated in my 'The conversations with the Syrian Orthodox under Justinian (532)', *Orientalia Christiana Periodica* 47 (1981), pp. 113-17.

43. E.g. Metropolitan Paulos Mar Gregorios, 'The Christological consensus reached in Vienna', *Wort und Wahrheit*, Suppl. 3 (1976), pp. 21-2. Compare also note 45.

44. See, for example, A. Grillmeier in *Wort und Wahrheit*, Suppl. 2 (1974), pp. 28-40.

45. Thus on Severus' understanding of what φύσις meant, the Chalcedonian definition would have seemed objectionable to Chalcedonians themselves.

46. Babai draws attention to this in his *Liber de Unione* (ed. Vaschalde), pp. 233, 249-50. At the other end of the theolo-

Any atomistic approach, then, which concentrates on individual formulae, images or analogies, will inevitably lead to a static and unsatisfactory perception of a particular Christological tradition, such as that of the Church of the East. What is needed, rather, is an approach which seeks to understand that tradition against the backdrop of its theology and anthropology as a whole (especially its understanding of the nature of the Fall), for only then will the full dynamic of the tradition become apparent.

Translations.[47]

(a) *Synod of* 410.

(It was pointed out above (I.a.1) that we have two texts claiming to be the declaration of faith made at this synod, of which the West Syrian recension has recently been shown to be the original, while the text preserved in the East Syrian Synodicon must date at the earliest from the sixth century. Both forms of text are translated here; in the West Syrian recension verbal agreements with the East Syrian (which represents the 'pure' Nicene symbol) are italicized).

(1) *West Syrian recension.*[48]

We believe in one God, Father, who in his Son, made *heaven and earth;* and in him were established the worlds above and below; and in him he effected the resurrection and renovation for all creation. And in his *Son,* the *Only-Begotten who was born* from him, *that is, from the essence (ituta) of his Father, God from God, Light from God, true God from true God; he was born and was not made; who is of the same* nature *(bar kyaneh)*[49] *as his Father; who, for the sake of us human beings* who were created through him, *and for the sake of our salvation, descended* and put on a body and became man, *and suffered and rose* on the third *day, and ascended to heaven* and took his seat at the right hand of his Father; *and he is coming* in order to *judge* the *dead* and the *living.*

And we confess the living and *holy Spirit,,*[50] the living Paraclete who (is) from the Father and the Son;[51];

And in one Trinity and in one Essence *(ituta)* and in one will *(sebyana)*.

(2) *East Syrian recension.*[52]

We believe in one God, Father Almighty, maker of heaven and of earth, and of all that is seen and that is not seen.

And in one Lord Jesus Christ, Son of God, who was born from the Father, the Only-Begotten, that is, from the Essence *(ituta)* of the Father; God from God and Light from Light, true God from true God, who was born and was not made, of the same essence *(bar ituta)* as the Father, through whom everything came into being that is in heaven and on earth; who for the sake of us human beings and for the sake of our salvation came down from heaven and was embodied and inhominated *(etgasham w-etbarnash)*; and he suffered and rose after three days, and ascended to heaven; and he is coming to judge the living and the dead.

And in the Holy Spirit.

Those who say that there is (a time) when he was not, and that before he was born he was not, or that he came into being from nothing; or who say that he is from (another) *qnoma* or from another essence; or who consider that the Son of God is subject to change and alteration *(meshtahlpana w-meshtagnyana)*: such people the Catholic and Apostolic Church anathematizes.

(b) *Synod of* 486[53]

Let the faith of us all be in the single confession of the one divine nature which exists in the three complete *qnome* of the single true and eternal Trinity of the Father and of the Son and of the Holy Spirit, (a confession) by which paganism is vanquished and Judaism judged.

(p. 55) Further, let our faith in the dispensation of Christ be in the confession of the two natures, of the divinity and of the humanity, while none of us shall dare to introduce mixture, mingling or confusion *(muzzaga aw hultana aw bulbala)* into the differences *(shuhlape)* of these two natures; rather, while the divinity remains preserved in what belongs to it, and the humanity in what belongs to it, it is to a single Lordship and to a single (object of) worship that we gather together *(mkannshinan)* the exemplars *(parshagne)*[54] of these two natures, because of the

---

gical spectrum Philoxenus makes the same point in *Tractatus Tres de Trinitate et Incarnatione* (Corpus Scriptorum Christianorum Orientalium 9, pp. 152–5).

47. The translations are deliberately on the literal side; brackets denote words added by myself for the sake of the sense, or occasionally, where it has been thought helpful, the corresponding Syriac term. Annotation is kept to a minimum and only direct biblical quotations are noted; each of the passages deserves a full commentary, but that would be out of place here. Much shorter extracts from these synods can also be found translated in W.A. Wigram, *An Introduction to the History of the Assyrian Church*, chapter 13.

48. Translated from Vööbus' edition (see note 5); the text is reproduced by de Halleux (title in note 5), with a few modifications (notably the addition of 'Almighty' in the first clause, on the basis of Paris syr. 62).

49. The standard early translation of ὁμοούσιος: see above II.c.

50. Syriac *ruha...qaddisha;* the East Syrian recension here retains the older terminology, *ruha d-qudsha.*

51. Note the absence of 'proceeds', which gives a different nuance; de Halleux (title in note 5) offers some pertinent observations on the wording here, pp. 172–3.

52. Translated from Chabot, *Synodicon Orientale* (henceforth *SO*), pp. 22_{14}–23_4.

53. Translated from *SO*, pp. 54_{29}–55_9.

54. This is not a term used elsewhere in a Christological context it seems; in translations from Greek the word usually represents ἀντίγραφον.

perfect and inseparable conjunction (nqiputa)[55] that has occurred for the divinity with respect to the humanity.

And if someone considers, or teaches others, that suffering and change (hashsha w-shuhlapa)[56] have attached (nqep) to the divinity of our Lord, and (if) he does not preserve, with respect to the union (hdayuta) of the prosopon of our Saviour, a confession of perfect God and perfect Man, let such a person be anathema.

(c) Synod of 544 (Letter of Mar Aba)[57]

We believe in one eternal God who has no beginning or end; and there was never a time when he was not, but (rather) he was continually and is always. Neither has death or change in any way ever had authority over him, nor will it; nor has he been, nor will he be, (involved) in it; and he alone is not made and not created: the maker and creator of all existing things and all natures. He alone has never been in need of anything, nor will (ever) be in need: he who fills all our needs. And he it is who, by his indication (remzeh), controls everything and guides everything, the provisioner of all. And he is the giver of the two testaments, of the Old and of the New. And there is no other God apart from him; he is the first and he is the last. He is omniscient and the giver of wisdom. And it was he who was preached to the ancients through the prophets in singleness of nature (ba-hdanayut kyana) 'in all sorts of ways and in all sorts of forms, and in the latter days he spoke with us in his Son whom he appointed as heir of everything' (Hebr 1:1–2) who is Christ our Lord, he who was born in the flesh from the holy Virgin Mary without intercourse with a man, by the power of the Holy Spirit, as was told her by the angel Gabriel: 'The Holy Spirit will come and the Power of the Most High will overshadow you' (Luke 1:35).[58] And this Son, Christ, was in the world for thirty years, in that he was making repayment on behalf of the debts of nature and of Adam, the head of our race, and of the law of Moses, as Scripture said: 'He was under the law', and 'he bought us (back) from the curse of the law by his perfect righteousness' (Gal. 4:4 and 3:13). At the age of thirty he approached and was baptized by the blessed John, and he sanctified our baptism by his baptism. And after he had been baptized and had contended with Satan and overcome him in the

fast of forty days in the wilderness, he chose the holy apostles and performed signs and wonders.

And when he had fulfilled on earth the work of him who had sent him, that is, his teaching, which he confirmed by various mighty deeds that he performed, and (after) he had handed over the mystery of his Body and his Blood to his disciples, then he sealed his dispensation by his passion and his death on the Cross. And on the third day he overpowered Death by the might of his divinity, and he rose after three days as he had told the reprobate Jews: 'Undo[59] this temple, and after three days I will raise it up', speaking of the temple of his body, as the Evangelist explained (John 2:19, 21). This (temple) which the Jews had undone, he rebuilt with immortal and immutable life.

And after he had arisen from the dead he appeared to his disciples and confirmed them concerning his resurrection, saying 'Touch me and recognize that a spirit does not have flesh (p. 542) and bones, such as you observe that I have (Luke 24:39). And after forty days he ascended to heaven while there were looking on (both) his disciples and those to whom it had been said by the angels 'This Jesus whom you have seen ascend to heaven' (Acts 1:11), (as if) to say that, as he ascended in his true body, that is, in his perfect humanity, 'thus is he going to come' at the end of the world in the glory of his angels in order to raise the dead and to judge the whole creation, as it is written 'God is going to judge all the earth in righteousness at the hands of a man whom he has separated out; and he has caused everyone to turn to faith in him, in that he has raised him from the dead' (Acts 17:31).

And at the end of the days of Pentecost he sent upon his disciples the Holy Spirit from heaven in the likeness of tongues of fire, just as he had told them: 'Do not leave Jerusalem until you have put on might from on high' (Luke 24:49). And when the grace of the Holy Spirit had rested upon the holy apostles, it taught them all truth, as our Lord had told them: 'When the Spirit, the Paraclete, comes upon you, he will teach you all truth' (John 16:13). And what truth did the Holy Spirit teach his disciples, if not concerning the holy Trinity, which was hidden from all created things, and had been spoken of in veiled terms (remzana'it) in the Old Testament, but at the baptism of our Lord was revealed as though in image in the Son who was recognised in him who was being baptized, and (in) the Father who was testifying concerning him, and in the Holy Spirit who rested upon him like a dove: this is the mystery of the Trinity to which he referred when speaking to the apostles

---

55. Corresponds to συνάφεια, another once respectable term which most Greek writers dropped after the 430s.

56. Note the combination; among East Syrian writers 'suffering' has something of the Stoic connotations of πάθος, hence their abhorrence of Theopaschite language.

57. Translated from SO, pp. 541₃–543₁.

58. Here, as is the norm in East Syrian exegetical tradition, the 'Power of the Most High' is associated with the Holy Spirit; this contrasts with West Syrian exegetical tradition which identifies the 'Power' as the Logos.

59. The word used here and elsewhere in these texts (shraw) is not that of the Peshitta or Old Syriac Gospels, but is evidently derived from the Syriac versions of Theodore's writings where shraw occurs (e.g. Commentary on the Creed, ed. Mingana in Woodbrooke Studies V, p. 200).

after his resurrection: 'Go, instruct and baptize in the name of the Father, Son and Holy Spirit' (Matt. 28:19). These things came to be known with exactitude by the gift of the Holy Spirit upon the disciples; for they learnt from the Holy Spirit that Christ is not an ordinary man, nor is he God naked of the garment of humanity[60] in which he had been revealed, but(that) he is Christ God and Man, that is, the humanity which has been anointed with the divinity which anointed it, as it is said: 'For this reason God your God has anointed you with the oil of gladness above your companions' (Ps. 44 (45):8). This indicates concerning his humanity.[61] And again: 'In the beginning was the Word' (John 1:1). This indicates his divinity, which exists eternally for ever, which created all that is visible and all that is invisible.

And (the divinity) exists in three *qnomin*, without beginning, without change, without suffering and without division, (the *qnome*) being the Father Son and Spirit, as our Lord said; for in him was the eternal Trinity made known, as he indicated concerning himself: 'Undo this temple' (John 2:19), that is, the humanity which he had put on; and again 'My Father who dwells in me performs these works' (John 14:10); and again, concerning the Holy Spirit who (was) in him, saying 'The Spirit of the Lord is upon me, for this reason he has anointed me' (Luke 14:18).

Thus from the name of Christ we have learnt concerning the Father and the Son and the Holy Spirit: and from this same (name) we have understood concerning his humanity. In it is (p. 543) the seal of the entire confession of Christianity.

(There follow various anathemas, including one aimed at the Theopashites).

(d) *Synod of 554*[62]

Before everything else we preserve the upright confession of two natures in Christ, that is, his divinity and his humanity. And we preserve (p. 98) the characteristics *(dilayata)* of the natures, by which (sc. the characteristics) we get rid of confusion and disturbance *(bulbala w-duwwada)*, alteration and change *(w-shugnaya w-shuhlapa)*.

We also preserve the number of the *qnome* of the Trinity as threefold, and we confess the single

true and ineffable union *(hdayuta)* in the single true Son of the one God, the Father of truth.

In the case of anyone who considers or speaks of two Christs, or two Sons, or who for one reason or another, and by some device or other, arouses (thought of) a quaternity, such a person have we anathematized and we do anathematize him, considering him to be a limb rejected by the entire body of Christianity.

(e) *Synod of 576*[63]

We have offered the worship of acknowledgement and thanksgiving to God, Lord of all dominions, whose nature is high and exalted, and glorified above all words of praise, the eternal Being *(itya)* who alone truly exists eternally, ineffably, hidden, unattainable, uncontained, without beginning and without end, having authority over all, maker of all created things, removed from all changes and alteration, distanced from all sufferings and stirrings *(hashsin w-zaw'in)*, in whom all exists while he exists outside everything and inside everything in the glory of his majesty; and with the indication *(remza)* of his authority and with the might of his power he controls and governs, provides for and performs everything; the giver of the Old and the fulfiller of the New (Testament); through his holy prophets he taught former (generations) concerning the singleness of his nature *(hdanayut kyaneh)*, and by various indications he manifests concerning the glorious *qnome* of his threefold being *(tlitayuteh,* Trinity).

While in latter days, according to the word of the universal apostle Paul (Hebr. 1:2) the elect, he was revealed to us and spoke with us in his Son Christ our Lord; in him the glorious *qnome* of his Father and of himself and of the Holy Spirit became known in a new way, when he taught and commanded his holy apostles, his true preachers, 'God, instruct all peoples, and baptize them in the name of the Father and the Son and the Holy Spirit. (Matt. 28:19); and when they have been reborn from baptism, give them sustenance appropriate to their requirement— the teaching and commandments and admonitions that I gave you, that they should keep them and meditate on them, for from them they are able to enter and enjoy the kingdom of heaven; and behold I am with you all the days until the end of the world (Matt. 28:20), amen'.

It is he who lowered himself of his own will for the salvation of our nature that had grown old and worn out through acts of sin; and he took for himself a perfect temple for the dwelling of his divinity, in an inseparable way, from Mary the holy virgin; and he was conceived and born from her by the power of the Most High: Christ who is in the flesh, who is recogni-

---

60. This is again archaic imagery (e.g. Ephrem *Hymns on Faith* 19:2) which Greek writers later tended to drop; it derives from a Christological interpretation of Genesis 49:11. (The phrase 'He put on the body' is the standard metaphor for the Incarnation in early Syriac tradition: see my 'Clothing metaphors as a means of theological expression in Syriac tradition', in ed. M. Schmidt, *Typus, Symbol Allegorie bei den östlichen Vätern und ihren Parallelen im Mittelalter,* Regensburg 1982), pp. 11–40).

61. In East Syrian tradition the 'anointing' of the humanity of Christ is understood as having taken place already at his very conception: for a specific statement to this effect see Babai, *Liber de Unione* (ed. Vaschalde), pp. 278–9.

62. Translated from *SO,* pp. 97$_{31}$–98$_7$.

63. Translated from *SO,* pp. 113$_7$–114$_8$. There are a number of reminiscences of Mar Aba's letter (III.c).

zed and confessed (as being) in two natures, God and Man, one Son. In him the oldness of our nature was renewed, and in the robe of his humanity the debt of our race was repaid, in his drawing close (*metqarrbanuteh*) to suffering and the death of the cross. And by the power of his divinity he rose from the dead after three days, as he had told the Jews: 'Undo this temple and after three days I will raise it' (John 2:19), which (p. 114) the evangelist interpreted, saying, 'Now he spoke of the temple of his body' (John 2:21). And in his resurrection he shattered the bars of death and broke down the walls of Sheol; he rendered ineffective the strength of sin and brought low the pride of Satan who had been roaring fiercely for the destruction of our nature. And he gave hope and a pledge of resurrection from the dead to all the world through his own resurrection and his going around with his disciples up to the time of his ascension...

(f) *Synod of* 585.

(1) Profession of faith at the synod:[64]

'We believe in one God, Father Almighty, and in one Lord Jesus Christ, the Son of God, and in one Holy Spirit who proceeds from the Father'. Even though the serial reading of the words places the names of the Holy Trinity at a distance (from each other), owing to the attachment (in each case) of those terms which particularly and properly attach to them, yet the sense and the meaning of this composition of the Fathers requires such an attachment in order to indicate that the Trinity is above number, so that it might be realized that the words 'one...one...one' point to the single nature of the (divine) essence; as it is said 'The Lord your God is one' (Deut. 6:4). The words 'Father, Son, and Holy Spirit' indicate the difference of the *qnome* of the essence, following the tradition of the Gospel of Christ our Saviour: 'Go forth, convert all peoples and baptize them in the name of the Father and the Son and the Holy Spirit' (Matt. 28: 19).

By adding 'God' and 'Lord' and 'Spirit' they also attached common terms to the individual names, 'Father', 'Son,' 'Holy Spirit'. The fathers clearly showed that these were common terms, each one of which, that is, (all) three, extend to the three *qnome*, for it is clear and without dispute that the Father is God and Lord and Spirit, and the Son is Lord and God and Spirit, and the Holy Spirit is Spirit and Lord and God. Our Fathers did well to utter the confession of the Trinity briefly; by it they taught wisely and fully the equality of nature and the equality of essence and the difference of the *qnome* and the singleness (*hdanayut*) of the Godhead. They proclaimed equality of essence

and equality of nature, then, as though to stop the crazy mouth of Arius who wickedly devised to split up the equality of essence of the Trinity. And our Fathers proclaimed the difference of the *qnome* of the Trinity to nullify the supposition of the obstinate Jews who suppose that God is one *qnoma*. As for the terms which are extended and are (held) in common, while being attached to the individual names that are not extended, our Fathers proclaimed 'one Godhead', 'one Lordship', 'one spiritual Being' as though to nullify and refute the doctrine of the pagans (p.134) who insanely acknowledge various godheads and lordships.

Having thus overthrown the wickedness of Arius by the proclamation of the equality of essence, and silenced the childishness of the Jews with the difference of the *qnome*, and muzzled the error of paganism too by the singleness of Lordship, then they went on to things which follow on from their confession, attaching 'Almighty' to the words 'one God', and saying 'maker of all that is visible and that is invisible', in that he is the maker and establisher and arranger of all in all.

Likewise they attached to the words 'one Lord' the (further) words 'Jesus Christ', and they showed that the word 'one' is common to the *qnome* of the Trinity, as hinted at above.

The fact that they did not add 'and in one Lord the Son', corresponding to the words 'one God the Father', but instead altered the order of their words and said 'in one Lord, Jesus Christ', will not escape the notice of right believers, for this abundantly points to the humanity of God the Word and it wisely proclaims the single union (*hdayuta*) of the divinity and the humanity of Christ, even though the Eutychians speak insanely, defrauding the humanity of the Son of God: for the name 'Christ' is an indicator of his Godhead from the Father and of his humanity from (his) mother indisputably, even though Eutyches and those in error with him may prattle away, defrauding and denying the taking of our humanity, or speaking of the suppression of the humanity of Christ. For the Fathers add, following on (this), 'the Only-Begotten and the First-Born of all created things', that is, Only-Begotten without brothers, with regard to the divinity, and Firstborn of many brothers, that is, Firstborn of all created things, as it is written (Col. 1:15).

And then they add 'Through whom the worlds were established and everything was created', showing that he is cause and maker of all, together with his Father. And again they show, concerning his (divine) essence, that 'he was born from his Father before all worlds, and he was not made: Light from Light, true God from true God', Jesus Christ in his divinity. Again they add, in refutation of Arius, putting 'the Word who is homoousios', that is, of the same nature and of the same essence (*bar kyaneh*

---

64. Translated from *SO*, pp. 133$_7$–136$_{20}$. The text is in the form of a running commentary on the Nicene–Constantinopolitan creed; there seem to be some reminiscences of Theodore's commentary (ed. Mingana in Woodbrooke Studies 5), and the last paragraph reflects the last paragraph of III.a.2 above.

w-bar ituteh) 'as the Father, through whom everything came into being', Jesus Christ in his divinity.

Thus, contesting with the invincible armour of true doctrine that they wore against the fantasies and imaginings of the false teachings of the Simonians and the Manichaeans, they say 'He who for the sake of us human beings and for the sake of our salvation came down from heaven, and was embodied *(etgas-hsham)* of the Holy Spirit and of Mary the Virgin and became man' –Jesus Christ in the unification of his natures *(ba-mhayydut kyanaw)* and in his manifestation in the flesh and in his embodiment. The unification of the natures, of the divinity and of the humanity, is an indication that he came down and was embodied and became man: (p. 135) it informs, without dispute, concerning the taking of our humanity, thus removing from all sides the empty fancies of the Simonians and Mani who deny the fleshly state *(besranuteh)* and the embodiment and manifestation of God the Word who took our humanity and resided *('mar)* in it, as (John) said: 'The word became[65] flesh and dwelt among us' (John 1:14) – in order that the magnitude of the grace of him who descended and resided in us might be all the more manifested. For the wicked Arius, by applying both the exalted and the lowly things to the nature of the Word's divinity, not knowing how to allocate them singly and individually as truth demands,[66] stumbled and fell on this point, going astray himself and leading (others) astray, (as a result of which) he was anathematized and driven out.

The Fathers add further and complete the wording about the dispensation: after the teaching on the divine nature of the Only–Begotten, and after the teaching on the unification of the natures of Christ– that is, of his unchanged and undying divinity and of his humanity that is not abused or absorbed–they attach teaching concerning his humanity. And, just as they showed clearly above concerning his divinity, (so) they will show openly concerning his humanity which was taken for our sakes and for our salvation, and for the renovation[67] of all created things, saying 'And he was crucified for us in the days of Pontius Pilate, and he suffered and died and was buried and rose after three days as the holy Scriptures say'. Jesus Christ in his humanity, or, to utter the truth, in his fleshly state *(besranuteh)* accepted the death of the cross for our sakes.

It is obvious to all who are orthodox in their confession that just as he did not suffer or die according to the nature of his divinity, neither did his soul receive the sentence *(apophasis)* of death, in that the nature of the soul is not constituted so that it is subject to the limit of death, (as) our Lord himself testifies: 'Do not fear those who kill the body; they are unable to kill the soul' (Matt. 10:28). Also testifying to this is the fact that after our Lord had been crucified and his holy body had died and been buried, in his soul he went to Paradise.

The blessed Fathers then go on: 'And he ascended to heaven and sat at the right hand of his Father' –Jesus Christ in his humanity: for it was in his humanity that he received exaltation and the seat at the right hand, and not in his divinity, for he had been eternally and without beginning with his Father.

'And he will come in glory to judge' the living and the dead; whose kingdom has no end' –Jesus Christ in his divinity and in his humanity.

After they had spoken against the ejected bands of the Anomoeans, they turned themselves to the wickedness of Macedonians who had blasphened against the Holy Spirit, and they said 'And in one Holy Spirit, Lord, life–giving, who proceeds from the Father and is worshipped with the Father and the Son; who spoke in the prophets and apostles'. Thus by their divine teaching the Fathers preached magnificently concerning (p.136) the *qnoma* of the Holy Spirit, showing him to be of the same essence and of the same nature as the Father and the Son. As it is said, 'He searches out everything, even the depths of God' (I Cor. 2:10).

This is the faith without corruption; this is its sense, put briefly, following the sequence of its phrases. By it the person *(prosopon)* of Christ and the natures of his divinity and his humanity are fully proclaimed, in opposition to those who confess his divinity but deny his humanity, and in opposition to those who confess his humanity but deny his divinity, and in opposition to those who deny his divinity and confess that he is an ordinary man, or who liken him to one of the just.

Because our blessed Fathers cause the baptized to inherit the wealth of their faith, they further add: 'And in one holy, catholic and apostolic Church, and in one baptism for the forgiveness of sins; and in the resurrection of the dead and in the new life, and in the world to come'.

After having thus richly and fully proclaimed the truth they turned from this to the anathema on Arius and those who had gone astray with him–on those who say 'There is a time when he was not' and 'Before he was begotten he was not', or 'He came into being out of nothing', or who say that he is from (another) *qnoma* or another essence, or who consider the Son of God to be subject to change and alteration: (all) these the catholic and apostolic Church anathematizes–heretics who in their stubborness have dared to attribute to the nature and *qnoma* of the

---

65. The Syriac can just as well mean 'was'.

66. It is worth noting that part of the Church of the East's abhorrence of Theopaschite language stems from this anti-Arian stance.

67. This interestingly reflects the wording of the West Syrian recension of the profession of faith of 410, confirming de Halleux's view that this recension preserves the original text; cp also Isho'yahb I's profession of faith, III.f.2 below.

divinity and (divine) essence of the Word the characteristics *(dilayata)* and sufferings of the nature of Christ's humanity, things which sometimes, because of the perfect union that took place for the humanity of Christ with his divinity, are allocated to God by economy, but not by nature.

(2) Confession of faith composed by Isho'yahb I[68]

We believe in one eternal God, uncontained, without beginning and without end;[69] a living spirit, hidden, unattainable, whose nature power and authority have no limit or boundary; who knows all prior to all, giver of wisdom, who alone is wise, maker and lord of all created things, visible and invisible, by the indication *(remza)* of whose will the worlds above and below were established and set up; the beneficent governor and upright judge, the wise provisioner of this world and the world to come, giver of all graces, who never wearies or proves lacking, who is not changed or subject to blame, the Being *(itya)* without cause, the cause of all, from whom is everything, because of whom is everything, belonging to whom is everthing, (directed) towards whom is everything; the one timeless Godhead, three *qnome* without any beginning which are perfect in everything and do not lack in anything; the one God who is known, confessed and worshipped in the three *qnome*, of the Father and of the Son and of the Holy Spirit, who are distinct and united in an ineffable wonder, equal, not confused, conjoined *(nqipin)*, not intermingled, alike but different: alike in their equality of nature, but distinct in the distinction of *qnome;* one Father, beside whom there is no other Father, who begat eternally without himself being born, cause that has no cause, (p. 194) maker of everything, from whom everthing was established; one Son, beside whom there is no other Son, who was born eternally, but did not beget, the causer *('elltana)* from the Cause *('ellta)*, the cause of everything with the Father, without whom there was not even a single thing that came into being; one Holy Spirit, beside whom there is no other Spirit, who proceeds, who did not beget and was not born, proceeding from the Father eternally, the causer *('elltana)* from the Cause, the cause of everything along with the Father and the Son, who 'searches out everything, even the depths of God' (1 Cor. 2:10).

One nature which is not reduplicated, three *qnome* who do not become four; (whose) fullness *(shumlaya)* is one-fold *(hdana'it)* and indication *(shudda'a)* is threefold *(tlita'it)*; one nature eternally, in which and with which are also the *qnome* eternally; and with it the Son is born eternally, and with it the Spirit proceeds eternally; at once nature, at once *qnome*,

at once Father, at once Son, at once Holy Spirit, one God and not three Gods–let the crazy Marcion wail; three *qnome* and not one *qnoma*-let the errant Sabellius wail, and along with him Paul of Samosata who denied the Essence *(ituta)* of the Word before the ages...

This is the Christianity that the Holy Spirit taught through the apostles and through the prophets concerning the revelation of God the Word and concerning his dispensation in the body, and concerning his embodiment for our sakes and for the sake of our salvation, and for the renovation and restoration of all created things.

Out of his great love with which he loved us he departed from the bosom of his Father voluntarily and without being changed, and he came to the world, while being in the world, as it is written (John 1:10); the hidden one who was revealed in the flesh: 'The Word became flesh and dwelt among us' (John 1:10). He became, but was not changed–he who is 'the form of God emptied himself and took the form of a servant' (Phil. 2.7);[70] 'he took', but did not add (to himself), for both in his 'becoming' and in his 'taking' his Essence remained without change or addition. Jesus Christ, Son of God, God the Word, Light from Light. He came down and was embodied and became man, by dispensation, above alteration and change, our Lord God, Jesus Christ. He who was born from the Father before all worlds in his divinity was born in the flesh from Mary the ever–Virgin in latter times, one and the same (Person), but not in the same (way) (p. 195). 'The Word became flesh'–in an indivisible union *(hdayuta)*-'and dwelt among us'. O profundity of the riches of faith! 'He became', but was not changed: let the Eutychians and Apollinarians wail; 'he took', but did not add (anything): let the Photinians and Paulinians wail.

Again I say, let the abusers and schimatics listen, and let them be united to the Church; let them not be like old rags cut off from the harmony of concord; let them not rend the perfect garment of faith and baptism, woven with divine craftsmanship by the operation of the Spirit, the Lord. The soldiers who crucified him did not dare, and were not able, to rend the garment of Christ (John 19:23–4[71]); so you (singular) should not tear the perfect garment of the harmony of the apostolic Church; rather, listen to the truth of the faith and remain inside the ecclesiastical sheepfolds, together with all the Church redeemed by the blood of the great Shepherd of the flock, Jesus Christ the Son of God, God over all, born in his divinity from the Father, without a mother, eternally;

---

68. Translated from *SO*, pp. 193$_{16}$–194$_{13}$, 194$_{21}$–195$_{34}$. There are some reminiscences of Mar Aba's letter (III.c) as well as of the profession of faith of 585 (III.f.l).

69. I omit here a phrase which is badly corrupted.

70. Isho'yahb in fact uses two different Syriac words corresponding to the repeated μορφή in Greek (in this he follows the Peshitta New Testament).

71. For the history of this exegesis of the passage see M. Aubineau, 'Dossier patristique sur Jean 19:23–4', *La Bible et les Pères* (Strasbourg 1971) pp. 9–50.

one and the same, but not in the same (way), he was born in his humanity from (his) mother, without a father, in latter times; and he suffered in the flesh and was crucified and died and was buried, in the days of Pontius Pilate; and he arose from the dead after three days.

He suffered in the flesh, Christ the Son of God, one and the same; but in the nature of his divinity Christ the Son of God is above sufferings: impassible and passible, Jesus Christ, creator of the worlds and recipient of sufferings, who for our sakes became poor, while being rich (2 Cor. 8:9). God the Word receives the abuse of sufferings in the temple of his body according to the dispensation in the supreme inseparable union, while in the nature of his divinity he does not suffer, as our Saviour himself said: 'Undo this temple and after three days I will raise it' (John 2:19). And because the Jews in their stubbornness imagined that he was speaking about the temple (made) of stones, the evangelist interprets the Saviour's utterance, saying 'He spoke concerning the temple of his body' (John 2:21). Our Lord himself indicates the sublimity [72] of the prosopic union *(hdayuta parsopayta)* unitedly and unconfusedly, when he says: 'No one has gone up to heaven except he who came down from heaven' (John 3: 13): the Son of Man is he who came down from heaven, the Son of Man is the one who is in heaven. Christ, who came down without any change in his divinity from heaven, being unembodied and in the limitlessness of his divinity in heaven, in his humanity is raised up to heaven, while not destroying his visible nature, following the angelic indication: 'This Jesus who has gone up from you to heaven, shall come in like fashion as you have seen him ascend to heaven' (Acts 1:11). Christ is Only–Begotten *(ihidaya)* and united *(mhayyda)* : Only–Begotten with respect to the Father, and united and unseparated (in the union), for his divinity does not die or get destroyed or changed, while his humanity is not stolen away or hidden or absorbed...

(g) *Synod of 596* [73]

(We profess the Nicene faith) which accurately and luminously teaches us the confession of the glorious nature of the holy Trinity, of the Father and of the Son and of the Holy Spirit; which reveals and manifests to us the glorious mysteries of the dispesation of God the Word which he perfected and fulfilled at the end of times in the nature of our humanity.

By this faith paganism, which confesses a plurality of gods, is vanquished, and Judaism, which does not confess the Trinity of *qnome*, is judged, and all (kinds) of heresy, which deny the divinity or humanity of our saviour Jesus Christ, are rebuked and condemned. We accept it in the precise sense of our holy Fathers, expounded by the glorious among the orthodox, the blessed Theodore of Antioch, bishop of the town of Mopsuestia, the Exegete of the divine Scriptures. [74] With it all the orthodox everywhere have agreed and do agree, and it has also been held by all our holy Fathers who governed this apostolic and patriarchal see of our government.

We anathematize and alienate from our company anyone who denies the nature of the divinity or the nature of the humanity of our Lord Jesus Christ; or anyone who (p. 198) introduces into the union of the Son of God any mixture, mingling, or composition or confusion; or anyone who (introduces) suffering or any of the base things of humanity in any way into the glorious nature of his divinity; or anyone who considers the dominical temple of God the Word to be ordinary man –(that temple) which, in an inexplicable mystery and in a union that cannot be understood, he united to himself from the womb of the holy virgin in a union which is for ever, indissoluble and inseparable.

We also abhor anyone who introduces a quaternity into the holy Trinity; or anyone who calls the one Christ Son of God two Sons or two Christs; or anyone who does not say that it was God the Word himself who perfected the passion for *(lit.* of) our salvation in the body of his humanity, being in it and with it and by it in the womb and on the cross and in the passion, and for ever, inseparably, while the glorious nature of his divinity did not share in any of the sufferings.

But we believe firmly, in accordance with the words and sense of the Scriptures and the traditions of our holy Fathers, in one Lord Jesus Christ, Only–Begotten Son of God, who was born before the foundations of the world in his divinity spiritually without a mother, and at the end of times was born of the holy virgin in the flesh *(besrana'it)* without intercourse of a man, by the power of the Holy Spirit. In his divinity that is from everlasting and in his humanity that is from Mary he is the one true Son of God, who, in the nature of his humanity, received for our sakes suffering and death. And by the power of his divinity he raised up his body without corruption after three days, and he promised resurrection from the dead and ascension to heaven, and a new world, indissoluble and lasting for ever.

With this true and apostolic faith do we agree, and both we and the flocks entrusted to us preserve it. And if anyone dares to tear up, or does not accept, this deposition of the true faith, we will make him an alien to the entire company of Christians, ejected and driven out, until he accepts correction and agrees to this true faith of the Church.

---

72. Reading *m'lywt'* for *m'lnwt'* ,entry'.
73. Translated from *SO*, pp. 197₁₉–198₂₄. There are some reminiscences of III. b. and f.l. above.

---

74. The reference will be to the text published by Mingana (see note 64).

(h) *Synod of* 605.[75]

One and the same (sc. with the creeds of Nicaea and Constantinople) is our opinion and faith in the holy Trinity and the mysteries of the dispensation of our Lord in the body. (It is the faith) which our Fathers have taught us and shown to us; it consists for us in the confession of the one divine nature, the eternal Being, Creator of all created things, cause of all, having no beginning and possessing no end, who exists continually without ending, who is above the limit and boundary of suffering, change and alteration of any sort. Never has anything had, nor will it ever have, authority over him: he controls all and governs all; for he is the first and the last, who indicated concerning our renovation through the prophets in the Old (Testament), and revealed it through the apostles in the New, by means of his beloved Son, whom he had made heir of everything and in whom he had made known concerning the Trinity of his *qnome*, which are without beginning and without change, a single Godhead, unattainable, a single eternal nature who is known in three *qnome*, of the Father and of the Son and of the Holy Spirit.

Who, through the Firstfruits from us (1 Cor. 15:23), effected the liberation and renovation of our race, for 'the form of God took the form of a servant', according to the apostolic utterance (Phil. 2:7), and in him he perfected and completed his exalted dispensation for the sake of our salvation: the form of God in the form (p. 201) of a servant, the single Son, our Lord Jesus Christ, through whom everything came into being, perfect God and perfect Man: perfect God in the nature of his divinity, and perfect Man in the nature of his humanity, two natures, of divinity and of humanity, the divinity being preserved in what belongs to it, and the humanity in what belongs to it; and they are united in a true union (*hdayuta*) of the one person (*prosopon*) of the Son, Christ. And the divinity perfected the humanity in the suffering, as it is written, while suffering change and alteration of any sort did not enter into the divinity.

This faith we have agreed to and have held. All the holy fathers have agreed to it, and we too hold it in the pure concurrence of our mind, concurring with it and anathematizing all who slip away from it in any way.

(i) *Assembly of bishops in* 612.[76]

(1) We believe in one divine nature which exists eternally, without beginning, living and life-giving, mighty, creating all powers, wise, providing all wisdom, simple spirit, unlimited, incomprehensible,

uncomposed and without parts, unembodied, invisible, unchangeable, impassible, immortal; neither in itself *(b-yateh)*, nor in another, nor with another, is it possible that any suffering or change should enter into it; rather, it is perfect in its essence (*ituteh*) and in all that belongs to it; and it cannot receive addition or subtraction, for it alone is Being (*itya*) and God over all, who is known and confessed in three holy *qnome*, Father, Son and Holy Spirit, a nature with three *qnome* essentially (*tlitay qnome itya'it*), *qnome* with a single eternal nature (*hdanay kyana mtomaya*), between whom there is no distinction apart from the distinct characteristics (*dilayata*) of their *qnome*, (namely) Fatherhood and Sonhood and Procession.

For the rest, everything that is confessed of the (divine) nature in common is likewise confessed of, and is the case with, each of the *qnome* individually, without subtraction. And in that the Father is passible and unchangeable, (so) too the Son and the Spirit are confessed as being without suffering and without change, along with him and like him. And just as the Father is believed (to be) unlimited and without parts, so too the Son and the Spirit are confessed (as being) without limit and without composition.

Three *qnome*, perfect in everything, in a single Godhead, in a single Power that is not weakened ever, a single knowledge which is not surpassed, a single will which is not deflected, a single authority which is not dissolved: for he creates the world in his grace and guides it with the indication *(remza)* of his will.

Having at the beginning instructed the human race with knowledge of his divinity in a small way, with respect to the measure of the greatness of knowledge of him, and having during the intermediary time (p. 565) been revealed in different visions and various forms to the saints, and having educated and given wisdom to human beings for the increase of their knowledge, by means of various laws; and then, at the end of times, it having pleased his unattainable wisdom that he reveal and make known to rational beings the wonderful mysteries of his glorious Trinity in order to magnify our nature and sow in it the true seed of resurrection from the dead and the new and incorruptible life that receives no alteration unto eternity, in accordance with his foreknowledge and will that is from eternity; therefore, for the sake of us human beings and for the sake of our salvation, the Son of God, the Word, without having departed from his Begetter, 'came to the world and was in the world, and the world came into being through him' (John 1:10).

And because created natures were unable to see the glorious nature of his divinity, he fashioned for himself in exalted manner, from the nature of the house of Adam, a holy temple from the blessed Virgin Mary, a complete man, who was completed without the intercourse with a man that follows the natural course (of events). And he put him on and united him to himself, and in him he was revealed to

---

75. Translated from *SO* pp. 209$_{20}$–210$_9$. There are reminiscences of III.b and perhaps of III.c and f.2.

76. Translated from *SO*, pp. 564$_{10}$–567$_8$. There are reminiscences of III.c,e and f. 1–2.

the world, in accordance with the utterance of the angel to the mother of our Saviour: 'The Holy Spirit shall come and the power of the Most High shall overshadow you; for this reason he who is going to be born from you is holy and shall be called the Son of God' (Luke 1: 35).

Concerning the wonderful conjunction (*neqpa*) and inseparable union (*hdayuta dla purshana*) that took place from the very beginning of its fashioning[77] for the human nature that was taken by God the Word, the 'taker', he taught us that from that point we should recognize as one person (prosopon) our Lord Jesus Christ, the Son of God, who was born from before the worlds, without beginning, from the Father in the nature of his divinity, and who was born latterly of the holy virgin, the daughter of David, in the nature of his humanity; just as God had previously promised to the blessed David: 'From the fruits of your womb shall I cause to sit upon your throne' (Ps. 131(132): 11). And after the outcome of the events the blessed Paul expounded the promise, saying to the Jews concerning David: 'From the seed of this man God has raised up, just as he promised, Jesus the Saviour' (Acts 13:23). And again, he wrote to the Philippians as follows: 'Ponder this in yourselves, that even Jesus Christ, although he is the form of God, took the form of a servant' (Phil. 2:6-7). For who was the one whom he calls 'form of God' if not Christ in the nature of his divinity; and whom again does he name 'form of a servant', if not Christ in his humanity? With respect of the former he says 'he took,' and to the latter 'was taken'; (Thus) it is not possible to confuse the characteristics (*dilayathon*) of the natures; for it is impossible that 'he who took' should become 'who was taken', and that 'he who was taken' should become ,the taker'. (But) it is possible for God the Word to be revealed in the human being whom he put on, and for his human nature to become visible to creation in the mode (*teksa*) of his humanity and in the inseparable union (as) the single Son of God, just as we have learnt and hold. (p. 566) That the divinity should be changed into humanity, or that the humanity should be altered to the nature of the divinity, is impossible; for it is not the case that Being (*itya*) can fall under the compulsion of change or of suffering, for if the divinity is changed, it is no longer a revelation, but a destruction, of the divinity. And if, again, the humanity should depart from its nature, salvation no longer obtains, but a wiping out of the humanity.

For this reason we believe with our hearts and we confess with our lips a single Lord Jesus Christ, Son of God, whose divinity is not hidden, and whose humanity was not stolen away, but who is perfect God and perfect Man. When we speak of Christ as

perfect God, we are not referring to the Trinity, but to one of the *qnome* of the Trinity, God the Word. And when again we call Christ perfect Man, we are not referring to all mankind, but to that single *qnoma* who was specifically taken, for our salvation, into union with the Word.

For this reason our Lord Jesus Christ, who was born in his divinity from his Father eternally, in latter times for our sakes was born the holy Virgin in his humanity. While he remained, in his divinity, without need and without suffering and without change, in his humanity after his nativity he was also circumcised and grew up, according to the testimony of Luke the evangelist: 'Jesus was growing in stature and in wisdom and in grace before God and mankind' (Luke 2:52); and he kept the law and was baptized in the Jordan by John; and then he began to preach the new covenant, performing wonders by the power of his divinity- the cleansing of lepers, the opening of the eyes of the blind, the chasing out of demons, the resurrection of dead people; while in the nature of his humanity he thirsted, he hungered, and he ate and drank, grew tired and slept; and last of all, for our sakes he gave himself up and was crucified, and he suffered and died–without his divinity having departed from him or having suffered; and his body was wrapped in a shroud and was laid in a place of burial; then after three days he rose, by the power of his divinity, just as he had told the Jews beforehand: 'Undo this temple, and after three days I will raise it up' (John 2:19), which the evangelist interprets, saying, 'He was speaking of the temple of his body, (John 2:21).

And after he arose, he went about on earth with his disciples for forty days, showing them his hands and his feet, saying: 'Feel me and know that a spirit does not have flesh and bones such as you see that I have' (Luke 24:39) – so that both by word and by actions he might assure them of his resurrection, and so that, from the assurance of his resurrection, he might assure in us a hope of our resurrection.

And after forty days he ascended to heaven in the sight of his disciples as they looked on, and a cloud received him, and he was concealed from their eyes, according to the testimony of Scripture (Acts 1:9).

And we confess that he is going to come from heaven in the power and glory of his angels, and he will effect a resurrection for all the race of humanity, and a judgement and examining (p. 567) for all rational beings, just as the angels told the apostles themselves at the time of his ascension: 'This Jesus, who has been taken up from you to heaven, will in like wise come just as you saw him go up to heaven' (Acts 1:11). And by this they openly taught us this too: 'He was taken up to heaven'–and the *qnoma* of his humanity was not dissolved and was not changed, but is preserved in the inseparable union with his divinity in the exalted glory in which he is going to behold, at his final revelation from heaven, the shame of those who cruci-

---

77. Here, as perhaps elsewhere in this document, we can identify the influence of Babai who isuses this phrase on many occasions (e.g. *Liber de Unione*, pp. 133, 278–9).

iied him and the glory and pride of those who believe fn him.

To him, and to his Father and to the Holy Spirit, be praise and honour, for ever.

(2) From the reply to questions posed by theological opponents:[78]

It is clearly apparent that Christ is perfect God and perfect Man. Now he is said to be God, being perfect in the nature and *qnoma* of divinity, and he is then said to be perfect Man, being perfect in the nature and *qnoma* of humanity. And just as it is made known, from the opposition (expressed in) the words just used, that Christ is two natures and two *qnome*, so too, from the fact that they refer to the one Christ, Son of God, it is made known that Christ is one— not in a oneness *(hdanayut)* of nature and of *qnoma*, but in an the single *prosopon* of Sonhip and the single (source of) authority and single governance and single power and single lordship.

---

78. Translated from *SO*, p. 575_{11-18}.

IMAGES OF EPHRAEM: THE SYRIAN HOLY MAN AND HIS CHURCH

By SIDNEY H. GRIFFITH

I

IMAGES OF EPHRAEM

Ephraem the Syrian is undoubtedly the best-known holy man of the Syriac-speaking world in the patristic period. Within fifty years of Ephraem's death, Palladius included a notice of him among the ascetic saints whose memory he celebrated in the *Lausiac History*.[1] Sozomen the historian celebrated Ephraem's memory as a popular ecclesiastical writer, some of whose works had been translated into Greek even during his lifetime.[2] Jerome claimed to recognize Ephraem's theological genius in a Greek translation he read of a book by Ephraem on the Holy Spirit.[3] And toward the end of the fifth century, Gennadius of Marseilles called attention to Ephraem as a composer of metrical psalms.[4] Well within the patristic era itself, therefore, Ephraem's reputation as holy man, theologian, and poet was secure.

Beyond these Greek and Latin testimonies, however, the image of Ephraem that has prevailed in the West, in both hagiography and iconography, has been a portrait of the saint as a monk, or even as a hermit of virtually Antonine proportions. The story of how this icon of the ascetic St. Ephraem was produced is the story of the growth of a hagiographic legend that had its beginnings in Greek appreciations of the saint, but which reached its full-bodied maturity in the Syriac narrative of the *Vita Ephraemi*, a work with its roots in the cosmopolitan culture of the Graeco-Syrian monastic communities of the fifth and sixth centuries.[5] Due to the popularity of the *Vita's* portrait of

---

[1] See C. Butler, *The Lausiac History of Palladius* (Texts and Studies 6; Cambridge 1898 and 1904) 2.126–27.

[2] See J. Bidez and G. H. Hansen (edd.), *Sozomenus, Kirchengeschichte* (GCS 50; Berlin 1960) 127–30.

[3] See E. C. Richardson (ed.), *Hieronymus, Liber de Viris Inlustribus* (TU 14; Leipzig 1896) 51.

[4] Gennadius was actually speaking of one Peter of Edessa, of whom he said that 'he composed metrical Psalms in the manner of Ephraem the deacon.' E. C. Richardson (ed.), *Gennadius, Liber de Viris Inlustribus* (TU 14; Leipzig 1896) 87.

[5] See now Joseph P. Amar, 'The Syriac *Vita* Tradition of Ephrem the Syrian' (Dissertation, The Catholic University of America 1988). A convenient summary in Latin of the traditional lives of St. Ephraem is readily available in 'De S. Ephrem Syro Edessae in Mesopotamia,' AS February 1 (Paris 1863) 49–78.

the saint as a retiring, ascetic hermit, with only a few dramatic intrusions into the church-life of his own day to his credit, the historical St. Ephraem, the teacher *par excellence* of the churches of fourth-century Nisibis and Edessa,[6] has disappeared into the 'golden mist of the unreal,' to borrow a phrase from Dom David Knowles.[7] From the *Vita* there emerges a stately icon of St. Ephraem as an ascetical ideal, which owes little or nothing to the historical reality of the Syrian holy man.

The seventh-century Graeco-Syrian writer of the Greek encomium of St. Ephraem that is atttributed to Gregory of Nyssa forthrightly admitted his uninterest in biographical details. Toward the beginning of the work he wrote:

> Neither the genealogy, nor the prosperous social visibility of the ancestors, nor the good name of the parents, nor the breeding, nor the education, nor any increase of stature, nor bodily fitness, nor fortune, nor arts, nor any of the other contributions of the chroniclers of externals that solemnly bespeak approval do we especially presume to bring forward here, because we do not undertake to commend godly men for such things.[8]

True to his principles, the author of the encomium went on to portray St. Ephraem in a glowing representation of the ascetical ideal that paid no attention at all to the facts of his life. For it was the icon itself that was important, not the historical St. Ephraem; and the icon was one that depicted the archetype of the monk according to the hagiographical canons of the Byzantine orthodox church,[9] not according to the role the saint actually played in the Syriac-speaking churches of the fourth century. What is wrong with this life of St. Ephraem is not its celebration of his sanctity, or the author's uninterest in biographical and historical details; rather, what one misses here is the model of the ascetic life that Ephraem himself actually lived. So one must distinguish between the icon of St. Ephraem Byzantinus and the portrait of St. Ephraem Syrus. The two are not unrelated; but their images are painted in colors from two different palettes, and the icon of the Byzantine ascetic has been painted over the portrait of the real man.

---

[6] In Syriac sources, as will appear below, Ephraem is consistently remembered as 'the great teacher' (*malpōnō rabbō*).

[7] David Knowles, *The Monastic Order in England* (2nd ed.; Cambridge 1966) 693.

[8] PG 46.824A–B. As Joseph Amar has argued in 'The Syriac *Vita* Tradition of Ephrem the Syrian' (above, n. 5) 21 n. 73, a seventh-century date for the *Encomium* is suggested by a reference at the end of the work to hostile action in Syria on the part of the 'Barbarian progeny of Ishmael' (849A).

[9] Classic studies of the pertinent hagiographical literary genre are H. Delehaye, *Les Légendes hagiographiques* (2nd ed.; Brussels 1906) and P. Peeters, *Orient et Byzance: Le tréfonds oriental de l'hagiographie byzantine* (Subsidia Hagiographica 26; Brussels 1950). See also P. Cox, *Biography in Late Antiquity: A Quest for the Holy Man* (Berkeley 1983).

A. *The Icon of Ephraem Byzantinus*

The icon of Ephraem Byzantinus owes its main features to writers in the Graeco-Syrian monastic communities of the fifth and sixth centuries. They transmitted Ephraem's works in both Greek and Syriac, even composing new hymns and homilies in his style and under his name;[10] they also composed the *Vita Ephraemi* and even a document called Ephraem's *Testament,* two works that together virtually completed the iconic profile of Ephraem Byzantinus.[11] During the fifth and sixth centuries there was a surge in the intellectual and religious power of proto-Byzantine culture in the oriental patriarchates, to the point that one can even plot the crescendo of Greek learning by the growing incidence of Greek vocabulary and syntax in texts composed in the Syriac language from this period.[12] Greek religious classics, such as Palladius' *Lausiac History* — to mention only the work most relevant to the present purpose — were readily translated into Syriac in these centuries, along with influential theological treatises such as the works of the Cappadocian fathers.[13] In some quarters there were continued efforts to bring the Syriac versions of the New Testament into an ever closer harmony with the Greek original, with the primary purpose of achieving a more accurate reading of the Bible.[14] A measure of the extent of this hellenization process might be seen in the crisis it provoked at the School of Nisibis under the Nestorian Church's auspices: in the last quarter of the sixth century, Henānā of Ḥadyab became the head of the famous catechetical school there, and precipitated a virtual revolution in the Nestorian church by his openness to a pluralistic religious culture that looked beyond the theology of Theodore of Mopsuestia toward the Byzantine West.[15]

---

[10] See André De Halleux, 'Une clé pour les hymnes d'Éphrem dans le MS Sinaï Syr. 10,' *Le Muséon* 85 (1972) 171–99; *id.,* 'La transmission des hymnes d'Éphrem d'après le MS. Sinaï Syr. 10. f. 165v–178a,' *Symposium Syriacum 1972* (Orientalia Christiana Analecta 197; Rome 1974), 21–63; B. Outtier, 'Contribution à l'étude de la préhistoire des collections d'hymnes d'Éphrem,' *Parole de l'Orient* 6–7 (1975–76) 49–61.

[11] On the *Vita Ephraemi* and its origins, see now J. P. Amar, 'The Syriac *Vita* Tradition of Ephrem the Syrian' (above n. 5). On the *Testament* of Ephraem, its inauthenticity, and its debt to the tradition that produced the *Vita,* see Amar, and E. Beck, *Des heiligen Ephraem des Syrers Sermones* IV (CSCO 335; Louvain 1973) xi–xiv.

[12] See Sebastian Brock, 'From Antagonism to Assimilation: Syriac Attitudes to Greek Learning,' in N. G. Garsoïan *et al.* (edd.), *East of Byzantium: Syria and Armenia in the Formative Period* (Washington 1982) 17–34.

[13] See R. Draguet, *Les formes syriaques de la matière de l'Histoire Lausiaque* (CSCO 389, 398; Louvain 1978). For Syriac translations of the works of the Cappadocians, beginning already in the fifth century, see Anton Baumstark, *Geschichte der syrischen Literatur* (Bonn 1922) 75–82.

[14] See Barbara Aland, 'Die philoxenianisch–harklenische Übersetzungstradition,' *Le Muséon* 94 (1981) 321–83.

[15] See Arthur Vööbus, *History of the School of Nisibis* (CSCO 266; Louvain 1965) 234–317.

301

The point is that, along with a greater Syrian participation in the intellectual and religious life of the Roman Empire in the early Byzantine period, the ascetic milieu in Syria developed in tandem with what was quickly becoming a cosmopolitan or 'international' ascetical culture in the fifth and sixth centuries.[16] While retaining elements of its own local tradition — including, as a primary feature, the memory of St. Ephraem — segments of this monastic culture soon adopted the classic Greek texts that set the tone for the cultivation of the ascetical life Empire-wide. Athanasius' *Vita Antonii*, the *Apophthegmata patrum*, Palladius' *Lausiac History*, as well as other works that breathed the spirit of Evagrius Ponticus, were all soon translated into Syriac;[17] and in the Syriac-speaking world this Evagrian, Byzantine model of asceticism eventually found its certificate of legitimacy in the ninth-century legend of St. Eugene, who was supposed to have brought the desert life of Nitria to Syria as early as the fourth century.[18]

It is within the largely monastic milieu of these cosmopolitan spiritual writers of the fifth and sixth centuries that one must look for the inspiration behind the Byzantine icon of the ascetic St. Ephraem. According to the *Vita*, Ephraem lived in a cave on a mountain near Edessa, from which he emerged only at the end of his life to help victims of the plague in that city. Incidentally, he is said to have composed some doctrinal hymns and exegetical homilies in Syriac, and then only to combat the popular heresy of Bar Dayṣān. In this account, Ephraem even ensured the authenticity of his style of ascetical life by a visit to the deserts of Egypt, where he is said to have met the Macarian hero, Bīshoi.[19] Afterward, according to the *Vita*, he guaranteed his

---

[16] For the spread of the ascetical culture in the West, see Philip Rousseau, *Ascetics, Authority, and the Church in the Age of Jerome and Cassian* (Oxford 1978). For the East, see P. Canivet, *Le Monachisme syrien selon Théodoret de Cyr* (Théologie historique 42; Paris 1977).

[17] See R. Draguet, 'L'Histoire Lausiaque — une œuvre écrite dans l'esprit d'Évagre,' *Revue d'histoire ecclésiastique* 41 (1946) 321–64; 42 (1947) 4–49; id., *Les Formes syriaques de la matière de l'Histoire Lausiaque* (CSCO 389–390; Louvain 1978); A. Guillaumont, 'Les versions syriaques de l'œuvre d'Évagre le Pontique et leur rôle dans la formation du vocabulaire ascétique syriaque,' in R. Lavenant (ed.), *IIIe Symposium Syriacum 1980* (Orientalia Christiana Analecta 221; Rome 1983), 35–41. The works of Evagrius enjoyed a special prestige in the Syriac-speaking world: see A. Guillaumont, *Les 'Kephalaia Gnostica' d'Évagre le Pontique* (Paris 1962) 196–99.

[18] See J.-M. Fiey, 'Aones, Awūn et Awgīn (Eugène), aux origines du monachisme mésopotamien,' *Analecta Bollandiana* 80 (1962) 52–81.

[19] On this incident in the *Vita*, see H. J. Polotsky, 'Ephraems Reise nach Aegypten,' *Orientalia* 2 (1933) 269–74. The late fourth-century Egyptian St. Bishoi came to play a special role in the spiritual life of the Syriac-speaking church, through his *Vita* and the liturgical celebration of the anchorite's accomplishments. In the present connection one should note that in all accounts, Egyptian and Syrian, Ephraem's visit is a dominant feature of the story. See the *Vita* in P. Bedjan (ed.), *Acta Martyrum et Sanctorum Syriace* 3 (Paris 1892) 572–620. See also E. R. Hambye, 'Pishay, anachorète — une commémoraison peu connue du calendrier de l'église syrienne d'Antioche,' *L'Orient syrien* 7 (1962) 255–58.

orthodoxy for the emperor's church by an *ad limina* visit to St. Basil of Caesarea, even fleeing priestly ordination at Basil's hands, in good Evagrian style, although accepting the diaconate.[20] Parallel to this account, Ephraem's *Testament* reflects the world-view of a true ascetic hero, a desert solitary of the stature of those holy men whose stories John of Ephesus or even Cyril of Scythopolis might have told. Ephraem's *Testament,* in fact, echoes many sentiments in common with the *Testament* of St. Sabas, of Palestinian monastic fame.[21]

The Graeco-Syrian monastic milieu from which the Syriac *Vita Ephraemi* and Ephraem's *Testament* come may most plausibly be associated with fifth- and sixth-century Edessa and its environs.[22] Both works present Ephraem almost exclusively as living near Edessa, virtually ignoring the fact that Ephraem was originally a member of the church of Nisibis;[23] he spent all but the last ten years of his life, in fact, in the metropolis whose surrender to the Persians under the emperor Jovian (363–364) he so poignantly lamented in his hymns *Against Julian.*[24] It is true that some of Ephraem's most important compositions come from the decade he later spent in Edessa. But the virtually exclusive attention to Edessa in the *Vita* and the *Testament* says more about the concerns of their authors to celebrate that 'Blessed City' than it does about Ephraem's actual career.

---

[20] See O. Rousseau, 'La rencontre de saint Ephrem et de saint Basile,' *L'Orient syrien* 2 (1957) 261–84; 3 (1958) 73–90.

[21] Ephraem's *Testament* was first published and translated into French by Rubens Duval, 'Le Testament de saint Éphrem,' *Journal asiatique* 9th series, 18 (1901) 234–319. The critical edition, with German translation, is by Edmund Beck, *Des heiligen Ephraem des Syrers Sermones* IV (CSCO 334–335; Louvain 1973) 334.43–69 (Syriac); 335.53–80 (German). Sabas' 'testament' is a reproach of himself for his sinfulness. The so far unpublished Arabic text is in Vatican Arabic MS 71, fols. 210–14.

[22] See J. B. Segal, *Edessa, 'the Blessed City'* (Oxford 1970); H. J. W. Drijvers, 'Edessa,' in *Theologische Realenzyklopädie* 9 (1982) 272–88, esp. 284–88.

[23] The *Vita* presents the 'story of Mar Ephrem, hermit and master of the Syrians, who was in Edessa in Mesopotamia': Amar, 'The Syriac *Vita* Tradition of Ephrem the Syrian' (above, n. 5) 1. The writer notes Ephraem's birth in Nisibis, and his association with the saintly bishop Jacob. But the *Vita* says nothing about Ephraem's ministry in his native city. In fact the *Vita* reports that Ephraem was baptized only after the surrender of Nisibis to the Persians, and just before his move to Edessa, where his career unfolds. See Amar 34ff. The *Testament* celebrates Edessa, Ephraem's home, as 'the mother of wise men.' See Beck, *Des heiligen Ephraem des Syrers Sermones* IV (CSCO 334) 50.234.

[24] Edmund Beck, *Des heiligen Ephraem des Syrers Hymnen de Paradiso und Contra Julianum* (CSCO 174–175; Louvain 1957). See also Samuel N. C. Lieu, *The Emperor Julian, Panegyric and Polemic* (Liverpool 1986) 90–134; Sidney H. Griffith, 'Ephraem the Syrian's Hymns "Against Julian," Meditations on History and Imperial Power,' *Vigiliae Christianae* 41 (1987) 238–66.

Edessa, in the fifth and sixth centuries, was the Byzantine capital of Syriac culture at a time when a distinctive 'West Syrian' style was coming to the fore. After the middle of the sixth century two hierarchies emerged in Syria, reflecting the distinct dyophysite and monophysite christologies; but both of them, Melkite or Jacobite, were heirs of the Graeco-Syrian culture we have already described. Among the classic literary products of this culture, in addition to the writings of preachers and poets, are such nationalistic compositions as the *Doctrina Addai* and the *Acts of Sharbel,* two works of the period that celebrate the fame of Edessa's native nobility and their early reception of Christianity. Both works also celebrate Edessa's Roman connections and reflect a virtually Eusebian ecclesiology — a Byzantine characteristic that further bespeaks the bilingual cast of the culture.[25] Nor were the cultural influences in this period only from Greek to Syriac; the accomplishments of Romanos the Melode (fl. ca. 540) remind one of how Syriac literary genres might pass westward into the Greek-speaking world. And behind Romanos, more than one researcher has discerned the inspiration of Ephraem the Syrian.[26]

This cosmopolitan, Graeco-Syrian monastic milieu was the setting from which we have inherited virtually all the numerous Greek hymns and sermons that go under the name of St. Ephraem. Sozomen recorded, with some surprise, that even while Ephraem lived, his works were being translated into Greek;[27] today, in the *Clavis Patrum Graecorum,* the number of pages required to list the works in Greek attributed to St. Ephraem is second only to the number of pages devoted to the works of St. John Chrysostom![28] But the fact is that, of all of them, only the popular *Sermo Asceticus* can be shown to have its roots in the genuine Syriac works of St. Ephraem.[29]

The influence of this independent corpus of 'St. Ephraem Graecus,' bolstered by the popularity of Ephraem's profile as a Byzantine ascetic and monk, has been enormous. In medieval Europe, these ascetical homilies found a home in

---

[25] On this subject see Sidney H. Griffith, 'History and the *Doctrina Addai,*' forthcoming.

[26] See now William L. Petersen, *The Diatessaron and Ephrem Syrus as Sources of Romanos the Melodist* (CSCO 475; Louvain 1985). See also S. P. Brock, 'Syriac and Greek Hymnography: Problems of Origins,' *Journal of the Iraqī Academy Syriac Corporation* 6 (1981–1982) 1–11; reprinted in *Studia Patristica* 16 (TU 129; Berlin 1985) 77–81.

[27] See n. 2 above.

[28] See M. Geerard, *Clavis Patrum Graecorum* 2 (Turnhout 1974) 366–468. See also J. Schamp, 'Éphrem de Nisibe et Photios: Pour une chasse aux textes à travers la bibliothèque,' *Le Muséon* 98 (1985) 293–314.

[29] See the Greek text and Latin translation in J. S. Assemani (ed.), *Ephraem Syri Opera Omnia* 1 (Rome 1732) 40–70. Concordances to this text and Syriac texts attributed to Ephraem, with further bibliography, are listed in Geerard, *Clavis Patrum Graecorum* 2. See also Schamp, 'Éphrem de Nisibe et Photios,' n. 28 above.

monastic libraries;[30] in Byzantium, so important a monastic figure as Theodore Studites held up the example of St. Ephraem for the inspiration of his monks in their own ascetical endeavors.[31] In the monasteries of the Holy Land after the Islamic conquest, the works of 'Ephraem Graecus' were among the earliest texts translated into Christian Arabic, and this by persons whose native speech may well have been Syriac.[32] In Kievan Rus', the works of 'Ephraem Graecus' were especially dear to the influential monk Abraham of Smolensk, whose principal disciple even adopted the religious name Ephraem.[33] In our own century, after the first publications of St. Ephraem's genuine Syriac works in the West, but still with the traditional view of him as a Byzantine ascetic in mind, Pope Benedict XV proclaimed St. Ephraem a doctor of the Universal Church, in an encyclical letter issued on 5 October 1920.[34] And finally, in Western Christian iconography, the best-known portrayal of the saint is in a composition known as the 'Dormition of Ephraem Syrus,' in which Ephraem's body lying on a funeral slab, surrounded by mourners, is the focal point of a tableau made up of other scenes from a cycle of hermits, stylites, and recluses. Exemplars of this composite scenario are in both the Vatican Gallery and the monastery of Dokheiariou on Mt. Athos. It is a perfect iconic presentation of what we have been calling the profile of St. Ephraem Byzantinus.[35]

B. *The Portrait of St. Ephraem Syrus*

There are two categories of documents that one might examine in search of information about St. Ephraem the Syrian — about his own life and times, and

---

[30] See G. Bardy, 'Le souvenir de saint Éphrem dans le haut moyen âge latin,' *Revue du moyen âge latin* 2 (1946) 297–300; J. Kirchmeyer and D. Hemmerdinger-Iliadou, 'Saint Ephrem et le "Liber Scintillarum",' *Recherches de science religieuse* 46 (1958) 545–50; T. S. Pattie, 'Ephraem the Syrian and the Latin Manuscripts of "De Paenitentia",' *The British Library Journal* 13 (1987) 1–24.

[31] In Sermon 42, Theodore proposed the ascetical example of St. John Chrysostom and of 'Ephraem, famous in song': *S. Theodori Studitae Parva Catechesis*, in A. Mai, *Nova Patrum Bibliotheca* 9 (Rome 1888) 102. In his *Testament*, Theodore confessed his acceptance of the example of the oriental monks, especially Barsanuphius, Anthony, Ephraem and others. See PG 99.1815. Another Studite monk, now anonymous, remarked that the portraits of these same 'oriental monks' were to be found in the Hagia Sophia in Constantinople: see 'De S. Barsanuphio,' AS April 2 (Paris and Rome 1866) 22.

[32] See J. M. Sauget, 'Le dossier Éphrémien du manuscrit arabe Strasbourg 4226 et de ses membra disiecta,' *Orientalia Christiana Periodica* 42 (1976) 426–58; Samir Khalil, 'L'Ephrem arabe, état des travaux,' *Symposium Syriacum 1976* (Orientalia Christiana Analecta 205; Rome 1978) 229–40.

[33] See G. P. Fedotov, *The Russian Religious Mind: Kievan Christianity, the 10th to the 13th Centuries* (New York 1960) 158–75; G. Podskalsky, *Christentum und theologische Literatur in der kiever Rus' (988–1237)* (Munich 1982) 50, 101–104, 140.

[34] Benedict XV, 'Principi apostolorum Petro,' *Acta Apostolicae Sedis* 12 (1920) 457–73.

[35] See John R. Martin, 'The *Death of Ephraim* in Byzantine and Early Italian Painting,' *The Art Bulletin* 33 (1951) 217–25.

about his reputation in later Syriac-speaking communities, outside of the monastic circles in which the icon of St. Ephraem Byzantinus was cherished. First of all, and most importantly, one must turn to the saint's genuine works in Syriac; secondly, one may consult the historical and hagiographical documents of the Syriac-speaking church to learn of the fame the saint enjoyed in the parochial and diocesan spheres that in fact composed the scene of his ministry. Few as they are, these hagiographical testimonies all celebrate not the memory of a retiring ascetic, but the career of a busy minister of the church.

The 'Chronicle of Edessa,' an annotated list of important events and persons in that city's history, barely mentions St. Ephraem; it simply records that 'in the year 684, on the ninth of the month Hazîrān, the man of wisdom, Mar Ephraem, left this world.'[36] (The Seleucid date can be translated into 9 June 373 on the Gregorian calendar.) This notice from the archives of the 'Blessed City' provides one of the few fixed points of chronology in Ephraem's life that is still recoverable. The other interesting feature of the entry in the *Chronicle* is that St. Ephraem is presented not as an ascetic, but as a man of learning, a wise man; this epithet accords well with the other title by which St. Ephraem is universally remembered in Syriac sources, including the otherwise Evagrian Syriac *Vita*, namely 'the Teacher' (*malpônô*).

The influential writer of Syriac verse homilies, Jacob of Serugh (ca. 451–521), during the very years when the icon of St. Ephraem Byzantinus was in production in the Graeco-Syrian monastic communities of east Byzantium, wrote a now justly famous homily on 'the holy man, Mar Ephraem, the Teacher.'[37] In it, Jacob — a bishop with all the cares of the pastor before his mind — presents Ephraem as a skilled preacher and composer of doctrinal hymns carefully wrought to commend right teaching and to refute error. Jacob celebrates Ephraem as:

> A marvelous rhetor, who surpassed the Greeks in declamation;
>   who could include a thousand subjects in a single speech.
> A divine citharist; he set his phrases to verse, to make a joyful sound
>   in mighty wonder.[38]

Moreover, Jacob goes on to say, Ephraem trained choirs to give praise to God in song; and the bishop makes a special point of the fact that the saint included women in this musical ministry:

---

[36] I. Guidi, *Chronica Minora* (CSCO 1; Paris 1903) 5.

[37] Text in P. Bedjan, *Acta Martyrum et Sanctorum Syriace* 3 (Paris–Leipzig 1892) 665–79. A new edition of this important text is in preparation by Joseph P. Amar, of the Diocese of St. Maron and the University of Notre Dame.

[38] Bedjan, *Acta Martyrum* 3.667.

The blessed one saw that the women
    were silent in the hymn of praise.
The wise man judged that it was right
    for them to sing Alleluia!

As Moses gave the young women tambourines,
    the discerning one composed doctrinal hymns,
    and gave them to the virgins to sing.[39]

Finally, one may quote another apt line from Jacob of Serugh's homily on Ephraem, a line perhaps also appropriate to the present essay:

It did not bore the eminent Ephraem to teach,
    may it not bore you to listen to a speech about him.[40]

Echoing Jacob of Serugh's celebration of Ephraem's pedagogical talents is Barḥadbshabbā's († before 650) record — probably somewhat anachronistic — of Ephraem's role in the catechetical schools of Nisibis and Edessa. Barḥadbshabbā accords Ephraem the title of 'Interpeter (*mpaššqōnô*),' an accolade that identifies him as the local church's chief biblical exegete, and the master of the city's school of religious education. In fact, Barḥadbshabbā says that Jacob of Nisibis († 337/8) put Ephraem into a position in Nisibis comparable to that which bishop Alexander of Alexandria accorded the young deacon Athanasius in his own city after the council of Nicaea (325).[41] And Barḥadbshabbā goes on to say that in later years in the church of the East, before the works of Theodore of Mopsuestia had been translated into Syriac, the then 'Interpreter' at the school of Nisibis was still passing on 'the traditions of Mar Ephraem.'[42] While one may be legitimately skeptical about Ephraem's role as founding master of the schools of Nisibis and Edessa,[43] what is clear is that, in the seventh century, Barḥadbshabbā was claiming a patristic authority for Ephraem in the Syriac-speaking community comparable to that of Athanasius in the Byzantine church. Ephraem's Syriac fame, therefore, was not so much that of an ascetic as that of a doctrinally correct teacher, a doctor of the church.

There is no greater mark of distinction for a teacher than for others to adopt and to transmit his teaching. By this measure, too, Ephraem was the *malpōnô*

---

[39] *Ibid.* 672.

[40] *Ibid.* 676.

[41] Addai Scher, 'Mar Barhadbšabba 'Arbaya: Cause de la fondation des écoles,' *Patrologia Orientalis* 4 (1908) 377. On the sense of *mpaššqōnô* as Barḥadbshabbā would have understood it, see A. Vööbus, *The Statutes of the School of Nisibis* (Stockholm 1961) 73.

[42] Scher, 'Mar Barhadbšabba,' 382.

[43] Ephraem was probably never an official *mpaššqōnô* at Nisibis or Edessa, although he was an important teacher in the pre-history of these famous schools. See A. Vööbus, *History of the School of Nisibis* (CSCO 266; Louvain 1965) 7–9.

of the Syrians, to judge by the evidence of the persistence of his doctrine in the works of later Syriac writers. Philoxenus of Mabbūg († 523), for example, preserves much of Ephraem's language in his own treatise *de Deo uno et trino*.[44] Biblical exegetes such as Theodore bar Kônî and the compiler of the *Gannat Bussāmê*, to name only two, cite Ephraem's interpretations of the scriptures as authoritative opinions, to which a special respect is due.[45] And it would be hard to over-estimate the influence of Ephraem's own commentary on the *Diatessaron*, always popular in the Syriac-speaking world.[46]

The memory of Ephraem, the authoritative interpreter of the Bible, can be found as late as the fourteenth century in Syriac texts. The Nestorian bio-bibliographer ʿAbdishōʿ bar Berīkā († 1318), for example, speaks of ʿEphraem the Great, the Prophet of the Syrians,ʾ[47] and he lists Ephraem's writings with an obvious preference for the biblical commentaries and the controversial pieces that had come down under the holy man's name. For by the fourteenth century the practice was already old by which Ephraem's name, like that of his contemporary Athanasius, was often affixed to a work simply to commend its contents to the Church,[48] a practice that also attests Ephraem's renown as a guarantor of right doctrine.

In testimony to Ephraem's renown as a teacher, it remains only to notice that among the Armenian versions of his works, the biblical commentaries attributed to him surpass all other categories of writings in number.[49] Although there are several important *madrōšê*, notably those on Nicomedia, which have survived largely only in Armenian, Bible commentaries, both genuine and spurious, predominate. The point is that, unlike the icon of Ephraem cherished in Byzantine circles, in Armenia it was the memory of a reliable teacher and interpreter of the scriptures that was prized.[50]

---

[44] See E. Beck, 'Philoxenos und Ephräm,' *Oriens Christianus* 46 (1962) 61–76.

[45] See Lutz Brade, *Untersuchungen zum Scholienbuch des Theodoros bar Konai* (Göttinger Orientforschungen 8; Wiesbaden 1975) 78–80, 121; G. J. Reinink, *Studien zur Quellen- und Traditionsgeschichte des Evangelienkommentars der Gannat Bussame* (CSCO 414; Louvain 1979) 21, 26 *et passim*.

[46] See L. Leloir, *S. Ephrem, commentaire de l'évangile concordant, version arménienne* (CSCO 137 and 145; Louvain 1953–1954); *id., S. Ephrem, commentaire de l'évangile concordant, texte syriaque* (*Manuscrit Chester Beatty 709*) (Dublin 1962); *id., L'évangile concordant ou le Diatessaron* (Sources chrétiennes 121; Paris 1966). See also the studies cited in n. 26 above.

[47] J. S. Assemani, *Bibliotheca Orientalis Clementino-Vaticana* 3.1 (Rome 1725) 61ff. See the English translation in G. P. Badger, *The Nestorians and their Rituals* II (London 1852) 328.

[48] For the Syriac works attributed to Ephraem that are of questionable authenticity, and for a list of misattributed works, see J. Melki, 'Saint Éphrem le Syrien, un bilan de l'édition critique,' *Parole de l'Orient* 11 (1983) 44–88.

[49] *Ibid.* 42–44.

[50] Eventually the documents that present Ephraem in the icon of the holy monk were translated into Armenian. The Syriac *Vita* appeared in the early 12th century; Ephraem's

But in the Syriac-speaking world, Ephraem was never only a teacher. He was also a melodist, a liturgical hymnographer, and this aspect of his fame, too, was celebrated early and late. Ephraem himself, as if in passing, often mentions his own metrical compositions. So he speaks of the 'garland of melodies' his choirs of chaste singers weave for the glory of God;[51] and in what he says to God at the end of his *Hymns against Heresies,* it is clear that he sees his roles as teacher and melodist as one vocation:

> May I have built, as I was able,
> Enclosures of *madrōšê*
> For the lambs of your flock.[52]

Ephraem's Syriac *madrōšê* were catalogued by their melody lines in the manuscript tradition,[53] and stanzas from many of them found a permanent home among the songs and chants in the liturgical books of the Syriac-speaking churches.[54] Indeed, the title by which St. Ephraem is still widely known, 'the Lyre of the Holy Spirit,' appears as early as in a letter of Theodoret of Cyrrhus († ca. 466) to the monks of Constantinople, in which the Syrian bishop names the orthodox teachers whom he accepts, Ephraem among them.[55] And Jacob of Serugh († 521) echoes Theodoret's image with his own sobriquet for Ephraem, 'God's Harpist.'[56] St. Ephraem, therefore, was by all accounts the leading master of both doctrine and verse in the Syriac-speaking church; he was a man of action — a bishop's man, in fact — and a doctor of the church.

II
The Syrian Holy Man and his Church

In contrast with these later portraits, St. Ephraem's genuine works in Syriac are by far the most reliable sources of information about his life and ministry. Scholars have long noticed the contrast between the profile of the withdrawn

---

Testament was translated from Greek in the 11th or 12th century, as was the encomium of Ephraem attributed to Gregory of Nyssa. See L. Ter-Pétrossian and B. Outtier, *Textes arméniens relatifs à s. Ephrem* (CSCO 473–474; Louvain 1985).

[51] E. Beck, *Des heiligen Ephraem des Syrers Paschahymnen* (CSCO 248; Louvain 1964) 82–83. See also p. 84, stanzas 8 & 9.

[52] E. Beck, *Des heiligen Ephraem des Syrers Hymnen contra Haereses* (CSCO 169; Louvain 1957) 211–12.

[53] See n. 10 above.

[54] See J. Gribomont, 'La tradition liturgique des hymnes pascales de S. Éphrem,' *Parole de l'Orient* 4 (1973) 191–246.

[55] Theodoret of Cyrrhus, Epistle 145 (PG 83.1345D).

[56] Bedjan, *Acta Martyrum* 3 (above n. 37) 667.

St. Ephraem that emerges in one's mind from reading the *Vita Ephraemi* and associated hagiographical texts, and the picture of a busy minister of the church that even a casual perusal of Ephraem's own works suggests. Accordingly, beginning early in the present century — after the Louvain Orientalist T. J. Lamy had brought out an important selection of the saint's authentic hymns and sermons between 1882 and 1902[57] — a number of studies have been published devoted to Ephraem's biography. The purpose has been to integrate the two divergent portraits of the saint.[58] Prior to the point in mid-century when Dom Edmund Beck, o.s.b. began his series of critical editions of the most important Syriac works attributed to St. Ephraem,[59] the tendency among most scholars was to accept the Byzantine icon of Ephraem the ascetic as correct in its essential affirmations about the style of his sanctity. Once the more improbable events in the Syriac *Vita* were discounted, such as the saint's visit to the Egyptian desert or his meeting with St. Basil in Cappadocia, one simply added what one learned of the busy minister in Nisibis from the *Carmina Nisibena*, to what one read in the *Vita* about the retiring anchorite on the mountain outside Edessa.[60]

What remained intact in this scenario was the vision of St. Ephraem as an ascetic holy man in the Evagrian style. What Beck's critical editions of the Syriac works ascribed to St. Ephraem makes possible is a new glimpse of the genuinely Syrian holy man, whose portrait resembles much more Aphrahat's *iḥîdōyô*, the member of the Syrian church's *bnay qyōmô*,[61] than it does Palladius' anchorite monk. It is the purpose of the second section of this essay to bring Ephraem the *iḥîdōyô* into sharper focus.

A. *Arthur Vööbus' Asceticism in the Syrian Orient*

Arthur Vööbus did most of his research into the biography of St. Ephraem, and conducted his studies of the asceticism Ephraem commends in his writings, prior to Edmund Beck's project to publish critical editions of the saint's genuine Syriac works. Vööbus was well aware of the problems

---

[57] T. J. Lamy, *Sancti Ephraem Syri Hymni et Sermones* (Malines 1882–1902). See Melki, 'S. Éphrem, un bilan' (above, n. 48) 18.

[58] See, e.g., E. Bouvy, 'Les sources historiques de la vie de saint Éphrem,' *Revue Augustinienne* 2 (1903) 155–64; S. Schiwietz, *Das morgenländische Mönchtum* III (Mödling bei Wien 1938) 93–165.

[59] For a summary account of Beck's editions between the years 1955 and 1975 see Melki, 'S. Éphrem, un bilan' (above n. 48) 23–41.

[60] So S. Schiwietz could speak of St. Ephraem, the Syrian doctor of the church, 'as an ascetic in Nisibis and later a monk outside Edessa': *Das morgenländische Mönchtum* III 93.

[61] See Aphrahat's exposition on the *bnay qyōmô* in I. Parisot, *Aphraatis Sapientis Persae Demonstrationes* (Patrologia Syriaca 1; Paris 1894) 239–312.

associated with establishing the authenticity of texts attributed to Ephraem, and he was duly skeptical of the Syriac *Vita Ephraemi* and associated hagiographical material.[62] In fact, at one point in his justly famous *History of Asceticism in the Syrian Orient,* he stated clearly what might be taken as the topic sentence of the present writer's own thesis: 'The picture of the historical Ephrem is quite different from the Ephrem of hagiography.'[63] Nevertheless, Vööbus did think that St. Ephraem was the author of the *Testament* that goes under his name and of five Syriac texts on the ascetical life that severally laud the anchoritic lifestyle of those 'mournful solitaries' and 'reclusive mountaineers' who were the *dramatis personae,* one knows now, of a penitential movement that gained popularity in Syria toward the end of the fourth and well into the fifth century.[64] Because of his conviction that St. Ephraem was the author of these pieces, Vööbus conceived of the saint's own ascetical ideals in terms that are prominent in the *Testament* and the five ascetical texts attributed to him. According to Vööbus,

> Ephrem believed the monastic life to be an institution of penitence, locally tied to the mountains and deserts as the locale in which one may recover his lost health. Those in the world, having fallen into sin, will find in the abandoned places a terrain in which they will experience God's judgment and renewal. . . . Ephrem's ideal of the monastic life is anchoritism.[65]

Leaving aside for the moment the understanding of the term 'monasticism' as it appears here, it is clear that for Vööbus, following the lead of texts he takes to be authentic, St. Ephraem cherished and promoted a spirit of *contemptus mundi* that is all but absolute. Vööbus goes on to say:

> It does not take long, after even the first acquaintance with Ephrem's authentic writings, to realize that here we are in the province of mortification. Asceticism with all its means is directed against the human body. A longing for the spiritual life is equated with the contempt for nature. . . . The ultimate

---

[62] See A. Vööbus, *Literary, Critical and Historical Studies in Ephrem the Syrian* (Stockholm 1958).

[63] A. Vööbus, *History of Asceticism in the Syrian Orient* (CSCO 197; Louvain 1960) 89.

[64] The titles of the five texts bespeak their themes: the 'Letter to the Mountaineers,' the homilies 'On the Solitude of the Anchorites,' 'On Anchorites, Hermits and Mourners,' 'On Anchorites, Mourners and Hermits,' and 'On the Solitaries, Mourners.' All of these texts, save the last one, have been edited, together with the *Testament,* in E. Beck, *Des heiligen Ephraem des Syrers Sermones* IV (CSCO 334; Louvain 1973). For Vööbus' discussion of them, see A. Vööbus, 'Beiträge zur kritischen Sichtung der asketischen Schriften, die unter dem Namen Ephraem des Syrers überliefert sind,' *Oriens Christianus* 39 (1955) 48–55; *id., Literary, Critical and Historical Studies* 59–86; *id., History of Asceticism* (above n. 63) 2–10. See now the studies of Edward G. Mathews, Jr., 'Isaac of Antioch, "On Solitaries, Mourners and Hermits"': A Translation and Commentary' (MA Thesis, The Catholic University of America 1987).

[65] Vööbus, *History of Asceticism* (above, n. 63) 93–94.

purpose of subjugation is the killing of bodily needs. Life is death for the monk.[66]

The ideal of asceticism evoked here is, in fact, faithful to the tenor of the Syriac texts on the solitary life that Vööbus took to be authentic works of St. Ephraem. One of the results of Beck's critical examination of these Syriac texts, however, was to show that the *Testament* and three of the four homiletic pieces on asceticism cited by Vööbus are inauthentic: St. Ephraem did not write them.[67] Rather, these texts and others were included among the saint's works by those who preserved and collected them in later times — the very communities of Graeco-Syrian monks from whose milieu Ephraem's Syriac *Vita* and *Testament* were to come.[68] As for St. Ephraem himself, it was only toward the end of his life, as we shall suggest below, that he perhaps adverted in his compositions to the new style of asceticism in Syria, and praised its principal Edessan exponent, St. Julian Saba.[69]

St. Ephraem himself was a Syrian holy man of the old style. He was a bishop's man, a 'single' in God's service, a minister in the local church, one of those with a special status in the community whom some Syriac writers called, collectively, *bnay qyōmô*. From Ephraem's own authentic works, one may catch a closer glimpse of his career.

B. *St. Ephraem's Career*

In recent years a number of prominent scholars have sketched the biography of St. Ephraem on the basis of what they could glean from a survey of his authentic compositions.[70] The resulting portrait is assuredly no more than a

---

[66] *Ibid.* 97.

[67] See E. Beck, 'Ein Beitrag zur Terminologie des ältesten syrischen "Monchtums," ' *Studia Anselmiana* 38 (1956) 254–67; *id.*, 'Asketentum und Mönchtum bei Ephraem,' in *Il Monachesimo Orientale* (Orientalia Christiana Analecta 153; Rome 1958) 341–62 (French translation in *L'Orient syrien* 3 [1958] 273–98). In these important articles, Beck was reacting principally not to Vööbus' studies, but to the provocative article of Alfred Adam, 'Grundbegriffe des Mönchtums in sprachlicher Sicht,' *Zeitschrift für Kirchengeschichte* 65 (1953/54) 209–39. Nevertheless, in these studies Beck developed the views that enabled him definitively to perceive the inauthenticity of the ascetical texts Vööbus took to be genuine works of St. Ephraem. See E. Beck, *Sermones* IV (above n. 11) v–xi. See also Melki, 'S. Éphrem, un bilan' 72–76, 80–82, 87–88.

[68] See nn. 10, 22, 23 above.

[69] See E. Beck, *Des heiligen Ephraem des Syrers Hymnen auf Abraham Kidunaya und Julianus Saba* (CSCO 322–323; Louvain 1972); Melki, 'S. Éphrem, un bilan' 38, 57–60.

[70] See E. Beck, 'Éphrem le Syrien (saint),' *Dictionnaire de spiritualité,* 4.788–800; *id.*, 'Ephraem Syrus,' *Reallexikon für Antike und Christentum* 5.520–31; R. P. Murray, 'Ephrem Syrus, St.,' *A Catholic Dictionary of Theology* 2.220–23; *id.*, 'Ephraem Syrus,' *Theologische Realenzyklopädie* 9.755–62; A. De Halleux, 'Saint Éphrem le Syrien,' *Revue théologique de Louvain* 14 (1983) 328–55.

sketch. But there is more than enough detail in it for us to see that the saint never enjoyed an interval in his busy pastoral career in which to engage in the kind of Evagrian-style ἀναχώρησις the Byzantine icon of him suggests, or the Syriac ascetical texts, mistakenly ascribed to him by Vööbus and others, commend in even more enthusiastic terms. Rather, the bare outline of Ephraem's career abundantly seconds the portrait of the contemplative teacher Syriac tradition has preserved in many documents that have no immediate connection with the Byzantine ascetical movements of the late fourth or fifth centuries.

It has become customary to reckon the year 306 as the year of Ephraem's birth, but the calculation is in fact purely conjectural, resting on estimates derived from no more solid a foundation than reports contained in the Syriac *Vita* of the saint.[71] One is on firmer ground in claiming that Ephraem was born a Christian, to a mother originally from the town of Amida, who presumably raised her son in the faith, since in his *Hymns on Virginity* he says, 'Your truth was with my youth, your reality by my old age.'[72] One no longer knows when Ephraem was baptized, although he refers to his own baptism in his *Hymns Against Heresies* (III 3) in terms that suggest he was old enough to profess as his own the Trinitarian faith.[73]

When he reached his majority, Ephraem came into the service of bishop Jacob of Nisibis (ca. 308-338), and he remained in the episcopal service of Nisibis through the tenure of the next three bishops, Babū († 346), Vologeses († 361), and Abraham († 363). Ephraem's diocesan service, therefore, lasted some forty years until the day in the reign of bishop Abraham, in the year 363, when he and other refugees left Nisibis on the occasion of her surrender to the Persians as part of the agreement Emperor Jovian (363-364) made after his predecessor Julian had met his death deep in Persian territory.[74]

After the surrender of Nisibis, and his flight from the city westward to the environs of Amida, Ephraem came eventually to Edessa; there he entered the service of bishop Barses (361-371), whom the Arianizing Emperor Valens (364-378) translated to the lesser see of Ḥarrān in 371.[75] Two years later — on

---

[71] This observation and the following points in the biography of Ephraem follow the scheme set forth in A. De Halleux, 'Saint Éphrem le Syrien,' 330-33.

[72] E. Beck, *Des heiligen Ephraem des Syrers Hymnen de Virginitate* 37.10 (CSCO 223 [Louvain 1962] 135).

[73] See E. Beck, *Des heiligen Ephraem des Syrers Hymnen contra Haereses* 3.3 (CSCO 169 [Louvain 1957] 11).

[74] See Ephraem's reflections in his Julian hymns in E. Beck, *Des heiligen Ephraem des Syrers Hymnen de Paradiso und Contra Julianum* (CSCO 174; Louvain 1957) 66-91. See also Sidney H. Griffith, 'Ephraem the Syrian's Hymns "Against Julian": Meditations on History and Imperial Power,' *Vigiliae Christianae* 41 (1987) 238-66.

[75] See E. Beck, *Des heiligen Ephraem des Syrers Carmina Nisibena, erster Teil* 33.7 (CSCO 218 [Louvain 1961] 79).

9 June 373, according to the *Chronicle of Edessa* — Ephraem died,[76] but not before, earlier in the year, according to Palladius, he had helped to organize relief services in Edessa for the victims of famine.[77]

It is readily apparent, then, that by far the major part of Ephraem's ministry was spent in Nisibis. Edessa looms so large in the hagiography of Ephraem only because his memory was cherished there. In the fifth and sixth centuries Edessa became the capital city, so to speak, of the Syriac-speaking Christians in the early Byzantine empire. And it was in the Graeco-Syrian monastic communities of Edessa and her environs that Ephraem's works were collected and preserved, and that the hagiographers burnished the icon of St. Ephraem Byzantinus that we have characterized above.[78] But it was his ministry in Nisibis that Ephraem himself celebrated in his *Carmina Nisibena*. It is clear in these compositions that with varying degrees of reverence, awe, and genuine affection the service of the bishops of Nisibis was uppermost in Ephraem's mind. For this reason, to couch the discussion in modern Western terms, it is worth recalling some of the *Leitmotive* of his ecclesiology,[79] with the view to highlighting his own position in diocesan life.

The twin poles of reference for Ephraem's ecclesiology were the Byzantine Roman emperor in Constantinople, whom Ephraem calls simply 'the king' (*malkô*), and the bishop of the local Christian community, whom Ephraem usually calls 'the shepherd' (*rō'yô*), but sometimes 'the priest' (*kōhnô*). His view of their relationship is thoroughly Eusebian; so in the *Carmina Nisibena* he states his position succinctly:

> Let the priests pray for the kings,
>   to be a wall for humankind:
> Victory for the kings;
>   the Faith for the priests.
> Victory preserves bodies,
>   the Faith souls.
> Kings should put a stop to fighting;
>   Priests should put a stop to speculation.[80]

---

[76] Guidi, *Chronica Minora* (above, n. 36) 5.

[77] Butler, *The Lausiac History* (above, n. 1) 2.127.

[78] See nn. 10 and 22 above. See also Joseph P. Amar, 'Monastic Influence and (Greek) Cultural Bias in the *Vita* Tradition of Ephraem the Syrian,' to appear.

[79] On Ephraem's ecclesiology, see J. Molitor, 'Die kirchlichen Ämter und Stände in der Paulusexegese des hl. Ephräm,' in *Die Kirche und ihre Ämter und Stände: Festgabe Kardinal Frings* (Cologne 1960) 379ff.; I. Ortiz de Urbina, 'L'évêque et son rôle d'après saint Ephrém,' *Parole de l'Orient* 4 (1973) 137–46; R. Murray, *Symbols of Church and Kingdom: A Study in Early Syriac Tradition* (Cambridge 1975); Sidney H. Griffith, 'Ephraem, the Deacon of Edessa, and the Church of the Empire,' in T. Halton and J. P. Williman (edd.), *Diakonia: Studies in Honor of Robert T. Meyer* (Washington, D.C. 1986) 22–52.

[80] Beck, *Carmina Nisibena* 21.23 (CSCO 218.59).

The church for Ephraem, therefore, is not a disembodied, withdrawn spirit; rather, the one flock lives in both the civil and the ecclesiastical spheres. But the purity of the faith is the business of the ecclesiastical sphere, within which the shepherd-priest is the 'conscience' (*re'yōnô*) from which the members of the church purchase the fresh bread of 'doctrine' (*yulpōnô*).[81] And it was in the province of doctrinal teaching (*yulpōnô*) that Ephraem the teacher (*malpōnô*) apparently saw himself to be of most service to his bishops — to judge only by what has come down to us from his pen.

The bishop, as shepherd-priest (*rō'yô – kōhnô*) of the sheep ('*ōnô*) in his flock (*mar'ītô*), tended his charges with the assistance of a 'fold of herdsmen' (*dayrô d'allōnê*), to use St. Ephraem's terminology.[82] Indeed, it was from the ranks of these 'herdsmen,' it seems, that the shepherd himself was chosen when the opportunity for a new appointment arose.[83] Significantly, Ephraem used the title 'herdsman' ('*allōnô*) to distinguish his own role in church life. In the last of his *Hymns Against Heresies* he wrote of himself,

> O Lord, may the works of your herdsman ('*allōnô*)
>   not be negated;
> I will not then have troubled your sheep,
>   but as far as I was able
> I will have kept the wolves away from them,
>   and I will have built, as far as I was capable,
> Enclosures of *madrōšê*
>   for the lambs of your flock.[84]

In the very next stanza of the poem, Ephraem goes on to say,

> I will have made a disciple
>   of the rude and the imbecile,
> And I will have given him a strong hold
>   on the herdsmen's ('*allōnê*) staff,
> the healers' medicine,
>   and the disputants' armor.[85]

It is clear from these lines that St. Ephraem included himself on the 'pastoral team' of the church of Nisibis. He was one of the 'herdsmen' ('*allōnê*) in the 'fold' (*dayrô*) of those who wielded the herdsman's staff (*ḥûṭrô*) over the flock. Presumably, these 'herdsmen' in the shepherd's retinue were the 'deacons' (*šammōšê, mšammšōnê*) and 'presbyters' (*qašîšê*) among the bishop's clergy, in

---

[81] *Ibid.* 17.3 (46).

[82] *Ibid.* The use of the word *dayrô* here is instructive. Later it will become the standard Syriac word for 'monastery.' Here it applies to a 'fold' of ministers, or 'herdsmen,' within the shepherd's flock, who assist him in his pastoral ministry.

[83] *Ibid.* 17.4 (46).

[84] Beck, *Hymnen contra Haereses* 56.10 (CSCO 169.211f.).

[85] *Ibid.* 66.11 (212).

another parlance. For the three bishops of Nisibis, Jacob, Babū, and Vologeses, had many 'herdsmen,' Ephraem claims. There were daughter churches spreading in every direction from mother Nisibis, he says, with their own sheepfolds (*dayrōtô*).[86] And of bishop Abraham of Nisibis (361–363) Ephraem says explicitly:

> You are the crown of the priesthood (*kûmrûtô*);
>   in you the ministry (*tešmeštô*) shines.
> You are a brother to the presbyters (*qašîšê*),
>   a superintendent to the deacons (*sàmmōšê*).
> You are a master for the youth,
>   a staff and a helping hand for the aged.
> You are a protective wall for the chaste women;
>   in your stand (*qawmōk*) the people of stature (*qyōmô*) achieve glory.
> The church is adorned with your beauty;
>   blest is the One who elected you
>   to fill the office of Priest (*tkahhen*).[87]

Ephraem is not more specific about his own position in the church. Palladius, writing from the point of view of the Byzantine church, calls Ephraem 'the deacon of the church at Edessa,'[88] a designation that has since become the standard epithet for the saint who in fact spent all but the last decade of his life in Nisibis! In any case, there is no reason to doubt the report that Ephraem was a deacon.

St. Ephraem's lengthy bibliography testifies to the pastoral work he actually did in the service of his bishops. He was a teacher, a preacher, a biblical exegete, a theologian-poet whose discourse was Aramaic to the core. In his own idiom he commended to his flock what one now recognizes to be the orthodox faith of Nicaea, including, I would argue, the justification in Syriac of the Cappadocian Trinitarian formula.[89] His style of religious discourse was not academic; it was deeply contemplative, based on a close reading of the scriptures, with an eye to the telling image or 'type' (*rôzô*) in terms of which God chose to make revelations to the church, and its object was to project for the believers truthful reality (*šrōrô*), both doctrinal and moral.[90] In the context of the fourth century, in the 'Church of the Empire,' St. Ephaem's

---

[86] See Beck, *Carmina Nisibena* 14.1 (CSCO 218.37).

[87] *Ibid.* 21.5 (55f.).

[88] Butler, *The Lausiac History* (above, n. 1) 2.126.

[89] On this subject see E. Beck, *Ephräms Trinitätslehre in Bild von Sonne/Feuer, Licht und Wärme* (CSCO 425; Louvain 1981), where there are references to Beck's and others' earlier studies on the Trinity in the works of Ephraem. See also Sidney H. Griffith, 'The Cappadocian Trinitarian Formula in Syriac,' forthcoming.

[90] See Murray, *Symbols of Church and Kingdom* (n. 79, above), and 'The Theory of Symbolism in St. Ephrem's Theology,' *Parole de l'Orient* 6/7 (1975/76) 1–20.

style of thought was archaic in the etymological sense of the word — it issued from the well-spring of what, in the monastic West, one would call *lectio divina*. The result was a colloquy with the Word of God, the mode of religious discourse that is prior to academic theology.

The contemplative cast of St. Ephraem's thought recalls another dimension of the pastoral life of the bishop's house in Nisibis as the saint celebrated it in his writings, and as he himself may have shared it. The bishop was to be a 'holy man,' almost in the sense of the word popularized by Peter Brown,[91] and he was to live in the ascetical style one had come to expect of those who occupied that station in life (*qyōmô*) characteristic of the 'singles' (*īḥīdōyê*) in God's service. St. Ephraem said of bishop Abraham, for example, that he was 'single' (*īḥīdōyô*) in both senses of the word, in himself and in his lifestyle:

Single in his everyday life, being
    within his own body 'holy' (*qadīšô*);
Single in his house, inwardly and
    outwardly chaste (*nakpô*).[92]

Ephraem is here speaking of the chaste celibacy that was the manner of life recommended for ministers of the church in his day, be they men or women, as we shall see below. In bishop Abraham's 'fold' (*dayrô*), the additional ascetic note of penance for sin was apparently regarded as an appropriate item for episcopal concern. Ephraem advised Abraham,

If you hear bad news,
    from trustworthy people who are undeceived,
Let your own tears flow to quench
    the fire that is kindled in others;
Discerning people will pray along with you.
    Decree a fast for those in the know,
And let your fold (*dayrōk*) be in pain
    for the one who is lost in sin,
That he might be restored by repentance;
    Blest is the One who found the sheep that was lost.[93]

Everything we know about St. Ephraem's career in Nisibis and in Edessa, most of it from his own pen, suggests that he participated wholeheartedly in the program of an ascetical, penitential single life for which he praised his bishops. There is every reason to believe that this self-styled 'herdsman' (*'allōnô*) on the shepherd-bishop's 'pastoral team' lived as a member of the 'fold of herdsmen' (*dayrô d'allōnê*) of which he spoke in his poem in praise of

---

[91] See Peter Brown, *Society and the Holy in Late Antiquity* (Berkeley 1982), esp. 103–65, and 'The Saint as Exemplar in Late Antiquity,' in J. Hawley (ed.), *Saint and Virtue* (Berkeley 1988) 3–14.
[92] Beck, *Carmina Nisibena* 15.9 (CSCO 219.41).
[93] *Ibid.* 21.12 (57).

bishop Abraham.[94] The best way to understand his style of holiness is to put it in the context of the ascetical institutions then current in the Syriac-speaking world, as one finds them mentioned in his own works: the presumed conditions of a life of consecration to the Lord's service.

C. *Asceticism and its Institutions in Ephraem's Day*

Almost everything that we know about the institutions of asceticism in the Syriac-speaking world in the fourth century depends on the discussion of them one finds in Aphrahat's *Demonstration VI*, written in 336/7, and adressed to 'my beloved singles' (*īḥīdōyê*).[95] These 'singles,' or 'celibates' as one might properly call them, Aphrahat also calls 'people of contract status (*bnay qyōmô*), virgins and holy people.'[96] He sets out a virtual 'rule of life' for them that lays an emphasis on true faith, fasting, prayer, humility, and modest personal deportment.[97] It is clear that Aphrahat sees this 'single' way of life as an imitation of the life of Christ; so at the end of the 'rule of life' he says:

> These things are fitting for the 'singles,' those who take on the heavenly yoke, to become disciples of Christ. So it is fitting for Christ's disciples to emulate Christ their Lord.[98]

Continence or virginity, depending on one's own personal history, is at the heart of this emulation. 'Virginity,' Aphrahat says, 'is the heavenly portion, a participation with the angelic Watchers of heaven.'[99] And he identifies the 'people of contract status' (*bnay qyōmô*) in the church as 'those who are the lovers of virginity.'[100] 'All of these "singles",' Aphrahat claims, 'the "Single One" who is from the bosom of the Father gladdens.'[101]

---

[94] *Ibid.* 17.3 (46).

[95] See I. Parisot, *Aphraatis Sapientis Persae Demonstrationes* (Patrologia Syriaca I; Paris 1894) 239–312. For bibliography see G. G. Blum, 'Afrahaṭ,' *Theologische Realenzyklopädie* 1 (1977) 625–35.

[96] Parisot, *Demonstrationes* 276. Here and on subsequent pages, e.g., cols. 292–97, Aphrahat exploits the multiple associations of words built on the root *q-w-m,* one of which, *qyōmô,* is usually translated 'covenant' in the present context. On this issue see R. H. Connolly, 'Aphraates and Monasticism,' *Journal of Theological Studies* 6 (1905) 522–39; R. Murray, 'The Exhortation to Candidates for Ascetical Vows at Baptism in the Ancient Syriac Church,' *New Testament Studies* 21 (1974–1975) 59–80; id., 'The Features of the Earliest Christian Asceticism,' in P. Brooks (ed.), *Christian Spirituality: Essays in Honor of Gordon Rupp* (London 1975), 65–77; G. Nedungatt, 'The Covenanters of the Early Syriac-Speaking Churches,' *Orientalia Christiana Periodica* 39 (1973) 191–215, 419–44.

[97] See Parisot, *Demonstrationes* (above, n. 95) 272–76.

[98] *Ibid.* 276.

[99] *Ibid.* 309; see also 268f.

[100] *Ibid.* 312.

[101] *Ibid.* 269. In the Syriac Peshitta, *īḥīdōyô* is the term used in place of the μονογενοῦς of John 1.14.

It is clear that for Aphrahat these 'singles' in the service of the Lord include both men and women. For in his *Demonstration VI* he found it necessary to admonish the lovers of the 'single state in life' (*īḥīdōyūtô*) that 'it is fitting for a woman to live with a woman, and it is right for a man to live with a man.'[102] It is wrong, even hypocritical, he argues, for men and women 'singles' to live together — an observation that suggests that by Aphrahat's day abuses in this regard were already a problem in the Syriac-speaking church. We shall see that St. Ephraem adverts to these abuses even more concretely than does Aphrahat.[103]

For the moment, what is important to notice in Aphrahat's discussion of the 'singles' is the assumption that the ministers in the church, the deacons and presbyters and teachers, if not all the baptized, would share this special status in the church.[104] This was the state of affairs that one might presume to have been familiar to Saint Ephraem. For Ephraem, as we have seen, the 'singles' in the church included a distinguishable 'fold of herdsmen' (*dayrô d'allônê*) within the bishop-shepherd's flock. Ephraem was himself presumably among their number, and from his works one might sketch a profile of the religious life characteristic of these 'singles' in the local ecclesiastical community, a way of life it has become customary to call 'premonastic' or 'protomonastic.'[105]

One must understand St. Ephraem's remarks about asceticism and the religious life within the general context of his 'spiritual world vision.'[106] Here

---

[102] *Ibid.* 260.

[103] One recalls in this connection the problem of the *virgines subintroductae*, evident already in the Pseudo-Clementine epistles, 'Ad virgines,' which are preserved entire only in Syriac. See the bibliography in J. Quasten, *Patrology* (Westminster, Md. 1950) 58–59.

[104] See Parisot, *Demonstrationes* (above, n. 95) 341, 356, 357. For the controversy regarding 'singleness' as a requirement even for baptism see the studies cited in n. 96 above, esp. R. Murray, 'The Exhortation to Candidates for Ascetical Vows' (n. 96, above).

[105] The most important studies of St. Ephraem's ascetic style of life, which a number of authors call 'premonastic' or 'protomonastic,' are the following: E. Beck, 'Ein Beitrag zur Terminologie des ältestens syrischen Mönchtums,' in B. Steidle (ed.), *Antonius Magnus Eremita (356–1956)* (Studia Anselmiana 38; Rome 1956) 254–67; id., 'Asketentum und Mönchtum bei Ephraem,' in *Il Monachesimo Orientale* (Orientalia Christiana Analecta 153; Rome 1958) 341–62. In these studies, Beck is reacting against ideas suggested by A. Adam, 'Grundbegriffe des Mönchtums in sprachlicher Sicht,' *Zeitschrift für Kirchengeschichte* 65 (1953) 209–39. For Ephraem see also L. Leloir, 'Saint Éphrem, moine et pasteur,' in *Théologie de la vie monastique* (Théologie 49; Paris 1961) 85–97; id., 'La pensée monastique d'Éphrem et Martyrius,' in *Symposium Syriacum 1972* (Orientalia Christiana Analecta 197; Rome 1974) 105–34. for the larger issues involved in these discussions see G. Kretschmar, 'Ein Beitrag zur Frage nach dem Ursprung frühchristlicher Askese,' *Zeitschrift für Theologie und Kirche* 61 (1964) 27–67; A. Guillaumont, *Aux origines du monachisme chrétien* (Spiritualité orientale 30; Bégrolles en Mauges 1979).

[106] The best book in English on this subject is now Sebastian Brock, *The Luminous Eye: The Spiritual World Vision of St. Ephrem* (Rome 1985).

is not the place to review this whole matter; one may simply mention some of the highlights of Ephraem's thought on the subject of asceticism, with the proviso that their full comprehension requires a much broader consideration.

To borrow André de Halleux' felicitous expression, 'Ephraem considered the church to be the sacramental situation of paradise restored.'[107] And it was the function of the dedicated virgins and celibates within the church, the 'singles' of both sexes, according to Ephraem, to transform the church into a new paradise by assuming the life-style of the first parents before the fall. In this way, the practice of virginity and sexual continence in the church had an ultimate eschatological significance for St. Ephraem: the 'singles' were a symbol, a prefiguring emblem (rôzô), of a future, angelic life in paradise, divinely ordained for faithful believers.[108]

The ascetical practices suitable to these 'singles,' who enjoyed a distinctive status in church life as bnay qyōmô, were the usual exercises of fasting, prayer, and vigilance. Other practices, such as abstaining from wine and cultivating a habit of quiet reserve and silence, Ephraem also commends. But there can be no doubt that for him virginity was the most basic condition of the holy person. He makes this idea perfectly clear in a stanza from the Hymns of Paradise:

> Whoever sensibly
>   abstains from wine,
> For him the grapevines of Paradise
>   are eagerly waiting.
> Each one stretches out
>   to offer him its cluster.
> And if he is also a virgin (btûlô),
>   they draw him in,
> Well within their embrace,
>   because being a 'single' (īḥîdōyô)
> He had not lain within an embrace,
>   nor on a bed of marriage.[109]

Clearly the single state here appears to enhance the value of another ascetical practice, abstention from wine; at the same time, it is clear that the single

---

[107] De Halleux, 'Saint Ephrem le Syrien' 353.

[108] See, e.g., the significance of virginity in Paradise in E. Beck, Des heiligen Ephraem des Syrers Hymnen de Paradiso und Contra Julianum 7.6,15 (CSCO 174 [Louvain 1957] 26f., 28f.).

[109] Beck, Hymnen de Paradiso 7.18 (CSCO 174.29). This verse has been the subject of some controversy, because some scholars see in it a background for the vision of paradise one finds in the Qur'ān, an idea Dom Edmund Beck summarily rejected. See the comment and bibliography in R. Lavenant, Éphrem de Nisibe, Hymnes sur le Paradis (Sources chrétiennes 137; Paris 1968) 103f. The present writer thinks that such ideas as Ephraem expressed were in fact among those that were 'in the air' in the Christian milieu with which Muḥammad was familiar.

state is the *sine qua non* of the ascetical style of life St. Ephraem commends to his readers.

In his own instance, of course, asceticism is at the service of pastoral ministry, which was the vocation of exegete, teacher, and controversialist rolled into one. In a passage in the *Hymns of the Church,* Ephraem expresses this ideal of a learned and pastorally active asceticism in more universal terms:

> Here is the best one can say
>   about a man,
> That if he is wise,
>   he tortures and scourges his body,
> With fasts and thirsts,
>   for it to become healthy in the drill.
> He should discipline his spirit in books,
>   until he is worn out.
> Comely in spirit and in body,
>   the two crucibles will have refined him.
> One whose crucibles are multiple,
>   the more enhanced will his comeliness have become.[110]

While St. Ephraem thus lauds the ascetical life, in his homilies he is also sternly critical of those who hypocritically adopt the forms of asceticism but not its substance. In his *Admonitory Homilies,* for example, he admonishes Nisibis:

> Your mothers have become loose,
>   your freeborn are dishonorable.
> Even your virgins are stubborn,
>   the chaste ones shameless.[111]

The context makes it clear that the 'virgins' and 'chaste ones' Ephraem mentions are those included among the 'singles' in God's service. A few lines farther on in the homily, he points to the paradoxical situation that religious declension has brought about in society:

> Married women have adopted abstinence,
>   'Chaste ones' are sleek!
> The outward appearance is sleek,
>   Within, the mind is defiled![112]

In his *Letter to Publius,* Ephraem points to the same hypocrisy. Describing his vision of the next world, he writes:

---

[110] E. Beck, *Des heiligen Ephraem des Syrers Hymnen de Ecclesia* 28.9 (CSCO 198 [Louvain 1960] 68).

[111] E. Beck, *Des heiligen Ephraem des Syrers Sermones I* 1.356–59 (CSCO 305 [Louvain 1970] 7).

[112] *Ibid.* 9.

> I saw there pure virgins whose virginity had been rejected because it had not
> been adorned with the good oil of excellent works. . . . I also saw there those
> who did not have the title of virginity, but who were crowned with victorious
> deeds, their conduct having filled the place of virginity. . . . Let no man trust
> any longer in the chaste reputation alone of virginity, when it is deprived of
> the works which constitute the oil of the lamps.[113]

Not only does St. Ephraem find fault with the virgins who are supposed to
be devoted to God, but who are merely clinging to their status in hypocritical
fashion; he also upbraids his own class of ministers for their moral failures. So,
in his *Admonitory Homilies,* he scores the behavior of bishops and their co-
ministers in the church:

> For who can admonish
>   the judges and the rulers?
> Who will dare to set aright
>   the herdsmen (ʿallōnê) and the shepherds (rōʿawōtô)?
> If the shepherds are sleeping,
>   there's a great banquet for the wolves.
> If the herdsmen slumber and sleep
>   there's a mighty rout for the sheep.[114]

St. Ephraem's own ascetical life, as an ʿallōnô, a 'herdsman' in the church,
and as an īḥīdōyô, a 'single' in God's service, after the example of Christ
himself, was probably thoroughly conventional, from the point of view of the
forms of asceticism customary in the Syriac-speaking churches of his day. But
he lived at a time when substantive changes were taking place in the church on
many fronts, and although he was personally conservative he did much to
ensure the success of the new ways. As we have suggested, he championed the
'Church of the Empire' in almost Eusebian terms,[115] and did as much as
anyone to establish Nicene orthodoxy in concepts close to the Cappadocian
formulae; yet he did so in conventional Syriac terms, all the while deprecating
'the poison of the wisdom of the Greeks.'[116] And this same irony is evident in
Ephraem's championing of the forms of asceticism.

Toward the end of his life, perhaps during the ten years he spent in the
service of the bishop of Edessa, Ephraem began to praise the new anchorite
movement among those Christians interested in the ascetical life. In a much-
quoted passage from the *Hymns of Virginity,* for example, Ephraem comments
on the significance of the statement in the Gospel of John that says of Jesus,
'He withdrew to a town called Ephraim in the region near the desert, where he

---

[113] S. P. Brock, 'Ephrem's Letter to Publius,' *Le Muséon* 89 (1976) 286f. There is an
allusion here to Jesus' parable of the wise and foolish virgins, Mt. 25.1–13.

[114] Beck, *Sermones I* 2.295–98, 348–52 (CSCO 305.18f.).

[115] See Griffith, 'Ephraem, the Deacon of Edessa' (above, n. 79).

[116] E. Beck, *Des heiligen Ephraem des Syrers Hymnen de Fide* (CSCO 154 [Louvain 1955] 7).

stayed with his disciples' (John 11.54). Addressing that town near the desert, which one supposes St. Ephraem likens to Edessa, he says of Jesus' withdrawal:

> In you He has painted a type (ṭûpsô) for the 'sorrowing
> anchorites' (abîlê), those who love the desert, the liberator of all.[117]

The 'sorrowing anchorites' (abîlê), as Syriac writers after Ephraem's time often called wandering ascetics, were those in the Eastern church who had been inspired by the ascetical practices of the monks in Egypt.[118] Their teaching, and the lore of their exploits, came to dominate the burgeoning monastic movement from the second half of the fourth century onward. Syriac writers as well as others in the churches of early Byzantium enthusiastically supported the new movement, often in the name of St. Ephraem.[119] As for the saint, it is not unlikely that he lauded the new movement in those hymns in praise of St. Julian Saba († 367) that are attributed to his pen. Here he praises the hermit who lived in a cave on the mountain outside Edessa, right where later hagiographical tradition would locate Ephraem himself, in pursuit of the same ideal. Of Julian Saba, Ephraem wrote:

> In his lifestyle (dûbōrawy) Jesus was ever depicted.
> And because he had seen the glory of the 'Single One,'
> He too became a 'single one' (îḥîdōyô).
> He had contempt for this life that passes away.
> He despised the beauty that fades.
> In humility he showed a 'type' for his own people.[120]

What is noteworthy here is Ephraem's use of the traditional term 'single one' — in the Syriac tradition a title both for Jesus himself and for the traditional ascetical follower of Jesus[121] — to describe the behavior of Julian Saba, an adept of the new style of anchoritic asceticism.

This new style of asceticism used many of the terms of the traditional ways of holiness, but there was a difference now: the holy man, the 'sorrowing anchorite' (abîlô), no longer lived within the heart of the local church, as did the traditional 'single one' (îḥîdōyô). Like Julian Saba, he lived alone outside

---

[117] Beck, *Hymnen de Virginitate* 21.2 (CSCO 223.71).

[118] On the significance of the term abîlô for Ephraem and later writers, see the articles by E. Beck cited in n. 105 above.

[119] See n. 64 above.

[120] E. Beck, *Des heiligen Ephraem des Syrers Hymnen auf Abraham Kidunaya und Julianus Saba* 2.13 (CSCO 322 [Louvain 1972] 41).

[121] On the double significance of the title 'single one' to mean both 'celibate' and 'only-begotten' see above, and n. 101. The present writer will have more to say on this issue in the forthcoming paper, ' "Singles" in God's Service: Celibacy in Early Syrian Asceticism,' Society for Biblical Literature Annual Meeting; Chicago 1988.

of town, perhaps in a loose community of separated anchorites. Townspeople
looked up to the new-style ascetics, and prayed to participate in their merits
and to emulate their virtues, but they did not live alongside them. One may
get a sense of this new arrangement in the prayer with which an anonymous
writer closed a homily of these new-style monks that later came to be attributed to St. Ephraem. In it, the author prays as one who celebrates the
victories of the ascetics, but he is not really one of them. He wants only to tell
the story of a glory others have won, and to have their prayers on the day of
judgment.

> Blessed is the one who is worthy to become
> > a colleague of those who have triumphed.
> Blessed is the one who loves them,
> > and imprints their manners on himself.
> Blessed is the one who takes his start with them,
> > and finishes his course with works of theirs.
> Blessed is the one who does not slide away
> > from the model of their manners.
> Blessed is the one who is not separated from them,
> > when they come to inherit their promises.
> Blessed is the one who finishes and perfects
> > his course, heartened like them.
> We, O Lord, love them,
> > those who have loved your intimacy.
> Do not separate us from their ranks,
> > when they come to stand in the kingdom.
> And since we have recounted their works in love,
> > so that their triumphs might be proclaimed,
> Make us worthy to receive together with them
> > delights that will never end.
> Since our whole congregation enjoys
> > the story of the sons of light,
> May we find mercy on the day of judgment,
> > by their prayers, yes, Amen![122]

One may venture the opinion that during the last years of his life, St.
Ephraem welcomed the new ascetical movement as a long-overdue reform of
the institutions of the religious life, whose abuses he had himself often decried,
as we have seen. The irony of it all is that St. Ephraem's late support of the
new monachism may have been so successful that in later times, even in Syriac
literature, the true-to-life portrait of the holy teacher, St. Ephraem Syrus, was
painted over with the ascetical colors of St. Ephraem Byzantinus. It was not
that the Syriac-speaking monks in the Graeco-Syrian communities of east

---

[122] E. Beck, *Des heiligen Ephraem des Syrers Sermones IV* 2.509–32 (CSCO 334 [Louvain
1973] 27f.).

Byzantium were deliberately trying to conceal St. Ephraem's true identity behind an Evagrian mask. Rather, their intention was doubtless to praise the virtues of their most famous holy man, in the newly popular Byzantine idiom of asceticism in which the citizens of fifth- and sixth-century Edessa were desperate to claim a place of pride for themselves and for their city. So it was that in popular piety, Ephraem the bishop's man became St. Ephraem, the model Byzantine monk, the deacon of Edessa.

The Catholic University of America

Asceticism in the Church of Syria:
The Hermeneutics of Early Syrian Monasticism

Sidney H. Griffith

Many commentators on the history of asceticism in the Syrian Orient in the early Christian period have highlighted what they often call its encratic features. They cite the harsh and seemingly bizarre forms of ascetic life that flourished there. And everyone who knows anything at all about asceticism in Syria knows that it was home to that peculiar ascetical institution, the stylite—the holy man or woman who passed his or her life elevated above the cares of contemporaries, dwelling on a platform secured to the top of a pillar, and served by a monastic community gathered below.[1] One might borrow a phrase from Peter Brown to say that in the popular scholarly imagination the Syrian tradition of asceticism "admitted more vivid gestures than it did in the Greek world."[2] Indeed, Brown goes on to characterize the Syrian conception of monasticism, or of the "angelic life," as its practitioners would call it, as a "freedom that resembled that of the beasts, wandering up the mountainsides to graze, with the sheep, on the natural grasses."[3] He calls attention to the Syria-based "Messalians," who "provoked genuine alarm in the late fourth and fifth centuries."[4] Brown concedes that "the world East of Antioch was no spiritual 'Wild West'";[5] but, nevertheless, he speaks of drastic measures and deep pessimism as characteristic of Syrian asceticism. This general impression of the severity, or at least of the peculiarity, of asceticism in the Syrian Orient has become almost a stereotype, comparable to the stereotype of Egyptian asceticism in the fourth century as unrelievedly that of the Antonian hermit or the Pachomian cenobite, with no finer distinctions required to understand what was, in fact, a more complicated social phenomenon.[6]

The history of the earliest forms of asceticism in the Syriac-speaking world is inevitably bound up with the study of such foundational documents as the *Odes of Solomon* and the *Acts of Judas Thomas*. The interpretation of these texts necessarily involves a further inquiry into the much discussed issue of the styles of Christianity that first flourished in the Syrian milieu. There is no doubt that the followers of Marcion, Mani, and Bar Daysan, for example, were major players in the drama that saw the unfolding of Christian intellectual and cultural life in the environs of Nisibis and Edessa, the two cities that became the foci of the Syriac-speaking world—the one always open to Persia, and the other, at least from the second century onward, a stalwart champion of the Roman empire.[7] But, by the early fourth century, those forces prevailed in the church in Syria, which brought it ever more intimately into the socio-political life of the "Church of the Empire."[8] It is during this period that one begins to find the appearance in inner Syria of institutions typical of the "Great Church," including one that would uniquely mark Christian life for centuries to come, the institution of monasticism. This institution was easily as powerful and significant at the time as the institution of the hierarchical episcopacy, which also appeared in Syria in the fourth century.

The history of monasticism as a style of the ascetical life in Syria needs renewed scholarly attention. In recent years, it has become increasingly clear that the hitherto prevailing view rests, at least in part, upon mistaken assumptions from two sources about its origins. One is the traditional, monastic hagiography deriving from the Greco-Syrian milieu itself. The other is a modern scholarly mistake about the date and the authorship of certain texts crucial to the case as documentary evidence.

The first problem that one encounters in attempting to write the history of the forms of monasticism in the Syriac-speaking communities is that the past has almost always been read through lenses supplied by such essentially Byzantine texts as Theodoret of Cyrrhus's *History of the Monks of Syria,* Palladius's *Historia Lausiaca,* and Sozomen's *Church History.* These texts, and others of their ilk, rather than native Syriac ones, have set the parameters within which commentators have long discussed the biographies of such principal figures as Jacob of Nisibis (fl. 303–338 CE) and Ephraem the Syrian (306–373 CE).[9] They present verbal icons of these saints that conform to an hagiographic profile much esteemed in fifth and sixth century Syro-Byzantine monastic circles. But they have nothing much to do with the historical portraits of these figures that more indigenous Syriac materials allow one to draw. The result has been that the origins of monasticism in the Syriac-speaking world were considered to be part of the general flowering of the monastic phenomenon—which is supposed to have begun in the deserts of Egypt in the days of Antony. This errant view found a currency even in native Syriac milieus, in the accounts of St. Awgin, which, in later centuries enjoyed a considerable popularity in Syria.[10]

The modern scholarly mistake regarding Syrian monasticism has been the attribution of five Syriac texts, which describe the exploits and present the thinking of Syriac-speaking ascetics who withdrew into the deserts and mountains of Syria in pursuit of the anchoritic ideal, to St. Ephraem. The texts have such titles as the "Letter to the Mountaineers"; "On the Solitary Life of the Anchorites"; "On Anchorites, Hermits and Mourners"; another work similarly titled, "On Anchorites, Hermits and Mourners"; and "On Solitaries."[11] The problem is that in his influential book *History of Asceticism in the Syrian Orient,* and elsewhere, Arthur Vööbus vigorously defends the authenticity of these texts as works of St. Ephraem.[12] The result has been that subsequent historians have, accordingly, thought of them as documents indicative of the ascetical and monastic theory current in Syria in St. Ephraem's time and earlier. They abound in descriptions of the vivid gestures of asceticism of which Peter Brown speaks in the passages from his book already quoted (p. 220). But, in fact, these works, some of which are in the manuscript tradition sometimes attributed to Isaac of Antioch (fifth century), date from well after the time of Ephraem.[13] They tell us next to nothing about the origins of monasticism within Syrian asceticism. Rather, they reflect developments of the anchoritic idea which come from a later time, no real traces of which appear in Ephraem's certainly genuine works.

When one reads the texts of the native Syriac writers of the formative fourth century without the presuppositions imposed by either the Byzantine icon of the monastic holy man leading the hermit life, or the *idée fixe* supplied by what one might call the Vööbus hypothesis, a portrait of the emerging monastic, or premonastic, life in Syria emerges that bears the stamp of originality. On the one hand, as we shall see, the outward style of life that the sources describe is very similar to what recent scholars find elsewhere, in Egypt, for instance.[14] On the other hand, in the Syriac-speaking world the terms of burgeoning monastic life have their own resonances and nuances which impart a distinctive conceptual flavor that they never completely lose throughout the course of later developments.

Briefly put, crucial texts by Aphrahat, "the Persian Sage" (died c.345 CE) and Ephraem the Syrian allow one a glimpse of the lifestyle within the church of Syria of communities of "singles" in God's service, whose way of life is parallel to that of the biblical widows and virgins and with whom the men and women "singles" will be bracketed in later canonical legislation.[15] Within the first quarter of the fourth century, however, the anchoritic life also makes its appearance in Syria in the person of Julian Saba (died c.367 CE), whose experience Ephraem the Syrian, among others, would celebrate in hymns that in Syria functioned literarily in much the same way that Athanasius's *Life of Antony* would function in Egypt and elsewhere. They present Julian's exploits in a religious vocabulary that had already become traditional, while at the same time they indicate a paradigm shift in the forms of asceticism that, in an uncanny way, transmutes traditional ascetical terminology.[16]

In the late fourth century, and throughout the fifth century, the church in Syria both eagerly adopted monasticism, the new ascetical fashion that went together with the hierarchical features of Eusebius's Constantinian "Great Church"; and at the same time developed the institution in accordance with its own temperament. That temperament manifests itself in the *Liber graduum,* a late fourth- or early fifth-century text that in many ways echoes traditional Syrian ascetical vocabulary, already long familiar from Manichaean as well as more mainstream Christian discourse.[17] The stylites, too, were expressions of the Syrian temperament, as were the "mourners," "solitaries," and "mountaineers" whose "vivid gestures" Peter Brown mentions. Later Syrians took eagerly to the monastic thought of Evagrius of Pontus: so much so that his thinking, and that of commentators under his influence, such as Palladius and even Theodoret of Cyrrhus, eventually came to dominate the theory of asceticism in the Syriac-speaking milieu.[18] The important point in connection with all of these figures is that they were not the original Syrian ascetics. Rather, their enthusiasms were the product of the change in ascetical fashion which began in the fourth century after the Constantinian peace of the church. "Monasticism" is the term which has come functionally to designate the new fashion, the hallmark of which, from a phenomenological point of view, was what the Greeks called *anachōrēsis*, the departure of individuals or groups of individuals from the life of the city's church community to an environment more suited to the practice of asceticism seemingly for its own sake, or at least free of the entanglements of day-to-day ecclesiastical life. But the church of Syria long preserved adepts of the old ways, who continued to live in the general community and to use the traditional ascetical vocabulary, although much of it was also adopted by the new enthusiasts.[19]

The purpose of the present essay is to look again at several key terms in the traditional Syriac vocabulary of asceticism and monasticism, with the intention of highlighting their denotations and connotations within the Syrian hermeneutical horizon. The focus of attention will be on two expressions, the term *iḥidāyâ*, and the phrase *bnay* (or *bnāt*) *qyāmâ*, especially in the works of Aphrahat and Ephraem, the two classical writers of Syriac in the fourth century. And there will be a brief discussion of the uniquely Syriac ascetical term, *abîlâ*. The assumption is that Aphrahat and Ephraem used these expressions in their traditional Syrian senses and that their works made them more readily available for those writers coming after them. It is hoped that the study will contrast and compare these typically Syrian conceptions with parallel Greek modes of expression that became increasingly important to the Syrians, especially in the fifth and sixth centuries. The final section of this essay returns to the discussion of the history and the forms of asceticism in Syria, in the light of the foregoing investigations.

Îḥîdāyâ

In the tradition of the Syriac-speaking churches, the term *îḥîdāyê* regularly appears in the earliest texts together with the terms *bnay qyāmâ*, *btûlê/btûlātâ*, and *qaddîšê* to designate a class of people in the believing community who occupied a special status in the church.[20] They were not ministers properly so-called, such as the *šammōšê*, *mšammšānê* (deacons) or the *qaššîšê* (presbyters) or the *rā'awwātâ* (shepherd-bishops); although, as we shall see, *îḥîdāyê* were sometimes to be found in the pastoral ministry among the minor officials, or *'allānê* (herdsmen), as they were sometimes called, in the service of a local bishop.[21] Rather, the *îḥîdāyê* occupied a position comparable to that assigned to widows and virgins already in the New Testament and in early ecclesiastical books of canons.[22] In fact, the term *îḥîdāyê*, in general came to include both male and female virgins, as well as persons who may once have been married, but who subsequently consecrated themselves in a special way and who then lived as consecrated celibates in the Christian community under the name *qaddîšê* (saints or holy ones).[23]

The earliest texts in Syriac to which one may turn for help in the effort to explore the meaning of the term *iḥidāyâ* in this sense are from the fourth century, the *Demonstrations* of Aphrahat, the Persian Sage (died c. 345 CE), and the hymns and

[Some of the material in this section appeared in an earlier form in S. H. Griffith, "Singles in God's Service: Thoughts on the *Iḥidāyê* from the Works of Aphrahat and Ephraem the Syrian," *The Harp* 4 (1991):145–159.]

homilies of Ephraem the Syrian (d. 373 CE). By the fourth century, one supposes, the term was already current in ecclesiastical circles. Were it not for what one can learn of its connotations in the writings of Aphrahat and Ephraem, one would be poorly prepared to understand it in the few places where it appears in the yet earlier texts that have survived.

Scholarly essays dedicated to exploring the denotation and the connotations of the term *iḥîdāyâ* have not been lacking, and during the twenty years between 1953 and 1973 there was a mini-debate on the subject in the periodical literature. The discussion began with the publication in 1953 and 1954 of Alfred Adam's influential article, "Grundbegriffe des Mönchtums in sprachlicher Sicht,"[24] and it achieved something approaching closure, at least for the time being, in 1974 and 1975, when Robert Murray reviewed the whole matter in summary fashion in another influential article, "The Exhortation to Candidates for Ascetical Vows at Baptism in the Ancient Syriac Church."[25] In the meantime, additional important contributions to the discussion came from such notable scholars as Dom Edmund Beck O.S.B.,[26] Gilles Quispel,[27] and Antoine Guillaumont,[28] all of whom have called attention to important aspects of the definition of the term *iḥîdāyâ*.

For a while, the discussion was complicated by the inability of scholars to decide whether the employment of the Syriac term in the earliest texts presumed the currency, and distinctively Christian sense, of the Greek word *monachos*, or vice versa. Arthur Vööbus, and to some extent even Edmund Beck, presumed that the Greek word was in fact primary, with its emphasis on the solitariness of the person described, to the effect that such a one lives alone, and is single, or celibate, that is to say unmarried and sexually continent.[29] Alfred Adam and Antoine Guillaumont, on the other hand, insisted that in the Syriac-speaking world the word *iḥîdāyâ* has a deeper primary sense than simply what the adjective "single" implies about the human lifestyle—married or single—even in the basic denotation of the word. To support their position, they appealed to Semitic philology, and to the use of the term *iḥîdāyâ* in the works of the classic writers of Syriac: Aphrahat, and particularly Ephraem. For in Syriac religious texts the term is not simply a designation for a Christian ascetic of some sort, but is first of all a title of Christ with biblical authority; and this is its primary point of reference for many Syriac writers.[30]

Robert Murray has summarized the meanings of the term *iḥîdāyâ* in reference to a Christian ascetic, as these meanings have become clear from the two decades and more of scholarly controversy on the subject. Murray sees three senses for the term: *monachos* (single from wife or family); *monotropos, monozōnos* (single in heart), not *dipsuchos* (doubleminded, as in *Jas.* 1.8); and *monogenēs* (united to the Only Begotten).[31] These three senses are, in fact, among the connotations of the term *monachos* that Eusebius of Caesarea had mentioned in connection with his discussion of the word *monotropous* as it occurs in *Psalm* 68.7 (LXX).[32] And Murray, following Guillaumont, was able to show that in Syriac and, particularly, in the writings of St. Ephraem these senses of the Greek term are also senses of the word *iḥîdāyâ* and are fundamental to the comprehension of the definition of the word as the Syriac fathers used it.

The practical corollary to this is, therefore, that in Syriac ascetical texts the denotation of the term *iḥîdāyâ* is not limited to the notion of singleness that bespeaks celibacy or religious bachelorhood. Rather, it includes the element of singleness of purpose (*monotropos*), along with the clear claim that a person called single for ascetical reasons is thereby also said to be in a special relationship with Jesus the Christ, the "Single One," the single son of God the Father (*John* 1.14, 18, 3.16, 18). This latter sense of the term may have been the primary one for the Syrians.

One must concede that in the Peshitta New Testament the adjective *iḥîdāyâ* appears to describe the single son not only of God the Father, but also the single son of the widow of Naim (*Luke* 7.12), the single son of the man whose boy was possessed (*Luke* 9.38), and the single daughter of Jairus (*Luke* 8.42). Nevertheless, the occurrence of the adjective five times to describe Jesus as God's "single son" was enough to ensure its currency in the Syriac-speaking world as a special Christological title.[33] In those texts in which Aphrahat and Ephraem speak of the "singles" in God's service in the church, they seldom fail to make this connection explicitly.

Aphrahat is the author most often quoted in discussions of the *iḥîdāyê*. Among his *Demonstrations,* one is in fact exclusively devoted to them, entitled *bnay qyāmâ,* the name for the *iḥîdāyê* that, in Aphrahat's day, was used to signify their position in the social organization of the church, as we shall see.[34] For Aphrahat, it is clear, the *iḥîdāyê* were certainly celibates. He says, "It is just, right and good for me to give this advice to myself, and to my beloved *iḥîdāyê:* they should not take wives."[35] And, just a few lines later, he describes the religious significance he attributes to this celibacy:

> For those who do not take wives will be served by the Watchers of heaven; the observers of consecrated holiness (*qaddîsûtâ*) will come to rest at the sanctuary of the Exalted One. The *iḥîdāyâ* who is from the bosom of the Father [*John* 1.14, 18] will gladden the *iḥîdāyê*. There will be there neither male nor female, neither slave nor free, but all are sons of the Most High [see *Galatians* 3.28].[36]

Finally, at the conclusion of that section of *Demonstration 6,* which some commentators call "Aphrahat's Rule," he writes:

> These things are fitting for the *iḥîdāyê,* those who take on the heavenly yoke, to become disciples to Christ. For so is it fitting for Christ's disciples to emulate Christ their Lord.[37]

Aphrahat's so-called rule stipulates for the *iḥîdāyê* such standard religious practices as faith, fasting, prayer, humility, simplicity; and the avoidance of hilarity, fancy dress, deceitful contention, avarice, and scorn. These are the practices that he calls suitable for the *iḥîdāyê,* the sons of the covenant, the virgins, and the *qaddîsê* (consecrated holy ones).[38] But what is of particular interest in the present discussion is Aphrahat's sense of the term *iḥîdāyâ* itself; it bespeaks the "one who is from the bosom of the Father," who "will gladden the *iḥîdāyê*." Clearly, for Aphrahat, Christ's title is of determining significance for the self-understanding of the *iḥîdāyê*. To become single after the image of the Father's only son, as Marie-Joseph Pierre has recently reminded readers of Aphrahat, had constituted the eschatological ideal for earlier writers in the Syrian milieu, such as the author of the *Gospel of Thomas*.[39]

Ephraem the Syrian's remarks are even more to the point. For him, of course, as for Aphrahat, the *iḥîdāyâ* is celibate. In the *Hymns of Paradise,* for example, Ephraem says of the ascetical person:

> Whoever sensibly
>   abstains from wine,
> For him the grapevines of Paradise
>   are eagerly awaiting.
> Each one stretches out
>   to offer him its cluster.
> And if he is also a virgin,
>   they draw him in,
> Well within their embrace,
>   because being an *iḥîdāyâ*
> He had not lain within an embrace,
>   nor on a bed of marriage.[40]

Clearly, for Ephraem, the *iḥîdāyâ* is a celibate person, and one need not adduce any further evidence here to make the point.[41] But it is also true that Ephraem invested the term *iḥîdāyâ* with an even deeper significance, given the fact that for him it not only describes someone living an ascetical, celibate life in the church, but it is also a title of Christ in the Syriac scriptures.[42] And for Ephraem, as for Aphrahat, an important element in the understanding of the ascetical *iḥîdāyâ* in the church here below is his relationship to the *iḥîdāyâ* from the bosom of the Father in heaven.

It has become clear during recent decades of scholarship that the occasion of the baptism of adults was also the occasion when prospective virgins and *qaddîsê* in the churches of Aphrahat and Ephraem entered the ranks of the *iḥîdāyê*.[43] Accordingly, it is not surprising that some of Ephraem's clearest language about the relationship between the earthly *iḥîdāyê* and the heavenly *Îḥîdāyâ* occurs in the metrical hymns he composed for the feast of the baptism of our Lord, the Epiphany. The clearest and most often quoted passages evoking this theme are the following lines:

> Here they are, coming to be baptized
>   and to become Virgins and Holy Ones.
> They step down, are baptized,
>   and they put on [*lbešw*] the one *Îḥîdāyâ*
>
> For whoever is baptized and puts on [*lābeš*]
>   the *Îḥîdāyâ*, the Lord of the many,
> has come to fill for Him the place of the many,
> and Christ becomes for him the greatest
>   treasure.[44]

In another Epiphany hymn Ephraem returns to the same theme:

> You to be baptized, who have found the kingdom
>   in the very bosom of Baptism,

Step down, put on [*lûbšûhy*] the *Îhîdāyâ*
   who is the Lord of the kingdom.
Blessed are you who have been crowned.[45]

It may well be the case that St. Ephraem envisions here not only ascetics, but every baptized person as one who has put on the heavenly *Îhîdāyâ*.[46] Nevertheless, the fact remains that the very synonymy of the titles for the only begotten Son of God and the celibate ascetics in Ephraem's ecclesial community bespeaks a special relationship between Christ and the celibate ascetic that is inherent in the very term designating them. For this reason, Dom Edmund Beck has now revised an earlier *dictum* that the two uses of the term *ihîdāyâ* have nothing to do with one another,[47] in favor of the suggestion that there is an indirect relationship between the two applications of the same term. The indirect connection, Beck suggests, bespeaks a higher rank in the community of the baptized for the ascetic, because "Christ becomes for him the greatest treasure," and the ascetic in turn comes "to fill the place of the many," as St. Ephraem says, in the presence of Christ, the heavenly *Îhîdāyâ*.[48]

It is interesting to observe the language St. Ephraem uses to express the inauguration of the special relationship between Christ the *Îhîdāyâ* and the ascetic *ihîdāyâ* at the sacrament of baptism. He speaks of the candidate putting on Christ the *Îhîdāyâ* in a way that reminds one of the clothing metaphor St. Ephraem and other Syriac writers so often used to express the doctrine of the Incarnation; they customarily spoke of the Word of God as "having put on the body (*lbeš pagrâ*)" of humanity for the sake of our salvation.[49] Further, it was a commonplace in baptismal contexts to speak of the baptized as putting on the robes of glory and light that Christ had left behind for them in the water at his own baptism in the Jordan.[50] Accordingly, when the divine *Îhîdāyâ* was put on at baptism, the ascetic was, in Ephraem's view, putting on divinity, in the name of the many in Christ the *Îhîdāyâ*, just as the "Word" of God had put on humanity in Christ at the Incarnation. In this view, the ascetic *ihîdāyâ* came to anticipate symbolically, almost in an iconic fashion, the situation of paradise restored;[51] he represented publicly and liturgically humanity's response to the salvation offered to them in the Incarnation (Passion, death, Resurrection) of God's only son.

There are yet further dimensions of meaning in the term *ihîdāyâ*. Scholars studying the history of the forms of asceticism in the early Christian communities have made reference in this connection to the parlance of the Jewish communitarians at Qumran, where the Hebrew word *yahad* described the community whose sometimes celibate members were described by the adjective *yahîd*.[52] Furthermore, this Hebrew term, especially in the biblical narratives where it occurs independently of any influence of Qumran, means not only "sole" or "single," to designate, for example, a single or only son or daughter. It also bespeaks an affective relationship that Greek translators of the Bible sometimes reflected by translating the Hebrew term *yahîd* with the Greek word *agapētos*. Greek translators also employed the word *monogenēs* to render the Hebrew word *yahîd*.[53] And so the multiple connotations of the term *ihîdāyâ* in Syriac versions of the Bible which can be used to translate all of these expressions, must be taken into account if one wants to hear how it echoes when describing an ascetical person in the Syriac-speaking early Christian community. Such a person is not only single in the sense of a celibate, but also singleminded, and has a special relationship with the beloved only son of the Father, which is assumed at baptism.[54] Baptism was thus not only the inauguration of a full life as a Christian, but of special status as *iḥîdāyâ*. All of these senses of the term have been discussed by earlier scholars; and Robert Murray has summarized them in his now classic article, "The Exhortation to Candidates for Ascetical Vows at Baptism in the Ancient Syriac Church."[55]

Yet another nuance in the meaning of the term *iḥîdāyâ* has come to light. In a study of the Christological title, *monogenēs unigenitus,* in the earliest patristic literature, Francesca Cocchini has shown that the scriptural passages that underlie this title most often employ the terms *yaḥîd/monogenēs/iḥîdāyâ, iḥîdāyûtâ* (Old Testament) and *monogenēs/iḥîdāyâ* (New Testament) in contexts that in the Old Testament involve the notion of sacrifice and in the New Testament describe an individual who experiences both death and resurrection: either Christ himself (*Jn.* 1.14, 18) or people whom Christ raised from the dead (*Lk.* 7.12, 8.42, 9.38).[56] So the title both fulfils a typological function (e.g. Isaac/Christ, those whom Christ raised/the resurrected Christ); and, with its sacrificial aura, it suggests that the Only One takes the place of the many, be he the Christ who saved the many by his Passion, death, and Resurrection, or be he the ascetic *iḥîdāyâ* who takes the place of the many as a *rāzâ* (token) of humanity restored to its pristine state in Paradise.

The conclusion to which the preceding discussion leads is that the Syriac term *iḥîdāyâ,* unlike the Greek term *monachos,* which shares part of its range of meaning, is a scriptural term[57] that in Christian usage applies first of all to Christ, with the full set of connotations that only the several Greek words used to interpret it will allow the non-Syriac speaker to discern.[58] Secondly, in Syriac this term is also used by writers such as Aphrahat and Ephraem to designate the so-called ascetics in the community, precisely because the intention of these ascetic celibates was publicly to put on the *persona* of the *Îḥîdāyâ* from the bosom of the Father. Their purpose was to imitate Christ. Aphrahat is perfectly clear on this point. At the end of his rule for the *iḥîdāyê* he says of them, "For so is it fitting for the disciples of Christ to imitate Christ, their Lord."[59]

With his accustomed poet's objectivity, St. Ephraem puts the same point well in the verses he composed in praise of a notable *iḥîdāyâ* of his own day, St. Julian Saba (d.367 CE). Of him Ephraem said,

> In his lifestyle, Jesus was ever depicted.
> Because he had seen the glory of the *iḥîdāyâ,*
> He too became an *iḥîdāyâ.* . . .
> In humility he showed a "type" to his own people.[60]

The senses of the term *iḥîdāyâ* as applied to holy men and women thus come before us in the works of two classical authors of the fourth century. The presumption is that, by their day, such ideas were already traditional in the Syriac-speaking world. The term *iḥîdāyâ* does not occur in the allegedly second-century

Odes of Solomon, nor in the *Acts of Judas Thomas,* where, nevertheless, themes closely associated with the institution of the *īḥīdāyûtâ* do occur.[61] But a number of scholars do think that the term *īḥīdāyâ* did appear among the *logia* (sayings) of Jesus in the presumably originally Syriac *Gospel of Thomas* that now survives only in Coptic.[62] There are at least seven *logia* in which the expression "single one" appears in Coptic, in some of which the Coptic translator actually used the Greek word *monachos* to render the original expression. For example, "Blessed are the solitary *(monachos)* and elect, for you shall find the kingdom" *(logion* 49), and "Many are standing at the door, but the solitary *(monachos)* are the ones who will enter the bridal chamber" *(logion* 75).[63] If the Syriac term *īḥīdāyâ* does in fact lie behind the term *monachos* in such passages as these, its occurrence would be the only remaining documentary evidence of the word *īḥīdāyâ* in a nonbiblical text from earlier than the fourth century to describe a celibate ascetic, or a spiritually elect person among the Christians. It is this presumption that has prompted some scholars to propose, further, that the Greek word *monachos,* which is first found in a papyrus fragment dated 6 June 324 to designate a Christian devotee, could have come into the Christian vocabulary in this sense as a calque on the Syriac word *īḥīdāyâ.*[64] If this proposal has any plausibility, it goes a long way toward explaining why Greek writers like Eusebius had to use so many different Greek words to summon up the several dimensions of meaning in the single Syriac word. Few of these dimensions leap readily to mind at the simple sight of the nonscriptural Greek word *monachos;* many of them are already evident in the senses of the Syriac word *īḥīdāyâ,* when it is read in the light of the traditional usages we have described.

Bnay Qyāmâ

Within the Syriac-speaking Christian communities of the fourth century, and presumably earlier, the *īḥīdāyê,* be they *btûlê* (virgins) or *qaddîšê* (consecrated holy ones), belonged to a somewhat informal class of believers in the church whom the early writers called *bnay* (or *bnāt) qyāmâ.*[65] It has become customary to render this phrase as "sons (or daughters) of the covenant," or simply as "covenanters." Scholars are increasingly aware, however, of the limitations of the customary translations of the phrase.[66] In fact, as we shall see, the term *qyāmâ* has connotations in Syriac that go far beyond what the word "covenant" alone suggests. These connotations are decisive for an understanding of the social standing of the *īḥīdāyê* in the church.

Aphrahat's *Demonstration 6,* devoted entirely to the concerns of the *bnay qyāmâ,* is the earliest and the most basic document we have even to mention the phrase. And here it is perfectly clear that for Aphrahat the *īḥīdāyê* are the *bnay qyāmâ.*[67] Furthermore, later in his book, in *Demonstration 8,* the author refers to *Demonstration 6,* "*Bnay Qyāmâ,*" as a discourse on the *īḥīdāyê,*[68] so there can be no doubt that, for Aphrahat, the two terms designate the same people in the community. What differentiates them, then, is their point of reference in regard to these same people. The term *īḥīdāyâ* bespeaks both the single, celibate condition of the individual so described, and the special relationship one assumes at baptism with the Son, the Îḥîdāyâ "from the bosom of the Father." The point of reference for the term *bar qyāmâ* turns on the senses of the word *qyāmâ* in Syriac, a noun derived from the verbal root *q-y-m,* which basically means "to rise," "to stand."[69]

The basic study of the significance of the expression *bar qyāmâ* is the influential article, "The Covenanters of the Early Syriac-Speaking Church," by George Nedungatt, S.J.[70] Here the author studies the seventy-seven occurrences of the word *qyāmâ* in the *Demonstrations* of Aphrahat, in nine basic usages. He notices that in almost half of its occurrences (thirty-five times), the term *qyāmâ* means "any religious covenant in the history of salvation."[71] And Nedungatt suggests that this is the basic sense of the term: that is, "pact" or "covenant." Accordingly, he understands the expression *bnay qyāmâ* to mean sons of the covenant or covenanters. His conclusion regarding the significance of this expression in the present context is as follows:

> In a typological or theological sense the whole Church was the Qyāmâ of God, but in the language of everyday life the *bnay qyāmâ* and the *bnāt qyāmâ* represented an inner circle of élite Christians.[72]

Nedungatt goes on to say that "consecrated virgins are partners in a *qyāmâ* with Christ,"[73] and that, in Aphrahat's day, "the *qyāmâ* of the Covenanters was the equivalent of a perpetual vow of chastity, by which they knew to be freely entering upon a higher state of life in the Church, regulated by its pastors."[74] Finally, he says, "their *qyāmâ* therefore, can be rightly called the covenant of celibacy."[75]

Having come to the conclusion that *qyāmâ* means covenant or pact, even when it is used to signify the state of the *îḥîdāyê* in the Syriac-speaking church, Nedungatt makes the connection between this Syriac usage and the parlance of the Greek and Latin speakers on the same subject. He says,

> The *qyāmâ* of the Covenanters does not differ from the *synthéke* and *pactum virginitatis* of the *monádzontes* in the Greco-Roman world of the early fourth century.[76]

With this allegation, Nedungatt expresses both what had become the conventional wisdom regarding the significance of the term *bnay qyāmâ,* and also brings it within the range of the familiar Western (Greek and Latin) frames of reference employed by most scholars of early Christianity. By doing so, however, he leaves unexplored the further connotations of the expression in Syriac—connotations that are equally significant for understanding what authors like Aphrahat and Ephraem actually have to say about the role in the life of the church of the *îḥîdāyê.*

The verbal root *q-w-m* means basically "to rise" and "to stand," and the noun derived from it, *qyāmâ,* means not only "covenant," but, depending on the context, it means "stand," or "status," "state," "station," (as in station in life); and even "resurrection," as in "standing up" from among the dead—although for the latter phenomenon the related noun *qyamtâ* is generally employed.[77] Accordingly, a number of scholars have now called attention to the further dimensions of meaning in the term, all the while abiding by the convention of translating it with the word "covenant."[78]

Scholars have been intrigued by the translated expression "sons of the covenant" because it is clear that in some passages Aphrahat used the word *qyâmâ* in the sense of covenant, to designate the church as a whole.[79] And to historically minded researchers this usage recalled the Hebrew term *bᵉrît* (covenant), as the Qumran covenanters used it to designate their own somewhat ascetically oriented community.[80] Once this Jewish/Christian connection was made, the way was open to the suggestion that comparably in the early Syriac-speaking Christian community, baptism, and consequently, full membership in the church/covenant, was open only to the celibate. Arthur Vööbus was the scholar whose works have most recently put this view into wide circulation, when he proposed that passages from Aphrahat's *Demonstrations* have preserved liturgical strains from earlier times in the Syriac milieu.[81] Vööbus's studies did much to highlight the baptismal setting of the initiation of an individual into the *îhîdâyûtâ*. But for the understanding of the ecclesial institution, the *bnay qyâmâ*, this line of inquiry proved to be something of a "red herring." For the attention of scholars was distracted from the investigation of the conditions and of the symbolic value of the station in life of those professing *îhîdâyûtâ*, to combat the notion that, in the early days in the Syriac-speaking community, only the celibate might receive the sacrament of baptism.[82]

As for the connotations of the Syriac term *qyâmâ*, once one gets beyond the implications of the translation word "covenant," one is free to follow the guidance of the senses of the word in the various contexts in which it appears. In the works of Aphrahat and Ephraem, there are two senses of the term that seem to be particularly significant. First there is the resurrection idea that is never far below the surface when the root *q-w-m* is deployed. Then there is the fact that a number of nouns derived from this root straightforwardly bespeak one's status or station in life in the church—exactly the nuance one wants to interpret the expression *bnay qyâmâ*.

A number of passages in Aphrahat's *Demonstrations* and elsewhere speak of the *îhîdâyê* or the *bnay qyâmâ* as human beings who have "taken on the likeness of the angels,"[83] for whom virginity is a "communion with the Watchers of heaven."[84] When one conjoins this idea with the gospel passage that speaks of those who have risen from the dead as being "equal to the angels, being the children of God, the children of the resurrection" (*Luke* 20.36), it is a short step to the suggestion that the phrase *bnay qyâmâ* means simply "sons of the resurrection." While one knows of no text in the works of Aphrahat or Ephraem that explicitly makes this connection, there are scholars who posit the connection on the grounds of its internal logic.[85] Peter Nagel, for example, says,

> To me the conclusion seems to be unavoidable, that by the designation *Bnay Qyâmâ*, the Syrian ascetics understood themselves as "Sons of the Resurrection," since in their *Askēsis* they realized the *Vita Angelica*.[86]

Only one scholar, Michael Breydy, has straightforwardly followed Nagel's suggestion that the phrase *bnay qyâmâ* means simply "sons of the resurrection."[87] Others have argued against the proposal, citing Aphrahat's failure to make such an understanding explicit, even when his context would seem to demand it.[88] Therefore it seems highly unlikely that the expression "sons of the resurrection" is itself an apt rendering of the phrase *bnay qyāmâ;* even though it might, strictly speaking, be lexically possible.

While "resurrection" is not by itself an apt translation of the word *qyāmâ* in the contexts we have been discussing, it is nevertheless unlikely that the resurrection concept was entirely absent from Aphrahat's mind in his discussion of the *bnay qyāmâ.* It is the nature of Semitic languages and their semantics to employ polyvalent terms. Given the presumption that all forms derive from a particular set of root consonants, they carry a reference to all the other lexical possibilities implicit in their shared roots.[89] Indeed, this feature of a language like Syriac is one of the means at the disposal of its writers to compose artful speech—*Kunstprosa,* one might call it. In this enterprise, Aphrahat the writer was a master, as more than one scholar has observed.[90] Accordingly, one cannot claim that no notion of resurrection lies behind the phrase *bnay qyāmâ.* Rather, one might most plausibly say that it is always present, at least by implication, and that sometimes, as in the following quotation from the *Demonstrations* on the *bnay qyāmâ,* the polyvalent possibilities of the root *q-w-m* are the very focus of the writer's artistry. The passage comes near the end of the *Demonstration* in question; and, in terms of Aphrahat's distinctive eschatology, it describes the final resurrection of the *îḥîdāyâ.* Aphrahat says,

> As for the one who keeps the Spirit of Christ in purity, when it comes into the presence of Christ, it will say to Him, the body into which I came, and which clothed me with the waters of Baptism, kept me in consecrated holiness *(qadîšûtâ).* And this Spirit of holiness will exhort Christ at the resurrection *(qyāmteh)* of the body which kept it in purity, and the Spirit will pray that it will be added to that body to rise *(danqûm)* in glory. . . . When the end time of completion comes, and the time of the resurrection *(qyāmtâ)* draws near, the Spirit of holiness which was kept in purity will hearken to the great power of its own nature, and it will come ahead of Christ, and it will stand *(qyāmâ)* at the gate of the cemetery, the location of the buried men who kept it in purity, and it will await the cry. And when the Watchers open the gates of heaven before the King, then the horn will call and the trumpets will blare, and the Spirit that is awaiting the cry will hear and rapidly it will open the graves and raise up *(wamqîmâ)* the bodies and everything concealed in them, and it will clothe in glory the one that will accompany it, and it will be within for the resurrection *(qyāmteh)* of the body, and the glory will be without for the ornamentation of the body.[91]

In this relatively short passage, three of the six occurrences of the root *q-w-m* are the customary word for "resurrection," *qyāmtâ.* The assemblage of six occurrences of the root in so abbreviated a space is obviously a stylistic feature of the artistry of the passage, given its subject matter. It would hardly escape the notice of the practiced reader of such a piece that it is part of a discourse on the eschatological future of the *bnay qyāmâ.* The connection between the words *qyāmtâ* and *qyāmâ* would, therefore, be implicit here and allusive. But they could in no way be declared to be utterly distinct from, and completely irrelevant to, one another.

In another passage, toward the beginning of *Demonstration 6,* the manuscripts themselves give variant readings, and it is unclear whether one is to read *qyāmtâ* or *qyāmâ* in a sentence which it seems best to translate, "Let us be partakers in his (i.e., Christ's) passion, so that we might live in his resurrection."[92] So one may plausibly say that the resurrection idea is inevitably implied in the term *qyāmâ* in the phrase *bnay qyāmâ*, without being the best choice, or even, by itself, the correct one for rendering the term in a Western language.

In addition to the valid translation word "covenant" for the Syriac term *qyāmâ* in the phrase *bnay qyāmâ*, and in addition, as well, to any allusion to resurrection, there is the rendering "status" or "station in life." There are a number of passages in which this sense of the word seems most plausible. Perhaps for the present purpose a single stanza from St. Ephraem's *Nisibene Hymns* will serve best to illustrate the point. Here Ephraem is praising Bishop Abraham of Nisibis (361–363 CE); and the stanza is rich for our understanding of the role of the *bnay qyāmâ* in Ephraem's conception of the ecclesiastical polity. He says to the bishop,

> You are the crown of the priesthood;
>   in you the ministry shines.
> You are a brother to the presbyters,
>   a superintendent to the deacons.
> You are a master for the youth,
>   a staff and a helping hand for the aged.
> You are a protective wall for the chaste women;
>   in the status you assume, the people of
>   station achieve glory.
> The church is adorned with your beauty;
>   blest is the One who elected you
>   to fill the office of priest.[93]

The interesting line here is the one that reads, "in the status you assume *(qawmāk)*, the people of station *(qyāmâ)* achieve glory." In the immediate context, Ephraem is speaking both of the bishop's own status in the church and that of the chaste women, presumably *bnāt qyāmâ*, whose station *(qyāmâ)* and that of others, presumably *bnay qyāmâ*, is enhanced by their relationship to the bishop's status. The status he assumes, and the station the others have, seems to be that of participants in the *îhîdāyûtâ*. For earlier in the same collection of hymns, Ephraem said of the same bishop Abraham that he was:

> Single *(îhîdāyâ)* in his everyday life,
>   being within his own body "holy" *(qadîsâ)*;
> Single *(îhîdāyâ)* in his house,
>   inwardly and outwardly chaste *(nakpâ)*.[94]

Accordingly, the expression *bnay qyāmâ* may be understood to express the station in life the *îhîdāyê* assume, by the extra step they take at baptism to put on the heavenly *Îhîdāyâ*, "the Lord of the many"—whereby they come, as St. Ephraem said in the Epiphany Hymn quoted earlier, "to fill for Him the place of the many, and Christ becomes [for them], the greatest treasure."[95] On this reading the status or the station in life the *îhîdāyê* take, by contract or covenant, is much more than just a pact of virginity or celibacy, as Nedungatt would have it. For the many, they stand for Christ, and for Christ they stand for the many, as Ephraem says. If this is their station in life, it may also be why they are called people of status in the community. It seems to have been not so much a matter of a spiritual élite, as Dom Edmund Beck would have it,[96] or a matter of a church within the church, as Robert Murray has suggested[97]; although neither of these characterizations is false. Rather, the active stance that the *îḥîdāyâ* was expected to take in the community consisted principally in serving as a type for his own people. This, as St. Ephraem said, was the accomplishment of Julian Saba in the passage quoted earlier.[98] This was the role of the *îḥîdāyâ* as a living icon of paradise restored. It determined his status within the ecclesial community.

Abîlâ

In one stanza of the third hymn in praise of Syria's first hermit/monk of record, St. Ephraem characterizes him in very traditional ascetical terms. He says,

> Saba is the champion, the virgin, the holy one,
> Who preserved chastity, virginity, without injury;
> Mournfulness without outrage;
> Humility without pride;
> And leadership without the troublesomeness of boasting.[99]

The only term not yet discussed in this string of traditional terms, or their abstract expressions, in which Ephraem customarily characterized the *îḥîdāyê* is "mournfulness." As St. Ephraem uses it, the term refers to that sorrow or compunction for sin that, in his day, led some ascetic Christians into the desert in mournful penitence, most likely in response to the Beatitude: "Blessed are they who mourn, for they shall be comforted" (*Mt.* 5.4). The term *abîlâ,* or "mourner," thus became one of the technical expressions which Ephraem and others used to describe a person who in another milieu might be called an anchorite.[100] In Syriac, however, the term accents the attitude of the penitent rather than the outward circumstances in which he lived out his compunction. Ephraem put the phrase in context in one of his hymns *On Virginity,* in which he speaks of the biblical town of Ephraim, "the neighbor of the desert," as he calls it, where, according to *John* 11.54, Jesus and his disciples took refuge from the Jews during the time before the Passion. Ephraem says in a verse of praise addressed to the town of Ephraim,

> In you is the type [God] depicted for the
>   mourners *(abîlê)* who love
> The all-freeing desert waste.[101]

He means that the penitential mourners in the Christian communities he knew were liable to seek the solitude of the desert for the exercise of their penitence. And there they were likely to neglect the amenities of civilized life, as a passage in one of Ephraem's hymns *On Paradise* suggests. He says in words addressed to such mourners,

Bear up, O life of mourning,
    so that you might attain to Paradise;
Its dew will wash off your squalor,
    while what it exudes will render you fragrant;
Its support will afford rest after your toil,
    its crown will give you comfort.[102]

The squalor spoken of in this verse is, of course, the squalor of sin; but given a desert setting for the life of penitent mourning, the squalor may just as well also be that actual dirt that attaches to one who lives in the desert among the animals after the model of the penitent king Nebuchadnezzar (*Dn.* 4.33–37), as St. Ephraem depicts in the thirteenth hymn *On Paradise.*[103]

For St. Ephraem, the term *abîlâ* (mourner) suggests a penitent ascetic with a penchant for living alone for a time in the desert. *Abîlûthâ* (mourning) and the *ihîdāyûthâ* (single lifestyle) for him unite to make up the profile of the ascetical life, as people in his milieu were inclined to live it. Julian Saba's principal difference from the traditional singles consisted in his role as the founding father of a community of hermits, whose style of life required a permanent withdrawal in a body from town and village ecclesiastical society. Later in the fourth and fifth centuries, the Syriac poets who sang the praises of the burgeoning movement of hermits in the church used the traditional ascetic term *abîlâ* as almost the equivalent of the word "hermit." In this sense it was a term unique to the Syrians, and it played no small role in presenting the tableau of vivid gestures that Peter Brown found to be characteristic of asceticism in the Syriac-speaking milieu. But in its traditional meaning, as St. Ephraem used it, it had nothing to do with anchoritic monks, and everything to do with the expression of ascetic penitence.

History and the Forms of Asceticism

For all practical purposes, the works of Aphrahat and St. Ephraem are the only documentary sources available to the modern scholar who wants to inquire into the history of the early organized forms of asceticism in the Syriac-speaking world. They both flourished in the fourth century. Even when earlier texts like the *Odes of Solomon* or the *Acts of Judas Thomas*[104] afford one some insight into the ascetical thinking of an earlier age, one almost always has to recast the scene in reference to what is learned from Aphrahat and Ephraem, who are primary witnesses to the institutions of their own day in Syria. By the fourth century, these institutions were already well enough established that certain abuses had crept into them, and currents of change and reform in the ascetical establishment were already afoot, prompted perhaps by the Peace of Constantine, which effectively removed one earlier form of complete self-giving, namely martyrdom.

Both Aphrahat and Ephraem addressed themselves to abuses among the *ihîdāyê* and the *bnay qyāmâ.* In *Demonstration 6* Aphrahat was forceful in his exhortation to both men and women celibates against their cohabitation. He said,

341

Any man, a *bar qyāmâ,* or a consecrated holy one who loves *iḥîdāyûtâ,* but wants a woman, a *bat qyāmâ* like himself, to live with him, it were better for him to take a woman openly and not be captivated in lust. And a woman too, it is also fitting for her, if she cannot separate from the man, the *iḥîdāyâ,* to belong to the man openly.[105]

Aphrahat goes on later in the *Demonstration* to give explicit advice to single, consecrated women who have received invitations of cohabitation from single men. It is worth translating the advice in full, because the terms Aphrahat uses fairly express his estimation of the values involved. He says,

O virgins, who have espoused yourselves to Christ, if one of the *bnay qyāmâ* should say to one of you, "May I live with you, and you serve me." You say to him, "I am betrothed to a man, the King, and him I serve. If I leave his service and come to serve you, my betrothed will be angry at me and he will write me a letter of divorce and he will dismiss me from his house. If you want to be held in honor by me, and if I am to be held in honor by you, so that no harm might reach me or you, do not put a fire in your bosom, lest you set your own clothes to burning. Rather, you stay honorably alone, and I will be honorably alone. Such things as the Bridegroom prepared for the eternities of his banquet get for yourself for a wedding gift and prepare yourself to meet Him. And I shall get oil ready for myself to enter with the wise ones, and not be left outside with the foolish virgins."[106]

Clearly there were abuses among the celibate men and women singles in the church in Aphrahat's day. And St. Ephraem, at a slightly later date, registered a similar complaint in similar language. In his *Letter to Publius* Ephraem contrasted the hypocrisy of publicly proclaimed virgins with the manifest virtue of those who did not bear the formal title of virginity. He made the comparison in the description of a vision of the next life. He said,

I saw there pure virgins whose virginity had been rejected because it had not been adorned with the good oil of excellent works. . . . I also saw there those who did not have the title of virginity, but who were crowned with victorious deeds, their conduct having filled the place of virginity. . . . Let no man any longer trust in the chaste reputation alone of virginity when it is deprived of the works which constitute the oil of the lamps.[107]

The evidences of a decline in the morals of some of the professional celibates in the fourth century are clear. Commentators generally suppose that both Aphrahat and Ephraem preserve the ideals of an earlier age, while they address the problems that had crept into the institution of the *bnay qyāmâ* in their own day. According to this reading, one might suppose that earlier (perhaps even as remote as the second century) enthusiastic, single Christians had led lives of consecrated virginity along the lines recommended in the *Acts of Judas Thomas.* One might further suppose that they had consecrated their virginity to God at baptism, along the lines suggested by Arthur Vööbus, and that their consecration was encouraged by the homiletic themes so evocatively studied by Robert Murray.[108] One also supposes that these singles were called *iḥîdāyê.* But these suppositions are all extrapolations from the fourth-century evidence we actually have in hand, which immediately testifies to a more easily imaginable set of human circumstances.

From the evidence we have in hand it seems that, at the dawn of the fourth century at least, both the men and the women celibates were free to choose their own living arrangements within their local communities. One does not yet hear of withdrawn individuals or communities of singles in desert or mountain areas in the Syriac-speaking world. This ascetical fashion appears in texts from Syria toward the end of St. Ephraem's lifetime. But St. Ephraem does offer evidence of some formal ecclesiastical organization among the *iḥîdāyê* of his day. He says that Bishop Abraham of Nisibis, for example, was the protector of the *bnay qyāmâ* of his diocese.[109] The bishop himself was an *iḥîdāyâ*,[110] so this status was not incompatible with formal office in the church. Moreover, he governed his diocese as the chief *rā'yâ* (shepherd) of the *mar'îtâ* (flock), with the help of what St. Ephraem called a *dayrâ d'allānê* (fold of herdsmen);[111] of which group he was himself a member, on his own testimony.[112] St. Ephraem says, further, that in his day there were daughter churches in every direction from Nisibis, each with their own *dayrôtô* (sheep folds)[113] and, one supposes, resident *iḥîdāyê*, in whose number would be the priests and deacons who were the *'allānê* (herdsmen) of the chief shepherd's larger flock.

One notices that St. Ephraem's vocabulary here includes traditional terms such as *iḥîdāyâ*, *qyāmâ*, and *dayrâ* that in Syriac would become the standard terms for "monk," monastic "status," and "monastery" in a later parlance. But modern scholars prefer to speak of the period of St. Ephraem's own Nisibene ministry, and of earlier times, as the period of premonasticism or protomonasticism.[114] The reason for this preference seems to be that in modern discourse the words "monk," "monastery," and "monasticism" bespeak the more organized forms of religious life that emerged in the course of the fourth century and that were based on an individual or collective physical withdrawal from the society of the baptized community as a whole, that is, *anachōrēsis* as a condition of a new form of ascetical life. St. Ephraem himself noticed and praised this development in the Syriac-speaking world in the accolades he penned in praise of the anchorite outside Edessa, St. Julian Saba. But it is noteworthy that the terms of St. Ephraem's praise are the traditional terms appropriate to the *bnay qyāmâ*. Thus, in the Syriac-speaking church the old and new forms of ascetical, celibate life lived on together.[115] Occasionally one even finds the traditional terms used to evoke an earlier day, to which the writer looks back with nostalgia. The sixth century writer of the *Doctrina Addai*, for example, portrays the early Syriac-speaking Christians of Mesopotamia as one and all worthy *iḥîdāyê*, members of the *qyāmâ*. The *Doctrina* says of the ministry of Aggai, the apostle Addai's successor:

> In the souls of the believers he enriched Christ's church. For the whole *qyāmâ* of men and women were chaste and resplendent. They were consecrated holy *(qadîšê)* and pure, and they were living singly *(iḥîdā'it)* and chastely without defilement.[116]

Of such language are ecclesiastical legends made—and of such suggestions are some, now legendary, scholarly theories constituted—about the origins of monastic asceticism in the Syriac-speaking orient. But the word studies presented here enable one to discern some of the most important ascetic, and, eventually, monastic vocabulary arising, in their traditional meanings, in the works of the classic writers of fourth-century Syria.

Bnay qyāmâ designated a group of celibate people belonging to a certain station in life in the community that in the early period of the history of the church in the Syriac-speaking world they assumed by covenant, or solemn pledge, at baptism. Such persons took their stand with an anticipatory view to the Resurrection, the goal of all Christians. Their status in the community served as a type for the expectations of all the baptized.

In the fourth century, and presumably earlier, *îḥîdāyâ* designated an individual member of the *bnay qyāmâ* in such a way that the term first of all invoked the person's special investiture in Christ Jesus, the Son of God, "God the *Îḥîdāyâ* in the bosom of the Father" (*John* 1.18)—to the effect that he stood out from the many sacrificially, and filled their place for the Lord of the many, as St. Ephraem put it.[117] Secondly, the *îḥîdāyâ*'s emulation of Jesus Christ meant that, like Christ, he was single as a celibate, and single in his lifestyle. It was neither right nor fitting, as Aphrahat would put it, for men or women *îḥîdāyê* even to take house companions of the opposite sex.[118] Later in the Syriac-speaking world the term *îḥîdāyâ* came to have the same range of meanings as did the Greek term *monachos,* the very Greek term that, if some modern scholars are correct in their surmises, writers in the early fourth century had first used in a Christian context to render the Syriac term *îḥîdāyâ!*[119] Jacob of Serug (d. 521 CE), for an example of the later Syriac usage, in his metric homilies "To the *îḥîdāyê,*" was clearly addressing people whom no modern scholar would hesitate to call monks.[120]

So the final question is whether, in what they had to say about the *îḥîdāyê,* or about the *bnay qyāmâ,* to use their institutional designation, Aphrahat and St. Ephraem were talking about monasticism, properly so called. Some modern scholars think that some such term as "protomonasticism" or "premonasticism" would be more appropriate.[121] But what we call monasticism in our Western languages is what grew out of the anchoritic and cenobitic experiences of many Christians in Egypt and Palestine in the fourth century. When these usages reached the Syriac-speaking world in the days of St. Ephraem, in the person of Julian Saba and his followers they assumed the proportions of a reform movement among the *bnay qyāmâ,* and eventually they all but supplanted the old ways. As for the term "monk," it is an etymologically correct term to render the Syriac *îḥîdāyâ* in Western languages. But like many translation words, it is essentially misleading, given the inevitable overtones of fourth-century Egypt that accompany the words "monk" and "monasticism" as we now actually use them. The *bnay qyāmâ* and the *abîlê* were not properly speaking monks, but their institutions and their traditional vocabulary were ready to contribute to the growth of monasticism when it appeared in Syria, together with the other institutions of the Great Church. And, as in many other instances, so in this one, while Ephraem the Syrian was not himself a monk, his life and his work did everything to provide for the success of monasticism in Syria in the fourth century—in its own distinctive style.

NOTES

1. See I. Peña et al., *Les stylites syriens* (Milan: Franciscan Printing Press, 1975); H.J.W. Drijvers, "Spätantike Parallelen zur altchristlichen Heiligenverehrung unter besonderer Berücksichtigung des syrischen Stylitenkultes," in *Aspekte frühchristlicher Heiligenverehrung*, Oikonomia 6 (Erlangen: University of Erlangen, 1977), pp. 54–76; Susan Ashbrook Harvey, "The Sense of a Stylite: Perspectives on Simeon the Elder," *Vigiliae Christianae* 42 (1988):376–394. See now Robert Doran, *The Lives of Simeon Stylites*, Cistercian Studies 112 (Kalamazoo, Mich.: Cistercian Publications, 1992).

2. Peter Brown, *The Body and Society; Men, Women and Sexual Renunciation in Early Christianity* (New York: Columbia University Press, 1988), p. 330.

3. Ibid., p. 332.

4. Ibid., p. 333.

5. Ibid., p. 334.

6. On this subject see E. A. Judge, "The Earliest Use of Monachos for 'Monk' (P. Coll. Youtie 77) and the Origins of Monasticism," *Jahrbuch für Antike und Christentum* 20 (1977):72–89; *idem*, "Fourth-Century Monasticism in the Papyri," in Roger S. Bagnall, ed., *Proceedings of the Sixteenth International Congress of Papyrology; New York, 24–31 July 1980*, American Studies in Papyrology 23 (Chico, Calif.: Scholars Press, 1981), pp. 613–620. See also James E. Goehring, "The World Engaged; the Social and Economic World of Early Egyptian Monasticism," in J. E. Goehring et al., eds., *Gnosticism and the Early Christian World; in Honor of James M. Robinson* (Sonoma, Calif.: Polebridge Press, 1990), pp. 134–144.

7. See particularly the studies of Han J. W. Drijvers, "The 19th Ode of Solomon: Its Interpretation and Place in Syrian Christianity," *Journal of Theological Studies* 31 (1980):337–355; *idem*, "Odes of Solomon and Psalms of Mani; Christians and Manichaeans in Third-Century Syria," in *Studies in Gnosticism and Hellenistic Religions: Festschrift G. Quispel* (Leiden: E. J. Brill, 1981), pp. 117–130; *idem*, "Die Legende des heiligen Alexius und der Typus des Gottesmannes im syrischen Christentum," in M. Schmidt, ed., *Typus, Symbol, Allegorie bei den östlichen Vätern und ihren Parallelen im Mittelalter*, Eichstatter Beiträge 4 (Regensburg: Pustet, 1981), pp. 187–217.

8. See S. H. Griffith, "Ephraem, the Deacon of Edessa, and the Church of the Empire," in T. Halton and J. P. Williman, eds., *Diakonia: Studies in Honor of Robert T. Meyer* (Washington: Catholic University of America Press, 1986), pp. 22–52; *idem*, "Ephraem the Syrian's Hymns 'Against Julian'; Meditations on History and Imperial Power," *Vigiliae Christianae* 41 (1987):238–266; *idem*, "Setting Right the Church of Syria; Ephraem's Hymns against Heresies," *Journal of Eastern Christian Studies*, to appear.

9. See P. Peeters, "La legende de saint Jacques de Nisibe," *Analecta Bollandiana* 38 (1920):285–373; David Bundy, "Jacob of Nisibis as a Model for the Episcopacy," *Le Muséon* 104 (1991):235–249; E. Mathews, "The *Vita* Tradition of Ephrem the Syrian," *Diakonia* 22 (1988–1989):15–42; S. H. Griffith, "Images of Ephraem: the Syrian Holy Man and his Church," *Traditio* 45 (1989–1990):7–33; Joseph P. Amar, "Byzantine Ascetic Monachism and Greek Bias in the *Vita* Tradition of Ephrem the Syrian," *Orientalia Christiana Periodica* 58 (1992):123–156.

10. See J.-M. Fiey, "Aonès, Awun et Awgin (Eugène) aux origines du monachisme mésopotamien," *Analecta Bollandiana* 80 (1962):52–81.

11. The "Letter to the Mountaineers" is most recently published in Edmund Beck, *Des heiligen Ephraem des Syrers Sermones IV*, Corpus scriptorum christianorum orientalium, vol. 334 (Louvain, 1973), pp. 28–43. The second text, too, is most recently edited

in Beck, *Sermones IV*, pp. 1–16, as well as the third text, pp. 16–28. The fourth text is most recently re-presented, with an English translation, in E. Mathews, "Isaac of Antioch: A Homily on Solitaries, Hermits, and Mourners," master's thesis, The Catholic University of America, Washington, D.C., 1987.

12. See Arthur Vööbus, "Beiträge zur kritischen Sichtung der asketischen Schriften, die unter dem Namen Ephraem des Syrers überliefert sind," *Oriens Christianus* 39 (1955):48–55; *idem, History of Asceticism in the Syrian Orient,* CSCO, vol. 197 (Louvain, 1960), 2:1–11; *idem, Literary Critical and Historical Studies in Ephraem the Syrian* (Stockholm, 1958), pp. 59–65, 69–86.

13. See the case presented with full bibliographical citations of earlier studies in E. Mathews, "'On Solitaries': Ephraem or Isaac?" *Le Muséon* 103 (1990):91–110.

14. See the studies cited in note 6 above, and Samuel Rubenson, *The Letters of St. Anthony; Origenist Theology, Monastic Tradition and the Making of a Saint* (Lund: Lund University Press, 1990).

15. One thinks in particular of the legislation attributed to Rabbula, the famous fifth-century bishop of Edessa. See Arthur Vööbus, *Syriac and Arabic Documents Regarding Legislation Relative to Syrian Asceticism,* Papers of the Estonian Theological Society in Exile (Stockholm, 1960), 11:24–50, 78–86; *idem, History of Asceticism in the Syrian Orient,* CSCO, vol. 500 (Louvain, 1988), 3:68–77. See also Susan Ashbrook Harvey, "Bishop Rabbula: Ascetic Tradition and Change in Fifth Century Edessa," to appear in a forthcoming issue of the *Journal of Eastern Christian Studies.*

16. See Sidney H. Griffith, "Hymns to Julian Saba; the Hermit/Monk of Syria," a forthcoming study of texts (already published in Edmund Beck, *Des heiligen Ephraem des Syrers: Hymnen auf Abraham Kidunaya und Julianos Saba,* CSCO, vols. 322 and 323 [Louvain, 1972]).

17. See Antoine Guillaumont, "Situation et signification du 'Liber Graduum' dans la spiritualité syriaque," in *Symposium Syriacum 1972,* Orientalia Christiana Analecta 197 (Rome, 1974), pp. 311–322; Aleksander Kowalski, *Perfezione e Giustizia di Adamo nel Liber Graduum,* Orientalia Christiana Analecta 232 (Rome, 1989); Columba Stewart, *'Working the Earth of the Heart'; The Messalian Controversy in History, Texts, and Language to AD 431* (Oxford, 1991).

18. See Antoine Guillaumont, *Les 'Kephalaia Gnostica' d'Evagre le Pontique et l'histoire de l'Origénisme chez les grecs et les syriens* (Paris, 1962); Pierre Canivet, *Le monachisme syrien sélon Theodoret de Cyr,* Théologie historique 42 (Paris, 1977). A still masterly study is that of Stephan Schiwietz, *Das morgenlandische Mönchtum,* vol. 3, *Das Mönchtum in Syrien und Mesopotamien und das Asketentum in Persien* (Mödling bei Wien, 1938).

19. The old ways persisted particularly in that segment of the Syriac-speaking world that would later be called the Syrian Orthodox church. See Arthur Vööbus, "The Institution of the *Benai Qeiama* and *Benat Qeiama* in the Ancient Syriac Church," *Church History* 30 (1961):19–27; Susan Ashbrook Harvey, *Asceticism and Society in Crisis; John of Ephesus and the Lives of the Eastern Saints* (Berkeley, Calif.: University of California Press, 1990).

20. See, for example, I. Parisot, ed., *Aphraatis Sapientis Persae Demonstrationes,* Patrologia Syriaca (Paris, 1894, 1907), 1.6.260, 272.

21. See below, and E. Beck, *Des heiligen Ephraem des Syrers Carmina Nisibena,* erster Teil, CSCO, vol. 218 (Louvain, 1961), 17.3–4, p. 46.

22. See, for example, *1 Timothy* 5.3–16; *1 Corinthians* 7.25–35; and I. E. Rahmani, ed., *Testamentum Domini Nostri Jesu Christi* (Moguntiae, 1899), pp. 104–109.

23. See A. Vööbus, *History of Asceticism in the Syrian Orient* 1:104–106; Marie-Joseph Pierre, trans., *Aphraate le Sage Persan, les Exposés*, Sources chrétiennes, vols. 349, 350 (Paris, 1988), 1:376, note 38.

24. A. Adam, "Grundbegriffe des Mönchtums in sprachlicher Sicht," *Zeitschrift für Kirchengeschichte* 64 (1953/54):209–239.

25. R. Murray, "The Exhortation to Candidates for Ascetical Vows at Baptism in the Ancient Syriac Church," *New Testament Studies* 21 (1974–1975):59–80.

26. E. Beck, "Ein Beitrag zur Terminologie des ältesten syrischen Mönchtums," in *Antonius Magnus Eremita*, Studia Anselmiana 38 (Rome, 1956), pp. 254–267; "Asketentum und Mönchtum bei Ephraem," in *Il Monachesimo Orientale*, Orientalia Christiana Analecta 153 (Rome, 1958), pp. 341–362. French translation in *L'Orient Syrien* 3 (1958):273–298.

27. G. Quispel, "L'Évangile selon Thomas et les origines de l'ascèse chrétienne," in *Gnostic Studies II* (Istanbul, 1975), pp. 98–112.

28. A. Guillaumont, "Monachisme et éthique judéo-chrétienne," *Recherches de science religieuse* 60 (1972):199–218; "Le nom des 'Agapètes,'" *Vigiliae Christianae* 23 (1969):30–37. Both articles appear in Guillaumont's collection of separately published pieces, *Aux origines du monachisme chrétien*, Spiritualité orientale 30 (Bégrolles en Mauges, 1979).

29. See Vööbus, *History of Asceticism* 1:6–8; Beck, "Ein Beitrag zur Terminologie," written expressly against the ideas advanced by Alfred Adam in "Grundbegriffe des Mönchtums." Adam replied in "Der Monachos Gedanke innerhalb der Spiritualität der alten Kirche," in *Glaube, Geist, Geschichte; Festschrift E. Benz* (Leiden, 1967), pp. 259–265.

30. See the articles cited in notes 24 and 28 above.

31. Murray, "Exhortation to Candidates," p. 67.

32. Eusebius of Caesarea, "Commentaria in Psalmos," *PG* 23,689,

33. R. Murray, *Symbols of Church and Kingdom: A Study in Early Syriac Tradition* (Cambridge, 1975), p. 355.

34. I. Parisot, *Aphraatis Sapientis Persae Demonstrationes*, Patrologia Syriaca (Paris, 1884), cols. 239–312. See A. J. Van der Aalst, "A l'origine du monachisme syrien; les 'ihidaye' chez Aphrahat," in A.A.R. Bastiaensen et al., eds., *Fructus Centesimus; Mélanges offerts à Gerard J. M. Bartelink*, Instrumenta Patristica 19 (Steenburg, 1989); pp. 315–324.

35. Parisot, *Aphraatis Demonstrationes*, col. 261.

36. Ibid., col. 269.

37. Ibid., col. 276.

38. Ibid., col. 272.

39. Pierre, *Aphraate, les exposés* 1:383, note 51.

40. E. Beck, *Des heiligen Ephraem des Syrers Hymnen de Paradiso und Contra Julianum*, CSCO, vol. 174 (Louvain, 1957), 7.18, p. 29. See now the English version of the Paradise hymns by Sebastian Brock, *St. Ephraem the Syrian: Hymns on Paradise* (Crestwood, N.Y., 1990), p. 125 for a slightly different translation.

41. Other Ephraem texts are discussed by Edmund Beck, O.S.B., in the articles cited in note 27 above.

42. In *John* 1.18, the term is *Îḥidāyâ* in the Peshitta; in the *Diatessaron*, as Ephraem commented on it, the term is *Yaḥîdâ*. See L. Leloir, *Saint Ephrem, Commentaire de l'Evangile concordant* (Dublin, 1963), p. 2. See also L. Leloir, *Le Temoignage d'Ephrem sur le Diatessaron*, CSCO, vol. 227 (Louvain, 1962), p. 100.

43. See Murray, "The Exhortation to Candidates," for bibliography regarding the earlier controversy over celibacy as a requirement for baptism in the Syriac-speaking church, and A. Vööbus, *Celibacy, a Requirement for Admission to Baptism in the Early Syrian Church* (Stockholm, 1951). See now Edmund Beck, *Dōrea und Charis, die Taufe,* CSCO, vol. 457 (Louvain, 1984), pp. 56–185.

44. Edmund Beck, *Des heiligen Ephraem des Syrers Hymnen de Nativitate (Epiphania),* CSCO, vol. 186 (Louvain, 1959), p. 173.

45. Beck, *Des heiligen Ephraem Hymnen de Nativitate (Epiphania),* p. 191.

46. Such is the interpretation of Beck, *Dōrea und Charis,* pp. 162–163.

47. See the earlier statement in Beck, "Asketentum und Mönchtum," p. 344.

48. See Beck, *Dōrea und Charis,* p. 157, note 78; and pp. 160–161.

49. See Sebastian Brock, "Clothing Metaphors as a Means of Theological Expression in Syriac Tradition," in M. Schmidt, ed., *Typus, Symbol, Allegorie bei den östlichen Vätern und ihren Parallelen im Mittelalter,* Eichstatter Beiträge, vol. 4 (Regensburg, 1981), pp. 15–16, 25–26. See, too, the fascinating study of an earlier use of clothing imagery in the Semitic world by N. M. Waldman, "The Imagery of Clothing, Covering and Overpowering," *The Journal of the Ancient Near Eastern Society* 19 (1989):161–170; also M. E. Vogelzang and W. J. van Bekkum, "Meaning and Symbolism of Clothing in Ancient Near Eastern Texts," in H.L.J. Vanstiphout et al., eds., *Scripta Signa Vocis: Studies about Scripts, Scriptures, Scribes and Languages in the Near East, Presented to J. H. Hospers by His Pupils, Colleagues and Friends* (Groningen: Egbert Forsten, 1986), pp. 265–284.

50. Brock, "Clothing Metaphors." See also Sebastian Brock, *The Luminous Eye: The Spiritual World Vision of St. Ephrem* (Rome, 1985), pp. 65–76; revised ed., Cistercian Studies 124 (Kalamazoo, Mich., 1992), pp. 85–94.

51. See A. de Halleux, "Saint Éphrem le Syrien," *Revue théologique de Louvain* 14 (1983):353, for a discussion of Ephraem's idea of the church as the sacramental situation of Paradise restored.

52. See Françoise-E. Morard, "Monachos, moine; histoire du terme grec jusqu'au 4ᵉ siècle," *Freiburger Zeitschrift für Philosophie und Theologie* 20 (1973):354–357; H. Fabry, "Yāḥad," in G. J. Botterweck and H. Ringgren, *Theologisches Wörterbuch zum alten Testament,* Band 3 (Stuttgart, 1982), cols. 595–603.

53. See A. Guillaumont, "Le nom des 'Agapètes,'" *Vigiliae Christianae* 23 (1969):30–37.

54. See A. Guillaumont, "Monachisme et éthique Judéo-Chrétienne," *Recherches de science religieuse* 60 (1972):199–218.

55. See note 5 above.

56. Francesca Cocchini, "Il Figlio Unigenito Sacrificato e Amato," *Studi Storico-Religiose* 1 (1977):201–323.

57. It is notable in this connection that in North Africa St. Augustine had to defend the use of the term *monachos/monachus* against the Donatist charge that the word is unscriptural. See St. Augustine's "Exposition of Psalm 132" in English translation in A. Zumkeller, *Augustine's Ideal of the Religious Life,* trans. E. Colledge (New York, 1986), pp. 398–401.

58. *Monogenēs, monotropos, monozōnos,* etc. See Murray, "Exhortation to Candidates"; and Guillaumont, "Monachisme et éthique."

59. Parisot, *Aphraatis Demonstrationes,* col. 276.

60. E. Beck, *Des heiligen Ephraem des Syrers: Hymnen auf Abraham Kidunaya und Julianus Saba,* CSCO, vol. 322 (Louvain, 1972), 2.13, p. 41.

61. See Murray, "Exhortation to Candidates."

62. See A. Guillaumont, "Sémitismes dans les Logia de Jesus retrouvés à Nag-Hamâdi," *Journal asiatique* 246 (1958):113–123; M. Harl, "A propos des *Logia* de Jésus: le sens du mot *MONAXOS*," *Revue des Études Grecques* 73 (1960):464–474; A.F.J. Klijn, "Das Thomasevangelium und das altsyrische Christentum," *Vigiliae Christianae* 15 (1961):146–159; idem, "The 'Single One' in the Gospel of Thomas," *Journal of Biblical Literature* 81 (1962):271–278; G. Quispel, "L'Evangile selon Thomas et les origines de l'ascese chrétienne," in G. Quispel, *Gnostic Studies II* (Istanbul, 1975), pp. 98–112; W. Vycichl, *Dictionnaire étymologique de la langue copte* (Leuven, 1983), pp. 173–174.

63. Klijn, "The 'Single One,'" p. 271.

64. See E. A. Judge, "The Earliest Use of Monachos," pp. 72, 86–87; F. E. Morard, "Monachos: Une importation sémitique en Égypte?' *Studia Patristica* 12 (1975):242–246; idem, "Encore quelques reflexions sur Monachos," *Vigiliae Christianae* 34 (1980):395–401.

65. The remarks that follow on this subject appear in an inchoate form in S. H. Griffith, "'Singles' and the 'Sons of the Covenant'; Reflections on Syriac Ascetic Terminology," in E. Carr et al., eds., *Eulogêma: Studies in Honor of Robert Taft, S.J.* (Rome: Pontificio Ateneo S. Anselmo, 1993).

66. See Murray, *Symbols of Church*, pp. 13–15; De Halleux, "Saint Éphrem le Syrien," p. 331. Pierre translates it "membres de l'Ordre." See the explanation in Pierre, *Aphraate, Exposés* 1:98, note 81.

67. See Parisot, *Aphraatis Demonstrationes,* 1.260, 272.

68. Ibid., col. 404.

69. R. Payne Smith, *Thesaurus Syriacus,* 2 vols. (Oxford, 1879–1883), pp. 3522–3538.

70. George Nedungatt, "The Covenanters of the Early Syriac-Speaking Church," *Orientalia Christiana Periodica* 39 (1973):191–215, 419–444.

71. Ibid., p. 195.

72. Ibid., p. 203.

73. Ibid., p. 433.

74. Ibid., p. 437.

75. Ibid., p. 438.

76. Ibid., p. 443.

77. Payne Smith, *Thesaurus Syriacus* 2:3533–3535.

78. See Murray, *Symbols of Church,* p. 13, note 5.

79. Nedungatt, "The Covenanters," pp. 196–199.

80. See Murray, *Symbols of Church,* p. 15, note 1.

81. See A. Vööbus, *Celibacy, a Requirement for Admission to Baptism in the Early Syrian Church* (Stockholm, 1951); idem, *History of Asceticism* 1:93–95, 175–178. The idea that Aphrahat's *Demonstrations* showed that the *bnay qyāmâ* were the baptized laity of the early Syriac-speaking church was put forward first by F. C. Burkitt, *Early Eastern Christianity* (London, 1904), pp. 129, 137–138.

82. Already, in 1905, R. H. Connolly reacted to Burkitt's proposals in his article, "Aphraates and Monasticism," *Journal of Theological Studies* 6 (1905):522–539. For an early review of Vööbus's proposals see J. Gribomont, "Le monachisme au sein de l'église en Syrie et en Cappadoce," *Studia Monastica* 7 (1965):7–24. Now Robert Murray's article, "Exhortation to Candidates" gives the best summary of the discussion and broadens the inquiry into the baptismal and liturgical circumstances of the inauguration of a prospective *bar gyāmâ.* Other studies not mentioned earlier that touch on the issues of the controversy are the following: A. Baker, "Syriac and the Origins of Monasti-

cism," *Downside Review* 86 (1968):342–353; *idem,* "Early Syriac Asceticism," *Downside Review* 88 (1970):393–409; S. Jargy, "Les 'fils et filles du pacte' dans la littérature monastique syriaque," *Orientalia Christiana Periodica* 17 (1951):304–320; *idem,* "Les origines du monachisme en Syrie et en Mésopotamie," *Proche-Orient Chrétien* 2 (1952):110–124; *idem,* "Les premiers instituts monastiques et les principaux representants du monachisme syrien au iv⁰ siècle," *Proche-Orient Chrétien* 4 (1954):106–117; M. M. Maude, "Who were the Bᶜnai Qᶜyama?" *Journal of Theological Studies* 36 (1935):13–21.

83. Parisot, *Aphraatis Demonstrationes* 1.248.
84. Ibid., col. 309. See R. Murray, "Some Themes and Problems of Early Syriac Angelology," in *V Symposium Syriacum,* Orientalia Christiana Analecta 236 (Rome, 1990), pp. 143–153.
85. See Pierre, *Aphraate, les Exposés* 1:361, note 7.
86. P. Nagel, *Die Motivierung der Askese in der alten Kirche und der Ursprung des Mönchtums,* Texte und Untersuchungen 95 (Berlin, 1966), p. 43. See also the author's earlier article, "Zum Problem der 'Bundessöhne' bei Afrahat," *Forschungen und Fortschritte* 36 (1962):152–154.
87. See Michael Breydy, "Les laics et les Bnay Qyomo dans l'ancienne tradition de l'église syrienne," *Kanon* 3 (1977):60–62.
88. See Nedungatt, "The Covenanters," p. 438, note 2.
89. See Louis Massignon, *Parole Donnée* (Paris, 1962), pp. 361–385.
90. See, for example, L. Hafeli, *Stilmittel bei Afrahat dem persischen Weisen* (Leipzig, 1932); M. Maude, "Rhythmic Patterns in the Homilies of Aphrahat," *Anglican Theological Review* 17 (1935):225–233.
91. Parisot, *Aphraatis Demonstrationes* 1.293–296. For the theological context of this passage see F. Gavin, "The Sleep of the Soul in the Early Syriac Church," *Journal of the American Oriental Society* 40 (1920):103–120.
92. Parisot, *Aphraatis Demonstrationes* 1.241. (See note for line 23.) See also Pierre, *Aphraate, les Exposés* 1:361, note 7.
93. E. Beck, *Des heiligen Ephraem des Syrers Carmina Nisibena, erster Teil,* CSCO, vol. 218 (Louvain, 1961), 21.5, pp. 55–56.
94. Beck, *Carmina Nisibena I* 15.9, p. 41.
95. Beck, *Hymnen de Nativitate (Epiphania)* 186:173.
96. See E. Beck, *Dōrea und Charis, die Taufe,* CSCO, vol. 457 (Louvain, 1984), p. 161.
97. See Murray, *Symbols of Church,* p. 13.
98. E. Beck, *Des heiligen Ephraem des Syrers: Hymnen auf Abraham Kidunaya und Julianus Saba,* CSCO, vol. 322 (Louvain, 1972), 2.13, p. 41.
99. Beck, *Hymnen auf Julianos Saba* 322.3.2, pp. 42–43.
100. See Beck, "Ein Beitrag zur Terminologie," pp. 262–263.
101. Edmund Beck, *Des heiligen Ephraem des Syrers Hymnen de Virginitate,* CSCO, vol. 223 (Louvain, 1962), 21.2, p. 71.
102. Edmund Beck, *Des heiligen Ephraem des Syrers: Hymnen de Paradiso und contra Julianum,* CSCO, vol. 174 (Louvain, 1957), 7.3, p. 26. The English translation here is that of Sebastian Brock, *Saint Ephrem; Hymns on Paradise* (Crestwood, N.Y., 1990), p. 119.
103. See Beck, *Hymnen de Paradiso* 174 esp. 13.2, 3, 4, 5, 6, 7, 8, 9, 10, 11, pp. 55–57. For a very insightful discussion of these stanzas in light of this theme, see the forthcoming study by Gary A. Anderson, "The Penitence of Adam in Early Judaism and Christianity."

104. See J. H. Charlesworth, ed., *Odes of Solomon* (Missoula, Montana, 1977); A.F.J. Klijn, *Acts of Thomas,* Novum Testamentum Supplements 5 (Leiden, 1962). In the present writer's opinion, the earlier currents of ascetical thought in the Syriac-speaking world can best be studied in the history of the origins of Manichaeism. See Han J. W. Drijvers, "Odes of Solomon and Psalms of Mani: Christians and Manichaeans in Third-Century Syria," in R. van den Broek and M. I. Vermaseren, eds., *Studies in Gnosticism and Hellenistic Religions Presented to Gilles Quispel* (Leiden, 1981), pp. 117–130; *idem,* "Conflict and Alliance in Manichaeism," in H. G. Kippenberg, ed., *Struggles of Gods* (Berlin, 1984), pp. 99–124; S.N.C. Lieu, *Manichaeism in the Later Roman Empire and Medieval China* (Manchester, 1985).

105. Parisot, *Aphraatis Demonstrationes* 1.260.

106. Ibid., col. 272.

107. S. Brock, "Ephrem's Letter to Publius," *Le Muséon* 89 (1976):286–287.

108. See Murray, "The Exhortation to Candidates" and *Symbols of Church.*

109. See Beck, *Carmina Nisibena,* CSCO, 218.21.5, pp. 55–56.

110. Ibid., 15.9, p. 41.

111. Ibid., 17.3, p. 46.

112. See E. Beck, *Des heiligen Ephraem des Syrers Hymnen contra Haereses* CSCO, vol. 169 (Louvain, 1957), 56.10, pp. 211–212.

113. See Beck, *Carmina Nisibena,* CSCO, 218.14.1, p. 37. See, also, Sidney H. Griffith, "Setting Right the Church of Syria: Saint Ephraem's Hymns against Heresies," forthcoming in *Middle Eastern Christian Studies* 1.

114. Some scholars, however, speak anachronistically of a monasticism in St. Ephraem's milieu, and of the saint himself as a monk. See the articles of S. Jargy in note 83 above, and L. Leloir, "Saint Éphrem, moine et pasteur," in *Théologie de la vie monastique* (Paris, 1961), pp. 85–97; *idem,* "La pensée monastique d'Éphrem et Martyrus," in *Symposium Syriacum 1972,* Orientalia Christiana Analecta 197 (Rome, 1974), pp. 105–134.

115. See the survey of Nedungatt, "The Covenanters," pp. 200–215.

116. G. Phillips, *The Doctrine of Addai, the Apostle* (London, 1876), p. 50 (Syriac).

117. See note 44 above.

118. See Parisot, *Aphraatis Demonstrationes* 1.260–272.

119. See E. A. Judge, "The Earliest Use of *Monachos,*" pp. 72, 86–87; E. Morard, "Monachos: une importation sémitique en Égypte?" *Studia Patristica* 12 (1975):242–246.

120. See P. Bedjan, *Homiliae Selectae Mar-Jacobi Sarugensis* (Paris, 1908), 4:818–871.

121. See A. Guillaumont, "Perspectives actuelles sur les origines du monachisme," in T. T. Segerstedt, ed., *The Frontiers of Human Knowledge* (Uppsala, 1978), pp. 111–123. Reprinted in the author's *Aux origines du monachisme chrétien* (Bégrolles en Mauges, 1979), pp. 215–227; *idem,* "Esquisse d'une phénoménologie du monachisme," *Numen* 25 (1978):40–51. Reprinted in *Aux origines,* pp. 228–239. On Aphrahat and his thought see the following works of Peter Bruns: *Das Christusbild Aphrahats des Persischen Weisen,* Studien zur alten Kirchengeschichte 4 (Bonn: Borengässer, 1990), which originally appeared as the author's 1988 doctoral dissertation, Katholisch-Theologischen Fakultat zu Bochum; and *Aphrahat, Unterweisungen; aus dem Syrischen übersetzt und eingeleitet,* Fontes Christiani 5/1 (Freiburg im Breisgau: Herder, 1991).

Acknowledgments

Louth, Andrew. "Unity and Diversity in the Church of the Fourth Century." *Studies in Church History* 32 (1996): 1–17. Reprinted with the permission of the Ecclesiastical History Society.

O'Donnell, James J. "Augustine's Idea of God." *Augustinian Studies* 25 (1994): 25–35. Reprinted with the permission of *Augustinian Studies*.

Williams, Rowan D. "'Good for Nothing'? Augustine on Creation." *Augustinian Studies* 25 (1994): 9–24. Reprinted with the permission of *Augustinian Studies*.

TeSelle, Eugene. "The Cross as Ransom." *Journal of Early Christian Studies* 4 (1996): 147–70. Reprinted with the permission of Johns Hopkins University Press.

Hallman, Joseph M. "The Seed of Fire: Divine Suffering in the Christology of Cyril of Alexandria and Nestorius of Constantinople." *Journal of Early Christian Studies* 5 (1997): 369–91. Reprinted with the permission of Johns Hopkins University Press.

Wilson, R. McL. "Half a Century of Gnosisforschung — in Retrospect." In *Gnosisforschung und Religionsgeschichte*, edited by Holger Preissler and Hubert Seiwert (Marburg: Diagonal-Verlag, 1994): 343–53. Reprinted with the permission of Diagonal-Verlag GbR.

Layton, Bentley. "Prolegomena to the Study of Ancient Gnosticism." In *The Social World of the First Christians: Essays in Honor of Wayne A. Meeks*, edited by L. Michael White and O. Larry Yarbrough (Minneapolis: Fortress Press, 1995): 334–50. Reprinted with the permission of Fortress Press, Subsidiary of Augsburg Fortress Publishers.

Stead, Christopher. "Arius in Modern Research." *Journal of Theological Studies*, n.s. 45 (1994): 24–36. Reprinted with the permission of Oxford University Press.

Ferreiro, Alberto. "Jerome's Polemic Against Priscillian in his *Letter* to Ctesiphon (133, 4)." *Revue des Études Augustiniennes* 39 (1993): 309–32. Reprinted with the permission of *Institut d'Études Augustiniennes*.

Tilley, Maureen A. "Dilatory Donatists or Procrastinating Catholics: The Trial at the Conference of Carthage." *Church History* 60 (1991): 7–19. Reprinted with permission from *Church History*.

Burns, J. Patout. "The Atmosphere of Election: Augustinianism as Common Sense." *Journal of Early Christian Studies* 2 (1994): 325–39. Reprinted with the permission of Johns Hopkins University Press.

Bonner, Gerald. "Pelagianism and Augustine." *Augustinian Studies* 23 (1992): 33–51. Reprinted with the permission of *Augustinian Studies*.

Bonner, Gerald. "Augustine and Pelagianism." *Augustinian Studies* 24 (1993): 27–47. Reprinted with the permission of *Augustinian Studies*.

Scheppard, Carol. "The Transmission of Sin in the Seed: A Debate Between Augustine of Hippo and Julian of Eclanum." *Augustinian Studies* 27 (1996): 97–106. Reprinted with the permission of *Augustinian Studies*.

Bundy, David. "The *Life of Abercius*: Its Significance for Early Syriac Christianity." *The Second Century* 7 (1989/90): 163–76. Reprinted with the permission of Johns Hopkins University Press.

Brock, Sebastian. "Eusebius and Syriac Christianity." In *Eusebius, Christianity, and Judaism*, edited by Harold W. Attridge and Gohei Hata (Detroit: Wayne State University Press, 1992): 212–34. Reprinted with the permission of Yamamoto Shoten Publishing House.

Brock, Sebastian. "The Christology of the Church of the East in the Synods of the Fifth to Early Seventh Centuries: Preliminary Considerations and Materials." In *Aksum-Thyateira: A Festschrift for Archbishop Methodios*, edited by George Dragas (London: Thyateira House, 1985): 125–42. Reprinted with the permission of Thyateira House.

Griffith, Sidney H. "Images of Ephraem: The Syrian Holy Man and His Church." *Traditio* 45 (1989/90): 7–33. Reprinted with the permission of Fordham University Press.

Griffith, Sidney H. "Asceticism in the Church of Syria: The Hermeneutics of Early Syrian Monasticism." In *Asceticism*, edited by Vincent L. Wimbush and Richard Valantasis (New York: Oxford University Press, 1995): 220–45. Reprinted with the permission of Oxford University Press.